Corn lands of Muiry Headless
Gordon of Buchyne

Wett Pasture Common of Insch 2 . 2 . 36

Drumrossie

Aberdeen Road

No 2 Doctor Beattie . 2 . 11

No 2 Doctor Innes . 2 . 16

Dr Innes 20 F

Dr Beattie 1 . 4

Wm Michie . 1 . 16

Infield Good Soil No 1 Robert Milne . 3 . 34

No 2 Wm Break . 3 . 17

No 1 Wm Robertson . 3 . 33

Inclosure Dr Beattie . 3 . 11

No 1

R Milne

Dr Beattie

Robt

INSCH

Mr John . 27

R Rodger 25 F

Wm Robertson 30 F

No 2 Bleachfield

No 4 Mr Adam Maitland 2 . . 11

Infield Alexander Roger 2 . . 3

No 1 Good Infield Wm Break . 3 . 29

Mr Hall and 29

Rob Alexander 34 F

Kirk

Kirk Yard . 2 . 11

No 1 The Old Glebe very good soil Mr Adam Maitland 4 . 1 . 2

Water of

No 1 John Webster 1 . 1 . 23

No 3 Good Infield Mr Adam Maitland 2 . . 22

Infield Fine Soil

No 2 John Webster 1 . 2 . 19

No 4 Wm Michie 1 . 2 . 22

No 1 Good Infield of Mill of Insch Doctor Beattie 2 . . 32

Garden 35 F

Pasture 2 . 23

No 2 Ditto good land 1 . 3 . 24

Mill of Insch

No 4 arable 30

No 3 J Webster 2 . 14

No 1 Infield Doctor Innes 2 . . 14

Wett Pasture

No 3 Good Infield 1 . 2 . 3

No 6 Arable 24

No 5 Flooded Haughs 1 . 1 . 27 in all

Wett 1 . 2

lock & Wett pasture 2 . . 4

No 7 ooded Haugh with Bank 3 . 12

Long Foord

Wett Pasture 1 . 2 . 37

Gordon Esq.

ROTHNEY

OF

Premnay Road

n Hall to Aberdeen

Scale of Scotch Chains

In the Shadow of Bennachie

In the Shadow of Bennachie

A Field Archaeology of Donside, Aberdeenshire

Royal Commission on the Ancient and
Historical Monuments of Scotland

Society of Antiquaries of Scotland

2008

Royal
Commission on the
Ancient and
Historical
Monuments of
Scotland

First published in 2007 by the Society of Antiquaries
of Scotland in association with the Royal Commission
on the Ancient and Historical Monuments of Scotland
(RCAHMS).

Second edition published by RCAHMS in 2008.

**Royal Commission on the Ancient
and Historical Monuments of Scotland**
John Sinclair House
16 Bernard Terrace, Edinburgh EH8 9NX
tel 0131 662 1456
fax 0131 662 1477
info@rcahms.gov.uk
www.rcahms.gov.uk
Registered Charity SC026749

Society of Antiquaries of Scotland
Royal Museum of Scotland
Chambers Street, Edinburgh EH1 1JF
tel 0131 247 4133
fax 0131 247 4163
admin@socantscot.org
www.socantscot.org
Registered Charity SC010240

British Library Cataloguing-in-Publication Data.
A catalogue record for this book is available from
the British Library.

ISBN: 978 1 902419 61 9

The Society and RCAHMS gratefully acknowledge
grant-aid towards the publication of this volume from
the Strathmartine Trust.

Typeset by Mitch Cosgrove.
Printed in Slovenia by MKT.

End papers: Plans of the villages and lands of Insch
(front) and Duncanstone (back) in 1797, from the
survey of the Leith Hall estate by George Brown. © NTS

Contents

Royal Commission on the Ancient
and Historical Monuments of Scotland

Preface

This survey of Donside, published in partnership with the Society of Antiquaries of Scotland, is the latest in a series of landscape studies carried out by the Royal Commission since 1987 (RCAHMS 1990; 1994; 1997a; 2001). Each has built upon its predecessor in some way, reflecting, on the one hand, the shift of emphasis from the classified lists of monuments that characterise the first county inventories to landscape recording projects, while on the other, the evolution of local and national sites and monuments records and their presentation in electronic media. Archaeological sites and monuments continue to be recorded and classified but, whereas once they were gathered into bound volumes, now they can be delivered via the World Wide Web to remote workstations for interactive use with other datasets. The purpose of this volume is in no way to duplicate that process, but rather to complement it. The volume sets out to provide an overall commentary on the archaeological monuments that have been recorded, setting them in a framework of topographical maps, and ranging across the history of archaeological recording in Aberdeenshire, the processes of survival, destruction and discovery, the evolution of the cultural landscape, and, where possible, the context of their contemporary landscapes. These are high ideals for any publication, and it is inevitable that some aspects have been explored in greater detail than others, if only because of the uneven character of the available information through time. Unlike its predecessors, this volume makes no attempt to present a gazetteer of all the monuments in the area, but the index supplies the map-based reference number (e.g. NJ62SE 1) that will allow the reader to find out further information by an online search of the national database, CANMORE, at www.rcahms.gov. uk. The assumption that underpins this approach is that web-based systems are now sufficiently accessible from home computers, public libraries and other facilities that the printed gazetteer no longer serves a useful purpose. Furthermore, the ongoing development of the delivery systems of online databases will allow the information to be interrogated interactively in ever more complex ways that simply cannot be achieved within the confines of the printed page.

The project was initiated in the autumn of 1995 with the drawn survey of the fort on Barra Hill, and fieldwork was largely complete by the end of 2001. The preparation of the publication has taken rather longer and, like the fieldwork, has spanned various changes of personnel, so much so that only one member of the team has worked full-time on the project from inception to completion. Nevertheless, the results of the analysis and synthesis of the information that has been gathered provide new insights into numerous aspects of the landscape, particularly in the medieval and later sections of the volume. Fieldwork for the volume was carried out by R Adam, J Borland, G Brown, P Corser, D C Cowley, P J Dixon, T Duncan, I Fraser, A R Gannon, R H Jones, A J Leith, S P Halliday, A Lamb, J Mackie, K H J Macleod, A P Martin, I G Parker, S Scott, R Shaw, J R Sherriff, H Stoddart, S Wallace and A Welfare; aerial survey was carried out by R Adam, M M Brown, D C Cowley and D Smart; photographic services have been provided by R Adam, C Brockley, A Lamb, J Mackie, A P Martin, T Duncan, D Smart and S Wallace; the text has been written by P J Dixon, I Fraser, A R Gannon, S P Halliday, R H Jones, J R Sherriff, R Tipping and A Welfare, and edited by S P Halliday and J B Stevenson; and the drawings and maps have been prepared by J Borland, G Brown, A J Leith, K H J Macleod, I G Parker and H Stoddart. The results of the survey have been incorporated into CANMORE by R J Mowat. Design and production work was carried out by O Brookes, M Cosgrove and L Law.

The Royal Commission wishes to acknowledge the assistance given by all the owners of the archaeological sites and monuments that have been surveyed, who allowed access for study and recording, and also the co-operation of the staffs of Aberdeenshire Council, the Forestry Commission, the University of Aberdeen, Inverurie Museum, Peterhead Museum, Aberdeen City Museum, the National Museums of Scotland, Historic Scotland, the National Library of Scotland, the National Archives of Scotland, and the National Trust for Scotland. Particular thanks are due to: J Harrison for carrying out documentary searches; R Tipping for preparing the sections on the environmental history and commenting on this aspect in the rest of the text; P Bray, F Lee and J Cauldwell, placement students from the University of Bradford, for their work collecting and analysing data; I A G Shepherd and M Greig of Aberdeenshire Council, who have also carried out an extensive programme of aerial reconnaissance in the North-east; I B M Ralston for making aerial photographs available; Bob Henry for access to a database of early medieval place-names; N Curtis of Marischal College Museum, and T Cowie and A Sheridan of the National Museum of Antiquities, for their assistance in collating records of artefacts found in the area; and last, but by no means least, former Commissioners Professors John Coles and Rosemary Cramp, for their enthusiasm and interest.

The Royal Commission also wishes to acknowledge the generous grant by the Strathmartine Trust to assist the publication of this volume.

Map and Plan Conventions

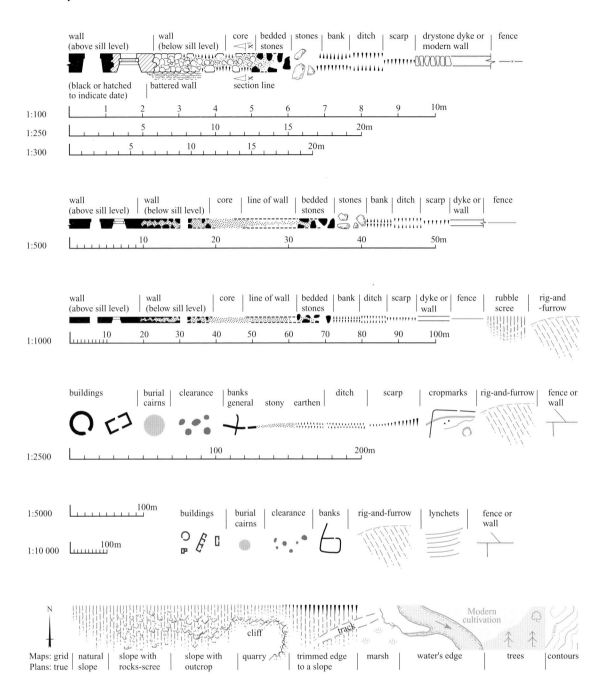

1:100   1   2   3   4   5   6   7   8   9   10m

1:250   5   10   15   20m

1:300   5   10   15   20m

Editorial Notes

The area that has been surveyed (Fig. 1.1) covers the whole of Donside but, for various operational reasons, it also embraces several neighbouring areas; these include the upper end of Strathbogie, the lowlands north of Aberdeen to the mouth of the River Ythan, the mouth of the River Dee and a small area on the north-west flank of the Howe of Cromar in Deeside. For the sake of clarity, this extended area is referred to as Donside in the text and, unless stated otherwise, general comments about the monuments of Donside refer to the whole area.

Site Names

All sites and monuments highlighted in bold in the text lie within this area of 'greater' Donside. They also appear in the index, where they are supplied with the record number (e.g. NJ62NE 1) in the national database, CANMORE, and the name of the parish within which they lie. The parish name serves as a general guide to the location of the monument within Donside, as does the OS 1:10,000 quarter sheet map reference that forms the root of the CANMORE number (e.g. NJ62NE); the parishes and the National Grid are shown on pp. 2–3, Fig. 1.1. The reader requiring more detailed information about the location of a monument can visit the RCAHMS public search room or interrogate CANMORE online at www.rcahms.gov.uk, where the National Grid Reference will be found, together with descriptive information, references and details of any archive material held in the RCAHMS collection. The archive includes numerous photographs, increasing numbers of which are available online. Archive items can be inspected in the RCAHMS public search room, which is open Monday to Friday from 9.30am to 4.30pm.

Monuments outside the area surveyed that are referred to in the text are cited in ordinary type. These too appear in the index, followed by the name of the administrative region within which they lie (e.g. Perth & Kinross) and the CANMORE record number.

Most of the visible sites and monuments are in private ownership, and the prospective visitor should seek permission for access locally. Great care is essential when visiting archaeological and historical monuments.

Bibliographical References

Harvard-style short titles are used throughout the text and are expanded in the full bibliography at the end of the volume. The main body of the text contains only those references that are relevant to the specific points under discussion; general references to individual sites will be found in the CANMORE record online. For journals cited in the bibliography, the volume number is highlighted in bold.

Index

The page references contained within the index will allow the reader to find named sites in the text, but the principal function of the index in the structure of the volume is to guide the reader to records in CANMORE on the RCAHMS website, which also provides access through PASTMAP to other sources of information held by Historic Scotland and local sites and monuments records. A general guide to the subjects covered in the volume is provided by the chapter subheadings, which are set out in the Contents.

Illustrations

All illustrations are treated as Figures and are presented as sub-numbers of the chapter in which they occur; for example, Fig. 6.3 refers to Figure 3 in Chapter 6, the Later Prehistoric Landscape.

The captions to the Figures include site names and National Grid References as appropriate; on composite pages of plans these appear adjacent to the relevant monument. A code number at the end of each caption (e.g. GV000185; SC872650; or DP011672) identifies the digital file for RCAHMS illustrations held in the archive and should be cited if the illustration is required for reproduction.

The introduction includes a map showing the principal settlements, roads and modern parishes at a scale of 1:250,000, and is provided to aid readers to understand the modern geography of the district. The distribution maps are presented at two scales, the larger simply showing the area of Donside (1:570,000), the smaller the whole of north-east Scotland (1:1,000,000). The density of the symbols on many of the maps has rendered it impractical to identify individual monuments cited in the text on the maps. Several other location maps and landscape plans are presented. All are aligned to Grid North, and the National Grid is marked along the margin. All maps are based on information derived from the Ordnance Survey and are reproduced by permission of Ordnance Survey on behalf of HMSO: Ordnance Survey Licence Number 100025406.

The plans in the volume are derived from three sources: surviving earthworks have been surveyed in the field by EDM, GPS or plane table with self-reducing microptic alidade; cropmark sites have been transcribed from oblique aerial photographs using computer-aided rectification techniques; and others have been taken from archive sources. Each plan is provided with a north point aligned on True North; where possible this points towards the top of the page. A legend to the conventions and scales used in the drawn illustration precedes these notes. The scale of reproduction is quoted as a representative fraction.

Copyright

Unless otherwise specified, the contents of this volume are Crown Copyright; copies of Royal Commission photographs and drawings (individually identifiable by reference to the figure-caption; see above) can be purchased on application to:

The Secretary
Royal Commission on the Ancient
and Historical Monuments of Scotland
John Sinclair House
16 Bernard Terrace
Edinburgh EH8 9NX
tel 0131 662 1456
fax 0131 662 1477
info@rcahms.gov.uk

The Royal Commission is grateful to: Aberdeen Archaeological Services for permission to reproduce Figures 1.5, 3.1, 5.7, 5.22, 6.19, 6.21, 6.22, 7.8 and 9.12; Historic Scotland for Figs 8.22 and 8.24; Sir Archibald Grant for Figs 8.65 and 8.68; the National Library of Scotland for Figs 8.8 and 8.54; the National Museums of Scotland for Figs 5.10 and 5.12; the National Trust for Scotland for Figs 8.55, 8.69, 8.70 and 9.2; and finally the University of Aberdeen for Figs 3.9, 5.13, and 5.45.

All maps are reproduced by permission of Ordnance Survey on behalf of HMSO. © Crown Copyright 2007. All rights reserved. Ordnance Survey Licence Number 100025406.

Further Information

Information about all Scotland's archaeological, architectural and maritime heritage can be found in CANMORE, the national database, and can be consulted at www.rcahms.gov.uk.

The public search room is open Monday to Friday from 9.30am to 4.30pm.

Chapter 1: Introduction

The River Don drains a huge tract of country, extending from the fringes of the Cairngorms down to the sea at Aberdeen, and along its way passing from heather-clad hills and mountains down through rolling farmland. Within its compass lies the heart of Aberdeenshire, which was traditionally one of three counties held to make up the North-east of Scotland, with Banffshire lying to the north-west and Kincardineshire to the south. In a later incarnation, as Grampian Region, Moray was also included and, with the most recent reorganisation of local government, it is shaped by the councils of Moray, Aberdeenshire, and the newly created City of Aberdeen. Within their stewardship falls about a tenth of the total landmass of Scotland, with distinct natural boundaries and a strong sense of identity and individuality. To the north lies the Moray Firth, to the east the grey North Sea shore, while to the south and west an imposing mountain barrier – the Grampian Mountains – cuts off the corner to define a triangle of open rolling country sweeping out of the highland glens up onto the Buchan plain.

The Mounth, as the southern arm of the Grampians is known, has always barred the way from Perthshire and Angus, the easiest roads lying out towards the coast. This was the route the Roman army took, its line of march into the Don marked by camps at Raedykes, **Normandykes**, **Kintore** and **Logie Durno** (p. 113), the latter in the shadow of the distinctive silhouette of the Mither Tap o' Bennachie (518m OD). More direct routes traverse the mountains through passes from the Angus Glens or over the Cairn o' Mount above Fettercairn in the Mearns, but these cross much more difficult terrain, and in most cases are only passable on foot today. Hemmed in by this mountain rampart, small wonder that the prosperity of Aberdeen, the *'granite city'*, sitting astride the mouth of the Don and its southern neighbour the Dee, has been intimately bound up with maritime trade.

The Don is only one of a number of rivers draining this triangle of land behind the Mounth, but the landscape along its course has all the essential character of the North-east, forming the middle ground between the rugged glens of Deeside and the sluggish meanders of the Ythan. While the Dee retains the sense of a mountain glen almost to the sea, the Don quickly debouches into more open country, with improved farmland extending inland well into the hill ground above Kildrummy, some 50km from the sea. This land is patently rich and fertile as we see it today, the contrast with the Dee cast in a popular rhyme dating from at least the 19th century – *'a mile of Don's worth two of Dee, except for salmon, stone and tree'*.

The landscape itself is particularly ancient and the underlying topography of mountains, hills and basins is inherited from long before the last glaciation. Nevertheless, the imprint of its glacial history is all too evident and, while the Dee was deeply scoured by the principal flow of ice, the lowlands of the Don are choked with thick deposits of glacial till. These underpin the area's wealth, for they are mineral rich, giving rise to the fertile, if stony, soils.

Fertility and stones are twin themes in the history of this landscape. On the one hand settlement has evidently flourished along the banks of the Don, but on the other it has been hard won. The earliest traces of agriculture visible in the landscape are simple heaps of stones, and the same people who cleared them from their fields also set up standing stones and stone circles (p. 68), and piled up large cairns to commemorate their dead (p. 48). The massive later forts that command the skylines are also largely built of stones, in some cases so fused and melted in catastrophic fires that early antiquaries mistook them for volcanoes (p. 96). The Picts too have left their mark, erecting stone pillars carved with symbols and crosses (p. 116), most of them standing on these same rich soils in the heart of Aberdeenshire.

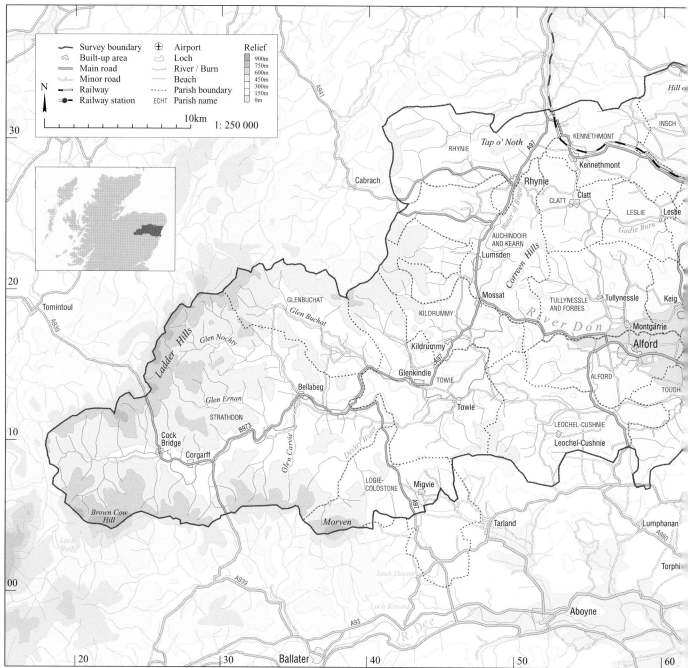

Fig. 1.1 Map of Donside and the area surveyed. GV000102

Likewise in the medieval period, this relationship with the land is perpetuated in the pattern of castles (p. 150), churches (p. 164), villages and farms (p. 183). More recent still, the very framework of the modern landscape is built of stones, most spectacularly with the massive consumption dykes of stones carted from the land around Kingswells, west of Aberdeen, during the agricultural improvements of late 18th and early 19th centuries.

The soils are perhaps not the richest to be found in Scotland, but they are largely freely draining, and the ground is capable of producing a moderate range of arable crops with high yields. The controlling factors are essentially climatic, depending on temperature, exposure and rainfall. The barrier created by the Grampian Mountains affords some degree of shelter from the high rainfall associated with the moist south-westerly winds that sweep across Scotland from the Atlantic. In the shadow of these mountains, rainfall tends to decrease towards the North Sea coast, but with more than half of the annual rainfall coming in the last six months of the year, the dry spells of early spring that promote germination and quick growth are counterbalanced by wet weather come autumn, often delaying the harvest relative to adjacent areas of Scotland by a matter of weeks. The coastal lowlands are also shielded from prolonged periods of frost by the ameliorating influence

of the North Sea, but in spring and early summer, easterly winds often bring the haar (sea fog) in from the sea, drifting inland and penetrating up the valley floor. Further inland, cold air collects in the basins, creating frost pockets that also conspire to inhibit the growing season.

Cereals are grown throughout the lower valley of the Don, as well as in the broad open basins around Insch, Kildrummy, Alford and upper Strathbogie – the basin around Insch, or the Garioch as it is known, is reputed to be the *'meal girnal of Aberdeenshire'*. With increasing altitude and exposure, however, farming enterprises have concentrated on raising beef cattle, though in the upper glens, under still more extreme conditions, the

options are reduced to rough grazing for sheep, shooting and forestry. Here the moors are regularly burnt over, the traditional method of managing heather for sheep and grouse.

While the greater part of the landscape is given over to agriculture, some of the higher ground is heavily forested with commercial plantations of coniferous woodland. On the north-east-facing slopes of Glenbuchat, for instance, or on what was the Candacraig estate, planting has been carried up to a height of 500m OD. Most of the land that has been planted here was rough pasture, but along the Kirkney Water, to the north-west of Rhynie in Clashindarroch Forest, at least half the ground had been improved by the 19th

Fig. 1.2 An oblique aerial view of the River Don as it flows through farmland and forestry around the foot of Bennachie. SC872650

century. Other coniferous plantations clothe the flanks of outlying hills along the middle reaches of the Don, but in this lower ground mixed plantations of hardwoods can also be found. These were laid out during 18th and 19th centuries by landowners such as Sir Archibald Grant of Monymusk (p. 219), a distinguished pioneer of agricultural reform in Scotland, who initiated a major tree-planting programme on his estate from as early as 1719 and is credited with planting some 50 million trees in under fifty years. His legacy is still visible in and around Monymusk, and the older trees on the south bank of the Don in Paradise Wood (NJ 675 184) are testimony to his foresight and vision.

The survey is principally concerned with the evolution of this rural landscape and its archaeology, but no volume on Donside would be complete without at least some comment about Aberdeen itself, for the city is unquestionably a key component of the landscape of the North-east. That is not to suggest that the urban origins of the city can be traced back into prehistory in any meaningful sense, but certainly over the last millennium the twin settlements of Old and New Aberdeen have been important foci of activity (see Dennison et al. 2002). Through the greater part of that time the two towns maintained distinct identities. New Aberdeen, at the mouth of the Dee, probably achieved burghal status in the reign of David I (1124–53), but before that it was evidently a trading centre, and was certainly in a position to dominate northern sea trade.

Fig. 1.3 An oblique aerial view looking inland from the mouth of the River Don. SC872641

On record in 1151 as the *'market town that is called Apardjon'* it was attacked and plundered by Eystein of Norway (Anderson 1922, ii, 216), and its role in royal government is underlined in 1154, when Swein Asleifsson stayed there for a month as a guest of Malcolm IV (Anderson 1922, ii, 236, n. 4). The complex street plan that had developed by the 14th century is redolent of its prosperity, and by the late Middle Ages it was one of the four wealthiest burghs in Scotland. Old Aberdeen, at the mouth of the Don, traditionally originated as an early medieval ecclesiastical centre and, in the 12th century, it became the episcopal seat of the diocese of Aberdeen. The town essentially straggled out southwards from St Machar's Cathedral along a single street leading to New Aberdeen, and was not to become a burgh until 1489.

The lands of New Aberdeen, known as the Freedom Lands, expanded in a series of stages, eventually extending well inland from the coast (p. 142). In 1313 the hunting reserve of Stocket Forest was granted to the burgh by Robert I (1306–29), while the lands of Rubislaw were purchased in 1379, and Cruives (modern Woodside) in 1459. By at least 1525 the marches of the Freedom Lands were marked by stones (Cruickshank and Gunn 1929, 6). Typically the surviving examples are low boulders about 1m across, the upper surface of which bears a single cup-shaped depression between 100mm and 150mm in diameter by at least 30mm in depth.

*Fig. 1.4 **Westfield Farm** (NJ 8520 0342). One of the markers of the Freedom Lands. The earliest of the markers were simply boulders bearing a single large cup-shaped depression. SC873287*

There is no space here to detail the surviving medieval buildings and monuments of Aberdeen (see RCAHMS 1997b; Brogden 1998) but, by the mid- to late 18th century the townscape was being reshaped. This was initiated with Marischal Street, built in 1766–73 to provide direct access down to the harbour, which itself underwent a series of improvements from 1788 onwards. The key to the expansion of Aberdeen, however, was the improved links to its hinterland brought about by the new turnpike roads. This led the County Road Trustees to propose a new street layout and, from 1800, the city was transformed, beginning with the construction of Union Street, which was carried on arched viaducts across the burns and gullies that had constrained earlier developments. Other changes were to follow, creating the basic framework of the city as it is today. The expansion of industry in the first half of the 19th century, and particularly textiles, which employed some 12,000 people at its peak in the 1840s, also demanded a massive expansion of housing in the city.

With the collapse of the textile industry in the mid-19th century, a more balanced economy emerged, drawing on the resources that lay in its improved hinterland, amongst them cattle and granite. These were exported through the port in considerable quantities, and in general sea-borne trade continued to increase throughout the 19th century. The port was also host to

a ship-building industry and, from the 1880s, a huge fishing fleet. Granite production steadily increased, but this was not simply to sustain the export market, for the city continued to expand until the turn of the century. This use of granite has given Aberdeen an unique character, for it has not only been employed in the creation of public monuments, but in the façades of so much of its housing.

In the chapters that follow various aspects of the history of the landscape in the hinterland of Aberdeen are explored, beginning with the factors that have shaped its archaeological record – patterns of survival, destruction and discovery, and the development of antiquarian thought in Aberdeen. Sections dealing with the prehistoric and medieval landscape follow, prefaced by an overview of the palaeoenvironmental evidence. The human veneer that frames the Don today may have been created in the last 200 years or so, but a significant part of its character is of much greater antiquity, embedded in a spectacular set of distinctly north-eastern monuments.

*Fig. 1.5 **Rubislaw Quarry** (NJ 911 054). Much of the stone used in the construction of the 'Granite City' came from the gaping chasm of Rubislaw Quarry, which lies in the western suburbs of Aberdeen. Though it closed in the 1970s, the quarry is said to have produced some six million tonnes of granite over its 230 years of operation. © AAS 97–11–CT20*

Chapter 2: The Antiquarian Tradition

Adam Welfare

There is little to suggest that the field monuments of Donside kindled any curiosity before the 16th century, yet Aberdeen is an important seat of learning, and it has played a significant part in the evolution of historical and archaeological studies. During the second half of the 14th century, John Fordun, a chaplain of the cathedral, attempted the first major synthesis of Scottish history, the *Chronica Gentis Scottorum* (Skene 1871–2), while in 1527 Hector Boece, the first Principal of Aberdeen University, published the first history of Scotland constructed upon renaissance principals (Royan 1999).

In writing his history, the *Scottorum Historia,* it was sometimes necessary for Boece to draw on his own local knowledge. Thus he enlisted folklore and classical sources to explain the recumbent stone circles, stating that *'ye gretest stane suld be erectit towart ye south, to be usit for ane altare',* and that *'Apoun ye samyn to immortall goddis suld hoistis be offerit and sacrifice be brynt* (Watson 1946). This religious imagery proved tenacious, for when Dr James Garden, Professor of Theology at King's College, Aberdeen, wrote to John Aubrey, more than a hundred and fifty years later, he reiterated that the recumbent *'was called by the vulgar the altar stone'* (Garden 1770, 315).

Boece's history relied for much of its credibility on narrative flow, but the serious study of antiquities depended on a historiographical methodology that was more rigorously founded upon accuracy, authenticity and authority. This more demanding approach was initially stimulated by the desire to understand the worlds described by Greek and Roman historians, but it was also encouraged in the opening years of the 15th century by the circulation of Latin versions of Ptolemy's *Geographia*. This embraced a wealth of names and geographical co-ordinates, although it was not perhaps until the appearance of the fine copperplate maps prepared by Gerardus Mercator (1578) and Abraham Ortelius (1590) that the nascent discipline began to inspire a new breed of British antiquary.

This was the climate in which William Camden produced the *Britannia*, a topographical study of the British Isles that was first published in 1586. His study was divided into two parts: a historical section constructed mainly from literary accounts that detailed the successive invasions of Britain; and a topographical section modelled largely upon the ancient Ptolemaic geography. And it is this that discloses the key aspiration of the work – to recover and investigate the topography of Roman Britain. The earlier part included sections on the Britons, the Picts, and the Scots, but Camden was at some disadvantage in writing about Scotland, as he had never travelled north of the border. Indeed, his knowledge of Aberdeenshire was so poor that even as late as 1607, the only place of historical interest that he could cite was **Kildrummy Castle**. Nevertheless, the *Britannia* succeeded in nourishing interest in Scottish antiquities, and, as the 17th century progressed, a network of correspondents continued to contribute to successive editions of the work.

That such correspondence could have a far-reaching impact upon antiquarian studies is illustrated by the nine letters that passed between James Garden, Professor of Theology at King's College, Aberdeen and John Aubrey, the Wiltshire antiquary, towards the end of the 17th century (Hunter 2001). Aubrey's queries embraced many aspects of Scottish folklore, but he was especially concerned to establish his hypothesis that stone circles were the temples of the druids and so looked to Garden for both evidence and support (Hunter 1975, 182–3). Despite the contradictions that seemed to be apparent in the Aberdeenshire evidence, Garden did all in his power to accommodate Aubrey's wishes, not only by making a special visit to a number of stone circles in the neighbourhood of Aberdeen, but also through soliciting his own acquaintances for information (Gordon 1960).

Aubrey evidently placed great value upon this correspondence, circulating copies amongst his friends and transcribing extensive extracts into the manuscript of his *Monumenta Britannica* (Aubrey 1980, 170–220; Hunter 2001, 24). However, it was only following the appearance of his theory in a new edition of the *Britannia* (Camden 1695) that the supposed link between stone circles and the Druids was broadcast more widely. This link, which has maintained its hold on popular imagination to this day, can be traced back directly to Aubrey (Hunter 2001, 22–3), yet Garden must shoulder some of the blame, for even then he had recognised the flaws in his friend's argument.

Gibson's edition of the *Britannia* made extensive use of correspondents, and Sir Robert Sibbald, Cartographer Royal for Scotland, was placed in charge of the revision of the Scottish material. Yet the section on the antiquities of Aberdeenshire is very disappointing, for in two short paragraphs it does little more than paraphrase a piece by the cartographer Sir Robert Gordon of Straloch that had first appeared in the 1662 edition of Blaeu's atlas. Sibbald was to make a more significant contribution to the development of Roman studies in Scotland, an area of interest pursued by a younger contemporary from Aberdeen, Alexander Gordon, who was also a graduate of the university. Gordon's best-known work, *Iter Septentrionale*, is largely devoted to Roman Scotland (Gordon 1726; Wilson and Laing 1874), but the second part deals with the *'Danish'* invasions of Scotland, relying heavily on George Buchanan for its historical narrative. Like Boece before him, Buchanan correlated Pictish stones depicting figures (i.e. Class II stones) with the graves of Danes slain by Scots in battles, but Gordon broke new ground and provided a series of comparative illustrations, amongst them the **Maiden Stone**.

As the 18th century progressed, so references to antiquities in Donside become more common, often noted in passing by travellers en route for Aberdeen. Thus William Maitland inspected the henge and megalithic monuments standing at **Broomend of Crichie** (Maitland 1757, 154), while in 1760 Richard Pococke made a special excursion to visit the vitrified fort on **Tap o' Noth** (Kemp 1887, 201). Vitrifaction was also noted at **Dunnideer** by the economist James Anderson of Monkshill, who published a fine plan of the fort and a figure illustrating the burnt rampart (Anderson 1782). His careful analysis of the chronological relationship between the fort and the medieval tower within its interior is still impressive, and his discussion is notably free of the highly coloured language that increasingly romanticised such ruins at the expense of their historicity. This same freedom from fancy also characterises his discussion of recumbent

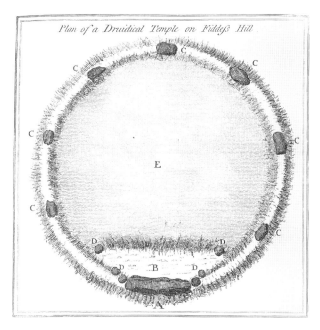

Fig. 2.1 **Hill of Fiddes** (NJ 9350 2432). When James Anderson prepared this plan and a description of the recumbent stone circle on the Hill of Fiddes it was 'very intire'. Anderson identified a raised platform behind the recumbent as a stage upon which the priest officiated, 'the large stone supplying the place of the altar' – this model continued to influence interpretations into the early 20th century. SC898654

stone circles in another influential paper that included an invaluable plan of the circle on the **Hill of Fiddes** (Fig. 2.1; Anderson 1779).

Anderson's conception of these *'temples'* is realised in a vignette on the title page of Charles Cordiner's *Antiquities and Scenery of the North of Scotland* (1780). Cordiner had made a series of sketching tours through Aberdeenshire, but in his opinion stone circles yielded *'small recompense for encountering the rough ways that lead to them'*. Although he refers to the example at **Dunnideer**, he found the vitrifaction on **Tap o' Noth** more stimulating, and was fascinated by the souterrains in the vicinity of the *'noble ruin'* of **Kildrummy Castle**. His real enthusiasm, however, was reserved for the mysterious symbol stones, which continued to excite his imagination for the rest of his life, leading to his second major work, the posthumous *Remarkable Ruins, and Romantic Prospects, of North Britain* (Fig. 2.2; 1795).

Both Cordiner and Anderson were early Corresponding Members of the Society of Antiquaries of Scotland, which was formed in 1780 under the aegis of the 11th Earl of Buchan (Smellie 1782; Smellie 1792; Bell 1981). This institution was destined to become the most important channel of Scottish antiquarian enquiry. In his opening address, Buchan had stressed that the Society of Antiquaries should encourage the investigation of Scotland's *'natural history'* parish by parish. Such a project was essentially statistical rather than historical, and it was eventually brought to fruition through the energy of Sir John Sinclair, who edited the results and published them in the *Statistical Account of*

*Fig. 2.2 **The Maiden Stone** (NJ /03/ 24/1). The puzzling 'hieroglyphics' of Pictish sculpture became an abiding interest of Charles Cordiner and this fine copperplate engraving published in 1795 is an elegant example of his artistry. SC871658*

Scotland (1791–9). The sections devoted to antiquities in this remarkable work are of variable quality, but they have the merit of providing the first source of information on field-monuments and stray finds that covers the whole country.

The quickening tempo in antiquarian studies during the last quarter of the 18th century is epitomised by the publication of yet another edition of Camden's *Britannia* (Gough 1789) and William Roy's research on the Roman military field monuments of Scotland (Roy 1793). Both initiated an upsurge of interest in the recovery of further evidence relating to the Roman advance into Scotland, and in 1801 led Colonel Alexander Shand to recognise the true character of the Roman temporary camp at **Normandykes** (Stuart 1868).

Some indication of the excitement resulting from this discovery at **Normandykes** can be gauged from the fact that a plan of the camp by Captain Patrick Henderson of the 29th Regiment of Foot appears in the first volume of George Chalmers' *Caledonia* (Fig. 2.3; Chalmers 1807). Chalmers had a particular interest in Aberdeenshire,

having been educated at King's College, and it is something of a loss that the section devoted to the county is plainly incomplete. Like the *Britannia,* which provided much of the inspiration behind the *Caledonia,* its contents depended on an extensive network of correspondents, one of whom was presumably responsible for supplying the fine illustration depicting the plan and profile of the fort on **Barra Hill**.

Another of Chalmers' correspondents was John Stuart of Inchbreck, sometime Professor of Greek at Aberdeen University. Stuart placed great emphasis upon field remains, believing them to be *'the surest foundation for establishing any opinion in regard to the early inhabitants of Scotland'*. He had helped with the survey of **Normandykes** (Stuart 1822b), and had discovered a dense scatter of hut-circles north of the Dee nearby (Stuart 1822a). He also published a new description of the souterrains in the Kildrummy area to correct errors in earlier reports. However, the theme that linked all his writings was his concern with the wanton destruction of antiquities without record (Stuart 1846). At a time when few in Scotland understood the value of field archaeology, his was the solitary voice that urged the Society of Antiquaries to employ a small team to record antiquities as a means of preserving history.

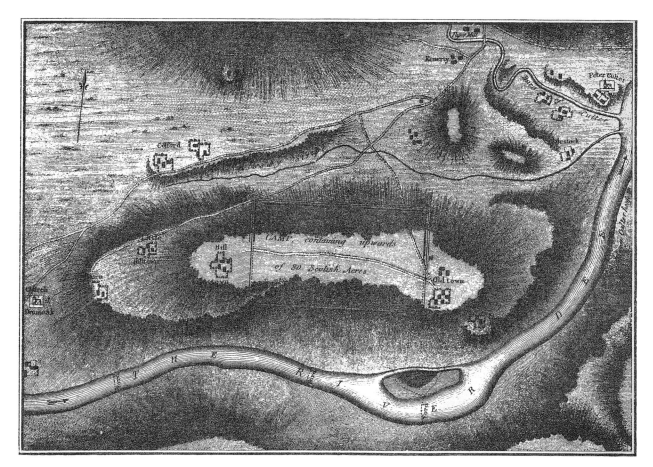

*Fig. 2.3 **Normandykes** (NO 8297 9938). The military character of Normandykes was recognised by the Reverend George Mark by 1795, but it was not identified as Roman until Henderson's excellent survey of 1801. SC898729*

Stuart also wrote a paper on symbol stones that is notable for its good sense and restraint, especially in comparison to Cordiner's more esoteric explanations (Stuart 1822c). He illustrated it with engravings of several examples from Donside, including the **Maiden Stone** and those at **Newton House**, **Dyce** and **Kinellar**. Although he followed his friend, John Pinkerton, in stressing the need for a corpus of the stones, if only to preserve a record of them, it is curious that he offers no comment on Pinkerton's inspired, yet lucid argument correlating the symbol stones with the *'Pikish'* (Pictish) people (Pinkerton 1814).

The destruction of antiquities was a concern that Stuart shared with James Skene of Rubislaw. It was this that impelled Skene to visit the fort on the **Barmekin of Echt** shortly after it had been planted with trees (Fig. 2.4; Skene 1822), and his sketch book shows that he was also collecting a corpus of drawings of Pictish stones in response to Stuart's plea (RCAHMS ABD 501). Within its pages are the sketches of the **Maiden Stone** and the symbol stones from **Dyce** and **Kinellar** that illustrated Stuart's paper, but he also recorded a series of other monuments. Those within Donside include the recumbent stone circles of **Wester Echt**, **Balquhain**, **Dunnideer**, **Hatton of Ardoyne**,

Stonehead and probably **Sunhoney**, the now destroyed cairn on the summit of **Calton Hill**, and **Luath's Stone**, most of which were to remain unpublished.

Skene's interest in sketching was shared by his Aberdonian compatriot, James Logan, who began to investigate the antiquities of his native county during a convalescence following illness. Although much of his manuscript material is now lost, many of his earlier efforts were devoted to *'Druidical Circles'*, providing descriptions, views and plans of the stone circle at **Cullerlie** and the recumbent stone circle of **Tyrebagger** in one paper (1829a, 409–11), and **Old Keig**, **Balquhain**, **Castle Fraser** ('Balgorkar') and **Sunhoney** in another (1829b).

Logan is now best remembered for *The Scottish Gael,* his miscellany of Highland traditions and customs (Logan 1831a). The cultural acquisitiveness that permeates this synthesis, however, had its genesis in his early antiquarian wanderings in Aberdeenshire, when he was content to record faithfully with pen and watercolour all that struck him as curious. The results are best represented in Basire's fine engravings that accompany his paper on the symbol stones (Logan 1829c).

Further gleanings from his Aberdeenshire rambles were published by the Society of Antiquaries of Scotland during his lifetime (Logan 1831b), but others were only issued posthumously by the Third Spalding Club in a volume largely devoted to ecclesiastical remains (Cruickshank 1941). Until this period, little attention had

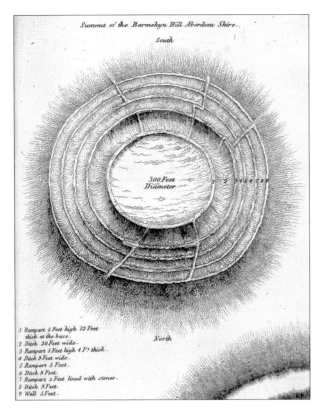

*Fig. 2.4 **Barmekin of Echt** (NJ 7260 0714). This drawing by Skene accompanied his published description of the earthworks, which he prepared in the belief that they would be lost to forestry. SC898701*

been paid to this subject, although standing buildings such as St Machar's Cathedral, King's College Chapel, the Church of St Nicholas, Grey Friars and Bishop Dunbar's Hospital had attracted notice previously. Logan's great strength was his inclination to record the fabric and architectural detail from even the most humble and ruinous of chapels, together with medieval or post-medieval grave monuments, coats of arms and church furniture. Moreover, an antiquarian's taste for gothic romanticism is apparent in a delightful colour-wash in his sketch-book of the façade dignifying the Elphinstone burial-enclosure at **Logie Durno** (Fig. 2.5).

The huge changes that were taking place in the landscape at this time were greatly influenced by the publications of agricultural societies (p. 225), and there is little doubt that a wider appetite for knowledge and information was developing. This appetite underwrote the success of the *New Statistical Account,* the Aberdeenshire volume of which was published in 1845, and is mirrored in the success of the contemporary Scottish publishing societies, such as the Roxburghe and Bannatyne Clubs, which were largely devoted to editing and printing important historical manuscripts. And what these accomplished at the national level, the Spalding Club emulated for the North-east. Named after the 17th-century Aberdonian historian John Spalding, the club was founded at Aberdeen in 1839 by the newspaper editor Joseph Robertson and the advocate John Stuart. Within less than a year the developing interest in

medieval and post-medieval times had swelled the membership of the club to more than 500 (Stuart 1871). Notable contributors included James Giles and Sir Andrew Leith-Hay, who began to compile studies of castles and tower-houses, although only the latter's work was published at the time (Leith-Hay 1849; Giles 1936).

In practice, only one of the Spalding Club's publications in the thirty years of its first manifestation was directly concerned with archaeological sites and monuments. This was John Stuart's own magisterial study of Pictish and Early Christian monuments, *The Sculptured Stones of Scotland* (1856; 1867). From the outset, the study was recognised as a landmark, and the corpus is notable for Stuart's modern handling of the data and his use of comparative analysis as an aid to classification. His interest in their artistic, functional and chronological evolution led him to solicit Charles Dalrymple and Andrew Jervise to oversee a series of excavations at certain standing-stones and stone circles. It fell to Dalrymple to conduct this research north of the River Dee, where, apart from an investigation around the base of the **Picardy Stone**, he seems to have confined his interest to the stone circles. In all he examined at least five recumbent stone circles, namely **Ardlair**, **Castle Fraser**, **Hatton of Ardoyne**, **Old Rayne** and **Sunhoney**, as well as the enclosure on **Tuach Hill** and the henge at **Broomend of Crichie**. As for the symbol stones, Stuart's first volume included a series of newly discovered stones in Donside, namely **Daviot**, **Clatt**, **Drimmies**, **Dyce**, **Keith Hall** and **Kintore**, while **Newbigging** and **Migvie** (Jervise 1864, 306) were added in the second.

This was a period of momentous change in archaeological studies in Scotland. The key event, whose significance cannot be overstated (Ash 1981; Clarke 1981; Ash 1999), was the publication of *The Archaeology and Prehistoric Annals of Scotland* by Daniel Wilson (1851; 1863). This was a national

Fig. 2.5 Dalrymple Horn Elphinstone burial-enclosure, Logie Durno (NJ 70408 2639). This colourwash of 1822 by James Logan was sketched during his wanderings of 1818. Its splendidly gothic character will have appealed to Logan's antiquarian sentiment. SC898677

synthesis, which provided a systematic framework that drew on the Scandinavian Three Age System and was largely independent of earlier antiquarian preconceptions. As such, Wilson's work marks the watershed between the old topographical tradition and the new *'scientific'* archaeology of the late 19th century.

But if these new approaches were to revolutionise contemporary understanding of the past, the mapping of Scotland by the Ordnance Survey was of especial significance in disclosing the fragments of earlier landscapes. The Society of Antiquaries of Scotland had petitioned the government for field monuments to be actively sought and plotted (*Proc Soc Antiq Scot,* 2, 1857, 129–31), but the sheer numbers that the Survey recovered were a revelation. In Donside the most spectacular new discovery was the Roman temporary camp at **Kintore**, which was located by Captain Edward Courtenay roughly a day's march north of **Normandykes**. Unusually, this was the subject of a contemporary paper in the *Proceedings of the Society of Antiquaries of Scotland,* which included a detailed plan (Courtenay 1868).

Although the Ordnance Survey had plotted large numbers of stone circles, these excited little new work before the turn of the century. Indeed, there was a dearth of comparative illustrations of these monuments, which was a problem for anyone interested in them. So much so, Sir Henry Dryden, the noted surveyor of the megaliths at Carnac, Brittany, found it expedient to copy plans as and when they came to hand, such as those of **Cothiemuir Wood** and **Sunhoney** (RCAHMS MS:SAS 39). This lacuna was so well-recognised that his colleague, W C Lukis, later surveyed **Tyrebagger** and **Sunhoney** as part of a short-lived, national project on behalf of the Society of Antiquaries of London (Lukis 1885).

That said, an important series of comparative sketch plans depicting ten recumbent stone circles was published by Christian Maclagan (Maclagan 1875, pls xxvii, xxviii and xxx). Unfortunately the accuracy of these plans is not always as flawless as she claimed, and her theorising interpretations were met with derision amongst her contemporaries. Nevertheless, they form an interesting body of work today, and she also included useful illustrated descriptions of some Aberdonian hillforts, amongst them the **Mither Tap o' Bennachie** and the **Barmekin of Echt**.

Excavation was becoming an increasingly common pursuit in the late 19th century, but the methods that were employed remained crude. Yet by the mid-1860s, Dalrymple and Stuart were aware of the value of stratigraphy in geological studies as a means of establishing a relative chronology. Both witnessed its use in the Sands of Forvie, when they accompanied Thomas Jamieson, the notable quaternary geologist from Ellon, and his colleague, the Reverend Samuel King, in the sectioning of two shell-middens (Dalrymple

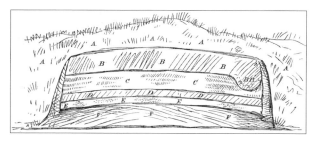

Fig. 2.6 Sands of Forvie (NJ 0115 2563). Charles Dalrymple investigated two mounds in the Sands of Forvie with the quaternary geologist Thomas Jamieson. His sketch of the section, probably under the influence of Jamieson, shows that they understood the relative chronology revealed by the stratigraphy. It was to be many years before the significance of such illustrations became generally accepted by archaeologists. SC898711

1866; B. 1913). The strong influence of the sister discipline can also be detected in the composition of Dalrymple's subsequent report, which is reinforced by two annotated sections (Fig. 2.6). Comparable drawings are few and far between in Donside, the exceptions being the annotated plans, sections and elevations of the stonework of several souterrains, including those at **Buchaam**, **Glenkindie** and **Clova** (Mitchell 1862; Lumsden 1878).

If excavation showed little sign of significant development, increasing emphasis was placed on artefact-based studies throughout the second half of the 19th century. The doyen of these studies was Joseph Anderson, who had been appointed Keeper of the National Museum in 1869 (Graham 1976). However, he did more than simply analyse this material. Taking up the mantle of Sir Daniel Wilson, he used the Rhind Lectures of 1879–82 to reintegrate the artefactual record with the sites and monuments from which so much of it derived. He also took the opportunity to emphasise the importance of accurate drawings to a proper understanding of the past (Anderson 1883, 276).

Anderson's most celebrated work lay in the field of Early Christian antiquities. New discoveries had continued to appear in the survey area, including further additions to the stones from **Rhynie** (Maclagan 1880) and the Pictish silver chain from **Parkhill** (Smith 1874, 330–2). Anderson now recognised the subtle relationships in the designs appearing on the metalwork and the stones, and compared them with those on the Monymusk reliquary (Anderson 1880). He explored the symbol stones under the broad remit of Early Christian art (Anderson 1881b), sharing the same perspective as Romilly Allen, whose precision and attention to detail led to new insights into the relationship between British and Irish art (Allen 1883). Supported by the Society of Antiquaries of Scotland, Allen compiled a new corpus, which Anderson used in 1892 to confirm that the distribution of the symbol stones suggested an origin in Aberdeenshire and, hence, their correlation with the Kingdom of the Picts (Clarke 2002, 14–15). However, Allen's corpus, which included only three new additions from Donside, namely **Clatt**, **Ardlair** and **Brandsbutt**, was far from complete and the study was not finally issued until 1903 (Allen and Anderson 1903).

Allen's comments on the location of the individual stones, and his concern for their care and preservation, are a notable feature of the corpus. A particular worry involved *'ancient monuments being treated as private property'*, which was the case with several stones in Donside. Anderson almost certainly shared these sentiments, and argued passionately that the preservation and protection of all Scotland's monuments was of the utmost national importance when the first Ancient Monuments Act of 1882 was under consideration (Anderson 1881a, 8–12). Allen, however, could only report that the two stones at **Dyce** had been scheduled under the Act, though he must have been aware that those at **Newton House** had also been registered (Chippindale 1983). The wider picture was equally bleak, for up to 1900 **Tap o' Noth** and the **Bass of Inverurie** were the only other monuments in Aberdeenshire that had been accorded statutory protection.

Archaeologists were not the only group to express a concern for conservation and preservation during the latter part of 19th century, for certain architects were equally disturbed by the general ignorance of Scottish architecture and its casual neglect. As in other disciplines, sound historical knowledge of the evolution and development of Scottish architecture depended on the collection and analysis of field data, and its correlation with literary evidence. This was the approach adopted by David MacGibbon and Thomas Ross, who, with the aid of analytical plans and elevations, not only established a classification and chronology for Scottish medieval and post-medieval architecture, but also disclosed its unique character within the European context (MacGibbon and Ross 1887–92; 1896–7). As elsewhere, their studies in Donside embraced the most significant castles, tower-houses and churches.

It was left to others, such as David Christison and Frederick Coles, to identify the earthworks of the earliest Norman castles in Scotland. Christison's contribution to Donside is relatively slight, though it was he who recognised the mottes at the **Doune of Invernochty** and **Keith Hall** (Christison 1898). More importantly, he devoted a whole chapter in his *Early Fortifications in Scotland* to vitrified forts, bringing the results of James Macdonald's excavations at **Tap o' Noth** in 1886 to the attention of a wider audience (Macdonald 1891).

By contrast, Coles became intimately involved in the archaeology of Donside. An Assistant Keeper at the National Museum, he was offered a bursary by the Society of Antiquaries of Scotland to compile a corpus of the stone circles in the neighbourhood of Banchory (Christison 1900, 11–12). Though the area straddled the River Dee, nine of the twenty-three rings he recorded fall within the Donside survey, and the descriptions he composed not only embrace his own observations, but also much oral history (Coles 1900). The recumbent stone circles of **Auld Kirk o' Tough**, **Tomnagorn**, **Midmar Kirk**, **Sunhoney** and **Tyrebagger** were all included, richly illustrated with numerous sketches, sections, and carefully measured plans at a common scale.

Coles' report must have been well received, for the grant was renewed the following year, allowing him to extend the study northwards into the heart of Donside (Coles 1901). In succeeding years he covered the whole of the area, creating an invaluable inventory of the recumbent stone circles, many of which were already sadly dilapidated (Coles 1902). He followed this up with papers on certain standing-stones of the Kintore area (Coles 1903a), and the cupmarked rocks that he had encountered (Coles 1903b). With the completion of the fifth season of survey in Buchan, he offered a provisional assessment of the circles of the North-east, and went on to excavate the recumbent stone circle at Garrol Wood, Kincardine (Coles 1905a). In almost his last remarks upon the circles of Aberdeenshire, Coles stressed their Bronze Age date and sepulchral function, and concluded that there was nothing about their design to justify any astronomical speculations or theories of sacred numbers (Coles 1910). This volley was plainly directed at A L Lewis and Sir Norman Lockyer, the Astronomer Royal. Lockyer was sympathetic to Lewis's ideas about the ritual functions of the circles and the influence of astronomical phenomena (Lewis 1888; 1900), and put them to the test in 1906 at **Easter Aquhorthies**, **Midmar Kirk** and **Sunhoney**. He eventually concluded that up to sixteen of the Donside recumbent stone circles appeared to be *'Star Clocks'* by which the time could be told at night, while three may have divined the solstice and two highlighted May Day (Lockyer 1909; see also p. 66).

Lockyer included a long quotation from a letter he had received from James Ritchie of Port Elphinstone, a Corresponding Member of the Society of Antiquaries who had embarked on a personal project to photograph all the Aberdeenshire stone circles (Fig. 2.7; Ritchie 1927; Ritchie 1998). The results of this work not only accompany his own papers on the subject, but also illustrate the lavish guide to local antiquities that was prepared by Bishop G F Browne for the amusement and instruction of Lord Cowdray's guests at Dunecht House (Browne 1921).

Ritchie's own writings on the stone circles were intended as a supplement to Coles and were largely restricted to describing the lesser-known sites, such as **Potterton** and **Nether Coullie** (Ritchie 1917; 1919). He also reported cupmarks and Pictish symbols that had not been noted on the stones before (Ritchie 1915; 1918). Yet his interests were far wider, and he

*Fig. 2.7 **Midmar Kirk** (NJ 6994 0649). The photographic collection of the prehistoric monuments of North-East Scotland taken by James Ritchie between 1899 and 1922 is one of the most important of its kind. Photography allowed him to combine his scientific and antiquarian interests; and by 1902 he was concentrating on photographing Pictish stones and stone circles. SC679948*

published important papers on a variety of subjects. These included: the antiquities at **Broomend of Crichie** (1920); the folklore of the stone circles (1926); the Pictish stones at **Clatt** and **Newton of Lewesk** (1910; 1916); the sculptured and engraved crosses of the county (1911; 1915; 1916); the structures found within its graveyards (1912; 1921); and whin mills (1925).

Other corresponding members of the Society of Antiquaries of Scotland at this time included F C Eeles of Stonehaven (Scott 1956) and J G Callander, who had been brought up on a farm near Insch (Simpson 1938). Eeles published several prehistoric discoveries, but his real passion was ecclesiastical remains, reflected in his note on the incised medieval grave slab of the two knights at **Foveran**, which had once engaged Logan's interest (Eeles 1909).

Callander was the most prolific of the Society's North-eastern correspondents. He published his first paper on a collection of small finds from the Garioch (1903) and assiduously followed up other discoveries to accumulate a mass of information. His papers report

burials at **Seggiecrook** (1905; 1908), **Pittodrie** (1906), Whitehouse (now **Whitestone**; 1906), **Mains of Leslie** (1907; 1909; 1912), **Mill of Wardes** (1907), **East Law** (1907) and **Newlands of Oyne** (1933), and he commissioned scientific reports on the skeletal material by Dr Alexander Low of Aberdeen University. He also reported other chance finds from Donside as they came to his notice. These include an axe mould from **Hill of Foudland**, Insch (1904), the bronze hoard from **Grassieslack**, Daviot (1907; 1913; 1923) and the stone cups from a cairn on Hill of Skares, near **Woodside Cottage** (1916). To these he added accounts of earlier discoveries, such as the Beaker from **Newhills** and the Iron Age hoard from **Crichie** (1925; 1927). The conscientious approach that informed all his studies enabled him to recognise the unusual character of a sherd of pottery at **Fernybrae** (1907), which eventually found its rightful place alongside fragments from **Den of Craig** (Auchindoir) and **East Finnercy** in his seminal catalogue of Scottish Neolithic pottery (1929).

Some of his discoveries resulted from scouring ploughed fields for artefacts, and included the flint-working sites at **Hill of Skares**, **Broomhill** and **Wraes** (Callander 1917). The surviving monuments did not excite his interest in quite the same way, yet, like Ritchie, he had accompanied Lockyer during the latter's second season of observations at various recumbent stone circles. His reports also include a description of the Neolithic cairn at **Longcairn** (Callander 1925).

At about the time that Callander was first engaging his interest in artefacts, one of his contemporaries in the North-east, Sir Alexander Ogston, was carrying out a remarkable study of the field monuments of the Howe of Cromar in Deeside. This work is unique for the period, focusing on the remains of ancient landscapes preserved on moorland around Loch Kinord (Ogston 1931). Although the present survey only takes in the north-west corner of the Howe of Cromar, these remarkable groups of hut-circles and field-systems provide a glimpse of an unimproved landscape that has largely disappeared from Donside (pp. 79–81).

The son of one of Ogston's neighbours was Alexander Keiller. Keiller is best known for his work in Wiltshire, at Windmill Hill and Avebury (Smith 1965; Murray 1999), but his initial interests were fired by the monuments of the Aberdeenshire landscape, in particular the recumbent stone circles, for which he prepared neatly inked plans, with innovative, carefully measured, unrolled elevations of silhouetted stones. These were never published, though his scathing assessments of the condition into which so many of them had fallen were widely known (Keiller 1927; 1928), and may account for the fact that twenty recumbent stone circles in Donside were scheduled in 1925 under the revised Ancient Monuments Act of 1913.

Interest in the recumbent stone circles also lay behind a flurry of work undertaken in Donside during the 1930s, beginning with the excavation of **Old Keig** by Gordon Childe (1933), the leading prehistorian of his day (Childe 1933; 1934). Soon afterwards, a second opportunity to explore their character and chronology was offered to one of Childe's students, H E Kilbride-Jones, when plans were made by the Ancient Monuments Department of the Commission of Works to restore **Loanhead of Daviot** and the small ring at **Cullerlie** (Kilbride-Jones 1935). Although **Loanhead of Daviot** was dilapidated, it was much better preserved than **Old Keig**, and allowed many of the typical constructional features of these stone circles to be observed for the first time. These excavations were not only of national importance, but were to influence perceptions of Aberdeenshire stone circles until the end of the 20th century.

This interwar period also saw the beginning of a concerted campaign by W Douglas Simpson of the University of Aberdeen to improve the understanding of medieval Aberdeenshire. Since the identification of the **Bass of Inverurie** as a motte by A O Curle (1919), little progress had been made in this field. Starting with the **Doune of Invernochty**, at Strathdon (Simpson 1919), Simpson set out to provide scholarly descriptions accompanied by new plans, sections, sketches and photographs of the major medieval monuments. Thus, his intelligent and imaginative

eye was brought to bear upon a series of castles and tower-houses in Donside, including the vital *caput* of the earldom of Mar, **Kildrummy Castle** (various papers from 1920 to 1944). He also produced important studies on the **Barmekin of Echt**, **Lulach's Stone**, the chapel of St Moluag of Lismore at **Clova**, the priory at **Monymusk**, and the churches at **Auchindoir** and **Essie**.

These, however, were no more than pieces in a larger jigsaw and perhaps his most significant achievement lies with his wider syntheses. *The Province of Mar* traced the history of the area from the Mesolithic to the 13th century AD, carefully integrating new information with earlier interpretations, and even today its later chapters on the conversion to Christianity and the introduction of the feudal milieu retain much of their value (Simpson 1943). *The Earldom of Mar* followed, dealing with the origin and development of the medieval earldom, before continuing the story up to the mid-18th century (Simpson 1949).

Simpson's contribution to the historiography of the North-east was not restricted to his own studies, for he was also one of the moving forces behind the third incarnation of the Spalding Club. Its immediate progenitor, the New Spalding Club (1886–1926), had largely restricted its output to scholarly texts, but under Simpson's editorship the Third Spalding Club issued a string of more topographically based works. These included Ogston's *Prehistoric Antiquities of the Howe of Cromar* (1931), Logan's *Collections* (Cruickshank 1941), Giles' *Drawings of Aberdeenshire Castles* (1936), Barclay's *Book of Glenbuchat* (Simpson 1942b) and Diack's *Inscriptions of Pictland* (1944); and by the time the third series was brought to a close in 1960, the list also included Alexander's *Place-Names of Aberdeenshire* (1952), together with Simpson's own account of **Castle Fraser** (1960) and Gordon's text and commentary on Garden's correspondence with Aubrey (1960).

Most archaeological fieldwork came to a halt with the outbreak of war in 1939, though Gordon Childe and Angus Graham managed to visit almost forty sites in Donside in the space of a fortnight in 1943 for the *'Emergency War Survey'*. Since then survey in the area has been fairly limited. In the 1950s RCAHMS visited and planned several of the forts for the survey of Marginal Lands (RCAHMS 1956, xxvi; *DES 1957*, 39), but the triple palisade on the summit of the **Hill of Christ's Kirk**, recorded as an unfinished fort, was the only new discovery (RCAHMS 1963, xxv). Revision survey by the Archaeology Division of the Ordnance Survey covered Donside in the course of the 1960s, but this too was mainly concerned with consolidating existing knowledge. A small number of excavations during this period can be traced through *Discovery and Excavation in Scotland,* but, sad to say, few have been fully published. Notable are the ring-cairn and round-houses in the **Sands of Forvie** (Kirk 1954), and the work associated with the conservation of **Kildrummy Castle** (Apted 1963).

For a long time the chief source of new information on this landscape has been provided by aerial photography. The first recorded flight was by the Master of Semple, who at the behest of Childe examined the area around **Old Keig** (Childe 1934, 386). O G S Crawford, the head of the Ordnance Survey's Archaeology Division, had also flown as far north as Aberdeen in 1939 (Crawford 1939), but regular flights did not take place until 1948, when the Cambridge University Committee for Aerial Photography assumed sponsorship of the work of J K St Joseph. Their chief purpose, like so many of the antiquaries before them, was to trace the progress of Roman arms north of the Forth, a subject that Crawford had addressed for the Society of Antiquaries of Scotland in 1943 (Crawford 1949). In 1976 RCAHMS initiated a wide-ranging reconnaissance programme with funding from the Rescue Budget of the Inspectorate of Ancient Monuments. Since then, however, most of this important work north of the Mounth has been carried out by

archaeologists based in Aberdeen, firstly Ian Shepherd and Ian Ralston, and more recently Moira Greig. The results of this work have dramatically altered perceptions of the archaeological record throughout the North-east and are graphically displayed by the photographs published in *Grampian's Past* (Shepherd and Greig 1996).

The 1970s also saw the beginnings of important changes in the structure of archaeological activity, and in 1975, the newly formed Grampian Council established an Archaeological Service under Ian Shepherd, who became the first regional archaeologist to be appointed in Scotland. At its heart lay a regional Sites and Monuments Record, which has continued to play an important role at the centre of the planning process of the more recently established Aberdeenshire Council. Apart from creating measured responses to projected developments, it maintains an active archaeological presence throughout the region, encouraging researchers and the public alike to explore the extraordinary wealth of evidence that is to be found in the North-east.

Chapter 3: Survival, Destruction and Discovery

Angela Gannon

Relatively few monuments identifiable in the countryside today appear in any published sources before the end of the 18th century. At that date the parish entries for the *Statistical Account* were prepared, followed in the 1840s by the *New Statistical Account,* providing the first systematic overviews of what were then considered antiquities. In many cases, however, the locations of the monuments are lost, and it is not until the 1860s and 1870s, and the completion of the detailed mapping programme of the Ordnance Survey, that any of them are recorded in their correct geographical and topographical positions. Taken together, these are the primary sources from which the archaeological record has been drawn, firstly by the Ordnance Survey in the revision of the maps from the 1950s to the early 1980s, and subsequently by the National Monuments Record of Scotland and the Sites and Monuments Record of Aberdeenshire Council.

The diversity of these sources, accumulated over a period of some 200 years, poses many problems. At face value they provide a remarkably rich record of the past, not only of monuments that are still impressive, but also of sites where nothing is now visible, or where artefacts, often now lost, first came to light. Yet these discoveries and records must be set against a process of continual change and evolution that has transformed the Aberdeenshire landscape (pp. 215–26). Today, it is almost impossible to find anywhere that has not been altered by human hands. From any local vantage point, such as the **Barmekin of Echt**, the **Mither Tap o' Bennachie**, **Dunnideer** or **Tap o' Noth**, man's impact is starkly visible, stretching away in the panorama of fields, farms and villages. This is a relatively modern landscape, a product of agricultural improvements that brought about sweeping changes in the countryside from the late 18th century onwards. Large areas of ground were cleared of stone and brought under plough, and the formal framework of enclosed fields that remains

to this day was imposed upon the landscape. This is the backdrop against which the archaeological record must be viewed, for it was during this transformation that monuments were preserved or destroyed, that sites and artefacts were found and lost.

Broadly speaking, the landscape within Donside can be divided into two zones, the first mainly occupying the lower ground and under permanent or intermittent cultivation, the second largely unimproved and extending up into the higher hills and mountains. It is in this basic division, that the archaeological record has been formed. The areas that have been regularly cultivated for the last 200 years contain on the one hand the fewest visible monuments, and on the other, by far the majority of records of monuments that have been removed or sites where artefacts have been discovered. Conversely, the areas of unimproved pasture and moorland offer the opportunity for upstanding monuments to survive undisturbed, though by the same token subterranean features and stray artefacts are rarely detected. This basic division in the landscape effectively dictates the distribution patterns of the various types of site. Whereas souterrains (pp. 88–92), cists, urns (pp. 52–5), and all types of artefacts are generally limited to the lower tracts of agricultural land, settlements of prehistoric hut-circles, field-systems and scatters of small cairns are found only in unimproved locations, and these are usually on higher ground (pp. 79–81).

In general terms, these observations hold true, but Donside is remarkable for the pockets of unimproved pasture that have survived throughout its length, in several instances almost down to sea level. Plantations established in the lowlands during the 18th and 19th centuries have also complicated the picture, particularly as many of these have reverted to rough pasture. In these gaps in the patchwork of fields, both in open ground and beneath the canopy of trees, prehistoric monuments have occasionally survived, but more often than not the

*Fig. 3.1 **Ardlair** (NJ 5527 2794). The survival of visible archaeological remains depends on subsequent patterns of land-use. This fine oblique aerial view, taken under low winter sunlight with the ground under a mantle of snow, reveals how a recumbent stone circle on the summit of the hill stands in a gap amidst the furlongs of later rig-and-furrow cultivation. The rig-and-furrow owes its own survival to an old plantation, long since felled, that once occupied the surrounding enclosure. © AAS 81–12–CT10*

gaps contain rig-and-furrow cultivation of medieval or later date. The latter is as much a component of the archaeological record as any prehistoric cairn or hut-circle (pp. 227–9), but it also shows that the archaeological record was being shaped by earlier episodes of cultivation extending back long before the agricultural improvements of the 18th and 19th centuries. The limits of cultivation have advanced or retreated as conditions allowed, and those prehistoric settlements on the best agricultural land were probably levelled during the medieval period, if not before. As such, they are effectively invisible in the landscape, though cropmarks have revealed the positions of a few settlements on freely draining soils in the lower reaches of the Don and around Insch and Alford (pp. 86; 93–6).

The impact of these earlier episodes of agricultural expansion on the archaeological record is almost impossible to assess, but the transformation of the landscape from the late 18th century into the 19th century is charted in the descriptions of the parishes in the *Statistical Accounts* (pp. 215–26). Before the improvements, the general appearance of the landscape was probably much as it had been several hundred years earlier, closely resembling the pattern of unenclosed rig-and-furrow and clusters of buildings shown on General Roy's Military map (1747–55). Many landowners, such as Grant of Monymusk, Gordon of Cluny and Forbes of Brux, had already introduced measures to improve their estates, but by and large these were fairly localised and restricted to the policies of their country houses and attendant home farms. This is certainly the impression gained from the parish descriptions of the *Statistical Account,* the minister of Strathdon commenting that *'the mode of farming has undergone little variation here, except among the gentlemen'* (*Stat. Acct.*, xiii, 1794, 174), while the incumbent at Auchindoir and

Kearn remarks that *'Improvements in this parish, and indeed all this country, have made little progress'* (*Stat. Acct.,* xii, 1794, 495).

By the time of the publication of the *New Statistical Account* some fifty years later, the commentaries are quite different and it is obvious that the character of the landscape had been altered in a wholesale and radical manner. The speed of this is remarked upon on numerous occasions, the minister of Strathdon writing that *'Within the last twenty years, very great and rapid progress has been made in agricultural improvement'*, while some measure of the scale can be gauged in Kintore where *'During the last thirty years, 300 acres at least have been thoroughly improved, by trenching, draining, and enclosing, entirely by the tenants'* (*NSA*, xii, Aberdeenshire, 551, 661).

The impact of this dramatic and rapid change in the countryside is reflected in the character of the descriptions of antiquities in the *Statistical Account* and the *New Statistical Account.* Whereas only a handful of the parish entries in the *Statistical Account* record the discoveries of stray coins, graves and souterrains, those of the *New Statistical Account* frequently mention coin hoards, urns, arrowheads and battle-axes. Without exception, the circumstances surrounding these later discoveries are allied to agricultural improvements, such as a bag of silver coins *'found some years ago in trenching the hill called Cockmuir'* in Kennethmont parish (*NSA*, xii, Aberdeenshire, 585), a gold piece of James I of Scotland found *'In digging a drain'* in Culsalmond parish (*NSA*, xii, Aberdeenshire, 731), and the cist containing a broken urn and human bones *'accidentally uncovered by the plough'* in Kemnay parish (*NSA*, xii, Aberdeenshire, 818).

It also appears to be the case that most of the earlier discoveries noted in the *Statistical Account* come from waste ground or moorland. Some of these may have been made in the course of agricultural improvements, such as the souterrains near Kildrummy, but other finds came about through peat cutting. A human body with a sword and a shilling of Queen Elizabeth, for instance, were found in a moss in the parish of Tough, near to the supposed site of the Battle of Alford *(Stat. Acct.*, viii, 1793, 268–9), while *'the body of a man on horseback and in complete armour'* was found alongside *'pieces of money'* while *'casting peats'* on moorland in the parish of Alford (*Stat. Acct.*, xv, 1795, 473). For the greater part of the population, peats were the only available fuel, but many of the mosses had been exhausted by the end of the 18th century and this source of archaeological discoveries largely disappeared with them.

The spirit that pushed forward the agricultural improvements also generated an interest in the past and in an age *'long prior to the Roman invasion'* (*NSA*, xii, Aberdeenshire, 782). The museum at Marischal College in Aberdeen had been founded in 1786, but it would seem that the majority of artefacts found

*Fig. 3.2 **Kemnay** (NJ 7286 1500). The agricultural improvements of the 19th century created the broad pattern of fields and farms that can be seen today. Taken in March 2003, this oblique aerial view looks north-north-west across Kemnay Golf Course towards Bennachie. SC872646*

locally fell into the hands of private collectors. The collection of Sir Alexander Leith of Freefield House in the parish of Rayne, for instance, included axes from the parishes of Culsalmond and Insch, which were held in what was known locally as the *'Freefield Cabinet'* (*NSA*, xii, Aberdeenshire, 731–2). Some of these collectors had evidently ventured much further afield than Aberdeenshire. James Byres of Tonley, for instance, *'a gentleman highly distinguished for his profound knowledge of architectural antiquities'*, had lived in Rome (*NSA*, xii, Aberdeenshire, 614), and is

listed as a corresponding member of the Society of Antiquaries of Scotland in 1781, where his profession is stated as *'Painter, Rome'* (*Archaeol Scot*, iii, appendix I, 21). During his life, he had amassed many *'articles of curiosity'*, some no doubt brought back from his travels abroad. The house at Tonley is now derelict and his collection appears to have been dispersed.

In addition to describing some of the discoveries that had found their way into these collections, the *Statistical Account* and the *New Statistical Account* also provide some insight into the impact of the Improvements on other types of monument. The deterioration in the condition of the Roman temporary camp at **Normandykes**, on the north side of the River Dee near Peterculter, is a particularly pertinent example, with a lengthy description appearing in the

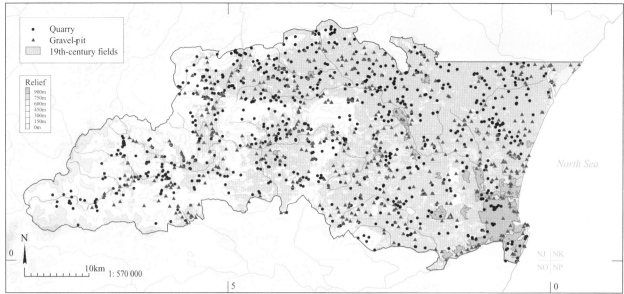

Fig. 3.3 This map shows the distribution of quarries and gravel-pits against the extent of 19th-century arable ground and urban areas. Agricultural improvement, quarrying and urban expansion are the principal mechanisms through which artefacts are discovered and archaeological sites are lost. GV000108

1795 Account, when three sides of the camp were still visible (*Stat. Acct.*, xvi, 1795, 380). By 1840, however, the description was shortened to a few lines, and the destruction of the ramparts was all but complete. The minister remarks that *'The remains of the military work mentioned in the former Statistical Account of this parish are now almost entirely obliterated: a small part of the dike and ditch still remains, and forms part of the fence of an adjoining field'* (*NSA*, xii, Aberdeenshire, 108). This is as it is depicted some thirty years later on the 1st edition of the OS 6-inch map, which shows the greater part of the northern side beneath the field boundaries (Aberdeenshire 1869, sheet lxxxv). Sadly, little more than the north-eastern angle can be detected today, surviving where it has been incorporated into the boundary of a plantation occupying part of the interior of the camp (Fig. 6.37).

A similar fate seems to have befallen many other monuments, with scant regard having been paid for either their form or date. The ruins of buildings around the **Doune of Invernochty** in Strathdon parish, first mentioned in a footnote in the *Statistical Account* in 1794, are by 1840 *'long since obliterated by the plough'* (*Stat. Acct.*, xiii, 1794, 182; *NSA*, xii, Aberdeenshire, 545), while, in the parish of Rayne, the residence of the Bishop of Aberdeen *'the foundation of which was discernible in the last century, has since been effaced, and the ground brought under tillage'* (*NSA*, xii, Aberdeenshire, 424). The latter is surrounded by a moat, which is depicted on the 1st edition of the OS 6-inch map (Aberdeenshire 1870, sheet xliv), but today modern buildings and a road obscure its western half.

Of the earlier monuments, the stone circles (pp. 70–2) and burial cairns (pp. 48–9) appear to have suffered the most damage, though this may be no more than a reflection of their numbers in the countryside. Prior to the Improvements, the sheer size of the larger examples had probably ensured their survival, but now they stood in the face of progress, and provided convenient quarries for the *'stone fences'* of the new field enclosures (*NSA*, xii, Aberdeenshire, 744). A large cairn at **Hill of Boghead** in Kintore, for instance, was robbed to build fences (*Stat. Acct.*, xiii, 1794, 92), while several had already been destroyed in Leochel-Cushnie parish to provide stone for *'building houses and fold-dykes'* (*Stat. Acct.*, vi, 1793, 221). By the 1840s many more had been removed, the minister of Leochel-Cushnie parish commenting that *'At one time these were numerous. Nine are specified in the former account of Leochel; but in the progress of cultivation and building, most of them have disappeared'* (*NSA*, xii, Aberdeenshire, 1121). In general the cairns that were spared tend to be in more elevated positions, above the upper limit of cultivated ground, though it was sometimes as convenient to incorporate one into the design of the new landscape as to remove it. Most of the latter are nonetheless heavily disturbed, though a few have not only survived relatively intact, but have escaped notice until the present survey. These include the cairns at **Donald's Hillock** near Hatton of Fintray, and at **Home Farm of Potterton**, both of which lie within arable land but were enclosed and planted with trees.

Stone circles, or Druidic temples as many of them are described, are listed in nineteen of the parish entries in the *Statistical Account*, giving a combined total of at least forty-three. Of these, some degree of damage can be inferred at eight sites, ranging from the *'less complete'* description of **The Candy Stone**, Cults, in Kennethmont parish (*Stat. Acct.*, xiii, 1794, 77), to the

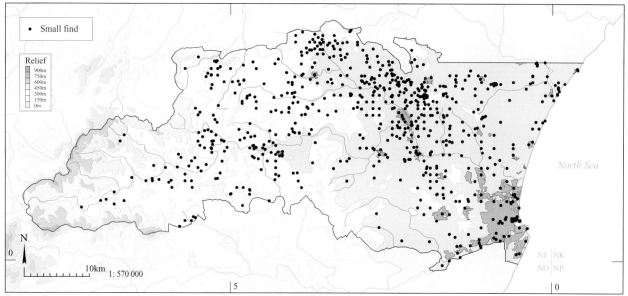

Fig. 3.4 This map shows the distribution of provenanced artefacts. Though few have recorded findspots, attribution to the name of farm allows them to be placed sufficiently accurately on the map to reveal the overall pattern. GV000110

complete removal of two in Foveran parish, *'one of which was very complete'* (*Stat. Acct.*, vi, 1793, 67n). One of the latter may be that on the **Hill of Fiddes**, which is shown as complete on a plan published in 1777, but is now represented by only the recumbent and its western flanker. In a few instances, such as the two recorded in Skene parish, and two of the three from Bourtie parish, the writer volunteers that they are *'pretty entire'* (*Stat. Acct.*, iv, 1792, 62; ix, 1793, 437). Unfortunately the descriptions of these circles are rarely supplied with any place-name and it is virtually impossible to reconcile them with the sites known from other sources.

Some fifty years later, a similar number of stone circles is recorded in the *New Statistical Account,* but this is by accident rather than design. At least twenty of a total of forty-six come from ten parishes where the previous account makes no mention of any *'Druidical temples'*, while references to fifteen circles in seven other parishes have disappeared. It would be misleading to view the latter as an index of their destruction, for entries in the *New Statistical Account* for three of the seven parishes concerned do not contain any section on antiquities. By the same token, fifteen of those circles that are mentioned for the first time, fall in parishes that had no antiquities section included in the previous account. Nevertheless, where comparisons can be drawn between the two accounts, they invariably include comment about the deterioration or demolition of the stone circles. Of the two *'Druidical temples'* in Leslie parish, both of which were acknowledged as incomplete in 1793, one had been removed by 1842 and the stones used *'in building fences'*, while the other receives no mention at all (*Stat. Acct.*, viii, 1793, 518;

NSA, xii, Aberdeenshire, 1022). Likewise in Keithhall & Kinkell parish, three are recorded in the *Statistical Account* (ii, 1792, 541), but by 1842 only a single stone remained (*NSA*, xii, Aberdeenshire, 744).

In addition to these major monuments, scatters of prehistoric hut-circles and small cairns were disappearing too, although the present survey has revealed numerous examples surviving in lowland plantations (pp. 79–80). The majority of the small cairns are probably no more than field clearance heaps, but they often became associated in folklore with memorials raised where men had fallen in battle. As a result many were attached to some event known from local history, such as the cairns on the **Hill of Milduan**, near Rhynie, attributed to a battle between Macduff and Lulach in 1057 (*NSA*, xii, Aberdeenshire, 1015–16), or those from *'a muir'* in Cluny parish assigned to an *'engagement in the reign of Charles I between the Irvines and Forbeses ... wherein some upon both sides fell'* (*Stat. Acct.*, x, 1794, 249). Many more examples are recorded in the *Statistical Accounts*, yet it would seem that this was not enough to save them, and most were simply swept away.

From the evidence presented in the two *Statistical Accounts,* it is clear that a great deal of damage was inflicted on the upstanding archaeological remains during the first half of the 19th century, largely as a result of agricultural improvements. This did not go unnoticed, and in 1855, appalled by the *'progressive and active destruction of many remains'*, the Society of Antiquaries of Scotland exchanged a series of communications with the Ordnance Survey, venturing the view that *'it would be of consequence to have all such historical monuments laid down on the Ordnance Survey of Scotland in the course of preparation'* (*Proc Soc Antiq Scot*, 2, 1857, 129–30). The Ordnance Survey agreed to meet this request, but there is little

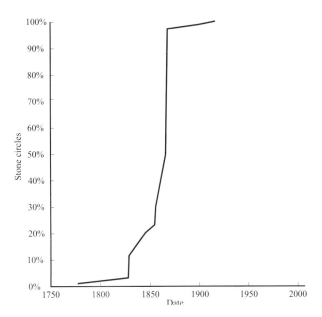

Fig. 3.5 This graph charts the dates when stone circles first appear in published sources. GV000128

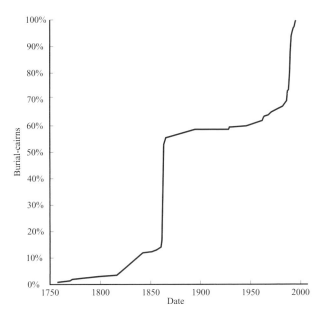

Fig. 3.6 This graph charts the dates when burial-cairns first appear in published sources. GV000126

way of gauging how persuasive the efforts of the Society may have been in preventing the destruction of individual monuments. In general, it is quite clear that archaeological remains continued to be removed; this is shown both by comments written in the Ordnance Survey Name Book, which accompanied the preparation of the 1st edition of the OS 6-inch map, and by a comparison of the numbers of monuments depicted on the 1st and 2nd editions of the map.

The preparation of the 1st edition OS map and the compilation of the Name Book mark an important watershed in the formation of the modern archaeological record. For the first time monuments were depicted in their correct positions in the landscape, coupled with some rudimentary record of their character and state of preservation. From these two sources it becomes possible to trace the history of discovery and destruction of individual monuments in more detail.

Surprisingly perhaps, the patterns of discovery are not uniform for all classes of monument. By way of example, the dates at which stone circles and burial-cairns are first recorded in published sources have been collated (Figs 3.5–6). Whereas virtually all of the stone circles accepted today were recorded by 1875, the discoveries of cairns merely plateau at this point, before rising slowly until the steep increase with the present survey. However, thirty-seven of the ninety-seven cairns shown on the 1st edition of the map were already annotated *'site of'*, and a further sixteen had apparently been removed by 1900, a trend that continued into the 20th century. Despite this continued attrition, it is remarkable to report that no less than forty-three burial-cairns have been discovered in the course of fieldwork, ranging from the large isolated cairns already mentioned at **Home Farm of Potterton** and **Donald's**

Hillock, to rather smaller examples found amongst scatters of what otherwise appear to be clearance heaps (p. 49). It is disappointing that no new examples of stone circles have been recorded in the area, but this is probably explained by the long-standing awareness and interest in standing stones and stone circles evident in the antiquarian sources.

Similar patterns can be detected in types of monuments that were not so prominent in the landscape. Souterrains, for example, which first aroused antiquarian attention in the late 18th century, show a relatively steady rise in the number of discoveries in the early 19th century, and again a rapid acceleration

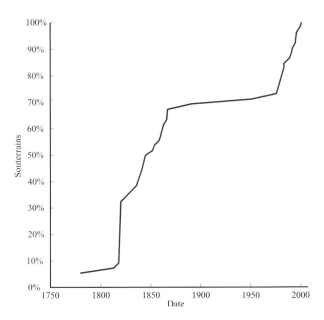

Fig. 3.7 This graph charts the dates when souterrains are discovered. GV000127

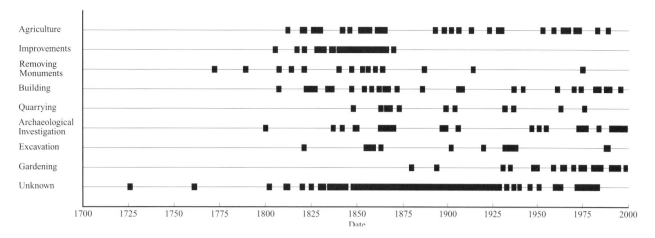

Fig. 3.8 This chart shows those artefacts from Donside for which the dates and methods of discovery are known. General agricultural operations, mainly ploughing, are separated from other activities to improve the land, the latter clearly confined to the period before 1870. The Excavation category should probably be distributed across those of Improvement, Building and Quarrying. GV000125

with the compilation of the Name Book (Fig. 3.7). Thereafter, few examples of these underground passages are recorded until the 1980s, when they were first recognised as cropmarks on aerial photographs. The capstones of these structures were often only just below the surrounding ground-level (p. 88), and it is not surprising that so many were discovered as a result of land improvement. Lesser subterranean structures, such as cist-burials, show a more even pattern of discovery throughout the 19th century, the frequency only tailing off after the First World War.

The 1st edition of the OS 6-inch map also shows findspots, ranging from coins and stone axes to urn-burials and human remains. With one or two exceptions, these relate to discoveries made in the 19th century, rather than the 18th century, and those that were relatively recent discoveries tend to be most detailed, often supplying the year in which the item was found. It is also clear that the character of a discovery coloured the way in which it was reported in the Name Book, burials receiving particular attention. By way of example, the Name Book entry for the site of **Elspet's Cairn, Irelandbrae**, in the parish of Rayne, records that it was *'trenched in 1849'* revealing two axes, together with a stone cist containing a skull and two decorated urns (Name Book, Aberdeenshire, No. 77, p. 77); the site of the cairn is indicated on the map, and an axe from Irelandbrae is now held in Marischal Museum.

As a result of this selective interest, the years in which 70% of Beakers and Cinerary Urns were discovered are known. No other class of artefact or discovery matches this figure, though discovery dates are known for quite a number of gold and silver items – coins, rings, pins and torcs – presumably because their intrinsic value would have been immediately recognised by the population at large. In contrast, the dates at which

bronze metalwork, carved stone balls and, to a certain extent, stone axes, were discovered are known for a mere 25%. These were highly prized by collectors, and the majority appear to have remained in local hands.

At the height of the agricultural improvements very few Aberdeenshire artefacts were donated to the collections of either the Society of Antiquaries of Scotland or Marischal College in Aberdeen. A dozen leaf-shaped arrowheads donated to Marischal College Museum in 1824 by John Stuart, Professor of Greek at Aberdeen University, is a notable exception. The first published notification of a discovery is often an entry in a sale catalogue following the death of a collector. More often than not this led to the dispersal of the collection, and by the time any of the artefacts found their way into a museum any notes about their discovery were irretrievably lost. Many items of Bronze Age metalwork, for example, are first recorded in the sale of the collection amassed by John Rae, which took place by auction in Edinburgh over three days in November 1892. Numerous bronze artefacts in museum collections are simply provenanced to Aberdeenshire.

While the information surrounding the retrieval of objects varies from category to category, in overall terms the circumstances of discovery are known for about 40% of the objects that have been discovered in Donside. As with the destruction of cairns and stone circles, and the discovery of cists and souterrains, analysis of this information reveals that the patterns of discovery are inextricably linked to the changes that were taking place with the improvements. Discoveries made by trenching, levelling, digging drains and land reclamation (included under the general heading of Improvements in Fig. 3.8), tend to fall within a fifty-year period spanning 1815 to 1865. The Name Book, for example, records that a stone axe was found in about 1842 by the tenant of **Milton of Lesmore** while *'trenching turf'* (Aberdeenshire, No. 78, p. 96); at **Cloisterseat**, a carved stone ball was found in 1858 *'whilst improving a barren piece of land'* (Aberdeenshire, No. 91, p. 53).

Building work and quarrying are other facets of the improvements that have played their part in the patterns

Fig. 3.9 ***Hill of Foudland*** *(NJ 60 33). In 1902, ploughing on the south side of the Hill of Foudland unearthed this sandstone block, which carries moulds for six bronze flat axes of several different sizes and two bars.* © *University of Aberdeen*

of discovery, all of which reveal a clear break in the 1870s. Thereafter, no more discoveries are recorded by trenching, levelling, digging drains and land reclamation. After 1866, the next artefacts to be unearthed by the plough were a perforated stone from **Lochend of Barra**, found sometime at the turn of the century, and a stone mould for casting bronze flat axes found in 1902 on a farm on the **Hill of Foudland** (Fig. 3.9). At first sight, this hiatus reflects the onset of the agricultural recession in the 1870s, yet stone circles and cairns continued to be removed, and comparison of the 1st and 2nd editions of the OS 6-inch map reveals the consolidation of small patches of uncleared ground into large improved fields (see **Hill of Boghead**, pp. 81–2). In practice, the impact of the recession was not as far-reaching in the North-east as in other parts of the country, and the acreage of tilled ground continued to grow, expanding by a further 12% between 1866 and 1901 (Carter 1979, 33–97).

Confirmation that radical changes continued to take place at the end of the 19th century comes from the remains of the farms and cottages depicted on these maps. With the progressive rationalisation of the holdings (p. 196), many of these were abandoned in the late 19th century, but the old buildings were not simply left to fall into ruin, so much as removed wholesale. In numerous instances roofed buildings on the 1st edition of the map give way to open fields shown on the 2nd edition. At the same time the steadings of the consolidated holdings were often extensively remodelled. This is not only detectable in the plans of the steadings between the two editions of the map, but can also be seen in the walls of many still in use today.

In the light of this evidence, the agricultural recession cannot in itself be responsible for the hiatus in the pattern of discoveries, though subtle shifts in the balance between arable and pasture may have played some part. In particular the gradual expansion of the proportion of ground under grass at the expense of other crops (Carter

1979, 80–3) may have created fewer opportunities for new discoveries. More importantly, however, the beginning of the hiatus coincides with the preparation of the 1st edition map and the Name Books, which proved to be the last systematic survey of this type. Thus the hiatus has probably as much to do with information supply as with rate of discovery, as the unbroken sequence of discoveries of unknown type implies. A steady trickle of artefacts were found through ploughing during the first three decades of the 20th century, but the depression and the mechanisation of farming effectively brought this to an end. Not only were fewer people required to work the land, but those who remained were one step removed from the ground. The only small objects found through agricultural operations after 1960 are a carved stone ball in 1964 and a bronze axe in 1967.

One final aspect of the pattern of discovery of artefacts remains to be considered, namely gardening, which is not only labour-intensive, but brings the gardener in close contact with the soil. The earliest recorded finds from gardening date to the late 19th century, amongst them a decorated stone cup found in **Park Street, Aberdeen**, in 1880, and a Roman coin dug up at **Port Elphinstone** shortly before 1894. Since the 1950s a steady flow of discoveries has been made in this way, almost half of them from Aberdeen itself. The finds include two stone axes, a handful of carved stone balls, flint arrowheads and a few coins. In Kintore, a Pictish symbol stone was found with a broken saddle quern in cleared top-soil. Whereas such discoveries are scattered throughout the countryside, there are recognisable concentrations of findspots in urban and suburban areas. This presumably reflects the concentration of modern gardeners in these areas rather than any ancient preference for such locations.

In summary, the complex strands of evidence that have been explored above show that the present archaeological record for Donside is intimately related to the formation of the modern landscape. As such it tends to reflect the way that information has been collected, before casting any light on any ancient patterns of activity lying behind the construction of ancient monuments, or the deposition of artefacts. Comparison of the various sources of information reveals that the agricultural improvements were the most important factor in physically shaping the archaeological record, on the one hand uncovering numerous artefacts and burials, while on the other destroying countless structures, from cairns and stone circles to hut-circles and clearance heaps. Today, archaeological surveys range far wider than these prehistoric remains, encompassing the abandoned farmsteads and cottages that in their day were the cutting edge of improved agriculture. It is ironic that these are now amongst the most threatened components of the modern landscape, as vulnerable to changes in agricultural practice as the monuments that they themselves replaced.

Chapter 4: Environmental History

Richard Tipping

The valley of the River Don spans a series of clearly defined topographical settings from its source above Corgarff down to the sea at Aberdeen. These were largely formed before the end of the last glaciation (30,000–11,600 years ago). Over the period since, known as the Holocene, the present land surfaces have been for the most part only modified, developing a succession of ecosystems which have been variously changed and destroyed through combinations of climatic and human (anthropogenic) agency. These agencies coexist with each other in dynamic relationships, so much so that it is rarely possible to entirely isolate one from another. The following sections in this chapter deal with specific aspects of the environmental evidence and some of the events that can be identified. Later sections are more heavily weighted to anthropogenic impacts, ordered both chronologically and in their topographical settings. For the purposes of clarity, the study sites discussed here are referenced in Table 2 (pp. 30–1) rather than in the text, and radiocarbon assays of the events that are described are expressed as mean dates calibrated Before Present using CALIB 3.03, for the Holocene followed by the date BC or AD. Assays relating to the Devensian Lateglacial and the earliest Holocene organic sediments appear in full in Table 1 (p. 29), and previously uncalibrated dates relating to other Holocene organic sediments are provided in Table 3 (pp. 32–3).

Landforms and their Long-term Evolution

Much of the topography of the Don valley is an expression of the bedrock geology and the long history of erosion and weathering that took place before the last glaciation. In this sense, both the Don valley and Buchan

Fig. 4.1 The 'solid' geology underlying Donside. GV000122

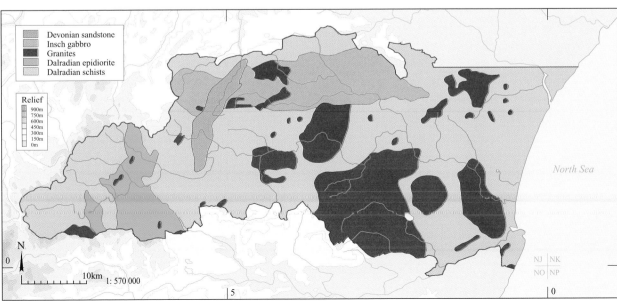

are exceptional in Scotland, for many of the landforms are inherited from before the Pleistocene Stage (the last 2.3 million years), and have only been modified by subsequent glaciations (Hall 1991; 1997). The isolation of the region from the main ice streams localised glacial erosion, while glacial deposition is marked only in the lowland valleys. Extraordinarily for Scotland, some 'soft' (unconsolidated) sediment bodies persist from before the Pleistocene.

The bedrock or solid geology is complicated, but essentially comprises three main components. The earliest of these is a mass of very old (Dalradian) metamorphosed sediments (metasediments) and igneous lithologies, into which large bodies of granite (batholiths) were intruded during a late stage in Caledonoid mountain building around 450–400 million years ago. The third and latest component, which includes coarse gravels, sands and shales of terrestrial origin, was deposited in the Devonian

Period (Lower Old Red Sandstone), between 400 and 360 million years ago.

The metamorphosed Dalradian metasediments and igneous lithologies forming the earliest rocks are in general of late pre-Cambrian and Cambrian age. They occur throughout the Don valley, and exhibit an exceedingly diverse range of lithologies and chemistries, reflecting several factors, principally the parent sediments and the temperature and pressure that they were subjected to during metamorphism. The parent sediments ranged from gravels to muds, and from acid to alkali, and the most intensely metamorphosed rocks were 'cooked' at depths of 35–40km within the crust (Johnson 1983). Many of these rocks are schists, a type of fine-grained, highly cleaved metamorphic rock rich in micas and quartz.

Fig. 4.2 An oblique aerial view looking across the planned village of Monymusk towards the granite tor forming the distinctive silhouette of the Mither Tap o' Bennachie. SC872649

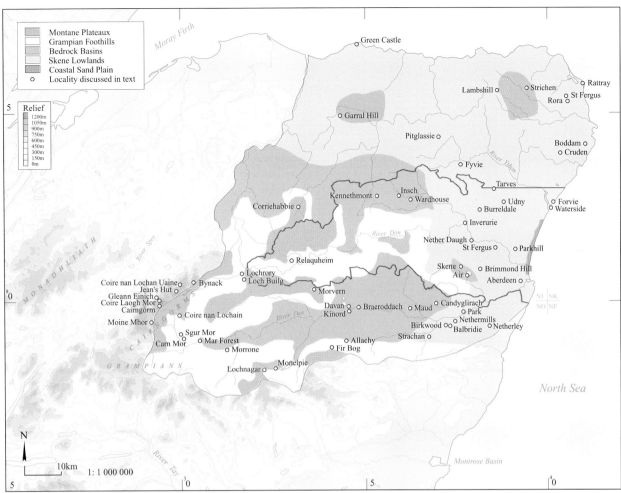

Fig. 4.3 The distribution within the former county of Aberdeenshire of landform elements, and sites and other localities of Devensian Lateglacial and Holocene age used in the reconstruction of the environmental history of the region. GV000124

In the Don valley, the Lower Old Red Sandstone strata that overlie these metamorphic and igneous rocks are found between Kildrummy and Rhynie, forming a narrow outcrop some 20km long, in which the well-known fossiliferous Rhynie Chert occurs. Almost no other pre-Quaternary deposits are found onshore, though immediately off the eastern coast there are thick successions of Permo-Triassic sandstones and mudstones, Jurassic mudstones, and Upper Cretaceous chalk. The Buchan Gravels, near Peterhead, are of Tertiary age, comprising isolated deposits of quartz- and flint-rich riverine and possibly marine gravels, which were a major source of material for flint tools in prehistory (Saville 1995). Elsewhere, extensive areas of rotted granite, gabbro and schist were weathered *in situ* during this period. Erosion has now exposed the upper domed surfaces of the granite batholiths, and these have been extensively quarried for building stone.

The resistance to weathering of the different rock types over long periods and in different climates determines in part whether they now form hills, basins or valleys. Other factors include more subtle interrelationships between rock type, deep weathering in pre-glacial times, pre-glacial fluvial incision, and glacial erosion (Bremner 1942; Fitzpatrick 1963; Hall 1984; 1986; 1987; 1991; 1996). These have given rise to a variety of landforms, five of which are defined on Fig. 4.3. The Montane Plateaux at the head of the catchment, above 700m OD, are erosional surfaces formed predominantly by chemical weathering in the Tertiary period (Fleet 1938; Sissons 1976; Hall 1991). Pre-glacial rivers flowed across these surfaces (Gibb 1910; Bremner 1942; Linton 1951; 1954; Sissons 1967; Hall 1996) and were responsible for the deposition of the Buchan Gravels to the north of the Don valley. The Montane Plateaux lead downslope and downstream to a second type of landform, the Grampian Foothills, and then into a third, the Bedrock Basins. This last is a very different type of landscape of isolated hills and deep fertile basins.

The fourth landform, the Skene Lowland (Glentworth and Muir 1963), includes the lower courses of both the Rivers Don and Dee. Areas of deep weathering here are apparently rare (Hall 1986), reflecting the intensity of glacial and fluvioglacial scouring and the subsequent burial of the eroded surface beneath thick masses of glacial till. The extent of fresh rock at the surface in the valley of the Dee reveals that this was the more intensely scoured and, therefore, the more significant ice stream (Clapperton and Sugden 1975; 1977; Murdoch 1975; Sutherland 1984; Munro 1986; Hall 1997; Merritt *et al.* 2000). Outwash terraces along the valleys in the Skene Lowland (Aitken 1991; Maizels and Aitken 1991) were deposited by gravel-rich braided rivers, contrasting with meandering single-channel rivers found there today. The Skene Lowland is separated from the North Sea by the fifth type of landform, the Coastal Sand Plain, which was formed almost entirely within the Holocene Stage. These five regions make up the basic components of the landscape as it was when the first Mesolithic communities colonised Scotland after the last phase of Pleistocene glaciation, the Younger Dryas Stadial.

The Devensian Lateglacial Stage

The Late Devensian ice-sheets reached their maximum extent between 25,000 and 15,000 cal BP. The onset of the present interglacial climate was not until around 11,500 cal BP. The period of deglaciation between these dates is known as the Devensian Lateglacial (Gray and Lowe 1977), and is characterised by massive climatic fluctuations, though these may also have been typical of the Devensian glaciation as a whole (Bond *et al.* 1993; Lowe *et al.* 1995; Clapperton 1997; Lowe and Walker 1997; Bjorck *et al.* 1998). These fluctuations appear to have been determined by the periodic breakdown of ocean currents that redistribute heat around the planet.

The early part of this stage, the Lateglacial Interstadial, is marked by the first clear biological evidence for the amelioration of the climate (e.g. Atkinson *et al.* 1987). At about 14,700 cal BP mean summer temperatures probably rose abruptly from much less than 10°C to 14–15°C (Bjorck *et al.* 1998). Thermal amelioration led to landscape and soil stability, microbiological and chemical activity in pedogenesis (soil formation), and the accumulation of organic matter in soils and in lakes. Pollen assemblages from lake sediments show an abundance of thermophilous (warmth-preferring) aquatic plants that flourish in nutrient-rich water (Tipping 1991). They also reveal the colonisation of terrestrial soils by grasses and herbs, responding to pedogenesis, soil stability and longer growing seasons. In the North-east these changes can be seen in pollen diagrams from the uplands near Loch Builg and above Braemar at Morrone, and in the lowlands at Loch Kinord in the Muir of Dinnet, and the infilled Loch of Park west of Peterculter (Fig. 4.3).

Within Scotland, it is exceptionally rare to find terrestrial peats of Lateglacial age (Tipping 1991). In the North-east, however, four peat beds of this period are known (Table 1). These peats may have formed during a climatic deterioration, perhaps through increased precipitation, in the latter part of the Lateglacial Interstadial, between 14,300 and 12,700 cal BP (Durno 1970; Clapperton and Sugden 1975; 1977; Connell and Hall 1987). Peat also accumulated at 13,500 cal BP across well-drained sands and gravels on a floodplain near Dyce (Munro 1986).

Tree cover increased after 14,000 cal BP, though birch is the only tree taxon confidently attested from plant macrofossils. Two pine needles from Lateglacial sediments at Loch Kinord remain the only evidence in Scotland for the growth of pine at this time. The lowlands of eastern Scotland were generally characterised by the development of an open, grassy birch and juniper cover (Tipping 1991). In the North-east open heath vegetation rich in crowberry was maintained at Morrone, and expanded on drier, more exposed acid soils on Cairngorm and at Garral Hill. The Loch Kinord and Loch of Park sequences show that heath and woodland communities were intimately associated.

Towards the end of the Lateglacial period the climate probably deteriorated in a series of steps lasting only decades, culminating at about 12,650 cal BP (Bjorck *et al.* 1998) in what is known as the Younger Dryas Stadial (Walker *et al.* 1994; Alley 2000). On Cairngorm, the glaciers advanced again (the Loch Lomond Readvance) but they were of modest size (Sugden 1970; Sugden and Clapperton 1975; Sissons 1979a; Bennett and Glasser 1991; Brazier *et al.* 1996). Mean summer temperatures fell below 10°C, and mean winter temperatures as low as -20°C have been suggested (Atkinson *et al.* 1987): mean annual temperatures at sea level may have been only 1–2°C (Ballantyne and Harris 1994). Levels of precipitation are unknown, but need not have been excessive to generate the large ice sheets if snow fell much more frequently (Sissons 1979b).

As temperatures fell, the plant cover fragmented and disintegrated. Bare ground was probably prevalent throughout the landscape, though tussocky grasses, sedges and disturbed-ground herbs are attested in pollen diagrams (Vasari 1977; Huntley 1994). The earlier birch, juniper and crowberry communities were destroyed (Tipping 1991), but willow may have persisted, and included tall shrub species as well as the dwarf *Salix herbacea* (Vasari and Vasari 1968; Huntley 1994). Solifluction acted to erode many soils (Connell and Hall 1987), and those soils that survived were winnowed by water and frost action (Fitzpatrick 1963). On Garral Hill soliflucted sediment buried the peat to a depth of 1m after about 12,670 cal BP, and comparable silts buried the peat at Woodhead after about 12,700 cal BP. In Loch Kinord, about 0.4m of soliflucted but water-sorted clays spread across the floor of the loch after about 12,300 cal BP. No sedimentary or stratigraphic changes are apparent high in Deeside at Morrone. The intense cold relented only at about 11,600 cal BP (Bjorck *et al.* 1998).

Table 1 Calibrated radiocarbon assays from Devensian Lateglacial and earliest Holocene organic sediments in the region.

Depth cm	Sediment Type	Lab. No.	^{14}C Age BP ± 1σ	Calibrated Age Range BP ± 2σ	Mean Age BP
Loch Kinord (Vasari 1977)					
465–475	gyttja	HEL-421	9820 ± 250	12150–10349	11250
496–506	gyttja	HEL-420	10101 ± 220	12339–10868	11600
550–560	gyttja–clay	HEL-419	10640 ± 260	13129–11499	12300
580–590	clay–gyttja	HEL-418	11520 ± 220	13975–12987	13500
Loch of Park (Vasari 1977)					
245–255	clay–gyttja	HEL-416	10280 ± 220	12554–11072	11800
330–340	gyttja	HEL-417	11900 ± 260	14570–13286	13930
Morrone (Huntley 1994)					
140–145	gyttja	Q-1289	9830 ± 150	11795–10792	11300
230–235	organic silts/sands	Q-1344	10880 ± 100	13018–12579	12800
365–370	silty mud	Q-1290	11810 ± 150	14190–13397	13800
395–400	silty mud	Q-1291	12595 ± 210	15478–14180	14830
by Loch Builg (Clapperton *et al.* 1975)					
1076–1082	gyttja	SRR-305	11770 ± 87	14023–13458	13750
Garral Hill (Godwin & Willis 1959)					
200–205	silty moss peat	Q-104	10808 ± 230	13200–12140	12670
205–210	silty moss peat	Q-103	11090 ± 235	13515–12528	13020
210–215	silty moss peat	Q-102	11300 ± 245	13771–12730	13250
215–220	silty moss peat	Q-101	11880 ± 300	14454–13331	13900
c.230	organic mud	Q-100	11350 ± 300	13955–12675	13315
Moss-side Farm, Tarves (Connell & Hall 1987)					
unknown	peat	I-6969	12200 ± 170	14782–13781	14300
Woodhead, Fyvie (Connell & Hall 1987)					
unknown	peat	SRR-1723	10780 ± 50	12851–12556	12700
St Fergus, Dyce (Harkness & Wilson 1979, 254)					
unknown	organic mud	SRR-762	11550 ± 80	13733–13257	13500
unknown	organic mud	SRR-763	11640 ± 70	13827–13358	13600

This rise in temperature at the end of the Younger Dryas Stadial marks the beginning of the Holocene Interglacial Stage, when mean summer temperatures returned to values of 16–18°C (Atkinson *et al.* 1987). In the North-east, the soliflucted deposits in lakes were replaced by organic sediments (Vasari 1977; Huntley 1994). Radiocarbon dates on slowly accumulating terrestrial sediments, however, cannot describe the astonishing abruptness of the switch from full glacial to full interglacial climate recorded in the GRIP ice core (Alley 2000). It is likely that the temperature increase from glacial to interglacial conditions took place in about ten years across almost the whole of the northern hemisphere.

Holocene
Sources and Limitations of Data
The impact of the Younger Dryas Stadial was to create a blank slate on the landscape at the beginning of the Holocene. The parent materials of the soils were once more exposed, vegetation cover was set back to tundra, and there was no significant animal life.

Within Aberdeenshire the data from which to reconstruct the environment that developed on this blank slate appears comparatively abundant. The distribution of study sites and localities known to the author is shown on Fig. 4.3, and Table 2 lists them in relation to the landforms identified on Fig. 4.3 and the types of information obtained.

Table 2 Sources of Holocene palaeoenvironmental data in the North-east defined by landform and type of information.

Site (* ¹⁴C assays)	Author	Information
Montane Plateaux		
Monelpie Hill	Durno 1959; Durno & Romans 1969	vegetation history; soil development
Morven	Durno & Romans 1969	soil development
Corriehabbie Hill	Durno & Romans 1969	soil development
Cairngorm **	Sugden 1971	fluvial & colluvial processes
by Loch Builg	Clapperton *et al.* 1975	vegetation history
Carn Mor **	Pears 1975b	soil development; vegetation history
Sgur Mor *	Pears 1975b	soil development; vegetation history
Meall a' Bhuachaille **	Pears 1975b	soil development; vegetation history
Jean's Hut *	Pears 1975b	soil development; vegetation history
Coire Laogh Mor: CLM *	Pears 1975b	soil development; vegetation history
Bynack *	Pears 1975b; Dubois & Ferguson 1985, 1988	soil development; vegetation history
Inchrory *	Preece, Bennett & Robinson 1984	soil development; vegetation history; climate change
Cairn Gorm *****	Dubois & Ferguson 1985, 1988	vegetation history; climate change
Coire nan Lochan Uaine *	Rapson 1985; Brooks 1996	vegetation history
Lochnagar *****	Rapson 1985; Jones *et al.* 1993	vegetation history; soil development
Coire nan Lochain: CL	Rapson 1985	vegetation history
Gleann Einich ****	Binney 1997	soil development; vegetation history; climate change
Moine Mhor	Barber *et al.* 2000	soil development; climate change
Grampian Foothills		
Fir Bog	Durno 1961	soil development
Morrone *****	Huntley 1994	vegetation history
Relaquheim **	Davies & Tipping 2001	vegetation history
Mar Forest *	Paterson unpublished	vegetation history
Bedrock Basin Landscapes		
Insch	Walton 1950	soil development; land-use
Loch Kinord **	Vasari & Vasari 1968	vegetation history
Braeroddach Loch *****	Edwards 1978a, 1979a & b, 1989; Edwards & Rowntree 1980; Edwards & Ralston 1984; Edwards & Whittington 2001; Whittington & Edwards 1993	vegetation history; fluvial & colluvial processes
Loch Davan *****	Edwards 1978a & b, 1989, 1990; Edwards & Ralston 1984; Edwards & Whittington 2001; Whittington & Edwards 1993	vegetation history; soil development; fluvial & colluvial processes
Kinord *	Edwards 1978b	soil development; land-use
Castle of Wardhouse	Yeoman 1998	land-use
Kennethmont	Dawson 1997	vegetation history

Table 2 *continued*

Site (* ¹⁴C assays)	Author	Information
Skene Lowlands		
Birkwood, Banchory	Paterson & Lacaille 1936	fluvial & colluvial processes
Strichen	Fraser & Godwin 1955	vegetation history; soil development
Netherley	Durno 1956, 1957, 1961	vegetation history; soil development
St Fergus, Peterhead	Durno 1956, 1957, 1976; Glentworth & Muir 1963	vegetation history; soil development
Skene	Durno 1957, 1976; Glentworth & Muir 1963	vegetation history; soil development
Candyglirach	Durno 1957; Glentworth & Muir 1963	vegetation history; soil development
Rora	Durno 1957	vegetation history; soil development
Burreldale	Durno 1957; Glentworth & Muir 1963; Edwards 1990	vegetation history; soil development
Maud	Durno 1961	soil development
Lambshill, New Pitsligo	Glentworth & Muir 1963; Dugmore, Larsen & Newton 1995	soil development
Moss of Air	Glentworth & Muir 1963	soil development
Parkhill	Glentworth & Muir 1963	soil development
Loch of Park	Vasari & Vasari 1968	vegetation history
Moss of Cruden *	Glentworth & Muir 1963; Stewart & Durno 1969	vegetation history; soil development
Nelson St., Aberdeen	Durno 1970	vegetation history
Meston Walk, Aberdeen	Durno 1970	vegetation history
Brimmond Hill	Durno 1970	vegetation history; fluvial & colluvial processes
Green Castle	Ralston 1980	land-use
Nethermills Farm	Ewan 1981; Boyd & Kenworthy 1992	vegetation history; fluvial & colluvial processes
Nether Daugh, Kintore *	Aitken 1991	fluvial & colluvial processes
Balbridie *****	Romans & Robertson 1983; Edwards & Ralston 1984; Fairweather & Ralston 1993	soil development; land-use
Castlehill of Strachan	Yeoman 1984	land-use; fluvial & colluvial processes
Pitglassie, Auchterless	Shepherd 1996	vegetation history
Inverurie	Carter 1999	fluvial & colluvial processes
Den of Boddam *****	Tipping & Milburn 2000a	vegetation history
Udny, near Methlick	Davies & Tipping unpublished	land-use
Coastal Sand Plain		
Waterside, Ythan estuary *****	Smith *et al.* 1992, 1999	coastal change; vegetation history; fluvial & colluvial processes
Forvie *	Gimingham 1964; Ritchie 1992	coastal change; land-use
Rattray Head *	Murray *et al.* 1992; Murray & Murray 1993	coastal change; land-use

Table 3 Previously uncalibrated radiocarbon assays from Holocene organic sediments in the order of their publication.

Depth & Sediment cm	Lab. No.	¹⁴C Age BP ± 1σ	Calibrated Age Range BP ± 2σ	Mean Age BP	Significance
Moss of Cruden (Stewart & Durno 1969)					
c. 210; peat	NPL-94	5020 ± 95	5938–5590	5760	blanket peat inception
Cairngorm solifluction lobes (reported in Sugden 1971)					
c. 40–70; peat/soil	unknown	2680 ± 120	3070–2430	2750	peat beneath solifluction lobe
c. 40–70; peat/soil	unknown	4480 ± 135	5477–4825	5150	peat beneath solifluction lobe
Cairngorm: wood remains in peat (Pears 1975a & b)					
Carn Mor: 20; pine wood	Gak-2006	6700 ± 300	8017–6920	7470	*Pinus* stump in peat
: 100; pine wood	Gak-2003	2880 ± 220	3488–2461	2975	*Pinus* stump in peat
Meall a' Bhuachaille: 20; pine wood	Gak-2539	6150 ± 150	7292–6708	7000	*Pinus* stump in peat
: 80; pine wood	Gak-2541	4400 ± 120	5323–4808	5065	*Pinus* stump in peat
Jean's Hut: 102; pine wood	Gak-2005	4630 ± 210	5596–4980	5290	*Pinus* stump in peat
Coire Laogh Mor: 84; birch wood	Gak-2538	4040 ± 120	4837–4225	4530	*Pinus* stump in peat
Barns of Bynack: 152; pine wood	Gak-2540	5110 ± 150	6266–6205	6235	*Pinus* stump in peat
Sgur Mor: 90; pine wood	Gak-2004	4140 ± 120	4879–4345	4610	*Pinus* stump in peat
Kinord, by Loch Davan (Edwards 1978b)					
c. 30; peat	UB-2084	455 ± 95	570–300	435	peat filling interstices of clearance cairn
Inchrory (Preece et al. 1984)					
345–350; soil in tufa	Q-2355	7360 ± 60	8207–7972	8090	soil formation within tufa precipitation
Cairngorm peats (Dubois & Ferguson 1985)					
unknown; basal peat	IRPA-361	5230 ± 260	6548–5453	6000	peat inception
unknown; basal peat	IRPA-366	5670 ± 250	7022–5924	6475	peat inception
unknown; twigs at base of peat	IRPA-362	6090 ± 300	7468–6385	6925	peat inception
Lochnagar (Rapson 1985)					
49–56; lake mud	SRR-2270	2680 ± 70	2953–2710	2830	*Ulmus* decline
110–120; lake mud	SRR-2271	7110 ± 90	8017–7684	7850	*Alnus* rise
125–135; lake mud	SRR-2272	7170 ± 80	8121–7794	7960	*Pinus* rise
100–110; blanket peat	SRR-2269	3150 ± 50	3467–3250	3360	*Ulmus* decline
150; pine wood	SRR-1808	6080 ± 50	7031–6845	6940	*Pinus-Betula* pollen assemblage zone
Coire nan Lochan Uaine (Rapson 1985)					
28–34; lake mud	SRR-2268	3320 ± 80	3714–3368	3540	*Ulmus* decline
Nether Daugh, Kintore (Aitken 1991)					
490–510; plant debris	SRR-3718 (i)	3855 ± 50	4410–4137	4275	peat within fluvial aggradation
490–510; organic silt	SRR-3718 (ii)	4120 ± 50	4825–4514	4670	
Rattray Head (Murray et al. 1992)					
Wood *(Salix)*	GU-2719	3130 ± 50	3351–3074	3210	hurdle associated with cultivation

Table 3 *continued*

Depth & Sediment cm	Lab. No.	¹⁴C Age BP ± 1σ	Calibrated Age Range BP ± 2σ	Mean Age BP	Significance
Sands of Forvie (Ralston, reported in Murray *et al.* 1992)					
unknown	GU-1827	3070 ± 140	3560–2879	3175	midden associated with ard marks
Morrone (Huntley 1994)					
47.5–52.5; organic mud	Q-1287	3300 ± 75	3659–3372	3515	*Pinus:* date reversal – rejected (Huntley 1994)
75–80; organic mud	Q-2317	2330 ± 30	2363–2309	2340	*Pinus*
85–90; organic mud	Q-2318	3950 ± 30	4446–4341	4395	*Pinus*
97.5–102.5; organic mud	Q-1288	6620 ± 100	7614–7321	7470	*Pinus*
115–120; organic mud	Q-2319	9730 ± 95	11047–10536	10790	prior to the *Betula* rise
125–130; organic mud	Q-2316	9830 ± 120	11682–10801	11240	prior to the *Betula* rise
Gleann Einich (Binney 1997)					
Site MNM: 147; peat	unknown	4270 ± 70	4989–4601	4795	basal peat formation
Site CPG: 175; peat	unknown	7240 ± 80	8160–7896	8030	basal peat formation
Site APB: 260; peat	unknown	7420 ± 80	8355–8062	8210	basal peat formation
Site LOD: 250; peat	unknown	7970 ± 60	8981–8587	8785	basal peat formation
Waterside, Ythan estuary (Smith *et al.* 1992)					
144–145; *Phragmites – Carex* peat	SRR-1192	3816 ± 55	4358–4080	4200	peat above marine clay
144–145; *Phragmites – Carex* peat	SRR-1769	4000 ± 80	4651–4229	4440	peat above marine clay
223–225; *Phragmites – Carex* peat	SRR-1193	6189 ± 95	7246–6854	7050	marine silt inwashing across peat
242–244; *Phragmites – Carex* peat	SRR-1565	6850 ± 140	7909–7427	7670	sand layer within peat

The length of this list conceals several deficiencies, however. Firstly, a number of analyses represent brief periods of time and do not provide a continuity of record. Secondly, because many analyses pertain to specific locations, it is significant in the region how frequently it has to be assumed that these represent the region as a whole. Thirdly, some records are described from comparatively few individual analyses.

Many analyses in the region, because of their comparative antiquity, are unsupported by 'absolute' dating controls provided by, for instance, radiocarbon dating. Sites with such controls are asterisked in Table 2. Many assays obtained are unsatisfactory by modern standards, being derived from thick sediment slices which provide very imprecise age and sediment accumulation estimates. Prior to the routine application of radiocarbon dating, pollen analyses could be 'dated' from changes in tree pollen across a region, which is abundantly produced and well dispersed. Such data can be misinterpreted, particularly when marker events are not unique in a sequence, and at some sites in this review, most importantly at Loch Kinord (Vasari and Vasari 1968), it is considered that the original zonation scheme is incorrect. Nevertheless, the increasing number of radiocarbon assays available has shown a reassuring regional synchroneity in some of the events, even though the timings of others, such as the rise in alder pollen, have proved highly variable (Birks 1989; Tipping 1994). The scheme adopted here to assign ages to pollen stratigraphic events is, with one difference, that of Birks (1989):

1. migration of birch *(Betula)* took place by *c.*11,500 cal BP;
2. hazel *(Corylus/Myrica pollen)* had colonised by 10,000 cal BP;
3. elm *(Ulmus)* migrated to the region by or at 9500 cal BP;
4. oak *(Quercus)* colonised significantly later, perhaps as late as 8500 cal BP;
5. pine *(Pinus)* expanded in parts of the region between 7500 and 6800 cal BP;
6. the elm decline occurred at *c.*6200 cal BP (Parker *et al.* 2001).

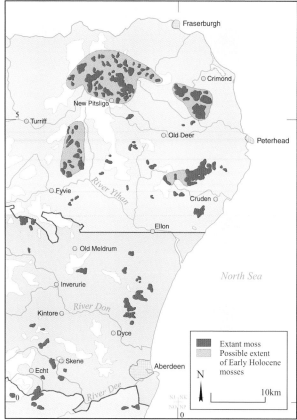

Fig. 4.4 Map showing the distribution and possible extent of raised mosses of probable early Holocene age, and of later Holocene blanket peats in the Aberdeenshire lowlands (modified from Stewart & Durno 1969). GV000123

Early Holocene Peat Formation in the Lowlands

Several large raised mosses probably began to form very early in the Holocene. These are not radiocarbon dated, but pollen stratigraphic correlation suggests this at Strichen, possibly at St Fergus, at Skene and south of the Dee at Netherley Moss. Raised mosses are prominent features in the lowland landscape and are shown in outline on Fig. 4.4, albeit in the 1960s after several centuries of sustained reduction by drainage, cultivation and cutting (Glentworth and Muir 1963; Stewart and Durno 1969). Most sediment stratigraphies in the region show they began to form in confined basins over earlier open water sediments on bedrock or till (Durno 1957). Being very large, not all parts of a moss need have formed at the same time, and in heavily cut-over mosses the point sampled, usually the thickest peat, need not be the earliest. In effect, however, these are random samples, and the consistency in their ages argues against any significant diachroneity in the formation and spread of the mosses. The full extent of the very largest mosses may have existed from the date of their inception.

Raised mosses initially supported open vegetation, with grass and sedge communities on drier ground surrounded by *Sphagnum* lawns and pools (Durno 1957;

Glentworth and Muir 1963); *Calluna* (ling heather) was initially a subsidiary component. Trees like birch and willow frequently colonised moss edges and could establish on domes when groundwater changes permitted. Raised mosses may have been important foci for Mesolithic hunter-gatherer activity (Clarke 1978), though in Aberdeenshire there is little spatial correlation between the findspots of Mesolithic artefacts (Kenworthy 1975) and raised mosses.

Peat accumulation in raised mosses, infilling shallow lakes in basins, need have no climatic significance. Away from these confined basins, however, early Holocene peat formation on formerly free-draining surfaces suggests some significant environmental change, perhaps linked to changing precipitation. On the floor of the impressive glacial meltwater channel at the Den of Boddam, near Peterhead, peat formed across fluvial sands and silts at *c.*10,625 cal BP (8675 BC), and accumulated rapidly until *c.*10,170 cal BP (8220 BC) in a nutrient-rich grass-sedge fen as groundwater levels rose but fluvial erosion ceased. Further south, the Netherley Moss pollen stratigraphy shows an extraordinary decline in tree pollen, and increases in grass and sedge pollen at and after the appearance of hazel between *c.*10,000 and 9200 cal BP (8050–7250 BC), which may also represent shifts in groundwater affecting bog communities. Elsewhere, on the steep westerly slope of Brimmond Hill near Aberdeen, peat grew after 11,500 cal BP (9550 BC) and before 10,000 cal BP (8050 BC), and on well-drained gravels in lower Glen Derry, basin peat formed at *c.*9850 cal BP (7900 BC). Peat inception in the early Holocene did not happen everywhere, or even over the major part of the landscape, but this reconstruction indicates that gleyed soils associated with waterlogging may have developed in some areas at the same time and rate as better-drained brown forest soils elsewhere. These gleyed soils were always unattractive to early human settlement.

Blanket Peat Development on the Montane Plateaux and the Grampian Foothills

The growth of blanket peat can have considerable constraints on human activities. The dominant model of blanket peat accumulation in the uplands is still that of Durno and Romans (1969). This has no dating controls, but suggests that surfaces between 300m and 700m OD were covered in blanket peat earlier than lower and higher surfaces. In this model the peat principally spread downhill from a few initial foci, though the slopes in the Grampian Mountains tend to steepen downwards, increasing water flow in soils and reducing the likelihood of peat forming. Unfortunately the radiocarbon dates in more recent analyses do not necessarily clarify interpretation. Not only are most of the dated sequences from basins rather than free-draining slopes (Clapperton *et al.* 1975; Huntley 1994; Binney 1997), but almost all the radiocarbon dates

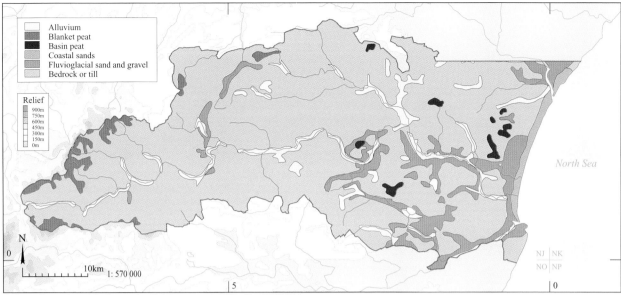

Fig. 4.5 Map showing the surficial cover of major accumulations of 'drift' and organic sediments in Donside, showing significant thicknesses of glacial, fluvioglacial, fluvial and peat deposits. GV000121

in the region are from single locations and cannot in themselves define the progress of peat spread in the vicinity. Many assays are also on wood preserved in peat rather than peat itself. Dubois and Ferguson (1985) suggested that blanket peat inception occurred extensively at 550m to 650m OD between 6900 and 6000 cal BP (4950 and 4050 BC), yet other assays on basal peat in valleyside mires (Binney 1997) and on wood in peat (Pears 1975a; 1975b) show that in some places it was forming by 8200–8000 cal BP (6250–6050 BC). Binney (1997) endorsed Durno and Romans' (1969) speculations that blanket peat formed earlier at altitudes between 500 and 700m OD, but peat inception can also be much later (Pears 1975a; Rapson 1985; Binney 1997). Without further work, it can be assumed only that most upland and montane surfaces mapped now as blanket peat (Fig. 4.5) were covered before 3000 cal BP (1050 BC).

Climatic Changes Expressed in Upland Environments

Recent work has explored the development of high-altitude blanket peats as a source of information about climate change. Changes in the peats after their inception, it is proposed, may have been promoted by climate change, either in alterations to precipitation or temperature, or indeed in complex combinations of both (Blackford 1993). Peat accumulation rates might be expected to change in response to climatic variables, but little conclusive data has been recorded. Unsurprisingly, lowland raised mosses grow more rapidly than hill peats, because of the greater warmth at lower altitudes (Durno 1961; Pears 1975b). However, peat decomposition

rates also vary under different hydrological conditions, slowing when waterlogged and increasing when drier (Blackford 1993; Binney 1997), and these suggest that montane peats in the region were wetter between 7700 and 7000 cal BP (5750–5050 BC), drier for a short period around 6700 cal BP (4750 BC), and possibly wetter in the earliest part of the Neolithic (Binney 1997; see also Tipping and Tisdall 2004).

Dubois and Ferguson attempted to define changing precipitation patterns using chemical analyses of radiocarbon-dated pine stumps. They argued that changing ratios of heavy to light water (deuterium: hydrogen) in the stumps represented responses of trees to relative aridity (1985; Dubois 1984). From these a series of wetter phases called pluvials were identified at c.8100 cal BP, between 7000 and 6700 cal BP (5050–4750 BC), between 4400 and 4200 cal BP (2450–2250 BC) and after 3550 cal BP (1600 BC). Some of these correspond to Binney's (1997) data for peat decomposition, but others do not. However, the use of deuterium:hydrogen ratios as a precipitation indicator has long been doubted. It is most often seen to indicate changing temperature (Epstein and Yapp 1977), and it is in this context that Dubois and Ferguson's (1985) data may need to be interpreted.

Later in prehistory peat decomposition signals are inconsistent between individual sites (Binney 1997), but it is not known why. One explanation is that blanket peat surfaces became less stable. Certainly radiocarbon assays from soils buried by solifluction on the high Cairngorm suggest slope and soil instability at c.5150 cal BP (3200 BC) and again at c.2750 cal BP (800 BC). For the last 2000 years, Barber *et al.* (2000) have produced a record of relative aridity from detailed and precisely dated changes in mosses forming a layered blanket peat at 920m OD on the Moine Mhor. This shows that the climate became gradually wetter or colder from *c*.1400 cal BP to *c*.850 cal BP (AD 550–1100), conditions becoming most intense after *c*.950 cal BP (AD 1000), before a return to relative aridity or warmth between *c*.750 and *c*.350 cal BP (AD 1200–1600). This last episode is a local expression of the much debated medieval warm period (Hughes and Diaz 1994; Broecker 2001), and was followed by the little ice age (Bradley and Jones 1995), which is marked in the data from Moine Mhor by an intense and abrupt climatic deterioration between *c*.350 and 150 cal BP (AD 1600–1800). Many blanket peats are now degraded and heavily gullied (Grieve *et al* 1995). Dubois and Ferguson (1985) suggested that this is a feature only of the last few hundred years, but whether this relates to climatic change or to overgrazing by deer and upland sheep populations is unclear.

Fluvial Change and Floodplain Terraces

The floodplains of most British rivers developed after about 6000 cal BP (4050 BC; Brown 1997; Macklin 1999), but the sequence recorded in the Dee suggests a different pattern. Nethermills, in the middle reaches of the Dee east of Crathes, is a critical locality, for here archaeological excavations have revealed a Mesolithic flint assemblage on a former floodplain at *c*.34m OD. The excavations have yet to be published, and published environmental analyses focused only on vegetation history (Ewan 1981), but the interpretation here suggests that this floodplain was built up by fluvial sediments before or during this earliest human occupation.

The deposits comprise some 1.2m of uniform coarse sands overlying coarse gravels, the latter perhaps a truncated surface of Late Devensian date (Brown 1993). The floodplain terrace surface here is 30–40m wide, and several palaeochannels on its surface run roughly parallel to the present river. Slightly sinuous, they bifurcate around sand islands, and at their widest they are about two thirds the width of the present river. There may be several generations of channels. The oldest preserved is 20m wide and 0.7m deep. A thin organic clay lines this channel, and must have been laid down in still water when the channel was inactive. The clay prevented free drainage and the channel filled with a peat that received numerous bands of inwashed minerogenic sediment from flood events. The aggradation of the floodplain with coarse sand was probably contemporary with the infilling of the palaeochannel by peat. Pollen analyses (Ewan 1981) suggest that peat inception occurred very early in the Holocene, close to the Younger Dryas-Holocene boundary, given the occurrence of open ground juniper and crowberry communities as birch trees became established.

In the Don valley at St Fergus, fluvial sands overlying Lateglacial Interstadial organic sediments are probably also of Younger Dryas age, but they form the surface of a higher terrace rather than the floodplain terrace (Munro 1986). This is different to the Dee sequence, and it is difficult to reconcile the two, except by suggesting that incision on both rivers took place at or towards the end of the Younger Dryas Stadial, as suggested for other valleys in northern Britain (Tipping 1998a).

The floodplain terrace on the Dee between Banchory and Crathes, then, is an ancient landscape feature formed very early in the Holocene. At Nethermills, the palaeochannel continued to receive peat and sediment until after the local colonisation of the floodplain by alder trees, after *c*.7500 cal BP (5550 BC). What happened thereafter is not clear because the Mesolithic artefact scatters recorded across the terrace surface to the bank above the Dee lie within a ploughsoil, and they cannot be shown to be *in situ.* This is also true for other surface collections along this reach of the river. At Birkwood, however, immediately upstream, Paterson and Lacaille (1936) excavated *in situ* late Mesolithic flint assemblages from towards the top of the sand fill of the same terrace, and in the middle of its surface. Thus, the deposits laid down in this terrace belong entirely within the Mesolithic. It is not known when the terrace surface ceased to be regularly inundated by floods.

There is little evidence in the region to suggest significant amounts of subsequent geomorphic activity. Lacustrine sequences should be sensitive to sediment inputs, as exemplified at Braeroddach, but these invariably indicate stability of the landscape from the earliest Holocene to after 6000 cal BP (4050 BC). At Castle of Wardhouse, where the present floodplain of the Shevock burn appears to have formed at the very beginning of the Holocene, a pond or lake formed from *c*.11,500 cal BP (9550 BC) until after *c*.6200 cal BP (4250 BC), but despite the narrow confines of the valley floor there is no evidence of any accelerated fluvial activity or even channel migration.

Each type of topographical setting probably has a different chronology of geomorphic activity, but data are too few to show that any of the recorded changes are of regional significance. Something major happened in the Late Neolithic period to the fluvial system of the Don between Inverurie and Hatton of Fintray, but it is not known what caused the change, nor the extent of its impact. The evidence was recovered from beneath the floodplain surface at Nether Daugh, near Kintore, where nearly 5m of fluvial sediments lie unconformably on glacial lake deposits. Near the base of this sequence, a peat some 20cm thick formed in the Late Neolithic, before minerogenic fluvial sediments were deposited once more in floods. Aitken (1991) saw this as the only major geomorphic disturbance to the fluvial regime in the Holocene, though whether caused by climatic instability or land-use change is unclear.

Along the Ythan, east of Ellon, the floodplain surface is graded to a sea level below that of the highest postglacial sea (Smith *et al.* 1992), indicating that the fluvial activity that formed it occurred after *c.*4400 cal BP (2450 BC). The substantial soil erosion dating from the Middle Bronze Age at Braeroddach Loch provides further evidence of fluvial activity, though it does not appear to be contemporary with the events in the Don or the Ythan.

Later activity is recorded at Relaquheim in the Ernan Water, a tributary of the upper Don and a typical high-gradient gravel-rich upland valley. Here the oldest preserved palaeochannel, which was formed during valley widening, was abandoned and infilled with peat *c.*1700 cal years ago (AD 250). Since then no flood sediment has been deposited.

The active aggradation of the floodplain of the Don at Kintore continued into the Middle Ages, and the alluvial deposits containing medieval pottery at The Stanners, Inverurie, imply that this was also the case upstream (Carter 1999, 654). Medieval fluvial activity is also recorded in the lower reaches of the Water of Feugh at Castlehill of Strachan, where the 13th-century channel was probably less constrained than at present, and possibly also multi-coursed. Such shifts in the plan of the channels may have been comparatively common where there were no embankments to constrain them. More importantly, these sequences demonstrate that parts of these valley floors are very young, in contrast to the youngest terraces in the middle reaches of the Dee.

Tree Migration in the Early Holocene

Landscape stability in the early Holocene is suggested from the absence of evidence for soil erosion in stratigraphic sequences. This quiescence was generated through the establishment of closed canopy grasslands at the beginning of the Holocene, and by the subsequent colonisation of trees. Juniper communities were abundant throughout the region before tree migration, irrespective of location (Vasari and Vasari 1968; Clapperton *et al.* 1975; Edwards and Rowntree 1980; Edwards and Ralston 1984; Huntley 1994).

Birch colonised slopes around Loch Kinord very soon after 11,250 cal BP (9300 BC), but, in contrast, had not become abundant some 30 kilometres upstream at Morrone by 10,800 cal BP (8850 BC), at which point the sequence is truncated. Elsewhere, birch woodland is described as having entirely replaced juniper and crowberry communities around Loch Builg at 525m OD, and to have been established in corries on Lochnagar. Birch pollen was already abundant before 10,000 cal BP (8050 BC) in the earliest pollen analyses at Braeroddach Loch, and at *c.*10,625 cal BP (8675 BC) was growing on the channel floor in the Den of Boddam.

Hazel followed on, comprehensively colonising the Ythan estuary at *c.*9500 cal BP (7550 BC), the slopes around Braeroddach at *c.*9925 cal BP (7975 BC), and

the high ground of Glen Avon around Loch Builg and Inchrory. Although it has been suggested that hazel colonisation was promoted by burning (Smith 1970; Huntley 1993), there is no consistent evidence that this was the case (Edwards 1990; Tipping 1994, 10).

The lowlands, from the coastal plain to the bedrock basins in the interior, were then colonised by elm trees, dated to around 8700 cal BP (6750 BC) at Braeroddach, where oak first appears at *c.*8300 cal BP (6350 BC). Variations in the sources of pollen to raised mosses, valley-floor peats and open water make it difficult to compare the proportions of different trees recorded. Nevertheless, around Strichen in the north, and Wardhouse near Insch, oak and elm pollen are represented in equal proportions. Elsewhere, on the coast at Aberdeen and at the mouth of the Ythan near Newburgh, elm is more common than oak, but in lower and mid-Deeside, at Loch of Park and in the Howe of Cromar, oak is much more common than elm. At Nethermills oak pollen is extraordinarily abundant and suggests that oak trees dominated the valley-floor woods. There were periods, very poorly defined, when the raised moss surfaces dried out sufficiently to be colonised by oak trees, and Durno (1957) quotes 19th-century descriptions of bog oaks 1m in diameter and 12m in length before branching, suggesting that they grew in closed woodland canopies, even on peat.

Pine Woodlands in the Montane Plateaux and the Grampian Foothills

Pine woodland in the Holocene was highly dynamic, its extent and density probably driven by climatic fluctuations (Birks 1975; Bennett 1984; Bridge, Haggart and Lowe 1990). The earliest Holocene pine colonisation is recorded before 10,000 cal BP (8050 BC) at Loch Kinord, where pine needles were found in the lake muds. However, the absence of significant amounts of pine pollen when the tree was probably growing so close by is a significant problem (Fossitt 1994; Bennett, Birks and Willis 1998). No less easy to interpret is the over-representation of pine pollen. At Morrone, for example, pine pollen contributes >40% of the terrestrial pollen throughout the last 7500 years, but Huntley (1994) did not find any macroscopic remains of the trees themselves. He concluded that pine trees had probably not grown on this hillslope, which is only a few kilometres from the present-day pine woods of Mar Forest. It is not possible to provide confident estimates of the chronology and extent of pine growth from pollen records alone, though analyses based on radiocarbon-dated wood remains in the peats are also disputed, largely because wood decays in dry peat, and the absence of wood need not, therefore, be of significance (Dubois and Ferguson 1988; Pears 1988).

Pears (1975b) demonstrated from a handful of radiocarbon assays in high-altitude peats that wood remains, principally pine, were of very different ages, ranging from 8000 to 2500 cal BP (6050–550 BC). Further analyses by Dubois and Ferguson (1985) collated a sample of forty radiocarbon-assayed pine trees. The oldest is calibrated to around 8100 cal years ago (6150 BC), and grew at 750m OD. Between c.7000 and 6000 cal BP (5050–4050 BC) radiocarbon-dated pine trees are not found higher than c.620m OD, but subsequently they grew at both high and low altitudes until shortly after c.4000 cal BP (2050 BC). Fewer pine remains were recovered after this, and only at altitudes below 500m OD. If these changes represent shifts in the altitude of the tree line it would probably reflect significant changes in temperature (cf. Kullman 1988), but Dubois and Ferguson (1985) maintained that the pattern signifies only the fortuitous preservation of tree remains. In order to explore this problem, Binney (1997) used pollen analyses at high altitudes in the Cairngorm. This showed that pine woods at high altitudes were never dense, but pine trees were more abundant before 7300 cal BP (5350 BC), and between 7000 and 6800 cal BP (5050–4850 BC). Rapson (1985) also suggested that pine colonised the high corries of Lochnagar around 7950 cal years ago (6000 BC). These data may define the warmest period of the mid-Holocene climate. Trees also became less common at the very end of the Mesolithic between 6700 and 6300 cal BP (4750–4350 BC), and after c.4500 cal BP (2550 BC) at the end of the Late Neolithic (Binney 1997). High-altitude woodlands were permanently more fragmentary after 6300 cal BP (4350 BC) and may have declined in response to falling temperatures.

The fragmentation of pine woodlands in the mountains through climatic stresses has considerable significance for the stability of woodlands in lowland contexts. Similar responses in the lowlands may be misinterpreted as anthropogenic clearance, though few analyses are detailed enough to evaluate this. The pine woodlands in the foothills and basins were established synchronously with those in the mountains. On the floor of Glen Derry, at 300m OD, pine probably represented the only tree of any significance after c.8400 cal BP (6450 BC). About a century later, it had also colonised the Braeroddach catchment, seemingly very rapidly, and at more or less the same time as oak. The two competed successfully, probably on different soils, but pine contributed no more than c.30 % tlp, which suggests that the tree was not abundant. However, some 4km west, pine was established as the dominant tree around Loch Kinord by c.7500 cal BP (5550 BC), and around nearby Loch Davan after c.7760 cal BP (5810 BC). This synchroneity in different settings across the region is not well understood, but pine gained a competitive advantage for a short time in all environments. This was probably aided by major climatic shifts, and there are suggestions that a lowering of the level of Loch Kinord, and some climatic aridity, coincided with this rise to dominance in the vicinity.

Pine woodlands below the mountains had the characteristics of present Cairngorm pine woods (Steven and Carlisle 1959) and supported an undergrowth of juniper. At their fullest range, they may have reached down to the hills above the lowlands, such as the Hill of Fare above Loch of Park and the east flank of Glen Tanar. Vasari and Vasari (1968) suggested that pine was for a time in the early Holocene an important tree around Strichen Moss in the north, and it may have colonised the acid soils here and around New Pitsligo before they were covered by extensive lowland blanket peats (below). There is no evidence that pine trees colonised the lowlands or the coastal plain in significant numbers or for sustained periods.

The Alder Rise
Alder is competitively inferior to the deciduous trees that had already colonised lowland soils, but it was able to outcompete pine in the interior. Most pollen sequences in the region suggest that the expansion of alder was rapid, though occurring at different times, at c.8000 cal BP (6050 BC) at Loch of Park, c.7700 cal BP (5750 BC) at Den of Boddam, c.7330 cal BP (5380 BC) at Braeroddach Loch, and between 7300 and 6800 cal BP (5350–4850 BC) at sites in Aberdeen. Sometimes, however, its establishment as a significant tree in the landscape is separated by a long interval from its colonisation. The Loch Kinord sequence typifies this. Alder trees probably grew here from around 7500 cal BP (5550 BC), and only expanded in any numbers around the time of the elm decline at c.6200 cal BP (4250 BC): the decline in elm may have allowed alder to spread. At nearby Loch Davan, alder may have grown locally from before 8000 cal BP (6050 BC), but it only became significant after 7500 cal BP (5550 BC). These extraordinary differences over such short distances have to be explained by different triggering mechanisms at each site, either through pedological or geomorphic shifts, or through mechanisms to reduce the competitiveness of other trees (Bennett and Birks 1990). Whatever else, the alder rise is not attributable simply to a wetter climate (Godwin 1975). The evidence for raised moss formation and soil gleying long before the alder rise suggests that few new niches were created by changing soil conditions in the mid-Holocene. In this respect, the Ythan estuary is perhaps a special case, where the exposure of salt marsh peats during sea-level fall after c.4200 cal BP (2250 BC) probably allowed alder to become established in the vicinity (Smith et al. 1983; 1999).

Human Disturbance to Woodlands in the Mesolithic
Evidence of Mesolithic activity in the North-east is only fleetingly represented in the palaeoecological record. At Burreldale, analyses reported by Edwards (1990) seem to suggest that local colonisation by alder was

Fig. 4.6 Den of Boddam (NJ 114 414). This oblique aerial view shows the reservoir that now occupies part of the floor of the den. Traces of the Neolithic flint-workings and their attendant spoil dumps can be seen on the slope rising up from the water's edge on the right of the picture. DP011672

accompanied by increased burning, although a causal link was not developed and anthropogenic activity is only one cause of any increase in the frequency of fire (Tipping 1996). The insubstantial character of the impact of Mesolithic communities in the lowlands is, perhaps, surprising. Even at the exposures of flint-rich Buchan Gravels at Den of Boddam, which were exploited on an industrial scale during the Neolithic (Saville 1995), there is little to indicate their presence. Edwards and Ralston (1984) were critical of the palynological evidence for late Mesolithic anthropogenic disturbance suggested at Loch of Park, and the plant macrofossil records for open ground are interpreted here as probably deriving from post-elm decline sediments. Similarly, the single anomalous pollen spectrum interpreted by Ewan (1981) to indicate late Mesolithic woodland disturbance at nearby Nethermills is unconvincing, perhaps made because of the artefactual evidence for Mesolithic occupation nearby (Paterson and Lacaille 1936; Kenworthy 1975).

The Elm Decline
The elm decline, which is often assumed to mark the boundary between the Mesolithic and the Neolithic

(Smith and Pilcher 1973), is recognised at most pollen sequences in the region, though it is securely radiocarbon dated only at Lochs Braeroddach and Davan in the Howe of Cromar. At Loch Davan, an initial decline dates to *c*.5800 cal BP (3850 BC), but a second, more substantial loss happened at around 4800 cal BP (2850 BC; Hirons and Edwards 1986). Two declines are also recorded at Braeroddach Loch. The first dates to *c*.6000 cal BP (4050 BC), but elm trees rapidly regenerated. The second, at 5000–4800 cal BP (3050–2850 BC), is accompanied by the first increases in the grazing indicator, ribwort plantain *(Plantago lanceolata)*. Oak pollen percentages increase temporarily at this time, suggesting that oak trees occupied ground ceded by elm (Edwards and Rowntree 1980). In contrast, alder seems to have colonised as elm trees died at Loch Kinord. The first elm decline around the Howe of Cromar is closely comparable in date with this event elsewhere in the British Isles (Parker *et al.* 2001), but here there is no evidence in the pollen record for contemporary human activity.

It has been argued that the elm decline need not occupy the critical position at the Mesolithic-Neolithic boundary, because agriculture may have predated the fall in elm (Edwards 1989; Edwards and Hirons 1984). This is not certain (Tipping 1994), and is not evident at sites in eastern Scotland. As Edwards and Ralston (1984) observed, vegetation changes in the hundreds of years after the first elm decline in the Howe of

Cromar are more akin to hunter-gatherer impacts. Thus, an anthropogenic origin for the first decline in elm values has not been established, and recent explanations have returned to the possibility of a brief climatic deterioration mediating pedological change (Tipping and Milburn 2000b). The probable climatic impacts on pine populations in the Cairngorm at *c.*6000 cal BP (4050 BC) may be part of this short-lived deterioration (Tipping and Tisdall 2004).

The Landscape Context of Neolithic Settlement

While no anthropogenic link with the elm decline has been demonstrated in the region, there is no doubt that farming communities were settling in the North-east at this time (pp. 45–7). Neolithic long cairns are recorded across the region, and two large rectangular buildings excavated at Balbridie and Crathes in lower Deeside are of this date. That at Balbridie was erected on a Late Devensian river terrace above the Holocene floodplain, and all but one of the many radiocarbon assays overlap between 5900 and 5650 cal BP (3950–3700 BC). About 20,000 carbonised cereal grains were recovered, the largest assemblage of Neolithic date in the British Isles. Emmer wheat *(Triticum dicoccum)* predominates at 80% of the cereal assemblage, with naked barley *(Hordeum vulgare* L. var *nudum)* at 18% and a bread-wheat type *(T. aestivum)* at 2%, but bread-wheat was recovered almost alone in one cache and so is argued to have been grown as a crop (Fairweather and Ralston 1993). Two charred grains of oat *(Avena* sp.) were retrieved, but probably represent a weed within fields. Flax *(Linum usitatissimum)* is also thought to have been cultivated. This extraordinary evidence for cultivation leads to speculation as to where the crops were being grown. Edwards (1989) found that the turves at the site, which were presumably cut locally, contained macroscopic remains of emmer and cereal-type pollen, though the charred plant analyses revealed no evidence for crop processing on the site. Similar cereal plant remains are now known from the building across the River Dee at Crathes (Timpany pers. com.). The landscape there was devoid of trees except hazel, and the relative abundance of cereal-type pollen and the absence of pollen indicators for grazing suggest this building to have been the focus of crop growing (Davies and Tipping unpublished).

The environmental context for early Neolithic activity elsewhere in the lowlands is very poorly understood, though at Wardhouse, in the Don valley, undated and poorly resolved pollen analyses suggest the replacement of birch-hazel woodland by grazed grassland at or soon after the elm decline. This general lack of data from lower Deeside and the Skene Lowland led Edwards and Ralston (1984; Edwards 1989) to look at the basin landscapes of upper Deeside, but it is hard to identify from pollen analyses in the Howe of Cromar a landscape that resembles the arable fields conjured by the plant macrofossils at Balbridie. Indeed,

Vasari and Vasari (1968) dismissed the likelihood of Neolithic setlement around Loch Kinord on grounds of soil impoverishment, and Edwards and Ralston also considered the conditions marginal.

The Neolithic period in the Howe of Cromar is characterised by what Edwards (1979a) defined as 'mainly regional activity', or evidence for the disturbance of tree taxa but with minimal indications of changes in herb pollen. Open-ground herbs recorded in the Neolithic at Braeroddach Loch were also recorded in earlier sediments. Disturbance of woodlands was recorded at *c.*6040 cal BP (4090 BC). Further disturbance occurred at *c.*5320 cal BP (3370 BC), slightly later (*c.*3100 BC) at Loch Davan. These are interference phases, in which the types of human activity are very difficult to discern, perhaps because they occurred some distance from the pollen site. However, in the absence of positive indicators of anthropogenic activity, such as the presence of cereal pollen or, less assuredly, grazing indicators (Behre 1981), it is not possible to demonstrate human causation. They do not necessarily represent settlement even if they represent human activities. These phases are, indeed, as ephemeral and ambiguous as Mesolithic disturbances in other parts of the country (Edwards and Ralston 1984). Two interpretations are either that hunter-gatherers in upper Deeside lived contemporaneously with early agriculturalists further downstream, or more likely that Mesolithic lifestyles were perpetuated by early farmers (Edwards and Ralston 1984; Edwards 1989).

Soil Acidification from the Early Neolithic

In addition to these small disturbances in the woodland cover, there is also some evidence that soil quality deteriorated at the beginning of the Neolithic. In Buchan, the soils across extensive areas of the landscape had probably already become podsolised and were being covered in a lowland form of blanket peat (Stewart and Durno 1969). At the Moss of Cruden, blanket peat inception seems to have occurred at around 5760 cal BP (3810 BC). *Calluna* (ling heather) dominated on this peat, and probably on the earlier podsol too. Charcoal is common throughout the profile, and the fires were interpreted as *'widespread and frequent'* (Stewart and Durno 1969, 178), though the burning need not have been causal in peat formation. Comparable blanket peats developed at Lambshill Moss, near New Pitsligo, although these are not dated directly. Tephra horizons in the sequence show only that inception predated *c.*4400 cal BP (2450 BC; Dugmore *et al.* 1995).

On raised mosses at Strichen in the north and Netherley in the south, substantial increases in heather pollen are indicated in post-elm decline peats at *c.*5700–5500 cal BP (3750–3550 BC). By the end of the Late Neolithic, after *c.*4600 cal BP (2650 BC), *Calluna* also grew abundantly on podsols on the increasingly stable channel slopes at the Den of Boddam, and, in close comparison to the Moss of Cruden sequence, microscopic charcoal records suggest that fires were frequent from this time until the last 1000 years. Similarly around Braeroddach Loch, from *c.*4600 cal BP (2650 BC) *Calluna* grew both on increasingly podsolised soils in the catchment, and with *Sphagnum* on blanket peats. Fire frequency or intensity increased with the rise in *Calluna* (Edwards 1979b).

The acidification of soils and the rise of heather are also reflected in data from archaeological monuments. At Balbridie, for example, turves used in the construction of the building were from acid brown forest soils, tending to podsols (Romans and Robertson 1983; Fairweather and Ralston 1993). The scant pollen data from the Neolithic barrow at Midtown of Pitglassie, radiocarbon dated to *c.*5710 cal BP (3760 BC), show that the immediate area was a rather monotonous *Calluna* heath (Shepherd 1996). The monument seems to have been constructed away from any arable farmland.

Later Holocene Human Activities on the Montane Plateaux and Grampian Foothills Landscapes

Few sequences provide more than a schematic outline of woodland loss. On high-altitude Cairngorm peats, heath had been significant throughout the Holocene (Binney 1997), but *Calluna* increased its ground cover gradually from the mid-Holocene, and more rapidly after *c.*4000 cal BP (2050 BC) as the remaining pine woodlands fragmented. At high altitudes in Lochnagar and the Cairngorm, the replacement of local tree communities by grassland and heath is recorded in the Middle to Late Bronze Age, between 3360 and 2830 cal BP (1410–880 BC), and in Glen Derry pine woodland seems to have gradually disintegrated at around the same time as *Calluna* heath began to dominate. At Morrone, however, on a north-facing blanket- and mire-clad hillslope at over 400m OD, there is no clear evidence of any woodland loss. Birch rather than pine woods may have persisted here from *c.*7500 cal BP (5550 BC), and the only significant change recorded in this landscape was not until an increase in the extent of wet flushes and surface water fed mires *c.*1500 years ago (AD 450).

These gradual declines in the extent of woodland are difficult to interpret. Viewed from the montane summits, a sustained fragmentation of woodland and its substitution by moor might reflect climatic deterioration. Looking up to the foothills from the basins of the middle Dee and Don, the same features might be interpreted as a product of low-intensity but sustained grazing pressures. Differentiating between these remains a central question in the Scottish Highlands (Davies, Tisdall and Tipping 2004).

The absence of clear evidence of human impact on the slopes at Morrone may relate only to wetter slopes in the uplands. Elsewhere, at Relaquheim, in the Ernan Water above Strathdon, slopes under podsols and brown forest soils at over 350m OD have had a rich agricultural

history in the last *c.*1700 years. This particular upland landscape was tended with care, managed and invested in, and never abandoned in the historic period (pp. 229–31). The Ernan valley was almost treeless at the inception of the sequence *c.*1700 years ago (AD 250), but it was grazed, and barley type and oats/wheat pollen suggest cultivation. Arable activity may have declined after *c.*1300 cal BP (AD 650), but the slopes continued to be a pastoral resource, and were more intensively exploited after *c.*850 cal BP (AD 1100). The survival of natural plant communities seems unlikely, and increases in the pollen of juniper on the dry slopes after *c.*350 cal BP (AD 1600) suggests the maintenance of this unpalatable shrub as hedges in a landscape increasingly compartmentalised and organised. Barley and oats/wheat (probably oats) began again to be cultivated *c.*270 years ago (AD 1680), in apparent disregard of the climatic deterioration known as the little ice age (Barber *et al.* 2000; see Tipping 1998b). Fields under permanent pasture may have been sown with nitrogen-fixing legumes some 200 years ago.

Human Activities in the Bedrock Basin Landscape

Edwards distinguishes *'small-scale activity'* (1979a) around Braeroddach after *c.*4250 cal BP (2300 BC), at the beginning of the Early Bronze Age. This shift, perhaps to a more permanent human presence in one part of the landscape, is dated to *c.*3840 cal BP (1890 BC) at Loch Davan. It is not clear precisely what this means, but from then on phases of woodland reduction can be assigned an anthropogenic cause, probably principally through grazing pressures. The impression is one of only limited impacts on the environment, but Edwards describes *'massive inroads into the woodland cover'* (1979b, 36) derived from pollen concentration data. These certainly show that the amounts of tree pollen were significantly reduced, and soils continued to be eroded from the catchment (Edwards 1979b). Changes recorded in lake sediment chemistry also suggest that the erosion of leached topsoils in the catchment may have resulted in soils that were richer in nutrients (Edwards and Rowntree 1980). However, it is very difficult to identify major increases in the absolute amounts of herb pollen at this time.

Ongoing activity around Lochs Davan and Braeroddach seems to have been small in spatial scale and short-lived, although some soil erosion indicators increased from *c.*4000 cal BP (2050 BC). Accepting the imprecision of radiocarbon assays, these clearance events persist for 100–300 years. Subsequent activities around both lochs were more extensive. Cereal pollen (barley-type) is recorded from *c.*3300–3100 cal BP (1350–1150 BC) at Braeroddach Loch, and after 2400 cal BP (450 BC) at Loch Davan. This phase is seen as a major clearance around Braeroddach at least, where lake sediments from this time until *c.*2000 cal BP (50 BC)

Fig. 4.7 This oblique aerial view taken from above Kildrummy Castle (foreground) looks northwards across a Bedrock Basin Landscape to Rhynie and the Hill of Noth. SC674805

show reversals in the chronological sequence of radiocarbon dates, indicating significant transfers of old organic matter to the lake from eroding soils. This instability is most readily ascribed to comparatively intense settlement and arable agriculture.

Interpretation of the subsequent sequence at Braeroddach over the last *c.*2000 years is complicated by uncertainties in the chronology and the possible truncation of the sediments (Edwards and Rowntree 1980). The cause of the former lies with a further intensification of soil erosion, again causing radiocarbon age reversals. The latter is, perhaps, implied by the absence of conifer pollen from 18th- and 19th-century planting (Durno 1956). At least two radiocarbon assays in the Davan sequence are also affected by the deposition of older organic matter between 1500 cal BP (AD 450) and the present day, but here a clear increase in pine percentages strongly suggests this sequence to be complete.

From before 2100 cal BP (150 BC) until, perhaps, 370 cal BP (AD 1580), the pollen sequence at Braeroddach has abundant birch. Comparable increases in birch and, more particularly, in hazel-type pollen, are seen at Davan from *c.*1900 cal BP (AD 50) until *c.*800 cal BP (AD 1150). Edwards and Rowntree (1980) suggested that this may represent woodland regeneration within a largely abandoned landscape, though crop growing persisted at Braeroddach. Whittington and Edwards have gone on to describe this change as an *'apparently massive abandonment of farmed land'* (1993, 18) around Loch Davan, linking it to a widespread abandonment as a result of Roman military campaigns (pp. 111–14). However, no reduction in agricultural activity is seen at more remote locations, such as at Relaqheim. Heightened agricultural activity was not recognised again around Loch Davan until after *c.*800 cal BP (AD 1150), but thereafter it was maintained to the present day.

Other sources of palaeoenvironmental information relating the exploitation of the basin landscapes are essentially archaeological. Deposits at the 13th-century **Castle of Wardhouse**, west of Insch, for example, contained charred cereal remains of barley, oats and one grain of wheat (Boardman in Yeoman 1998). This is perhaps no more than should be expected in the heart of the Garioch, though there was no evidence of on-site processing to confirm that these were from local crops. The importance of the Garioch and the Insch Depression in the later settlement pattern has been elegantly demonstrated by Walton (1950), who mapped the rural population recorded in the Poll Tax return of 1696. This shows how the pattern of settlement of 1696 in the Insch Depression closely coincides with the extent of deep phase soils of the Insch Series of brown forest soils mapped by Glentworth (1944). The larger settlements frequently occupy small patches of thickened topsoil, seldom more than a couple of hundred metres across. These would today be described as plaggen soils (Davidson and Simpson 1994), artificially created soils that have received high inputs of household and farmyard manure. The patterns of cultivation reflected in the creation of these soils are likely to have earlier origins.

Human Activities in the Lowland Landscape

In the lowlands, at Strichen and Netherley, it is also possible to trace woodland decline, but all events are undated and poorly resolved. Woodland reduction at Strichen appears to have been gradual, with no significant regeneration phases, but at Netherley the first significant and sharp woodland reduction is estimated to have occurred in the Early Bronze Age, and there were several woodland regeneration phases thereafter.

On the floor of the meltwater channel at Den of Boddam, and perhaps on the till plateau away from it, populations of birch trees were sharply reduced after 4600 cal BP (2650 BC). This date is neatly bracketed by radiocarbon assays from one of the adjacent flint mines. Samples taken from the humic surface of a podsol beneath the spoil from one of the pits, and from a basal peat in the top of the fill of the same pit, returned dates between 5460–5000 cal BP (3510–3050 BC) and 4250–3990 cal BP (2300–2040 BC) (Saville 1995). Low-intensity grazing pressures occurred at the same time, and some cereal-type pollen is recorded, but these are arguably not in proportion to the scale or intensity of woodland loss. It seems likely that woodland loss represents an indirect effect of the mining, though direct impacts cannot be demonstrated. Despite the density of small circular pits on the steep slopes directly above the channel-floor peats, there was apparently no soil erosion.

Subsequent records of agricultural activity elsewhere in the lowlands are fragmentary, probably reflecting the scarcity of sediment sequences that have survived agricultural improvements, the limitations of early analyses, and the Neolithic focus of some projects. Several snapshots are available, but these provide little evidence of the wider development of the landscape. At Kintore, for example, the pollen assemblage from the Late Neolithic valley-floor peat beneath the floodplain at Nether Daugh is dominated by alder. This is unsurprising in such a location, but the insect fauna are of open-ground character, and Aitken (1991) argued that this represented an arable landscape. An even briefer glimpse of part of the Early Bronze Age landscape comes from a Beaker cist at Udny Green, near Methlick, where pollen data suggest an open, almost treeless agrarian landscape (Davies and Tipping unpublished). These analyses depict a very small area around the cist, probably only measured in tens of metres, and for a very short time, perhaps only when the cist was open, but the area was grazed, and Hordeum-type pollen suggests the local cultivation of barley. These data are interesting for showing that the burial interred in this cist lay within the agricultural landscape, rather than beyond its edges.

Renewed woodland clearance is recorded at Den of Boddam after c.2600 cal BP (650 BC, apparently for the gradual expansion of grazed ground, and this may be true at nearby St Fergus Moss also. It may have been that by the time some of the large timber-laced forts were being constructed (pp. 97–105), suitable local timber was in short supply. Tipping, Davies and McCulloch (2006) have linked the development of managed oak woodland in the early centuries AD north of the Great Glen to the demands of such high-status sites.

The Coastal Sand Plain

The coastal sand plain contains deposits relating to the Devensian Lateglacial sea-level fall, but the formation of the sand dunes and links owes more to Holocene sea-level change. Current models emphasise the role of rising sea level in the early Holocene in driving sediment onshore from the seabed (Hansom 1998), but none of the early to mid-Holocene coastal sediments in the Ythan and Philorth estuaries contain wind-blown sands (Smith et al. 1983; 1992; 1999). Much of the data in the region imply that the subsequent fall in sea level was more significant in exposing sand to wind (Ritchie 1992; below).

In the Ythan estuary, relative sea level was below -9m OD at c.11,740 cal BP. Subsequent sea-level rise is represented by a grey silt, formed as a saltmarsh, which thins as it penetrates inland, successively burying peat at -7.85m OD after 9240 cal BP (7290 BC), and at +3.38m OD after 6770 cal BP (4820 BC; Smith et al. 1999). The deposition of these saltmarsh muds was interrupted by a coarser layer at between 8160 and 7900 cal BP (6210–5950 BC), which is believed to represent the incursion of the now well-known tsunami that struck eastern Scotland (Smith 2002). The tsunami sediments are found up to +3.2m OD, but this is a considerable underestimate of the probable height of the wave. The highest relative sea level was around 4m OD, and may have persisted until c.4440–4200 cal BP (2490–2250 BC; Smith et al. 1992), roughly the beginning of the Early Bronze Age. After this sea level fell again, with at least one sustained pause, to present levels slightly above Ordnance Datum.

Wind-blown sands are first recorded in the Ythan and Philorth estuaries some considerable time after 4200 cal BP (2250 BC; Smith et al. 1999). On the Sands of Forvie, however, and also at Menie Links south of Newburgh, Hawke-Smith reported surface collections made in the early 20th century of late Mesolithic microlithic flint assemblages 'in blown sand' (1980, 497). If this is correct, these are the earliest archaeological contexts that imply blowing sand. Further south, Durno's (1970) brief description of the sediment stratigraphy just inland of the coast at Nelson Street, Aberdeen, shows that peat was overlain after c.6000 cal BP (4050 BC) by 4m of sand. The origin of this sand is not discussed by Durno, and it may not be wind-blown, but this thickness of sediment is difficult to understand in such a context by fluvial processes.

At both Forvie and Rattray, the dune sands form a comparatively thin veneer over bedrock and Late Devensian sediments (Steers 1976). The precise way in which the present morphology of the dunes at Forvie was reached is unclear (Ritchie 1992), but the dominant movement of sand appears to have been northward from South Forvie, and it does not appear to have blown across the Ythan in great quantities (Smith et al. 1999). Archaeological deposits have been used to provide a chronology of major sand-blowing events (Landsberg, cited by Gimingham 1964; Ritchie 1992), though this has sometimes involved assumptions about the dates of some types of monument. For example a line of shell middens overlooking the Ythan estuary (Hawke-Smith

1980) lies parallel to the highest postglacial marine sediments (Smith *et al.* 1992), suggesting that they are either Late Neolithic to Early Bronze Age in date, or an earlier distribution shaped by marine erosion at this time. One, however, has now been radiocarbon dated to *c.*3170 cal BP (1220 BC) and lies in the Middle Bronze Age (cited in Murray *et al.* 1992). Ardmarks were found both here and in probable dune sands at Rattray, the latter associated with a wooden hurdle fence dated to *c.*3210 cal BP (1260 BC), again in the Middle Bronze Age (Murray *et al.* 1992). The palaeoenvironmental interpretation of the sandy soil cultivated at Rattray is ambiguous. The charred plant assemblage suggests that cereals were not being cultivated (Boardman in Murray *et al.* 1992), but the pollen analyses (Coles in Murray

et al. 1992) record *Hordeum*-type (cf. barley) pollen, though this pollen-type includes many wild grass taxa at home in sand dunes.

It is difficult to identify any specific sand-blowing events between *c.*3000 cal BP (1050 BC) and the medieval period, when dune-building is apparently contemporary with the 13th-century settlement at Rattray (Murray *et al.* 1992, Murray and Murray 1993). At Forvie the sand was pushed successively further north, but an exceptional event is documented in AD 1413, at which time sand inundated Forvie Kirk and covered ploughland. However, it is difficult to establish the significance of an individual event such as this, and to discriminate between climatic factors or overgrazing as its driving forces (Ritchie 1992).

Chapter 5: The Neolithic and Bronze Age Landscape

Angela Gannon, Stratford Halliday, John Sherriff and Adam Welfare

Neolithic and Early Bronze Age burial mounds and megaliths are often the most visible and tangible links to prehistory in the Scottish countryside. This was certainly the case in Aberdeenshire prior to the transformation of the landscape at the end of the 18th century. In Donside alone, at least fifty-three burial-cairns are known to have been removed by the end of the 19th century (p. 22), and standing stones and stone circles have suffered no less. Despite these losses, such monuments continue to form an important component of the countryside, the recumbent stone circles in particular, with a massive slab set between flanking uprights, contributing to the unique character of north-east Scotland.

The briefest examination of any of these monuments reveals some role in relationship to the landscape, from conspicuous burial-cairns heaped up on skylines, to the more subtle sitings of recumbent stone circles, often commanding spectacular vistas from less prominent positions. The architecture of the monuments also

plays its part, the recurrent features in the design of the recumbent stone circles, for instance, conveying a sense of order in the lives of the people who built them. But vestiges of their settlements are few and far between, and the Neolithic and Early Bronze Age landscape that is visible today is largely one of burial and ritual. As a result, the division between early and later prehistory in this volume is essentially drawn between funerary and ceremonial monuments on the one hand, and settlement remains on the other. For the purposes of this chapter, this division has been further refined, the first section dealing with the funerary sites in roughly chronological order, and the second the various categories of ceremonial monuments.

Fig. 5.1 This map shows the distribution of a selection of monuments and artefacts in Donside that are thought to be broadly Neolithic in date. The densest concentration of artefacts comes from the Garioch, mainly found as a result of intensive cultivation in the 19th century, but a thin scatter also penetrates into the uplands. GV000185

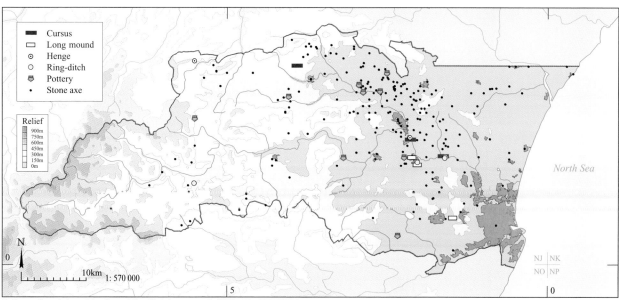

*Fig. 5.2 **Ardlair** (NJ 5527 2794). Photographed from some 15m above the ground, this view shows the landscape setting of this recumbent stone circle, which occupies the summit of a hill with panoramic views all around. SC851603*

Despite the difficulties of identifying early prehistoric settlement remains, there is little doubt that communities have flourished in Donside since at least the Neolithic. The distribution of stone axes, the key type-fossil of this period, extends throughout the most fertile land in the region, and there is a particularly dense concentration of finds in the Garioch. Few of these discoveries can be pinned down precisely in the landscape (p. 23), but pottery and other artefacts have also been found in the same general areas. Early Neolithic pottery has been identified at no less than ten locations, at six of them as a result of excavation – **Loanhead of Daviot**, Easterton (**Logie Durno**), **East Finnercy**, **Greenbogs**, **Deer's Den**, and **Forest Road**, Kintore – and at four as stray finds – **Legatesden Quarry**, **Fernybrae**, **Bin Hill** and **Clova Estates**. The hemispherical bowl, said to have been found in a short cist at **Den of Craig** and previously catalogued as Neolithic (Callander 1929, Fig. 40; Henshall 1983, 43), has not been included in this list, and is more likely to be Bronze Age in date.

Most of the Neolithic sherds are from round-bottomed carinated bowls, some of which are lugged, and some adorned with fingertip fluting at the rims. The shape and decoration of the vessels is in keeping with the 'north-east style' identified by Henshall (1983), for which radiocarbon dates within the first half of the 4th millennium BC have been attained from four sites in Aberdeenshire and Moray (Sheridan 2002, 87; Shannon Fraser, pers. com.). These are the barrows at Midtown of Pitglassie and Boghead, and the large, rectangular, timber buildings situated on opposite banks of the River Dee at Balbridie and Crathes.

Some of the pottery from Donside may well be derived from settlements, though most of the contexts from which they came are, at best, obscure. At **East Finnercy**, for example, following his re-excavation of the cairn in 1952, Atkinson believed the sherds were associated with hearths (*DES 1952*, 4), but subsequent writers have been more sceptical about the nature of the pre-cairn activity (Leivers, Roberts and Peterson 2000, 194). More recent discoveries, such as those at **Greenbogs**, near Monymusk (*DES 1996*, 9–10), and **Deer's Den**, Kintore (Alexander 2000), have come from scatters of what are probably domestic pits, and the only definite buildings so far located north of the Mounth are those at at Balbridie and Crathes (Ralston 1982; *DES 2005*, 12–13). The analysis of the 20,000 carbonised cereal grains recovered from Balbridie has revealed considerable detail of the crops that were being grown in the Neolithic Period, though the absence of any crop-processing debris from these deposits perhaps suggests the crops were not grown in the immediate vicinity. At Crathes, however, analyses suggest that the building was the focus for an area of crop cultivation (see Tipping above p. 40).

Early Bronze Age settlements are equally difficult to identify, though some are probably represented by scatters of stone tools identified in arable fields. With this in mind, a field-walking project was commissioned as part of the survey of Donside. The work was undertaken by a team from Reading University under the direction of Dr T Phillips (2003; 2005), and focused on the valley of the Brindy Burn, which flows southwards into the Don south of the recumbent stone circle at **Cothiemuir Wood**. A wide distribution of struck pieces of flint and quartz and a handful of tools was discovered in the fields then under cultivation. These were mainly on the middle and lower slopes along the valley of the Brindy Burn, and generally not far above the stream. The main exception was one of four discrete clusters of material, which was on the first terrace above the Don.

Translating this into patterns of settlement is difficult, as much as anything because the activities by which the general scatters of stone tools and waste were deposited are by no means clear. Nevertheless, these activities do not appear to have been focused on **Cothiemuir Wood**, reflecting a pattern previously discovered around the recumbent stone circle at Tomnaverie, Deeside (Phillips 2003; 2005, 97). However, at **Kirkton of Bourtie** field-walking has recovered several clusters of flint tools and debitage in the field immediately surrounding a recumbent stone circle (*DES 1994*, 25; *1995*, 31; *1996*, 7; *1997*, 7–8).

The uncertainties in interpreting this material are compounded by the loss of so many other components of the prehistoric landscape. Today, many recumbent stone circles appear to be isolated monuments, but this is essentially a product of agricultural improvement, which has had a particularly acute impact in Donside. Elsewhere, notably at the eastern end of Deeside, recumbent stone circles and ring-cairns survive in areas that have not been improved. In every case – Nine Stanes, Garrol Wood; Campstone Hill, Raedykes; Clune Wood; and Upper Balfour – they stand amongst scatters of clearance heaps, field banks and occasional hut-circles. Antiquarian records and the depictions of destroyed monuments on the 1st edition of the OS 6-inch map hint that this was also the case in Donside, for example on **Bin Hill**, near Leslie, where the Neolithic sherds were found. Here the recumbent of

Fig. 5.3 Crathes (NO 7393 9670). A Neolithic timber hall in lower Deeside under excavation in June 2005. SC991161

a stone circle is the sole surviving feature of a group of burial-cairns and other *'tumuli'*. In the valley of the Brindy Burn a probable hut-circle group lay in the field immediately north of the recumbent stone circle at **Druidstone**, and yet this location produced no artefacts in the course of the field-walking survey.

Funerary Monuments

In contrast to the scatter of Neolithic artefacts throughout the area (Fig. 5.1), Donside has fewer recognisable Neolithic funerary monuments than any of the neighbouring catchments. The discovery of a long mound at **Forest Road**, Kintore (Cook and Dunbar 2004) goes a little way to rectifying this situation, and perhaps implies that the overall pattern has been created by the agricultural improvements, both in the sense of the discovery of the artefacts and the destruction of the monuments. Nevertheless, there may well be other factors in play, and it would be a mistake to assume that every area should have its complement of long cairns and barrows, if only because there are good reasons to suppose that some Neolithic burial mounds were circular rather than long. This was first demonstrated at Pitnacree, in Strath Tay (Coles and Simpson 1965), and several other circular Neolithic barrows have been excavated since, including Boghead, in Moray (Burl 1985), and Fordhouse, in Angus (*DES 1994*, 81; *1995*, 93; *1996*, 12: *1997*, 13; *1999*, 111). In the light of this evidence, the lack of Neolithic funerary monuments across large parts of eastern Scotland is probably more apparent than real.

Neolithic Long Cairns and Barrows

Only three monuments in Donside can be considered in this category. The first is situated on **Longcairn** farm, which strictly speaking falls in the catchment of the River Dee, while the second lies at **Midmill**, some 9.5km to the north-west near Kintore. The third is the recently discovered structure at **Forest Road**, which lies a little farther north again, and has yet to be fully published.

The very name of **Longcairn** farm describes the character of the monument, although the bulk of the mound there today is probably made up of field-gathered stones. The cairn lies along the leading edge of a terrace and, despite being relatively low-lying, it commands extensive views to the south and west across the Brodiach Burn. In contrast, the mound at **Midmill** is situated within a large basin surrounded by the low hills that separate it from the coastal plain to the east, the catchment of the Dee to the south, and the Howe of Alford to the west. Thus, it commands no outlook over the surrounding countryside.

Rising 3.5m out of the leading edge of a gravel terrace, the greater part of the **Midmill** mound is almost certainly natural. Its eastern end was dug for gravel in the 19th century, which probably accounts for the discovery of a cist containing an inhumation and an *'urn'* (Name Book, Aberdeenshire No. 51, p.111). This part of the mound is separated from the west end by an artificial cleft across the axis, and the two ends are evidently on slightly different alignments. Overall the mound is some 60m in length, and the western end tapers from 20m to 16m over a distance of 27m from east-south-east to west-north-west.

The mound at **Forest Road**, which was at least 42m in length, also enhances a natural feature, and its broader east end has again been quarried away. Nevertheless, the excavations have revealed a complex sequence of events, from the first construction of the mound with material dug from the flanking ditches to its enclosure with timber walls (Cook and Dunbar 2004).

Neolithic Round Barrows

Several of the 165 circular cairns and barrows recorded in Donside are probably Neolithic in date, but without excavation it is impossible to identify them with any confidence. South of the Mounth it has been suggested that such mounds may display a lower, flatter profile than their Bronze Age counterparts (Barclay and Maxwell 1998, 115–16), but few barrows in the lowlands of Donside are sufficiently well preserved to allow such a judgement. The evidence to the north of the survey area is slightly better. In addition to the Boghead barrow, an unprepossessing mound excavated at Midtown of Pitglassie, near Auchterless, also dates from the Neolithic (Shepherd 1996). The mound measured only 10.5m in diameter by 0.5m in height, but excavation revealed a sequence of events that began in the early Neolithic with the removal of turf from the site and its use for a funeral pyre. Several pits were then dug and backfilled; one of them contained five sherds of what was probably a Neolithic carinated bowl. The site of the pyre was subsequently enclosed by a low bank of earth, stones and turf, which appears to have formed an oval ring-bank with an opening on the north-north-west (Shepherd 1996, 25, Illus 7). A broadly similar structure was found beneath the barrow at Pitnacree in Strath Tay.

The barrow at Boghead also overlay what was probably the remains of a pyre containing early

Fig. 5.4 Knapperty Hillock (NJ 9460 5032). Viewed from the air, the plan of this horned long cairn is easy to recognise as a Neolithic burial mound. Though it lies just below the crest of the hill, it forms an impressive skyline profile when approached from the west. SC976161

Neolithic pottery and fragments of burnt bone (Burl 1985). There was no mortuary structure, but three irregular piles of boulders were placed over parts of the pyre before being capped with a thick layer of sand. This capping also contained Neolithic pottery, and formed a mound about 15m in diameter.

A third example from the area to the north of the survey area was discovered in the 19th century at Atherb, not far from the long cairn at Knapperty Hillock (Milne 1892). Here, large amounts of burnt human bone and several flint arrowheads were intermixed with the cairn material. The mound stood only 0.9m high, but the stones at the centre were *'run and fused by intense heat'*. Sherds of both plain and carinated bowls were found in close proximity to the pyre (Henshall 1983, 39–40).

Possible examples of Neolithic round barrows from within Donside are more equivocal. For example, the assemblage of Neolithic pottery associated with areas of burning beneath the large cairn at **East Finnercy** may also have included a later sherd of Beaker pottery (Leivers, Roberts and Peterson 2000). Other possible pyres beneath cairns are described in antiquarian records as layers of black *'unctuous'* earth; they sometimes contained fragments of human bone, flint arrowheads, or broken pottery. Such a deposit was found in 1863 when a large cairn at **Cairnmore**, in Logie-Coldstone parish, was removed (Name Book, Aberdeenshire, No. 56, p. 61), and about 1846 another was noted at **Braehead**, near Leslie (Name Book, Aberdeenshire, No. 54, p. 23). Notwithstanding the pyres that have been discovered beneath Bronze Age monuments (see below), some of these mounds may well have been Neolithic.

Early Bronze Age Round Cairns and Barrows

There are records of over 650 round burial mounds in the three counties that traditionally made up the North-east, but only about 300 are still visible. Many of these are heavily disturbed, resulting in the discovery of

*Fig. 5.5 **Donald's Hillock** (NJ 8400 1609). One of a number of new discoveries made during the course of the survey, this burial-cairn is surmounted by the war memorial at Hatton of Fintray. SC674807*

burials in forty-six. These figures are broadly reflected in Donside, where 165 cairns and barrows have now been recorded, of which seventy-one have been removed. However, forty-three are new discoveries, mainly surviving in isolated patches of uncultivated ground or in old plantations within the present arable zone. This has increased the density of burial mounds in the eastern part of the survey area, but it has also pushed the distribution westwards into areas where the pattern was considerably thinner before. Upstream from Kildrummy, for example, several large cairns have come to light, including two at **Upper Culquoich** measuring 24m and 25m in diameter respectively, one on **Cairnbeg Hill** some 20m in diameter, and another on **Deskry Hill** about 17.5m in diameter.

The cairns noted above are amongst the larger cairns in the area, but many of the others are considerably smaller, so much so that it is sometimes difficult to distinguish a burial cairn from a field clearance heap. For example, the cairn some 6.5m in diameter on the summit of a low spur of **Cardlunchart Hill**, near Towie, has been identified as a probable funerary monument, whereas the small mounds of stones near the two hut-circles 200m to the north-east are classified as field clearance heaps. This does not exclude the possibility that some of the latter may also have served as burial monuments, but simply identifies their likely

origin. In several cases, one or two heaps in a group are considerably larger than their neighbours, though this is by no means a reliable guide that they had a different function. In **Garlogie Wood** the cairns around the hut-circle group include several measuring between 6m and 8m in diameter, while at **Drum Hill** three are about 7m in diameter, which is twice the size of any of the others in the group.

The locations in which Bronze Age settlement, agriculture and burial took place were in any case intimately related. In Donside this is implicit in some of the antiquarian descriptions of the removal of groups of small cairns. Many were evidently featureless,

*Fig. 5.6 **Cairn Ley** (NJ 4612 1463). Photographed by James Ritchie in 1915, Cairn Ley is amongst the largest cairns in Donside, measuring 33m by 24m and up to 3m in height. SC680091*

*Fig. 5.7 **Boat of Hatton** (NJ 8375 1622). Aerial photography has revealed the cropmarks of this large uninterrupted ring-ditch. © AAS 88–7–CT5*

but others contained burials. The **Hill of Boghead** (p. 81, Fig. 6.4) is a case in point, where there was an extensive landscape of cairns and hut-circles. Some of the cairns cleared in the early 19th century contained bones and skulls, and others covered Cinerary Urns and deposits of cremated bone (*NSA*, xii, Aberdeenshire, 114–15). In a few cases it is possible that an early medieval barrow cemetery is being described. For instance, on **Braehead Farm**, at least fifteen mounds on Bin Hill apparently covered cists containing inhumations and the place where they were found was known as *'The Old Grave Yard'* (Name Book, Aberdeenshire, No. 54, p. 25).

Most of the larger burial-cairns are now individual, isolated monuments, but in a few cases they form small groups, such as the two discovered at **Upper Culquoich**. A more spectacular cluster is strung out along Tullos Hill, to the south of Aberdeen. Prior to the survey four were known on the ridge, but a fifth has

been discovered partly subsumed into a consumption dyke towards the south-west end, and a possible barrow some 25m in diameter has been located on the north-east end. Four of the cairns stand on the spine of the ridge, and are silhouetted on the skyline from the south-east. In contrast, **Tullos Cairn** is situated on a slight spur about half-way down the north-west flank, and is only clearly visible from the other side of the valley, some 500m to the north-west. The barrow on the other hand is in an unusual position, enclosed by rising ground everywhere but the north-east. The cairns range from 11m to 19m in diameter and the largest still stands up to 2.5m in height.

The barrow on Tullos Hill is a relatively unusual monument in Donside, where most of the burial mounds are composed of stones. Occasionally, however, an enclosing ditch is visible, revealing that at least part of the mound was probably earthen. One example has been identified around the uphill side of the **Black Cairn**, which stands on a false crest on the Hill of Rothmaise. Here the remains of the mound measures about 21m in diameter and the ditch is at least 3.5m in breadth. Some of the ring-ditches recorded as cropmarks may also be barrows, though none approaches the diameter of the **Black Cairn**. The largest of the ring-ditches is at **Boat of Hatton**, but this measures only 13m in diameter, and there is no hint that the area enclosed by the broad ditch was ever mounded (p. 59). Others at **Collyhill** and **Fullerton**, measure about 10m in diameter within ditches 2m in breadth.

Other than occasional traces of kerbs, few of the cairns display any structural detail. Some of the kerbs, however, were evidently impressive, such as the larger of the cairns discovered at **Upper Culquoich**, where at least twenty-six kerbstones are visible, the tallest of them standing 0.6m in height. At **Chapel o' Sink** (Fig. 5.8), the kerb is graded, with the largest stones standing up to 0.6m in height on the south-west. In the case of **South Brideswell**, a kerb retains a stony platform some 4m in breadth, which encircles a central mound of cairn material about 14m in diameter. Platforms of this sort are more commonly found enclosing the cairns within recumbent stone circles (p. 63).

The cairns were clearly designed to present a range of profiles, and while some were piled high with stones, others were much flatter structures. This latter group includes a cairn on the summit of the **Hill of Knockollochie**, near Oyne, which qualifies as a kerb cairn, a type of small cairn with a disproportionately large kerb (Lynch and Ritchie 1975, 30). The cairn was excavated in 1961 (*DES 1961*, 3; Lynch and Ritchie 1975, 31), revealing that it was oval, measuring 4.9m by 3.7m overall and 0.6m in height. Other low cairns are also edged with kerbs, but they have much larger diameters, such as the pair in **Monael Wood** (Fig. 5.8),

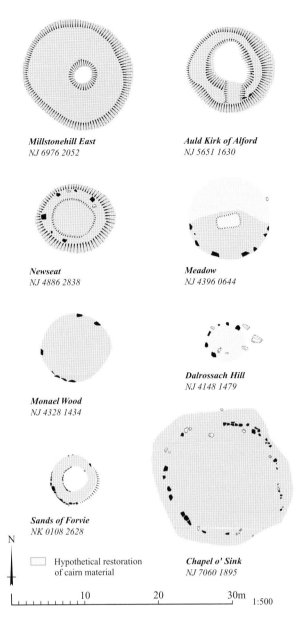

Millstonehill East
NJ 6976 2052

Auld Kirk of Alford
NJ 5651 1630

Newseat
NJ 4886 2838

Meadow
NJ 4396 0644

Dalrossach Hill
NJ 4148 1479

Monael Wood
NJ 4328 1434

Sands of Forvie
NK 0108 2628

N

Hypothetical restoration
of cairn material

Chapel o' Sink
NJ 7060 1895

10   20   30m   1:500

Fig. 5.8 Plans of a selection of cairns and ring-cairns in Donside.
GV000144

Glenkindie. The western of these two cairns measures up to 9.3m in diameter and its kerb of boulders and upright slabs is up to 0.45m in height. The kerb of the eastern cairn is largely obscured, but the top of a possible cist slab can be seen close to its centre. Another low cairn, on **Meadow** farm, near Migvie, measures 10.8m in diameter and the kerbstones are up to 0.65m high (Fig. 5.8).

Small kerb cairns are relatively rare in the North-east, apart from the unique cluster of eight within the stone circle at **Cullerlie** on the southern fringes of the survey area (p. 71); nevertheless, three have been excavated in the **Sands of Forvie** (Ralston and Sabine 2000). A small circular setting of stones on the south face of **Dalrossach Hill**, west of Glenkindie House, may be another, despite the absence of any visible cairn material (Fig. 5.8). It certainly has no parallels amongst

stone circles, either in size or character. Of the seven erect stones, the two tallest are about 0.5m high and oppose each other on the west-south-west and east-north-east arcs.

Some of the cairns with low profiles may prove on excavation to be ring-cairns. The most clearly defined ring-cairn in the area was uncovered in the **Sands of Forvie**, but the inner courts of these monuments are usually sealed with cairn material, and they are seldom visible unless the mound has been robbed or excavated. This certainly accounts for the discovery of a court in the cairn on **Hill of Selbie**, of which there was no trace before excavation, and indeed none today. In this respect, the probable ring-cairn in Bennachie Forest at **Millstonehill East** is unusual. No kerbstones are visible, but the low domed mound, some 15m in diameter, encloses a sharply defined court about 3.5m across (Fig. 5.8). Another possible example has been discovered at **Newseat**, near Rhynie, where a ring of six boulders protrudes from a raised lip forming the edge of a cairn about 9.8m in diameter, but here the centre may have been robbed (Fig. 5.8).

The excavation of the **Hill of Selbie** has yet to be published, but at 12m in overall diameter it is much larger than the small ring-cairn in the **Sands of Forvie** (Fig. 5.8). Excavated by Kirk in the eroding sand-dunes (1954, 158–61), this measures only 6.3m in diameter overall. Its inner kerb is constructed of thin closely fitting slabs, but the outer kerb includes a wider range of stones, the larger of which are placed around the south-west. A square setting of four small upright stones found on the floor is no longer visible, but its sides were set out square to an axial line drawn through the largest of the outer kerbstones on the south-west. Black *'greasy'* deposits covered this setting and contained fragments of charcoal and burnt bone. This is one of the smallest ring-cairns known, and is rivalled only by a group of five at Mowat Newton in Deeside.

Little is recorded about the burials in any of these monuments and the excavation at **Hill of Knockollochie** revealed little more than a rock-cut hollow beneath the centre of the cairn. Traces of a burial were limited to a few fragments of burnt bone amongst the white quartz scattered at various places beneath the southern half of the cairn (*DES 1961*, 3). The discovery of cists and urns are referred to in the antiquarian record, yet the only cist that remains visible today is at **Knocksoul**, near Migvie, and more properly in Deeside. Layers of blackened earth are occasionally mentioned, perhaps indicating the sites of pyres, and in one case, at **Backhill**, near Kinellar, three concentric rings of stones (*Stat. Acct.*, iii, 1792, 504). One of the most intriguing discoveries was at **Law Hillock**, near Kirkton of Culsalmond, where in 1812 a sophisticated timber cist or chamber was uncovered on the site of a large mound that had been removed about thirty years before (*NSA*, xii, Aberdeenshire, 732–3).

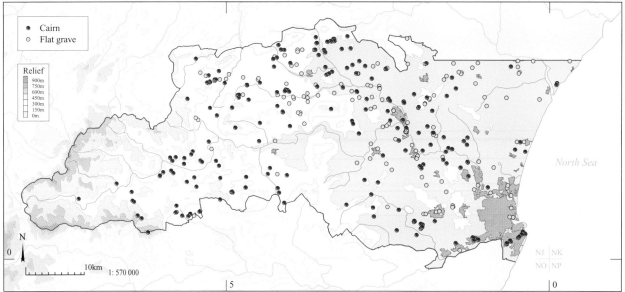

Fig. 5.9 Bronze Age burial sites are found throughout Donside. The distribution of burial-cairns extends well into the uplands, but flat graves are mainly confined to the cultivated lowlands, notably along the valley of the River Urie and into the Garioch. GV000180

Flat Cemeteries

In addition to the cists and urns found in cairns and barrows, numerous others have been discovered in locations where there are no records of any covering mound. In all, about 440 are known from north-east Scotland, comprising both individual burials and what may be cemeteries. By far the majority have come to light as a result of agricultural operations (p. 17), but they are by no means evenly distributed within the area of modern arable land and improved pasture. In Donside, the majority are scattered along the lower and middle reaches of the Don and up the River Urie into the Garioch (Fig. 5.9).

In general, these types of burial are described as flat graves, though this means no more than that there is no record of a cairn or barrow at the site. Most burials were probably marked in some way, if only by a low tump above the burial pit. As much is implied in cemeteries where the individual graves appear to have been interred successively, but without disturbing their neighbours. Ephemeral markers may have been ploughed away long before any trace of a burial was found, but in some cases quite substantial barrows or cairns may also have been removed before a cist or urn drew the attention of antiquarians to the spot.

The locations in which cists and urns are found are broadly similar to those occupied by cairns and barrows. Some are situated on level gravel terraces in the bottoms of valleys, others in more elevated positions, and yet others have been inserted into natural knolls, perhaps mimicking secondary interments in cairns or barrows. In some instances, burials appear to have been inserted into earlier monuments, such as the inverted urns containing cremations found within the interior of the henge monument at **Broomend of Crichie**, and possibly those recovered from within the ditched enclosure at **Tuach Hill** (see below). Though generally considered to have been built as ceremonial monuments, henges and other Late Neolithic and Early Bronze Age enclosures almost invariably contain burials. In the case of **Broomend of Crichie**, this included an inhumation in a cist at the bottom of a deep pit at the centre of the interior, while other burials have been found to either side of the avenue of standing stones that extended across the terrace to the south.

The character of the individual burials varies widely, from token deposits of cremated bones placed either in shallow pits or covered by inverted urns, to stone-lined cists containing inhumations or cremations. The form of cists ranges from relatively slight structures, designed to protect an inverted urn covering a cremation or to enclose a tightly crouched inhumation, to others which are significantly larger, built with thick side-slabs and covered by massive capstones.

The range of Early Bronze Age burials is well illustrated by those revealed in the 19th century during excavations in and around the henge at **Broomend of Crichie**. In 1855 Charles Dalrymple (1884), when excavating in the interior of the henge, found a series of cremation burials: two were set in simple, circular pits; one in a stone-lined pit (about 0.2m in diameter and 0.3m deep); and three contained within inverted urns, placed on stone slabs and protected by cover stones. One of the urns was set in a stone-lined pit, another stood in a small cist (0.28m by 0.23m and 0.4m deep). At the centre of the henge lay a complex of burials set in a deep pit some 4.5m in diameter. At the bottom there was a cist, the capstones of which lay 2.1m below the surface. In the cist were an inhumation and cremation

Fig. 5.10 **Broomend of Crichie** *(NJ 7789 1924). This horn spoon was found inside a Beaker in one of the cist burials discovered during road construction in 1866. © NMS E2967*

deposits; and further cremation deposits were recovered from the fill towards the top of the pit.

Evidence for other Bronze Age burial practices has been found close to the stone avenue associated with the henge. Excavations in 1993 in the garden of the house (**Allanshaw**) about 180m to the south of the henge revealed a cist (*DES 1993*, 34); it was empty but its joints had been sealed with a clay luting. In 1866, close to the southernmost stone of the avenue, four cists were found (Davidson 1870, 561–2). One was massive, measuring 1.6m by 0.75m and up to 0.9m in depth, and contained

two inhumations covered by a hide and accompanied by two Beakers. Adjacent to this cist lay another, smaller, clay-luted cist; it also contained two inhumations covered by a hide but, in this case, accompanied by a single Beaker in which stood a horn spoon (Fig. 5.10). Close by two small cists were uncovered, one containing an inhumation accompanied by a small pottery vessel. The final burial found, so far, in the area around the henge lay farther to the south and comprised an urn set into a natural, sandy knoll, which, it is assumed, accompanied a cremation (Name Book, Aberdeenshire, No. 52, p. 106).

This range of burials is fairly representative of those found throughout the North-east, though there are almost certainly significant biases in the proportions of the different types. The slabs of a cist, for example, are more likely to have caught the attention of a ploughman than an urn, leading to under-representation of urn-burials in antiquarian records. For the same reasons, cremations and inhumations in simple pits represent a relatively small proportion of the existing record. Many of the single burials discovered through ploughing may also have belonged to cemeteries in which other burials have either passed unnoticed, or are so deeply buried they have yet to come to light. This is to a certain extent confirmed by the cumulative nature of some of the discoveries, such as the three cists containing Beakers found in 1906 and 1908 at **Mains of Leslie** (Callander 1907, 116–22; 1912, 344–8), and most recently the six cists at **Borrowstone** (*DES 1977*, 4; *1980*, 9).

Despite these caveats, the funerary record from the North-east is remarkably rich. Grave goods include no less than 127 Beakers from Aberdeenshire alone (Fig. 5.11; Shepherd 1986), whereas Food Vessels are comparatively rare, accompanying only about thirty-six burials. With such a remarkable collection of Beaker

Fig. 5.11 This map shows the overall distribution of Bronze Age burial sites (cairns and flat graves) and highlights those where Beakers have been found. GV000177

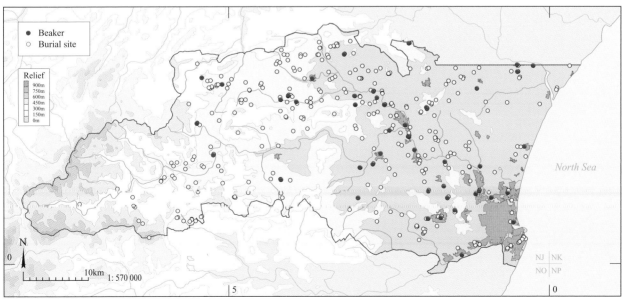

Fig. 5.12 Orbliston (NJ 3019 5859). The only surviving hair ornament of a pair found in a cist in 1863. © NMS E2024

burials, however, it is perhaps surprising that none is associated with any items of gold (Eogan 1994, 20, Fig. 5). Only one gold lunula (NMS X.FE 2) has been recorded from the North-east, from Orbliston, in Moray, though it was found close to the site of a cist in which a pair of gold hair-ornaments had been found five years previously (Fig. 5.12; Taylor 1980, 22, 25, 34, 36, pls 3, 16–17).

Other classes of object notably absent from burials in the area bounded by the River Spey on the west and the River Dee on the south include bronze daggers and jet necklaces (Morrison 1979, 31, Fig. 4; Cowie 1988, 25). The surviving metal daggers recovered in the North-east are copper rather than bronze, such as one from a cist containing an inhumation at **Tavelty**, near Kintore, which was also accompanied by a Beaker, two

*Fig. 5.13 **Newlands of Oyne** (NJ 6949 2533). This grave group, which accompanied a crouched inhumation, comes from one of two cists discovered during the 1930s at Newlands. © University of Aberdeen*

barbed-and-tanged arrowheads, further pieces of worked flint, a quartz pebble, and a strike-a-light (Ralston 1996, 141–51). Of the jet necklaces, only one has been found in Donside. This was at **Boghead**, Kintore (NMS X.EQ 80), and was discovered when a cairn was being removed (*Stat. Acct.*, vii, 1793, 92). A second comes from further north, at Blindmills, Auchterless (NMS X.EQ 85), and was found with an *'urn'* and two amber beads accompanying a probable inhumation in a cist in a cairn (NMS X.EQ 85 & 86; Stuart 1866, 217–8). Jet necklaces are almost invariably associated with Food Vessels, so this general absence may simply reflect the relatively small number of such burials in the North-east.

Despite this general lack of objects that intrinsically convey wealth and status, there can be little doubt that a Beaker placed in a grave was in itself a significant item (see Shepherd 1986), and the same may be said of some of the other objects that have been found with them. For example, a cist discovered at **Newlands of Oyne** also contained two archer's wristguards, together with a barbed-and-tanged arrowhead, two flint knives, two flint flakes, and three large worked flints (Fig. 5.13; Low 1936). Similarly, of the six cists containing Beakers at **Borrowstone**, two of them contained stone wristguards and flint arrowheads (Shepherd 1986, 13–15). Another Beaker grave, discovered in a sand-pit at **Clinterty** in 1897, was accompanied by a mica-schist axe-head, a flint knife, five flint scrapers, two barbed-and-tanged flint arrowheads, a topaz crystal, a bone ring and a bone needle.

Despite being under-represented, *'urns'* have been discovered at about ninety locations within Donside, occurring both singly and in cemeteries. However, antiquaries used the term indiscriminately to describe any vessel found with a burial, and it is now almost impossible to get an impression of the true number of Cinerary Urn burials (Fig. 5.14). Of those recorded in Donside, about fifty were found singly, and another thirteen in pairs. Thereafter the numbers in the cemeteries fall away rapidly, three urns in five instances, four in two, and occasionally between six and eight. By far the majority (fifty) are apparently from flat graves, but it is striking how many have come from cairns or other monuments, which account for no less than twenty. A further ten were found in what are described as knolls or hillocks. While some of these may have been barrows also, it is perhaps the mound that is of significance rather than whether it had been constructed as a burial monument.

With the exception of an enclosed cemetery excavated at **Loanhead of Daviot** (Fig. 5.15; Kilbride-Jones 1936), none of the groups of flat graves found in Donside betrays any hint of a formal monument. The same is true elsewhere in the North-east, and the account of a cremation cemetery at Middlethird, Methlick, some way north of Donside, is unusual for its description of a ring of eight pits beneath a cairn, with a ninth lying at its

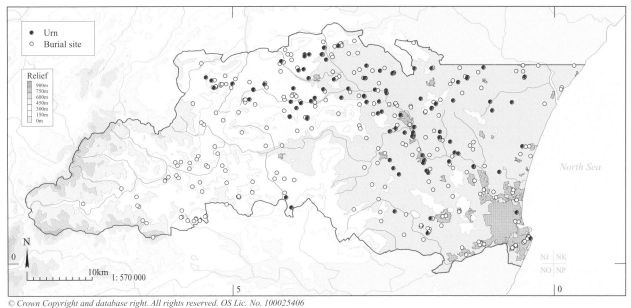

Fig. 5.14 This map shows the overall distribution of Bronze Age burial sites (cairns and flat graves) and highlights those where Cinerary Urns have been found. GV000191

centre (Name Book, Aberdeenshire, No. 61, p. 42). The pits forming the ring were filled with cremation deposits, and only two contained urns.

The rarity of such observations probably reflects no more than the haphazard way in which cemeteries were usually found, and it is quite likely that others were set out in formal ways. At **Loanhead of Daviot**, the burials lay within a small enclosure defined by a *'drystone dyke ... the stones of which were vertically placed'* in a shallow ditch (Kilbride-Jones 1936, 281), and there were opposed entrances on the north-east and south-west. Rather than a free-standing stone structure, the description of the perimeter of the enclosure sounds more like the packing for a timber wall, and areas of burning recorded along its line probably indicate that it was burnt down (Brück 2004, 183). Another area of intense burning at the centre of the enclosure was probably the site of successive pyres, and the cremated remains of no less than thirty-one individuals were disposed amongst twelve urns and thirteen pits within the interior. The sole grave goods were a stone pendant from a central pit, and a bone toggle from one of the urns.

The paucity of grave goods with the burials at **Loanhead of Daviot** repeats a pattern found elsewhere. Nevertheless, an inverted urn ploughed up about 1863 at **Backhill**, in the parish of Tullynessle and Forbes, contained *'a necklace'* (now lost) that was *'rudely ornamented, made of clay or some sort of light stone and which resembles a Romanist's rosary'* (Name Book, Aberdeenshire, No. 88, p. 25). At **Drumdurno**, Chapel of Garioch, another inverted Cinerary Urn contained a claystone pendant or amulet (*DES 1960*, 2), while a slate pendant was found beneath one of four Cinerary

Urns found in 1904 in a road-menders' gravel-pit at **Seggiecrook**, near Kennethmont. Finds from the other urns included six flint flakes, seven burnt clay objects – possibly pinheads – and a bobbin-shaped bead or toggle (Callander 1905; 1908; Cowie 1988, 50). Occasionally urns contain bronze artefacts, such as the decorated razor (ABDUA: 19688) from an urn discovered in a cairn at **Green Howe**, near Tullochvenus, Tough (*NSA*, xii, Aberdeenshire, 613).

Small Accessory Vessels sometimes accompany cremations, though few now survive from Donside. Two fine examples came from a *'tumulus or cairn'* near the foot of **Bennachie** (NMS X.EC 9 & 10; *Proc Soc Antiq Scot* 5, 1862–4, 13), and another from the **Hill of Keir**, Skene. The latter was apparently a surface find containing an ammonite, and a flint arrowhead lay nearby (ABDUA: 19721: Reid 1924). Others have been lost, such as the small *'oval shaped cup, resembling a sugar basin'* found in an urn at **Gordonstown**, one of several cremation deposits discovered in a sand-pit near Clatt (Name Book, Aberdeenshire, No. 14, p. 44).

Fig. 5.15 **Loanhead of Daviot** *(NJ 7478 2884). This cremation cemetery is one of only a handful that are known to have been enclosed. The bank of stones that forms the perimeter of the enclosure is probably the displaced packing that once supported a timber wall. SC336070*

Ceremonial Monuments

Neolithic ceremonial monuments in Donside are almost as scarce as long cairns and barrows. Nevertheless, two cursus monuments have been revealed as cropmarks and at least two henges have survived as earthworks, that at **Broomend of Crichie** apparently forming one element of a wider array of monuments, including a stone-lined avenue. To these may be added some of the other standing stones, though none has been dated (p. 68), and also many of the cupmarked stones that have been incorporated into Early Bronze Age monuments. The latter include a series of megalithic monuments, principally recumbent stone circles (p. 74). Each of these categories is discussed in separate sections below.

Cursus Monuments

The two cursus monuments identified in Donside display the main characteristics of these long, narrow enclosures, the majority of which in Scotland lie to the south of the Mounth and in Dumfries & Galloway. Some are defined by ditches, others by lines of pits, and the sides usually return at the ends to form either square or rounded terminals. The possible example at **Myreton**, in the Garioch, has a ditch, and the only end that has been photographed, so far, has a square terminal. The second, at **Mill of Fintray**, is altogether more complex, and is subdivided into at least three sections extending over a distance of about 130m. The sections are variously

*Fig. 5.16 **Mill of Fintray** (NJ 8357 1633). The cursus is divided into three compartments, each of which lies on a slightly different axis. Nevertheless, at least two monuments in the vicinity, one of them the large ring-ditch shown here, the other the cairn at Donald's Hillock (Fig. 5.5), fall on the projection of its general alignment to the east-south-east. GV004128*

defined by lines of pits and ditches, but each is set on a slightly different alignment, obscuring the overall axis of the monument. Nevertheless, the east-south-east end is aligned roughly with a large ring-ditch at **Boat of Hatton** (Fig. 5.16), some 140m beyond its terminal, and possibly also on the cairn at **Donald's Hillock** a further 400m away beside the road south of Hatton of Fintray.

Cursus monuments are not the only linear enclosures that have been recorded in Donside. At **Broomend of Crichie** there was an avenue of standing stones approaching the henge monument. Only four stones remain to mark its course today, strung out over a distance of some 450m to the south of the henge; however, in the mid-18th century there was *'a row of large stones erected on each side'* (Maitland 1757, i, 154), and the presence of further stone-holes has been confirmed by geophysical survey and trial excavation (*DES 2001*, 11). At first sight, this is perhaps a rather different type of monument, but it has been shown that many of the pit-defined features recorded as cropmarks once held settings of timber uprights. As such, some of the pit-defined cursus monuments are simply timber avenues.

Henge Monuments

The henge at **Broomend of Crichie** is itself a rare monument in the North-east, where **Wormy Hillock** is the only other convincing example of this class of Late Neolithic enclosure (p. 95). **Broomend of Crichie** stands on a gravel terrace overlooking the confluence of the Rivers Don and Urie, which is a characteristic location for a henge monument (Malone 2001, 169–70), but this contrasts sharply with the position of **Wormy Hillock**. Situated in the hills north-west of Rhynie, the latter lies in a remarkably hidden and secluded location.

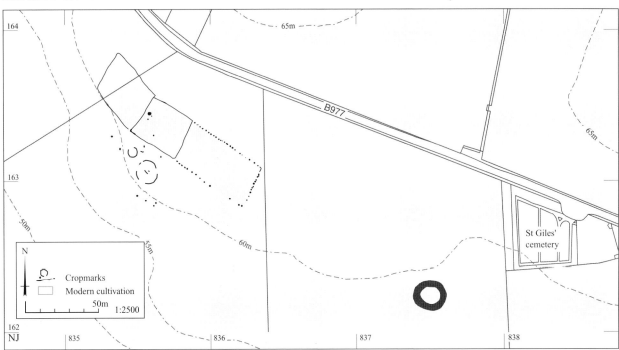

Not only is the bottom of the valley here narrow, hemmed in by steep hills, but the enclosure is set at the foot of a prominent natural ridge that snakes back up the gully to its rear and gives the enclosure its name. The interior measures only 6m in diameter within the ditch, making it one of the smaller examples of this type of monument, but it has the typical characteristics, with a thick bank on the outer lip of the ditch. The ditch, which is up to 4.5m in breadth, is interrupted by a causeway opposite the narrow gap in the external bank on the south-east. Several other causeway-like features are visible in the ditch, but these may be unexcavated baulks between pits dug into the fill in the course of the late-19th-century *'investigations'* (MacDonald 1891, 259). Nothing was found within the henge at the time but, in 1947, a hoard of eight Early Bronze Age flat axes was found under a stone at the foot of **Finglenny Hill**, no more than 80m away to the south-east (Stevenson 1948).

In comparison, **Broomend of Crichie** is a far more substantial monument, measuring 17m in diameter within a ditch 6m in breadth and 2m in depth (Fig. 5.19). It has two well-defined entrance causeways, which are opposed on the north and south arcs, though they are not matched by clear breaks in the external bank. Of the three stones now standing in the interior, only the two on the north are in their original positions, supposedly belonging to a circle of six stones that enclosed a seventh at the centre (Dalrymple 1884, 319). Whether this arrangement ever existed is less clear, for all bar the two northern stones had been removed before the excavations undertaken by Charles Dalrymple in the mid-19th century. Dalrymple dug extensively within the interior of the henge, discovering a fine perforated macehead and a number of burial deposits (pp. 52–3). One of these was placed in a cist in the bottom of a large central pit, and another three were covered by inverted urns (Dalrymple 1884). The stone presently at the centre is a Pictish symbol stone, which was moved into the henge for its safe-keeping.

Despite extensive aerial reconnaissance, few other henges can be identified with any confidence. Two

Fig. 5.17 ***Broomend of Crichie*** *(NJ 7792 1967). This oblique aerial photograph shows the henge monument in the foreground and, standing in the field beyond it, one of the surviving stones of an avenue that once approached from the south. SC342763*

Fig. 5.18 ***Wormy Hillock*** *(NJ 4498 3077). The interior and the bank on the outer lip of the ditch are clearly picked out in the heather in this view of the henge monument taken from the natural mound immediately to the north-west. SC344621*

Broomend of Crichie NJ 7792 1967

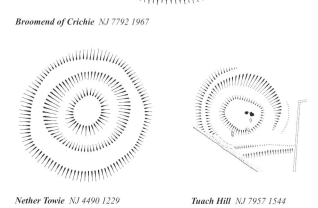

Nether Towie NJ 4490 1229

Tuach Hill NJ 7957 1544

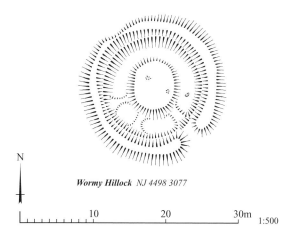

Wormy Hillock NJ 4498 3077

N

| 10 | 20 | 30m | 1:500 |

*Fig. 5.19 Plans of the henge monuments at **Broomend of Crichie** and **Wormy Hillock**, together with two other enclosures with external banks at **Nether Towie** and **Tuach Hill**. The entrances at Broomend of Crichie are apparently blocked by the external bank but, in its present form, the latter may be no more than the remains of a decorative roundel constructed as part of the improved landscape. GV000163*

*Fig. 5.20 **Nether Towie** (NJ 4490 1229). Situated on rocky ground, this unusual enclosure has escaped cultivation in an improved field. Taken in summer, the parching of the grass reveals the line of the external bank and the central tump within the ditch. SC958192*

contenders have been claimed in Donside, though neither is particularly convincing. The first, at **Whitestripes**, north of Aberdeen, was first recognised on vertical aerial photographs in 1961, but, measuring some 30m in internal diameter, there is little to distinguish this circular, ditched enclosure from those others that have been recorded in the area as a result of more recent aerial survey, most of which are probably Iron Age settlements (pp. 93–5). Likewise, an enclosure situated in the bottom of a shallow natural basin at **Middleton**, west of Inverurie, is perhaps more likely to be a later settlement (p. 95).

To confuse the picture further, several other small enclosures bear some superficial resemblance to henges, notably two with ditches surrounded by external banks, one on **Tuach Hill**, south of Kintore, and another at **Nether Towie**. **Tuach Hill** is situated at the foot of a steep wooded slope and measures a little over 7m in diameter. According to earlier accounts (Watt 1865, 152–3), the enclosing ditch was originally continuous, though both it and the external bank are more fragmentary today (Fig. 5.19). Of a setting of up to six stones within the interior noted by Watt, only one irregular block is certainly upright, and the others have evidently been moved, possibly in the course of excavations in the 19th century. These revealed a series of cremation burials, including three urns inverted at the foot of stones, two of them accompanied by small fragments of bronze (Dalrymple 1884). In contrast, **Nether Towie** has survived relatively unscathed, fortunately occupying a rocky outcrop that has escaped improvement on the crest of a ridge. The interior is only 4.5m in diameter, and the shallow flat-bottomed ditch is clearly continuous, providing sufficient material for a thick external bank (Figs 5.19–20).

The absence of an entrance causeway at either **Nether Towie** or **Tuach Hill** demonstrates that neither is a henge in any conventional sense, even though **Tuach Hill** evidently dates from at least the Early Bronze Age. This raises the possibility that other types of small ceremonial enclosure may be represented in the cropmark record. For

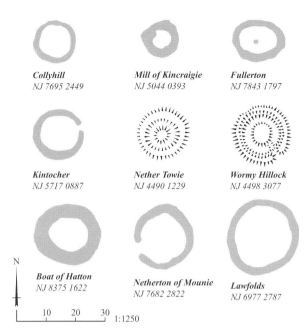

Collyhill
NJ 7695 2449

Mill of Kincraigie
NJ 5044 0393

Fullerton
NJ 7843 1797

Kintocher
NJ 5717 0887

Nether Towie
NJ 4490 1229

Wormy Hillock
NJ 4498 3077

Boat of Hatton
NJ 8375 1622

Netherton of Mounie
NJ 7682 2822

Lawfolds
NJ 6977 2787

N

10   20   30   1:1250

*Fig. 5.21 These plans illustrate at the same scale a selection of ring-ditches identified from cropmarks and two comparable enclosures with external banks recorded by ground survey at **Nether Towie** and **Wormy Hillock**. GV000170*

*Fig. 5.22 **Loanhead of Daviot** (NJ 7477 2885). This recumbent stone circle, which was excavated and restored after it was taken into Guardianship, displays many of the features found in other examples of this group of monuments; the recumbent setting on the south-south-west, the ring of graded stones, and the kerbed internal cairn. SC851585*

the purposes of comparison, several small ring-ditches have been set side by side here with plans of **Nether Towie** and **Wormy Hillock** (Fig. 5.21). At the latter the surface of the entrance causeway dips below the surrounding ground level and the ditch would probably form a continuous ring if it were reduced to a cropmark. Of those illustrated, the proportions of the diameter of the interior to the breadth of the ditch are much greater at **Fullerton** and **Collyhill** than at **Boat of Hatton** and Mill of Kincraigie. In this respect the latter two more closely approach **Nether Towie** and **Wormy Hillock**, possibly indicating these are enclosures, whereas the other two are barrows (p. 50). The **Boat of Hatton** ring-ditch, however, dwarfs them all and measures some 13m in diameter within a ditch up to 4m in breadth (Fig. 5.7).

Recumbent Stone Circles

The recumbent stone circles of north-east Scotland are one of the most distinctive categories of megalithic monuments in the British Isles. Unlike any other form of circle, they are characterised by the presence of a setting on the southern arc comprising a large horizontal boulder (the recumbent) flanked by a pair of tall stones (the flankers). Typically, the rest of the orthostats are graded in height, and in many instances there is evidence of an internal cairn. These cairns are often retained by graded kerbs of boulders or upright slabs, outside which a low platform extends to the foot of the surrounding circle. In well-preserved examples, the cairns expand to meet

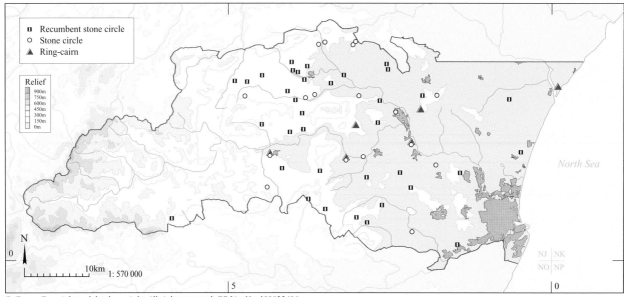

Fig. 5.23 Map showing the distributions of recumbent stone circles and other stone circles in Donside. GV000187

the back of the recumbent setting. While these are the features most often found, the circles in Donside display considerable variety, and in some cases the orthostats are apparently embedded in an unbroken circle of rubble, enclosing an open space, or no more than a thin spread of stones.

Donside lies at the core of the overall distribution of recumbent stone circles, but time has dealt severely with many of them, and only thirty-six examples can be identified within the survey area today (pp. 20–1). These are widely scattered, from **Potterton** and **Binghill** in the rolling coastal lowlands, to **Blue Cairn of Ladieswell** and **Corrstone Wood** in the foothills of the mountains to the west. Most are located between 100m and 300m OD, although exceptions include **Auld Kirk o' Tough** at 362m OD. For the most part, however, they lie on moderately fertile, well-drained soils, and they always command extensive outlooks.

*Fig. 5.24 **Braehead** (NJ 5926 2556). This isolated boulder, standing on the edge of a low swelling in the surface of an improved field, is all that remains visible of this recumbent stone circle. SC880897*

*Fig. 5.25 **Old Rayne** (NJ 6798 2798). The fractured profile of this orthostat results from the efforts of stone-breakers. Several of the iron wedges used to split the stone remain where they were driven into fissures in its surface. SC880905*

Fig. 5.26 Plans of a selection of recumbent stone circles in Donside. GV000142

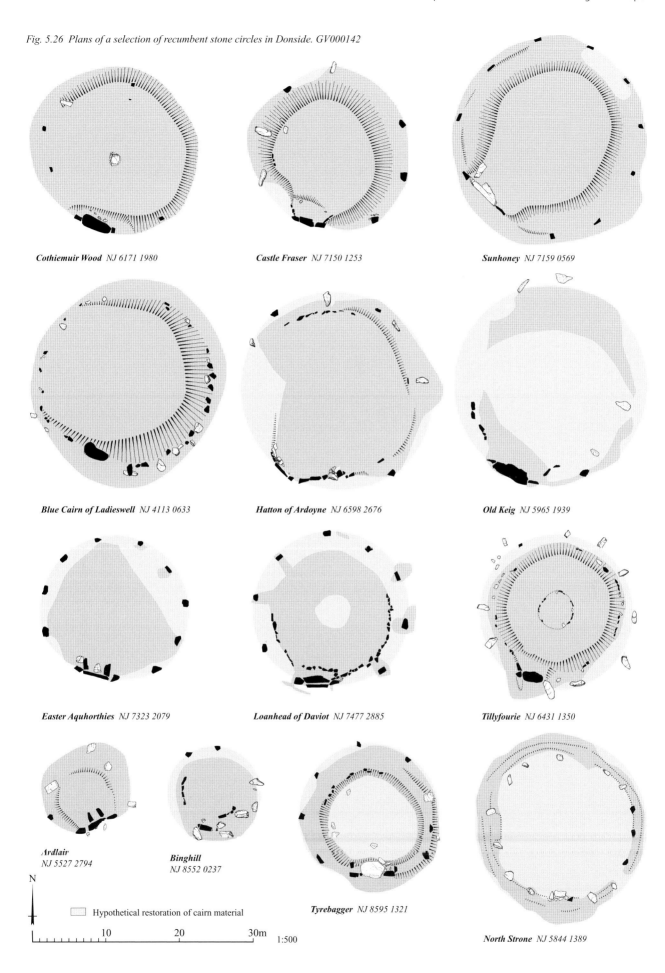

Cothiemuir Wood *NJ 6171 1980*

Castle Fraser *NJ 7150 1253*

Sunhoney *NJ 7159 0569*

Blue Cairn of Ladieswell *NJ 4113 0633*

Hatton of Ardoyne *NJ 6598 2676*

Old Keig *NJ 5965 1939*

Easter Aquhorthies *NJ 7323 2079*

Loanhead of Daviot *NJ 7477 2885*

Tillyfourie *NJ 6431 1350*

Ardlair
NJ 5527 2794

Binghill
NJ 8552 0237

Tyrebagger *NJ 8595 1321*

North Strone *NJ 5844 1389*

N

Hypothetical restoration of cairn material

10   20   30m   1:500

Fig. 5.27 **North Strone** *(NJ 5844 1389). This recumbent stone circle is unusual for the number of stones that make up the circle and their size. Most of the eighteen stones now lie prone, but none has stood more than 1.4m high. SC880909*

The consequence of this concentration on the better land is that recumbent stone circles have been at persistent risk of damage and total loss. Nevertheless, detailed survey has revealed much about their architecture (Figs 5.26; 5.29). Most are roughly circular on plan, and their diameters range between 11m overall at **Binghill** to 26m at **Sunhoney** and **Hatton of Ardoyne**. In a number of instances the circle is perceptibly flattened at the recumbent setting, suggesting that this feature was intended to be the centrepiece of a monumental façade. This is especially notable at **Tyrebagger**.

With the exception of **North Strone**, which has seventeen stones, the circles usually contain between nine and thirteen orthostats, but only **Easter Aquhorthies**, **Loanhead of Daviot**, **Sunhoney**, **Tomnagorn** and **Tyrebagger** still retain their full complement. As might be expected, the larger circles, such as **Sunhoney**, **Hatton of Ardoyne** and **Corrstone Wood**, tend to have a greater number of stones. For the most part, their broader, flatter and more regular sides face outwards, an arrangement that is sufficiently persistent to point up the general rule. Like the façade formed by the recumbent setting, this implies that the circle was to be viewed from without, rather than from within. The grading of the circle, which is so apparent at all of the better-preserved examples, also stresses the importance of the recumbent

setting, though close measurement shows that the actual height of the stones mattered less than the illusion conveyed.

It is clear that the recumbent setting was intended to make an imposing visual statement. This much is evident from the sheer size of the recumbents, which survive at thirty-two of the circles in Donside. The smaller ones weigh as little as 1.5 tons, as at **North Strone**, while the largest, at **Kirkton of Bourtie**, is as much as 43 tons. Yet weight alone is less important than the dimensions of its face. Thus, while the fallen 14-ton recumbent at **Sunhoney** is in the midst of the weight range, its length of 5.2m is second only to that at **Old Keig**, which weighs about 40 tons and is 5.45m long.

The arrangement of the recumbent setting also plays its part. Some form a roughly straight line, as at **Castle Fraser** and **Loanhead of Daviot**, but in others the flankers are set at a slight angle to the recumbent, as at **Easter Aquhorthies**, apparently to emphasise the curve of the circle. This may also have been the intention at **Cothiemuir Wood** and **Old Keig**, where the flankers are set slightly back from the face of the recumbent.

The smallest flankers are at **North Strone**, where the prone western stone measures no more than 1m in length, and its pair is only 0.75m high. These may be contrasted with those standing at **Tyrebagger**, where they are 3.25m and 2.8m high. Some of the stones appear to curve and arch over the recumbent, as at **Midmar Kirk** and **Tillyfourie**, and this general profile can also be seen in the more stunted profile of those at **Ardlair** and

*Fig. 5.28 **Kirkton of Bourtie** (NJ 8009 2488). This view shows the massive boulder that has been used in the recumbent setting. SC880907*

elsewhere. Where both flankers survive, they are always of different height, and there is often a marked contrast in their shape, one being essentially stout, the other slender. This is well illustrated at **Castle Fraser** and **Cothiemuir Wood**, and there was evidently no intention of achieving a symmetrical arrangement.

In addition to size and shape, it is also clear that colour and texture played a part in the visual statement. As with the orthostats in the rest of the circle, the irregular scarring of a sheared face usually faces inwards, though an exceptionally smooth split plane on the recumbent at **Balquhain** is turned outwards. Similarly most of the spectacular feldspar-flecked outer face of the recumbent at **Easter Aquhorthies** is a sheared surface. Similar choices were exercised for colour, and the recumbents, flankers and orthostats commonly display a wide range of combinations in shades of blue, grey and red.

In some cases the colour of the flankers matches the recumbent, as with the greys at **Candle Hill**, or the pinky reds at **Hatton of Ardoyne**, but in others they offer a contrast. At **Easter Aquhorthies**, for example, the creamy grey of the flankers contrasts with the pale grey-white surface of the recumbent, while at **Midmar Kirk** and **Sunhoney** the unweathered pinky-red flankers stand out boldly from their greyish recumbents. The contrast at **Stonehead** and **Tillyfourie** is more unusual, for here the two flankers appear to be different colours.

Large mineral inclusions also seem to have been prized, commonly occurring on both the recumbents and their flankers, while the external faces of the darker recumbents are frequently shot through with quartz or feldspar. A striking example is provided by the recumbent at **Easter Aquhorthies**, where the pale grey-white, external face exhibits not only thin veneers of quartz, but also numerous large flecks of feldspar. An equally spectacular contrast occurs at **Hatton of Ardoyne**, where a broad horizontal band of pale feldspar is splashed across the face of the red recumbent.

Although the stones of the recumbent setting and the circle are the most striking elements of these monuments, in most cases there is evidence that they incorporate a cairn or ring-cairn, and this may also have employed colour in its design (Bradley 2002b, 844). Undisturbed, the typical profile of these cairns is probably relatively low and flat-topped, one of the best-preserved examples being **Sunhoney**. Now grass-grown within a small plantation ring, the cairn measures about 20m in diameter and is encircled by a low platform extending out to the foot of the orthostats of the circle. This has created a tiered profile in which the lip of the encircling platform is emphasised by a low bank linking the orthostats of the circle.

This type of stony platform was also uncovered in the recent excavations at Tomnaverie, in Deeside, and **Cothiemuir Wood**, where they were of one-build with the cairns (Bradley 2002b, 843–4). Others can be inferred from earlier excavations at **Castle Fraser**

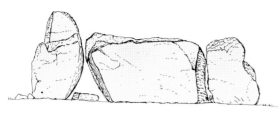

Loanhead of Daviot NJ 7477 2885

Old Keig NJ 5965 1939

Wantonwells NJ 6187 2729

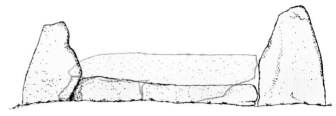

Sunhoney NJ 7159 0569

Tyrebagger NJ 8595 1321

Stonehead NJ 6010 2869

Castle Fraser NJ 7150 1253

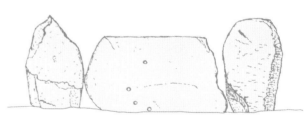

Old Rayne NJ 6798 2798

Hatton of Ardoyne NJ 6598 2676

New Craig NJ 7455 2966

Tomnagorn NJ 6514 0775

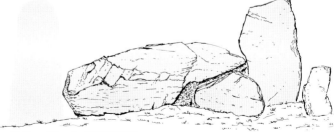

Kirkton of Bourtie NJ 8008 2487

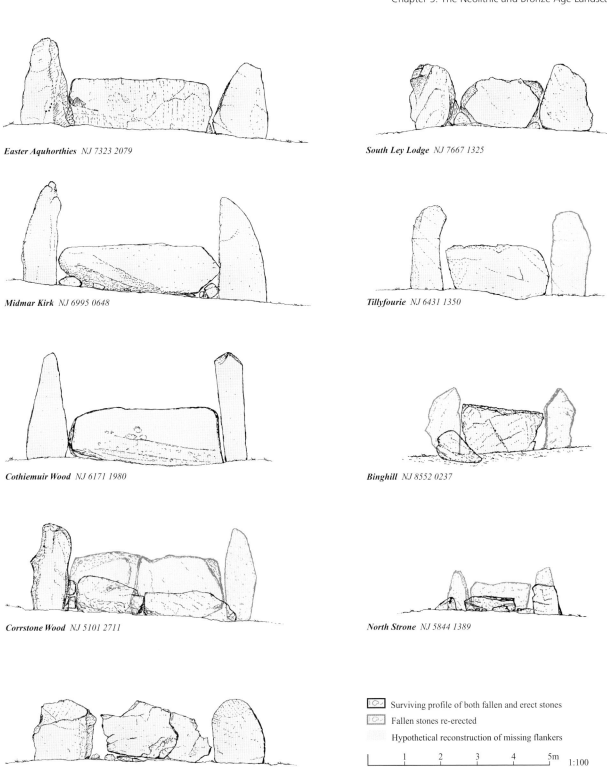

Easter Aquhorthies NJ 7323 2079

South Ley Lodge NJ 7667 1325

Midmar Kirk NJ 6995 0648

Tillyfourie NJ 6431 1350

Cothiemuir Wood NJ 6171 1980

Binghill NJ 8552 0237

Corrstone Wood NJ 5101 2711

North Strone NJ 5844 1389

Ardlair NJ 5527 2794

Surviving profile of both fallen and erect stones

Fallen stones re-erected

Hypothetical reconstruction of missing flankers

1   2   3   4   5m
1:100

Balquhain NJ 7350 2408

Fig. 5.29 The recumbent setting creates an impressive visual statement facing out from the circle. For the purposes of this illustration, the surviving profile of each setting is shown in black, but where a stone is fallen it is shown re-erected in brown, and in four cases a missing flanker is shown as a toned 'ghost' of what is estimated to be the likely size. While there is no way of confirming the original profiles of these flankers, this device suggests that even the most heavily ruined setting was as impressive as its better-preserved counterparts. GV000143

(Slade 1978, 271; Mercer 1978, 275), **Loanhead of Daviot** (Kilbride-Jones 1935, 172–3) and **Old Keig** (Childe 1934, 379). The expansion of the main body of the cairn to meet the back of the recumbent setting is another recurring feature, and is particularly clear where there is an external kerb. In every case the kerbstones are clearly graded, mimicking the surrounding circle. The kerbstones at **Old Keig** are the tallest in Donside, reflecting the massive scale of this particular circle.

These same features are found in ring-cairns within recumbent stone circles (pp. 51; 71–2). In Donside, an inner court is only visible at **Tillyfourie**, but earlier accounts reveal others at **Auld Kirk o' Tough** and **Castle Fraser**. At **Tillyfourie** roughly half the inner kerbstones are exposed, each carefully selected to fit closely with its neighbours. Not all ring-cairns were as formally constructed and some were probably defined by no more than a band of rubble. This was perhaps the case at **Cothiemuir Wood**, where a bank of boulders found in the body of the cairn was interpreted as the boundary of a broad central court (Bradley 2002b, 846). The supposed courts at **Loanhead of Daviot** and **Old Keig** lack any clear definition and their identification as ring-cairns is far from convincing (Bradley 2002b, 847–8), but several other reports describe cairns containing probable ring-banks, notably at **Corrie Cairn** and **Hatton of Ardoyne** (Stuart 1868, 24; Stuart 1856, xxii). The construction of later dykes around both **Easter Aquhorthies** and **Tyrebagger** is unfortunate, for it creates the misleading impression that these too are ring-cairns.

Excavation has also shown that the surface beneath a cairn was often levelled-up prior to its construction, most recently at Tomnaverie (Bradley 2002b, 843), but also at **Castle Fraser** and **Loanhead of Daviot** (Mercer 1978, 275; Kilbride-Jones 1935, 172–3). The truncation of the soil-profile beneath **Old Keig** and **Cothiemuir** may also indicate that the topsoil was stripped before construction of the cairn began (Childe 1934, 388; Bradley 2001, 3). However, burnt residues from beneath cairns, which are believed to originate from funeral pyres (pp. 48; 51), have been found persistently since at least the 17th century (Garden 1770, 320), occurring at **Castle Fraser**, **Corrie Cairn**, **Cothiemuir Wood**, **Hatton of Ardoyne**, **Loanhead of Daviot**, **Old Keig**, **Old Rayne** and **Sunhoney**. The three zones of burnt subsoil detected by Childe at **Old Keig** are sufficiently widely spread to suggest that multiple firings had taken place (Childe 1934, 381).

The results of Bradley's more recent campaign of small-scale excavation at **Cothiemuir Wood**, Aikey Brae and Tomnaverie have proved remarkably informative, showing that the same general sequence of construction recurs from site to site (Bradley 2002b). Whereas recumbent stone circles were previously thought to have originated as open circles, it is now clear that the sequence is the reverse, culminating in the erection of the stone circle and, finally, the emplacement of the

recumbent stone itself. The initial use of so many of the sites for pyres possibly provides a clue to why the elevated positions chosen for recumbent stone circles were selected in the first place. Modern study necessarily focuses on the monuments themselves, but this in turn places an undue emphasis on the outlook from the positions they occupy. This, perhaps, is to miss the point, for they are equally positions that can be seen from the landscape, particularly if a funeral pyre burned at night.

The evidence of multiple firings may indicate that this phase of use persisted for some time, whereas the construction first of a cairn and then a circle, represent relatively short phases of activity, in which the earlier usage was physically and symbolically foreclosed. Thus, the recumbent stone circle does not locate an area where activity continued to take place, so much as an area where activity had already taken place. In this respect, the recumbent setting can be understood as a portal that leads to this numinous space, but one that has been blocked by a massive stone door (Keiller 1934, 15–16; Burl 2000, 218; Bradley 2002a, 136). The expansion of the cairn up to the back of the recumbent forms a symbolically blocked passageway to its rear – a feature that is also indicated by the paired slabs at the rear of the recumbents at **Ardlair** and **Easter Aquhorthies**. But the fact that the portal faces outwards clearly indicates that the monument was designed to confront the living.

The southern aspect of this portal, which forms the focal point of the whole design, is also manifest in more subtle features, such as the distribution of stones of different sizes, and the concentration of quartz. Moreover, the incidence of cupmarks is also concentrated in this sector (Burl 1970, 65–6), being especially common on the recumbent setting, as at **Corrie Cairn** and **Easter Aquhorthies**, or upon stones in their immediate vicinity, as at **Balquhain** or **Ardlair** (p. 74). Some of these cupmarks may be earlier carvings that have been deliberately collected and put to reuse, but others, such as those upon the summit of the recumbent at **Loanend**, are probably contemporary with the erection of the monument.

This emphasis on the southern quadrant signifies an important geographical dimension to the rituals that were played out at these monuments, leading many to look to astronomy by way of explanation (p. 13). Recently, inspired by a statement made by Boece and the beguiling notion of quartz as a metaphor for moonlight, a serious attempt has been made to correlate them with lunar transits (Burl 1980; Ruggles 1999). And yet, in their completed forms, recumbent stone circles can seldom have lent themselves to celestial observations, and there is no convincing evidence that individual circles enshrine alignments on any lunar event. At best, the moon might shine over the recumbent on a favourable mid-summer night (Ruggles 1999; 97). Nevertheless, these monuments may incorporate other alignments, for the cairn at Tomnaverie contained subtle radial divisions

*Fig. 5.30 **Easter Aquhorthies** (NJ 7323 2079). This recumbent stone circle stands within a circular enclosure. Built some time before the late 1830s, the latter creates a misleading impression of the character of the stone circle, which originally enclosed some form of cairn. SC712491*

that not only appear to have anticipated the position of orthostats, but also the recumbent setting (Bradley 2002b, 847).

Until recently, the dating evidence for these monuments has been very poor. An archer's wristguard comparable to those from Beaker graves (p. 54) had been found at **Old Rayne**, but its stratigraphical context was unknown (Stuart 1856, xxi). The undiagnostic character of the plain wares from the excavation of **Old Keig** and **Loanhead of Daviot** was of little help, but the significance of the Beaker sherds from potentially early contexts was not lost upon Kilbride-Jones (1935,

193; 1994, 139). To date radiocarbon assays have been obtained from stratified contexts at only five recumbent stone circles – Aikey Brae (*DES 2002*, 142–3), Berrybrae (Burl 1979, 29), **Cothiemuir Wood**, Strichen (Burl 1995, 109) and Tomnaverie (Bradley 2002c, 142–3) – though an old discovery from **Old Rayne** has also been dated (Sheridan 2003, 167). At the time of writing only those from Tomnaverie have been published in any detail. There, dates from charcoal retrieved from a pit probably dug and infilled during the preparation for the construction of the cairn fall at about 2500 BC. In addition, Beaker sherds were found deposited against the kerb of the cairn. Taking into account the Beaker pottery also recovered from **Loanhead of Daviot**, Berrybrae, **Old Keig**, **Old Rayne**, and **Corrie Cairn**, there can be little doubt that this remarkable group of monuments is essentially Early Bronze Age in date.

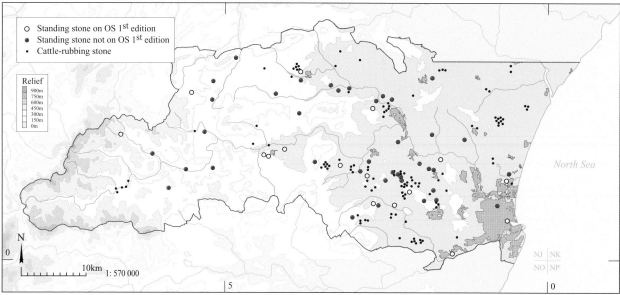

Fig. 5.31 This map shows the distribution of all the recorded standing stones in Donside. Those shown on the 1st edition of the OS 6-inch map are likely to be prehistoric monuments, as are some of those found since, but by far the majority of the stones standing in Donside are probably cattle-rubbing stones. GV000192

*Fig. 5.32 **The Lang Stane o' Craigearn** (NJ 7238 1493). This is one of the tallest standing stones in Donside. SC957511*

Standing Stones and Stone Circles

In addition to the recumbent stone circles, there has been a long tradition of erecting standing stones in the North-east. Many large standing stones were set up in the Neolithic or Early Bronze Age, but there are others dating from the early medieval period (pp. 116–24), and yet others that have been set up since the late 18th century to provide rubbing posts for cattle.

Distinguishing one type of standing stone from another is not as straightforward as it may appear, although many cattle-rubbing stones are plainly modern erections, marked on maps or exhibiting telltale evidence of modern quarrying. Certainly, such stones have caused confusion in the past. Callander, for example, described a standing stone north of **Clinterty Home Farm** in 1925, but it does not appear on either the 1st or 2nd edition of the OS 6-inch map, despite standing in a landscape of enclosed fields. It is inherently unlikely that this was an unrecorded prehistoric stone, but to confuse matters further the stone itself has now been removed. The same case can be made for a stone at **Foot o' Hill**, above Blackburn, and another at **Nether Mains of Tertowie**, the latter also displaying two quarried faces. Any stone standing within an improved field dating from the 19th century, but not shown on the 1st edition of the OS 6-inch map, should probably be treated as suspect.

Despite these difficulties, there are several fine monoliths that are likely to be of prehistoric date. Tradition often alleges that these are the sole survivors of circles or other settings, but there is seldom any visible evidence that this was the case. Unlike the recumbent stone circles, lone standing stones are also found in the upper reaches of the Don, broadly reflecting the distribution of burial-cairns. At **Glenkindie**, for example, there is an irregular block some 2.3m in height, though by tradition this belongs to a circle; it

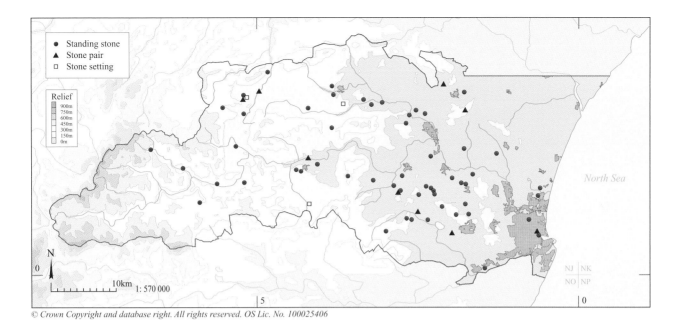

Fig. 5.33 This map shows the distribution of probable prehistoric standing stones, stone pairs and other stone settings. GV000190

*Fig. 5.34 **Balblair** (NJ 6987 0661). This flesh-pink granite pillar, which is said to be the sole surviving member of a stone circle, stands in a strip of woodland some 120m to the north-west of the recumbent stone circle at Midmar Kirk. SC958187*

fell in 1991 but has been re-erected. The larger stones in Donside are tall and imposing, including **The Lang Stane o' Craigearn** (3.4m high), **Woodend of Cluny** (3.3m), **Luath's Stone** (2.8m) and **The Gouk Stone** (2.9m). At least two stones are cupmarked, namely **The Ringing Stone** and **Balhalgardy**.

In addition to these single monoliths, there have evidently been other settings of stones, ranging from close-set pairs to the avenue at **Broomend of Crichie** (p. 56). They include at least one four-poster, at **Howemill**, and what may have been a second at **Broomend**, where the Name Book describes a circle that was removed about 1835 as *'composed of four stones'* (Aberdeenshire, No. 75, p. 12). Three stones of the four-poster at **Howemill** still survive, though two are no more than stumps, and there is a fallen outlier some 20m to the south. The setting measures about 6m by 5.5m, the south stone standing 1.1m high. One of the fragments lying beside the stump of the east stone bears six cupmarks.

Close-set pairs can be seen at **Mill of Noth**, north of Rhynie, and possibly **Nether Corskie** at Echt, and there are also two stones standing at right-angles to each other at **Upper Ord** near Rhynie. Other pairs are more widely set, such as at **Castle Fraser**, where two stones in the same field as the recumbent stone circle stand about 13m apart. Curiously, one of this pair is aligned along the axis of the alignment, roughly north-west and south-east, and the other lies across it. This arrangement is also repeated at **Mill of Noth**. Another spaced pair stands immediately east of the stone circle at **Shelden** (Fig. 5.37), but here the stones face each other along the general axis of the alignment, which lies north-west and south-east.

*Fig. 5.35 **Druidstone**, Premnay (NJ 6153 2219). This recumbent stone circle, and its outlier standing on the right of the picture, are the sole survivors of an ancient landscape of prehistoric hut-circles and burial mounds. SC880898*

The juxtaposition of standing stones and stone circles has long been recognised. In addition to **Castle Fraser**, such stones can still be seen in proximity to at least four other Donside recumbent stone circles – **Balquhain**, **Druidstone**, **Wester Echt** and **Midmar Kirk** – and others may have existed elsewhere, such as the *'massive'* stone that was blown up about 100m west-south-west of **Wantonwells** (Coles 1902, 536–7). In addition to these, there is the pair at **Shelden**, one of the few surviving circles that does not appear to have included a recumbent setting. The stone near Midmar Kirk (**Balblair**) is an impressive pillar of pink granite some 2.6m high, which stands in woodland about 110m north-north-west of the recumbent stone circle in the churchyard, but the others are in much closer proximity, at **Balquhain** lying 6m south-east, at **Druidstone** 8m north, and at **Wester Echt** probably about 6m east. Each is an imposing stone, at **Balquhain** composed of white quartz and standing 3.3m in height. Such stones are usually regarded as outliers to the stone circles, implying that they are either contemporary or secondary components of these monuments, but if this is the case it is difficult to detect any rhyme or reason in their placing. It is equally likely that these large and impressive stones are earlier, related to the previous use of the site, which was finally closed with the erection of the recumbent stone circle (p. 66).

Apart from the thirty-six recumbent stone circles, there are records of at least forty-seven other monuments that have been described as stone circles (pp. 20–1). Doubtless some of these were recumbent stone circles also, but most of them had already been removed by the time the 1st edition of the OS 6-inch map was prepared in the 1870s, and their classification should be treated fairly circumspectly. In some cases the annotation *'stone circle'* on the map was evidently applied to some other type of monument, such as the stone-walled enclosure on **White Hill** (Name Book, Aberdeenshire, No. 14, p. 56), or the circles at **Cothill**. The latter are even described as enclosures with

entrances in the Name Book (Aberdeenshire, No. 30, p. 31) and they were probably hut-circles rather than rings of standing stones. In another case, a description of a circle implies that the interior was levelled into the slope, claiming that the stones were on the top of the encircling bank and that a paved road stretched away for a distance of 600 yards to the south-east (*NSA*, xii, Aberdeenshire, 449). Later in the 19th century, the OS surveyors correlated this circle with the standing stones at **Druidsfield**, but they were evidently dealing with conflicting accounts from various sources (Name Book, Aberdeenshire, No. 88, p. 90). It is certainly difficult to reconcile the description with the two stones at **Druidsfield** today.

Causeways or paved roads recur in several descriptions of stone circles, and it is usually assumed that they are some form of early prehistoric ceremonial monument. Most are quite short, such as the stretch of paving about 18m in length found approaching a *'stone circle'* at **Nether Balfour** (Name Book, Aberdeenshire, No. 88, p. 107), and another two near Clatt, at **Bankhead** and **Newbigging** (Name Book, Aberdeenshire, No. 14, p. 23). The descriptions of the last two also display the tendency for such discoveries to become exaggerated. In both cases, the causeways were

*Fig. 5.36 **Balquhain** (NJ 7350 2408). The outlying standing stone to this recumbent stone circle is an impressive monolith of white quartz. SC961117*

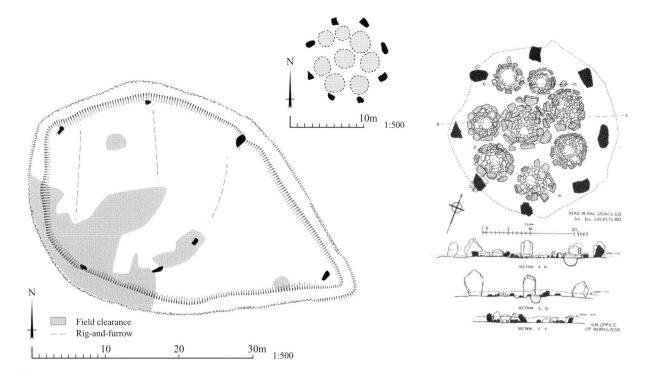

Fig. 5.37 **Shelden** *(NJ 8229 2493) and* **Cullerlie** *(NJ 7850 0428). The plans of these two stone circles, which are presented at the same scale, convey their differences in size and architecture. The excavation plan prepared by Kilbride-Jones in 1934 is also reproduced here. GV004125*

only exposed for short distances, but the proprietor, a Mr Booth, believed they extended much further, in the case of **Newbigging** linking the circle to a group of *'tumuli'* he had removed about 185m to the south-east. Rather than an observation of its course, however, this was surely part of Mr Booth's explanation of the ancient features in his landscape. And if the *'beautifully paved'* circle at **Bankhead** was not a megalithic monument but a hut-circle, then the adjacent causeway is more likely to have been a domestic structure, perhaps a shallow souterrain of the type that can still be seen at Kinord, in the Howe of Cromar (Abercromby 1904; Ogston 1931).

Leaving aside such records, there are still about twenty-four that have claim to be some form of stone circle, amongst them the stones standing within the henge monument at **Broomend of Crichie** (p. 57), and the enclosure at **Tuach Hill** (p. 58). The rest probably range from open rings of free-standing orthostats to those that formed components of cairns or ring-cairns. Included with the latter is the small circle at **Cullerlie**, Echt, with its unique cluster of small kerb cairns within the interior (Figs 5.37–8). Excavated by Kilbride-Jones (1935), the circle is now in the care of the state. As a counterpoint to the recumbent stone circles, **Cullerlie** presents an interesting contrast, demonstrating the presence of a completely different style of megalithic architecture in the region. The absence of any recumbent setting, and indeed of any focal point in the southern arc, is perhaps the most striking feature, but there is

no comparable grading in the stones either. With the exception of a stone about 1.8m in height on the north-west, the stones are comparatively small, ranging in height between 1.1m and 1.35m. Before the erection of the stones, the ground-surface was levelled, but thereafter the interior had been extensively burnt, apparently scorching some of the stones. The cairns within the interior had been built upon this burnt surface. Only one was undisturbed, but deposits of charcoal and calcined bone were recovered from pits or rough cists beneath most of them.

At least five other possible circles – **Fullerton, Deer Park, The Ringing Stone, The Auld Kirk of Alford**, and **The Sunken Kirk, Seggieden** – enclosed cairns or ring-cairns, and six if the curious description of a circle of stones connected by a wall found beneath

Fig. 5.38 **Cullerlie** *(NJ 7850 0428). Excavated by Kilbride-Jones in the 1930s, this stone circle is unique for the small kerbed cairns that stand within the ring. SC958750*

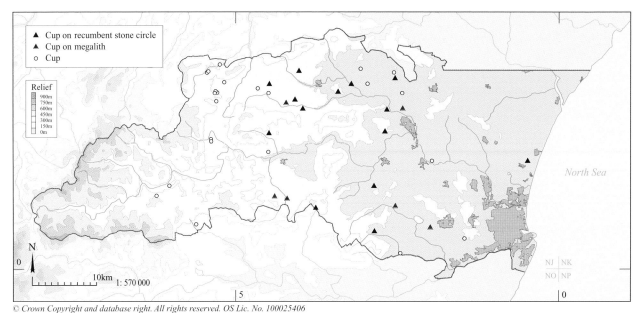

Fig. 5.39 This map shows the distribution of cupmarks on the stones of megalithic monuments. GV000184

the motte at **Kintore** is included (Watt 1865, 140–2). In the cases of **The Ringing Stone** and **The Sunken Kirk**, these cairns appear to have been quite large, the demolition of **The Sunken Kirk** entailing the removal of 500 cartloads of stones (Name Book, Aberdeenshire, No. 15, pp. 13–14). All that now remains of either is **The Ringing Stone** itself, a claw-shaped granite pillar some 2m high, which bears at least four shallow cupmarks on its south-west face. **Fullerton**, **The Auld Kirk of Alford** (Fig. 5.8) and **Deer Park** have fared slightly better, having been enclosed in small roundels, but all are heavily disturbed and obscured by field-cleared stones. In so far as it is now possible to tell, the first two have comprised a ring of orthostats set in a kerbed ring-bank, but most of the orthostats have been removed and the ring-banks are obscured by the later roundels. A pit containing both an inhumation and a cremation lay beneath an area of burning at the centre of the **Fullerton** ring-bank, and seven other cremation deposits were found around it (Coles 1901, 218–19). At **Deer Park** three stones remain upright, set in an oval mound measuring a maximum of 10m in diameter by 0.4m in height. Coles believed this to be the remains of a small circle surrounding a central monolith (1901, 201–3).

The circle at **Shelden** may also have enclosed a cairn, although there is no trace of one there today (Fig. 5.37). Enclosed by a later dyke and littered with field clearance, it appears to be an open ring, but the Name Book notes that a cist was discovered in the remains of the cairn in about 1820 (Aberdeenshire, No. 10, pp. 43, 48). The circle measures about 23m and provides another interesting contrast to the recumbent stone circles. Not only is there no sign of the grading

that is so typical of recumbent stone circles, but the more regular faces of the stones are set facing inwards.

Of the other circles little trace now remains. At best one or two standing stones survive, such as the two standing on a low ridge at **Druidsfield**, or the single stones at **Drumfours** and **Gask**. The rest were simply broken up during the Improvements and used for building stone, their removal to some extent catalogued in the Name Book. One of the few for which there is any record of its size was at **Gordonstown**. Removed in 1851, the circle *'was about twenty yards* [18m] *in diameter and some of the stones were of great size and weight'* (Name Book, Aberdeenshire, No. 14, p. 33). Other entries mention the number of stones in a circle, though these do not necessarily reflect their original complements. Thus, a circle removed at **Newton** apparently comprised seven or eight stones (Name Book, Aberdeenshire, No. 75, p. 34), while another on **Husband Hillock** had seven (Name Book, Aberdeenshire, No. 75, p. 41). Despite the litany of demolition, the stone holes and other features of such sites may well survive in the subsoil, as was demonstrated at **Brandsbutt**, where Ian Shepherd was able to identify five stone holes of a circle about 25m in diameter (Shepherd 1983).

With so little information available it is difficult to draw any firm conclusions about the character of any of these stone circles and settings. Nevertheless, it seems reasonable to suggest that the way in which recumbent stone circles apparently dominate the megalithic architecture of north-eastern Scotland is largely a reflection of the durability of the recumbent settings, even in the face of determined assault. Several other strands in the megalithic repertoire can be detected in Donside, ranging from pairs of standing stones and the four-poster at **Howemill**, to the circle at **Shelden** and the unique configuration of orthostats and small kerb cairns at **Cullerlie**.

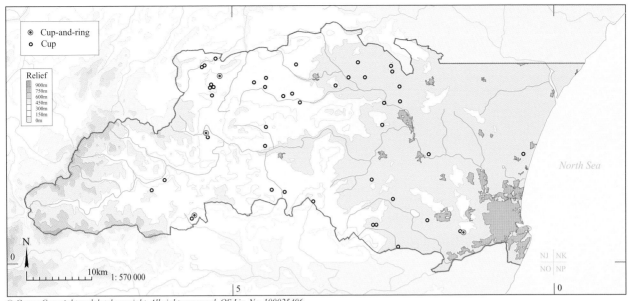

Fig. 5.40 This map shows the distribution of rock art recorded in Donside. GV000183

Rock Art

Fifty-nine cupmarked stones have been recorded in Donside, eleven of them noted for the first time during the present survey. Twelve, however, are now lost, including two on small portable boulders said to have been found in a cist (Callander 1907, 125–6). With one exception carved in living rock, the **Bowman Stone** at Kirkton of Rayne, they are all carved on slabs or boulders and are scattered widely throughout the area. The densest concentration extends from the Garioch into upper Strathbogie at Rhynie (Fig. 5.40) and contains no fewer than thirty-four examples, nine of them forming a notable cluster in the relatively poor ground on the hills to the west of Rhynie. This cluster has been enhanced by the discovery of three new stones, but it also includes one of the few ring-marked stones from the area, a slab discovered in the 19th century at **Scurdargue** (now lost). The stones are more scattered in the richer farmland to the east of the Water of Bogie, but here the majority are found incorporated into recumbent stone circles.

Elsewhere, cupmarked boulders are spread more thinly, extending up the Don from Inverurie as far as Strathdon, but virtually absent from the lower reaches of the valley. A single example lies out towards the coast at the recumbent stone circle at **Potterton**, north of Aberdeen, while those along the southern fringes of the survey area technically lie within the catchment of the River Dee. Those in the upper Don include four slabs incorporated into souterrains at **Clova**. Like the distribution in the Garioch, however, a remarkable proportion of the stones come from recumbent stone circles or other stone settings (Fig. 5.39).

Compared with neighbouring areas in Angus (Sherriff 1995; 1999) and Strath Tay (Hale 2003), the repertoire of motifs in Donside is disappointing. Nine of the stones bear but a single cup, and there are only ten stones with more than twenty, the most heavily cupmarked being a boulder bearing forty-two at **Migvie** (Fig. 5.41). Only six of the designs display any complexity, including four that have ring-marks. A lost boulder from **Deskry Hill** described by the Ordnance Survey, had six of the seven cups disposed in a cross-shaped arrangement, and the boulder from **Migvie** has a similar feature, though in this case short channels link the cups forming the cross. One small boulder, apparently found in a stone circle at **Skene** but now in the National Museum of Scotland (NMS X. IA 15), is carved with cups on opposing faces.

*Fig. 5.41 **Migvie** (NJ 4373 0675). Heavily cupmarked stones are rare in Donside and this particular example comes from the edge of the survey area in the Howe of Cromar. SC958181*

The four ring-marked stones are not elaborately decorated, but they include two of the most heavily cupmarked examples. The first of these comes from **Blacktop**. It is a rounded erratic boulder about 1m across, and has at least thirty-six cupmarks on one face, seven of which are ringed. The other, from **Tom Dubh**, on Meadow Farm, has forty cupmarks, but only one is ringed. Of the other two, the lost stone from **Scurdargue** (Jolly 1882, 343–4) had two of its thirteen cups ringed, while the last is a largely hidden slab in the roof of a souterrain at **Clova**.

The most remarkable aspect of the cupmarks in Donside is the apparent association with recumbent stone circles, thirteen of the circles accounting for no less than twenty-three of the carvings. Typically, they occur in the southern half of the circles and are often on the recumbent or its flankers (Burl 1970, 66), but it is difficult to demonstrate whether they have been incorporated by accident or design. The cups on the recumbent at **Loanend** seem to represent design, cut into the very apex of the stone some 2.2m above the ground, and may have been freshly carved when the stone was set upright. In other cases, however, the carvings were hidden from the view of the casual observer standing in front of the recumbent setting. At **Sunhoney**, for example, where the upper face of the fallen recumbent bears at least thirty cups, the carved

Fig. 5.42 **Balquhain** *(NJ 7350 2408). This cupmarked stone, photographed in 1911 by James Ritchie, is one of the monoliths on the west side of the recumbent stone circle. SC678940*

surface is on the back of the slab and would have faced onto the cairn. The same is true of the nine cups on the recumbent at **Corrie Cairn**. Such carved stones may well be in reuse, particularly as this form of decoration is known to date from the Neolithic, one small cupmarked boulder occurring in the mortuary structure beneath the long barrow at Dalladies, in the Mearns (Piggott 1972).

Even in reuse, these stones may have been selected for their symbolic significance, but it is worth sounding a note of caution. After all, the presence of the carved stones can hardly be considered a typical feature of recumbent stone circles, occurring in only thirteen of the thirty-six circles in the area. By far the majority of them have yet to reveal any evidence of rock art. Furthermore, the intensive clearance of stones from the lowland landscape has skewed the distribution of surviving cupmarkings to those incorporated into other monuments. Of these, recumbent stone circles have proved the most durable (pp. 20–1). Despite the wholesale removal of stones from every field, in some cases with the assistance of gunpowder, one or two of the larger stones at virtually every recumbent stone circle has survived. Typically, these include the recumbent, and often at least one flanker, which are the very stones upon which the majority of cupmarks have been observed (p. 66). It is difficult to escape the conclusion that the improvement of the lowlands has not only skewed the survival of cupmarks to the recumbent stone circles, but also to their southern arcs.

The surviving cupmarked stones are probably a tiny proportion of those that originally existed throughout the valley, and it is no coincidence that the cluster of nine around Rhynie occurs on ground that has been less heavily improved than the adjacent area in the Garioch. Ring-markings, however, are evidently much rarer, and it is interesting to note that no example has yet been discovered in the Garioch, nor at a recumbent stone circle. Only time will tell if these patterns are of any significance.

Wider Context

The assemblage of Neolithic and Bronze Age monuments along the Don is by no means unique and broadly reflects the range of archaeological remains that is to be found all over the North-east of Scotland. In this sense, the archaeological dimension of the Don catchment has no particular identity of its own in early prehistory. Nevertheless, Donside not only forms the topographical core of the North-east, but also embraces the densest concentrations of many of its monuments and artefacts. So much so, the sheer numbers of Neolithic and Bronze Age artefacts and monuments within its bounds, particularly within the Garioch, suggest a preference for settlement here that is only matched in the area to the north-east of the River Ythan.

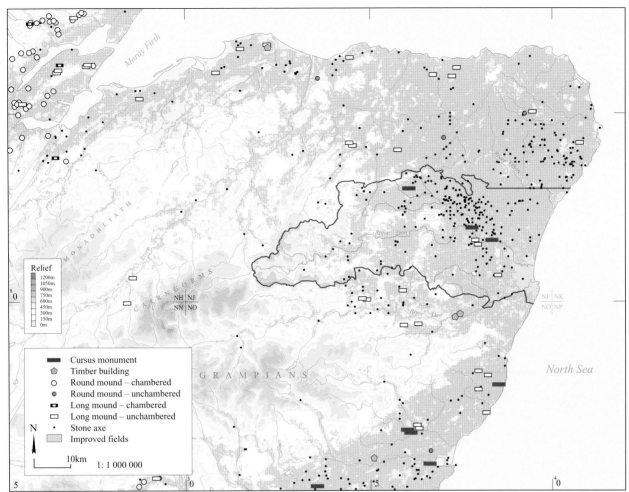

Fig. 5.43 This maps shows the distributions of a selection of Neolithic monuments and artefacts in north-east Scotland. The Garioch in Donside boasts the densest concentration of stone axes found anywhere in the North-east. GV000234

With few exceptions, distributions of artefacts within Donside display a rash of discoveries through the Garioch and into the top of Strathbogie at Rhynie, while lesser scatters extend through the Howe of Alford and into the narrower highland glens. To a certain extent this simply reflects the pattern of intensive arable farming over the last 200–300 years, but the proximity of a seat of learning in Aberdeen may also have played its part in the recording of discoveries. Nevertheless, the Garioch stands out in the whole of the North-east, and there can be little doubt that this concentration of finds is also a reflection of the intensity of prehistoric activity.

The extent of this activity in the Neolithic is immediately apparent in the distributions of artefacts and monuments (Fig. 5.43). The stone axes for example, which are a characteristic fossil of this period, reveal a massive concentration in the Garioch, even taking into account some of the problems involved in the provenances of axes found in the 19th century. The scatter in the upper reaches of the Don, however, does not include records of three axes from the general

area of Strathdon. The distribution of the axes is complemented by other discoveries, such as carved stone balls and Early Neolithic pottery, and is doubtless reflected in some of the flint tools that have been collected from ploughed fields. In contrast, long cairns and barrows are few and far between, though the long mound discovered in the excavations at **Forest Road**, Kintore, suggests that others may have been lost to later ploughing. What is perhaps surprising is that no unrecorded long cairns have come to light during the present survey in the upper reaches of the valley, where standing monuments are consistently better preserved.

The evidence from charred cereal grains at Balbridie provides a remarkable insight into some aspects of Neolithic exploitation of the landscape, but as yet this is not complemented from other palaeoenvironmental sources (p. 40). On the one hand, there is the general lack of palynological data for the Neolithic from the lowlands of either Deeside or Donside; on the other, the difficulty of discerning any clearly defined types of human activity at this date from pollen analyses higher up the Dee in the Howe of Cromar. The distribution of Neolithic artefacts implies that clearings were made in the woodland throughout the catchment, and some of these may have been of considerable size, if only to

Fig. 5.44 Howford Bridge (NH 8782 5384). Though no long enclosures of this type have been found in Donside, the closest parallels for this example from near Nairn, at the west end of the Moray Plain, lie south of the Mounth in Perth & Kinross. SC957512

accommodate a linear monument such as the cursus at **Mill of Fintray**. This not only occupies quite a large space but, if it was to be any more than a narrow corridor through the contemporary woodland (Loveday 2006, 36–7), would have required extensive clearance to allow any outlook along or across its axis.

The pace of woodland clearance and soil erosion recorded in the Howe of Cromar picks up in the Early Bronze Age (p. 41). This complements the distribution of Early Bronze Age funerary monuments, which in Donside penetrates into the headwaters of the river. Contemporary artefacts are also found in the upper reaches of the valley, seen, for example, in the scatter of flat axes, which includes a hoard from **Finglenny Hill** at the head of the Kirkney Water (Stevenson 1948, 292–3), close to the small henge monument at **Wormy Hillock**. The density of burial-cairns in upper Donside almost rivals that in the Garioch, while the general absence of flat graves presumably reflects the emphasis on pasture here, which conversely accounts for the survival of so many large cairns. These distributions, however, present a curious anomaly in the pattern of Early Bronze Age monuments, for while the survey has recorded several new and substantial burial-cairns in the upper part of the valley, recumbent stone circles have remained stubbornly absent. With the possible exception

of the standing stone at **Glenkindie**, by tradition the lone survivor of a circle, there are no circles of any sort along the Don west of the Howe of Alford. Within the area surveyed, the westernmost is the **Blue Cairn of Ladieswell**, a recumbent stone circle, but this is in the Howe of Cromar in Deeside rather than in Donside. In respect to Deeside, the Howe of Cromar occupies a similar position to the Howe of Alford in Donside. It is the last major basin in the hills before the strath adopts a narrower highland character. While the recumbent stone circles are generally in locally elevated positions, they are essentially lowland monuments.

Taking a broader view of the distributions of different types of monuments and artefacts tends to suggest that the Mounth was not the barrier in the earlier part of the Neolithic that it was to become in later periods. Certainly, local materials were routinely employed in the manufacture of stone axes (Ritchie and Scott 1988, 90), and yet there is also a scatter of exotic items from much further afield, such as porcellanite axes from Antrim, and flint adzes and axes from Yorkshire. The only hint of a regional identity at this stage is the identification of a 'north-east style' of early Neolithic pottery (above p. 46), though Sheridan has pointed out that it has yet to be demonstrated whether this style is an early regional development away from the tradition of carinated bowl pottery, or simply a variant within it (Sheridan 2002, 86).

No such regional pattern can be detected in the character of the local types of Neolithic monuments found in the North-east. The overall distribution of long barrows and cairns spans the Mounth, though the north-eastern group appears to peter out in the Mearns (RCAHMS 1994, 37–40), leaving a large gap in the distribution in Angus. Barclay has played down the significance of this gap (Barclay and Maxwell 1998, 115–17), and suggests not only that new examples of long barrows may remain to be discovered, but also that a proportion of the round barrows in the area are likely to be Neolithic. Of the latter there is little doubt, demonstrated most recently at Fordhouse, on the northern shores of the Montrose Basin (*DES 1999*, 111). In this respect, it may not matter whether there are gaps in the distribution of long barrows in the lowlands, for the overall pattern of funerary monuments north and south of the Mounth would be broadly similar, with a mixed assemblage of circular and long mounds. Rather than a general mixed scatter, however, these monuments are possibly disposed in highly localised, discrete clusters of long or circular mounds. This may provide a better explanation of the peripheral clusters of some of the long cairns and barrows rather than simply attributing the gaps to later agricultural attrition. It should also be borne in mind, however, that some of these monuments may well have been erected in peripheral locations; this seems to be the implication of the pollen data from beneath the barrow at Midtown of Pitglassie (p. 41).

Other components of the monumental vocabulary that the North-east shares with the rest of eastern Scotland include the presence of large timber buildings, long mortuary enclosures and cursus monuments. Admittedly, they do not occur in any numbers, but this has more to do with the general incidence of cropmarks than any underlying cultural factors (p. 82). The cursus monument at **Mill of Fintray**, for example, with its pit-defined sides and sub-divisions, is typical of examples in Angus and Perth & Kinross, as is the probable mortuary enclosure on the southern shore of the Moray Firth at Howford Bridge, near Nairn.

By the mid-3rd millennium BC, however, at the transition from the Late Neolithic into the Bronze Age, some of the distinctive aspects of a North-eastern identity were emerging, though these must be set against the backdrop of Bronze Age funerary practices and burial monuments that have a much wider currency. Nevertheless, the distribution of megalithic monuments displays a clear bias towards the North-east, while the flowering of the Migdale tradition of bronze-working at the beginning of the Bronze Age is also apparently focused in the North-east (Needham 2004). Carved stone balls are another type of artefact thought to be of this date that is particularly common in the North-east, though, like the Migdale metalwork, they are also scattered more widely. The Aberdeenshire examples are generally of local manufacture, and thirteen of the fifteen in Inverurie Museum are made of granite from its hinterland (Marshall 1977, 55).

Fig. 5.45 **Kildrummy** *(NJ 45 18). These carved stone balls from the general area of Kildrummy represent a type of artefact that is apparently associated with the North-east. Very few have accurately recorded findspots or contexts.* © *University of Aberdeen*

The concentration of stone circles in the North-east shows a regional pattern at this date more reliably, displaying the densest distribution of such monuments to be found anywhere in the British Isles (see Burl 2000, 2). The recumbent stone circles form the mainstay of this concentration, although, as has been shown (pp. 70–2), a significant proportion of the circles in the area probably did not have a recumbent setting. The distribution of recumbent stone circles peters out to the south of the Mounth, roughly coinciding with the pattern of surviving long barrows and cairns in the Mearns, while to the west it marches with the Clava group. Bradley has shown how aspects of the architecture of the Clava cairns draw on Late Neolithic traditions, such as the grading of rings of monoliths, which is evidently present in henge architecture (2000, 218–20). The same must equally apply to the recumbent stone circles, but whereas Bradley would see the Clava group as the product of the mixing of different cultural traditions from north, east and south-west, this would imply a derivative position in the expression of the ideas that lie behind the architecture.

There can be little doubt that the Great Glen has been an important thoroughfare in the evolution of Scottish history and prehistory, but the discrete regions occupied by the Clava cairns and the recumbent stone circles, both of which are Early Bronze Age in date (Bradley 2000; 2005), tend to suggest that they reflect components in a regional structure. Bradley has drawn attention to the secondary reuse of Orkney-Cromarty chambered tombs during the Early Bronze Age, which defines a regional practice to the north, albeit one that is limited by default to the distribution of the chambered tombs (2000, 221–3), while Barclay has identified the apparently exclusive distributions of henge monuments and recumbent stone circles on the eastern seaboard (Barclay 2000, 278, Fig. 24.2). For these purposes, however, the henges are not the most useful group of monuments to employ. Not only is their distribution based on untested interpretations of enclosures recorded as cropmarks, but the general distribution of cropmarks in any case falls off to the north of the Mounth (Fig. 6.15). In addition to the surviving henges at **Wormy Hillock** and **Broomend of Crichie**, there are several penannular enclosures and ring-ditches that may also belong in this category, such as Kintocher on Deeside (Fig. 6.20), and others almost certainly remain to be found. On these grounds, henges are probably at least as common as anywhere else in eastern Scotland.

Rather than cropmark categories, the distribution of recumbent stone circles is better set against other types of stone monuments, where the factors that have governed their survival and destruction are broadly similar. Perth & Kinross, and to a lesser extent

Angus, are particularly rich in a range of megalithic monuments, and it is arguable that these are also hinting at the existence of a regional pattern. Formally built ring-cairns with graded kerbs, for instance, are found all along the fringes of the hills between Perth and the Mearns, while the area around Perth also has a notable group of small graded circles (RCAHMS 1994, 30–3). Like the recumbent stone circles, the largest stones of these circles are usually in the south-western quadrant, a feature also encountered at burial-cairns with formal kerbs. Graded four-poster stone settings might be considered in this light too. They are mainly concentrated west of Forfar and up Strath Tay and Strath Earn, but in this case there are a few outliers north of the Mounth (p. 69).

Perth & Kinross also contains a concentration of stone alignments, the smaller ones comprising a simple pair of close-set stones (RCAHMS 1994, 31; Burl 1993). Such pairings display considerable variety in their design, so much so that their integrity as a single category may be questioned. Nevertheless, the stones of the pairs often display the same thick and thin character that has been observed in the flankers of recumbent stone circles, and they often face southwards over wide open views. While Burl was inclined to reject this link (1993, 199), it is worth considering that they drew upon the same ideas for their construction, even though the *'doorway'* they frame is open, rather than closed.

While it may be possible to detect some pale reflection of Neolithic and Bronze Age geography in the distributions of various types of funerary and ceremonial monument, these shed little light on the character of contemporary settlements. By the beginning of the Bronze Age, at about 2500 BC, it is likely that people were mainly living in circular houses (pp. 87; 108), but the evidence of earlier settlements is more sketchy. The large rectangular timber building excavated at Balbridie, on the southern bank of the Dee, has been used as a model for the character of Neolithic settlements (p. 40; Shepherd 1987, 120–1), but, despite more recent discoveries of similar Neolithic structures (Barclay *et al.* 2002; *DES 2005*, 12–13), it is far from certain that these are typical settlements. Usually, there is little more than a cluster of pits containing Neolithic pottery and other artefacts to indicate that a site has been occupied at this time, such as was found at **Deer's Den** and **Forest Road**, Kintore (Alexander 2000, 65–7; Cook *et al.* forthcoming). At **Deer's Den** the pits were clustered into a roughly rectangular area, and yet there was nothing to indicate that this was the remains of a building. The typical Neolithic settlement was perhaps characterised by much flimsier structures than the large buildings discovered at Balbridie and Crathes.

Chapter 6: The Later Prehistoric Landscape

Stratford Halliday

The most enduring symbols of the later prehistoric landscape in Aberdeenshire are undoubtedly the forts that occupy several of the most prominent landmarks in the district. Powerful centres such as these, for there can be little doubt that they do represent foci of secular and political authority, cannot have existed in isolation, but the landscape that they now dominate is essentially modern, enclosed within stone dykes and planted with crops or trees.

In this sense, the landscape of Donside presents a remarkable contrast to the valleys of other major rivers draining east and south from the Cairngorms. In the glens of Angus and north-eastern Perthshire, and to a certain extent along the Dee, a relict landscape of unenclosed settlements and clearance heaps can be found across large swathes of the uplands. Nominally, at least, the upper reaches of these glens contain what appear to be *'prehistoric landscapes'*, albeit ones that are composed of monuments spanning 4000 years or so.

In contrast, enclosure and cultivation over the last three hundred years have penetrated far more deeply into the hills of Donside, taking in the majority of the gentler slopes below 400m OD.

Despite this attrition, unenclosed settlements can be found throughout the valley, from the foot of the Lecht in the west to the arable lowlands around Aberdeen in the east. Those in the uplands are still visible on the ground, whereas the lowland settlements appear mostly as cropmarks. Such a pattern is no more than should be anticipated, but one of the most unusual aspects of this part of the Aberdeenshire landscape, and indeed of Deeside too, is the way in which small patches of ground in the lowlands have survived unploughed since prehistory. Here, in small niches of stony ground, often enclosed within plantations laid out at the time of the

*Fig. 6.1 **Barra Hill** (NJ 8025 2570). Rising above farmland to the south of Old Meldrum, this multivallate fort is preserved amidst furlongs of later rig-and-furrow cultivation. SC773003*

Fig. 6.2 Pockets of prehistoric and medieval landscape remains have survived the agricultural improvements to the east of Kintore, around and within what is now Balbithan Wood. The pattern of surviving hut-circles implies the density of prehistoric settlement remains that once existed in the lowlands of Donside. In this area, no fewer than twenty-five hut-circles have been recorded in rough pasture and woodland. GV000176

agricultural improvements, occasional relicts of this earlier landscape are still visible, including some quite extensive groups of hut-circles, such as those preserved in **Garlogie Wood** or at **Benthoul** (Fig. 6.3).

In several areas these relicts are sufficiently close together to provide some idea of the density of prehistoric settlement that must once have existed. A good example lies on the north-east side of the Don to the east of Kintore (Fig. 6.2), where hut-circles, burial-cairns, and scatters of field clearance heaps occupy the gaps between later patches of rig-and-furrow and modern fields over a distance of 2km. Situated between the 70m and 100m contours, these are only 25m to 55m above the floor of the valley. Some of the hut-circles and scatters of small cairns lie in small patches of rough pasture, but the major group lies beneath Balbithan Wood (**Greenlands**). Cropmarks in the fields to the south reveal the sites of other elements in this landscape, including several enclosures (see **Suttie**, Fig. 6.20) and timber round-houses, the latter visible as discs or crescents in crops of wheat and barley. Other hut-circle groups recorded in

this part of the valley in the 19th century are now largely cleared away. On the **Hill of Boghead**, for example, on the opposite side of the Don to the south-east of Kintore (Fig. 6.4), scatters of *'tumuli'* and three *'camps'* are depicted in some detail on the 1st edition of the OS 6-inch map (Aberdeenshire 1869, lxv), but by the end of the century many of the cairns had been removed (1901, lxv.nw & sw) and little survives today.

A similar pattern can be pieced together throughout Donside, even though several of the antiquarian accounts almost certainly misinterpreted the remains they described. At **Damil**, for example, the *New Statistical Account* for the parish of Alford describes a *'camp'* covering an area of about 10ha, which was enclosed by *'an earthen wall and ditch, strengthened, at intervals of one hundred yards, by round buildings, also of earth, of about fifty feet diameter'* (1845, Aberdeenshire, 499). At least one of two stone cups or lamps provenanced to **Damil** in Marischal College Museum, Aberdeen (ABDUA: 17418 & 17419) was found *'on levelling a turret'* (Gillan 1863, 499), and the site is annotated *'Site of Fort'* on the 1st edition of the OS 6-inch map (Aberdeenshire 1869, lxii). Thus, **Damil** has passed into the archaeological record as a fort. The *'round buildings'*, however, have no parallel amongst forts in the North-east, whereas large hut-circles are relatively common. The same confusion is evident with the hut-

circles depicted in **Garlogie Wood**, which are annotated
Remains of Supposed Camp. Two of the hut-circles are
shown on the perimeters of large enclosures, giving the
impression of *'turrets'* along a rampart (Aberdeenshire
1869, lxxiv).

The antiquarian records also describe another element
of the later prehistoric settlement pattern, namely
souterrains found in the course of cultivation (pp. 22–3;
88–92). These subterranean chambers hidden beneath
huge capstones seem to have caught the imagination of
ploughman and antiquarian alike, and the locations of
many earlier discoveries were still remembered when the
1st edition of the OS 6-inch map was prepared. The sites
of others have now been revealed by aerial photography
(Figs 6.8; 6.14).

The visible remains of hut-circles and cairnfields now
occupy locations that were marginal to agriculture in the
19th century. That much is evident from comparing the
depictions of the **Hill of Boghead** on the 1st and 2nd
editions of the OS 6-inch map (Aberdeenshire 1869,
lxv; 1901, lxv.nw & sw). Surveyed at an interval of
only thirty years, these two maps clearly reveal how the
surviving monuments were marginalised in the expansion
and formalisation of the improved intakes. However,
the extent of rig-and-furrow shown on 18th-century
estate plans, fragments of which can be found beneath
numerous old plantations in the lowlands (Fig. 9.11),
shows that huge inroads into the prehistoric landscape had
already been made long before. In many places virtually
all the land under cultivation today had been ploughed in
rigs during the 18th century. On the richest farmland, this
was probably the case at a much earlier date.

In these areas the best guide to the general locations
that were occupied in later prehistory is provided by the
more durable Bronze Age monuments, such as recumbent
stone circles and large burial-cairns. Most of those in
the lowlands only stand in isolation today because the
lesser structures that once surrounded them have been
cleared away. This is confirmed by the incidence of burial
monuments preserved within hut-circle groups, and
indeed of recumbent stone circles and ring-cairns, as can
be seen in eastern Deeside. Most of the recumbent stone
circles and ring-cairns there have been subsumed into the
pattern of improved fields, but those that have not usually
stand amongst groups of small cairns – Clune Wood;
The Nine Stanes, Garrol Wood; Upper Balfour; and
Campstone Hill, Raedykes.

When the various distributions are pieced together,
they reveal that later prehistoric settlement in Donside
was extensive. The only areas of modern improved fields
that may have been avoided are those where the soils
are poorly drained, such as in the bottom of the Howe of
Alford (p. 34).

*Fig. 6.3 **Benthoul** (NJ 788 034 to 794 035). The hut-circles and stone
clearance heaps of this prehistoric settlement were incorporated first
into a system of rig-and-furrow cultivation, and subsequently into a
plantation in the improved landscape. GV000233*

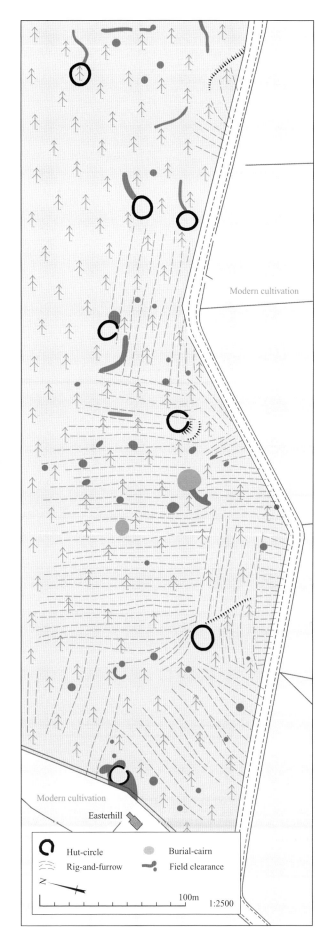

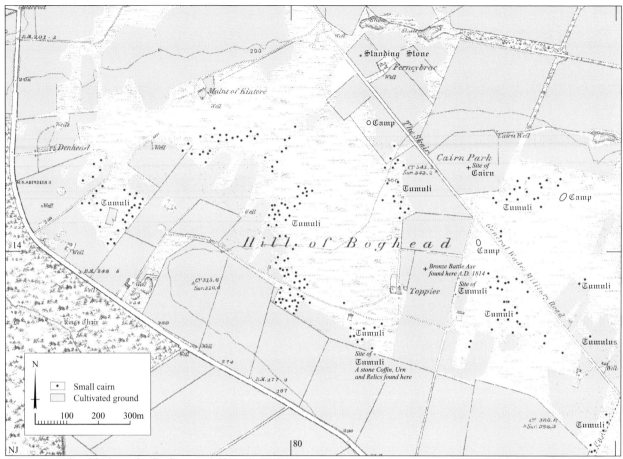

*Fig. 6.4 **Hill of Boghead** (NJ 800 140). Comparison of successive editions of the OS 6-inch map reveals the way in which extensive traces of prehistoric settlement were cleared away during the 19th century. In this case, on the Hill of Boghead, only a handful of the cairns and enclosures depicted on the 1st edition of the OS 6-inch map (Aberdeenshire 1869, lxv) remain visible. GV000175*

Unenclosed Hut-circles and Round-houses

In the course of the survey, no less than ninety-one new hut-circles have been identified, bringing the total for the survey area to at least 187. These new discoveries are scattered throughout the valley, some of them occurring in the groups that are already known, but the majority lying in moorland in the upper reaches of the valley (Fig. 6.5). Six have been identified in Glenbuchat, for instance; another ten in three or four groups in the unforested, east side of the Deskry Water; and a clutch of others close to the watershed separating Donside from the Howe of Cromar.

To these can be added the remains of round-houses recorded as cropmarks – mainly disc- and crescent-shaped marks – and by excavation (Fig. 6.7). In proportion to those that must once have existed in the lowlands, round-houses are almost certainly under-represented in the cropmark record, in part reflecting the general reduction in the density of cropmark evidence

north of the Mounth (Fig. 6.15). That is not to say that the same dense concentrations of unenclosed settlement remains that have been recorded in Fife and Angus do not exist north of the Mounth; it is simply that the factors that govern the formation of cropmarks – the extent of wheat or barley cultivation and freely draining soils, coupled with long spells of dry weather – do not work in favour of their discovery. The excavations in advance of a housing development at **Forest Road**, Kintore neatly demonstrate the case. There, numerous round-houses have been uncovered, only one of which was previously recorded as a cropmark (Cook and Dunbar 2004, 86).

The hut-circles and round-houses that are still visible today can be divided into several categories. The first of these comprises what may be termed typical hut-circles, essentially indistinguishable in character from those found in moorland locations in many other parts of Scotland. In Donside these measure from 3m to 16m in internal diameter, and their walls are anywhere from 1m to 3m in thickness, although in many cases the facing-stones have been robbed and the hut-circle has been reduced to little more than a low stony ring-bank. By far the majority (125) fall between 7m and 11m in diameter, and almost half of these (61) between 8m and 10m. In one or two instances the ring-bank is no more than 0.1m in height and shows no signs that it is

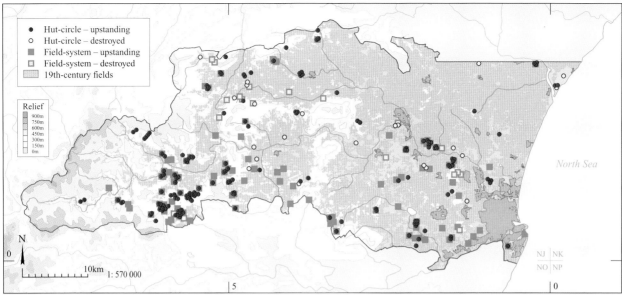

Fig. 6.5 This map shows the overall distribution of all the upstanding remains of round-houses, here covered by the term hut-circle, that have been recorded since the mid-19th century in Donside. Although a number of those known from the lowlands are now ploughed out, the distribution is remarkable for the examples that are still visible in low-lying contexts. A similar pattern emerges for the scatters of clearance cairns that form the mainstay of evidence for prehistoric field-systems. GV000253

the remains of a degraded stone wall. A hut-circle in the headwaters of the **Drumquhil Burn**, for example, measures 7m in diameter within a bank spread some 1.7m in thickness, and it is only visible today on account of the low carpet of young heather regenerating upon its site. In some cases these ring-banks may mark the sites of timber round-houses. Suffice it to say that such remains are very vulnerable to any change in land-use, and a single episode of cultivation or land improvement would probably erase all trace of them from the surface of the moor.

The second category of round-house that has been recognised in the field is essentially a type of hut-circle, but one in which the wall is formed by a thick bank, rarely with any trace of a stone face, and there is a concentric ring-ditch immediately within the interior. At least fourteen have been identified within Donside itself (Fig. 6.7), but this is a distinctive type of round-house, known as a ring-ditch house, and has a wide geographical distribution in eastern Scotland. Most of the surviving examples in Donside are situated in relatively high moorland, such as six discovered in Glenbuchat (**Creag an Sgor**, **Craigies** and **Creagandubh**), and another two at the foot of the Lecht (**The Luib**). They measure between 7m and 11m in diameter over the ditch, and the banks can be as much as 3m in thickness. Some of the ring-ditches are quite shallow, but in others the ditch may be as much as 0.7m in depth, and in the case of two in the forestry at **Woodend of Braco** (Fig. 6.6), the whole of the interior

has been sunk beneath the surrounding ground level. In these examples at least, the partly or wholly sunken character of the floor is evidently inherent in the design of the round-house.

The third category is only recognisable by virtue of a circular or oval platform that has been dug into the slope to provide a level foundation. In Aberdeenshire such platforms are but a minor component of the settlement record, so much so that the only examples identified within Donside are those scattered around the flanks of **Dunnideer** (Figs 6.6; 6.25). The larger ones measure between 9.5m and 12m in diameter, and are much the same size as the typical hut-circles in the North-east. Indeed, it would be unwise to suppose any chronological or functional distinction between stone-walled and timber-walled round-houses, the only real difference being in the materials from which the walls were constructed. Furthermore, where hut-circles are sited on hillsides, they too are terraced into the slope, although in these cases it is usually only the area within the wall that has been levelled up.

While these three categories may not carry any cultural or chronological significance, they have an important bearing on the interpretation of the cropmark record, which is too often seen as a separate category of evidence. In some cases cropmarks reveal types of settlement that are otherwise unrecorded, but in many others they record the sites of unenclosed round-houses scattered in much the same way as those of any hut-circle group. In effect, the unenclosed settlements recorded upstanding on the ground and as cropmarks from the air are facets of the same pattern, the datasets merely reflecting differential preservation and the application of different survey techniques to discover them.

Having asserted that these two datasets are one and the same, the question arises as to whether they

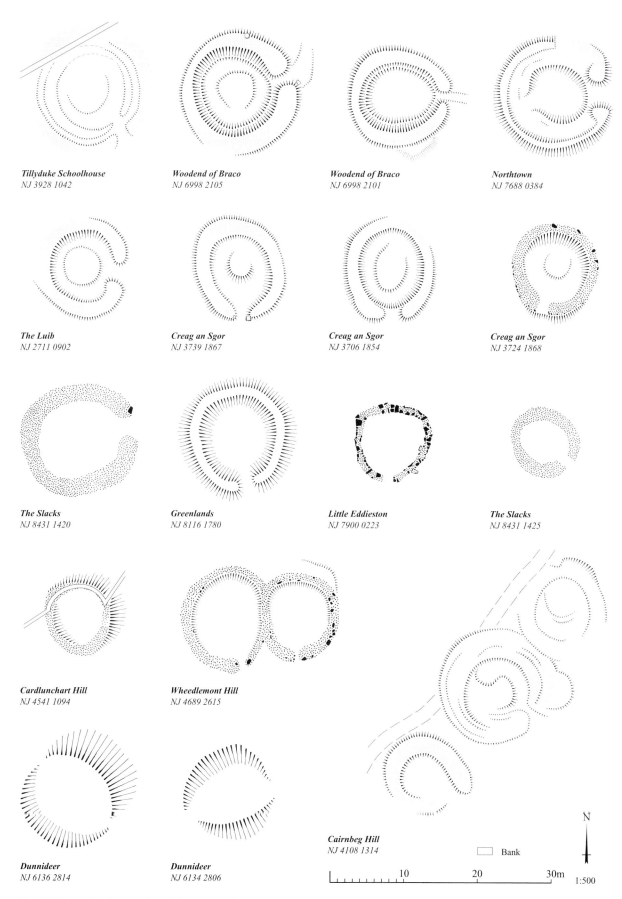

Tillyduke Schoolhouse
NJ 3928 1042

Woodend of Braco
NJ 6998 2105

Woodend of Braco
NJ 6998 2101

Northtown
NJ 7688 0384

The Luib
NJ 2711 0902

Creag an Sgor
NJ 3739 1867

Creag an Sgor
NJ 3706 1854

Creag an Sgor
NJ 3724 1868

The Slacks
NJ 8431 1420

Greenlands
NJ 8116 1780

Little Eddieston
NJ 7900 0223

The Slacks
NJ 8431 1425

Cardlunchart Hill
NJ 4541 1094

Wheedlemont Hill
NJ 4689 2615

Dunnideer
NJ 6136 2814

Dunnideer
NJ 6134 2806

Cairnbeg Hill
NJ 4108 1314

Bank

N

10   20   30m

1:500

Fig. 6.6 Plans of a selection of round-houses recorded in Donside. GV000145

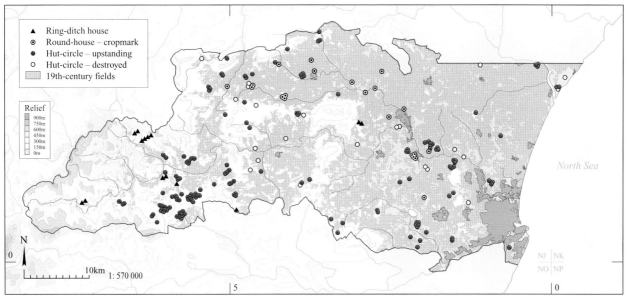

Fig. 6.7 This map shows the distributions of all the different types of round-house recorded in Donside, ranging from stony ring-banks – conventional hut-circles – to ring-ditch structures and cropmark remains. The addition of the cropmarks does little to alter the overall distribution, reflecting the general paucity of the cropmark record in Donside. GV000250

can be married into a single set of categories. The simple answer is no, because one is based solely on shape derived from the images on aerial photographs, while the other incorporates a wider range of visible characteristics. Nevertheless, it is important to consider which elements from this wider range of characteristics contribute directly to the shapes recorded on aerial photographs. All trace of a stone or turf wall, for instance, will normally be removed by a sustained period of cultivation, while internal rings of roof supports or the posts of the doorway are only revealed by cropmarks under exceptional circumstances, and then only on the most freely draining soils. In practice, the only round-houses that can be expected to appear in the cropmark record are those where the floor is wholly or partly sunk below the level of the subsoil. Roughly transposed to the upstanding remains, these comprise: levelled hut-circle or timber round-house stances, where the back of a platform may be preserved below the ploughsoil; ring-ditch houses, where the whole circuit of the ditch, or at least the deeper portions, may survive (e.g. **Woodend of Braco**); and round-houses where the whole interior is sunken (e.g. **Woodend of Braco**). These have the potential to form cropmark maculae ranging in shape from complete discs to crescents, and from annular and penannular rings to short arcs of ditch.

This approach is borne out by the cropmarks that have been photographed to date. Although relatively few of these lie in Donside itself, from the Mearns to the Moray Plain the cropmarks of unenclosed

settlements are dominated by disc- and crescent-shaped markings, and annular or penannular rings. From the markings alone, however, it is almost impossible to distinguish the crescentic and semi-circular shapes that indicate the backs of platforms from those that have formed over arcs of ring-ditches. Discs, too, may obscure the presence of a ring-ditch, as was discovered by excavation at **Deer's Den**, Kintore (pp. 86–7; Alexander 2000). This is again implicit in the upstanding remains, for the central area of the round-house with the well-developed ring-ditch at **Woodend of Braco** lies below the surrounding ground level (Fig. 6.6).

Rather than shrouding the detailed interpretation of these cropmarks with caveats, the more important point to emphasise is that most of these markings indicate the sites of round-houses, in particular round-houses where some portion of the floor is sunken. The typical hut-circle on level ground, comprising a circular wall and an internal post-ring, is probably largely unrepresented, though such buildings may be recoverable by excavation, as shown by the post-rings discovered at **Forest Road**, Kintore (Cook and Dunbar 2004). The few post-rings that have been identified as cropmarks to the north of the Mounth mainly occur on gravels at the mouths of the major rivers debouching along the Moray Plain (see Jones *et al.* 1993, 59). Excavation of several post-rings at Romancamp Gate, Bellie, has confirmed that they are probably the remains of round-houses (Barclay 1993), while others occur in conjunction with crescentic markings and wall trenches. Closer to Donside, an exceptionally clear example has been identified in Deeside, amongst a cluster of souterrains at Mains of Balfour, but in this instance the ring possibly lies at the centre of a concentric enclosure (p. 95; Shepherd and Greig 1996, 52, nos 70–1). For the greater part of Aberdeenshire,

Fig. 6.8 Mains of Balfour (NO 555 964). This oblique aerial photograph reveals unusually detailed cropmarks of the post-ring of a round-house adjacent to one of three souterrains at Mains of Balfour, near Birse on the south side of the River Dee. © AAS 94–15–CT14

however, including Donside, such details do not appear, and the cropmarks of unenclosed round-houses are probably disproportionately weighted towards buildings that included a ring-ditch in their design.

Despite the paucity of settlement cropmarks within Donside, those that have been discovered fit broadly into the pattern that has been revealed elsewhere in the North-east. On the one hand, a number of single discs, crescents and rings have been recorded; on the other, there are several clusters of six or more. Examples of the former are a boldly defined disc on the floodplain of the Urie at **Portstown**, or a crescent at **Newton**, near Kennethmont. A penannular ring-ditch at **Logie**, Chapel of Garioch, may also fall into this category. Amongst the latter there are at least seven discs, crescents and rings in a field at **Littlemill**, Leslie, and the site excavated on the line of the Kintore bypass at **Deer's Den** (Alexander 2000). At **Deer's Den** the aerial photographs had revealed at least six round-houses in all, including one well-defined disc that turned out to be a ring-ditch house with a heavily worn entrance passage. In its immediate vicinity, however, there were another three round-houses that are unrecognisable as such on the aerial photographs.

With so few examples of these cropmark settlements falling within Donside, estimated diameters have been collected across the whole of the North-east, amounting to at least 100 discs and crescents in all. These reveal a much wider range of diameters than the hut-circles from the same area, the largest of which is about 17m. In contrast, at least twelve discs and crescents measure between 18m and 22m in diameter, and one disc is as much as 24m in diameter. The majority, however, are between 8m and 16m in diameter. A few smaller examples have also been identified, though none is less than 5m in diameter. When compared with the range of diameters of the upstanding hut-circles, the discs and crescents tend to fall in the upper range, to the point where they appear to form a disproportionate number of the larger round-houses. Thus, while discs and crescents make up only 6% of all round-houses measuring 8m to 10m in diameter, this rises to 25% of the 12m to 14m range, and 50% of the 14m to 17m span. Adding other ring-ditches and enclosures into the graph swings the balance even more heavily towards the cropmarks, though their interpretation as the remains of round-houses is open to question. The largest discs are too big to be considered as the remains of single round-houses, and it is likely that these are masking small enclosed settlements (pp. 93–5). The absence from the cropmarks of discs or crescents of the equivalent size to the 3m to 5m diameter hut-circles is possibly more apparent than real, and is essentially a problem of cropmark interpretation. On the one hand a disc only 3m in diameter is almost impossible to distinguish from the larger pits that occur on so many aerial photographs, while on the other, it is likely that the minimum diameter of a crescent that can be identified with any confidence will be at least 5m in diameter, if not larger still.

In addition to the round-houses that have been identified by survey and aerial photography in Donside, excavations on two sites have revealed types of building that are otherwise unrepresented. These are on **Candle Hill**, near Insch, and **Greenbogs**, near Monymusk. The first of these was a chance discovery adjacent to a recumbent stone circle, and comprised part of a bedding trench about 15m in diameter and several internal rings of post-holes (Cameron 1999). It was interpreted by the excavator as a single building, but the rings of post-holes are not precisely concentric and it is possible that at least two large buildings are represented, one of them superimposed almost concentrically upon the other. The two structures at **Greenbogs** were of a rather different design (*DES 1996*, 9–10), measuring about 9.7m and 7.7m in diameter respectively, and each comprising a ring of spaced posts surrounding a setting of four posts some 3m square. The posts of the larger ring were set about 1m apart, while those of the smaller were at intervals of about 0.5m. Buildings of this design are unusual,

Fig. 6.9 Chapelton, Angus (NO 6289 4798). The soils of Angus are especially conducive to the formation of cropmarks and occasionally reveal fine detail of timber structures. In this oblique aerial view, taken in the summer of 1995, a group of what are probably post-built structures can be seen, each comprising a ring of small pits encircling a square setting of four larger pits. Round-houses of this type have been excavated at Greenbogs in Donside. SC503739

but others have been photographed as cropmarks south of the Mounth, at Chapelton and Balcathie in Angus, and Green of Invermay in Perth & Kinross. Some of the four-post settings revealed by cropmarks and by excavation may also be the remains of structures of this type (RCAHMS 1994, 29; Russell-White 1995; Alexander 2000, 24–6).

The chronology of these settlements can only be sketched in outline. There has been only one modern excavation of a hut-circle within Donside, on **Berry Hill**, near Oyne (Murray 2002), and only one hut-circle group in the North-east has even been sampled, that being Tulloch Wood, Moray. The chronology of Tulloch Wood, however, conforms to a pattern recovered from hut-circle groups over a wide area of the Highlands, the majority of the dates lying in the 2nd millennium BC or in the late 1st millennium BC to early 1st millennium AD (Carter 1993). To a certain extent this same pattern is also reflected in dates from round-houses excavated in the lowlands. At **Deer's Den**, for example, the dates from the ring-ditch house lie firmly in the 2nd millennium BC, and most of the others lie before the plateau in the radiocarbon calibration curve in the first

half of the 1st millennium BC (Alexander 2000). The round-house excavated at **Tavelty**, on the other hand, and those from Romancamp Gate, all fall in the later bracket (Alexander 2000; Barclay 1993). The dates from the more recent excavations at **Forest Road**, Kintore, however, are more evenly spread, the major hiatus in the sequence of round-houses apparently lying at the end of the 1st millennium BC (M Cook, pers. com.). Further consideration of this important site must await full publication. The large round-houses on **Candle Hill** also lie in the first half of the 1st millennium BC (Cameron 1999), as do one or two of the dates from a multi-period settlement at Wardend of Durris, Deeside (Russell-White 1995).

Fig. 6.10 Balcathie, Angus (NO 606 391). As can be seen in this oblique aerial photograph taken in 1994, four-poster settings occur amongst the cropmark disks and crescents that indicate settlements of timber round-houses in the lowlands of eastern Scotland. SC958175

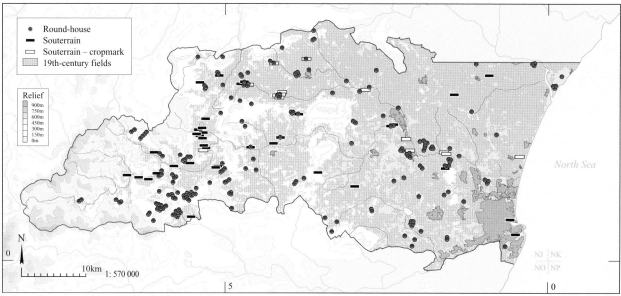

Fig. 6.11 This map shows the distribution of souterrains in Donside in relation to other settlements of round-houses, the latter taken to include all the hut-circles, ring-ditch houses and cropmark remains shown on Figs 6.5 & 6.7. For the souterrains, a distinction is drawn between those revealed as cropmarks and those found by other means. GV000254

Souterrains

The main concentration of souterrains in Donside lies around Kildrummy, and extends westwards up the valley to Strathdon itself (Fig. 6.11). Two unconfirmed reports from Aberdeen and a handful of cropmarks serve to cast the distribution more widely, and there are also several cryptic antiquarian descriptions of structures that are likely to have been souterrains (pp. 70–1) in the eastern part of the area. By far the majority were discovered, filled in, and put back under plough in a matter of days, but within Donside four are still accessible – **Clova** (2), **Glenkindie House** and **Buchaam** (Fig. 6.12) – and a fifth can be seen at Culsh, just across the southern boundary of the survey on the northern edge of the Howe of Cromar. The drawn plans of the four within Donside, coupled with the antiquarian records and descriptions gathered from a wider area north of the Mounth, reveal the range of architectural features displayed by these curious subterranean structures. Typically built in a trench dug into a freely draining slope, the passages usually describe shallow arcs on plan and measure from 10m to 20m in length. The broader passages are up to 2.5m across at floor level, and the walls are corbelled to reduce the span of the stone lintels of the roofs (Fig. 6.16), which stand between 1m and 2.2m above the floor. The entrances are often on the axis at one end, and, where intact, are framed by upright stone jambs. In some cases there are upright pillars at the junction between a relatively narrow entrance-passage and the main chamber. Several appear to have small subsidiary

chambers, and two of the antiquarian accounts – one at **Netherton of Drumnahoy**, and the other at **Mill of Torry** – record that the souterrains terminated in circular chambers. The latter, however, may be no more than a description of the rounded terminals that are preserved in the accessible examples.

To all intents and purposes, the features displayed by these Aberdeenshire souterrains are indistinguishable from those of Angus, Perth & Kinross and Fife, and the antiquarian account of those found in the Kildrummy area (Stuart 1822a, 56–7) might as easily be describing the souterrains at Mudhall in Perth & Kinross (Pennant 1776, 448–9; *Stat. Acct.*, xix, 1797, 359). That said, the stone-built souterrains south of the Mounth that are accessible today appear to be rather larger than their Aberdeenshire cousins, which has undoubtedly fostered the long-held belief that the souterrains south of the Mounth form a separate group, with a discrete distribution. However, the 18th- and 19th-century descriptions from Perth & Kinross and Angus (conveniently summarised in Wainwright 1963) plainly show that the discoveries south of the Mounth included a wide range of sizes. The large souterrains amongst them were probably the exception rather than the rule, and it is no more than chance that they make up the majority of those visible today. This is essentially confirmed by the cropmark evidence, for while this includes some large stone-built souterrains, both singly and in spectacular clusters, by far the majority are much smaller structures, and in their original form many of them were little more than narrow timber-lined creeps. In the face of the wealth of cropmark evidence, it is increasingly difficult to sustain the idea of a typical souterrain anywhere in eastern Scotland.

While there is probably no material difference in the range of subterranean structures north and south of the Mounth, aerial reconnaissance has not dramatically

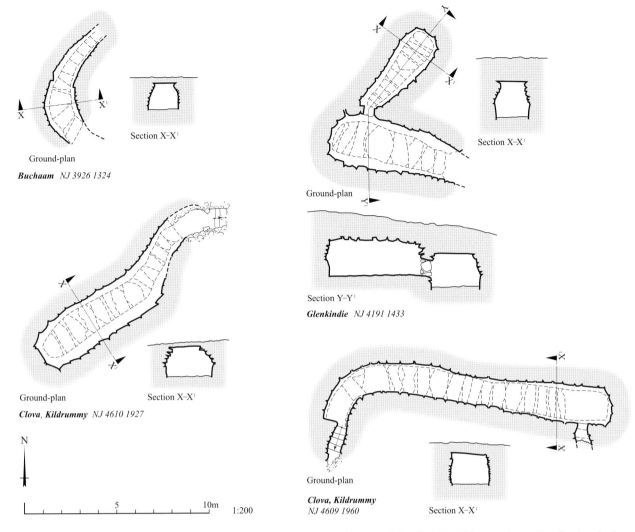

Ground-plan

Section X–X¹

Buchaam NJ 3926 1324

Ground-plan

Section X–X¹

Clova, Kildrummy NJ 4610 1927

N

5   10m   1:200

Ground-plan

Section X–X¹

Glenkindie NJ 4191 1433

Section Y–Y¹

Ground-plan

Clova, Kildrummy
NJ 4609 1960

Section X–X¹

Fig. 6.12 The plans and sections of the four souterrains in Donside that are still accessible. GV000237

*Fig. 6.13 **Clova, Kildrummy** (NJ 4609 1960). This view towards the east end of the souterrain reveals the character of its construction, with random rubble walls and a roof of massive slabs. SC958179*

increased the density of the northern distribution in the way that has happened to the south. To a certain extent, this is a function of the lower incidence of cropmarks north of the Mounth (Fig. 6.15). Nevertheless, aerial survey has extended the distribution along the Moray coast, an area where relatively few discoveries caught the attention of antiquaries.

There is also a more subtle difference in the patterns of discovery north and south of the Mounth. All the antiquarian accounts to the south are apparently of souterrains that were entirely hidden beneath the ground at the time of their discovery. The most likely reason for this is that the majority lie in good arable land and had been under cultivation since long before the improvements. The same may be observed of many cropmark examples, which as often as not lie in fields traversed by rig-and-furrow.

In contrast, the Aberdeenshire examples include several at New Kinord, in the Howe of Cromar, that are still visible as unroofed components of hut-circle settlements, while several others now under plough were first recorded adjacent to surface structures. Some of the latter lie within Donside, for example at **Clova**, and are described by John Stuart:

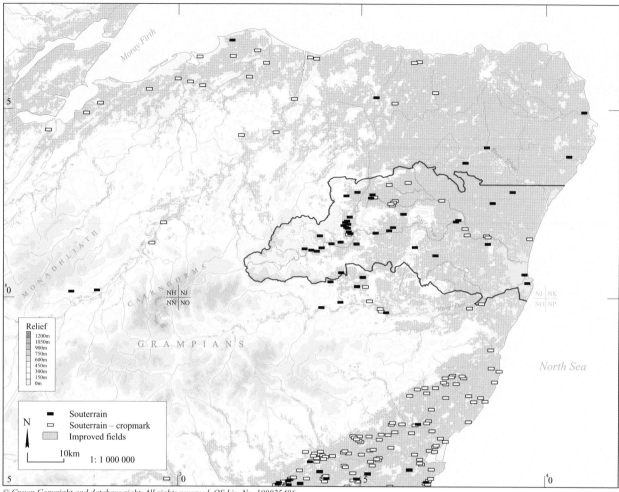

Fig. 6.14 This map shows the overall distribution of souterrains across north-east Scotland, which coincides with the extent of improved agricultural land. The majority of recent finds result from aerial survey programmes and are concentrated in Angus and Perth & Kinross. As the overall distribution of cropmarks shows, this probably reflects the poorer conditions for the formation of cropmarks north of the Mounth rather than any underlying pattern in the distribution of souterrains. GV000235

'a small fold or inclosure (sic) of a square form, about ten or fifteen paces each way, dug a foot or two deep, with the earth thrown outwards, which is uniformly found in a certain direction, and almost adjoining to each separate cavern' (1822a, 57).

These souterrains survived in undisturbed moorland, and were well-known locally at the end of the 18th century. They only came to wider notice as they were cleared in the course of agricultural improvements (*Stat. Acct.*, xviii, 1796, 419–20). This suggests that the pattern of expansion of arable land, and the development of antiquarian studies, have both played some part in creating the uneven distribution of souterrains that has been recorded north of the Mounth (Fig. 6.14). The concentration in the upper reaches of Donside, for example, may be explained by the expansion of arable land there at a time when antiquarian records were becoming more numerous. Conversely, the sparse

scatter in the lower Don simply reflects the area that had been most heavily cultivated before the improvements, where any discoveries were long forgotten by the end of the 18th century.

The cluster around **Clova**, however, is remarkable by any standards. Within a distance of little more than 1km, the sites of no less than fourteen are identified on the 1st edition of the OS 6-inch map (Aberdeenshire 1870, li), disposed in four clusters; and the querns ploughed up at five locations in the same area may mark the sites of others. Most had already disappeared beneath the plough by the time the map was surveyed in 1866–7, but two were still visible and are depicted with open rectangles. Both were cleared out shortly after in the autumn of 1875 by Hugh Lumsden of Auchindoir (Lumsden 1878) and are still accessible today. They are impressive monuments, the drystone masonry rising from large grounders and capped with a massive roof of stone slabs (Fig. 6.13). As is so often the case to the south of the Mounth, they incorporate several stones carved with cupmarks.

The southern passage dug by Lumsden, which forms a shallow S-shape in plan, now measures about 10.5m in length, varying in breadth from 1.2m at the entrance on the north-east to a maximum of 2.5m, but Lumsden's

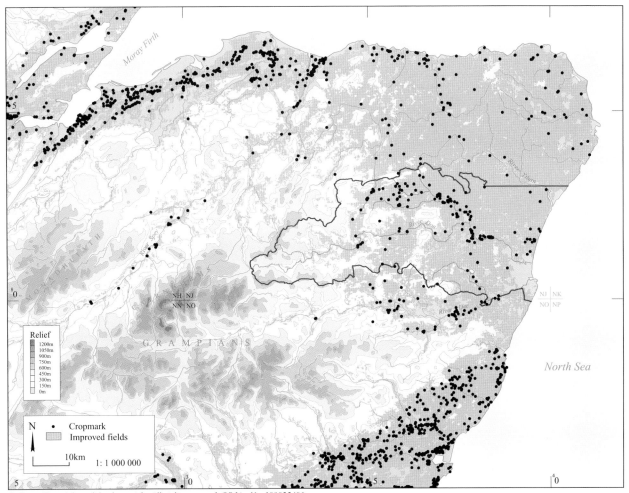

Fig. 6.15 The general incidence of cropmarks south of the Mount is three to four times that of Donside. GV000182

excavation showed that it extended at least 3m farther to the north-east. The walls, which are up to 1.6m in height, are corbelled to such an extent that along the south-east side the top of the wall overhangs the basal grounders by as much as 0.6m. Any prospective visitor would be wise not to enter the chamber; several stones appear to have slipped out of position and are now propped up with fence-posts. Two stone jambs 0.8m in height frame the present entrance and mark the junction of the entrance passage with the chamber. An outer pair of jambs located by Lumsden is now hidden by the modern steps that descend into the mouth of the chamber.

The northern souterrain is rather longer, measuring about 16m in length, but the western end, which hooks sharply southwards, had been destroyed prior to Lumsden's excavations. The masonry at this end has been reconstructed and the flight of steps that descends into the souterrain is a modern insertion. As a result no distinction can be made here between an entrance passage and the main chamber, which in this case ranges in width from 1.3m at the west end to 1.9m at the east end. The walls are up to 1.7m in height, rising

almost vertically to the roof for much of its length. At the eastern end, where the roof has been removed, the entrance to a subsidiary passage can be seen in the south wall, but it is entirely choked with soil and rubble. Lumsden thought that it led to the surface, but a similar feature at **Glenkindie House** opens into a small chamber set at a slightly higher level (Fig. 6.12).

Large sections of the roofs at **Clova** are still in place, and these reveal the construction in some detail, showing that they comprise at least two sets of lintels. The lintels of the first set span the wallheads, while those of the second are laid transversely across them. Gaps between lintels are plugged with rounded boulders, and the whole roof is covered with a mound of soil and stones rising up to 0.6m above the surrounding ground level. Most of this material was probably derived from the construction trench, and it is reasonable to suppose that such mounds were typical of most souterrains. Thus these structures were buried rather than hidden, and the presence of a souterrain in a settlement would have been perfectly plain when it was in use.

In the course of the antiquarian explorations several artefacts have been recovered from souterrains, but the contexts of these discoveries are at best uncertain, and their deposition may not relate to the occupation of

Fig. 6.16 **Glenkindie House** *(NJ 4191 1433). This view of the terminal of the souterrain clearly shows the corbelled walls rising from a basal course of large boulders. SC958180*

the structure at all. The descriptions of ten souterrains north of the Mounth mention artefacts of one sort or another, including: pottery at **Bogfechel**, **Mill of Torry**, **Buchaam**, Culsh and Milton of Whitehouse; stone lamps at **Clova** and **Milton of Migvie**; a stone ball from **Loch Kinord**; beads from Culsh and **Castle Newe**; iron objects from **Buchaam** and **Milton of Migvie**; a piece of bronze wire from Milton of Whitehouse; a bronze ring from **Milton of Migvie**; a coin of Nerva (AD 96–8) from **Castle Newe**; and, finally, a pair of massive bronze armlets from **Castle Newe** and another three from Aboyne. Of these, only the coin of Nerva (now lost) and the bronze armlets are closely dateable, in both cases indicating activity, if not occupation, in the 1st and 2nd centuries AD. At Aboyne, however, the armlets were only found when two large circular enclosures close by were removed, while at **Castle Newe** the armlets were recovered from the soil above the mouth of the passage, and the coin of Nerva was simply found nearby.

Enclosed Settlements

The visible remains tend to suggest that the prehistoric settlement record north of the Mounth is mainly composed of unenclosed round-houses and souterrains, but a small number of what are probably enclosed settlements is also scattered across this area (Fig. 6.26). As they survive today, these enclosures do not form a coherent group and, in the absence of excavation, it is difficult to provide any context for them. Some have banks and ditches, others thick stone walls, but none has had sufficient stature that it might be included amongst the forts (pp. 96–103). In several instances,

the existence of an enclosure is merely known from antiquarian references, and the true character of the work is uncertain. With the advent of aerial photography, however, it is evident that enclosed settlements are far more numerous than had been thought previously.

The most striking settlements are those with stoutly constructed stone walls, now generally reduced to bands of rubble from 3m to 6m in thickness. Within the survey area itself, **White Hill**, **Hill of Keir** and the inner enclosure at **Maiden Castle** (Fig. 6.25) certainly fall within this category, and the enclosures on **Cairnmore** and the **Barmkyn of North Keig** (Fig. 6.25), both of which are in hilltop positions and are usually described as small forts, might possibly be included. Neither of the latter is particularly strongly sited, and, like Stot Hill, in Deeside, the perception of their strength rests on the thickness of the perimeter wall rather than the defensive qualities of the location. Farther afield, what may have been an enclosure with a thick stone wall was removed in 1824 from Widdie Hillock, near Turriff; described as measuring *'70 yards in circumference'* (about 21m in diameter), human remains, bronze implements and finger rings were said to have been found in the course of its demolition (Name Book, Aberdeenshire, No. 89, p. 119).

Apart from a thick stone wall, these enclosures share little else in common and display a wide range of sizes. **Maiden Castle**, for example, is only about 20m in internal diameter, perhaps bearing comparison with Widdie Hillock, but it is not much bigger than some

Fig. 6.17 **Pyke** *(NJ 6197 2914). Discovered in 2003, this possible settlement is one of a number of enclosures revealed by cropmarks on oblique aerial photographs. SC958186*

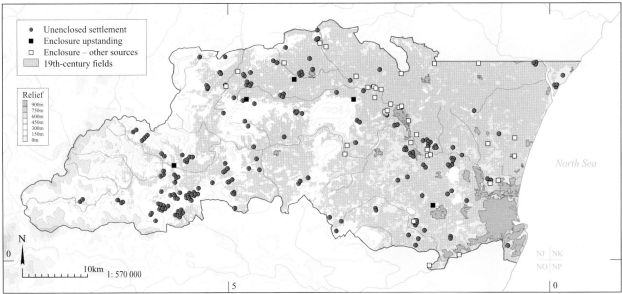

Fig. 6.18 This map shows the distribution of enclosures in Donside, most of which have been discovered through aerial survey programmes. This has added a new dimension to the prehistoric settlement in Donside, which was previously dominated by souterrains and unenclosed round-houses. GV000251

of the enclosures occurring amongst the hut-circle groups in the Howe of Cromar. One at New Kinord is slightly larger, measuring 23m by 21m internally. **Hill of Keir** and the **Barmkyn of North Keig** are a little over 30m across internally, while **White Hill** measures 39m by 33m, and **Cairnmore** 50m in diameter. Stot Hill is larger still at about 60m by 40m. Several other enclosures have less substantial walls, and these similarly exhibit a wide range of sizes. One, some 27m in diameter, occupies a shelf on Little Hill, in Deeside; another, measuring some 40m by 38m internally, is situated on sloping ground at Wester Tulloch, Moray.

Of the rest of the enclosures, by far the majority are cropmarks, but for reasons already outlined (p. 82), relatively few of them lie within Donside itself. As with the unenclosed settlements, the analysis presented here takes a broader perspective, reviewing all the enclosures that have been photographed to date between the Mounth and the shores of the Moray Firth (Figs 6.20; 6.35). With the exception of a handful of rectilinear examples (Fig. 6.23), these are mainly circular or oval, enclosed by single ditches from 2m to 5m in breadth, and ranging from 20m to 80m in internal diameter. One or two larger enclosures have been recorded, such as one 140m in diameter at Easter Calcots, Moray, but these are unusual. Smaller enclosures are far more typical, and of the sixty or so for which measurements can be estimated, sixteen are about 20m in diameter, contributing to a total of thirty-nine between 20m and 30m in diameter. This figure is further increased by the inclusion of the inner palisaded enclosure still visible on the summit of the **Hill of Christ's Kirk** (p. 103),

and the larger cropmark discs (p. 86), at least thirteen of which are in excess of 18m in diameter. A further twelve enclosures are a little over 30m across, and there are twenty-three in all between 30m and 40m in diameter. This same pattern appears to extend along the southern shore of the Moray Firth to the area around Inverness.

The aerial photographs reveal few details about the character of these enclosures, or of their interiors. In one or two cases the perimeter is so narrow that it is almost certainly a palisade trench, such as the two at Templestone, Moray, one measuring 25m in diameter and the other 30m. The enclosures at Millbank, near Maryculter, and **Colpy**, near Culsalmond (Fig. 6.20),

*Fig. 6.19 **Middleton** (NJ 7443 2217). Revealed as a cropmark by aerial photography, this circular enclosure has previously been interpreted as a henge monument but it is more likely to be the ploughed-down remains of a settlement. © AAS 95–06–CT98*

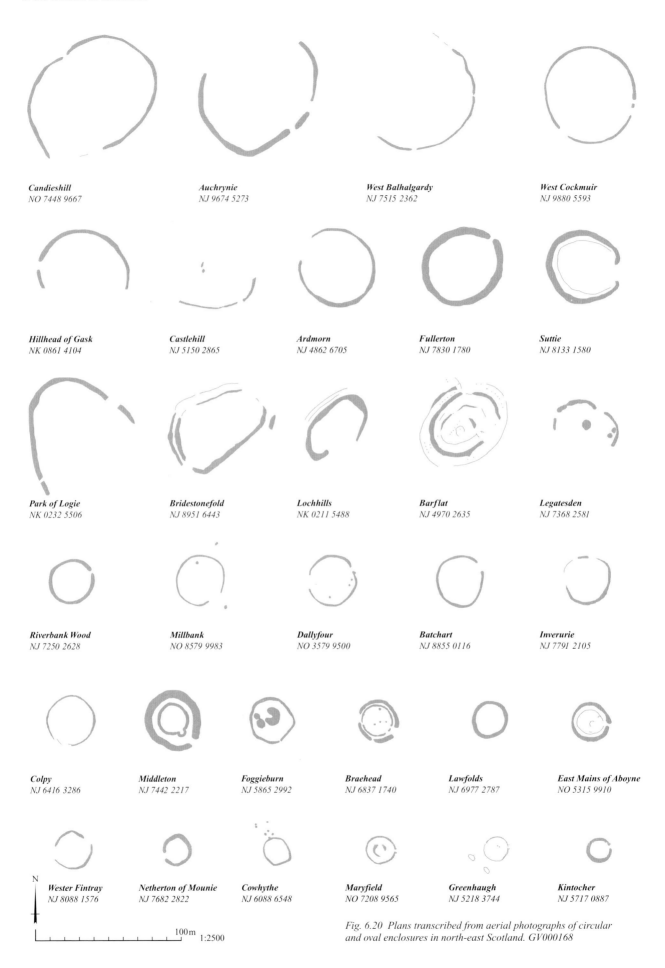

Candieshill
NO 7448 9667

Auchrynie
NJ 9674 5273

West Balhalgardy
NJ 7515 2362

West Cockmuir
NJ 9880 5593

Hillhead of Gask
NK 0861 4104

Castlehill
NJ 5150 2865

Ardmorn
NJ 4862 6705

Fullerton
NJ 7830 1780

Suttie
NJ 8133 1580

Park of Logie
NK 0232 5506

Bridestonefold
NJ 8951 6443

Lochhills
NK 0211 5488

Barflat
NJ 4970 2635

Legatesden
NJ 7368 2581

Riverbank Wood
NJ 7250 2628

Millbank
NO 8579 9983

Dallyfour
NO 3579 9500

Batchart
NJ 8855 0116

Inverurie
NJ 7791 2105

Colpy
NJ 6416 3286

Middleton
NJ 7442 2217

Foggieburn
NJ 5865 2992

Braehead
NJ 6837 1740

Lawfolds
NJ 6977 2787

East Mains of Aboyne
NO 5315 9910

Wester Fintray
NJ 8088 1576

Netherton of Mounie
NJ 7682 2822

Cowhythe
NJ 6088 6548

Maryfield
NO 7208 9565

Greenhaugh
NJ 5218 3744

Kintocher
NJ 5717 0887

N

100m   1:2500

Fig. 6.20 Plans transcribed from aerial photographs of circular and oval enclosures in north-east Scotland. GV000168

*Fig. 6.21 **Braehead** (NJ 6837 1740). The cropmarks of this small settlement were photographed during 1989. Measuring some 20m in internal diameter, they reveal that the settlement was enclosed by a timber palisade set in a narrow foundation trench behind a broader external ditch. © AAS 89–09–CT35*

*Fig. 6.22 **Riverbank Wood** (NJ 7250 2628). This ditched enclosure, which is slightly larger than the enclosure at Braehead (Fig. 6.21) but has no trace of an internal palisade, is probably another small settlement. © AAS 89–09–CT37*

are also likely to have been free-standing palisades, while other palisade trenches are set roughly concentrically within ditched enclosures. Three such enclosures are included on Figure 6.20, those at **Suttie** and **Braehead** lying within Donside, and East Mains of Aboyne in Deeside. The **Suttie** enclosure measures 35m within its palisade, and 42m within its ditch, which is broken by a broad entrance on the east. **Braehead**

and East Mains of Aboyne are amongst the smaller enclosures, and the palisade trench might be mistaken for the wall-trench of a large timber round-house within the interior. At **Braehead**, however, the palisade trench describes a circle about 20m in diameter, and, as far as is known, is too large to be the remains of a round-house. The ditch lies no more than 2m outside the palisade, and there would have been little room for an internal bank (see Quarry Wood, below). The East Mains of Aboyne enclosure is remarkably similar, if a little smaller, and enclosures such as **Riverbank Wood** near Pitcaple (Fig. 6.22) are quite likely to have had a similar format. This may also explain the unique arrangement of features recorded at **Middleton**, near Inverurie (Fig. 6.19), an enclosure which has been claimed as a henge monument (p. 58). It measures about 28m in diameter within a broad ditch and contains a concentrically placed inner enclosure some 18m in internal diameter. The cropmark forming this inner enclosure is up to 2m in breadth and exhibits a curious porch-like feature roughly aligned on the entrance on the south-east.

Traces of round-houses within these enclosures are few and far between. Nevertheless, a small ditched enclosure 26m in internal diameter at **Foggieburn**, near Insch, contains a crescent-shaped macula about 12m across, placed to one side of the interior (Fig. 6.20), while a possible palisaded enclosure 20m in diameter at Maryfield, on the south side of the Dee near Banchory, contains traces of a central round-house about 8m across. In Moray, both of the Templestone enclosures are also concentrically arranged around a central round-house, but in these cases the crescentic macula is 16m in diameter. This same format can be seen farther westwards along the Moray plain, where there are several pit-circles lying within concentric palisaded enclosures. It is also found in the complex of palisaded enclosures and round-houses excavated at Wardend of Durris, near Banchory (Russell-White 1995). Farther up the Dee, the pit-circle photographed amongst a cluster of three souterrains at Mains of Balfour, Birse (Fig. 6.8), may also lie at the centre of a concentric enclosure. In this last case the course of the enclosure is marked by little more than a faint halo some 28m in diameter, two large pits on its line possibly marking the position of an entrance. The combination of a souterrain immediately adjacent to the circle of pits, and a surrounding enclosure, recalls the arrangement of the souterrain and a substantial stone-built enclosure at New Kinord, in the Howe of Cromar. It is worth considering that some of the larger structures included as hut-circles may in reality have been walled enclosures surrounding timber round-houses. Such an arrangement would be virtually unrecognisable as a cropmark.

While the bulk of the evidence for enclosed settlement is drawn from cropmarks, several earthworks have survived unploughed in the fringes of the improved landscape. In Donside, this includes the **Hill of Christ's Kirk**, which has already been mentioned, and an enclosure near **Glenkindie House**, situated on a low spur overlooking the site of the souterrain from the north-west. Measuring about 32m in internal diameter, the low bank forming its perimeter is overlain by an old plantation boundary on the east, but elsewhere the ground falls away quite steeply, creating a scarp up to 1.8m in height. The only other earthworks of note are in Moray; one in Sleepieshill Wood, a forestry plantation in the low-lying ground to the east of Lhanbryde, the other in Quarry Wood on the rising ground west of Elgin. Sleepieshill Wood measures about 72m by 60m within a ditch with an external bank, and compares with the larger of the enclosures recorded as cropmarks. Quarry Wood is smaller, measuring 47m by 42m internally, and it too has a ditch with an external bank, so much so that it has been interpreted as a henge monument. In the light of the cropmarks that have now been recorded, Quarry Wood is more likely to be the sole upstanding survivor of this wider group of small settlement enclosures, closely matching some of those shown on Figure 6.20, such as **Fullerton**, **Suttie** and Ardmorn. The presence of an external bank might also explain the position of the palisade trench immediately within the ditch at **Suttie**.

The final enclosures that need to be mentioned are rectilinear. Although about forty have been recorded north of the Mounth, only eight of them lie within Donside. Two of these are illustrated on Figure 6.23; one of them at **Newton of Lewesk**, east of Old Rayne, and the other a possible example at **Middleton**, west of Inverurie. For the purposes of comparison, three other enclosures are shown, two farther south in Kincardineshire, at Hindwells and Chapelton, and one less regular example to the north at Auchtydonald, near Mintlaw. These are in the middle range of rectilinear enclosures, the smaller examples measuring as little as 20m by 15m internally, and the larger as much as 100m by 70m. **Newton of Lewesk**, which is one of the better-defined examples, measures about 60m by 48m within its ditch, and there is at least one entrance in the south side.

In southern Scotland enclosures such as this form a recognisable category of later prehistoric settlements, but there is little excavated evidence to draw upon this far to the north. An unstratified sherd of Roman pottery was recovered from within an enclosure at Boyndie, near Banff, and at Easter Galcantray, on the banks of the River Nairn, a deposit of charcoal in the upper levels of the ditch has been dated to cal AD 80–220 (1880±20 BP: GrN-14643; Gregory 2001). Even if some of the rectilinear enclosures are of late Iron Age date, others may be more recent, ranging from old folds to medieval moated sites (p. 154). Several of the latter can be recognised amongst the cropmarks

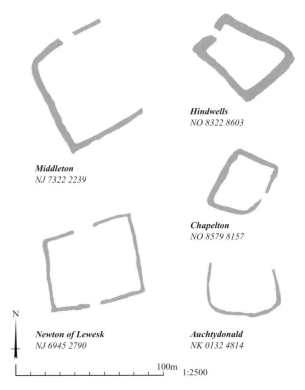

Fig. 6.23 These plans transcribed from oblique aerial photographs depict a selection of rectilinear enclosures that have been recorded in north-east Scotland. GV000169

on the Moray Plain, for example at Barmuckity and Collie near Elgin. Two widely spaced ditches forming an inner and outer enclosure around the old parish church of St Andrews Lhanbryde at Kirkhill are also likely to be medieval, and the enclosure at Chapelton, Kincardineshire (Fig. 6.23), was pointed out in the 19th century as the position of a chapel from which the farm had taken its name, though there is no other evidence to sustain this identification.

The dating of the circular and oval enclosures is equally uncertain. The closest parallels for the stone-walled enclosures lie in Angus and Perthshire (Feachem 1955, 71–6), those on Turin Hill apparently overlying a lozenge-shaped fort, but this provides no more than a relative sequence of construction (p. 101). Even less can be said about the cropmark enclosures, the only excavated examples lying in the cluster of structures, round-houses and successive palisaded enclosures at Wardend of Durris. Here, the radiocarbon dates for various enclosed and unenclosed elements of the settlement span the second half of the 1st millennium BC (Russell-White 1995).

Forts

The forts that break the skylines of Donside provide some of the most dramatic images of later prehistory that can be found anywhere in eastern Scotland. The positions alone are often spectacular, **Tap o' Noth** and the **Mither Tap o' Bennachie** dominating the landscape

*Fig. 6.24 **Tap o' Noth** (NJ 4845 2930). As the second highest fort in Scotland, Tap o' Noth casts a formidable shadow over Strathbogie. The massive wall that crowns the summit is clearly visible from the surrounding countryside. SC958177*

for miles around, but others, such as **Dunnideer**, **Barra Hill**, **Bruce's Camp** and the **Barmekin of Echt**, are equally commanding in their localities.

These positions convey an impression of power, a message also projected by the scale of some of the defensive systems that have been constructed. At **Tap o' Noth** the scree of tumbled rubble dropping away from the wall around the summit is in excess of 10m high (Fig. 6.24), and huge chunks of vitrified stone protrude from its crest. The sheer quantity of stones speaks for itself, while the vitrifaction bears witness to a violent and catastrophic end. This is truly a fort in a sense invoking images of military and political strongpoints.

But the range of enclosures that appear to display some measure of defence in their perimeters is far more disparate than this definition allows, as can be seen on Figure 6.25. Indeed, the compact, oblong forts with vitrified walls on the summits of **Tap o' Noth** (0.3ha) and **Dunnideer** (0.15ha) are perhaps the only forts within the survey area that conform to this description, although the massive outer wall taking in the **Mither Tap o' Bennachie** (0.7ha) is equally impressive (Fig. 6.31). Of the others, there is a huge disparity in the strength of their defences and the extent of the ground they enclose. At one end of the spectrum there is the tiny fort known as the **Maiden Castle** (0.07ha), while at the other there is the enclosure of 16.4ha taking in the slopes below the vitrified fort on **Tap o' Noth**.

The distribution is equally uneven (Fig. 6.26), thinly spread in the middle reaches of Donside. No forts have

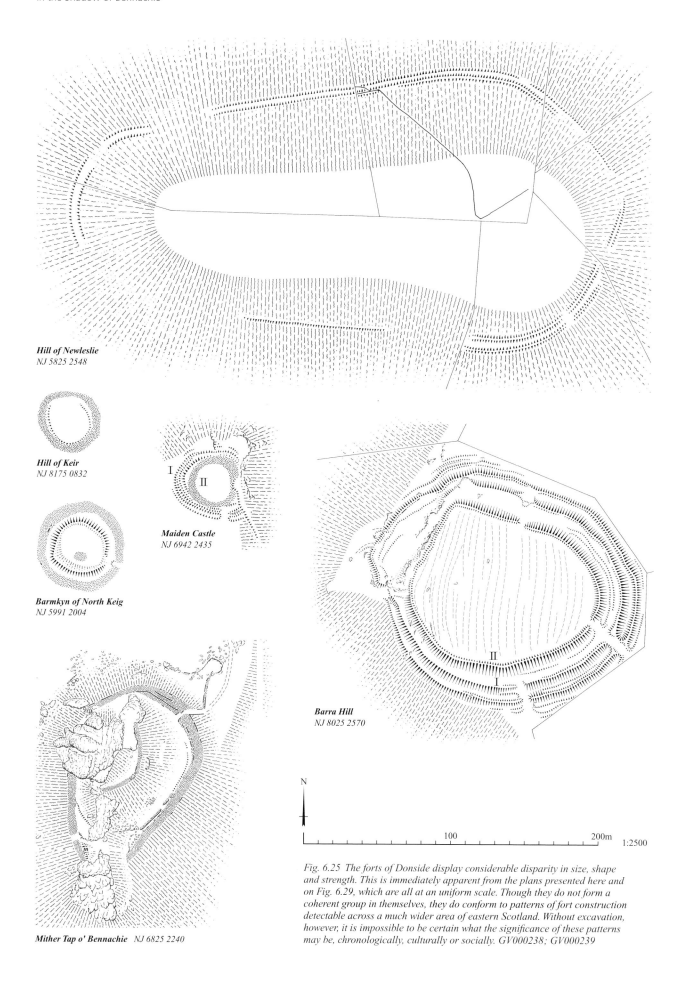

Hill of Newleslie
NJ 5825 2548

Hill of Keir
NJ 8175 0832

Barmkyn of North Keig
NJ 5991 2004

Maiden Castle
NJ 6942 2435

Barra Hill
NJ 8025 2570

Mither Tap o' Bennachie NJ 6825 2240

N

100   200m

1:2500

Fig. 6.25 The forts of Donside display considerable disparity in size, shape and strength. This is immediately apparent from the plans presented here and on Fig. 6.29, which are all at an uniform scale. Though they do not form a coherent group in themselves, they do conform to patterns of fort construction detectable across a much wider area of eastern Scotland. Without excavation, however, it is impossible to be certain what the significance of these patterns may be, chronologically, culturally or socially. GV000238; GV000239

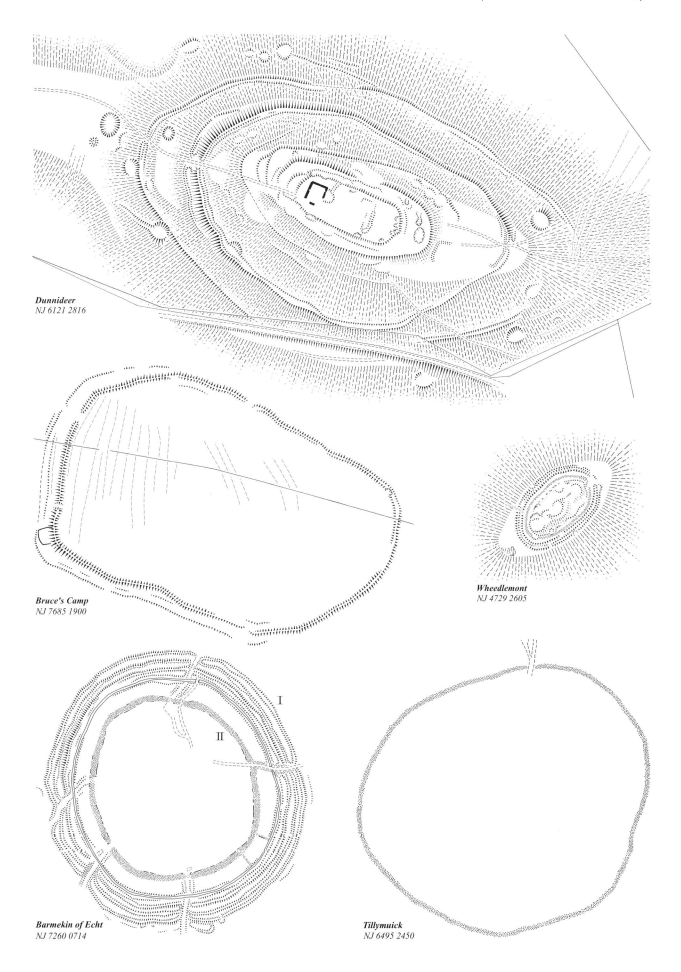

Dunnideer
NJ 6121 2816

Bruce's Camp
NJ 7685 1900

Wheedlemont
NJ 4729 2605

Barmekin of Echt
NJ 7260 0714

I

II

Tillymuick
NJ 6495 2450

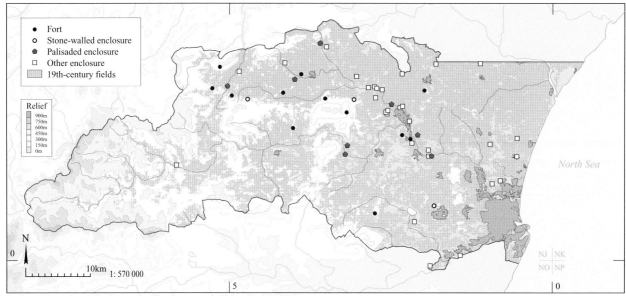

Fig. 6.26 This map shows the thin scatter of forts and other types of enclosure in Donside. GV000252

been recorded within 20km of the sea, though this is probably an accident of preservation and the lack of fortifiable promontories on the coast, and there are none in the upper reaches of the valley. In this respect, Donside matches most of the other glens opening eastwards and southwards out of the Grampians, where the forts tend to lie along the Highland edge. In neighbouring Deeside, there are no forts farther west than the Howe of Cromar, though in Strathbogie **Tap o' Noth** occupies such a position.

Despite the disparity in the character and distribution of the forts within Donside, they nonetheless fall into six rough groups that can be recognised elsewhere in eastern Scotland. The first of these groups is composed of the massively constructed oblong forts, such as **Tap o' Noth** and **Dunnideer**, which also commonly exhibit evidence of extensive vitrifaction. These have long been recognised as a group, other examples to the north including Knock of Alves, Craig Phadrig and Knock Farril, while to the south there are Green Cairn, Balbegno in Kincardineshire, Finavon and Turin Hill in Angus, and Barry Hill and Castle Law, Forgandenny in Perth & Kinross (Feachem 1966, 68). In Aberdeenshire, as elsewhere, the oblong forts often form one phase of construction in a sequence of defences.

The forts of the second group present an impression of strength in depth, and include **Barra Hill** and the **Barmekin of Echt**. Both are about 1ha in extent, but the impression of strength may be more apparent than real, for in each case the innermost wall or rampart has been inserted concentrically into the interior of a larger multivallate fort of about 1.5ha. Of the multivallate forts to the south of the Mounth, one revealed by

cropmarks at Auchray (1.9ha), near Dundee, has no less than four concentric ditches.

The third group is made up of two large forts with relatively slight defensive systems, namely the outer fort at **Dunnideer** (2.1ha) and **Bruce's Camp** (2.7ha). The enclosure on the rounded summit of **Tillymuick** (2.4ha) is perhaps another, although its perimeter now forms little more than a low bank some 4m in thickness and 0.5m in height. Comparable forts to the south include Knockargety Hill in Deeside, and a large enclosure revealed by cropmarks at Craigend of Careston, near Brechin, Angus.

The fourth group contains only two examples, but these are extensive enclosures that far outstrip any others in their extent. These are the **Hill of Newleslie** (5ha) and the outer fort on **Tap o' Noth** (16.4ha). These too find their parallels to the south, such as Kinpurney Hill in Angus.

In the fifth group, the forts are relatively small enclosures defended by ramparts and ditches. **Wheedlemont** (0.1ha) and **Maiden Castle** (0.07ha) fall into this group, and it should probably include the ploughed-out earthwork at **Barflat** (Figs 6.20; 7.8), its site on the rising ground south of Rhynie marked by the **Craw Stane**, a Pictish symbol stone (pp. 119–22). Known only from cropmarks, this enclosure has at least two concentric lines of defence, the inner a ditch up to 4m in breadth, and the outer probably a palisade trench. A third concentric mark within the line of the inner ditch probably marks the rear of the rampart rather than another defensive ditch, indicating that the interior measured only 32m by 20m, an area of some 0.05ha. The most notable feature of this group is their small size, putting them on a par with some of the small promontory forts found along the coast.

The final group is composed of small enclosures defended by a thick stone wall. In Donside this category

Fig. 6.27 ***Dunnideer*** *(NJ 6121 2816). The sequence of prehistoric defences here, where an oblong fort with a vitrified wall probably succeeded a larger defended enclosure, is found throughout eastern Scotland. Dunnideer also became an important medieval centre, and the castle on its summit is built of stones robbed from the earlier vitrified wall. SC958189*

includes **Cairnmore** (0.37ha) and the **Barmkyn of North Keig** (0.42ha), which are both in hilltop positions, but it might also include several of the stone-walled enclosures that have already been discussed – **White Hill** (0.19ha), **Hill of Keir** (0.14ha) and the inner enclosure at **Maiden Castle** (0.07ha; pp. 92–3). While these may not be forts in any strict sense, the examples at both **Maiden Castle** in Donside, and Turin Hill in Angus, figure in fortified sequences.

While the various fortifications can be grouped in this way, the small numbers that make up each of the categories, and the limited criteria upon which they are defined, offer little scope for the detection of any underlying patterns. More informative are the sequences of construction that have been identified. These reveal general trends in fort construction in the North-east that broadly mirror sequences observed elsewhere in eastern

Scotland. This is illustrated by the small stone-walled enclosures that form the last phase of occupation on several forts. This sequence is represented in Donside by the enclosure inserted into the interior of the **Maiden Castle**, and in Angus by the three overlying the oblong fort on Turin Hill. Farther south it involves the construction of brochs in the 1st and 2nd centuries AD. Radiocarbon dates from stone-walled enclosures excavated at Aldclune, near Blair Atholl, Perth & Kinross, span the end of the 1st millennium BC and the beginning of the 1st millennium AD (Hingley *et al.* 1997). Whether this same chronology can be applied north of the Mounth is uncertain.

The stratigraphic relationships of the oblong forts reveal other aspects of the general trend of fortification in eastern Scotland, for most of them represent the final stage of construction in a sequence in which there is a much more extensive earlier fortification (Alexander and Ralston 1999, 46). In Perth & Kinross examples can be seen at Barry Hill, Dunsinane Hill, and Castle Law, Forgandenny. This same succession can also be seen at Turin Hill, and is the most likely sequence at both **Dunnideer** and **Tap o' Noth**. At **Dunnideer**,

*Fig. 6.28 **Hill of Newleslie** (NJ 584 254). Discovered in the course of aerial survey by Aberdeen Archaeological Services, the defences of this large enclosure are relatively slight; where best preserved they comprise two low banks with a medial ditch. SC958191*

the vitrified wall of the oblong fort, which has been extensively robbed to build the medieval castle, takes in most of the level ground on the summit of the hill, while the relatively slight lines of defence lower down the slope appear to form a discrete enclosure (Figs 6.25; 6.27). At **Tap o' Noth**, where the outer line takes in an area of 16.4ha (Fig. 6.29), the sequence between the two schemes of defence is implied by the contrast between the heavily robbed outer fort, and the massive scree of rubble from the inner on the summit.

In view of the similarities in the shape and design of the oblong forts, it is tempting to see them as part of a single period of fort construction in eastern Scotland. However, dating them has proved difficult, and their chronology is fraught with uncertainties. Childe's

excavation in the 1930s at Finavon, in Angus, failed to recover any distinctive artefacts from the interior (1935; 1936), but subsequent work by Mackie in 1966 obtained three radiocarbon determinations spanning the early and mid-1st millennium BC (1969), which were thought to relate to occupation immediately within the wall. More recently a programme of thermoluminescent dating has been applied to a series of vitrified forts, including both Finavon and **Tap o' Noth**. In contrast to the radiocarbon dating of charcoal from timbers used in the construction of the forts, the thermoluminescence technique is applied to the vitrifaction itself, dating the conflagration in which the wall or rampart was burnt and destroyed. Unfortunately the dates that have been obtained are widely spread and are in some cases in conflict with the radiocarbon dates. The date for Finavon falls in the 7th century AD, up to 1000 years after the latest of the radiocarbon dates, while that for **Tap o' Noth** lies before 2000 BC (Sanderson *et al.* 1988, 315, Table 3).

The dates from two other oblong forts near Inverness, namely Craig Phadrig and Knock Farril, are equally diverse, those from the latter falling at the end of the 2nd millennium BC. Resolution of the problems posed by these dates is possibly offered by the application of yet another dating technique – archaeo-magnetism – to the vitrifaction. This has returned a more consistent group of dates, placing the destruction of these four forts in the final centuries of the 1st millennium BC (Gentles 1993). Such a dating has the advantage of corresponding with the consistently late position of oblong forts in the observed defensive sequences.

If the stone-walled enclosures and the oblong forts give some pretence of recurrent designs, no such claim can be advanced for the rest. They not only range widely in their size, but also in the scale of their defences. In the case of **Dunnideer**, the ramparts are so slight that it has even been suggested that the outer ramparts are unfinished (Feachem 1966, 69–70; 1977, 105), though this ignores the way they progressively increase in height and thickness to either side of the western entrance. This same feature may be observed at Knockargety Hill, in the Howe of Cromar, another supposedly unfinished fort, and implies some level of deliberation in their form.

The slight stature of these ramparts raises the question as to the true character of some of these enclosures and whether they were really intended as defensive works at all. In the case of the massive walls of the oblong forts at **Tap o' Noth** and **Dunnideer**, or those of the **Mither Tap o' Bennachie** and the **Barmekin of Echt**, there can be little doubt that these were once formidable barriers, but it is hard to believe this of the outer perimeter of **Dunnideer**, unless the slight earthworks are masking evidence of a substantial timber superstructure. This is certainly a possibility, for there are several enclosures in the North-east that resemble the timber-built fortifications more commonly found in the Border counties (Halliday 1995, 33–4). In Donside, these include an enclosure on **Hill of Christ's Kirk**, which has been described as the marker trenches of an unfinished fort. In all, three shallow trenches with low external banks enclose the summit of the hill, each measuring from 1m to 1.2m in breadth by 0.2m in depth. Superficially, at least, these are typical of the palisade trenches found in the Borders. The innermost, which lies eccentrically within the two outer lines, probably represents an independent phase of enclosure, and at 21m in internal diameter finds its parallels with small palisaded enclosures in the cropmark record (p. 93). The outer enclosure, which measures 40m by 30m internally, takes in an area of 0.1ha and should perhaps be considered as a small fort in its own right.

Other probable palisaded forts in the North-east were much larger than **Hill of Christ's Kirk**. On Durn Hill, near Portsoy, for example, the two concentric marker trenches of another supposedly unfinished fort (Feachem

1971, 27–8) are again more likely to be palisade trenches. In this case they take in an area of about 1.9ha. This not only approaches the size of **Dunnideer**, but the trenches clearly increase in breadth to either side of the entrance on the south-west, suggesting that this sector of the perimeter was deliberately enhanced.

Two other hilltop enclosures have been included with the forts on Figure 6.25 – **Tillymuick** (2.7ha) and **Hill of Newleslie** (5ha) – but it is far from clear whether either belongs in this category. **Tillymuick** is bounded by little more than a low stony bank, apparently grubbed up from a shallow internal quarry scoop some 5m broad, while at **Hill of Newleslie** the perimeter comprises a low bank fronted by a shallow ditch and traces of a counterscarp bank (Fig. 6.28). Neither perimeter can ever have been of any stature. Indeed, but for the entrance approached by a hollow trackway on the north side of **Tillymuick**, this enclosure might be considered as an old plantation boundary rather than a possible prehistoric settlement. This impression is strengthened by the lack of any convincing evidence for the fifty-six hut-circles that were identified within its interior in 1957 (RCAHMS Marginal Lands Survey).

Despite the disparate character of the forts in Donside, there can be little doubt that they include a series of key centres of power. Amongst them, there are three worth considering in a little more detail – **Tap o' Noth**, the **Mither Tap o' Bennachie**, and the **Barmekin of Echt** – illustrating not only the sheer scale of some of the fortifications, but also the commanding positions that they occupy.

Tap o' Noth

Without question this is one of the most spectacular forts in Scotland. The summit of the hill lies at a height of 563m OD, rising up from the south-west end of a whale-backed ridge above Rhynie, and the view from the top commands a huge sweep of north-east Scotland. On a clear day the North Sea can be seen to the east, while the southern shore of the Moray Firth lies to the north, its far coast extending into the distance to Sutherland and Caithness.

The fort itself comprises two main components, one represented by the massive vitrified wall around the summit, and the other by a stone rampart set much farther down the slope. The vitrified wall, which encloses an area measuring about 85m from north-west to south-east by 30m transversely, now forms a mound of rubble at least 15m thick, although it has evidently been quarried for stone internally at a relatively recent date. Despite the quarrying, the rubble is piled up between 2m and 3m above the level of the interior, but its external talus of debris forms an even more impressive feature, spreading up to 30m down the slope. At various points around the circuit substantial masses of vitrifaction can also be seen, in part exposed by the quarrying, but demonstrating that the wall was constructed with an

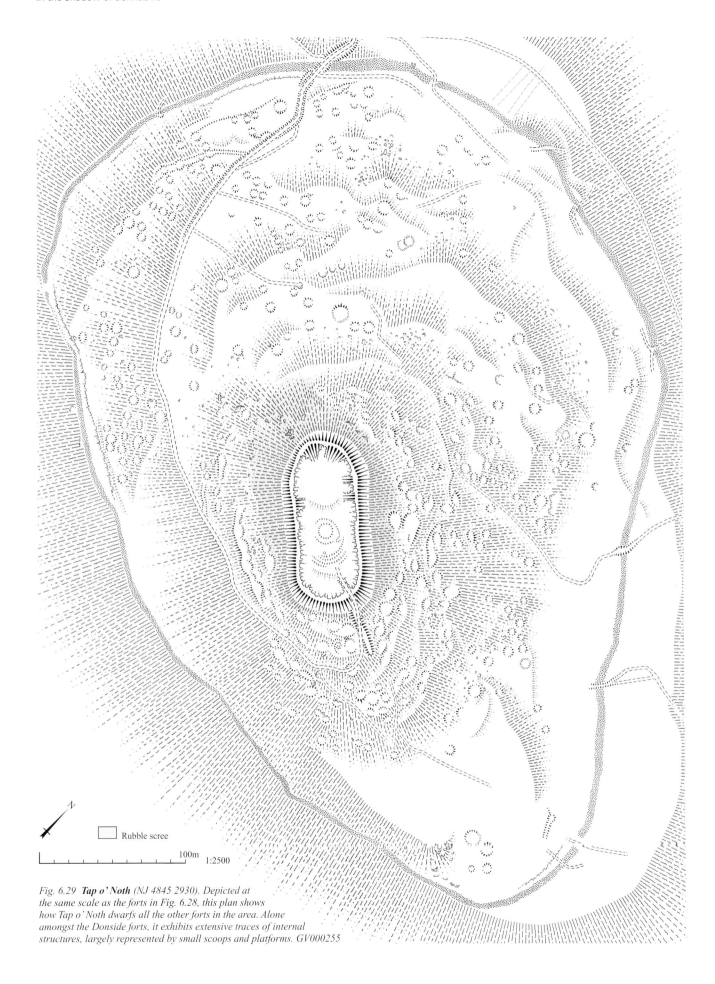

Fig. 6.29 **Tap o' Noth** *(NJ 4845 2930). Depicted at
the same scale as the forts in Fig. 6.28, this plan shows
how Tap o' Noth dwarfs all the other forts in the area. Alone
amongst the Donside forts, it exhibits extensive traces of internal
structures, largely represented by small scoops and platforms. GV000255*

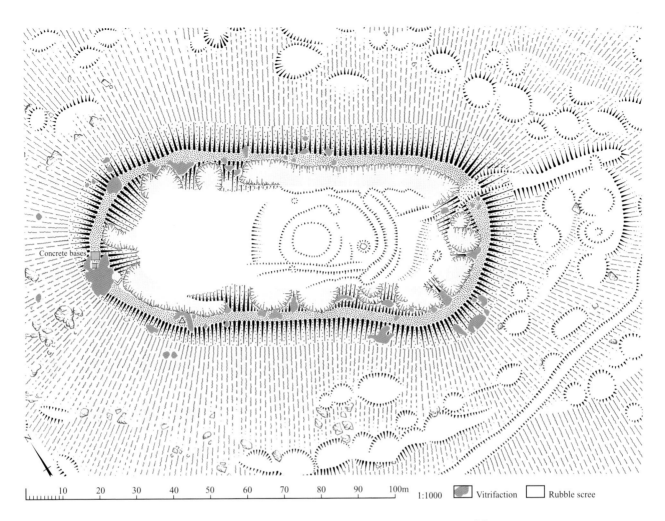

10   20   30   40   50   60   70   80   90   100m

1:1000   [shaded] Vitrifaction   [white] Rubble scree

Fig. 6.30 **Tap o' Noth** *(NJ 4845 2930). This detailed plan of the inner fort shows the extent of visible vitrifaction in the wall. The mound of rubble from the wall was once considerably larger than it is today, and there are extensive quarries dug in around its inner margin. This has obscured the relationship between the main wall and the traces of a small enclosed settlement which is visible within the interior. GV004133*

internal timber framework and destroyed in a massive conflagration. No entrance is visible and the present access, which can be seen in a 19th-century illustration of the fort (Hibbert 1857), rides over the debris at the south-east end. Two low banks with a medial ditch cut across the south-east end of the interior, presumably indicating the presence of an earlier enclosure on the summit. The only other features visible within the interior are a possible well or cistern, and what may be traces of a large round-house.

The outer fort is defended by a single rampart, though this has been largely wrecked by stone-robbing, and in some places, particularly on the steepest slopes above Rhynie, its line is barely perceptible. Ten gaps in the rampart can be identified, mainly around the northern half of the circuit, though not all are original entrances. Nevertheless, several short lengths of trackway within the interior are probably ancient, servicing the clusters of small circular house-platforms that pockmark its surface.

Mither Tap o' Bennachie

As a landmark, the stark and craggy profile of the Mither Tap is far more imposing than Tap o' Noth, an ever-present reference point in the landscape of central and eastern Aberdeenshire. The fort too is a remarkable structure, its defences again reduced to massive screes of rubble. Approached from the north-east, the visitor is at once confronted with the sheer scale of the outermost wall, with what appears to be a stone-faced entrance-way climbing the slope into the interior. On closer inspection, however, this stone facing is holding back the tumbled debris from the wall itself, and can only have been constructed after the wall had become ruinous. That said, some of the stones facing the inner end of the entrance passage are possibly original, forming the terminals of a wall at least 8m in thickness. A long run of the outer face can be seen in the rubble extending south from the entrance, while substantial portions of the inner face still stands some nine courses high to the north, with an upper tier of masonry some five courses high stepped back above it. The facing of the inner end of the entrance passage also extends beyond the line of the inner face, apparently turning to either side to form the edge of a stony plinth at the foot of the wall in the interior. At the entrance at least, the inner face of the wall has thus been raised in a series

Fig. 6.31 ***Mither Tap o' Bennachie*** *(NJ 6825 2240). Occupying the easternmost of the summits of the Bennachie range, this fort has been a spectacular landmark throughout central Aberdeenshire. SC636483*

of steps or tiers, presumably culminating in a parapet, though this was probably at least one tier above the level of the surviving masonry.

The scale of this wall suggests that at some stage it was the principal line of defence for the fort, presumably spanning the rock outcrops on the south and resting on the precipitous outcrops on the west. However, it evidently succeeded an earlier rampart following roughly the same line. This rampart is best-preserved on the south, where it forms an artificial terrace faced with large blocks to a height of at least 1.2m immediately behind the wall. Northwards this terrace tails off into a low scarp, but to the south it appears to turn, as if

to cut over the spine of the summit, disappearing in a scatter of large blocks on the slope. This corresponds to the position of a slight break in slope to the west of the spine, but on this side of the fort there is also a heather-grown rampart behind the southern end of the outer wall.

Within the interior, which rises steeply into the rocky boss that forms the distinctive summit of the hill, at least two further lines of defence can be seen, the lower represented by another long scree of rubble, the upper by a few facing-stones set on ledges on the outcrops above a small band of debris. These are presumably the remains of walls backing onto the edge of the cliff to the west to form a citadel on the summit. Today the summit is simply bare rock, riven with natural clefts, and it is difficult to conceive that it could ever have been occupied.

Fig. 6.32 **Mither Tap o' Bennachie**
*(NJ 6825 2240). The massive rampart
around the foot of this granite tor has been
a formidable barrier and preserves evidence
of what may be a drystone parapet along part of
its crest. The central tor has also been fortified, and
may have formed an inner citadel. GV004132*

N

Rubble scree

10   20   30   40   50   60   70   80m   1:1000

Without excavation the sequence and arrangement of these defences cannot be fully understood, but it is likely that in at least one period they comprised an inner citadel surrounded by an outer enclosure. Curiously, however, for all the huge effort that has been expended in the construction of the defences, little of the space enclosed, a maximum of 0.65ha, lends itself to occupation. Rather than providing secure accommodation for a community, the walls give the impression that they were more concerned with power and prestige.

*Fig. 6.33 **Barmekin of Echt** (NJ 7260 0714). A light dusting of snow on the deep heather helps pick out the concentric ramparts and ditches of the fort on this oblique aerial photograph taken in 1999. SC958176*

Barmekin of Echt

The contrast between the position of the **Mither Tap o' Bennachie** and the third of the forts to be considered in detail, the **Barmekin of Echt**, could not be more complete. This is not to say that the fort is not in a commanding position, but it is much more difficult to pick out from the surrounding countryside, particularly now that the defences are encumbered with deep heather. Previous interpretations have seen at least two phases of fortification here, the earlier comprising an outer system of three close-set ramparts, and the later an inner circuit of two concentric stone walls, which blocked three of the five earlier entrances (Feachem 1966, 72; 1977, 104). As a result of the present survey, it is clear that the outer scheme comprises no less than four ramparts, the fourth lying beneath the supposed outer wall of the inner fort. This outer wall, however, blocks at least four of the entrances in the outer ramparts, all of which correspond to original gaps in the innermost wall, and the fifth has been obscured by the trackway that is thought to have served an observatory set up in 1822 to track the planet Venus. This relationship with the other four entrances implies that the outer wall is of relatively late date, and probably confirms antiquarian opinion that it was built in the 17th century to enclose a plantation on the summit of the hill (*Stat. Acct.*, xii, 1794, 620–1, note). The stones for its construction were robbed from the inner wall, causing the inner face to collapse across the remaining core like fallen dominoes.

The Wider Landscape

The identity of the North-east expressed in the recumbent stone circles in the Early Bronze Age (pp. 77–8) is not perpetuated in the later settlement remains. The various types of round-houses that have been recorded (pp. 82–7) are found north and south of the Mounth, and the souterrains in Donside would pass muster anywhere in Angus. Equally, the oblong forts represented by **Tap o' Noth** and **Dunnideer** are scattered northwards from Perth and along the Moray Plain to Easter Ross (p. 100), while the smaller stone-walled enclosures, such as **Hill of Keir** and **White Hill**, find their closest parallels in Angus (p. 101). The cropmark record in the North-east is similarly representative of a wider area, though some types of settlement, such as the interrupted ring-ditches (RCAHMS 1994, 59–62), have yet to be recognised north of the Mounth.

Even in this wider setting it is difficult to make much sense of the settlements. Most of the excavations taking place are commercially led, inevitably falling in the lowlands, and there is a dearth of equivalent work in the adjacent uplands. This dichotomy creates considerable difficulties in any attempt to integrate the upstanding settlements recorded by survey on the fringes of the improved landscape in the uplands with those known only from cropmarks in the lowlands. Nevertheless, these are facets of the same history of settlement, one still visible, the other buried (p. 83). In essence, the settlement excavated at **Forest Road**, Kintore (Cook and Dunbar 2004), is a hut-circle group.

Excavation of upstanding hut-circles elsewhere in Scotland has shown that most date from the 2nd millennium BC, though a small number were occupied much later in the 1st millennium BC (e.g. Lairg, Sutherland; McCullagh and Tipping 1998). This was the case at both Tulloch Wood in Moray (Carter 1993) and Carn Dubh in Perth & Kinross (Rideout 1995), the nearest groups of hut-circles to Donside for which dates are available. There is no reason to suppose that those in the uplands of Donside will behave differently, but the chronology of the round-houses in the lowland setting of **Forest Road** covers a much broader range, continuing through much of the 1st millennium BC (Cook and Dunbar 2004, 86–7). At the end of the millennium, however, this particular location is abandoned, and is apparently not settled again during the first half of the 1st millennium AD. Other settlements dating from this period have been found nearby, but the abandonment of **Forest Road** may well signify some wider reorganisation of the landscape.

Elsewhere in eastern Scotland, the presence of a souterrain usually serves as a marker for late Iron Age occupation on a settlement, typically producing Roman artefacts dating from the 1st and 2nd centuries AD (Halliday 2006, 16). Aberdeenshire is no exception, but here a handful of such settlements survive upstanding, as can be seen at New Kinord in the Howe of Cromar, with its cluster of large hut-circles and enclosures lying at the core of a surrounding field-system. Other souterrains found in the lowlands were probably components of similar settlements, though none of the hut-circle groups in Donside bears any resemblance to that at New Kinord. The site of the *'Druidical village'* at **Druidstone**, Premnay, with antiquarian descriptions of linking alleys or causeways (Laing 1828, 277–8; Low 1866, 221), may have been one, while the clusters of souterrains at **Clova** may have included others.

Despite the density of settlement remains that must once have existed (p. 80), there is little evidence to show how the wider landscape was organised. The field-systems at **Damil** or **Garlogie Wood** probably covered no more than 10ha, and the only hint that the landscape may have been more extensively enclosed comes from outside the survey area at New Kinord (Ogston 1931). The long raking field-banks on the northern flank of **Deskry Hill**, in the upper reaches of the valley opposite Buchaam, are perhaps a fragment of a large system, but, even if this took in all the improved ground on the spur, it cannot have covered more than 60ha. Enclosure on this scale is notoriously rare anywhere in eastern Scotland, either upstanding or amongst the cropmarks, so much so that if the landscape that survives around New Kinord was once typical, it is now unique. With so little evidence of any extensive landscape enclosures, it is perhaps more likely that settlement was typically scattered in smaller pockets, though these may well have lain within a mosaic of open pasture and woodland. The system on **Deskry Hill** was certainly cultivated, and traces of narrow cultivation rigs – cord rig – can be seen between the banks that divide up the hillside. Occasional patches of cord rig have been recorded elsewhere, but, by and large, the visible evidence of prehistoric agriculture is composed of clusters of clearance heaps spread over a hectare or so. This is the pattern recorded on the depiction of the **Hill of Boghead** (Fig. 6.4), and it is found widely elsewhere. Even where the scatters of cairns appear to merge and cover a much larger area, such as Balnabroich in Perth & Kinross (RCAHMS 1990, 34–6, no. 108), this pattern of smaller clusters can still be detected.

With such a fragmentary range of evidence to draw upon, it is difficult to reconstruct the settlement landscape at any particular point during prehistory. All that is known for certain is that round-houses, singly and in groups, formed the mainstay of the settlement pattern from the beginning of the 2nd millennium BC until the early centuries of the 1st millennium AD, and that forts were built at various times from at least the end of the Late Bronze Age (*c.*800 BC) until probably the end of the early medieval period (*c.*AD 1000). The

smaller forts appear to be the strongholds of relatively small groups, while others, such as the lower enclosure on the summit of **Tap o' Noth**, or perhaps **Hill of Newleslie** and **Tillymuick**, were presumably the foci for substantial populations.

The stratigraphic sequences displayed by the defences of other forts in eastern Scotland tend to suggest that the largest defensive enclosures are of relatively early date. If the evidence from southern Scotland has any bearing on the matter they are possibly as early as the Late Bronze Age, following on from the period at which so many hut-circle groups in the Highlands were apparently abandoned. The defensive sequences also suggest that forts became progressively smaller. Thus, several of the oblong series can be shown to succeed these large forts, and were succeeded in their turn by even smaller structures (p. 101). If there is any direct relationship between the size of fortifications and their social or political significance, in the course of the 1st millennium BC power appears to have been focused in the hands of progressively smaller groups of people.

The hut-circle groups themselves are essentially composite monuments, in which relatively few of the visible features are contemporary. This has been amply demonstrated by excavation on Arran and in Sutherland (Barber 1997; McCullagh and Tipping 1998), and the general picture that has emerged from the excavation of hut-circles throughout Scotland is of episodic occupation broken by intervals of abandonment (Barber and Crone 2001; Halliday 2000; Halliday 2007). There is, therefore, some doubt that any hut-circle groups were continuously occupied over long periods of time. Rather than sedentary settlement, these groups may reflect a more dynamic system, in which the locations that were occupied were shifted at short intervals. The major period of abandonment that has been identified in the uplands at the end of the 2nd millennium BC, coinciding with the appearance of large fortified enclosures, may signal a major change in the structure of the settlement landscape, but in practice there is little to show that Iron Age settlements were occupied any more continuously than their Bronze Age predecessors. The only notable difference between the two periods is the greater frequency with which Iron Age settlements are enclosed by banks or palisades.

The souterrains represent the first period in which the overall extent of the settlement pattern can be assessed. They reveal that at the beginning of the 1st millennium AD settlement had penetrated deep into the Highland glens. The four clusters of souterrains within the space of 1km at **Clova** also imply a dense pattern of settlement, inviting comparison with that on the free-draining soils around the edges of the Carse of Gowrie, Perth & Kinross (RCAHMS 1994, 64–7). If these examples are in any way representative, large numbers of souterrains remain to be discovered in the lowlands of Aberdeenshire.

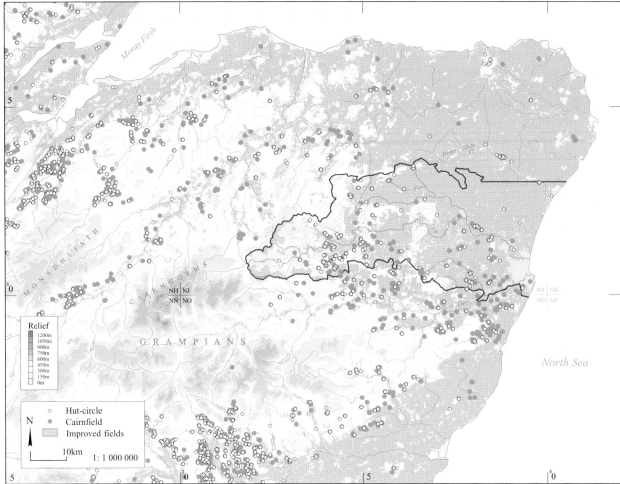

Fig. 6.34 This map shows how the distribution of hut-circles and cairnfields across north-east Scotland has been confined largely to the uplands by later agriculture. In this respect lower Donside and Deeside are unusual, the remains of hut-circle settlements extending down into the lowlands. Many of the gaps in the upland distribution probably reflect the uneven pattern of archaeological field survey. GV000186

In the Howe of Cromar (pp. 41–2), extensive soil erosion is recorded during this period, which probably provides an index of the intensity of agriculture in some places. Palaeoenvironmental information elsewhere is scarce, but it is likely that large tracts of woodland had been cleared throughout Donside. This seems to have been the case in Glen Ernan, near the top of the Don, where the peat at the base of a pollen diagram was laid down in an almost treeless landscape some 1700 years ago (p. 41). At some stage woodland in parts of the Howe of Cromar started to regenerate, which has been attributed by Whittington and Edwards (1993) to the impact of successive Roman campaigns against the northern tribes (p. 42). However, such correlations are dangerous, and the resolution of the chronology of the palaeoenvironmental sources against calendrical events is no more convincing here than elsewhere (RCAHMS 1997a, 21–2).

Roman sources shed little further light on the character of settlement at this date, though a chain of Roman temporary camps extends well north of the Mounth. The written accounts are more concerned to paint a picture of the difficult terrain in *Caledonia*, presumably to enhance the feat of arms that had taken the Romans to the extremities of Britain. According to Ptolemy, the Alexandrian geographer writing in the 2nd century AD, the *Taexali* occupied Aberdeenshire, and a place named *Devona* lay within their territory. This name is probably linked to the Don (Rivet and Smith 1979, 338). To other writers, including Tacitus, the biographer of Gnaeus Julius Agricola, Governor of the province of *Britannia* in about AD 77–83, the northern peoples were simply the inhabitants of *Caledonia*. The first reference to the people who became known as the Picts only comes in AD 297. Of society at large, there is barely a mention.

The precise date of the first intervention of the Roman army into Donside is uncertain, but it has been argued that the battle of *Mons Graupius,* the deciding encounter of Agricola's campaigns in about AD 83, was fought in the shadow of Bennachie (St Joseph 1978; see also Maxwell 1990, 91–110). If this is indeed correct, Tacitus' account of the

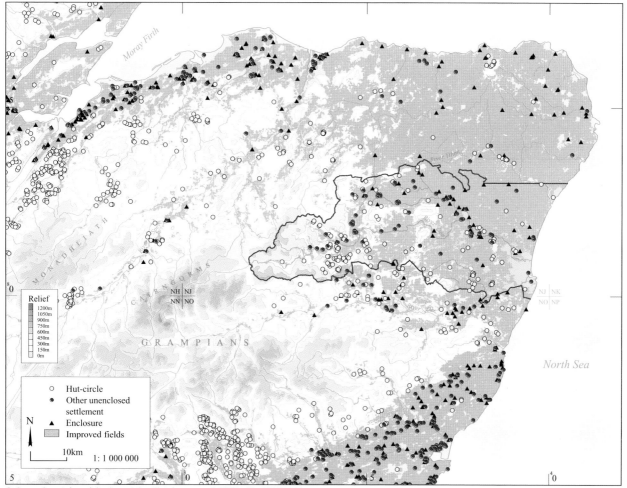

Fig. 6.35 This map shows the impact of aerial survey programmes on the pattern of evidence for prehistoric settlement across north-east Scotland since 1976. Cropmarks have revealed large numbers of unenclosed and enclosed settlements in the arable zone, an area where previously only souterrains were known. A significant proportion of the unenclosed settlements revealed by cropmarks include the distinctive markings of souterrains, and for the purposes of this map this category of settlement includes all the souterrains that have been discovered by other means. The cropmarks are particularly dense in Angus and at the western end of the Moray Plain, where the conditions are more favourable for the formation of cropmarks. GV000189

battle is describing the landscape of Donside and its people. Presumably, there must have been sufficient open ground for the opposing forces to manoeuvre, but more importantly the battlefield must have lain at or close by some recognised place of assembly. The bleak pinnacle of rock that forms the summit of the Mither Tap is certainly the most instantly recognisable landmark in Aberdeenshire. Unfortunately Tacitus leaves his readership none the wiser as to whether the status of *Calgacus*, the leader of the native host, should be translated into a fort such as that on the summit. The defensive sequences already outlined perhaps point to the small ring-fort in the interior of the **Maiden Castle** as a more likely candidate.

Roman Intervention
– Rebecca Jones

Followers of Tacitus' biography of Agricola would place the earliest intervention of the Roman army in the affairs of north-eastern Scotland in the Flavian period, about AD 82–3, during the sixth or seventh season of his campaigns in northern Britain. In the sixth season it is reported that Agricola advanced on the tribes beyond (north of) the Forth (*Agricola* 25–6), while in the seventh and final season he decisively defeated the Caledonians at the battle of *Mons Graupius* (*Agricola* 29ff). Despite the subjugation of the Caledonian tribes, Tacitus reports bitterly that Britain was immediately thrown away (*Histories* 1.2), and the northern conquests were abandoned shortly afterwards.

The presence of this biography of Agricola has often skewed the interpretation of Roman monuments in Scotland, which have been made to fit into the chronology presented by Tacitus. However, it is now known that one of Agricola's predecessors, Petillius Cerialis (AD 71–4), had reached at least as far as the Solway some ten years previously, constructing a fort at Carlisle in about AD 72 (Frere 1990, 320; Caruana 1992, 101–3). In effect, Agricola's predecessors may

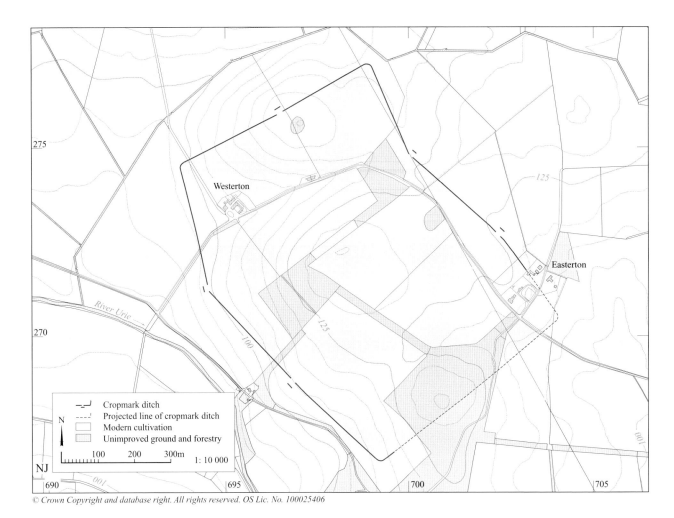

Fig. 6.36 **Logie Durno** *(NJ 6985 2718). Lying on uneven ground to the north-east of the River Urie, the plan of this camp is transcribed from cropmarks on oblique aerial photographs. GV004094*

have paved the way for his rapid envelopment of southern Scotland, while his successor was probably responsible for the dispositions of at least some of the garrisons established farther north.

It is equally clear that the evolution of the northern frontier was more complex than Tacitus' account suggests. This has been evident since the discovery of a fort and fortlet some 250m apart at Cargill, in south-eastern Perthshire (RCAHMS 1994, 84). In addition, several of the watchtowers along the Gask Ridge, west of Perth, are now known to have two phases (Woolliscroft 2002, 7; Glendinning and Dunwell 2000, 273–6), as has the fort at Cardean, in Angus. In view of these discoveries, it is likely that the occupation of eastern Scotland was more complex than traditional interpretations have allowed.

Following the withdrawal from southern Scotland towards the end of the 1st century AD, the frontier of the province was established on the Tyne-Solway line in northern England, firstly on the road known as the Stanegate, and later with Hadrian's Wall. There it was to remain until the reign of Antoninus Pius

(AD 138–61), when Lollius Urbicus, who became Governor of Britain in about AD 139, erected a new frontier work, the Antonine Wall, on the Forth-Clyde isthmus. There were undoubtedly campaigns to secure the approaches to the new frontier, and a series of outposts were built northwards as far as Bertha, near Perth. By the AD 160s, however, the frontier was back on the line of Hadrian's Wall.

Despite this later withdrawal from Scotland, the Romans attempted to exercise some control over the northern tribes. On occasion, such as in the AD 180s, this involved warfare, but the events recorded at the end of the century reveal two other aspects of Roman policy, namely treaties and bribes. The tribes, named as the *Maeatae* and the Caledonians by Cassius Dio, had broken the terms of these agreements, and in the short term the Governor, Virius Lupus, bought them off. The distribution of large sums of money beyond the frontier is manifested in late 2nd- and early 3rd-century hoards of Roman coins discovered in Scotland, most recently at Birnie, in Moray, where no less than two have been recovered by excavation (Hunter 2002b).

The situation in the north continued to deteriorate, leading to an imperial expedition by the Emperor Septimius Severus in AD 208–11. According to the contemporary Greek historians Cassius Dio and

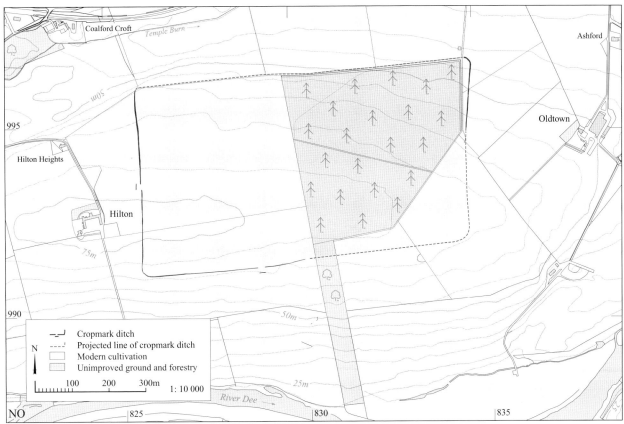

*Fig. 6.37 **Normandykes** (NO 8297 9938). Little is now visible of this camp and the plan is transcribed from cropmarks on oblique aerial photographs. GV004095*

Herodian, Severus campaigned to the farthest point of the island (*Cassius Dio* LXXVI, 13), and there can be little doubt that he penetrated north of the Mounth before his death at York in AD 211. The Caledonians proved elusive opponents, however, and there was to be no decisive victory to match Agricola's triumph. Nevertheless, despite the hasty conclusion of the campaign by Severus' son, Caracalla, little more is heard of the northern frontier until the campaigns by Constantius Chlorus into the territory of the 'Picts' almost a century later in AD 305 (*Pan Lat Vet* 7, 1–2). Further trouble with the Picts is attested in the AD 360s (Ammianus Marcellinus xx, 1) and in the AD 390s (Miller 1975).

This literary backdrop to the archaeological evidence led Professor J K St Joseph to postulate that individual military campaigns might be recognised in the temporary fortifications or marching camps that marked the lines of advance northwards. These camps had long been recognised as earthworks, including both **Kintore** (Fig. 6.38) and **Normandykes** (Fig. 6.37; pp. 9; 12), and St Joseph himself identified a number of others as cropmarks, including **Logie Durno** in Donside (Fig. 6.36). An analysis of their sizes, their morphological characteristics, and the marching distances between them, led him to define several series

of camps. Those of the 'Stracathro' series, for instance, have a distinctive type of gateway, and were attributed a Flavian date. The larger camps in north-eastern Scotland were initially grouped into a '120-acre' (*c*.49ha) series and identified as probably of Severan date (St Joseph 1958, 93; 1969, 118), but later this group was refined into a '110-acre' (*c*.45ha) and a '130-acre' (*c*.52ha) series and attached to the Flavian and Severan campaigns respectively (St Joseph 1973, 231). The camps at **Kintore** and **Normandykes**, at about 44.5ha (110 acres), fitted into the former group, alongside those of Glenmailen I and Muiryfold, all of them lying at intervals of about one day's march.

Some 14km north of **Kintore**, at **Logie Durno**, St Joseph discovered the largest camp yet recorded north of the Forth-Clyde isthmus, which he proposed as the gathering ground for Agricola's forces before the battle of *Mons Graupius* weaving Tacitus' account of the battle into countryside around Bennachie (St Joseph 1978). The camp encloses some 57ha (144 acres), and he observed that a camp of these dimensions might neatly hold a combined force that had occupied camps belonging to his '30-acre' (12ha) and '110-acre' (44.5ha) series (St Joseph 1977, 144). Again, the literary evidence afforded by Tacitus was brought into play, for in the sixth season Agricola had marched forward in three divisions (*Agricola* 25; St Joseph 1973, 229). This prompted the suggestion that the force gathered for the battle had operated in at least two divisions

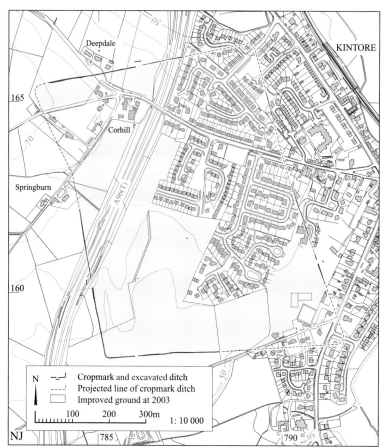

Fig. 6.38 **Kintore** *(NJ 7869 1619). This camp, which is depicted on the 1st edition of the OS 6-inch map (Aberdeenshire 1869, sheet lxv), is now largely destroyed by modern development. The line of the ditch is known through a combination of cropmarks on aerial photographs and excavation. GV004093*

(St Joseph 1978, 280), one of them occupying his '30-acre' series, which included Bellie, Auchinhove, Burnfield and Glenmailen II. St Joseph proposed another example closer to hand at Cairnhall, just to the north of **Kintore** (1977, 140), but this still requires confirmation.

The various series proposed by St Joseph represent an ingenious piece of deduction, but they are not all supported by other lines of evidence. For example, the camps included in his '30-acre' series exhibit a much wider range of sizes (Jones 2006, 170–1). In addition, the sequence between the two camps at Glenmailen (Ythan Wells) has variously been interpreted in support of both a Severan and Flavian date for the '110-acre' series (St Joseph 1969, 118–9; 1973, 231–2). While the excavations here established that the larger '110-acre' camp succeeded a smaller Stracathro-type camp, the elapse of time between them is unknown. This highlights the difficulties of obtaining dating evidence from any camp without extensive excavations, as have now taken place at **Kintore**.

Excavations at temporary camps usually concentrate on the perimeter ditch rather than the interior (see Leslie 1995). At **Kintore** a total of over 35ha of the interior has now been stripped, revealing in excess of 180 bipartite field ovens and sixty rubbish pits (Shepherd 1986, 207; Alexander 2000, 31–3; Cook and Dunbar 2004; Cook *et al.* forthcoming). The ovens are apparently scattered throughout the interior of the camp and have been subjected to an extensive programme of radiocarbon dating. As might be expected, the majority of the dates simply bracket the period from the 1st to the 3rd century, but cluster in the late 1st century; an iron axehead of probable 3rd-century date was also found in one of the ovens (Cook and Dunbar 2004). Radiocarbon dates from ovens excavated in 1996 (Alexander 2000, 31–2) also include two late assays, one of cal AD 330–550 (1620 ± 40 BP: OxA-8180) and the other of cal AD 410–610 (1540 ± 50 BP: OxA-8244). As revealed by the ovens, the camp was probably used on a number of occasions over a very long period of time, though sections through the perimeter ditch have revealed no evidence of any reconstruction or refurbishment.

Despite this wide range of dating evidence from **Kintore**, the camp appears to have been a Flavian foundation. However, this does not necessarily support St Joseph's contention that **Logie Durno** was where Agricola marshalled his troops for the Battle of *Mons Graupius*. Others have preferred different locations (see Maxwell 1990, 104–10; Fraser 2005), though the North-east is the most likely scene of these momentous events. Whether the battlefield itself will ever be located remains to be seen. The discovery in the late 1980s of the battlefield where three legions under P. Quinctilius Varus were destroyed in AD 9 in the Teutoburg Forest, Germany (Schlüter 1999; Wells 2003), at least holds this prospect for *Mons Graupius*.

Chapter 7: The Early Medieval Landscape

Iain Fraser and Stratford Halliday

The transition from the late Iron Age into the early medieval period is rarely manifested in any clear-cut manner. So much so that in many areas of Scotland, particularly in the south and east, there is little tangible evidence in the landscape for a period of settlement that was to last for almost 1000 years. The last recognisable settlement types of the late Iron Age were apparently abandoned by or during the 3rd century AD (Halliday 2006), while the first medieval castles and churches only come on record in the 12th century. Some of the forts are known to have been occupied (Ralston 2004), but to all intents and purposes the people – peasants and kings alike – disappear from view. In eastern Scotland this coincides with the era of the Picts, key players in the history of northern Britain, who only succumbed with the emergence of Alba in the 10th century. The Picts, however, have maintained a resonance to this day, if only for their symbols, which so excited antiquarian imagination (pp. 8–11) and continue to shroud them with an alluring mystery in the public eye.

While the settlements remain elusive, there is substantially more evidence for the political and social organisation during this period than at any time before. Historical sources are available for the first time, and these shed a fitful light upon events and organisation unavailable from any archaeological evidence. The advent of Christianity, and indeed the evolution of the parochial structure of the medieval landscape (pp. 143–5), add further dimensions, while the place-names recorded in medieval documents and on later maps implicitly retain clues to earlier patterns of settlement and land-use. To these can be added more immediate sources of evidence, including Pictish symbol stones and cross-slabs, simple Christian cross-stones, and cemeteries of square barrows.

In so far as they tell us of Aberdeenshire, the historical sources are both scanty and late, so much so that it is sometimes contended that this was never

an important district in Pictland (Henderson 1958, 55; 1972, 166). Nevertheless, one of these later sources, the Irish version of the *Historia Brittonum*, tells of Pictland's division among the seven sons of the legendary king Cruithne, by which the North-east became the province of *Ce* (Henderson 1972, 166). A second source, the 12th-century *de situ Albaniae*, also relates that Pictland was divided into seven provinces, the North-east encompassed by *Marr cum Buchen*. However, both were medieval earldoms, and this is perhaps best viewed as an attempt to explain the origin of the contemporary situation in the 12th century rather than the political geography of Pictland (Broun 2000). These general references aside, little is known until the death of Macbeth, who was killed in 1057 at Lumphanan, on Deeside (Anderson 1922, i, 600), and his stepson, Lulach the Fatuous, killed the following year at Essie in upper Strathbogie, presumably by supporters of Malcolm III (Anderson 1922, i, 603–4).

To some extent the silence of early historical sources may be no more than a consequence of the distance of Aberdeenshire from Irish scriptoria. Thus, the Irish sources refer to centres of power further west and south, such as Burghead in Moray, Dunnottar in the old county of Kincardineshire, and Dundurn and Forteviot in Perth & Kinross, but make no mention of any equivalent centres in the North-east, despite the best efforts of later historians. These latter tend to be unreliable, often basing their identifications upon misreadings of the earlier sources. According to the 14th-century historian Fordun, for instance, Giric, king of the Picts, died at Dunnideer (Skene 1871–2, ii, 152, 409). Local tradition absorbed this story, and named the ruined castle on the summit *Gregory's Wall* (Robertson 1843, 553; Name Book, Aberdeenshire, No. 41, p. 55; Laing 1828, 245). Fordun's *Dunideer*, however, is a misreading of Dundurn, in Perth & Kinross (Anderson 1922, i, 364, 368). Similarly, the *'city'* of *Nrurim*, where Giric's

*Fig. 7.1 **Maiden Stone** (NJ 7037 2471). The east face of this spectacular Class II cross-slab is divided into four panels and bears, from top to bottom, a centaur, a notched rectangle and Z-rod, a 'beast', and a mirror and comb. SC337196*

predecessor, Aed, met his death in 878, is identified by Chalmers with Inverurie (1887–94, i, 383n), yet other references place his death in Strathallan, again in Perth & Kinross (Anderson 1922, i, 356–8).

This lack of authentic references to any important political centres or events in the North-east is compounded by the absence of the physical evidence of secular patronage at any comparable level to that implied by the large collections of highly developed Christian sculpture found at several sites in Perth & Kinross, Angus, Moray and Easter Ross. The impression is left of a peripheral zone between the two power blocs of Moray and southern Pictland.

If the division of Pictland into provinces has any veracity, then this part of Aberdeenshire lay within *Ce*, and must surely have been served by its own centres of power. To this extent the suggestion that the title of the Pict Artbranan, *primarius Geonae cohortis*, who was encountered by Columba on Skye, should be interpreted as *'leader of a warband in the region of Ce'* provides an intriguing, if tantalising reference to the area (Dumville 1981, 130–1; Sharpe 1995, 136, 294). Identifying such centres on purely archaeological grounds, however, is fraught with difficulties. It is salutary to reflect that the reason that the Pictish sculpture and the cropmarks at Forteviot now bulk so large in interpretations of southern Pictland rests largely on the survival of written references. Similarly, the significance of the Celtic monastery at Old Deer in studies of the early medieval church lies in the chance survival of the 9th-century Gospel book, the *Book of Deer*, and the 12th-century Gaelic notes it contains. The monastery presumably stood in the vicinity of this Buchan village, but there are no visible remains to identify its site.

The Pictish Symbol Stones

Whatever the shortcomings of the historical record for Aberdeenshire, the Pictish symbol stones provide a direct link to the landscape, the valleys of the lower Don and its tributaries the Urie and the Gadie containing no fewer than forty-one Class I stones – bearing only symbols – some 22% of the total known nationally (Fig. 7.3). Another two Class I stones occur in the southern portion of the survey area, where it crosses the watershed into the Howe of Cromar. To these can be added four Class II stones – bearing both symbols and a cross – one of these also lying in the Howe of Cromar.

Conventional dating of the symbol stones is largely dependent upon art-historical comparisons. These show a close relationship in stylistic detail with insular manuscript painting of the 7th century (Henderson 1967, 121–34). It has also been suggested that, in comparison with those of the Moray Firth area, the Aberdeenshire symbols display decadent characteristics indicative of a relatively late date (Stevenson 1955; Henderson 1958). It is important to realise, however, that nothing is known of the application and evolution of the symbols on more perishable media, such as wood and fabrics, which might radically alter our understanding of both their chronology and distribution. The possibility that the chronology of the symbols may be considerably longer than is usually accepted, is demonstrated at Pool, on Sanday, Orkney, where deposits incorporating a stone bearing a crude double disc have been dated to the 5th to 6th centuries AD (Hunter 1997).

By far the majority of the Aberdeenshire stones were first recorded by antiquaries in the 18th and 19th centuries (pp. 8–13), but further examples continue to

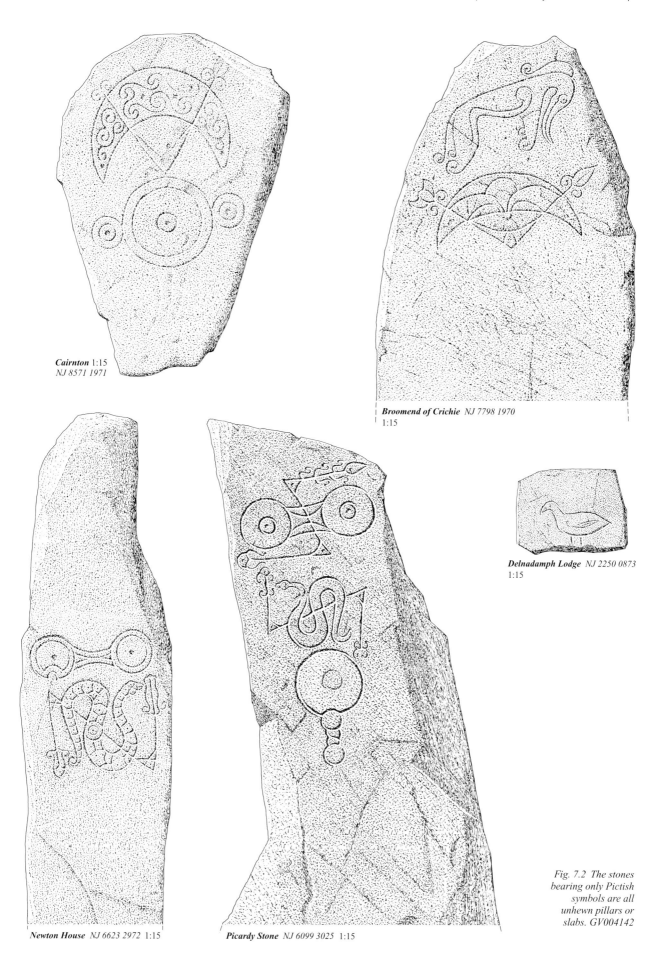

Cairnton 1:15
NJ 8571 1971

Broomend of Crichie *NJ 7798 1970*
1:15

Delnadamph Lodge *NJ 2250 0873*
1:15

Newton House *NJ 6623 2972* 1:15

Picardy Stone *NJ 6099 3025* 1:15

Fig. 7.2 The stones bearing only Pictish symbols are all unhewn pillars or slabs. GV004142

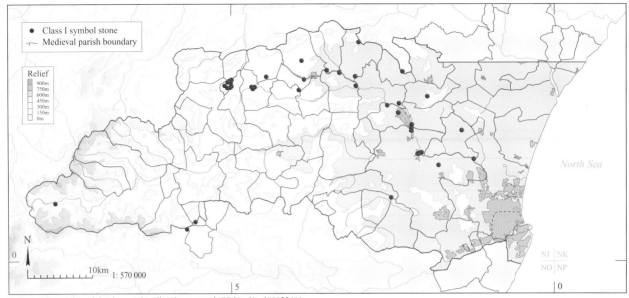

Fig. 7.3 The distribution of Class I symbol stones in Donside reveals a close proximity to watercourses, many of which coincide with the boundaries of medieval parishes. The lower reaches of the Don and its tributaries account for the vast majority of finds, surpassed only by the group from Rhynie in upper Strathbogie. GV000248

come to light. Most recently a stone bearing a possible goose has turned up at **Delnadamph Lodge** (Fig. 7.2), at the top of the Don, while at **Cairnton** (Figs 7.2; 7.4), Fintray, a large slab bearing a crescent and V-rod, and a triple disc, was discovered on a heap of field-gathered stones. More surprisingly, the present survey has revealed a mirror symbol on the **Newton Stone**. This stone (Fig. 7.11), with its well-known inscriptions in ogham and an unintelligible script, has been much studied, and yet this symbol has passed undetected beneath moss and lichen.

Of the forty-three Class I stones in the survey area, only four – **Ardlair**, **Nether Corskie**, the **Craw Stane** (Fig. 7.5), and the **Picardy Stone** (Fig. 7.2) – now stand in their original locations. A fifth stone, the spectacularly carved Class II cross-slab known as the **Maiden Stone** (Fig. 7.1), was moved a short distance during road construction. Fortunately, however, it is known roughly where most of the others were first found, if not precisely where they originally stood. About half of them were found singly, but the rest belong to larger groups. Indeed, given the loss and destruction of stones that is known to have taken place, it is likely that many of the single stones are the sole survivors of larger groups, which, as at **Ardlair**, may have included both inscribed and uninscribed slabs. **Rhynie** has the largest collection, with at least eight scattered southwards from the village, including two from the site of the parish church (see below). Other groups include: a mixture of Pictish and Christian stones from the kirkyard at **Dyce** (Fig. 7.18); four symbol stones on the **Moor of Carden**, three of which were removed to **Logie Elphinstone**; four from

Kintore, two of which were found in the **Castle Hill**, and a third probably in the nearby kirkyard; three from the kirkyard at **Clatt**; and four from the fabric of the old parish church in **Inverurie** kirkyard (Fig. 7.9).

*Fig. 7.4 **Cairnton** (NJ 8571 1971). This Class I symbol stone is one of two recent discoveries in Donside. It bears a crescent and V-rod, and a large triple-disc. SC958185*

The sites of parish churches figure remarkably prominently in this list, a total of thirteen stones having been found in reuse in the walls of a church or its kirkyard – **Dyce**, **Kinellar**, **Kintore**, **Bourtie**, **Clatt**, **Inverurie** and **Rhynie** – and a further five nearby. Inevitably some will argue that these stones have been moved from their original positions, possibly some distance, but equally most of the rubble for the walls of these churches and their enclosures has come from close at hand. Such records must be analysed cautiously, yet this pattern is repeated throughout the North-east, accounting for about 75% of the symbol stones in Moray and along the River Spey. This figure is surely too great to be ignored, and there can be little doubt of some causal relationship between the placing of these symbol stones and the positions of parish churches in the landscape (Alcock 1991, 9).

The Siting of Symbol Stones

By and large, the surviving stones and the find-spots fall between 50m and 260m OD, with an easterly aspect ranging from the north-east round to the south-south-west. Overwhelmingly, however, they show a preference for a south-easterly or open outlook. The single stone that fails to conform to this pattern, **Wantonwells**, was ploughed up at the foot of a steep slope facing north-west, but in this case it has been suggested that the stone may have stood at the top of the slope (Inglis 1987, 75).

The topographical features favoured as sites for the stones show a wide variation. Some of them are in elevated positions with broad views, and there is a preference for low knolls that form relatively prominent local features. The **Craw Stane** falls in the first category, standing just below the crest of a shoulder of rising ground with a fine prospect around Rhynie in upper Strathbogie. Similarly, the **Ardlair** stone and its companion look out across a broad valley from a terrace below the summit of a ridge, the latter occupied by a recumbent stone circle. The findspots of several other stones lie in comparable positions, as can be seen at **Kinellar** or the **Moor of Carden**. The **Kinellar** stone was recovered from the foundations of a hilltop church overlooking a broad swathe of the Don valley. The **Moor of Carden** is an area of rising ground above the confluence of the Gadie and the Urie. In other cases the outlook is not so extensive, such as at the **Picardy Stone**, which stands in an expanse of level open fields, with rising ground to the north and west, and an arc of low hills to the east. Less conspicuous sites include **Clatt** church, from which three stones are known, though here the church occupies a pronounced rise beside the Gadie Burn. In the case of **Inverurie**, four stones were discovered in reuse in the fabric of the old parish church, which stood on the haugland at the confluence of the Don and the Urie, and a fifth (now at **Keith Hall**) was recovered from the River Urie some 400m to the south.

Despite this wide range of topographical locations, the presence of water nearby is a recurring theme. This association is not limited to Donside, but is found throughout the North-east, from the Dee round to the Spey (Inglis 1987, 76). Within the Garioch, the distribution not only closely follows the line of the lower Don, the Gadie and the Urie, but also displays a noticeable bias towards the confluence of lesser tributaries with the main stream. Curiously, however, whereas the valley of the lower Don contains numerous stones, with the exception of the possible new stone from **Delnadamph** and the cross-slab at **Monymusk**, none has been recorded in the middle and upper reaches of the Don above Inverurie.

In addition to topographical features, the people who erected these stones also appear to have been attracted to earlier man-made components of the landscape, particularly Neolithic and Bronze Age monuments incorporating standing stones. This was apparently first noted by Charles Cordiner (1795), and has been examined by several more recent studies (Alcock 1991, 9; Mack 1997). Within the survey area symbols have been carved upon a slab belonging to a stone circle at **Brandsbutt** (Fig. 7.19), and one of a pair of upright stones at **Nether Corskie**. A similar reuse can be postulated at **Kinellar**, where in 1801 a symbol stone was found in the foundations of the old parish church, while the kirkyard dyke still incorporates several large stones that are believed to be from a recumbent stone circle (Coles 1902, 503–4). At **Kintore** too, the two symbol stones found beneath the medieval motte, **Castle Hill**, appear to have belonged to some form of stone monument. This interest in earlier monuments is also reflected in other discoveries that have been made in the North-east and includes a hoard of Pictish silver found adjacent to a stone circle at Ley (Gaulcross) in the old county of Banffshire (Stevenson 1964, 206–11).

Rhynie

Before discussing the role of the symbol stones in the landscape, it is worth considering the concentration of stones from **Rhynie** in more detail (Fig. 7.5). Only one of the eight stones, the **Craw Stane (Rhynie no. 1)**, is still in its original position, standing on the rising ground to the south of the village, but, in addition to two recovered from the foundations of the old parish church, the findspots for another five are known in some detail. Thus they offer insights into the siting of symbol stones that are otherwise lacking in the general descriptions of many stray finds from elsewhere.

The presence of so many symbol stones here almost certainly reflects the significance of this part of Strathbogie in the early medieval period, a significance signalled at an earlier date by the fort crowning **Tap o' Noth** (pp. 103–5). Then, as now, it was presumably a major routeway through the hills from north to south,

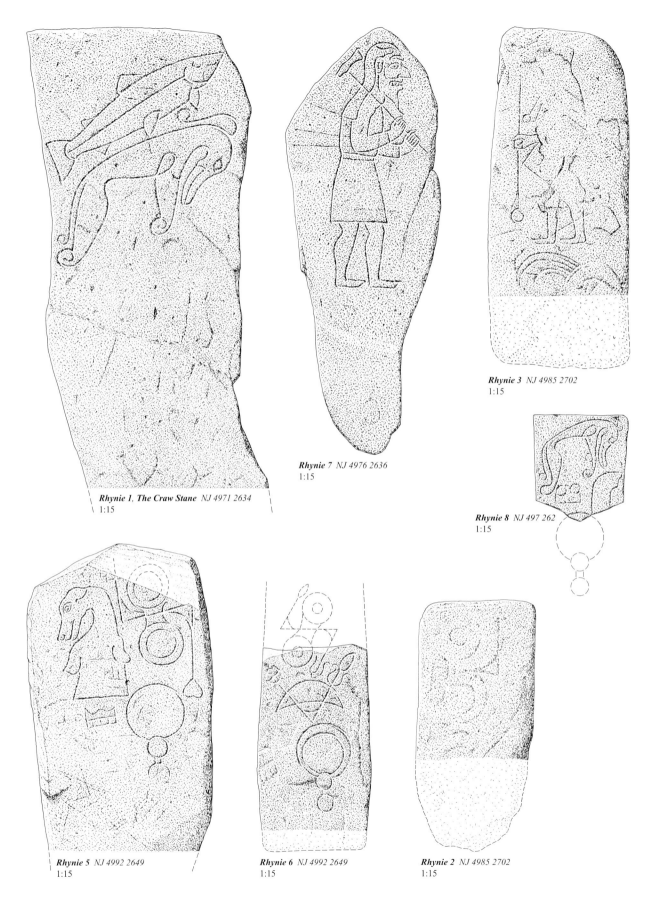

Rhynie 3 NJ 4985 2702
1:15

Rhynie 7 NJ 4976 2636
1:15

Rhynie 1, **The Craw Stane** NJ 4971 2634
1:15

Rhynie 8 NJ 497 262
1:15

Rhynie 5 NJ 4992 2649
1:15

Rhynie 6 NJ 4992 2649
1:15

Rhynie 2 NJ 4985 2702
1:15

Fig. 7.5 This remarkable collection of stones includes carvings of human figures on
Rhynie 3 *and 7. These are the least common carvings on Class I stones. GV004148*

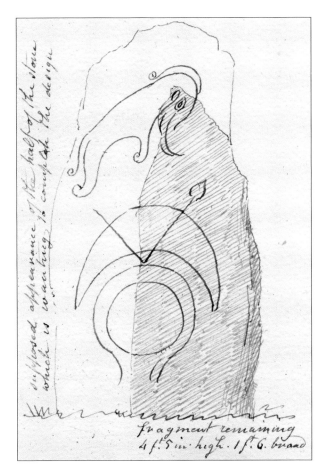

Fig. 7.6 **Rhynie 4** *(NJ 4892 2700). This stone is now broken up and lost, but a sketch by Skene depicts the head of a Pictish beast, a crescent and V-rod, and a mirror. SC1043213*

of the square about 100m north-east of the Plough Inn. Of a similar size and appearance to **Rhynie nos 2–3**, they too stand in the square.

The rest of the symbol stones have been found to the south of the village, two of them (**Rhynie nos 5–6**) recovered in 1878 from the foundations of the old parish church (Maclagan 1880, 11–13), and two others (**Rhynie nos 7–8**) in 1978 from the farm of Barflat (Shepherd and Shepherd 1978). These were ploughed up on the slope dropping away from the **Craw Stane** towards the west bank of the Water of Bogie. The old parish church stands within its burial-ground on a terrace at the foot of this slope, while a prominent Bronze Age cairn, known as the **Bell Knowe**, stands on a knoll overlooking the burial-ground some 200m north of the **Craw Stane**.

So far the positions and find-spots of the **Rhynie** stones display all the characteristics that have been discussed already – an extensive outlook from a prominent local feature, proximity to a water course, the presence of a large Bronze Age monument nearby, and the recovery of stones from the walls of a parish church. A further dimension to this landscape has emerged from aerial photography. This has not only revealed two square enclosures, possibly square barrows, at **Mains of Rhynie** (Fig. 7.7), no more than 150m to the south of the stones found at the Plough Inn,

Fig. 7.7 This map shows the location of sites and monuments around the village of Rhynie. GV000245

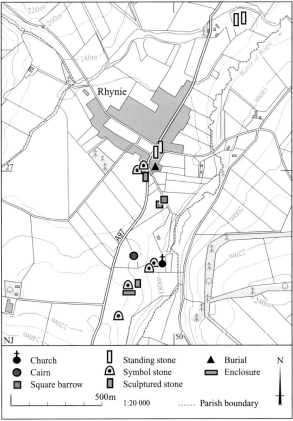

providing direct access between the Moray coast, the upper reaches of the Don, and numerous routes into Deeside and over the Mounth. Other routes strike off east and west, on the one hand to cross the watershed into the Garioch and the lower Don, on the other through Essie and over the hills to the Deveron and Moray. It may not be a coincidence that Lulach was killed at Essie, not far from this important crossroads on the way to the relative safety of Moray.

The modern village of Rhynie, which was established on its present site in the early 19th century, occupies the former Muir of Rhynie, a low spur, bounded on the east by the course of the Bogie, and to the west by the Ord Burn. Southwards the ground rises in a series of gentle knolls towards Quarry Hill, which closes off the southern end of the valley. Two of the stones (**Rhynie nos 2–3**), which now stand in the village square, were found about 1836 at the Plough Inn. This occupies the first of the low knolls at the south end of the village, but is now largely concealed by buildings. Human remains were also found nearby. A third stone (**Rhynie no. 4**) stood some 50m to the south-west, but was broken up about 1803 and is now entirely lost. In addition to these stones, two small uninscribed slabs were recorded in 1866, standing in the garden of the Free Church manse, on the south-east side

*Fig. 7.8 **Barflat** (NJ 4970 2635). Cropmarks on aerial photographs reveal that the Pictish stone known as the Craw Stane stands at the entrance to a complex earthwork overlooking the Water of Bogie. © AAS 92–CT15*

but has also shown that the **Craw Stane** stands at the entrance to a substantial earthwork enclosure (**Barflat**). This earthwork is unusual and there are no immediate parallels for it in the cropmark record (Fig. 6.20). Its perimeter probably comprised a thick wall or rampart fronted by a broad ditch, and the line of an outer palisade trench can also be seen on the aerial photographs. The interior, however, is remarkably small, measuring no more than 32m by 20m (0.05ha).

The records of Rhynie, collected over a period of about 200 years, probably indicate that the stones were originally disposed in two groups, one focused on the knoll at the south end of the village, the other around the **Craw Stane**, the latter the likely source for the two found in the foundations of the parish church. Interestingly, each group includes a stone bearing an incised human figure, which is one of the least common carvings on Class I symbol stones.

The Function of Symbol Stones

The reasons behind the erection of Pictish symbol stones and the interpretation of the symbols have been hotly debated. Some have seen them as boundary markers, others as memorials, and it has also been suggested that some of the smaller slabs may be fragments of architectural friezes. The meaning of the symbols themselves is probably beyond resolution,

though the range of interpretations includes statements of lineage or marriage alliances.

No single explanation may fit all of the stones, but modern excavation is beginning to confirm that one of their functions was to mark the sites of burials, either individually or in cemeteries. Furthermore, it has been shown that many of the cemeteries of this date include circular and square cairns and barrows. Thus, symbol stones were found on square cairns at Garbeg in the Great Glen, and Dunrobin in Sutherland (Ashmore 1981, 352; Close-Brooks 1981, 334–6; Mack 1997). On Donaldstone's Haugh at Tillytarmont, some way north of the survey area, one of five stones known from the site was ploughed up above a spread of stones adjacent to a square cairn (*DES 1975*, 6). Not all the cairn and barrow cemeteries were necessarily marked with symbol stones, and no evidence of any stone-holes was recovered from those at Red Castle in Angus, and Lundin Links in Fife (Alexander 2005; Greig, Greig and Ashmore 2000). At Boysack Mills, also in Angus, there was a stone-hole in the top of the grave-pit at the centre of a square barrow, but here the burial appears to have been rather earlier, and was accompanied by an iron pin probably dating from the 1st century AD (Murray and Ralston 1997).

Armed with this more modern data, some of the earlier discoveries of probable burials in the immediate vicinity of symbol stones fall into place. These often came to light in the course of agricultural improvements, such as those identified at the original site of the **Newton Stone** at Pitmachie, but in some cases also involved crude excavations by antiquaries. In Aberdeenshire, Charles Dalrymple carried out several such investigations, apparently at the behest of John Stuart in the preparation of the *Sculptured Stones of Scotland* (1856, xx). Digging around the **Broomend of Crichie** symbol stone (Fig. 7.2), which then stood outside the henge to the east, proved inconclusive, but at the **Picardy Stone** (Fig. 7.2) he discovered that the stone stood upon a small cairn some 1.8m in diameter. About 1m from the south (symbol-bearing) side of the stone there was a pit measuring some 2.1m in length from east to west, though no human remains were identified in it (Stuart 1856, xxiv).

It is also clear that Neolithic and Bronze Age monuments sometimes acted as the foci for burials in the early medieval period. This is better known from English excavations, such as the cemetery at the site of the royal palace at Yeavering, Northumberland (Hope-Taylor 1977, 83–5, 108–6), or the late-7th- or 8th-century inhumations inserted into the nearby henge of Milfield South (Scull and Harding 1990). A Scottish example is provided by the small inhumation cemetery discovered in the henge monument at North Mains, in Perthshire (Barclay 1983, 145). The presence of a cemetery may also account for the finds made in the 19th century in a sand-pit close to a stone circle at Waulkmill, on Deeside

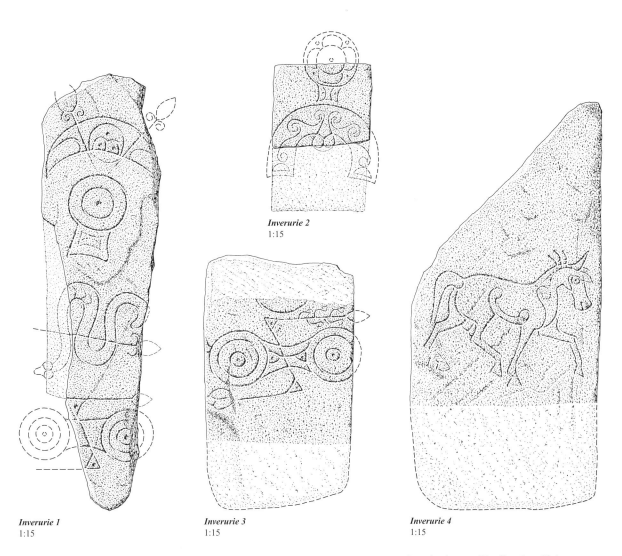

Inverurie 2
1:15

Inverurie 1
1:15

Inverurie 3
1:15

Inverurie 4
1:15

*Fig. 7.9 **Inverurie** (NJ 7802 2062). The symbols on these four stones from Inverurie include the mirror-case symbol, the double-disc and Z-rod, and the figure of a horse in motion. The stones are all said to have come from the foundations of the old church, and Nos 2 and 3 have both been trimmed into rectangular blocks. GV004146*

near Tarland. There a probable cist was found, along with a bronze cauldron, a silver penannular brooch, and glass and stone 'playing pieces', the finds albeit dating from the 1st and 2nd centuries AD, rather than later in the 1st millennium AD (Inglis 1987, 77).

Returning to **Rhynie**, the discovery of the human remains in the village group, coupled with the two possible square barrows to the south, points to the existence of a cemetery here, perhaps focused on the symbol stones. Including the two uninscribed stones to the north, the cemetery may have been strung out over at least 300m, possibly lining a recognised routeway along the strath (Fig. 7.7). For what it may be worth, a local tradition, recorded by the Ordnance Survey in 1866, told that the sculptured stones belonged to a line of standing stones extending from the pair at **Mill of Noth** to the **Craw Stane** (Name Book, Aberdeenshire No. 78, p. 146). No trace of a burial was discovered when the stone bearing the figure of

a man was ploughed up at Barflat, but if the cemetery extended as far as the **Craw Stane**, the graves were presumably on the terrace above the crest of the slope. However, the presence of the enclosure here raises another possibility, in which the **Craw Stane** and Barflat man were two of a series of emblems raised on the approaches to the entrance.

Leaving this last possibility to one side, several common strands can be identified in the findspots of Pictish symbol stones and the siting of barrow cemeteries. The latter often appear to occupy locally prominent positions with open outlooks, but include cemeteries such as Donaldstone's Haugh, Tillytarmont, which lies on haughland at the confluence of the Rivers Isla and Deveron. This position bears a striking similarity to the location in which the stones at **Inverurie** (Fig. 7.9) were found, both locations comprising a spur of haughland in the angle between two major rivers. It is also noticeable that many of the square barrows recorded on aerial photographs are set on gravel terraces close to burns and rivers, although this must be qualified, since these are locations favoured for the formation of cropmarks. The Red Castle cemetery, however, occupies a position overlooking the

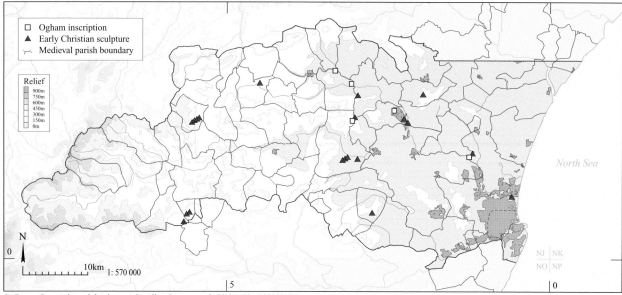

Fig. 7.10 Like the Class I stones, Early Christian sculpture and stones bearing ogham inscriptions are often sited close to watercourses and parish boundaries. GV000249

mouth of the Lunan Water on the Angus coast, and is thus at a major confluence. Attention has recently been drawn to the possible significance of these sorts of places, identified in the P-Celtic place-name element *aber*, 'confluence' or 'river-mouth', and it has been suggested they may have functioned as cult centres (Nicolaisen 1997). Here perhaps is one of the factors dictating the siting of Pictish symbol stones and cemeteries.

Red Castle, however, is far more than a confluence, for its position overlooking Lunan Bay places it at the boundary between the land and the sea. In this case, the boundary may have been between the realms of gods and men, but the landscape in which the symbol stones stood was almost certainly framed with boundaries too. Like so many of the parish and estate boundaries of the medieval period, these would not have been marked with banks and ditches, but rather by burns, rivers, and other distinctive natural features, supplemented by man-made reference points drawn from earlier ages. Herein lie other factors that may have driven the siting of symbol stones and cemeteries alike, mirroring the relationship between pagan burials and estate boundaries that has been observed in some parts of southern England (Bonney 1972, 171–2). Here too is an explanation of the role of some Neolithic and Bronze Age monuments in the distribution of the symbol stones, acting as visible reference points in the framework of the landscape. While the cemetery at **Rhynie** may have lined an important thoroughfare running up past the **Bell Knowe** cairn, equally the Water of Bogie to its east may have been a boundary. Like so many of the

other watercourses near the sites of symbol stones, this boundary is also one that is enshrined in the marches of a medieval parish.

Drawing links between the siting of symbol stones and cemeteries on the one hand, and boundaries and cult centres on the other, is certainly an attractive hypothesis. It is all the more so for the recurrent discoveries of symbol stones in or close to the sites of parish churches, and perhaps more specifically the incorporation of such stones into the very fabric of so many churches. Is this simply chance use or is it a deliberate act in the sanctification of pagan cemeteries and cult centres, involving not only the breaking and reshaping of the original stone, but also its subjection to Christian tradition? The incidence of Pictish stones discovered at the sites of parish churches in Aberdeenshire may not be as high as in neighbouring Moray (Alcock 1991, 9), but this provides a tentative route for the evolution of at least a few of the sites of local churches, some of which, like **Rhynie**, are situated adjacent to the parish boundary.

Christianity

The adoption of Christianity by the Picts, or at least by a powerful section of Pictish society, is amply borne out by spectacular cross-slabs combining Pictish symbols with crosses and other Christian iconography. The conversion of the Picts, however, was a long drawn-out process, perhaps beginning in the early 5th century and certainly not completed until at least the 8th century. The broad outline of events over this period is recorded by the Venerable Bede, writing in the early decades of the 8th century, but to what extent they relate to the conversion of the Picts living in what is now Aberdeenshire is far from clear. Here the evidence must be drawn from other sources, particularly the

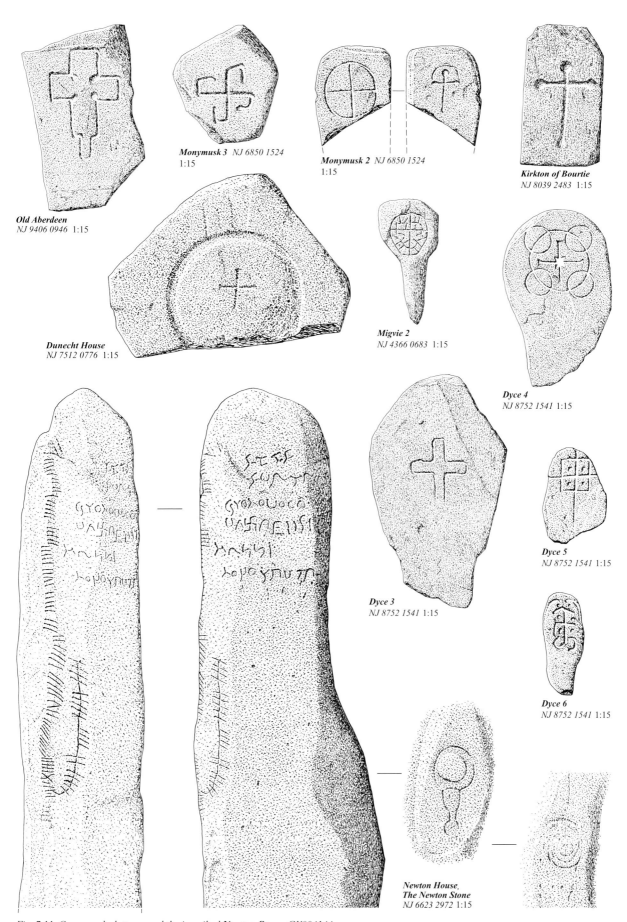

Old Aberdeen
NJ 9406 0946 1:15

Monymusk 3 *NJ 6850 1524*
1:15

Monymusk 2 *NJ 6850 1524*
1:15

Kirkton of Bourtie
NJ 8039 2483 1:15

Dunecht House
NJ 7512 0776 1:15

Migvie 2
NJ 4366 0683 1:15

Dyce 4
NJ 8752 1541 1:15

Dyce 3
NJ 8752 1541 1:15

Dyce 5
NJ 8752 1541 1:15

Dyce 6
NJ 8752 1541 1:15

Newton House,
The Newton Stone
NJ 6623 2972 1:15

Fig. 7.11 Cross-marked stones and the inscribed **Newton Stone**. *GV004144*

Fig. 7.12 **Migvie Church** *(NJ 4366 0682). The deeply inscribed cross on this Class II stone is accompanied by symbols in each quadrant: a double-disc and Z-rod (upper left); a horseshoe and V-rod (upper right); a pair of shears (lower left); and a mounted horseman (lower right). A second mounted horseman is carved in low relief on the reverse of the stone. SC627191*

stone monuments – symbol stones, Pictish cross-slabs, inscribed crosses and ogham inscriptions – and place-names (Fig. 7.10).

The conversion of the Picts, however, was bound up as much with intertribal politics as with any new religious belief, and it is probably this political dimension that explains some of the patterns evident in the distributions of the sculpture and the place-names. In north-east Scotland, for instance, the preponderance of Class I symbol stones to Class II cross-slabs is overwhelming – of sixty-four of the latter known

nationally, only seven fall within the modern bounds of Aberdeenshire Council – compared with the concentrations of Class II stones south of the Mounth. This hints at the political unity of this north-eastern province of Pictland, the contrast with neighbouring areas to the south and west placing geographical bounds on the manner in which the trappings of patronage were overtly displayed through Christian sculpture. This is not to say that the North-east was not exposed to the same Christian influences as its neighbours, for this same area contains a remarkable group of stones bearing ogham inscriptions, to say nothing of other cross-marked stones (Fig. 7.11).

The adoption of new religious practices is likely to have elicited complex responses from the more conservative sections of Pictish society. This in itself may explain the relatively sudden appearance of the symbol stones in the archaeological record, in effect a reaction to the threat posed by Christianity to traditional religious practices and their role in secular power (cf. Foster 1996, 78–9). A similar hypothesis has been advanced for the appearance of pagan barrow-cemeteries in southern England (Carver 1998). Like the symbol stones, the locations of the various Christian stones and place-names may also reveal something of the contemporary landscape within which they lay.

Four Class II cross-slabs have been recorded in the present survey, though one, at **Migvie Church** (Fig. 7.12), is in the Howe of Cromar, and more properly belongs in Deeside. Of the other three, the spectacularly carved **Maiden Stone** (Fig. 7.1) stands in isolation, and the slab now in the church at **Monymusk** was first reported in about 1800, lying in a field near the Don, about a mile east of Monymusk House (*NSA*, xii, Aberdeen, 463–64). The remaining cross-slab, which also bears an ogham inscription on its reverse, comes from **Dyce**, where there are not only a Class I symbol stone but also at least four cross-marked stones of various designs (Fig. 7.18). Eight other cross-marked stones have been recorded in Donside, including three from the parish church at **Monymusk**, but none of them is closely datable (Fig. 7.11).

The ogham inscription from **Dyce** is one of a small group of such inscriptions in north-eastern Scotland. Originally devised in Ireland in about the 5th century AD, and probably introduced into Scotland in the 7th century, ogham is a simple alphabet conveyed in short strokes cut to either side of a line. Reading the Scottish inscriptions poses many problems, though some record recognisable personal names (Forsyth 1997, 31–6). The **Dyce** ogham, which was discovered in the course of conservation work, is one of two that have come to light in the course of the survey. The other is on a boulder reported in 1994 in a forestry plantation near **Mains of Afforsk** (Fig. 7.13), and is an addition to the cluster of inscriptions known around the eastern end of

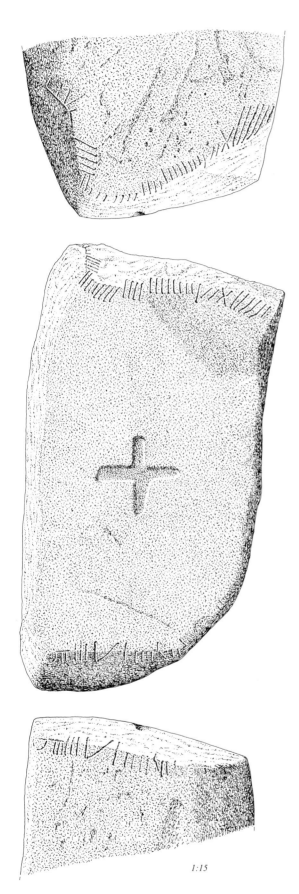

*Fig. 7.13 **Mains of Afforsk** (NJ 6956 2085). The topographical position of this cross-incised boulder with its two ogham inscriptions suggests that it was probably a boundary marker. GV004147*

1:15

the Bennachie range. The other inscriptions in this group comprise one of the three surviving symbol stones from **Moor of Carden** (Fig. 7.14), the symbol stone forming part of the **Brandsbutt** stone circle (Fig. 7.19), and the enigmatic **Newton Stone** (Fig. 7.11).

The **Mains of Afforsk** stone is unusual, for while the other inscriptions are on stones that have been set upright, in this case the unshaped boulder appears to be lying undisturbed, just off the crest of a ridge adjacent to what is probably a Bronze Age burial-cairn. Originally reported for the simple equal-armed sunken cross upon its upper surface and the notches of a possible inscription along one edge, closer examination of this granite block reveals that the notches belong to a much longer ogham inscription extending round the edges of the west face. Furthermore, a second inscription runs along the opposite edge of the upper surface. The inscriptions and the cross need not be contemporary, but both indicate creation in a Christian milieu.

Despite being hemmed in by the modern forestry plantation, the **Mains of Afforsk** stone lies in a striking topographical position, which appears to shed further light on the positioning of sculptured stone monuments in the early medieval landscape. The adjacent cairn lies on the crest of a low ridge that drops in a south-easterly direction from an outlier of Bennachie named Millstone Hill. The cairn must have formed an easily recognisable, if not prominent, landmark before it was subsumed into the plantation. As such, the juxtaposition of what is evidently a Christian carving with a much earlier monument recalls the relationship that has already been discussed with respect to some of the symbol stones. Potentially, the cairn is one of those earlier monuments that served as reference points in the framework of the early medieval landscape, placing the inscribed and cross-marked stone on or close to a boundary. While it cannot be shown that the stone itself was incorporated into any later boundary, this ridge evidently figures in subsequent divisions in the landscape. Several boundaries are documented in the vicinity, namely the medieval bounds of the lands of Monymusk, the late 18th-century march of the fermtoun of Deuchries, and the 19th-century parish boundary between Oyne and Chapel of Garioch.

At three other locations ogham inscriptions are applied to Class I symbol stones – **Brandsbutt**, **Moor of Carden** and the **Newton Stone** – though whether the ogham is applied to the symbol stone or *vice versa* cannot be demonstrated. More importantly, the identification of the **Mains of Afforsk** stone as a probable boundary marker raises the question of the function of these other inscriptions occurring on stones which, it has already been argued, probably lie close to boundaries. In the case of **Brandsbutt**, the stone also forms part of an earlier prehistoric monument. Possibly these three stones are simply witness to a process by which pagan monuments were sanctified, but it seems

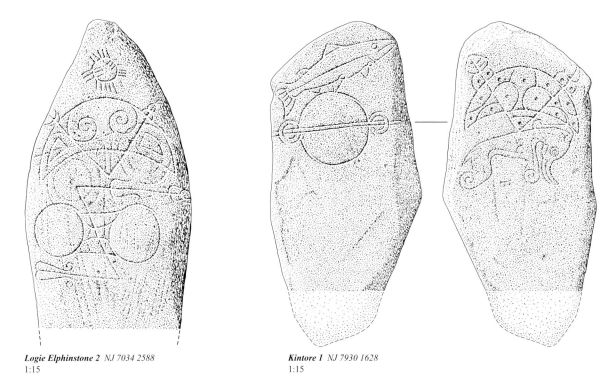

Logie Elphinstone 2 NJ 7034 2588
1:15

Kintore 1 NJ 7930 1628
1:15

Fig. 7.14 **Logie Elphinstone 2** *bears two sets of symbols, one superimposed upon the other, as well as a circular ogham inscription. The later set, a crescent and V-rod with a double-disc and Z-rod, is more sharply defined, cutting across a partly erased double-disc and Z-rod. The reinscription of other stones in Donside is recorded at* **Inverurie** *and* **Kintore***, and possibly accounts for the presence of symbols on both faces of* **Kintore I***. GV004141*

much more likely that the symbols and ogham inscriptions are essentially serving the same functions at specific locations in the landscape, locations lying at the edges of territories. While the stones visibly identify the presence of a boundary, the symbols and inscriptions – the latter probably naming individuals or groups – visually identify the territories. The addition of an ogham to an existing symbol stone possibly carries the same message as the addition of a fresh set of symbols, as seen at **Kintore**, **Inverurie** (Fig. 7.9 no. 1), and one of the **Moor of Carden** stones now at **Logie Elphinstone** (Fig. 7.14). This re-inscription is unlikely to be simple chance reuse, and is likely to have carried an important message, perhaps recording that the territory had changed hands. At both **Inverurie** and **Kintore**, however, the stone was turned upside down before its reinscription, possibly implying a more dramatic political statement.

The precise site at which the **Dyce** cross-slab with its ogham inscription stood is unknown, but the church itself is set on a terrace overlooking the Don, which here forms the parish boundary. As such, its location conforms to the patterns already outlined. In this case, however, the cross-slab forms part of a more varied collection of sculpture, including a symbol stone and several cross-marked stones (Fig. 7.18). While the primary function of the site here may have been as a

cemetery or cult centre at the edge of a territory, the range of sculpture appears to represent its transition into a Christian burial-ground. Neither of the other cross-slabs from Donside – the **Maiden Stone** and **Monymusk** – comes from a kirkyard, though both seem to have stood adjacent to well-defined natural features. The Monymusk stone is first recorded lying recumbent near the River Don, while the Maiden Stone stands on the leading edge of a terrace above a steep-sided den.

In addition to the **Mains of Afforsk** stone, there are several other cross-marked stones that may have been set up on boundaries. The possible stone now at **Dunecht House**, for instance, was found on the upper slopes of the Barmekin Hill in about 1840 (Fig. 7.11). This hill, crowned with its presumably Iron Age fort (p. 108), forms part of a prominent ridge extending from north to south over a distance of about 4km. As such the ridge is an obvious boundary in the landscape, though not one recognised in recorded boundaries, the old parish boundary lying at the western foot of the ridge. The stone from **Tofthills**, near Clatt, which is also cupmarked, may be another example, though there is some uncertainty as to the precise site of its discovery. When it was first noted, the stone was already at **Tofthills**, but it was supposed to have come from a prehistoric cairn or stone circle known as the *'sunken kirk'* (Ritchie 1910, 213). This has been completely removed now, but its site lies within 30m of a parish boundary, recalling those same ingredients that have already been cited in the discussion of the locations of symbol stones and ogham inscriptions – a prominent prehistoric monument, a natural boundary and a medieval parish boundary.

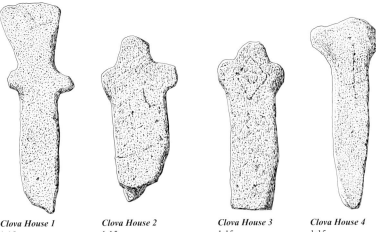

Clova House 1
1:15

Clova House 2
1:15

Clova House 3
1:15

Clova House 4
1:15

*Fig. 7.15 **St Luke's Chapel** (NJ 4557 2124). The four cross-shaped stones from St Luke's Chapel are now at Clova House. GV004143*

These stone monuments are only one of two principal strands of evidence for the introduction of Christianity into this part of north-eastern Scotland. The other strand is provided by place-names, which, at face value, point to locations that have been of some significance in the organisation of the ecclesiastical landscape. The place-name element *annait* has long been recognised as signifying a church of early date, although its precise significance has been the subject of debate (Watson 1926, 250; MacDonald 1973). A recent study has identified it as indicating a mother church, providing pastoral care for a secular estate, and therefore of some local significance (Clancy 1995, 114). Three such place-names occur within Donside, while two others – Andet, near Methlick, and Ennets, in Lumphanan parish – fall just outside. Two of those in Donside are current names in the valley of the Deskry Water, one being Ennot Hillocks beside the river, and the other the Burn of Badnahannet, one of its tributaries (Alexander 1952, 271). The location of the *annait* is presumably indicated by the farmsteads of **East** and **West Chapelton**, both now removed. The church or chapel itself had evidently disappeared by the early 19th century, when Laing refers to it as the former site of a Roman Catholic chapel (Laing 1828, 65). The Burn of Badaglerack (clump or hamlet of the clerics), another tributary nearby, either supports or draws upon this tradition. In addition to these current names, the obsolete *Anit Hill*, a shoulder of the Hill of Christ's Kirk, clearly refers to the former parish church of **Rathmuriel** at the foot of the slope below (NAS RHP 5199/3).

The use of *cill*, the most common word for a church in Ireland and the west of Scotland, is more problematic in Aberdeenshire. Its use as an active element in the creation of place-names has been attributed to the period between AD 550 and 900, prior to and overlapping with the absorption of Pictland by the Scots of Dalriada and the introduction of Gaelic into eastern Scotland. Thereafter, its use in the creation of place-names appears to have dwindled, and other

than a small group in Fife, is comparatively rare on the east coast (Nicolaisen 1976, 129–33; Taylor 1995, 10–13; 1996, 93–104). Suggested occurrences in Aberdeenshire include Kennethmont, early forms of which are recorded as *Kilalckmunith* and *Kelalcmund* (Robertson 1843, 625; Barrow 1973, 51), and Kilblean, in Meldrum parish (Watson 1926, 165, 273), but such names are not necessarily genuine examples of *cill*-names. The parish of Towie, for example, appears as *Kelbethok* in 1507, but in an earlier reference (*c.*1275) as *Kynbethok* (Innes 1845, ii, 52). Another example, *Kilwalauch*, now lost but apparently in the vicinity of Badenyon in Glenbuchat (Robertson and Grubb 1847–62, iv, 219), may incorporate the Gaelic *coille* 'wood' and *bealach* 'pass'. In this case, however, prior to gaining parochial status in the late 15th century, Glenbuchat formed a detached portion of the parish of Logie in Cromar, where the church was dedicated to St Wallach (Simpson 1942b, 9). Problems such as these have lead Taylor to cast doubt on the authenticity of all the examples in the North-east (1996, 95). Nevertheless, some of the identifications are reasonably convincing, including the lost *Kilmaclome* in the parish of Fyvie (Barrow 1973, 61; Robertson 1843, 246).

A third group of names possibly indicating the sites of churches are those including the element *eccles*, ultimately drawn from the Latin *ecclesia*. These names, which occur widely throughout England, are scattered across southern Scotland and up the east coast to Aberdeenshire, where a single example occurs in Donside. Professor Barrow has argued that the adoption of *eccles* as a P-Celtic word for church must be attributable to the period between the conversion to Christianity and the take-over by Q-Celtic and Germanic speakers. The *eccles* names in Pictland south of the Mounth are thus placed in the period between AD 450 and 800 (Barrow 1983, 6). The sole occurrence of this P-Celtic form north of the Mounth is *Eglismenythok*, a property recorded in 1210 as associated with the monastery of **Monymusk** (Macpherson 1895, 94; Barrow 1983, 8). This later appears as *Abersnithock*, and is now **Braehead** (Alexander 1952, 136). Intriguingly, the grass-grown remains of a small church or chapel of probable medieval date overlook the River Don nearby.

In addition to the place-names, several elements of the ecclesiastical organisation documented in 12th-century and later sources provide glimpses of earlier arrangements, though when they were first established is unknown. The principal of these are minsters – churches with dependent lands and chapels – but they also include a community of *Celi De* or Culdees at **Monymusk**. The latter is first documented in the early 12th century and may have survived until 1245, when a house of Augustinian canons was established there (Simpson 1925; Cowan and Easson 1976, 51, 93–4). This may account for the group of three cross-marked stones recorded at **Monymusk**, though one of these is now lost (Fig. 7.11).

The sole minster documented in Donside is at **Clova**, identified in 1157 as the *monasterium de Cloveth*, at which time it was confirmed to the bishop of Aberdeen, apparently as one of five churches belonging to the *monasterium de murthillach*, now known as Mortlach (Cowan and Easson 1976, 51). This in itself implies some form of hierarchical structure in the early organisation of the church in Aberdeenshire. In later documentation Clova also appears as Cabrach or Strathdeveron, indicating that its *parochia* crossed the watershed between the Don and the Deveron. Two of its dependent chapels serving this huge area presumably lay at Cabrach and Strathdeveron, both of which were later to be erected as parish churches in their own right, possibly in a reorganisation of 1362/3, when Clova was united to Kildrummy. The location of the *monasterium* may be marked by the grass-grown foundations of **St Luke's Chapel**. Lying on the lands of Littlemill, these are probably of late medieval date, but the four cross-shaped stones now at Clova House were found here (Fig. 7.15).

Although **Clova** is the only documented minster, what may be a second example can be identified at **Kinkell**, which in the 15th century had six dependent chapels (Cowan and Easson 1976, 52). These were at **Dyce**, **Kinellar**, **Kintore**, **Kemnay**, **Skene** and Drumblade, and all became parish churches. With the exception of Drumblade, these *parochia* also made up the lands of the secular estates that appear in the documentary record as the thanage of Kintore. As we have seen, a Class I symbol stone, a Class II cross-slab bearing an ogham inscription, and at least four cross-marked stones have been found at **Dyce**, while symbol stones have also been found at **Kinellar** and **Kintore**. Such discoveries may be no more than coincidence, but they hint that substantial components of the early medieval landscape have been passed down in the ecclesiastical organisation documented in medieval sources (see below).

Place-names and the Pattern of Settlement

While elements in the division of the early medieval landscape can be detected in the various strands of evidence that have been discussed so far (see above), little of it illuminates the pattern of settlement and land-use. Nor is there any archaeological evidence north of the Mounth to fill this gap, though excavation has revealed that a number of fortified promontories along the southern shore of the Moray Firth – Burghead, Green Castle at Portknockie, and Cullykhan, Troup – were occupied at this time (Ralston 1987; 2004). Place-name studies, however, most notably by Watson (1926) at the beginning of the last century and more recently by Nicolaisen (1976), have shown that the names of many farms and villages in eastern Scotland may have evolved during this period, albeit mainly towards its very end. In eastern Scotland two languages – P-Celtic Pictish and Q-Celtic Gaelic – were active in the creation and development of place-names, Q-Celtic gradually replacing P-Celtic from perhaps the middle of the 9th century.

As might be expected, relatively few names containing P-Celtic elements survive in comparison to those of Q-Celtic origin. The largest group comprises those prefixed with *pit-*, a cognate of the Welsh *peth*, 'thing', and Breton *pez*, 'piece', meaning a 'portion' of land or an 'estate' (Watson 1926, 408; Nicolaisen 1976, 151–8), but there is also a small group of names that refer more specifically to features in the landscape. The word *tref-*, for instance, meaning 'homestead', is combined with a Gaelic first element in the place-names Clinterty and Fintray (Nicolaisen 1976, 169–70). What may be another example of a *tref*-name is the obsolete *Trenechinen*, in the vicinity of Bograxie, which appears in a medieval account of the bounds of the lands of Monymusk and Keig (Low 1866, 222; Robertson 1843, 171; Alexander 1952, 403). This last would be unusual, however, examples of *tref* as a first element otherwise occurring exclusively in southern Scotland (Nicolaisen 1976, 170). Other names include elements referring to woodland, such as the Moor of Carden, which preserves a P-Celtic word cognate with the Welsh *cardden*, 'thicket'.

Of the small group of place-names that have been identified as P-Celtic in origin, the most studied, and the most important for our purposes here, are the *pit*-names, the vast majority of which occur in the eastern lowlands of Scotland, from the Firth of Forth to the margins of Sutherland. The distribution is not exclusive to the lowlands, however, and they are also found scattered in the adjacent highlands, with conspicuous concentrations occurring along the Tay, the Garry, and the Spey.

It has long been recognised that most of the farms and settlements that currently bear *pit*-names occur

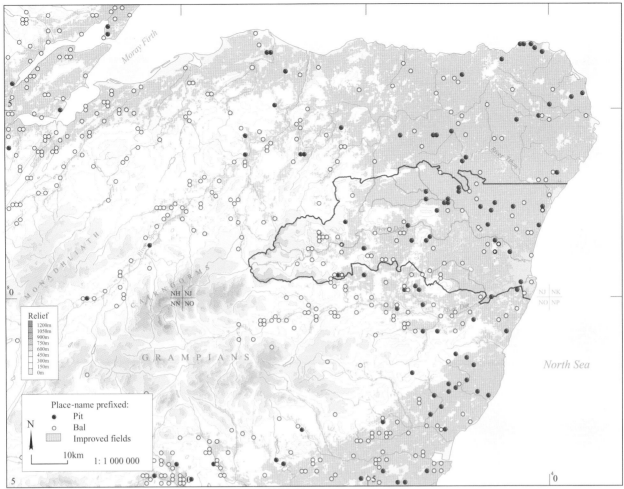

Fig. 7.16 This map shows the distribution of place-names prefixed 'Pit-' and 'Bal-' in north-eastern Scotland. GV000244

on the better agricultural land (Watson 1926, 407). More recent studies tend to confirm this observation (Whittington and Soulsby 1968; Whittington 1975; Fraser 1998), showing that by far the majority lie on the best soils, in well-sheltered and well-drained locations. Donside is no exception to this pattern, the lowest examples occurring at about 30m OD at Pitscaff and Pitmillan in the coastal parish of Foveran, and the highest at 280m at Pitcandlich in Towie parish in the upper valley of the Don. The great majority, however, fall below 200m, and lie within the lowland portion of the survey area. All are on land that has been cultivated since the improvements, and their outlook is overwhelmingly open, or southern, although a few face east.

The precise significance of the *pit*-names has precipitated intense argument, as has the chronology of their formation. Although the prefix *pit-* is P-Celtic, in the majority of cases the qualifying suffix is Q-Celtic, and the name thus belongs to the period after the takeover of the Pictish kingdom. Nicolaisen proposed that such hybrids were coined during a period of Picto-Gaelic bilingualism that followed in its wake (1976,

156), but Taylor has suggested that in Fife the *pit-* prefix continued to function as an appelative until the very end of the Gaelic-speaking period (Taylor 1994, 3). If so, the use of these names to study early medieval settlement patterns is seriously undermined. Nevertheless, there is no question that the *pit-* element is P-Celtic. After all, this is what has lead scholars to focus on the process of formation and subsequent evolution, rather than concentrating on the mechanisms that have lead to the conservation and survival of an archaic term in the way that is postulated in Fife. This mechanism is evidently crucial to any interpretation of the role of these names in the landscape. The relationship to good agricultural land, for instance, is not that this land was favoured in the creation of estates bearing *pit*-names, thus identifying land preferred by the Picts, but that the mechanism that conserved these names in use was one generally confined to good agricultural land.

The most likely route for the continuing use of the *pit-* prefix lies in the character of the estate administration where they survived from the takeover of Pictland until the 12th century. Rather than substituting a Q-Celtic equivalent, usually considered to be *bal-* (see below), these estates appear to have retained the *pit-* terminology in the vocabulary of their administration

131

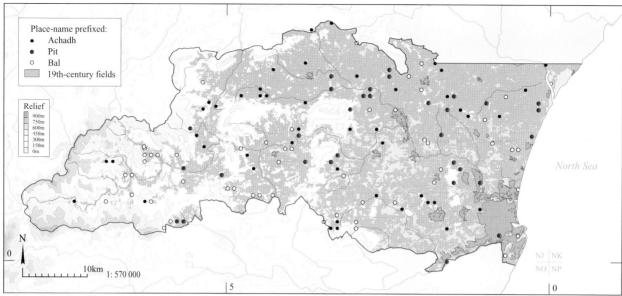

Fig. 7.17 This map shows the distribution of place-names prefixed 'Pit-', 'Bal-' and 'Achadh-'. The greater majority of these fall below 200m OD, with a marked preference for open south-facing locations. GV000246

long after P-Celtic had been more generally supplanted by Q-Celtic. Thus, the *pit*-names are a manifestation of a conservative administration, and it is this that is related to the best agricultural land. At present it is not possible to identify the reasons for this conservatism with confidence, but it is noticeable that in Donside a significant proportion of these names is concentrated on what were royal estates. Some of the concentrations recorded elsewhere are also on royal lands, while others are on estates in the hands of the church, as witnessed by Dunfermline in Fife, and Abernethy in Perth & Kinross (Barrow 1973, 34, 42). The clustering of *pit*-names on such estates may well indicate the most likely forces involved – the crown and the church – at the end of the early medieval period.

If this is correct, the *pit*-names may yet reveal aspects of early medieval estate structure. Of particular note are those that imply a sub-division of a larger administrative unit, seen within Donside in names such as *Pitmeadhon*, 'the middle pit', a name which occurs in the parishes of Dyce, Oyne and Udny. Equally, the absence of the *pit*- prefix from any medieval parish name has led to the suggestion that some of the parishes of the subsequent ecclesiastical structure may embody examples of these larger administrative units (Cowan 1967, 164; Barrow 1973, 59–60). A number of such units also emerge in later records as thanages or shires, which Barrow has identified as survivals of a type of early medieval territorial unit known as a multiple estate. He suggested that the *pit*-names identified some of the component elements of these multiple estates (Barrow 1973, 64–8). Donside contains three recorded thanages, one of which, Kintore, is of particular interest for the hints

of its structure contained in later documentation. With the exception of the parish of Drumblade, the marches of Kintore appear to be those of the postulated minster based on Kinkell, with its dependent chapels (p. 145). Both lines of argument point to the origin of this thanage as a single large territorial unit divided into six 'parish-sized' estates, each of these subdivided yet again into the units represented by the *pit*-names.

From about the mid-9th century Gaelic names were being coined across eastern Scotland, the most numerous relating to settlement being those prefixed with *bal*-, a contraction of *baile*, meaning 'town' or 'farm'. These are common throughout north-east Scotland, appearing in some numbers in the upper reaches of the Don, and also in neighbouring Deeside. To a certain extent *bal*- was probably interchangeable with *pit*-, and several cases are known in which a *pit*-name has been replaced by a *bal*-name, or in which the two forms appear to have coexisted for a considerable period. Pitgersie, in the parish of Foveran, for instance, variously appears on record between 1514 and 1815 as *Ballgirschaw*, *Petgeirscho*, *Balgeirso* and *Pitgerso* (Alexander 1952, 102). With the late survival of the Gaelic language in some of the highland areas of Aberdeenshire, *bal*- continued as an active element of place-name formation, possibly accounting for the dense concentration of *bal*-names in the upper Don and Deeside (Fraser 1998).

A second Gaelic element in place-names that relates to settlement is the word *achadh*, meaning 'field'. The distribution of these names slightly expands upon both the national and local distributions of *baile*, and they are thought to denote secondary settlements, usually lying in less fertile, upland areas (Nicolaisen 1976, 127, 141; Fraser 1986, 27). The name also occurs frequently throughout the lowlands of Aberdeenshire, notably in Buchan, where it may indeed reflect less favourable conditions on poorer soils (Fraser 1998).

In the course of the survey the topographical positions in which *pit-*, *bal-* and *achadh* names are found within Donside have been analysed. Some 83% of the *pit-*names lie below 200m OD, compared with 60% of the *bal-*names and 74% of *achadhs*. The disparity between the *pit-* and *bal-*names is largely accounted for by the preponderance of the latter in the upper reaches of the valley. Within the lowland area there is little to distinguish the locations of the *bal-*names from those of the *pit-*names. Most of the farms now bearing these names apparently occupy a similar range of open or southerly-facing positions. Many of the names incorporating *achadh* are in similar positions, but others occupy what are evidently less favourable spots. In the parish of Midmar, for instance, Auchorrie, Auchintoul and Auchmore all lie in an area of exposed and broken terrain at the foot of the northern slopes of the Hill of Fare. In the parish of Kinellar, Aquhorsk and Auchronie occupy sites on north-east facing slopes. In the upland areas the *bal-*names are more numerous than *achadh* names, but even here both tend to occupy similar positions, though in some cases, notably in the parish of Strathdon, *achadh* names do seem to fall in more marginal locations. To this extent, the most marginal locations occupied by any of these three types of name are *achadh* names. Auchernach, for instance, lies at 390m on a steep south-east-facing slope, while Aldachie (Alexander 1952; *allt achaidh*, meaning burn of the field) is situated at 340m on another steeply sloping site. Several *bal-*names occur at similar altitudes, but while Auchernach and Aldachie are tucked up narrow side-glens and are now forested, these others are still working farms, lying at the boundary between cultivated ground and rough grazing.

There is, of course, no way of demonstrating when the majority of these names came into existence. The first mention of a name often dates from after 1500, and in some cases the sole record may be on the 1st editions of OS maps. In areas where Gaelic continued in use, such as the upper Don and Deeside, some of the names may be comparatively recent creations. Nevertheless, the approach that has been employed in the course of this survey shows that *pit-* and *bal-* names tend to occupy the most favourable locations available. Thus, even in the more confined valleys in the upper reaches of the Don, the *bal-*names occupy the prime sites with access to a good range of natural resources. In this respect their claim to antiquity is as good as any farm bearing a *pit-*name. Despite the absence of *pit-*names and Pictish symbol stones from the uppermost part of the Don, this area was probably occupied from at least the late Iron Age. Not only are Iron Age settlements with souterrains found in the vicinity of Strathdon itself, but a pollen diagram from Edinglassie reveals an open landscape which was continuously farmed throughout the 1st millennium AD (see p. 41).

The Wider Landscape

Despite the general silence in contemporary texts about events in this north-eastern corner of Scotland, Aberdeenshire has much to offer the student of Pictland, and the distribution of carved stone monuments alone hints at the political integrity and independence of the area from its immediate neighbours. As such, it may not in itself have been the seat of power north of the Mounth, but as a province it had its place in the structure of that power.

Perhaps the most striking result of the analysis of the monuments in Donside, is that they all relate to the landscape and its organisation. In some respects, this simply reflects the objectives of the survey, to record the landscape, but the primary role of the sculptured stones was to communicate with people in their contemporary landscape. The landscape was the arena in which they were erected, and should therefore provide the main framework for their study. By taking this approach, common strands can be detected in the way in which the various categories of stone monuments – Class I symbol stones, ogham inscriptions, and Class II cross-slabs – were being used. Rather than intellectual puzzles marking the boundaries of modern expertise and knowledge, these are the identifiers of territory in the landscape.

The *caputs* of these territories, and indeed the remains of any settlements, continue to elude us, but there can be little doubt of their existence, nor of the social status of some of their occupants. Two massive silver chains that have been found within the area, one in **Nigg** parish, the other near **Parkhill**, in the parish of New Machar, are thought to have conferred the status of their owners. The first is plain, composed of a silver-bronze alloy, but the **Parkhill** chain, which has twenty-three double links, has a penannular terminal ring engraved with the 'S' symbol. Unfortunately little is known of the circumstances of these discoveries, though many such items appear to have been deposited as offerings to the gods.

While the stone monuments and these chains represent the tangible evidence of the Picts, the other forms of evidence are more esoteric, drawn from later documentary sources. But these too point to the structure of the landscape. The place-names, for instance, are not referring to places as such, but to units of land, units furthermore that are implicitly components of larger territories. The ecclesiastical structure is also bound up with land, the confirmation of the minster at **Clova** to the bishops of Aberdeen again revealing the presence of some hierarchical structure.

The problem facing historians and archaeologists alike is to show how these various strands are woven together. In southern Pictland the later organisation of secular estates and ecclesiastical parishes has provided historians with a tool to explore the structure of the early medieval landscape (Barrow 1973, 7–68; Rogers 1992), though

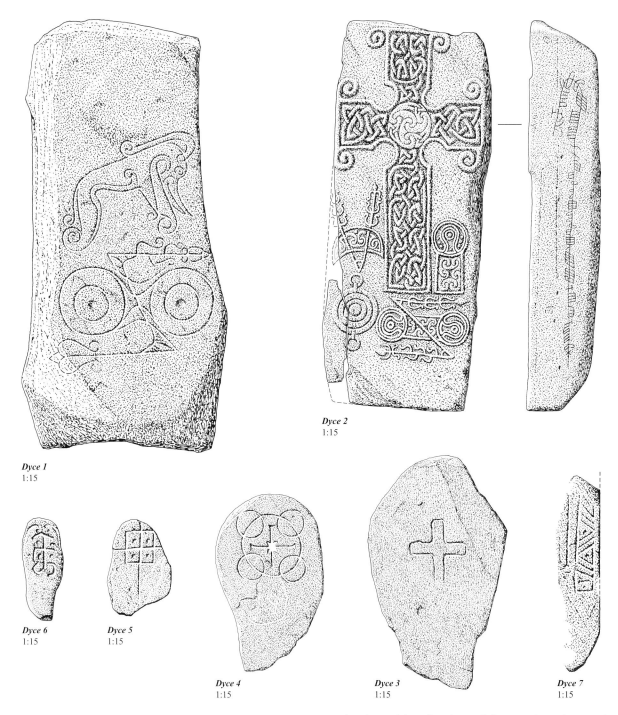

Dyce 1
1:15

Dyce 2
1:15

Dyce 6
1:15

Dyce 5
1:15

Dyce 4
1:15

Dyce 3
1:15

Dyce 7
1:15

Fig. 7.18 **Dyce** *(NJ 8752 1541). The collection of sculptured stones from this churchyard includes a Class I stone bearing a Pictish beast above a double-disc and Z-rod, a Class II cross-slab with symbols and an ogham inscription, and four small stones bearing crosses. GV004145*

attempts to manifest this in archaeological evidence are rather less convincing (see Driscoll 1987; Driscoll 1991, 91–109). Much of this work has focused on the origin of thanages (Barrow 1973), a source of information that is also available further north. Of six thanages recorded in Aberdeenshire, three lie in Donside – Kintore, Aberdeen and Belhelvie – and one of them, Kintore, contains a range of evidence comparable to any cited from southern Pictland. The division of its lands between

the six parishes that formed the putative minster of Kinkell probably reveals the major estates of which it was composed, the *pit*-names a tier of smaller estates below them.

This sort of evidence is by no means limited to Kintore. A grant between 1172 and 1185 of an estate forming the greater part of the parish of Leslie, for example, came with rights more normally associated with thanes (pp. 145–6). It was also one of at least six parishes – Culsalmond, Insch, Rathmuriel, Kennethmont, Leslie and Premnay – that made up *Garviach*, a discrete unit of the lordship of Garioch granted to Earl David of Huntingdon (p. 140), and one of a similar size to the thanage of Kintore. As we have seen, the church of **Rathmuriel** is apparently associated with an *annait* place-name (p. 129), signifying a mother church. **Rathmuriel**, perhaps, held the same relationship to *Garviach* as **Kinkell** to the thanage of Kintore, though there is no evidence here that the churches in the other parishes of *Garviach* originate as dependent chapels. Another large block comparable to Kintore can be detected in the parish boundaries of Invernochty and the detached portions of Tarland, Logie Mar, Migvie and Coldstone. One of these detached portions, Glen Ernan, is recorded as a *dabhach*; another, Glen Buchat, was eventually erected as an independent parish (p. 144), and there can be little doubt that these subdivisions reflect a tier of lesser holdings in a large territory taking in the headwaters of the Don. Here too there are two *annait* place-names close to the 19th-century farms of **East** and **West Chapelton** in the Deskry Water.

Seeking the origin of ecclesiastical parishes and their boundaries in secular estates is fundamental to this case, though demonstrating the antiquity of these units is nigh impossible. The Garioch, however, may prove the exception, for if the Pictish symbol stones are placed on or close to territorial boundaries, then their recurring juxtaposition to parish boundaries suggests that at least some sectors of these marches served the same purpose in the structure of the Pictish landscape. The utilisation of prehistoric monuments in the identification of these marches also provides an explanation of the apparent attraction of early medieval activity to such monuments that has been noted elsewhere.

A further link between the division into parishes and the structure of the Pictish landscape is provided by the incidence of symbol stones from kirkyards, which is surely greater than can be attributed to mere chance. The evidence from Donside hints at an evolutionary path in which the siting of a Pictish cemetery or cult centre at the edge of a territory is ultimately preserved in the location of the parish church, thus placing it to the periphery of the parish and not its centre. At **Dyce**, for instance, one of the components of the thanage of Kintore, the site of the kirkyard at the head of the brae overlooking the Don, is first marked by a Class I symbol stone, and subsequently reaffirmed with the Class II cross-slab with its ogham, at least four cross-marked stones, and finally by a medieval parish church. Assuming that each estate had no more than one cult centre and one cemetery, then the disposition of the stones may also indicate the division of parish-sized units into smaller estates. The parish of Inverurie, for instance, not only yields a clutch of stones from the site of the 12th-century church, but also a single stone from the **Brandsbutt** stone circle, 2.7km to the north-west, and another at the farmsteading of **Drimmies**, a further 2km north-west on the parish's northern boundary.

Despite the uncertainties posed by this sort of evidence, it is difficult to escape the conclusion that the

Fig. 7.19 **Brandsbutt** *(NJ 7599 2240). The ogham inscription on this shattered stone occurs on a face bearing a crescent and V-rod incised above a serpent and Z-rod. The stone originally belonged to a stone circle but was broken up in the 19th century. SC336079*

structure of Donside in the 12th century is deeply rooted in the Pictish landscape. This would repay a systematic examination, including not only the parishes and place-names, but also the units of land known as *dabhachs*, which have not been dealt with here (p. 183). As far as can be seen, however, the evidence drawn from later documentary sources and place-names indicates that this landscape was divided into a hierarchy of estates and territorial units, which ultimately sustained the identity of the province of *Ce*. The distribution of symbol stones probably played a direct role in this structure, both marking and identifying some of the component estates along the course of the lower Don, the Urie, the Gadie, the Shevock and the upper end of Strathbogie. But the concentration in the Garioch also highlights the relative dearth of stones in neighbouring Buchan and Mar.

Buchan lies well outside the area dealt with by the survey, but the whole of the upper Don lies within Mar. The Class I sculpture is not the only form of evidence that is thinly spread in Mar, for the *pit-* place-names are equally sparse, whereas the *bal-*names are notable for their concentration in the upper Don and the Dee (Fig. 7.16). Many of the latter may have been substituted for *pit-*names, but the general absence of Class I sculpture from the upper Don is unlikely to be simply an accident of survival and discovery. An alternative is that the contrasting distributions imply differences in tradition or land tenure that are more deeply rooted, perhaps indicating that the tract of lands held by the crown in the 12th century from the upper Garioch down to Aberdeen (Fig. 8.3) had much earlier origins as a discrete entity. If this is the case, these distributions are not only mapping out elements in the lower tiers of estate organisation in the landscape, but also the major units that made up the province of *Ce*.

Chapter 8: The Medieval and Later Landscape

Piers Dixon and Iain Fraser

Donside is dominated to this day by relics of its medieval landscape. The dramatic silhouette of the castle on **Dunnideer**, for example, presides over the Garioch, while the seat of royal power at Inverurie is manifested in the great mound of the **Bass of Inverurie** behind the modern centre of the town. Save for a scatter of castles and ruined churches, however, the character of medieval settlement and land-use can only be pieced together from documentary sources, and it is not until the 18th century that visible settlement remains survive in any numbers.

The earliest documentary records are limited and mainly comprise land grants to the bishop of Aberdeen (Innes 1845) or to reformed monasteries, such as Lindores Abbey, Fife (Dowden 1903). From the 14th century onwards, however, the number and variety of records increases. Of particular value are royal muniments, such as the Exchequer Rolls and the Register of the Great Seal. From the 15th century this range widens further still, with increasing numbers of estate documents, many of them gathered into the *Collections for a history of the shires of Aberdeen and Banff* and *Illustrations of the topography and antiquities of the shires of Aberdeen and Banff* (Robertson 1843; Robertson and Grubb 1847–62). Yet it is not until the 17th century that a complete pattern of settlement can be reconstructed, based firstly upon early maps, such as those of Robert Gordon (*c.*1636–52, NLS Gordon MS 27 & 32), and secondly on the Poll Tax returns of 1696 (Stuart 1844). From the 17th century information on land-use and settlement also proliferates with the expansion of estate records.

Come the end of the 18th century the *Statistical Account* (*Stat. Acct.,* 1791–9) provides commentaries for every parish, and its successor, *The New Statistical Account* (*NSA,* xii, Aberdeenshire, 1845), charts the changes in the countryside over the intervening thirty years or so. Thereafter, the 1st and 2nd editions of the OS 6-inch map (Aberdeenshire 1864–71; 1899–1901) preserve a remarkable record of the continuing evolution of the landscape.

With such a large survey area, it is impractical to examine all of this later documentation. Thus, while examples for the period between the 12th and the 17th century have been drawn from throughout Donside, the discussion of the changes thereafter is more selective, focusing not only on the published material for Monymusk estate (Hamilton 1945; 1946) but also on the documentary archives for Glen Ernan, a side glen at the top of the Don, as well as the parish of Rhynie at the top of Strathbogie (Harrison 2001a; 2001b).

The principal monuments dating from the beginning of the period are the earthworks of the timber castles and the burial-grounds of the parish churches. Though few of the churches themselves survive, these and the parochial structure provide some of the framework of the estates recorded in the earliest land grants. The earthwork castles found at the most important estate centres were the seats of the nobility, marking a new departure in military architecture, introduced with the influx of Anglo-Continental adventurers in the wake of King David's accession to the throne in 1124. From as early as the 13th century, however, stone-built tower-houses or keeps began to appear, built by the new baronial class that Robert I created with the grants of free barony in the aftermath of the Wars of Independence (Grant 1996, 201–3).

Donside contains a remarkable series of tower-houses, many of which are incorporated into mansion houses. Despite their importance as architectural monuments, these spectacular buildings have largely fallen outside the scope of this survey, which has necessarily focused on an archaeological and topographical approach to the estate centres that they represent. That said, several ruined towers have been recorded in detail, and these serve as a mirror

Fig. 8.1 **Dunnideer** *(NJ 6124 2815). Crowning the summit of this prominent conical hill, the castle commands the countryside around the village of Insch. SC970317*

to the changing architectural requirements of the late medieval nobility, from the grim defensive qualities of **Hallforest** to the Renaissance influence in the more comfortable and decorative establishments at **Esslemont** and **Balquhain**. The wider community of standing medieval structures in Aberdeenshire has been exhaustively discussed elsewhere (e.g. Leith-Hay 1849; MacGibbon and Ross 1887–92; Cruden 1960; Slade 1967; 1978; 1982; 1985; Fawcett 1994; Howard 1995; McKean 2001).

Beyond the formal monuments that identify the centres of power and influence in the landscape, the main thrust of the survey has concentrated on the visible deserted rural settlements and land-use remains. These are largely confined to the upper margins of the highland glens, where the progressive retreat from the high point of post-medieval settlement in the late 18th century can be traced in the ruined townships and farmsteads that lie scattered across the landscape. These, however, are but a handful in comparison with the numbers that have been lost. Of the 2300 deserted rural settlement sites

that have been identified in the course of the survey, over half have been destroyed by modern changes in land-use and leave no visible trace. In practice, far more have been lost, for the majority of pre-improvement settlements included in this total come from a limited number of estate maps, mainly covering the parishes of Rhynie, Clatt, Kennethmont and Leslie. Equivalent maps elsewhere would reveal a similar mass of pre-improvement settlements. Indeed, the Poll Tax returns of 1696 contain hundreds of such sites throughout the lowlands (Fig. 8.61). For the purposes of the survey, these have only been employed to reveal the broad character of the settlement pattern throughout Donside at the end of the 17th century.

With the agricultural improvements, two main phases of settlement change can be detected. In the first, there were many changes in the overall pattern of settlement and land-use, including the replacement of pre-improvement *touns* with improved steadings, the final collapse of the shieling system, the complete loss of many dependent crofts, and the creation of a rash of new crofts as independent holdings on marginal land. In the second, there was widespread abandonment of the new crofts, and indeed of many improved steadings. The cottages on the crofts represent about 65% of the abandoned sites that have been recorded (Fig. 8.86), and many of the rest are improved farmsteads. In overall terms, some 80% of the settlement remains that have been recorded originate in the agricultural improvements of the early 19th century and are depicted as roofed or unroofed buildings on the 1st or 2nd edition of the OS 6-inch maps.

Most of the remainder are likely to be earlier, pre-dating the agricultural improvements, and mainly lie in the upland-edge parishes of Strathdon, Logie-Coldstone, Glenbuchat, Kildrummy, Auchindoir, Towie and Rhynie. Relatively few are pre-improvement touns, which in itself is an indication of the sweeping extent of the reforms that occurred during the 19th century, but numerous shieling groups have been identified in the upper reaches of the side glens. These were finally abandoned in the late 18th century, but there are numerous other single huts and small buildings scattered in the same areas, their functions probably ranging from illicit stills to shepherds' and cattle herders' bothies, or foresters' lodges.

The contents of this chapter follow the broad outline presented above. The first sections deal with the structure of the medieval landscape revealed by documentary sources, and include the castles, towers and churches that are found within it. In the earliest stages at least, the pattern of lordship and the organisation of the church were indivisible. Thus, the parochial structure is dealt with as part of the discussion of the 12th- and 13th-century estates, while the churches and chapels are treated as monuments of lordship. The twin strands of church and state provide the broad framework for the collage of pastoral and temporal interests that made up the medieval landscape. The later sections detail the available evidence for settlement and land-use. This is divided fairly strictly between the evolution of the settlement pattern revealed in documentary sources since the 12th century, the archaeology of the settlements that have survived, and the transformation of the landscape that has taken place from the late medieval period to the present day.

The Medieval Lordships

The **Bass of Inverurie** (Fig. 8.2) is a potent monument to the civil and military power of medieval lordship, but it is also a manifestation of royal power in the landscape, as successive Scottish kings in the 12th century strove to extend and strengthen their authority. Under David I and his successors, a raft of innovations and reforms were introduced in southern Scotland, including feudal tenure, the intensive settlement of loyal Anglo-French, the introduction of new religious orders, and the establishment of the parish system. For much of the 12th and early 13th century royal policy in the north was in part dictated by the hostile reaction to this process, mainly emanating from the province of Moray. Despite the defeat of its last *mormaer*, Angus, at Stracathro in 1130, Moray repeatedly rebelled against David's successors (Barrow 1975). Set against this background, the royal lands in the Garioch were of immense strategic importance, straddling a major routeway to the troublesome north, and forming a corridor of economically valuable land between the two other powerful and unpredictable appanages of the North-east, the earldoms of Mar and Buchan.

Royal Lands and the Garioch

Holdings of royal demesne in central Aberdeenshire were extensive (Fig. 8.3; Barrow 1960, 43). Royal thanages are recorded in the 13th century at Aberdeen, Kintore and Belhelvie, but these appear to have formed part of a much larger tract of royal lands between Aberdeen and Strathbogie (Grant 1993, 46). Their original extent may later have been perpetuated in the bounds of the 13th-century deanery of the Garioch, which encompassed a much more extensive area between Dyce and Drumblade than the lordship of Garioch itself (Stringer 1985, 65–6). In addition to these lands in Donside, there were royal thanages at Fyvie on the River Ythan, and at Aboyne and Kincardine O'Neil in Deeside (Grant 1993, 74).

These lands provided a base from which royal influence could be promoted and exercised in the North-east. As an agency of royal policy, the church was a particular beneficiary, and in 1157 the bishop of Aberdeen received confirmation from Pope Adrian of extensive lands and revenues, including the *vills* and

Fig. 8.2 **Bass of Inverurie** *(NJ 7809 2059). Now lying within the cemetery on the outskirts of the town, this important motte-and-bailey castle stands at the confluence of the Rivers Don and Urie. SC976848*

churches of Rayne, Clatt, Tullynessle and Fetternear, and the churches of Daviot and Auchterless (Innes 1845, i, 5–7). The early charters of Aberdeen Cathedral were unfortunately lost, but a 14th-century cleric attempted to supply the deficiency, forging grants and confirmations by David I and Malcolm IV. For all their spurious nature, these forged charters may represent contemporary belief in the identity of the Cathedral's benefactor (Barrow 1960, 43). That the endowments listed in the Papal Bull of 1157 include the church of what later appears as the royal thanage of Belhelvie and the royal tenth from the burgh of Aberdeen, confirms the Crown's interest in the Cathedral (Innes 1845, i, 6; Grant 1993, 74).

The lands and rights of a number of other religious corporations also point to royal patronage in the area. The bishop of St Andrews held the lands of Monymusk and Keig, other lands in Kinkell and Dyce, and rights to *cain* from Monkegie, Culsalmond, Echt and Muchall (Cluny) (Robertson 1843, 171–2, 178–9; Dowden 1903, 10–11; Ash 1976, 108). The Knights Templar, who are believed to have been introduced to Scotland by David I, are later found holding land in Rayne, one of the bishop of Aberdeen's shires, which is again strongly suggestive of this royal patronage (Robertson and Grubb 1847–62, iii, 435–8).

Although David I and Malcolm utilised the resources of the Garioch, it was only under William the Lion that the lordship was consolidated as a northern bastion of royal authority with the grant of the lordship of Garioch to Earl David of Huntingdon. In this, William was following existing policy, by which trusted allies were endowed with major estates along the geographical fringes of royal authority, such as those of Robert de Brus in Annandale (Stringer 1985, 31–2). This situation, however, did not survive for long, and following the death in 1237 of Earl David's son and successor, John, the lands of the lordship were divided between his three heiresses, passing to the families of Balliol, Bruce and de Hastings (Dowden 1903, xxv; Stringer 1985, 180–1).

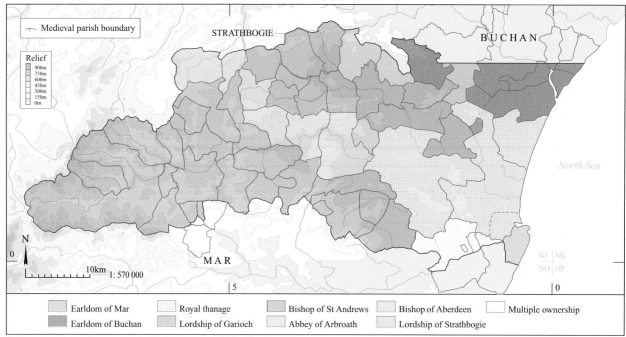

Fig. 8.3 This map shows the principal land-holdings in Donside at the end of the 12th century. GV004091

The Garioch first appears by name in a charter, which has been dated to between 1178 and 1182 (Dowden 1903, 1–2). By this William granted to his younger brother David the earldom of Lennox, together with lands and properties in eastern and north-eastern Scotland, including Fintray, *Rothiod*, Inverurie, Monkegie, Bourtie, Durno, Oyne, Ardoyne, and *Garviach*. At this time it appears that the name *Garviach* applied to a much smaller district than the lordship that came to bear its name. The same implication can be drawn from its appearance in a subsequent grant to the bishop of Aberdeen datable to before 1190 (Stringer 1985, 220).

A comparison between the lands mentioned in these grants, and the lands and churches specified in Earl David's subsequent endowments of the Lindores Abbey, suggests that *Garviach* originally comprised Culsalmond, Insch, Rathmuriel, Kennethmont, Leslie and Premnay (Dowden 1903, 2–5; Stringer 1985, 65–7). To this might also be added Clatt, by then already held by the bishop. With the creation of the lordship, the Garioch's name came to be applied to a much wider area extending down to the lower Don, and, by the late 13th century, to the ecclesiastical deanery within which its parishes were organised (Stringer 1985, 66; Cowan, 1967).

Under Earl David, Anglo-French settlement of the Garioch was pursued intensively. This is particularly evident in contemporary documents, which contain a striking frequency of English, French, Norman, Breton and Flemish names, but there is also a layer of place-names in the modern landscape that are of English and Continental origin, and some at least can be traced back

to this period. Williamston, in Culsalmond parish, for example, is probably the *villa Willelmi* granted by Sir Robert de Brus in 1261 to the abbey of Lindores (Dowden 1903, 146), while the farm of Ingliston, about 1km north-east of Keith Hall, presumably received its name from a settlement of colonisers associated with the estate of **Caskieben** (Alexander 1952, 71). Flinder, in Kennethmont parish, now divided between the farms of Old, New and Little Flinder, appears as *Flandres* in a grant of about the same date, signifying the presence of Flemings in the area (Alexander 1952, 278). One of them was perhaps *Bartholomeus flandrensis*, who in the 1230s held the **Castle of Wardhouse**, just across the Shevock Water from Flinder (Dowden 1903, 65). The legacy of this period of colonisation persists in the charter evidence as late as 1358, and can be seen in David II's confirmation of a grant by Thomas, Earl of Mar, of his lands of Courtestown, in Leslie parish, to his cleric, John de Mar, canon of Aberdeen, with all rights, customs and rightful pertinents, *'unacum lege Fleminga que dicitur Fleming lauch'* – with the law of the Flemings, which is called Fleming Law (Robertson 1843, 548–9).

By the same token, the native population in Donside scarcely appears in the written record of the 12th and 13th centuries, and then only in a subservient role. One of the few is *Gillandres Buch*, referred to in one of Earl David's charters (*c.*1208–1214; Dowden 1903, 167; Stringer 1985, 227), and his name is preserved in the place-name Glanderston, a farm immediately adjacent to Flinder. Whether this imbalance is a genuine reflection of the overwhelming predominance of Anglo-French landowners settled in the Garioch in this period, or simply a consequence of the selective nature of the surviving documentation, remains unclear (Stringer

1985, 81), but there is no evidence that native Scots were shown any favour by the earl (Stringer 1985, 82–3, 160–1).

Mar

In contrast to the open, undulating landscape of the Garioch, the earldom of Mar stretched westwards up into the highland glens of the Don and the Dee. The roots of the earldom lie in the early medieval period, falling under the jurisdiction of a *mormaer*. The first *mormaer* of Mar to be attested was Donald, son of Emhinn, son of Cainnech, who was killed in 1014 at the Battle of Clontarf, in Ireland (Anderson 1922, i, 536; Simpson 1949, 62; Paul 1908, 566–89). A coherent succession, however, only begins with Ruadri, who appears in charters between 1114 and 1132 both as earl and as *mormaer* of Mar. Ruadri was probably succeeded by Morgrund, from whom the subsequent line of earls descended until the late 14th century.

Reflecting its semi-autonomous state, the earldom of Mar was not subject to such intensive colonisation as the Garioch. Nevertheless, it too was opened to Anglo-French influence, not least through the marriage of Earl Gilchrist (d. *c.*1211) to Orabila, former wife of Robert de Quincy, a cousin of Kings Malcolm and William, and Earl David, and mother of Saher de Quincy, the earl of Winchester (Barrow 1980, 22–3; Simpson 1943, 115). Mar also provides several examples of an earthwork castle, juxtaposed to a parish church, a relationship familiar from the heartlands of Anglo-French settlement.

At the beginning of the 13th century the earldom's eastern boundary appears to have encompassed the parishes of Auchindoir, Forbes, Alford, Tough, Cluny and Echt (Cowan 1967, 5, 9, 32, 58, 67, 199), but the loss to the Durwards of a great block of land centred on Lumphanan heralded a general retreat westwards. The last heiress of the direct line, Isabella, Countess of Mar, died in 1408, although her husband, Alexander Stewart, retained the title of earl until his death in 1435. Thereafter, the earldom was annexed to the Crown and became a source of repeated gifts by the king to his close kin and intimates.

The Crown organised the payment of the accounts of the earldom between the lordships of Strathdon, Cromar and Strathdee (Burnett 1882, 459–460). Cromar and Strathdee largely fall outside the area that has been surveyed, but the lordship of Strathdon encompassed most of the upper reaches of the Don, from Skellater in the west to Auld Auchindoir and Ardhuncart in the east, taking in the parishes of Invernochty, Kildrummy, Kinbattoch and Glenbuchat, and parts of Auchindoir and Migvie. This arrangement appears to reflect the earlier organisation of the earldom, for 14th-century land grants also refer to the lordship of Strathdon, such as that of the lands of Over and Nether Towy and Culfork in 1359 by Thomas Earl of Mar to William de Fentoun (Robertson and Grubb 1847–62, 718).

Buchan

The earldom of Buchan lay mainly to the north of the River Ythan, and well to the north of Donside itself, but the area that has been surveyed encompasses the lands on its southern march, including a detached portion of the earldom in the parish of Bethelnie (Young 1993, 183–5). Like Mar, Buchan was formerly governed by a *mormaer*, but in the early 13th century it passed by marriage to the powerful Anglo-Norman Comyn family and came to form their main bastion in northern Scotland (Young 1993, 174–202). By an exchange of lands with King John between 1292 and 1296, the earldom gained the royal thanage of Formartine, and probably also Belhelvie (Young 1993, 184–5; Grant 1993, 65), but the Comyns' support of John Balliol was to lead to their overthrow shortly afterwards in 1308, when they were defeated by Robert I at the Battle of Barra. In the ensuing Herschip of Buchan, their lands were laid waste and the earldom was dismembered to provide estates with which the king could reward his followers.

Late Medieval Changes in the Pattern of Lordship

The turmoil that attended the Wars of Independence led to considerable change in the pattern of lordship. In 1320, in the wake of the defeat of the Comyns and the Herschip of Buchan, Robert I granted the earldom of Buchan to Robert de Keith, Marischal of Scotland, though it was no longer the large territorial power block it had been before. The lordship of Strathbogie, which lay to the west of the Garioch, went to Seton of Gordon in 1319, and the lordship of Garioch, split since 1237, was reunited and regranted to Robert's sister, Christina Bruce, Countess of Mar (Duncan 1988, 648). Upon her death in 1357, David II granted the lordship to Thomas, Earl of Mar. Thereafter the Garioch and its lands remained tied to the earldom (Webster 1982, 204), which, as we have seen, was itself annexed to the Crown in 1435.

Having been taken into the royal demesne, Mar and the Garioch became a source of patronage throughout the late medieval period until 1565, when Queen Mary finally recognised the inheritance rights of the long-frustrated claimants, the Erskine family. By then the earldom had been reduced to a mere rump of its former extent (Simpson 1949, 80), but its waning fortunes had seen the ascendancy of other families as the dominant powers of Mar and the Garioch. The Forbes family, former vassals of the earl of Mar, and barons in their own right from 1405, built their castle at **Druminnor** in Kearn, once a part of the parish of Forbes. Their relations and offspring acquired many holdings in the earldom, such as Brux in Kildrummy, and Glen Carvie, Glen Conrie and the Orde in Invernochty. James IV complicated matters further by establishing Lord Elphinstone as Baron of Invernochty in 1507, and of Kildrummy in 1513, with much of the Lordship of Strathdon as his domain. The Gordons of Strathbogie also spread their influence across the North-east by dint of their position as one of the foremost landowners. As such, they provided a useful counterweight to the Erskine claimants of Mar, and fought a bitter feud with the Forbes family during the 16th century. Other lesser families also became influential local landowners, such as the Skenes, Frasers and Leslies.

Estates and Parishes

Before examining the evidence for some of the estates that made up the various lordships and royal lands, it is important to grasp some of the difficulties that this presents, particularly in respect to locating them in the landscape. Place-names of the lands granted in charters allow the rough position and extent of many estates and baronies to be established, but it is generally more difficult to identify the boundaries of the individual holdings with any precision, even where contemporary perambulations and delineations survive. In Aberdeenshire these are relatively rare, and many of the place-names so tantalisingly enumerated, and often of Celtic origin, have been lost.

The character of the boundaries described in these sources varies, but typically they followed natural features, in particular watercourses, and these have largely remained unchanged to this day. Elsewhere they followed less permanent lines, such as roads and the edges of fields, or employed landmarks, ranging from large natural boulders to earlier monuments. Artificial boundary markers were also erected, but these appear less frequently in the documentation. A *'cross and great stone'* is one of the features of the boundary of Dyce parish and Cordyce forest noted in 1316 (Duncan 1988, 383; p. 147), while in 1523 the marches of the lands of Auchintoul, in Alford parish, included *crucem Sancte Catharine* (Robertson and Grubb 1847–62, iv, 143). Neither has been located in the course of the survey.

The fashion for setting up stones on the boundaries of estates seems to have been more prevalent in the 18th and 19th centuries (pp. 236–7), but a boulder incised with an equal-armed cross at the **Gallows Hill** of Aberdeen (now Trinity Cemetery) is probably a medieval marker (Cruickshank and Gunn 1929, 63). Some of the older boundary stones of the Freedom Lands of Aberdeen, which bear *'an sauser'* or large cupmark and are described in 1525 and 1698, also survive (p. 5). Four of those lying on the march between Old and New Aberdeen bore an incised key, the insignia of St Peter (Cruickshank and Gunn 1929, 33–4), but these are now lost. They either marked the lands of the 12th-century hospital of St Peter, or the bounds of St Peter's parish, which was erected in 1427, and united with St Machar's in 1583 (Haws 1972, 4; Cowan 1967, 2). The description of the march in 1698 also mentions that three of the boulders bore an incised letter P (Kennedy 1818, 382). A fourth P has now been found, carved on a rock outcrop on **North Westfield**

farm, but off the line of the march. If this new marker does indeed relate to the Freedom Lands, it lies on an undocumented line.

Documented boundary disputes can also provide a rich source of information. One such contentious march lay between the bishop's lands of Rayne and the Lindores Abbey's lands of Culsalmond, and concerned the boundaries of Threpland (now Freefield), its very name signifying a disputed territory. In 1259 an agreement was reached between Bishop de Potton and Abbot Thomas, fixing the boundaries of Threpland between the bishop's lands of Bonnyton and the abbey's lands of Newton (Innes 1845, i, 26; Robertson and Grubb 1847–62, iii, 429). The march was again a matter of dispute in 1521, when a meeting was arranged *'anent the debateable lands betwixt Rothmaiss and Tulymorgond and the peit moss callit off Malyngsyd and Bonytoune of Rayne'* (Dowden 1903, 294–300, 311; Innes 1845, i, 386). An unshaped boulder bearing a crudely incised equal-armed cross (Fig. 8.4), which is at the entrance to the quarry at **Cairnhill** (Ritchie 1916, 285–7), lies within 300m of the present parish boundary and is possibly a relic of these disputes.

Fortunately, the introduction of the parish system and its maintenance to the present day, albeit in an evolved form, provides another source from which to map some of the estates. The parochial structure was first established by David I, and was designed to maintain the church by a tax – *teinds* – levied on the land. This led to a close relationship between the parishes and the pattern of estates at the time. The earliest comprehensive depictions of the parish boundaries appear on the 1st edition of the Ordnance Survey maps of the 1870s, but, as will be shown below, this can also be supplemented with earlier written delineations, and compared with the modern locations of names that appear in charters. Such an approach suggests that many of the medieval estates granted throughout the Garioch and Mar were either coterminous with parishes, or formed lesser subdivisions.

No attempt has been made to map all the 12th- and 13th-century holdings that can be identified in the documentary record, but the parochial structure at about 1300 has been delineated (pp. 143–4; Fig. 8.5). Of the fifty-three medieval parishes that fall wholly or partly within Donside, fifteen or so are sufficiently well documented that it is not only possible to demonstrate that the extent of the secular and parochial lands was identical in the 12th century, but also that the original parish marches were still in use in the 1870s. Amongst others, the episcopal baronies of Clatt, Rayne and Tullynessle demonstrate this case, though only Clatt is presented here.

The church and lands of Clatt are first recorded in 1157, in the confirmation of the endowments of the bishop and cathedral church of Aberdeen (Innes 1845, i, 6). In later references the lands are referred to as

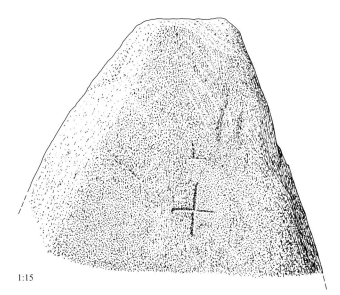

1:15

*Fig. 8.4 **Cairnhill** (NJ 6697 3261). The incised cross on this boulder is probably a medieval boundary marker. GV004149*

a shire, and latterly as a barony (Innes 1845, i, 218, 390). With two exceptions, the lands of the *Schira de Clat* enumerated in a series of 16th-century charters and rentals fall within the modern parish boundaries, and their names correspond with the major farms in operation today (Innes 1845, i, 360–4). It is also worth noting that, with the exception of Newbigging and Newton, the names of the principal 16th-century lands of the shire of Clatt are all Gaelic in origin. Of the lands of the shire lying outside the parish, the first comprised the two ploughgates of the lands of Ardlair, just across the boundary into the adjacent parish of Kennethmont. These two ploughgates serve to underline the survival of Clatt as a medieval parish unit, for Ardlair has always lain outside the parish, its association with Clatt deriving from the grant of this land to the bishop of Aberdeen by Earl David, prior to 1190, in exchange for Bishop Matthew's resignation of his rights to the second teinds of the earl's Garioch lands (Barrow and Scott 1971, 315; Innes 1845, i, 9–10). The adjacent lands of Seggieden, which form a conspicuous salient in the northern boundary of Clatt parish, also lay within Kennethmont as far back as a grant (probably 1185x1195) by Earl David, and help confirm that component elements of Clatt have remained unchanged since the 12th century (Stringer 1985, 263). The second area of lands belonging to the shire that lay outside the parish is *Clouetht*, which is probably to be identified with the church lands of the former parish of Clova, which was later united with Kildrummy (Innes 1845, i, 102; ii, 363). Although the Ardlair ploughgates and Clova were never incorporated into the parish of Clatt, it was logical that they should be administered as part of its shire.

In addition to this detailed enumeration of the lands of Clatt, the documentation also allows several sectors of its boundaries to be identified in detail.

Two brief notes exist of portions of the bounds of the bishop's lands of Clatt. The first defines the boundary between Auchlyne on the eastern side of the parish, and Courtestown in neighbouring Leslie parish (Innes 1845, i, 245–6), which then, as now, followed a tributary of the Gadie Burn. The second describes the parish's western march with the Forbes' lands of Kearn, following the Canny Burn from its confluence with the Water of Bogie to its head (Innes 1845, i, 249). For the modern parish boundary this description only holds true along the lower reach of the burn. Higher up, the burn forks, the west branch bearing the name of the Canny Burn, but the parish boundary following the east branch. The probable explanation of this lies in an agreement of 1391, between Bishop de Greenlaw and Sir John Forbes, by which the land of *Tulycoscheny* was to be held in common by the two parties (Innes 1845, i, 188). *Tulycoscheny* can be identified with the modern farm of Cushnie, which lies between the two branches of the stream. In its original form, the parish boundary almost certainly followed the western fork of the burn, but the common use of this land has been superseded by its cession to Kearn and a realignment of the boundary between the two parishes.

Parochial Structure

Of the fifty-three pre-Reformation parishes that lie wholly or partly within Donside, twenty-seven appear on record by the end of the 12th century. A further twenty-six are first recorded in the 13th century. The majority of these other parishes probably also date back to the 12th century and have simply escaped record, though it is equally clear that the parochial structure continued to evolve in response to changing patterns of settlement and authority. This is illustrated by the parish of *Rothket*. According to Pope Celestine's 1195 confirmation of the endowments of Lindores Abbey, Inverurie and Monkegie were both chapels of the church of *Rothket*, which has been identified with **St Apolinaris's Chapel** near Newseat of Manar (Dowden 1903, 103; Simpson 1949, 13). Shortly thereafter, however, Inverurie superseded *Rothket* as the parish church and as the mother church of Monkegie, probably as a result of the erection of **Inverurie** as a burgh and its new secular status as the *caput* of the Garioch (Cowan 1967, 90; Stringer 1985, 70, 94). Another example can be seen in the parish of Culter, which formerly straddled the River Dee. In 1287, following a lengthy dispute concerning the foundation of a house and chapel of the Knights Templar on the south side of the river, the parish was divided in two. The northern portion became the parish of Peterculter, and the southern half Maryculter (Cowan 1967, 143, 164).

In other cases the existence of large communities in remote parts of a parish seems to have been a determining factor. This was almost certainly the case

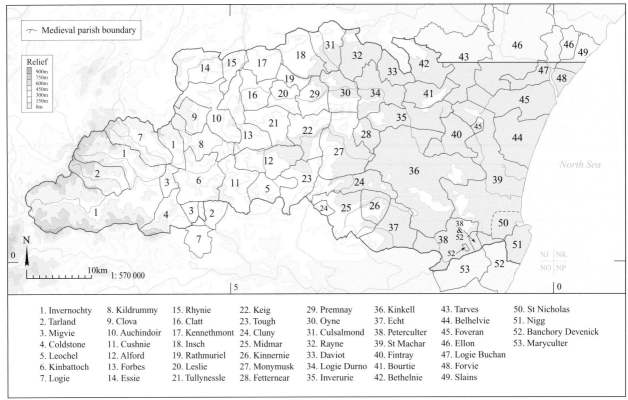

Medieval parish boundary

Relief
900m
750m
600m
450m
300m
150m
0m

North Sea

1. Invernochty	8. Kildrummy	15. Rhynie	22. Keig	29. Premnay	36. Kinkell	43. Tarves	50. St Nicholas
2. Tarland	9. Clova	16. Clatt	23. Tough	30. Oyne	37. Echt	44. Belhelvie	51. Nigg
3. Migvie	10. Auchindoir	17. Kennethmont	24. Cluny	31. Culsalmond	38. Peterculter	45. Foveran	52. Banchory Devenick
4. Coldstone	11. Cushnie	18. Insch	25. Midmar	32. Rayne	39. St Machar	46. Ellon	53. Maryculter
5. Leochel	12. Alford	19. Rathmuriel	26. Kinnernie	33. Daviot	40. Fintray	47. Logie Buchan	
6. Kinbattoch	13. Forbes	20. Leslie	27. Monymusk	34. Logie Durno	41. Bourtie	48. Forvie	
7. Logie	14. Essie	21. Tullynessle	28. Fetternear	35. Inverurie	42. Bethelnie	49. Slains	

Fig. 8.5 This map reconstructs the boundaries of the medieval parishes of Donside and their associated pendicles. GV000240

for the communities living in some of the detached portions of Cromar parishes in the upper reaches of the Don (p. 183) and were the grounds for the petition that saw the erection of Glenbuchat's chapel as a parish church in its own right in 1470 (Cowan 1967, 74–5; Innes 1845, i, 307–9).

The process was not wholly one of subdivision. In the charters of endowment of Lindores Abbey, Kennethmont and Rathmuriel are both named as churches, apparently of equal status (Dowden 1903, 3, 8, 103). By the Reformation, however, Rathmuriel was no more than a pendicle of Kennethmont (Cowan 1967, 168). The parish of Clova is another that disappeared as an independent entity, having been united with Kildrummy in 1363 (Innes 1845, i, 102–3; Cowan 1967, 24). The church of Clova first appears in 1157, when it is referred to as a *monasterium*, or minster. As such it was a relic of an earlier pattern of ecclesiastical organisation, and would have possessed a number of dependent chapels, probably in what is now the parish of Cabrach.

The disruption of pastoral care in the aftermath of the Reformation led to several major reorganisations of the parish structure. In 1583 the parish church of Logie Durno was transferred across the Urie to its former pendicle at Chapel of Garioch, possibly as a reflection of the increased importance of the Leslie barony of Balquhain (see p. 172). Subsequently, in 1655 (or

possibly 1599; Scott 1926, 151), Chapel of Garioch absorbed the small neighbouring parish of Fetternear (Davidson 1878, 311). This sort of amalgamation of several small, poorly-endowed parishes to create more viable parochial units was particularly common in the early 17th century. Rhynie and Essie in Strathbogie, for example, were united for this reason in about 1612 (Scott 1926, 329).

This period also saw the division of some of the more extensive parishes. In many instances these divisions followed pre-existing pastoral lines, providing existing dependent chapels of pre-Reformation origin with ministers of their own. The parish of St Machar illustrates the process. In 1607 its north-western portion was detached to form a new parish, at first centred upon **St Colm's Chapel**, Monykebbuck, which had served the area since at least 1256 (Innes 1845, ii, 48), and from 1639 on a new church built in what is now the village of New Machar (*Stat. Acct.*, vi, 1793, 465). A second portion of St Machar was detached in 1666, becoming the parish of Newhills with a new church built upon a greenfield site. In the case of the parish of Kinkell, which appears to have covered the whole of the thanage of Kintore (p. 145), in 1648 its six dependent chapelries were hived off as parishes in their own right (Davidson 1878, 302). The remaining rump of Kinkell, which straddled the Don, was further divided in 1754, the area west of the river passing to Kintore, that to the east to the neighbouring parish of Monkegie to form the new parish of Keithhall & Kinkell (*Stat. Acct.*, ii, 1792, 527). Other new parishes were more radical creations.

In 1597 Udny was erected from elements detached from the neighbouring parishes of Ellon, Foveran, Logie-Buchan and Tarves (Scott 1926, 206). Udny, however, was focused on a pre-Reformation chapel, and there is again some sense that most of these changes respected long-standing divisions in the temporal landscape.

Other changes were on a much smaller scale, rationalising the cures of ungainly parishes. Usually this involved part of a parish that was inconveniently remote from its church, such as the transfer in 1651 of the lands of Wraes from Insch to Kennethmont. In return the lands of Rathmuriel (now Wantonwells, Murrial and Priestwells) were annexed to Insch (Davidson 1878, 310). Not all such attempts were successful, vested interests and traditions resisting administrative reform. Prior to its union with Chapel of Garioch in 1655, an attempt had been made to annex Fetternear to Kemnay, but this was opposed by the minister of Kemnay (Davidson 1878, 311). Similarly, in 1623 an attempt had been made to have the minister of Daviot serve the inhabitants of Saphock in Fyvie, and of Lethenty in Chapel of Garioch, both remote districts of their respective parishes. Here too, however, the minister objected. The duties of these lands remained payable to the original churches, and he would have received no stipend in return (Davidson 1878, 309). A number of other unions proved only temporary: the parish of Bourtie was united to that of Bethelnie in 1618, but disjoined once more about 1650 (Scott 1926, 148). Even more brief was the union decreed by the Commissioners of Teinds between Tough and Keig in 1832, which was dissolved after only two years (Scott 1926, 140).

Despite this evolution of the parish system in response to new temporal and pastoral demands, nine parishes appear to have remained unchanged since the 12th century. At least another six apparently returned to their original limits following the dissolution of temporary or unsuccessful unions and boundary changes.

Medieval Estates

The medieval estates in Donside present a wide range of sizes, essentially reflecting the status of their holder. Thus, while Earl David was granted a huge tract of royal lands extending from Inverurie up into the upper Garioch, he in his turn granted out smaller estates to his supporters, ranging from parish-sized units such as Leslie (see below) to much smaller parcels of land, creating a mosaic of vested interest throughout his lordship. Though an equivalent range of estates must surely have existed in Mar, the lands in the Garioch and the lower Don are better documented and provide the examples discussed here.

The largest of the units that can be identified are those that remained in royal possession, such as the thanages of Kintore and Aberdeen. Thanages had an important fiscal role for the Crown, providing not

only a system in which royal demesne was exploited, and tribute collected, but also one that would sustain the king on progress through his realm (Grant 1993). Thanages, however, were also archaic units, derived from multiple estates, an early type of estate widely found in Britain and known by a variety of names, including shire (Barrow 1973; see pp. 132; 133–4).

The lands of the thanage of Kintore were certainly extensive, probably including the royal forest granted to Robert de Keith in 1324 (Duncan 1988, 524; Grant 1993, 74), and they evidently extended well beyond the limits of the modern parish of Kintore, for in 1368 the thanage drew *cain* from Kinkell and Dyce (Grant 1993, 74). This is one of several strands of evidence that allow its extent to be reconstructed, probably equating with the medieval parish of Kinkell. This was a remarkably large parish (Fig. 8.5), with its church on the opposite side of the River Don some 2.8km to the north-west of Kintore, but it was divided into six pendicles, each served by a dependent chapel and later erected as an independent parish (p. 144). This structure implies the origin of Kinkell as a minster, its *parochia* extending in a single block in the lower Don forming the later parishes of Dyce, Kinellar, Kintore, Kemnay and Skene, and a detached territory in the upper Garioch, namely the parish of Drumblade. The extent of the lands held by the Keiths in the 14th and 15th centuries also tallies with the *parochiam* of Kinkell. These links between the secular and ecclesiastical organisation of the landscape in this period are sufficiently close to indicate that the areas they took in are probably one and the same. The six pendicles of the mother church at Kinkell are equally likely to equate with a substructure of smaller estates within the thanage, and the *pit-* place-names provide some insight into yet another tier of lesser holdings (p. 132). It has also been suggested that Kintore and Kinkell may have served respectively as the regional administrative and ecclesiastical centres for the royal lands between the Don and Strathbogie, until superseded by Aberdeen (Stringer 1985, 65).

Few other estates within Donside were as large as the thanages of Kintore and Aberdeen, although the lands of *Garviach*, which formed part of the grant to Earl David, appear to have been another such unit in origin (p. 140). The charter evidence for the lordship, however, provides hints that most of the lands had already been divided into smaller discrete units by the late 12th century. For example, William the Lion endowed his brother with named blocks of land, *'per rectas divisas suas'* (by its proper boundaries; Dowden 1903, 2), and about a dozen such estates are preserved in the pattern of ecclesiastical parishes imposed upon the lordship of Garioch during the 12th century (Stringer 1985, 62). By and large, the lands granted by Earl David were not of this extent, though the greater part of the parish of Leslie was given to Malcolm, son of Bertolf, between 1172 and 1185 (Stringer 1985, 254). Malcolm's feu evidently did not include Duncanstone, which is listed among lands still held by the lordship in 1503 (Burnett 1889, 129–132), but it was still a substantial estate, requiring a whole knight's service. Its grant also came with the judicial rights of *sake*, *soke*, *toll*, *team* and *infangenthief*, terms more usually associated with thanes, and almost certainly a relic of Leslie's origins (Stringer 1985, 61–2, 88, 254–5).

While such grants are unusual among Earl David's known dispositions to his vassals, several other large estates of the size of Leslie can be identified elsewhere. As we have already seen (pp. 142–3), the shire of Clatt was coterminous with its parish, and the same may be said of the other shires confirmed by Malcolm IV to the bishop of Aberdeen in 1155 – Rayne, Tullynessle and Daviot (Innes 1845, i, 4). The bishop of St Andrews also held an extensive estate around Monymusk, where a Culdee community was replaced with a house of Augustinian canons in 1245 (Simpson 1925; Cowan and Easson 1976, 51, 93–4). The bounds of the estate are detailed in the 16th century and encompassed all the lands in the parishes of Keig and Monymusk (Robertson 1843, 171–2; Low 1866, 218–32). The thanage of Aberdeen, however, was clearly deemed too great a gift for the bishop of Aberdeen *en bloc*. The lands of the thanage confirmed to Bishop Edward in 1157 include Goule, Kinmundy, Malmeulah and Tulligreig (Innes 1845, i, 5), but Straloch and Monykebbuck were retained by the king, appearing in the rental of Alexander III (Innes 1845, i, 160).

The single greatest beneficiary of Earl David's largesse as lord of Garioch was the Tironensian abbey of Lindores, which he founded between 1191 and 1195. By 1207 the abbey had accumulated extensive properties and rights through the Earl's endowments, and through grants of lands and revenues by his *familia*. Those in Donside included: the lands and churches of Fintray, *Rothket* (*Rothiod* of William the Lion's original grant), Inverurie, Monkegie and Durno; the lands of Oyne, Ardoyne, Ledikin and Mellinsyde; and the churches of **Premnay**, **Rathmuriel**, **Insch**, **Culsalmond** and **Kennethmont** (Dowden 1903, 2–4). To this Norman, son of Malcolm, added the church of **Leslie** (Dowden 1903, 88). Smaller holdings included part of Rathmuriel parish, and properties and rents in **Inverurie** (Dowden 1903, 60, 21).

Others of Earl David's followers favoured by a grant, the majority of whom were lesser, often landless, knights, had to be content with a smaller holding (Stringer 1985, 86–7). Between 1199 and 1219, for instance, David de Audri received the whole *dabhach* of Resthivet, a component part of Durno parish, for the tenth part of one knight's service (Stringer 1985, 223–4). Robert de Billingham and his kinsman Simon are each known to have received a ploughgate in Durno, together with a toft in the burgh of **Inverurie** (Stringer 1985, 225).

Despite the fragmentary nature of the documentary record, it is possible to reconstruct some of these 12th- and early 13th-century sub-parochial-level estates. For instance, two estates occupying the eastern half of the medieval parish of Inverurie can be identified, one centred on **Caskieben**, now Keith Hall, the other on Crimond. These were served by the chapel of **Monkegie**, which was a pendicle of the parish church of Inverurie, and was granted to the abbey of Lindores with its lands as part of Earl David's endowment. The chapel stood near **Caskieben**, where an earthwork castle (p. 150) presumably served as the *caput* for the estate. The other estate was held by Simon de Garentuly, though what form the estate centre took and where it stood are not known. One charter simply refers to '*domum meam de Creymund*' (my house at Crimond), another to '*faciat sibi capellam intra septa curie sue*', granting permission to 'build a chapel within the enclosure of his court' (Dowden 1903, 62–5).

Other small estates and holdings are revealed by a peculiarity of the parochial structure at the top of the Don, where several of the Deeside parishes in the Howe of Cromar held remote subdivisions across the watershed as detached pendicles (pp. 135; 183). Glenbuchat was a pendicle of Logie Mar, served by its own chapel, and it was not until a petition reporting the inaccessibility of the parish church during floods that in 1470 it was erected as a parish in its own right. As late as the 19th century, the valley of the Deskry Water formed a detached element of Migvie parish, and Glen Ernan part of Tarland parish. Glen Ernan was also a territorial unit known as a *dabhach* (p. 183). These detached lands were interleaved with elements of the medieval parish of Invernochty, suggesting that by the 12th century the top of the Don was already divided into a series of small estates, each probably served by its own chapel (p. 193).

Hunting Forests and Woodlands

Designated hunting forests were an essential component of medieval lordship, and the chase was one of the pleasures of kings and nobles. As such, from the 12th century the creation of these game reserves formed an important aspect of the changing face of the rural landscape in Aberdeenshire. Grants of free forest were made throughout the lowlands of Donside (Gilbert 1979, 338–53) – Fintray (Lindores Abbey); Tarves and Nigg (Arbroath Abbey); Fetternear (bishop of Aberdeen); Kinkell (Humphrey de Berkeley); Leslie (Alformo, son of Norman); Aberdeen (Burgh thereof); Cordyce (James of Garioch); and Kintore (Robert de Keith) – some of them from the string of royal forests following the king's thanages up the River Don from Aberdeen to Kintore (Gilbert 1979, 360, 364). Hunting in these forests was presumably one of the attractions of this area for successive kings. William the Lion is recorded at Kintore in 1206, lying ill there in the winter of 1210–11, and Alexander III visited in 1264 (Barrow and Scott 1971, 103–4; Grant 1993, 64). Even when the forest of Kintore passed to Robert de Keith in 1324 (Duncan 1988, 524–5), a hunting park there was excluded from the grant. Later still, David II dated charters of 1362 and 1366 *'Apud forestam de Kyntor'* and *'Apud manerium nostrum foreste de Kyntor'* – 'At the forest of Kintore' and 'At our manor of the forest of Kintore' – respectively (Thomson 1984a, i, 115, 213, App. ii, 46).

The importance of hunting is underlined by the frequency with which the Old Irish word *elerc* (ambush) occurs in place-names, usually as the name Elrick and thought to signify the site of a hunting trap (Gilbert 1979, 8, 52). These reveal that hunting was carried out far more widely in the lowlands than the recorded forests, appearing in the parishes of Alford, New Machar, Skene, Newhills, Fetternear (latterly Chapel of Garioch) and Strathdon, of which those in the lowlands – Alford, New Machar and Skene – fall outside any known forest. In such circumstances, the traditional pre-Anglo-Norman rights of the landowner to the deer on his land were presumably being applied, together with the customary methods of driving or coursing the quarry (Gilbert 1979, 6–13). This was especially likely on the earl of Mar's lands before they fell into royal hands in the 14th and 15th centuries.

The creation of these designated hunting forests in the 13th century followed the Anglo-French model, and should not be equated with woodland *per se*. In this notion of a hunting forest, some tree cover was essential to maintain the deer stock, and the creation of a hunting reserve was usually carried out where there was already a mix of woodland and open uncultivated ground. The separation of the land reserved for hunting from farmland was also considered essential, and forest laws controlled any activity that might interfere with the habitat of the deer, including timber extraction, grazing, agriculture and settlement (Gilbert 1979). With the notable exception of Cordyce (see below), the boundaries of the forests in Donside are not described in detail, and in the lowlands it is difficult to get much idea of the landscape set aside. In the case of the royal forest of Kintore, it is only a handful of place-names – Park Burn, Harthills, Hallforest, Woodside, Woodhead and Woodend – that allow the rough position of the forest to be identified. These mark out about 15 square kilometres of undulating ground between 50m and 150m OD to the west of the burgh around the **Castle of Hallforest** (pp. 173–4). Now made up of mixed farmland, crofts, deciduous woodland and coniferous plantations, it is certainly not an area of prime agricultural land.

A better indication of the mixed terrain considered suitable for hunting is provided by the forest of Cordyce, which was also encompassed by the thanage of Kintore. Cordyce is first recorded in 1316, when it was granted by Robert I to James of Garioch, whose family held **Caskieben** (Duncan 1988, 382–3; p. 153). The grant is of particular interest in its detailed delineation of the bounds of the forest. The majority of the place-names

mentioned in the grant are now lost, but, combined with natural features and parish boundaries, there are sufficient clues to allow the boundary to be plotted in some detail (Fig. 8.6). The eastern boundary, for example, which ran south from Kirkton of Dyce, followed the *'via regia que ducit apud Abirden'* (the King's road which leads to Aberdeen). This can be identified with a field boundary and a farm track depicted on the 1st edition of the OS 6-inch map (Aberdeenshire 1869, sheet lxv), its line still perpetuated in Forties Road amidst the modern development around Dyce airport. The boundary then continued to the ford of *'Achynaterman'* (the field of the boundary), probably crossing a burn north-west of the former farm of Upper Farburn and joining the parish march. From there it ran to the *'crucem et magnum lapidem in via regia iuxta Huctereny'* (the cross and great stone on the King's road next to Huctereny). The cross in question is presumably commemorated in the name of Corsehill, though there have been attempts to identify it with what is probably a cruciform sheep shelter on the south-west side of the forest near Bishopton (Cruickshank 1926, 269–71). The detail with which the bounds are specified in the grant implies that this was not an enclosed reserve defined by a pale, but was essentially an area of upland on the fringes of settlement, rising up to 250m OD on the summit of Tyrebagger Hill. The survival of several groups of prehistoric hut-circles show that the thin rocky

Fig. 8.6 Place-names, topographic features and parish boundaries allow the boundary of the forest of Cordyce to be reconstructed. GV000241

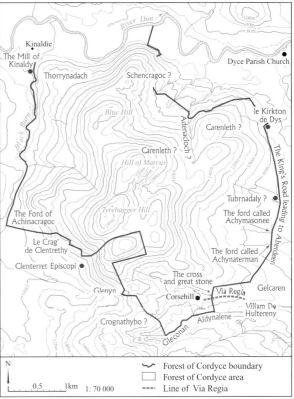

Fig. 8.7 **Allt Tuileach** *(NJ 21 08). By the mid-15th century areas set aside for hunting were probably already limited to the uplands at the head of the Don. SC961123*

soils on the upper slopes have largely escaped any later cultivation, and these hills are now clothed in coniferous plantations.

Nevertheless, not all the land within hunting forests was necessarily as bleak as the summit of Tyrebagger Hill, and even here the lower slopes would have been perfectly capable of sustaining settlement and agriculture. Settlement within the forests was strictly controlled, and could only take place under licence, or grants of assart. In southern Scotland there is evidence of such intakes, defined with dykes and ditches (RCAHMS 1997a, 36–7), but there is little sign of this in Aberdeenshire, though in the 13th or early 14th century most of the royal and free forests were in the more densely settled lowlands. This lack of documented assarts probably reflects no more than the uneven

character of the evidence. In short, the management of most of the forests passed out of royal hands with the grants of free forest and no documentation survives. In the case of the forest of Stocket, Robert I enshrined an assarting process in a grant to the burgh of Aberdeen, even if not naming it as such (Duncan 1988, 430–1). Initially, in 1313, he had simply granted custody of the Stocket to the burgh of Aberdeen (Duncan 1988, 326), but six years later he granted the forest to the burgh in feu, with the right to cultivate, build and gather fuel within its bounds. As at Kintore, however, a park was set aside as a royal hunting ground, and the wood of Stocket was excluded from the grant (Duncan 1988, 430–1). This was evidently an enclosed park, *'the der dyke'* of which was noted in 1446 in a delineation of boundaries between the lands of St Peter's Hospital and Cottown (Innes 1845, i, 245). The area of the Stocket and its park have long since been absorbed by the urban expansion of Aberdeen, its memory preserved by such place-names as Forresterhill.

With the acquisition of Mar by the Crown, various parts of upper Donside were granted as hunting forest. These were mainly in upland areas, where it may be inferred there was little or no settlement to interfere with the hunting. Royal visits in the late 14th century attest to the use of the mountainous parts of the earldom for hunting deer, though it is not clear if this included the upper parts of Donside. Nevertheless, there are grants of hunting forests relating to Kildrummy in 1342 and Bennachie in 1358 (Gilbert 1979, 341, 352), and during the late 15th century Mar and the Garioch were the subject of several grants of free forest to scions of the royal family. This was followed by a spate of grants to lesser mortals in the early 16th century, including: Corgarff at the head of the Don, and Badenyon in upper Glen Buchat to Lord Elphinstone in 1507; Glen Carvie and Glen Conrie to John and William Forbes in 1504–5; and Aldnakist and Lechery in Glenkindie to William Strathachin in 1511 (Gilbert 1979, 188–9, 350–1). A later charter of 1684 also refers to the forest of Glen Nochty (Harrison 2001a, 95–6), though this may have originated as part of Corgarff and Badenyon. The distribution of these forests suggests that by the mid-15th century the area available for hunting was already limited to the very top of Donside, or to uninhabited portions of the side valleys. Even these areas came under pressure with the post-medieval expansion in the population (pp. 192–3).

Little evidence of the use of these areas for hunting now survives, but a plan of Glen Carvie dating from 1766 annotates a boundary on the west side of the glen *'a found of stones called Deer Dyke'* (AUL MS 2769/I/131/6). Unfortunately much of this area is now afforested, except to the south of Lynemore, where a length of earthen dyke with a stone face on its west side can be seen crossing an area of boggy ground. Faced on one side like this, the dyke is certainly designed to prevent beasts from Glen Conrie crossing over into the farmland in Glen Carvie, but a fence is also depicted on this line on the 1st edition OS 6-inch map (Aberdeenshire 1869, sheet lx). The latter turns east towards its south end, essentially dividing the rough pasture in the southern half of the glen from the improved pasture and arable fields on the lower ground, and in its present form it may be no more than a head-dyke. Traces of a similar style of bank are to be seen in places along the head-dyke behind the farmsteads at **Bressachoil** and **Lynardoch** in Glen Ernan, but again there are the same uncertainties in its identification as a deer-dyke, in this case perhaps separating the two farms from the forest of Glen Nochty.

The extent of woodland, particularly pine woodland, within these hunting forests is also difficult to gauge, particularly as so much of the ground is now planted with modern forestry. Nevertheless, a few stands of native pine remain in Glenkindie and on Breda Hill, Alford. According to Gordon's map, there were many

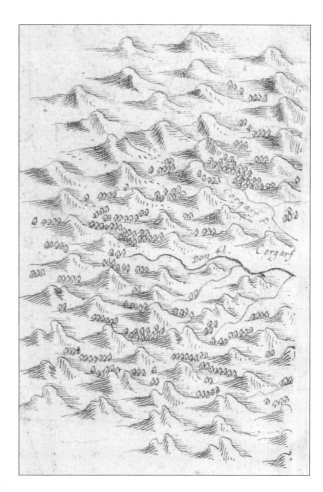

Fig. 8.8 **Corgarff** *(NJ 25 08). This extract of Gordon's map gives an impression of the extent of tree cover in the area around Corgarff during the first half of the 17th century. Apart from Corgarff itself, no other settlements are shown. © NLS*

stands of trees on the glen sides in the upper reaches of the Water of Nochty and the Water of Ernan, as well as the River Don above Corgarff, but little trace of these is in evidence today. The tops of Glen Nochty and Glen Ernan were used as shieling grounds until the late 18th century, before first being turned over to grazing, and latterly grouse shooting. Lower down the Don, Gordon shows woodland on the hillsides near Forbes and on the hills between Keig and Pitfichie (NLS Gordon MS 32), both areas that are now largely under modern plantations. The grants for Glen Carvie and Glen Conrie, and Lechory and Aldnakist in Glenkindie, also mention woods. There was little trace of any widespread woodland in the palaeoenvironmental core analysed in Glen Ernan (p. 41), and by the medieval period the woodland cover was probably already managed within relatively confined areas of the landscape. Any unmanaged woods would have quickly succumbed to grazing pressures as settlement expanded from the the medieval period onwards (pp. 190–3). The trend to deforestation was only reversed with the advent of the improvements, when new woodlands were planted and new sporting estates were established (e.g. Edinglassie and Delnadamph; p. 236).

Monuments of Lordship 1150–1700

Castles, Moated Sites and Manors

The handful of surviving earthworks that mark the sites of medieval estate centres dating from the 12th to the 15th century cannot be the complete corpus of manorial sites in Donside over this period. Indeed, based upon the documented landholdings of the late 12th and early 13th centuries, Stringer identifies some forty principal landholders in the lordship of Garioch alone, each of whom would have required some kind of administrative centre. While this may be so, few can be located with any confidence, leading to the temptation of equating a range of miscellaneous earthworks of uncertain date or character with documented landholders. The ploughed-down earthwork at **Whiteford**, for example, has been proposed as a 'medieval homestead', and even a castle, based simply upon its proximity to the tower-house on the opposite side of the River Urie at **Pitcaple** (Stringer 1985, 91; Yeoman 1998, 585). Other sites have been identified from place-names and unsubstantiated traditions, but these cannot be confirmed by survey alone. In this latter group are **Castle Hillock** near Kildrummy, '**Moathill**' at Insch, and **Castlehill**, Druminnor.

A more fruitful approach to the identification of estate centres is provided by the parochial structure, for the introduction of the parochial system (p. 142) led to the juxtaposition of many parish churches and the estate centres of their founders. This relationship can be observed in nineteen of the fifty-three medieval parishes falling wholly or partly in Donside. In each case the site of the medieval church lies within a short distance of some form of medieval estate centre,

*Fig. 8.10 **Leslie Castle** (NJ 5996 2483). Set in rich rolling farmland on the floor of the valley of the Gadie Burn, the moated site at Leslie Castle is a good example of the juxtaposition of a medieval estate centre and a parish church. SC961120*

whether it be an earthwork castle, a moated manor, or a tower-house. Examples in Donside include **Leslie**, **Midmar**, **Auchindoir** and **Monkegie** (**Caskieben**). At **Auchindoir** the earthwork castle lies immediately adjacent to the site of the medieval church, while at **Leslie** a tower stands within an earlier moated enclosure some 250m from the church (Fig. 8.10).

This relationship, however, is not quite as straightforward as these examples might indicate. Not only is the system of estates lying behind the parochial structure probably much older than the 12th century, but so are a significant proportion of the church sites (p. 135). In some instances the latter may well indicate the positions of earlier estate centres, though there is no evidence that this was the case. There are also parishes where there is no evidence for any estate centre in the medieval period. These include: Rathmuriel, now Christ Kirk in Kennethmont; Clova, later combined with Kildrummy; Forvie, now in Slains; Peterculter, split off from Maryculter; and Kinnernie, subsumed

Fig. 8.9 This map shows the locations of medieval estate centres in Donside that can be identified from the presence of a moated site, an earth and timber castle or a stone castle. GV000218

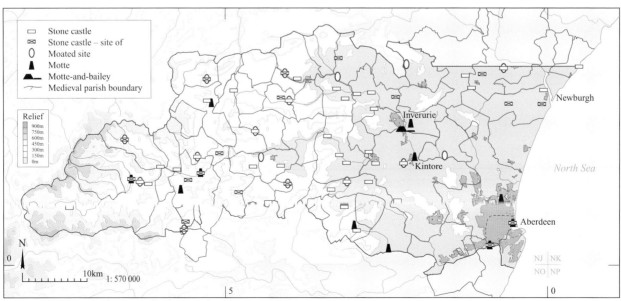

▢	Stone castle
⬚	Stone castle – site of
O	Moated site
◣	Motte
◣▬	Motte-and-bailey
⌒	Medieval parish boundary

Relief
900m
750m
600m
450m
300m
150m
0m

Newburgh

Inverurie

Kintore

North Sea

Aberdeen

N

0

10km   1: 570 000

NJ | NK
NO | NP

5

0

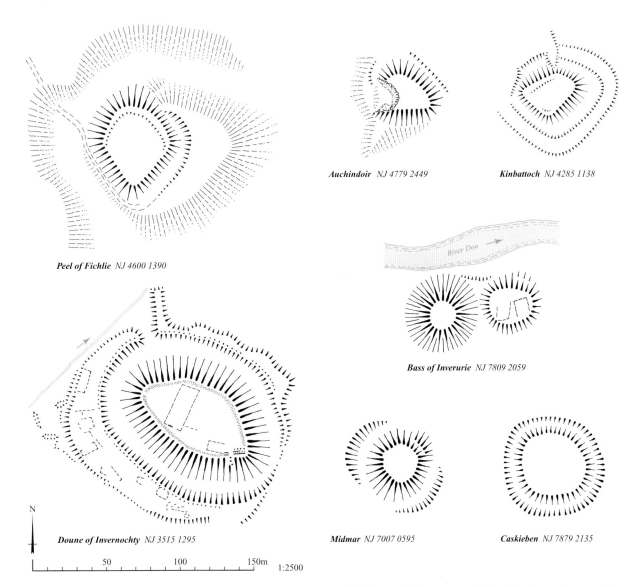

Peel of Fichlie NJ 4600 1390

Auchindoir NJ 4779 2449

Kinbattoch NJ 4285 1138

River Don

Bass of Inverurie NJ 7809 2059

Doune of Invernochty NJ 3515 1295

Midmar NJ 7007 0595

Caskieben NJ 7879 2135

N

50   100   150m

1:2500

Fig. 8.11 These plans depict the remains of the earth and timber castles that survive upstanding in Donside. The variety of forms illustrates the way several of them are tailored to the natural features of their locations. GV000211

in Midmar. In other cases the church is at some considerable distance from any known estate centre, such as that in the planned village of Insch, which is about 2km distant from the castle on the summit of **Dunnideer**. This begs the question as to the status of the castle on the summit, whether it was simply the estate centre of Insch, or perhaps the *caput* of a much larger unit (pp. 140; 155–6).

Not all the estates were in secular hands, but ecclesiastical estates were probably administered in much the same way, though again the estate centre may have been at some remove from the parish church. Thus, from the 14th century the bishop of Aberdeen administered his lands at Clatt and Tullynessle from the manor at **Old Rayne**, which is itself at a considerable distance from the church of Rayne. The bishops also built a separate palace at **Fetternear** some 0.9km from the site of the medieval parish church. Equally,

Lindores Abbey managed its Culsalmond estates from **Wrangham**, some 1.7km from the church, and Fintray from **Hatton of Fintray**, more than 3km from the church. These are discussed at greater length below.

The earthworks that are now visible at these estate centres take a range of different forms. Most are recognisable as ditched enclosures, but while some conform to the traditional notion of a rectangular moated site, with a shallow ditch and an open interior (e.g. Taylor 1983, 186–7, 190–1), others are more clearly defensive, with deep ditches enclosing an oval or subrectangular mound, and these have been classified as mottes (e.g. Kenyon 1990, 3). Not all the earthworks in Donside fit easily into this framework, but the important point for the purposes of this discussion is that they formed part of the framework of estate administration.

Raised earthwork castles, or mottes, characteristically take the form of a conical mound, sometimes accompanied by an outer earthwork or bailey enclosing a more extensive area of ground. The mound may be artificially raised, but most of the mottes in Donside (Fig. 8.11) appear to have been sculpted from

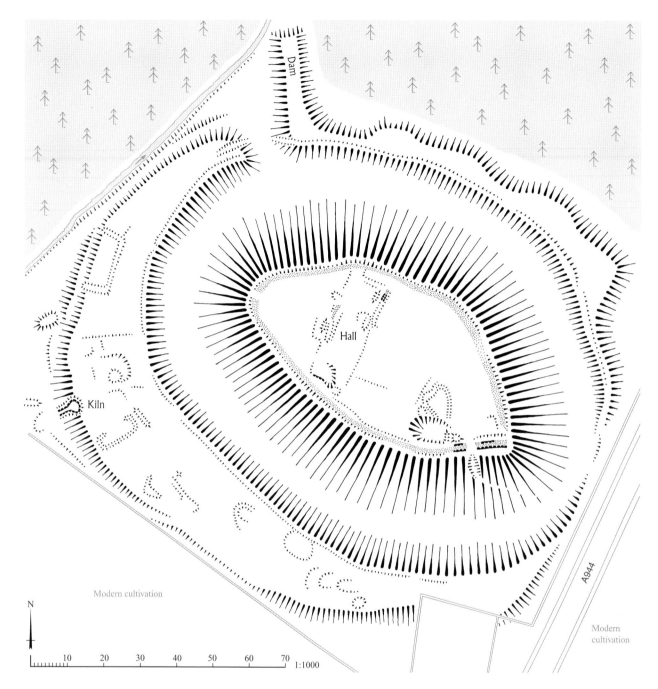

Fig. 8.12 ***Doune of Invernochty*** *(NJ 3515 1295). Undoubtedly one of the finest mottes in Scotland, the Doune of Invernochty dwarfs the other earth and timber castles in Donside. The motte was encircled with a wet ditch fed from a dammed loch to the north-west. The motte was subsequently refortified with a stone curtain wall, traces of which can be seen enclosing the summit. GV000196*

natural hillocks, a solution that is common enough in Scotland but rare in England (Kenyon 1990, 5). As such, they represent the application of the 'motte' concept to local conditions, possibly by local lairds rather than Anglo-Norman incomers.

Typically, the motte of a motte-and-bailey formed a compact strongpoint in the castle defences, the bailey housing most of the manorial buildings, which might include a hall, a chamber, a kitchen block and possibly outbuildings for storage and stabling. This cannot have been the case in Donside, where only the **Bass of Inverurie** has a bailey (Fig. 8.11), and the tops of most of the other mottes are larger than would be necessary for a strictly defensive function. Here the purpose of the earthwork was to combine both a defensible and imposing place with the space required for all the components of a manorial centre. Excavated sites of this type in the North-east include Castlehill of Strachan in Deeside (Yeoman 1984), and Rattray in Buchan (Murray and Murray 1993).

The **Bass of Inverurie** was the administrative centre of the lordship of Garioch during the late 12th and early 13th centuries and exhibits the classic profile of an earthwork castle. The motte is about 18m across

*Fig. 8.13 **Doune of Invernochty** (NJ 3515 1295). Taken under snow, the line of the curtain wall skirting the outer edge of the motte and the rectangular outline of a probable hall set across the summit can be picked out. SC961121*

at its top and stands some 12m high, while the bailey now forms a second mound, its flat oval top extending to about 30m by 23m across and about 5m in height. It is reported that the top of the Bass was levelled in the late 19th century, and a path was cut between the two mounds, presumably following the line of a ditch (Curle 1919). Two slightly raised rectangular mounds on the bailey, however, may indicate the sites of buildings.

In contrast to the **Bass of Inverurie**, the **Doune of Invernochty**, the presumed seat of the *mormaers* of Mar, displays none of the classic arrangements of a motte-and-bailey (Figs 8.12–13). Here a large natural hillock was fashioned into a massive motte, its oval summit measuring 80m by 43m and standing some 12m in height. The encircling ditch is up to 15m wide and 3m deep, and was evidently designed to hold water, which was fed from a small lake in a shallow basin to the north-west. The basin is at least 130m across, and was dammed with a thick earthen bank, though this has been breached long since, and the basin itself has been planted with conifers. Another curiosity of the earthworks here is a bold platform up to 25m in breadth around the south-west side of the castle, apparently constructed with upcast from the ditch and raised up above the level of the broad lake that must have lain out to the north-west. Whether this was intended as some form of bailey is uncertain, but there are traces of several buildings on it today, and a corn-drying kiln with a long flue has been let into the scarp on its leading edge. Of the manorial buildings that once stood on the summit of the motte, little is known, and the remains of a probable hall and an enclosing curtain wall probably belong to a later phase of occupation (p. 156). The waterworks were

probably not purely for defence, and to some extent must have been decorative. This is an unusual feature for castles of this period, and is rarely encountered in Scotland before the late medieval period. In this light, they emphasise the status of this castle, and it is interesting to note that another motte in the earldom, at Lumphanan, at the centre of the block of lands ceded in the 1220s to Thomas de Lundin (p. 141), has a broad flat-bottomed ditch that was also filled with water.

The **Doune of Invernochty** dwarfs the rest of the mottes in Donside. The next largest, at **Caskieben** (Fig. 8.11), on the east side of the Don opposite Inverurie, only measures about 44m by 41m. As we have already seen (p. 146), it was the *caput* of a relatively small estate, and was later succeeded by the Z-plan tower-house now incorporated within the country house of **Keith Hall**. Probably an artificial mound, this is also one of the lowest mottes, only rising about 1m above its surroundings, but the ditch is undeniably defensive, measuring some 12.5m in breadth and still 2m in depth.

The other earthwork castles of this order have exploited natural hillocks, which probably accounts for their range of sizes and shapes (Fig. 8.11). The motte at **Auchindoir**, for example, standing on the edge of the gully adjacent to the 13th-century parish church, is roughly triangular, its top measuring 34m by 22m, whereas those at **Kinbattoch** and the **Peel of Fichlie** are roughly subrectangular. **Kinbattoch** measures about 30m by 24m inside the ditch that cuts back into the sides of the knoll, while the **Peel of Fichlie** occupies the higher end of a natural ridge and is about 40m across (Figs 8.11; 8.14). Little is known of the ownership of **Kinbattoch**, which was the pre-Reformation name of the present parish of Towie. At the Reformation the patrons of the parish were the Knights of St John, and it is possible that the motte was the *caput* of a Templar property. Fichlie, on the other hand, is documented in the royal accounts of 1438 (Burnett 1882, 54ff.) as a grange of the Lordship of Strathdon, as is nearby Drumallochy, now a farmstead with no visible predecessor. In the mid-19th century *'the vitrified remains of a tower'* stood within the **Peel of Fichlie** (*NSA*, xii, Aberdeenshire, 417).

Not all the mottes are quite so irregular, and several display the conical shape of the **Bass of Inverurie**. At the larger end of the scale, there is the motte near **Midmar** church (Figs 8.11; 8.15), though the greater part of the mound has been removed by a gravel-pit and the enclosing ditch is now only visible on the east and west. Nevertheless, it must have stood at least 7m above its surroundings and the top measured about 24m by 22m before it was dug away. The destroyed motte at Kintore, presumably the seat of the thane of Kintore, also falls in this category, and in this case the upper part of the mound was man-made. This was revealed when it was removed to make way for the railway, leading to the discovery of a complex of earlier structures (Watt 1865).

Fig. 8.14 ***Peel of Fichlie*** *(NJ 4600 1390). Viewed from the north-east, this earthwork castle has been sculpted out of the end of a natural ridge. SC961134*

One possible motte is probably too small to have served in itself as a manorial centre. This is the hillock at **Tillydrone**, near Aberdeen Cathedral, which is less than 10m across the top, and stands 7m in height. Despite excavation, no enclosing ditch has been located, but it may still have served a military function, possibly supporting a timber tower like that found at Abinger in England (Kenyon 1990, 13–17). From this point of view, **Tillydrone** certainly occupies a strong position on a high bluff overlooking the Don, and with the bishop's palace nearby this was evidently the location of an important administrative centre (p. 163). Recent excavations on the mound, however, have failed to confirm that it is the remains of a motte (*DES 2002*, 7).

In addition to the mottes that are located close to parish churches, there are several earthworks that share the same characteristics, and yet lie in apparent isolation. One such has been revealed by aerial photography at **Tillyorn**, where a low rounded hillock is encircled by a broad ditch. Now standing only 2m high, the mound is heavily ploughed down, but its summit probably measured at least 41m by 22m.

Once ploughed to this extent, it becomes increasingly difficult to distinguish between mottes and moated sites. For example, the interior of an unprepossessing earthwork at **Roundabout**, near the church at Alford, now barely rises above its surroundings, but it is situated at the edge of a river terrace, which at least provides a measure of natural strength on one side, and elsewhere there are traces of a broad ditch. Its situation on a river-terrace recalls that of **Castle of Wardhouse**, probably the seat of Bartholomew the Fleming in the early 13th century (p. 140), where a low knoll on the edge of a shallow gully has been tailored to form a level platform measuring about 60m by 40m across. Cropmarks have revealed two ditches enclosing three sides of the platform, though traces of only the inner are visible on the ground today. A tower-house was subsequently built

within the interior, but this has since been completely demolished (Yeoman 1998). The same problems attend the character of the bishop's palace at **Old Rayne** (p. 163). Again it forms a low mound, surrounded by a ditch 6m wide and 2m deep, yet even before they were degraded, these earthworks would not have sat happily in any strict classification of mottes and moated sites.

There are, however, several more typical examples of moated manors in Donside. This is seen most clearly at **Leslie Castle**, where the 17th-century tower-house was constructed within an earlier moated enclosure. Although recently landscaped into a garden, the shallow gully of the moat is still traceable, forming a rectilinear enclosure measuring about 65m by 40m internally. A better-preserved example is the **Castle of Esslemont**, where the moated enclosure around an early 16th-century tower is roughly 35m square internally. In places the ditch is still up to 5m broad and 2m deep (pp. 174–5; Fig. 8.40). The tower at **Lynturk Castle**, the seat of the Strachans, Barons of Lynturk, also stood within a moated enclosure, traces of which can be seen around the farmhouse, and a 16th-century gun-loop is built into the adjacent steading. A ploughed-out rectangular enclosure at **Bethelnie**, in Meldrum, is another good candidate for a moated manor, despite lying some distance away from the site of the parish church.

During the 13th century, some of the greater landlords of Aberdeenshire invested in stone-built castles. More than any other, this trend is exemplified by **Kildrummy Castle**, but it is also manifested in the remains of the **Doune of Invernochty** and **Dunnideer**. The royal castle at **Aberdeen** also appears to have been at least partly built of stone by the mid-13th century, if the payment for work on it by the mason Richard Cementarius in 1266 is anything to go by (Stuart and Burnett 1878, 12). Such investments by the king and the nobility were presumably intended to secure their support and status, though they may also have been the result of the competing rivalries of neighbouring lords. Following the division of the earldom of Mar in the 1220s, for example, the Durwards built a new castle of enclosure at Coull, over the watershed from the Don into the Howe of Cromar (Simpson 1924), and it may have been to counter this, rather than to offset royal insecurity, that a new and more powerful castle was constructed in the heart of Donside at **Kildrummy** (pp. 156–61).

The earliest reference to a royal castle at **Aberdeen** dates from the reign of William the Lion (Barrow and Scott 1971, 473). It is thought to have stood on Castle Hill, where some *'subterranean vaults'* were still to be seen in the early 18th century, but there is also a possibility that an earlier timber castle stood on St Katherine's Hill. The payment to Richard Cementarius was presumably for work on Castle Hill. Having been ceded to the English Crown following the Treaty of

Fig. 8.15 **Midmar** *(NJ 7007 0595). This motte lies just over 100m from the old parish church and burial-ground. The circular crater in its summit is the result of quarrying. SC970879*

Birgham of 1291, the castle was to remain in English hands almost continuously until 1308, when it appears to have fallen to Bruce's supporters (Moir 1894, 16, 17; Fraser 1905, 1–41). It is believed to have been slighted thereafter, and never repaired.

The families of the three main claimants to the Scottish throne at the end of the 13th century – Robert Bruce, John Balliol and Lord Hastings – were inextricably linked by marriage with the descent of the lordship of Garioch. This had been split between the three daughters of Earl David following his death in 1237. The upper end of the Garioch came into the Balliol family, who invested in a new castle. In 1260 this was occupied by Joscelin de Balliol, as Lord

of Dunnideer, who granted the abbey of Lindores permission to construct a lade from the River Urie to the mill of Insch *'through the middle of his land on the east of his castle of Donidor'* (Dowden 1903, 152–3). That this castle is the ruin on **Dunnideer** seems the inescapable conclusion (Figs 6.25; 8.1). In any case, the ruin, which now has the appearance of some romantic folly, bears little resemblance to any conventional late medieval tower-house. Roughly rectangular on plan, it is a plain keep measuring about 15m by 12.5m overall and its walls are about 1.9m thick, but the apparent lack of vaulting, the arch-pointed first-floor window and the builder's skilful use of rubble all point to an early date. In addition to the tower, there would probably have been a curtain wall, but little trace of it can be detected. The whole circuit of the underlying vitrified fort has been extensively robbed, and there is certainly no trace of a

*Fig. 8.16 **Kildrummy Castle** (NJ 4548 1639). Taken in late autumn, the defences of the castle cast long shadows over the surrounding ground. SC636463*

mortared wall along its line today. However, a possible robber trench and a low bank cut across the interior of the fort to the east of the tower, and this may well mark its course.

The erection of a stone castle on the **Doune of Invernochty**, only for it to be superseded with the shift in the seat of power to **Kildrummy Castle**, presumably reflected the changing fortunes of the earldom of Mar. The summit of the great motte was enclosed with a mortared stone curtain wall and a tower-like building was erected just inside the entrance (Fig. 8.12). Sadly, the wall has been reduced to a grass-grown bank of rubble, and the tower to little more than its basement.

Nevertheless, the curtain would have made a strong shell-keep when standing, and another large, stone-founded building set across the interior was probably a hall. Simpson preferred this building as a chapel, largely on account of a Romanesque basin found nearby (Simpson 1936a, 12), but with its orientation almost north and south this is unlikely. At 30m by 11m overall, it was larger than the great hall at Kildrummy, itself one of the largest ground-floor halls in Scotland, and certainly a place that befitted an earl to entertain.

Kildrummy Castle embodies everything that the aristocratic castle should be. Its history spans the period from the 13th to the 18th century, but the main phases of construction lie at the beginning of this period, representing the technical peak of castle construction before the use of artillery changed the

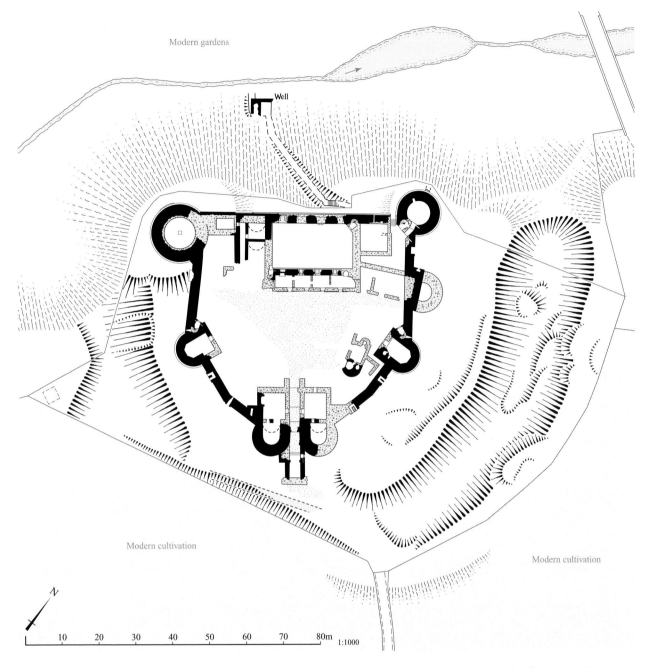

*Fig. 8.17 **Kildrummy Castle** (NJ 4548 1639). This stone castle superseded the Doune of Invernochty and became the key stronghold in the earldom of Mar, its importance reflected in successive rebuilds and modification from the 13th century until its abandonment following the Jacobite rising in 1715. GV000210*

design of fortifications at the end of the Middle Ages. Kildrummy first appears on record in 1296 in the possession of the earl of Mar, but there is a tradition recorded in the 17th century (Simpson 1920, 134; Simpson 1928a, 36) that the castle was built between 1223 and 1245 for Alexander II by Gilbert de Moravia, Bishop of Caithness. He was related to the Moravias who built the castle at Bothwell, perhaps explaining some of the similarities in the design of the two castles (Simpson 1920, 136). A further link to Alexander II is provided by the circular donjon at Kildrummy, the Snow

Tower, which makes architectural reference to the great 13th-century donjon at Coucy, in France. Alexander II married a daughter of the Sieur de Coucy. Whatever its origin, Kildrummy was a castle of the first rank, and the Crown was always keen to hold it in times of crisis, such as the Wars of Independence, even though it was a possession of the earl of Mar in 1296.

The castle comprises a D-shaped enclosure standing eccentrically within an earthwork defence (Fig. 8.17). The fine 13th-century donjon, now reduced to little more than foundations, occupies its west corner, and the main gateway lies midway round the arc on the south-east. On the north-west the castle backs on to the Back Den, a steep-sided gully, and the donjon, the main domestic structures – hall, solar and kitchen, and the Warden's Tower – all lie along its lip. Together with the

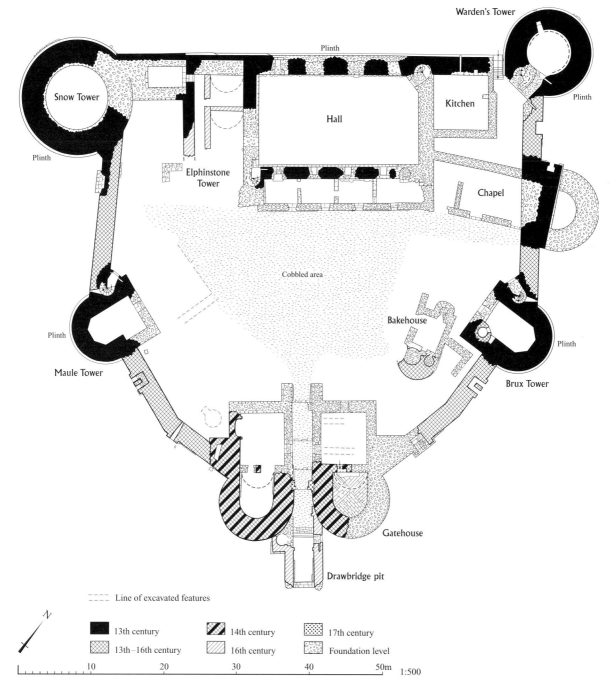

Fig. 8.18 **Kildrummy Castle** *(NJ 4548 1639). Plan showing the principal phases of construction. GV000208*

two mid-curtain towers to the east and south-west, they are also built with the same finely-dressed ashlar and a sloping external plinth, indicating that all belong to the same phase of construction.

The rest of the curtain is more roughly built, and has evidently been extensively rebuilt and repaired, but there is no evidence for any change in the basic design of the enclosure from the 13th to the 18th century, when it was finally abandoned. The only major changes appear to be: the 13th-century chapel projecting through the curtain wall on the north-east; the Edwardian-style

gatehouse on the south-east; the conversion in the 16th century of the solar block into a tower-house by the Elphinstones, barons of Kildrummy; and the addition of a range along the front of the great hall.

The construction of the chapel slighting the line of the east curtain is unique amongst castles. Simpson first showed that this was the result of a change in design (Simpson 1928a, 63–5 and 79–80), but Apted's excavations uncovered the base of a projecting semi-circular turret outside the east end of the chapel (1963, 214). This suggests that the weakness the chapel created here was recognised, and that steps were taken to improve the strength of the curtain in this sector. The foot of the tower is not

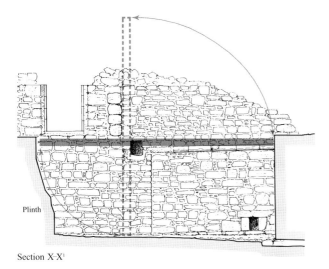

Section X–X¹

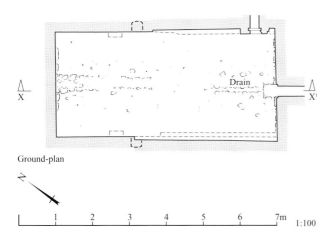

Ground-plan

1:100

Fig. 8.19 **Kildrummy Castle** (NJ 4548 1639). Plan and section of the drawbridge pit. GV000207

Fig. 8.20 **Kildrummy Castle** (NJ 4548 1639). The north end of the drawbridge pit. SC973803

1928a), and Apted's excavations failed to identify any trace of an earlier arrangement (Fig. 8.22; 1963, 213). Nevertheless, detailed examination of the drawbridge pit not only reveals that it has been rebuilt on at least two occasions, but that the primary masonry is of the same neatly dressed and squared ashlar as the earliest stonework found in the donjon and the other towers around the curtain (Figs 8.19–21). This masonry forms both ends of the pit and the outer return of the south-west side, and is particularly noticeable at the inner end, where the coursed blocks form a plinth below the sloping talus that accommodated the inner end of the drawbridge. The contrast between the ashlar here and the stonework of the Edwardian-style gatehouse implies that an earlier arrangement of the gateway was removed in the latter's construction.

The drawbridge itself was a turning bridge, pivoting on an axle set in a square socket some 2m from the north end of the pit. This type of bridge is similar to those at Hadleigh Castle, in Essex, which is dated to the 1360s (Kenyon 1990, 81–2, 92), and the Black Gate,

Fig. 8.21 **Kildrummy Castle** (NJ 4548 1639). The south end of the drawbridge pit. SC973802

bonded into the chapel wall, leading Apted to argue that only the foundations were laid, but this is such a weakness in the defences that it is likely to have been raised at least to the wallhead of the curtain. Indeed, the lack of any signs of siege damage to the lancet windows of the chapel would suggest that this was the case.

A close parallel to the layout of the castle is provided by the first phase of construction at Bothwell Castle (Kenyon 1990, 69), though at Bothwell the primary gateway was flanked by twin-towers and fronted with a drawbridge. The surviving gatehouse at Kildrummy is rather different, and displays close affinities with that at Harlech Castle in North Wales (Simpson 1928a, 71–75), suggesting that it was built during the Edwardian occupation in 1303 (Apted 1963, 208). This style of gatehouse was designed to turn the inherent weakness of an entrance into a virtue, creating a strongpoint capable of independent defence. This would have involved gates front and rear, though at Kildrummy such an arrangement has been obliterated by later changes.

Simpson argued that the visible gatehouse belonged to the initial construction of the castle (Simpson

*Fig. 8.22 **Kildrummy Castle** (NJ 4548 1639). The drawbridge pit under excavation by Apted in 1955. © Historic Scotland*

Newcastle-upon-Tyne, dating to 1247–50 (Harbottle and Ellison 1981, 80–5). At Kildrummy, the length of the pit remained constant at 6.4m throughout its life, suggesting that the same bridging system was employed until the pit was finally filled in. A curious feature of the pit, also seen at Hadleigh Castle (Kenyon 1990, Fig. 4.2) and at Newcastle-upon-Tyne Castle, is the way the walls of the barbican oversail its sides between the pivot sockets and the outer end. On the north-east of the pit at Kildrummy, the walls of the barbican and the pit are apparently of a piece, carried up on a

*Fig. 8.23 **Kildrummy Castle** (NJ 4548 1639). This plan schematically reconstructs the line of the outer curtain wall that probably stood immediately within the ditched defences. GV000209*

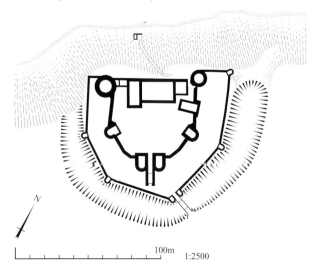

single course of corbels. On the south-west, however, there are two courses of corbels, and the side of the pit beneath them is not checked back in the same position as the check on the north-east (Fig. 8.19). The different treatment of the two sides indicates that the south-west side is of a different build and date, but it is bonded into the return of the 13th-century ashlar, and is more likely to be associated with the construction of the Edwardian-style gatehouse.

The barbican, which projects forwards on either side of the gate to protect the flanks of the drawbridge, clearly had a long history of repair and alteration. Its superstructure abuts the gatehouse, but the stair-turret that provided access to the winding chamber and a defensive platform above the gate appears to have been built on an earlier foundation, which forms a plinth of stone at its base. The date of this earlier foundation is unknown, though there must have been some kind of structure here to house the drawbridge mechanism ever since the 13th century. Simpson's argument that the barbican dates from the mid-15th century is based on unspecified building work documented at the castle by James II (Simpson 1920, 143; Apted 1963, 209) and cannot be sustained.

The main defences of the castle undoubtedly comprise the gatehouse, the donjon, and the towers along the curtain wall, but raggles on the donjon and the Warden's Tower raise the possiblity that there was

*Fig. 8.24 **Kildrummy Castle** (NJ 4548 1639). Excavations by Apted in 1955 outside the gatehouse uncovered the footings of an outer clay-bonded wall fronted by a broad ditch. © Historic Scotland*

*Fig. 8.25 **Kildrummy Castle** (NJ 4548 1639). Cordiner's romantic engraving of the castle in ruins appears to show the lower courses of an outer wall running eastwards (left) from the base of the Warden's Tower (centre). DP004531*

also an outer curtain. This is apparently shown on an 18th-century engraving, extending eastwards from the Warden's Tower along the edge of the Back Den (Fig. 8.25). Presumably an outer curtain would have been fronted by the visible earthwork defences, though test excavations by Apted along the inner edge of the ditch failed to locate its line. In front of the gatehouse, however, the foundation for a clay-bonded wall some 2.1m thick was uncovered (Fig. 8.24). While at first sight this apparently confirms the presence of an outer curtain, the drain from the drawbridge pit, its mouth apparently integral to the 13th-century masonry at the south end, had been cut through the surviving masonry and crudely covered back over. This places the clay-bonded wall in a yet earlier context, together with a ditch about 6m in breadth that lay in front of it. This strongly suggests that the great stone castle we know today was built within the defences of an earlier castle, its defences comprising a curtain wall and a ditch enclosing an area about 100m across. Any further resolution of the line of an outer curtain and the earlier defences must await further excavation.

Ecclesiastical Manors

Episcopal and monastic estates were interwoven in the fabric of secular lordship across great swathes of Donside, and were probably managed from local centres in much the same way as their secular counterparts. However, whereas the records of many secular estates have long since disappeared, some of those for the church lands have been preserved. In Donside, as elsewhere, these tend to provide a disproportionate source of information about medieval landscape in general. Nevertheless, the records of Aberdeen Cathedral (Innes 1845) and Lindores Abbey (Dowden 1903) allow something of the administrative hierarchy of the ecclesiastical estates and their centres to be discerned. Several have already been mentioned in connection with the broad discussion of the character of

mottes and moated sites in the area, but it is equally clear that the ecclesiastical centres also had characteristics of their own, those of the bishops of Aberdeen including palaces that were intended as the principal residences of the bishop in office.

Lindores was the single greatest recipient of patronage from Earl David of Huntingdon (p. 146), holding two distinct concentrations of lands in the lordship of Garioch. One of these was in the lower Don, comprising the parish of Fintray and lands in Monkegie, while the other was made up of the greater part of the parish of Culsalmond and smaller holdings in the parishes of Insch, Rathmuriel and Premnay. These outlying properties in the upper Garioch were probably managed from **Wrangham**, in Culsalmond, though no trace of an estate centre has been found there. The principal administrative centre for the abbey's lands was at **Hatton of Fintray**, its very name recalling the hall that stood there.

Fleeting contemporary references provide little clue to the overall character of the centre, though James IV visited on several occasions; in 1497 he is recorded staying *'in Fyntray, the Abbot of Lundoris place'*, in 1501 making a payment *'in Fintray, to the preist that kepis the Place'*, and in 1504 *'being in Fyntree'* when a payment was made to falconers in Inverurie (Dickson 1877, i, 375; Balfour 1900, ii, 124, 463, 467). The hall is thought to have been demolished in about 1680, to make way for a new parish church built in 1703, which is itself now little more than an ivy-clad gable (Cruickshank 1935, 7–8; Ritchie 1911, 337). In describing the surrounding burial-ground in the early 19th century, however, Logan observed that it was *'surrounded by a wall and ditch: both it is said, formerly of considerable height and depth'* (Cruickshank 1941, 5). In this sense, the estate centre appears to have been a moated site (p. 151), though the buildings were evidently of stone, for during the 19th century their foundations were encountered in both the glebe and the burial-ground; the enclosing dyke apparently contained at least one architectural fragment (*NSA*, xii, Aberdeenshire, 167–8), though this has not been located since.

The holdings of the bishops of Aberdeen in Donside were even more extensive than those of Lindores, in many cases its estates comprising entire parishes that had probably been granted by the king before the creation of the lordship of Garioch (p. 139). To the west of the lordship lay the shires of Clatt (pp. 142–3) and Tullynessle, to the north Rayne and Daviot, and to the south Fetternear. A substantial component of what had been the royal thanage of Aberdeen had also been granted to the bishop of Aberdeen. The maintenance of the identities of these shires, several ultimately becoming episcopal baronies, suggests that each had an independent administrative centre, but by the 15th century, the bishops of Aberdeen had centralised the running of their affairs in the upper Garioch at their manor of **Old Rayne** (Innes 1845, i, 217–8, 389).

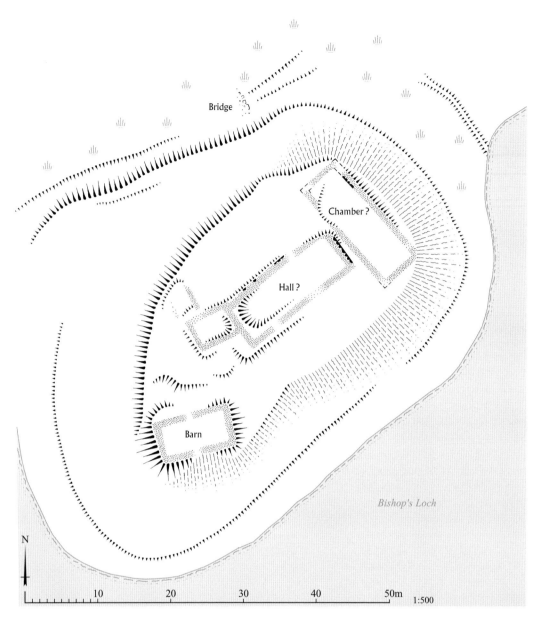

Fig. 8.26 **Bishop's Loch** *(NJ 9117 1427). The remains of this estate centre of the bishops of Aberdeen occupy what was formerly an island in Bishop's Loch. GV004134*

This rough territorial framework clearly provides scope for a wide range of estate centres, at one level serving an individual holding, at another one of the bishop's shires, and above that again a group of shires. But these estate centres were not simply to manage the land and collect the dues, they were also to provide a chain of residences appropriate to a bishop and his officials on their tours of inspection of the diocese. As such, they might be formal palaces, built in stone and projecting all the grandeur that the bishop's status demanded, but equally they might include much lesser structures. To some extent this is borne out by the documentary and archaeological sources, though it should be remembered that these reflect a wide range of dates. Something of the bishops' peripatetic existence is captured by the tradition related by Boece that Bishop Alexander Kinninmund (1329–44) moved around the diocese with the seasons, spending the winter at Mortlach, spring in Aberdeen, and

summer and autumn between **Fetternear** and **Old Rayne** (Moir 1894, 19). The choice of Aberdeen in the spring was on liturgical grounds, to instruct the Lenten crowds and spend Easter in greater solemnity. According to Boece the bishop began work on residences in these four locations, though he was only able to complete those at Aberdeen and **Fetternear**. As principal centres in the organisation of the episcopal estate, these were to become formal palaces, built in stone on an imposing scale (see below). Contrast this with the stipulation in the lease of the lands of **Terpersie** in Tullynessle in 1428, in which Bishop Henry de Lichton required John Clark to pay a rent of 8 merks and build an honest house in which the bishop might be lodged for one night each year (Innes 1845, i, 229). Clark was also charged with making a garden and planting it with trees. Unfortunately, nothing of this building and its garden remains visible, and the existing castle of **Terpersie** appears to date from no earlier than the 16th century (Simpson 1942a, 93–9).

Many of the lesser holdings perhaps had similar arrangements to those set out for **Terpersie**, but the main landward manors appear to have been ditched enclosures, and were probably indistinguishable from some of the secular estate centres that have already been described (pp. 153–4). At **Old Rayne**, for example, the bishop's manor occupied a low, oval mound enclosed by a ditch some 6m in breadth by 2m in depth. The recent excavations at **Fetternear** have also revealed a ditched enclosure containing stone buildings (*DES 2000*, 9; *2002*, 8), and in the early 18th century *'fosses'* were apparently visible at the site of the bishop's palace at Aberdeen (Orem 1830, 74). If enclosed by nothing else, the manor on the island in the **Bishop's Loch**, formerly Loch Goul, in New Machar parish, was surrounded by water, though now a peninsula with the lowering of the water-level.

Little is known of the internal layout of these manors, particularly in their early stages. Nevertheless, an informal T-shaped arrangement of buildings is visible on the island in the **Bishop's Loch** (Fig. 8.26). Its sole appearance on record is the death there of Bishop Benham in 1282, Boece claiming that the old bishop *'found such a delight in the pleasant groves adjoining [Loch Goul] that he sought no other retreat'* (Moir 1894, 15). It was presumably the *caput* for at least the lands of Goul. To Orem, in the early 18th century, the buildings comprised a large hall, with office houses to east and west, and an oratory to the south (Orem 1830, 89–90). This certainly tallies with the grass-grown walls visible today, though whether any were there in Bishop Benham's day is unknown.

In the 18th century the foundations of buildings were also visible within the interior of **Old Rayne**, but by 1840 the ground had been taken under the plough (*NSA*, xii, Aberdeenshire, 424) and it is now partly built over. Limited excavations in 1991 recovered 14th-century pottery from the bottom of the enclosing ditch and revealed evidence of mortared stone buildings with large stone roofing slabs within the interior (*DES 1991*, 31). One of these buildings was probably the *'capella dicti domini manerio suo de Rane'* (the chapel of his aforesaid manor of Rayne), which was the venue for the absolution of a number of the bishop's husbandmen in 1383 (Innes 1845, i, 164).

By the 15th century, the buildings at the episcopal seat of Aberdeen were laid out in a formal quadrangle. This is revealed by both the surviving remains, and the depiction of the buildings on Gordon of Rothiemay's map of Aberdeen in 1661. Although it had already been demolished by that date, the palace at Aberdeen is shown immediately east of St Machar's cathedral, in the area where the Dunbar Halls of Residence were erected in the 1960s. According to Gordon of Rothiemay, it had been abandoned in 1639, before being looted and

stripped by Covenanting forces, and in 1655 it was demolished by the occupying English army to provide building materials for the construction of the artillery fortification on Castlehill. The remaining stones were taken for new work at King's College (Gordon 1842, 23). Nevertheless, the palace appears to have been arranged around a quadrangular courtyard, with towers at the corners, ranges of buildings along the north and possibly east walls, and a gatehouse in the south wall.

Although nothing can be seen of the palace itself, part of the Chaplains' Court, which lay to the south-east, is incorporated into a later townhouse in **The Chanonry**. Built by Bishop Dunbar's executors, Alexander Galloway and Alexander Spittal, this too is shown on Gordon of Rothiemay's map as a quadrangular courtyard, again with corner towers, and buildings along each side. According to Keith in the 1730s, each of the towers was allocated to a chaplain. Wooden chambers were built around the court, including a hall and pantry, and there was a draw-well in the centre (Robertson 1843, 156–7). One of the towers and a section of wall containing the reconstituted gateway into the courtyard are incorporated into the house. A plaque bearing Dunbar's coat of arms surmounts the gateway.

The bishop's palace may have been constructed on similar lines, if at a rather earlier date, and the depiction on Gordon of Rothiemay's map broadly accords with the description of the palace erected in about 1459 by Bishop Spence. He is said to have demolished the old palace, and built it anew with towers and battlements (Moir 1894, 53). When the Dunbar Halls of Residence were built, a complex of walls indicating three separate periods of construction was exposed (*DES 1965*, 1). More recently, following the demolition of the Dunbar Halls, an assessment by the Aberdeen Archaeological Unit revealed foundations of what was probably a two-storey building and medieval occupation (*DES 2002*, 7).

While the palace is largely lost, an inventory compiled in 1519 of the belongings of Bishop Alexander Gordon provides some idea of the accommodation required by a major church dignitary. This lists *'the wairdrope, the chawmer abun ye wardrape, the chawmer wndir ye wardrope, the chapell waist, the chapell chaumer, the grit chaumer, the closait'*, together with the study, hall, pantry, cellar, kitchen, larder, brewhouse, bakehouse, and the south-west tower (Innes 1845, ii, 174). Outside the court a further enclosure held the offices and a beehive doocot. On the south, between the palace and the Chaplains' Court, lay an orchard, with on its west wall a three-storey summer-house, *'whence one had a prospect of the whole town'* (Robertson 1843, 152). The insight provided by Alexander Gordon's inventory is presumably equally as relevant at **Old Rayne** or **Fetternear**.

Churches and Chapels

With the establishment of the parish system in the 12th century, the church became self-sufficient within the structure of local lordship, sustained by *teinds* and endowments. In many cases the churches of these parishes were probably already in existence, and in Donside at least the minsters recorded at **Clova** and inferred at **Kinkell** (pp. 130; 145) suggest a local organisation of mother churches and dependent chapels. As we have seen, the disposition of these chapels in the parish of Kinkell probably relates to the pattern of secular estates, and the collection of cross-marked stones and a cross-slab at **Dyce** (Fig. 7.18) indicates that at least one was an early foundation. In the early 12th century, however, the see was moved from Mortlach to Aberdeen, presumably to attend the new administrative centre established there. With the exception of those in Strathbogie – essentially Rhynie and Essie – the parishes of Donside all lie within its diocese, and most of them in the deaneries of Garioch and Mar.

With the move of the see, Aberdeen was to become the focus of a remarkable concentration of churches, chapels, friaries and hospitals, and an extraordinarily large population of clerics. The description of these various institutions has no place here, but they include the two greatest churches of the region, namely the cathedral of St Machar in Old Aberdeen (Fig. 8.28), and the parish church of St Nicholas in New Aberdeen. These were imposing churches by any standards and dominated the skylines of the two burghs, as can be

Fig. 8.28 **St Machar's Cathedral** *(NJ 9395 0882). View from the south-west showing the nave and the two towers at the western end. SC447498*

seen in Gordon of Rothiemay's view of Aberdeen in 1661 (Fig. 8.27). The nave and western towers of the Cathedral remain in use and date from between the 14th and early 16th centuries. The remains of the transepts can also be seen, the stumps of its walls incorporating a number of medieval tombs, but the 16th-century choir has been removed. This was quarried during the 1650s to provide stone for the Cromwellian fort at Castlehill, apparently fatally weakening the great central tower, which collapsed in 1688 and crushed the transepts.

Fig. 8.27 Aberdeen (NJ 930 080). This engraving from Slezer's Theatrum Scotiae shows Old Aberdeen in the middle of the 17th century, with St Machar's Cathedral occupying the centre of the view. The main tower above the crossing fell down in 1688. SC958184

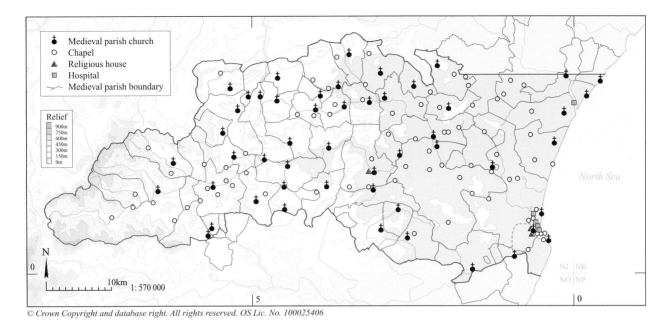

Fig. 8.29 This map shows the distribution of medieval parish churches, chapels and religious houses across Donside. GV000247

The parish church of St Nicholas appears on record in the early years of the 12th century, though the existing structure was extensively rebuilt in the 18th and 19th centuries, the nave in 1755, the choir in 1835, and the tower after a disastrous fire in 1874 (Cooper 1888–92; Cowan and Easson 1976, 214–15; Fraser 1989). Nevertheless, the medieval transepts, the crossing and the 15th-century undercroft still preserve an impression of the church's scale at the time of the Reformation. By then it had been considerably enlarged from the cruciform plan with an apsidal east end revealed by excavations in the 19th century. In the 14th century the nave, the aisles and the south transept were all extended, and in the early 15th century the undercroft chapel was added. Built on falling ground to the east, the undercroft served as the foundation to a great new choir with a polygonal apse. By the time of the Reformation the church of St Nicholas was the second longest parish church in Scotland, a church endowed by the families of burgesses and lairds, many of whom founded private chantries. Indeed, by the Reformation, over fifty chaplainries are documented at some thirty altars (Fraser 1989, 278–302). In the 1540s the church was formally established as a collegiate church.

In the hinterland of Aberdeen the transformation of the landscape that took place in the 18th and 19th centuries was matched stride for stride in the wholesale reconstruction and replacement of its parish churches. Of the churches in use today, only **Monymusk** overtly displays its medieval fabric (Fig. 8.31), while at **Clatt** the long, narrow ground-plan betrays a medieval predecessor beneath the harling. In addition to these two, the shells of but a handful of others remain – **Auchindoir**, **Kinkell**, **Forbes**, **Dyce** and **Nigg**

(Fig. 8.32). As they survive today, most of these are plain buildings, and it is only **Auchindoir** that preserves a more elaborate decorative repertoire. Nevertheless, surviving architectural fragments elsewhere suggest that the quality of the workmanship at **Auchindoir** was by no means unique, and reveal something of the sophistication that once existed amongst the rural churches that have been removed or are now represented only by mute footings.

With this wholesale reconstruction and replacement of the parish churches, the survival of the church of St Mary's at **Monymusk** is the more remarkable, for

*Fig. 8.30 **Kirk of St Nicholas** (NJ 9407 0629). A heavily eroded votive plaque, incorporated into the west wall of the Drum Aisle. SC949827*

*Fig. 8.31 **Monymusk** (NJ 6849 1524). The medieval fabric of the tower, nave and part of the chancel of St Mary's parish church survives largely intact. The east end of the chancel is lost in the burial-enclosure of the Grants of Monymusk. SC439422*

it is situated in a planned village established by Sir Archibald Grant in the early 18th century and rebuilt in the 19th century (p. 193). Over time the fabric has been considerably altered, but the tower, nave and existing chancel are substantially medieval in date. Built in neat granite ashlar, it is not only the largest of the rural parish churches in Donside, but it is also the only one with a tower. From the west a round-arched doorway with a hood moulding opens into the tower, from which an arch leads through to the nave. The plastered interior betrays little of its earlier history, but the chancel arch with its cushion capitals is evidently an original 12th-century feature. In its present form, the chancel has been shortened (Simpson 1925, 62–3), and its east end is lost in a burial-enclosure for the Grants of Monymusk bonded on to the east end of the church (Simpson 1943, 110). Monymusk is first recorded as a Culdee foundation, which may account for the various cross-marked stones that have been found here (Fig. 7.11). The lands of Monymusk and Keig, however, came into the possession of St Andrews Cathedral, traditionally by

royal grant, though the earl of Mar later appears as patron. By 1245 this link with St Andrews saw the replacement of the Culdee community with a house of Augustinian canons. Given the size of St Mary's, it is reasonable to presume that this is the priory church, but whether it also served the parish remains unclear (see discussion in Simpson 1925). If there was a separate parish church, it is now lost, along with the rest of the priory, which presumably included the administrative centre for the extensive monastic estate covering the parishes of Monymusk and Keig.

Of the other rural churches in Donside, **Auchindoir** (Figs 8.33–4) is perhaps more typical, and serves as an example of what may have been lost elsewhere. Standing hard by the tree-grown motte on the lip of the Den of Auchindoir, it displays the typical relationship to a secular estate centre so commonly encountered (p. 150), and the renovations of its fabric also reveal the role of wealthy patrons in its history. Now a roofless shell, in 1811 the church was replaced by a modern building on a new site some 500m to the east, though this too is now roofless.

The old church has undergone several phases of reconstruction, the most radical in the 16th and 17th centuries, but the core of the building dates from the beginning of the 13th century, at which time it measured

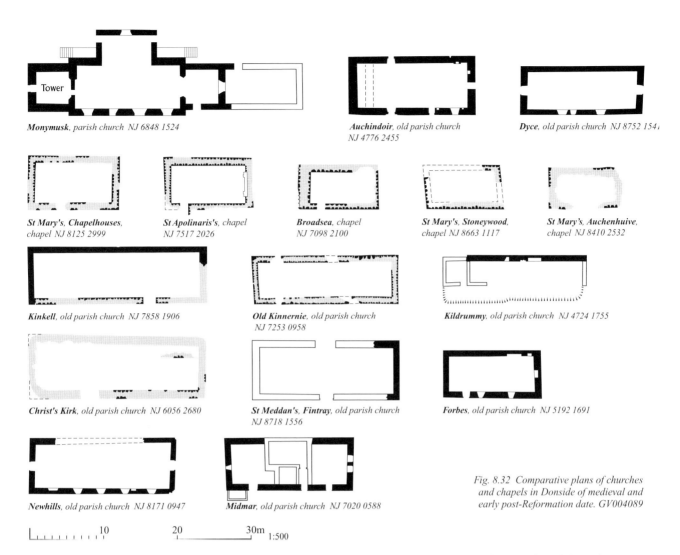

Monymusk, parish church NJ 6848 1524

Auchindoir, old parish church NJ 4776 2455

Dyce, old parish church NJ 8752 154|

St Mary's, Chapelhouses, chapel NJ 8125 2999

St Apolinaris's, chapel NJ 7517 2026

Broadsea, chapel NJ 7098 2100

St Mary's, Stoneywood, chapel NJ 8663 1117

St Mary's, Auchenhuive, chapel NJ 8410 2532

Kinkell, old parish church NJ 7858 1906

Old Kinnernie, old parish church NJ 7253 0958

Kildrummy, old parish church NJ 4724 1755

Christ's Kirk, old parish church NJ 6056 2680

St Meddan's, Fintray, old parish church NJ 8718 1556

Forbes, old parish church NJ 5192 1691

Newhills, old parish church NJ 8171 0947

Midmar, old parish church NJ 7020 0588

Fig. 8.32 Comparative plans of churches and chapels in Donside of medieval and early post-Reformation date. GV004089

10   20   30m 1:500

only 13.2m in internal length (Fig. 8.34). The church was subsequently lengthened, probably in the 17th century, and a new gable was built at the west end. The original position of the west gable is revealed by the quoins of the internal angles in both the north and south walls. Original openings include the fine late Romanesque doorway at the west end of the south wall, a plain arched doorway with a draw-bar hole in the north wall opposite it, and a blocked round-headed arch for a narrow window at the east end of the north wall.

In 1361 the parish revenues of Auchindoir were united with those of Invernochty (modern Strathdon) to support a canonry in Aberdeen Cathedral, and in 1514 Auchindoir was erected as a prebend in its own right, but of King's College rather than the Cathedral. If the standards of parochial cure suffered by this diversion of its revenues, the building itself was nevertheless to benefit from the College's patronage. About 1550 the window in the north wall was blocked with an elaborate sacrament house, and a new doorway was inserted into the east end of the south wall, together with an adjacent square-headed window to light the altar. The initials of the donor, M A S, appear repeatedly on the building: on the lintel of the doorway; in a shallow ogee recess

above it; on the sacrament house (Fig. 8.34); and on a graveslab of 1580 (Fig. 8.35). They can probably be identified with Master Alexander Strachan, a canon of the Cathedral (Simpson 1930, 63). Also of 16th-century date is a pair of armorial plaques built into the east gable, one bearing the three boars' heads, couped, of the Gordons of Craig and the date 1557, the other the Gordon arms impaled with those of the Cheynes.

*Fig. 8.33 **Auchindoir** (NJ 4776 2454). The ruins of the medieval parish church viewed from the south-east. SC447827*

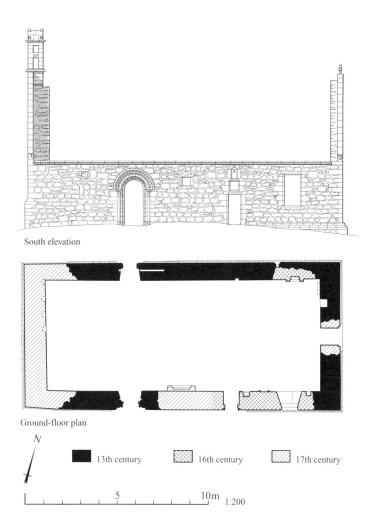

South elevation

Ground-floor plan

N

■ 13th century ▨ 16th century ▧ 17th century

5 10m 1:200

*Fig. 8.34 **Auchindoir** (NJ 4776 2455). Plan and south elevation
of the old parish church (GV004088), with photographs of the fine
13th-century doorway at the west end of the south wall (SC447829),
and the elaborate sacrament house inserted into the north wall in
the 16th century. SC447833*

The subsequent alterations in the 17th century were
more extensive, much of the work taking place during
the ministry of Mr William Davidson between 1621 and
1667. Several phases can be identified, beginning with
the insertion of a small rectangular window in the south
wall, probably to provide light for a pulpit constructed
in 1625, inscribed panels of which are still preserved
at **Craig Castle**. In 1638 a rectangular window was
inserted above the eastern door in the south wall, and the
legend NEC TIBI, NEC MIHI and the date, were added
to the ogee-headed panel. The date 1638 is also found
with Davidson's arms, on the southern skewput of the
east gable. This is presumably the date of a substantial
reconstruction of the gable, which involved the insertion
of a central doorway and a square window. It appears
that the gable was rebuilt from at least the level of an
internal ledge or scarcement that is visible immediately
above the top of the doorway.

The erection of the new west gable took place later
again, when the length of the church was increased
by 1.8m. The 13th-century basal plinth was extended
around the exterior of the new gable, but this work
is clearly inferior, and the gable itself incorporates
numerous fragments of earlier stonework, including a
roll-moulding of 16th-century date. A small rectangular
window in the gable probably lit a loft, the presence

of which is indicated by two rows of sockets in its inner face. The gable is capped with a belfry dated 1664, which is also the date at which Davidson was instructed to carry out repairs to the church. Whether these included the construction of the new gable is not known.

The pattern of renovation and reconstruction seen at **Auchindoir** was probably played out at many of the churches that were replaced in the 18th and 19th centuries, and can certainly be detected at **Kinkell** and **Dyce**. At **Kinkell** the reuse of the church as a private burial-aisle and the heavy consolidation of its walls have left few visible clues to the building's date, but in common with **Auchindoir**, the church was to benefit from the appropriation of **Kinkell** to a canonry, in this case of Aberdeen Cathedral, and in particular from the patronage of its parson, Master Alexander Galloway. Galloway was a close associate of Bishop Dunbar, serving as master of works for a number of major building projects, and his personal involvement in **Kinkell** can be seen in an elaborate, though now sadly weathered, sacrament house bearing his initials and the date 1524. The church itself is a remarkably long building, perhaps reflecting its inferred status as a minster (p. 145), but in the early 16th century the walls of the chancel were raised and the east gable was reconstructed to accommodate a large tracery window. Later benefactions include a mural plaque bearing a depiction of the Crucifixion, and a font, the latter now in St John's Episcopal Church, Aberdeen. The church also possessed a wooden chancel screen, now long vanished (Robertson 1843, 571–2).

Galloway's interest in the fabric of the churches under his care is again seen at **Dyce**, and probably at another of Kinkell's dependencies, **Kintore**. At **Dyce** the sill of a sacrament house bearing Galloway's arms is preserved, and the shell of the church itself appears to be substantially of 16th-century date, if considerably modified thereafter. All that remains of the medieval church at **Kintore** is a particularly elaborate sacrament house, which is also likely to be a product of Galloway's patronage.

Similar links back to Aberdeen Cathedral recur at **Clatt**, where the skewput at the south-east corner bears a shield and what appear to be the letters A S, the initials of Alexander Spittal, the 16th-century prebendary of Clatt. He was presumably responsible for a remodelling of the church immediately prior to the Reformation, and is noted with Alexander Galloway as Bishop Dunbar's executors in the building of the Chaplains' Court in Old Aberdeen (p. 163). At first sight the harled walls and tall round-headed windows of Clatt parish church give the appearance of a late 18th-century date, but it evidently incorporates the greater part of a medieval building. Not only is this implicit in the character of its narrow plan, but the level of an earlier wallhead is clearly revealed in the quoins at the corners,

and a painted and gilded sacrament house was exposed during rebuilding work in 1799. This was presumably the church with which Alexander Spittal was associated, its wall subsequently raised in the late 18th century to accommodate the new windows and the galleries.

Few features of note survive elsewhere, even at **Forbes** where the shell of another substantially pre-Reformation church stands within its burial-ground.

Fig. 8.35 **Auchindoir** *(NJ 4776 2454). The initials on the graveslab set up in the north-east corner of the church probably refer to Master Alexander Strachan. SC958183*

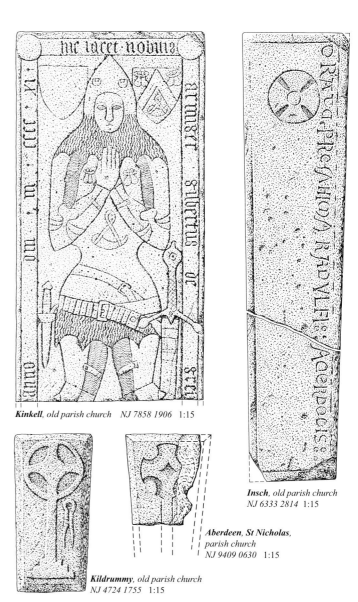

Foveran, parish church NJ 9849 2414 1:15

Kinkell, old parish church NJ 7858 1906 1:15

Kildrummy, old parish church
NJ 4724 1755 1:15

Aberdeen, St Nicholas,
parish church
NJ 9409 0630 1:15

Insch, old parish church
NJ 6333 2814 1:15

*Fig. 8.36 This selection of medieval graveslabs is drawn from a wider selection across Donside. The earlier of the slabs include that at **Insch** to a priest named Radulf, which is probably of 12th- to 14th-century date; the later, the slabs at **Foveran** to members of the Turing family, at **Kinkell** to Gilbert de Gren[lau], died 1411, and at **Kildrummy**. This last slab is carved in low relief, depicting a knight and his wife dressed in a style dating from the beginning of the 15th century, but the slab appears to have been reused in the 16th century and an inscription cut into its edge commemorates Alexander Forbes of Brux and his wife Mariota. These slabs are finely carved, and were probably originally painted, but there are also a series of much rougher stones, presumably cut by local masons, such as those from **St Meddan's, Fintray**. GV004150; GV004157*

At **Kildrummy** the much reworked north wall of the church incorporates a medieval tomb recess, and at St Meddan's, **Fintray**, a crudely carved sacrament house is preserved in the remaining fragment of the east end. Another tomb recess has been built into the wall of the burial-ground at **Rhynie**, and is accompanied by a monolithic sarcophagus of probable 12th- or 13th-century date.

Of the numerous private and dependent chapels documented, few remain visible. Where they do, such as at **Broadsea** (Chapel of Braco), **Stoneywood**, **Chapelhouses**, **St Apolinaris's Chapel**, and **Chapelton of Sinnahard**, they were simple rectangles on plan, and not much smaller than the church at **Auchindoir** (Fig. 8.32). Those at both **Stoneywood** and **Chapelhouses** were associated with a well. In the case of the latter, this was credited with beneficial properties and was still attracting pilgrims in the 17th century, much to the disquiet of the Presbytery.

Despite the loss of so many of the churches and chapels, a wide range of funerary monuments survives. The most impressive single collection is preserved in the church of St Nicholas, Aberdeen, where there are no fewer than seven 15th-century effigies: three male in armour; one male in civilian costume; and three female. Tradition identifies the men as Irvine of Drum, and Provosts Davidson, Collison and Menzies, but more importantly these effigies are testimony to the

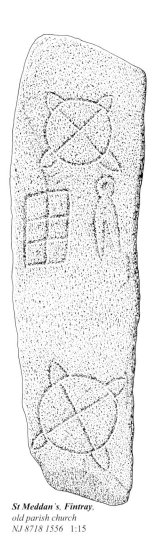

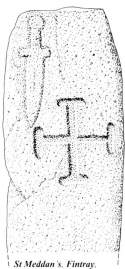

St Meddan's, *Fintray*,
old parish church
NJ 8718 1556 1:15

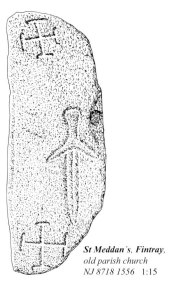

St Meddan's, *Fintray*,
old parish church
NJ 8718 1556 1:15

Kildrummy, old parish church NJ 4724 1755 1:15

St Meddan's, *Fintray*,
old parish church
NJ 8718 1556 1:15

prosperity and social aspirations of the burgesses of Aberdeen. Two monumental brasses, and a number of stone matrices for others, are all imports from the Low Countries, revealing the late medieval burgh's trading links with the Continent. Another collection of effigies is preserved at St Machar's Cathedral, though here they are of ecclesiastics dating from the late 14th and 15th centuries. There is also an unusual effigial mural plaque, and two robbed matrices for monumental brasses.

Accomplished funerary monuments were not restricted to the burghs, and are also found widely in the burial-grounds of country churches. At **Bourtie**, for example, the effigies of a knight and a lady can be seen, and there is another knight at **Insch**. These effigies can probably be dated to the late 13th century, and presumably commemorate the descendants of Anglo-French settlers in the Garioch. The most widespread form of medieval funerary monument, however, is the recumbent graveslab (Fig. 8.36). These survive in a

variety of forms, as can be seen from the collection in the church of St Nicholas, where they range from a possible 12th-century slab bearing a cross and elaborate chipwork decoration, to a stone with a crudely incised Latin cross. A calvary cross-slab from **Kildrummy** parish church is now preserved in Marischal College Museum, and further lost examples are known from **Kildrummy Castle** and **Towie** parish church. Early 15th-century incised slabs at **Kinkell** and **Foveran** depict military figures in the plate armour of the period.

The majority of these stones were the work of skilled masons employing readily worked freestone, and it is probably no accident that a cluster of such slabs is known from **Kildrummy** and **Towie**, close to an important source of sandstone. Not all the monuments are so accomplished, and some roughly shaped slabs at St Meddan's, **Fintray** (Fig. 8.36), and a diminutive calvary cross at **Chapel of Garioch**, are presumably the work of local cowans utilising less tractable country stones.

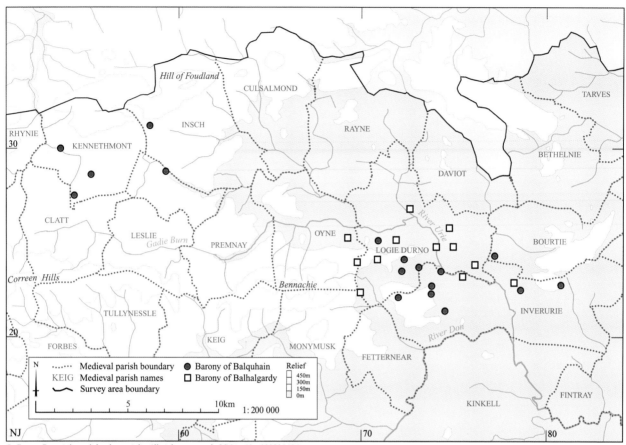

Fig. 8.37 This map shows the scattered holdings that made up the baronies of Balquhain and Balhalgardy. GV000258

Baronies

Baronies with judicial powers and a barony court became more common with the fragmentation of the regional lordships. Between the 14th and 17th centuries this led to the establishment of seventy-five or so baronies in Donside. Before that time such judicial powers are rarely attested. Nevertheless, the grant between 1172 and 1185 of Leslie by Earl David to Malcolm, son of Bertolf (pp. 145–6), included *sake, soke, toll, team* and *infangenthief* (Stringer 1985, 254), the judicial rights that came to be regarded as one of the measures of a barony (Duncan 1988, 41–4). Subsequently, by 1390, Leslie was granted baronial status (Robertson and Grubb 1847–62, iii, 393). The barony of Leslie is not alone in preserving a block of land that appears in an earlier grant, other examples including Strathbogie and the episcopal baronies of Clatt, Rayne and Tullynessle. In the case of Kintore and Belhelvie, the baronies were converted from old thanages, even if some of the lands were hived off (Grant 1993, 65ff.). While baronies such as these were relatively compact territories, as the regional lordships broke down many of the new creations were made up of scattered holdings. The examples illustrated here (Fig. 8.37) are Balhalgardy and Balquhain, but many of

the other new creations reveal the same pattern, such as Skene, Cluny and Pitfoddels.

Just as the earlier estates are often manifested in the remains of manorial centres and churches, so the principal monuments of the baronies are many of the tower-houses that are found in apparent profusion throughout the area (Fig. 8.9). Where there was an earlier manorial centre, a new tower-house might be built on or adjacent to its site, such as the tower standing within the moated enclosure at **Leslie Castle**. In other cases a tower was erected some distance away, as at **Midmar Castle**, which stands 800m to the south-east of the earlier motte. At **Auchindoir** too, the motte beside the old parish church was replaced by a tower, **Craig Castle**, which is set back up the Burn of Craig. Still others were apparently built *de novo*, such as **Balquhain Castle** in the parish of Chapel of Garioch, **Mains of Brux** in Kildrummy, and Muchall (**Castle Fraser**) in Cluny.

These towers apart, baronial status has also left a more subtle mark in the landscape, enshrined within *Court-* and *Gallow-* place-names rather than any visible monument. These are found throughout Donside and mark some of the locations where justice was exercised, though some of the *Court*-names may derive from the Gaelic *corthie*, meaning standing stone (e.g. *Courthillock*, an obsolete name recorded near a standing stone in Kennethmont parish). In some cases the barony courts utilised prominent, and possibly numinous, landmarks as their meeting places. In 1381 and 1382, for example, the bishop of Aberdeen's head courts were held *'apud montem capelle beati Thome Martiris iuxta canoniam de Aberdon'* – at the hill of the chapel of St Thomas the Martyr beside the canonry of Aberdeen (Innes 1845, i, 135). This is sometimes thought to be a reference to **Tillydrone** motte though it possibly refers to some other mound close by the Cathedral. Elsewhere, the bishop's court in 1389 was held at the standing stones of Rayne, possibly to be identified with the stone circle of **Old Rayne** (Innes 1845, i, 80), while in the mid-14th century Thomas, Earl of Mar, held his head court *'at the stone of Migvie in Cromar'* (Robertson and Grubb 1847–62, iv, 716). In 1468, 1548 and 1614 the barony court of Cluny was held *'apud lie Gray Stane de Cluny'* (Robertson and Grubb 1847–62, iv, 404; Browne 1923, 95; Huntly 1894, 225).

The *Gallow*-names are an altogether more menacing relic of these judicial powers. The power of *infangenthief*, granted to Malcolm, son of Bertolf, gave him the right to execute a criminal apprehended within the lands of Leslie. He was also licensed to maintain his own gallows, though whether this stood on the Gallow Hill about 1km north of Leslie Castle is not known. Elsewhere, there is anecdotal evidence of human remains encountered at several such sites during the agricultural improvements of the 18th and 19th centuries. More recently, in 1978, two extended and oriented graves containing the remains of three individuals were discovered on the top of a Gallows Hillock in Towie parish. Its name has changed more recently to **Bogneish Hillock**, but the burials have been interpreted as possible execution victims (*DES 1978*, 10).

In some cases, a *Gallow*-name lies close to the march of the baronial lands, but in others it is much closer to a tower at the centre of a barony. In a compact barony, this was presumably the normal venue for the court in session. The towers at three such centres are presented by way of illustration, but these have also been selected to reflect the architectural evolution of castles and tower-houses from the 14th to the 17th century, which saw defensive retreats transformed into elegant country houses standing within designed landscapes. **Castle of Hallforest** (Figs 8.38–9), situated within the bounds of what had been the Royal Forest of Kintore, and possibly on the site of a moated predecessor, represents the first stage in this progression, probably being the seat of a high-ranking member of the late medieval nobility and one of very few 14th-century stone keeps in the north-east of Scotland. **Balquhain Castle** (Figs 8.42–4), on the other hand, first documented as a barony in 1511, relates to the later stages, bridging the change from a 15th-century manor to a more comfortable mansion. The sequence from **Castle of Esslemont** (Fig. 8.40) is even longer, displaying the transition from 14th-century moated manor to late-medieval tower-house, and then post-medieval Renaissance-style tower-

Fig. 8.38 ***Castle of Hallforest*** *(NJ 7772 1541). The castle seen from the south. SC961137*

house, before it was finally abandoned in 1799 in favour of the country house that occupies the policies to the north-west (Simpson 1944, 100).

All that is visible at **Castle of Hallforest** today are the ruins of the keep, but this would not have stood alone, and the wall of an enclosure is depicted on an engraving of 1840 by James Giles (1936, pl. lxxiv). The only hint of an enclosure today, however, is a shallow gully about 35m to the west of the keep, which may mark the line of a ditch and perhaps the presence of an earlier moated manor or hunting lodge. The castle itself measures in excess of 14m by 9m overall, and its walls are some 2m in thickness, supporting two vaults. The lower of these formed the floor of the first-floor hall, and the upper the floor of a chamber above, but each vaulted compartment was also divided into two storeys by a wooden entresol floor. The principal entrance was evidently at the level of the first-floor hall, and was served by an external wooden stair. Whether there was ever an independent entrance into the basement is uncertain, though there is now a ragged breach near the south-east angle. At this level the walls are otherwise pierced only with narrow window loops. The kitchen occupied the entresol above the basement, where there is a fireplace and an oven in the east gable, but it is not clear how access between floors worked, either down into the basement, or up into the hall above. The latter has a fireplace flanked by two narrow windows in the west gable, but the hall was also lit by two large openings in the south wall, though these may not be in

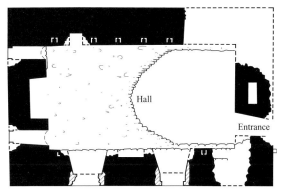

First-floor plan

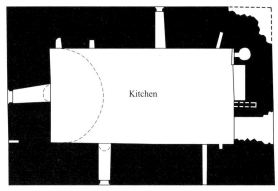

Entresol plan

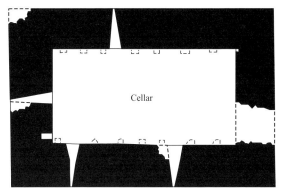

Ground-floor plan

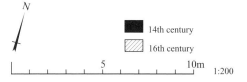

N

14th century

16th century

5   10m
                   1:200

*Fig. 8.39 **Castle of Hallforest** (NJ 7772 1541). GV000206*

their original form. The eastern retains the holes for an external iron grille. A gap in the wall adjacent to the entrance at the south-east angle presumably marks the position of a newel stair to the upper floors, but with the collapse of the eastern end, many details of these upper floors have been lost. However, whereas the entresol has no evidence of any openings, the chamber above the vault has two windows on the south and others on the north and west. Presumably there was also another floor

above this, with some sort of wall-walk and a parapet, but this has been entirely lost.

The date at which the keep was built is not recorded, and there is nothing in the structure that allows it to be dated closely. Nevertheless, its simple rectangular shape, with thick walls and two vaults, is a design that occurs in other probable 14th-century castles, from nearby Drum, on the Dee, to Balthayock in Perth & Kinross (RCAHMS 1994, 139) and Torthorwald in Dumfriesshire (RCAHMS 1997a, 201). Unfortunately the documentary record for **Castle of Hallforest** does not allow any greater precision. The Royal Forest of Kintore was included among other lands in the grant of the title of Marischal to Robert de Keith in 1324 (Duncan 1988, 524–5), which would certainly have provided a suitable occasion for the construction of a new tower, but the name does not appear until 1351, recorded in the formula *'in aula foreste mee de Kinto(re)'* (in the hall of my forest of Kintore) in a charter of William de Keith (Webster 1982, 163). This wording, however, perhaps implies no more than a hall, rather than the keep there today. As such it may have referred to an earlier building associated with the possible moated enclosure, though the latter might equally be the remains of a royal hunting lodge (pp. 146–7).

The documentation of **Castle of Esslemont** (Fig. 8.40), which stands in a plantation beside the A920 public road, is rather fuller. The lands of *'Essilmont'* appear as a separate holding in the late 14th century, when the Marischal family were in possession. In 1500, however, following a fire which destroyed the *'Place of Essilmont'* in 1493 (Robertson 1843, 304), the Cheyne family were given licence to build a tower and fortalice (Robertson, 1843, 317). Shortly afterwards, in a charter of 1515–16 to Patrick and Alexander Cheyne, Esslemont is described as a *'fortalice and manor'* (Paul and Thomson 1984, 13). In 1564 Patrick Cheyne was created Baron of Esslemont by Queen Mary, who stayed there during her campaign against the earl of Huntly, and a fortalice and tower are also recorded in 1575–6 (Thomson 1984b, 681).

The earliest element of the castle is a moated enclosure (Fig. 8.40), the interior of which was subsequently enclosed by a curtain wall with round corner turrets. The latter is probably late medieval in date, finding parallels at places like Craigmillar, near Edinburgh, and Threave in The Stewartry. Lying symmetrically at the centre of this enclosure are the ruins of an L-plan tower-house. This was excavated in 1938 (Simpson 1944) and, to judge from its plan and the thickness of the walls (2m), belongs in the late 15th or early 16th century, but a later wing also extends south and slights the line of the curtain wall, suggesting that by the time of the latter's construction defence was no longer an overriding concern. In addition to the central tower, the roofless shell of a 16th- or 17th-century tower-house stands on the line of the earlier curtain and the moat on the east. This is evidently the house that was in use when the new country house was built at the end of the 18th century. Standing side by side, the two towers are remarkably different in style and construction.

The L-plan tower at the centre had a ground-floor entrance in the re-entrant. This opened into a lobby, from which the main stairs led left to the first floor, and a doorway at the back led through into a basement room. This provided access to a service stair in its west corner, a store on the north, and the kitchen in the eastern wing. A second service stair rose from the south corner of the kitchen. The springers for a stone vault are still visible in the western block of the tower, where, like **Colquhonnie Castle** (Fig. 8.41), there was probably a first-floor hall. The wing added to the south is of much slighter construction and is more akin to that of the later three-storey tower-house standing to the east. The walls of the latter are comparatively insubstantial, and a large round turret at its eastern angle evidently displays architectural pretensions rather than any defensive merit. The entrance is again in a re-entrant, where a square staircase leads to the upper floors.

Fig. 8.40 **Castle of Esslemont** *(NJ 9321 2974). Plan of the moated enclosure (I) and the tower-houses successively built in the centre of the interior (II), and across the line of the perimeter on the east (III). These were replaced at the end of the 18th century by a country house on a new site to the north. GV000198*

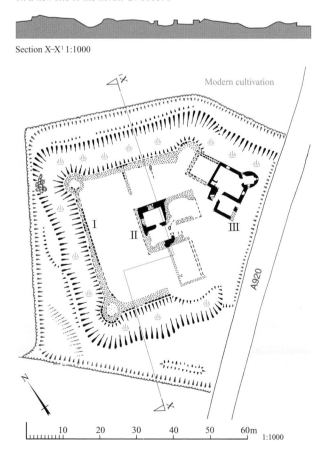

Section X–X¹ 1:1000

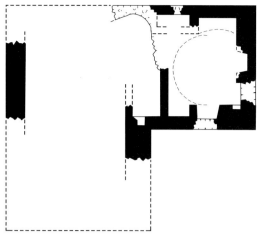

First-floor plan

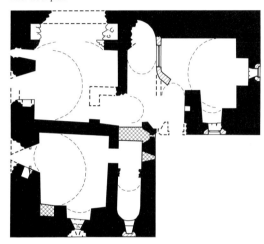

Ground-floor plan

N

■ 16th century
▨ 19th century
▨ later

5   10m
                    1:200

Fig. 8.41 **Colquhonnie Castle** *(NJ 3653 1258). GV000204*

According to Simpson there were extensive traces of fire in and around the central tower, leading him to conclude that this was the *'Place of Esslemont'* destroyed in 1493. Little sign of burning is evident on the stonework today, but in any case there is nothing in the reference to the *'Place of Esslemont'* to suggest a tower-house or a castellated structure. The buildings that were destroyed were more probably largely of timber, on the model of the late-medieval buildings excavated at the manor at Rattray (Murray and Murray 1993). In practice, the stump of the tower, which still stands about 2m high, would have proved very inconvenient for the occupants of the later house. Thus, it is more likely that the central tower is the fortalice built in the early 16th century, which, along with the wing added on the south, remained in use as an ancillary building to the later house.

A similar transition from defensive tower into mansion can be seen at **Balquhain Castle** (Fig. 8.42), where a tower and fortalice is first documented in 1545 (Paul and Thomson 1984, 734). The surviving ruins, however, incorporate the remains of a somewhat earlier three-storey tower with a crenellated parapet, which was probably built in the 15th century. The estate of Balquhain first appears as a barony in 1511 (Paul 1984, 775–6), but it had been the eponymous possession of Sir William Leslie of Balquhain as early as 1460 (Paul 1984, 157). As such, it is essentially an example of a baronial castle built *de novo*, and its lands are scattered through several parishes (Fig. 8.37). The castle was apparently destroyed in 1526, but rebuilt in 1530, and in 1562 Queen Mary spent the night there before the Battle of Corrichie. With the move to **Fetternear** by the Leslies in the late 17th century (p. 180), the fortunes of **Balquhain** were set to wane. In 1746 the tower and its ancillary buildings were burnt by the Duke of Cumberland, never to be repaired (Simpson 1936b).

The fabric of Balquhain reveals a complex history, in which the crenellated building incorporated into the tower is the earliest visible component. Subsequently a substantial stone range was added at the south-west corner of the early building (Figs 8.43–4), its accommodation probably comprising a first-floor hall with stores at basement level. Together, the two blocks provided a hall and chamber arrangement typical of the 15th or early 16th century.

*Fig. 8.42 **Balquhain Castle** (NJ 7315 2361). The castle viewed from the east bank of the Strathnaterick Burn. SC961138*

*Fig. 8.43 **Balquhain Castle** (NJ 7315 2361). General site plan of the tower-house and its surrounding buildings. GV000257*

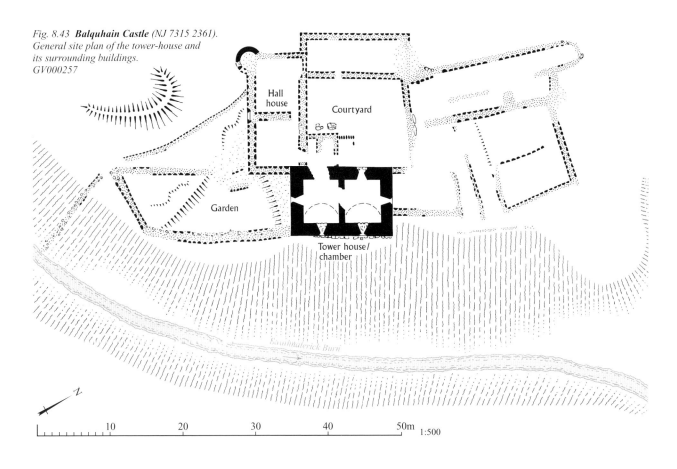

Hall house

Courtyard

Garden

Tower house / chamber

10   20   30   40   50m   1:500

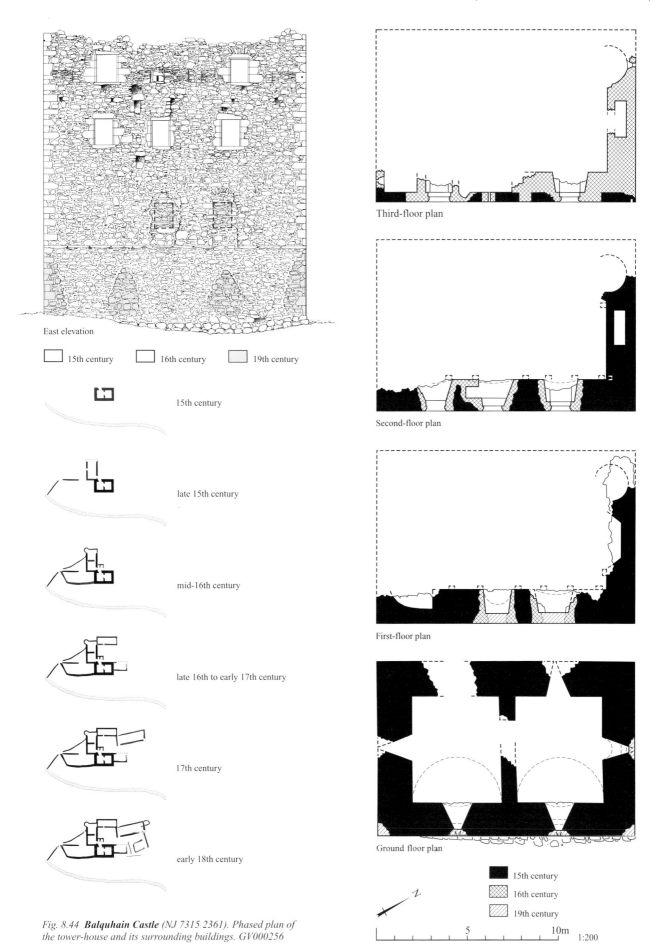

East elevation

☐ 15th century　　☐ 16th century　　▨ 19th century

15th century

late 15th century

mid-16th century

late 16th to early 17th century

17th century

early 18th century

Third-floor plan

Second-floor plan

First-floor plan

Ground floor plan

■ 15th century
▨ 16th century
▨ 19th century

5　　　　10m
1:200

*Fig. 8.44 **Balquhain Castle** (NJ 7315 2361). Phased plan of the tower-house and its surrounding buildings. GV000256*

*Fig. 8.45 **Tolquhon Castle** (NJ 8726 2862). Rather than providing a formidable defence, this late 16th-century gatehouse was intended to convey the status of its occupants. SC961133*

During the 16th century further modifications were carried out, with the addition of a stair-turret in the re-entrant between the tower and the range. This provided access to the first floors of both, and presumably linked the hall in the range, now the south wing, with the main private chambers in the tower. This phase of alterations may also have included the raising of the tower another storey, and the remodelling of the south wing, where the west end was rebuilt with a turret at its south-west corner, and a thick dividing wall was inserted into the interior, blocking the entrance in its south wall. A quirked roll-moulding in the turret window, and the style of the turret itself, suggest a date in the mid- to late 16th century for this work. Another building was butted onto the north wall of the tower, and, following the reconstruction of the south wing, yet another was added on the west to create a formal square courtyard. Several other features fit less easily into this sequence, including a possible garden enclosure on the south of the tower, and the remains of buildings to the north. The latter may have included stabling and stores, but they partly block the impressive approach to the courtyard and may relate to a later phase of occupation, after the family had moved to **Fetternear**.

The towers at **Balquhain** and **Hallforest** make an interesting comparison, for though they are roughly the same size on plan, the original tower at **Balquhain** never attained the height of **Hallforest**, and its walls are much thinner. The vaulted basement at **Balquhain** is also too low for an entresol, and is sub-divided into two small vaulted chambers by a central stone partition. If there was an original ground-floor entrance, it lay in the north-west wall, but it is more likely that the main entrance was at first-floor level, probably in the missing north-west wall. Two blocked first-floor openings in the south-east wall were probably windows to light the hall, though possibly in different phases. Little remains above this level, but the second floor presumably contained the private chambers. These were lit in the 16th century by three windows in the south-east wall, the middle opening also including a garderobe. The floor added above had only two windows in this wall.

There are some similarities here with the development of **Tolquhon Castle**, near Pitmedden (Fig. 8.45). This comprises a 15th-century tower, where a courtyard was added in the Renaissance style during the 16th century. As with all such developments, more ephemeral medieval predecessors may have been removed, but these substantially built 16th- and 17th-century additions reflect the changing demands and outlook of the upper classes. Even **Kildrummy Castle** was extensively modified in a Renaissance style. Not only was the chamber block restyled as a tower-house by the Elphinstones, but the south side of the great hall was reworked with a series of chambers.

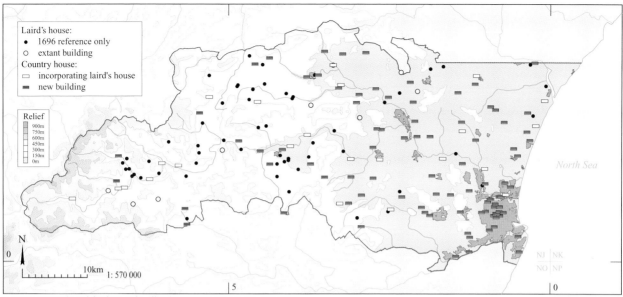

© Crown Copyright and database right. All rights reserved. OS Lic. No. 100025406

Fig. 8.46 Many of the laird's houses are only known from the Poll Tax returns of 1696 and are now lost, but others may have been incorporated into later country houses. GV000221

Gentlemen's Houses

Other gentlemen were not sufficiently important to be given rights of free barony, but they were wealthy enough to build a tower-house at their seat. The tower-house of **Colquhonnie** (Fig. 8.41) in the parish of Strathdon is one example, built as a seat of a branch of the Forbes family, **Tillycairn Castle** in Cluny, built by the Lumsden family, is another. Several other well-known tower-houses fall into this category, such as **Asloun Castle** and **Balfluig Castle** in Alford, **Pitfichie Castle** in Monymusk, and **Harthill Castle** in Oyne (Simpson 1921). While the remains of towers such as these serve to mark some of the family seats, it is clear from the Poll Tax return of 1696 and the parish descriptions dating from 1721–44 in Macfarlane's *Geographical Collections* that many others are lost. The Poll Tax return identifies no less than 128 gentlemen in Donside, though this figure includes notaries and ministers of the church, while Macfarlane's *Geographical Collections* lists in excess of 100 gentlemen's houses and a handful of *'old castles'*. The latter include **Kildrummy Castle**, **Badenyon**, **Corgarff Castle**, **Towie Castle**, **Dunnideer**, **Old Slains Castle** and **Dumbreck Castle**, but none of the more ancient earthwork castles, such as the **Doune of Invernochty** or the **Bass of Inverurie** (Mitchell and Clark 1906–8, i, 1–99). Many of the places referred to as *'old castles'* had already fallen into ruin, but their inclusion alongside **Kildrummy** and **Dunnideer** implies that they were regarded as ancient places of strength. **Badenyon**, which comprised a tower enclosed by a deep ditch (Name Book Aberdeenshire, No. 81, p. 40), had been abandoned by the Gordon family in about 1590 in favour of **Glenbuchat Castle**, a Z-plan tower-house at the mouth of the glen. **Old Slains Castle**, on a rocky

coastal promontory at the north edge of the survey area, had been blown up by order of James VI in 1594 and is described in Macfarlane's *Geographical Collections* as a ruin. **Corgarff Castle** had been burnt in 1571, though it was subsequently rebuilt by the earl of Mar. Later still, in the mid-18th century, **Corgarff** was converted into a barracks for a Hanoverian garrison and enclosed within the star-shaped curtain wall that surrounds the tower today (Fig. 8.47). Most of these *'old castles'* were no longer the seats of gentlemen, and their evident defensive qualities were at odds with the contemporary architectural fashions.

The great majority of earlier tower-houses, often modified during the 16th and 17th centuries, were now viewed primarily as houses. Thus, **Castle Fraser**, known as Muchall until the 17th century, is mentioned in Macfarlane's *Geographical Collections* as a house, as is **Druminnor Castle**, the seat of the family of Forbes. The change of name of Muchall to **Castle Fraser** was clearly to impress, and was not to be confused with any

*Fig. 8.47 **Corgarff Castle** (NJ 2545 0866) was converted into a garrison for Hanoverian troops in the mid-18th century and provided with a star-shaped curtain wall. SC961139*

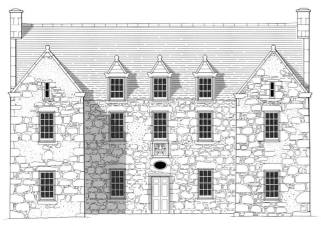

South-east elevation

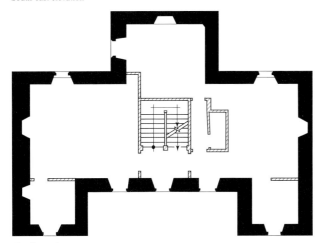

First-floor plan

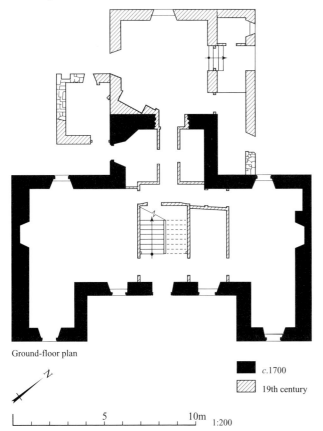

Ground-floor plan

■ *c*.1700

▨ 19th century

5   10m
1:200

fortified redoubt. This was after all a list of the houses of gentlemen. Many of the other houses listed, however, are also tower-houses, such as **Pitfichie Castle**, near Monymusk, renovated from a ruin in the 20th century, and in some cases, for example **Cluny Castle**, they have been incorporated into country houses. Yet others were built as country houses in their own right, such as the fine mansion of **Skellater** (Fig. 8.48) in the parish of Strathdon.

The general shift away from defensive architecture is nowhere better shown than at **Fetternear**, which was acquired by the Leslies of **Balquhain** after the Reformation. Whereas at **Balquhain** the transition into a mansion was managed by the erection of additional blocks, at **Fetternear** they created an integrated house in a single block (Fig. 8.49). This comprised a first-floor hall set between two three-storey towers. The stair-turret at the corner of the east tower provided access from a kitchen in the basement to the floors above. This symmetrical design of a central range with towers at either end is by no means unique to **Fetternear** and can also be seen at Kellie Castle, Fife (McKean 2001, 134–6). Subsequently, in the 1690s, with the removal of the family seat from **Balquhain**, Count Patrick Leslie enlarged **Fetternear** to create the familiar corner-turreted central block with wings that in essence survives today. His armorial, dated 1693, is displayed in the wall above the central doorway. In the course of these radical alterations he rebuilt the whole of the façade of the central block, building a second stair-turret to improve the symmetry and adding a third floor. This was probably surmounted with an attic floor lit by half dormers, but in 1818 the whole wallhead was revamped with crenellations in a mock baronial style similar to that at Taymouth Castle in Perth & Kinross. At the same time the windows were enlarged to suit more contemporary tastes.

Despite such extensive alteration, **Fetternear** survives substantially intact, but there are many others where the character of the building is largely unknown. At best, a few architectural fragments may be preserved in a garden or the walls of a steading, at worst they have gone without a trace. **Culquharrie**, on the south bank of the Don near Strathdon Parish Church, falls in this latter category, as do the houses of six lairds, all but one surnamed Forbes, listed in the Poll Tax return for Glen Nochty, at **Ledmacay**, **Invernettie**, **Corriebreck**, **Belnaboddach**, **Bellabeg** and **Invernochty** respectively. Some of these lairds may have built small tower-houses, for there can be little doubt that height was often used to impress, as can be seen at **Castle Fraser** and **Craigievar Castle** but, from the 17th century, gentlemen of lesser means often opted for less ostentatious houses laid out horizontally rather than

*Fig. 8.48 **Skellater House** (NJ 3146 1076). This fine house, dating from the late 17th or early 18th century, ably demonstrates the trend away from defensive architecture. GV004086*

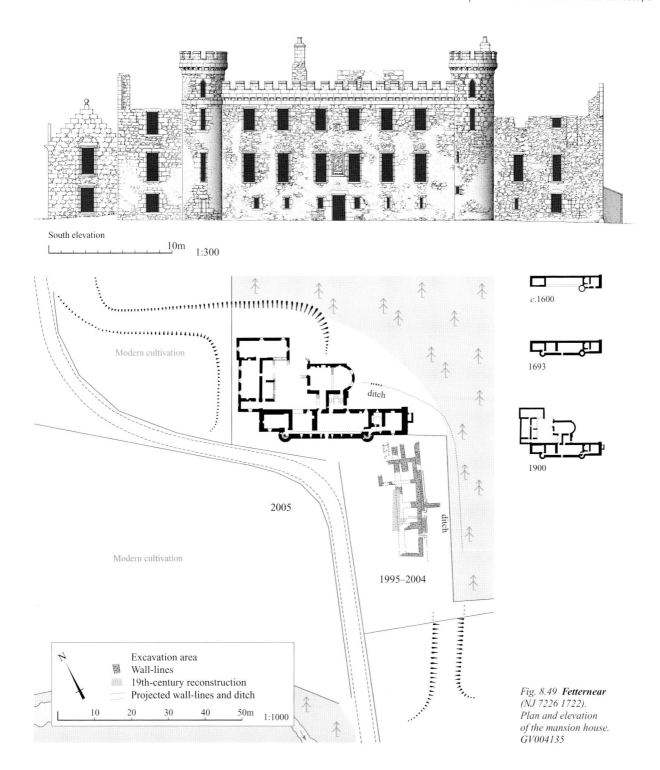

South elevation

10m   1:300

Modern cultivation

ditch

2005

Modern cultivation

1995–2004

ditch

*c.*1600

1693

1900

N

Excavation area
Wall-lines
19th-century reconstruction
Projected wall-lines and ditch

10   20   30   40   50m   1:1000

Fig. 8.49 **Fetternear**
(NJ 7226 1722).
Plan and elevation
of the mansion house.
GV004135

vertically. **Tullos House** in Chapel of Garioch parish is one such house, which appears in Macfarlane's lists but not in the Poll Tax return. Originally L-shaped on plan, with an entrance in the re-entrant, by 1973 it had been reduced to a rectangular ruin divided by a partition wall.

Examples of houses of this type are scattered throughout Aberdeenshire, such as at Balnacraig on Deeside, but in Donside **Tullos House** continues to be a relatively rare survival. Nevertheless, as a result of the survey several others have been identified, the best-preserved of which is incorporated into the old

farmhouse at **Mains of Brux** (Figs 8.50–1). Dating from the early 18th century, it measures almost 18m in overall length by 5.3m in breadth, and is only slightly smaller than the surviving block at **Tullos House**. The ground-floor openings are now almost entirely 19th century in character, but there was originally a symmetrical arrangement, with four equally spaced windows and a central entrance in the south-east façade. The interior was probably divided into at least three compartments, those at the ends served by fireplaces in the gables and the central one by a blocked fireplace on the rear wall.

Fig. 8.50 **Mains of Brux** *(NJ 4903 1692). The rear elevation and north-east gable of the now derelict farmhouse incorporates the shell of an early 18th-century laird's house. SC961135*

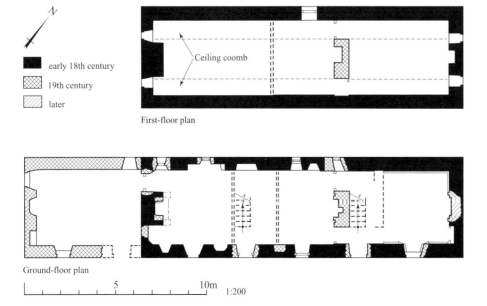

N

■ early 18th century

▨ 19th century

▧ later

Ceiling coomb

First-floor plan

Ground-floor plan

5   10m
1:200

Fig. 8.51 **Mains of Brux** *(NJ 4903 1692). Plan of the laird's house incorporated into the derelict farmhouse. GV000202*

The kitchen was probably at the south-west end, where the lintel of the early 18th-century fireplace is supported by reused corbels from a demolished tower-house of 16th-century date, and there is a recess in the rear wall with a small window opening in its centre. This recess is paralleled in the 18th-century laird's house at Balsarroch in Wigtownshire (Smith 1985).

Mains of Brux, or the tower-house that preceded it, is presumably the manor house of Brux listed in Macfarlane's *Geographical Collections*, but other small houses of this date have escaped without a mention. One of these was discovered at **Foggiemill**, in the Deskry Water, where the doorway was framed with roll-mouldings and the lintel bore the date 1717 and the initials CF·GF. Measuring 13.1m by 6.1m overall, the house was rebuilt as a cottage with two dormers at the turn of the 19th century, but until recently the ground floor appears to have retained its original openings, with a symmetrical façade on the south-east comprising a central doorway and two windows. Unfortunately, this doorway has been removed, and the datestone now forms the sill for a new window in the north-east gable. This small house is very similar in size to another possible example at **Lochans** (Fig. 8.52), in neighbouring Glen Carvie, at a spot annotated on an estate map of 1766 as *'A Cairn of Stones called the Old Hall of Lochans'* (AUL MS 2769/I/131/6). Reduced to little more than its footings, which measure 14.4m by 6.6m overall, it is difficult to be certain that this is not simply the remains of a later cottage, but its walls are substantial enough to have supported a second storey.

*Fig. 8.52 **Lochans** (NJ 3526 0868). General site plan showing the footings of the probable laird's house. GV000193*

Reconstructing the Medieval and Later Settlement Pattern

By the 12th century settlement extended into most parts of Donside, its presence in the uppermost reaches of the strath implied by a series of detached portions of parishes from across the watershed in the Howe of Cromar. Glen Ernan, for example, was a detached part of Tarland parish, and Glen Buchat was part of Logie Mar before becoming an independent parish in 1470, while the lower stretches of the Deskry Water fell to Migvie (Fig. 8.5). These detached portions, interspersed with elements of the medieval parish of Invernochty, probably reflect secular divisions in the landscape, suggesting that the lordship of Invernochty was divided into small estates, each probably supporting some form of administrative structure and settlement.

This pattern also suggests that Invernochty was intimately interrelated with Cromar, implying that there were dependent landholding units within the earldom of Mar, of which there are no other records. On the model of the examples above, such holdings were provided with a range of lowland and upland resources, and it is ultimately through this link that the detached upland glens supplied settlements in many lowland parishes with areas of summer grazing, a practice to which the minister of Tarland refers in the *Statistical Account* (vi, 1793, 226; Fig. 8.77).

Apart from being a detached portion of the parish of Tarland, Glen Ernan was also a type of land unit known as a *dabhach*. In Moray, it has been demonstrated that *dabhachs* operated as territorial units, presumably containing settlements with access to all the resources necessary for subsistence (Ross 2003, 135–6; 2006). There the *dabhachs* were the basic building blocks of the units that lie behind the parochial structure, and Ross has argued that they are evidence of a system of estate organisation that was already ancient by the time it first comes on record in the 12th century (Ross 2006). There is nothing to contradict this possibility in Donside, though only a handful of *dabhachs* have yet been identified in documentary sources. These occur widely in both lowland and upland contexts, as represented by Resthivet in Chapel of Garioch, and Glen Ernan in Strathdon; in the case of Resthivet, the boundaries of the *dabhach* are described in a charter of about 1219 (Stringer 1985, 223–4). Before the 12th century, *dabhachs* may well have covered most parts of Donside, but the existence of such a framework alongside that of the parishes provides little clue to the pattern or form of settlement at that time.

Burghs and Planned Villages 1150–1750

The influx of Anglo-Norman landowners during the 12th century led to a number of new settlements being founded, especially in the lordship of Garioch, which was granted to Earl David of Huntingdon, the brother of the King, in about 1178 (Stringer 1985, 30ff). These were

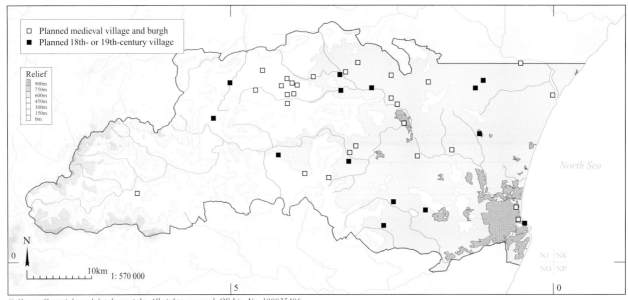

Fig. 8.53 This map shows the distribution of planned villages in Donside. GV000217

*Fig. 8.54 **Inverurie** (NJ 77 21) and **Kintore** (NJ 79 16). The plans of both burghs in the mid-17th century are represented on Robert Gordon's map. © NLS*

imposed on the pre-existing pattern of settlement and included both planned burghs and villages (Fig. 8.53).

The foundation of a burgh at **Inverurie** and the construction of the motte-and-bailey castle known as the **Bass of Inverurie** (pp. 152–3), together with the neighbouring royal foundation of a burgh and a castle (**Castle Hill**) at **Kintore**, were part of this Anglo-Norman settlement of the area, providing alternative administrative and market centres to Aberdeen. Their economic success, however, was overshadowed by Aberdeen and there is little archaeological evidence to reveal the character of either burgh at this time. Although often assumed to be trading centres, the excavators of Rattray have argued that many small burghs served as little more than agricultural markets (Murray and Murray 1993), while Carter, following his work at **Inverurie**, has suggested that some burghs were simply components of lordship (Carter 1999, 657–60).

Whatever their functions, medieval burgh foundations are typified by rows of adjoining burgage plots, or tofts, each of a similar breadth and depth. The plots fronted a street or marketplace, and were granted to burgesses to build their houses and conduct their business (e.g. Aberdeen; Dennison *et al.* 2002, 17–19). Both **Kintore** (1187x1200) and **Inverurie** (1178x1182) have roughly triangular marketplaces at the north ends of their high streets, which are lined by properties of similar size (Aberdeenshire 1869, sheets liv & lxv). The grant of a toft in the burgh of **Inverurie** to Robert de Billingham confirms that properties of this sort existed here in the late 12th century (Stringer 1985, 225), though confirmation of the layout of the burgh does not come until the late 15th century, when there are records that the burgh was parcelled into properties in the Upper

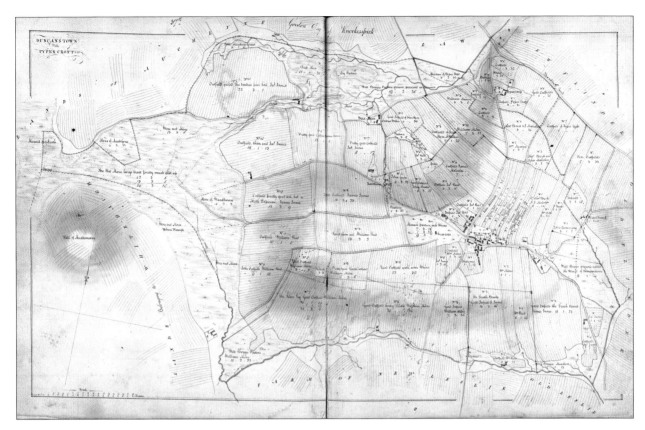

Fig. 8.55 **Duncanstone** *(NJ 5795 2663). This extract from the survey of the Leith Hall estate by George Brown in 1797 shows the village ranged along a single street. This layout is still preserved in the disposition of the houses there today.* © NTS

and Lower Roods, lying to the west and east of the high street respectively (Davidson 1878, 118–9; Carter 1999, 657). This gives a *terminus ante quem* for the layout of the burgh, which is most likely to have occurred at its foundation by Earl David in the late 12th century (Carter 1999, 657). In the mid-17th century Robert Gordon depicts both **Inverurie** and **Kintore** as two rows of houses on either side of a north–south street (Fig. 8.54; NLS Gordon MS 32), a layout that more or less matches the present high streets.

Also of this period is the 13th-century foundation of **Newburgh**, probably by Alexander Comyn (pre-1261), its position on the coast at the mouth of the Ythan bearing comparison with Rattray further north. A market cross is reported to have stood in the high street, although this may have been erected following its re-foundation as a burgh of barony in 1508–9, an event that perhaps signals that the earlier foundation was not a great success. Nevertheless, the origin of **Newburgh** as a medieval planned village is given some support from its depiction by Robert Gordon as a single row of houses along the north side of a creek that debouches into the Ythan estuary (NLS Gordon MS 32). Its economy was clearly biased to the sea, with twenty-eight seamen paying the Poll Tax in 1696 (Stuart 1844), and the 1st edition of the OS 6-inch map shows a densely built-up two-row village (Aberdeenshire 1870, sheet xlviii).

Rows of yards or *tofts* were not the sole preserve of burgh planning, and it is plain from 18th-century estate maps that a number of the lesser rural settlements or *touns* were organised in a similar fashion before the improvements. Such layouts typify medieval settlements elsewhere in eastern and southern Scotland, as well as many parts of England and Europe (Roberts and Glasscock 1983; Dixon 1998; Lewis *et al.* 2001, 172–7). In Scotland this concept of a village is usually attributed to the influx of a new class of Flemish or Anglo-French landholders during the 12th and 13th centuries, and suggests an element of planning of planted settlements.

In the Garioch a number of the incomers were granted land in return for service to Earl David of Huntingdon. Some of these grants were old holdings, or parts thereof, such as Bourtie, Durno, Ardoyne, Leslie and Resthivet, but they were often accompanied by the foundation of a new settlement. The names of these settlements typically combine the name of the founder with the English suffix *toun*, or *villa* as it appears in Latin in the charters. In the Garioch such names include Williamston in Culsalmond, Glanderston in Kennethmont, Johnston and Courtestown in Leslie, and Ingliston near Keithhall (Stringer 1985, 83ff). **Duncanstone** (*Duncanstoun*) in Leslie parish appears to be another example, although there is no contemporary record of its establishment. Flinder in Kennethmont is thought to be descriptive of its origin as a Flemish foundation from its 13th-century form, *Flandres* (Alexander 1952, 278).

*Fig. 8.56 **Duncanstone** (NJ 5795 2663). An oblique aerial view of this row village from the south-west. SC976824*

The original forms of these settlements are not known for certain, but by the time they make their appearance on 18th-century estate plans most appear to be row villages, where a row comprises three or more adjacent yards, usually laid out along a street. Indeed row villages are quite common on these maps, particularly in the Garioch. Estate maps of 1758 for the Leith Hall estate of Leslie, for example, depict **Duncanstone** (Fig. 8.55), **Old Leslie**, **Old Flinder** and **Christkirk** as row villages, comprising one or two rows of yards and houses along a street (NAS RHP 5199). Elsewhere there are single short rows of yards, as at **Bogs** (of Leslie; NAS RHP 5199/5) or **Belnagauld** (AUL MS 2769/I/131/6). Another short row of yards aligned from north to south on a map of the Monymusk estate in 1774 is labelled as the site of the ruins of **Delab** (Grant MS). Relatively few of these row villages are still occupied, but examples include **Duncanstone**, **Kirkton of Daviot** and **Kirkton of Rayne**, and possibly **Balhalgardy** and **Harlaw**. The main distribution of these modern survivals and those depicted on estate maps falls in the Garioch (Fig. 8.53), but a few isolated examples lie in Mar, such as **Blairdaff** and **Tillyfourie**

near Monymusk (Grant MS), and **Torries** near Tough (NAS RHP 232).

In Donside at least, the general coincidence of these planned villages with places where incomers were given land in the Garioch tends to support the idea that many of these settlements were laid out in the 12th or 13th century. This must be treated with some caution, however, for several settlements probably founded when *touns* were split in the post-medieval period are also shown on estate maps as row villages. These include **Little Flinder** (NAS RHP 5199), which appears on the series of estate plans relating to Leith Hall. This raises the question as to whether there was any material or chronological difference between the short rows that have been recorded and the fully developed street layout of the larger examples. The latter are relatively secure as medieval foundations and appear to lie at the core of many later burghs of barony (see below). There is no reason to believe that many of the smaller examples are not equally early, and it may simply be the size of the population and the resources available to a *toun* that dictates whether it developed a formal layout along a street. It should also be borne in mind that a short row depicted in the 18th century may have resulted from the shrinkage of a larger village following the post-medieval dispersal of settlement (pp. 190–3).

New burgh foundations again became common from the end of the 15th century, and burghs of barony, which gave benefits to the baronial landlord, continued to be created until the early 18th century. Few of these ever developed into significant settlements, but at some the elements of a planned village are combined with burgh architecture, such as a market cross or a tolbooth, betraying their mixed commercial and agricultural origins. The layout of **Old Meldrum**, for example, erected as a burgh in 1671, displays clear signs of

*Fig. 8.57 **Insch** (NJ 63 28). Though Insch has expanded well beyond the bounds of the 18th-century village, the core of its earlier layout and the main roads are easily detected. SC961132*

*Fig. 8.58 **Clatt** (NJ 5393 2594). The scattered houses in this oblique aerial view of the village from the west reflects its origin as a clustered township. SC906938*

its planned origins, comprising four rows of narrow properties fronting a rectangular market square, on the west side of which stood the tolbooth (Aberdeenshire 1870, sheet xlvi). The characteristic toft-rows are also apparent at the post-medieval burgh foundations of **Old Rayne** (1498) and **Insch** (1677). Of these, **Old Rayne** has an extant market cross in a small square at the junction of two streets lined by house-plots, and the site of the bishop's palace lies at the far end of the street leading to the north (Aberdeenshire 1870, sheet xliv). At **Insch** (Fig. 8.57) the layout comprises two rows along a street that widens slightly to form the marketplace between the church and the crossroads at the centre of the village. The intimate relationship of the settlement with agriculture is evident from an estate map of **Insch** drawn up in 1797 (Fig. 9.2), which shows that the tenants in the village held scattered blocks of land in the surrounding fields in runrig fashion (NTS Leith Hall MS). Indeed, the burgh of barony was often little more than a township with market rights where some of the tenants had a special tenurial status as burghers. As such, the element of planning detectable in some of them may indicate that any burgh architecture present was an addition to an earlier planned village.

Other burghs of barony in Donside include **Hatton of Fintray** and **Clatt** (Figs 8.58–9), though at first sight neither displays much evidence of planning or burgh architecture. At **Hatton of Fintray** (erected 1625), there is no obvious focus for a marketplace, but a tolbooth is situated on the east side of the street that leads through the village from north to south (Aberdeenshire 1869, sheet lxv). Furthermore, the regularity of this street, and the sharp turn east at the north end to avoid the churchyard and the site of the

administrative centre established here by Lindores Abbey (p. 161), hint at some planning, though this may be a relic of an earlier planned village rather than the post-medieval burgh. The burgh of **Clatt** (erected 1501) had a market cross on the east side of the churchyard, but by 1870 the marketplace had been shifted to the east edge of the village, where a new row of buildings called Hardgate was built (Aberdeenshire 1870, sheet xliii). **Clatt** retained its agricultural function after its erection as a burgh, for eight tenancies of bondland and eight burgages, including the mill and brewery, are recorded in 1511 (Innes 1845, i, 360–1). By the late 18th century, the village comprised over thirty houses and twenty yards clustered around the church, with streets leading out on the four quarters. Although the market cross stood by the church, there was no space within this framework for a marketplace (NAS RHP 14753). Despite the haphazard appearance of the village, elements of planning may be detected. The buildings and yards are aligned mainly from north to south or from east to west, and, more significantly, many

*Fig. 8.59 **Clatt** (NJ 5393 2594). These map extracts depict the village in c.1770 (upper) and 1870 (lower), the former derived from an estate map, the latter from the 1st edition of the OS 6-inch map. GV000260*

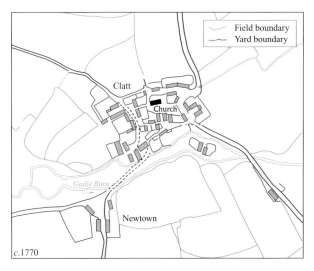

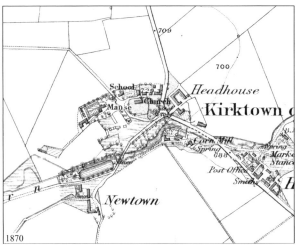

*Fig. 8.60 **Rhynie** (NJ 4990 2712). This oblique aerial view from the north-north-west shows the rectilinear layout of this early 19th-century planned village. SC961130*

of the yards are arranged in short rows of two or three around the central space occupied by the church in a fashion reminiscent of the more developed layout of **Old Meldrum**. At **Clatt** the clustered appearance of the village in the late 18th century may be the result of the failure of its market and its relative poverty (*Stat. Acct.,* viii, 1793, 535ff). This may also explain why there was no clearly defined marketplace at that time, its failure leading to encroachment by later buildings.

The rest of the burghs of barony have failed to leave any trace in the landscape, places like **Old Leslie**, **Strathdon** and **Balgownie** preserving no evidence of burgh architecture or planning. At **Kildrummy**, founded in 1509, the tolbooth is said to have lain at the site of Nether Kildrummy farm, though nothing is visible of it today. The Burgh Leys, the fields to the north, appear to preserve a memory of the status of the burgh and the location of its arable lands. In other cases a burgh has been replanned in modern times, as at **Echt**, **Rhynie**, **Monymusk** and **Alford**. The failure

of these burghs lends some weight to Carter's argument that their trading functions should be seen as an attribute of lordship rather than a commercial centre (1999, 657–9). In some cases, however, the erection of a burgh may have served to confirm an existing local market that was not necessarily focused upon an agricultural village. A good example is provided by the village of **Rhynie**, which was replanned in the early 19th century (Fig. 8.60). This was established as a burgh in 1684 and is shown on an estate map of 1776 as a small farm supporting a cluster of half a dozen houses and yards spread in a rough linear fashion along the road to Huntly (NAS RHP 2254). There is little here to suggest a successful market or service centre, and its very name, originally Muir of Rhynie, suggests an intake of rough pasture, but in this instance the market functions of the settlement are known to pre-date the establishment of the burgh (AUL MS 2499/15 and NAS GD 44/16/9/2).

Touns, Cottars and Crofts 1150–1750

Topographical descriptions of settlements dating from the medieval period are rare, and most contemporary sources use the Latin terms *villa de* and, more frequently, *terra de*, in effect referring to the units of land belonging to a settlement. From the 15th century, however, topographical details are mentioned more frequently and the suffix *toun* is applied to the name of the settlement of the farm (giving rise to many of the modern place-names ending in *-ton* and *-tone*). Here the tenant or tenants of the farm resided, thus giving rise to the term *fermtoun*. Such settlements usually formed the nucleus of a township, but the *fermtouns* were only one

Fig. 8.61 This map shows the distribution of touns recorded in the Poll Tax returns of 1696; a number of the names were already prefixed with 'Old'. Relatively few touns survived the process of improvement, though the plans of several can be detected in the layout of buildings depicted on later OS maps or, in a few cases, in the footings of buildings preserved in areas of rough pasture. See also Fig. 8.75 GV000225

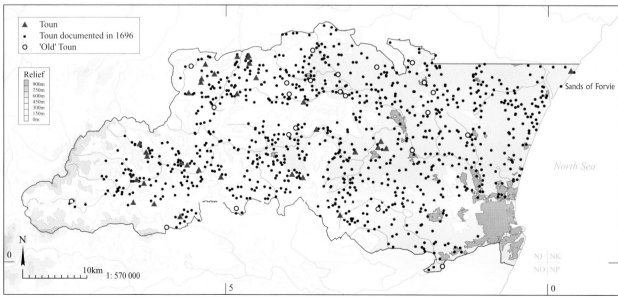

element in the overall settlement pattern that emerged in the late medieval period. At least three other forms of settlement are identifiable, four if manorial sites are also included. These are: *milltouns*; *cottowns* or *cottertouns*; and individual crofts.

In some cases *milltouns* and *cottertouns* were probably indistinguishable from *fermtouns*, but these terms reflect recognisable groups in the rural population who played a part in the evolution of the nucleated settlements that dominated the settlement pattern across Aberdeenshire. The estate mill, for instance, was an essential element in the pattern of rural settlement, its position dictated by a suitable source of water. In some cases this could be found adjacent to an existing *toun*, as at Clatt, but in others it lay some distance away, as at Mill of Leslie. Where it was separate, it sometimes developed the status of a farm in its own right, thus becoming the focus of an independent *toun*, as at **Milton of Noth**. Cottars, on the other hand, are the unseen class of rural medieval Aberdeenshire, essentially sub-tenants who barely appear in documentary records. The Poll Tax returns, however, indicate their frequency in the late 17th century. By and large they depended on their labour for their livelihood, but some were able to keep a cow and hold small plots in the cultivated lands of the township, as indeed can be seen at Monymusk in the 18th century (Hamilton 1945, xxv). Many cottars lived in the existing *touns*, but sometimes they formed separate settlements, hence the terms *cottown* or *cottertoun*. Examples are shown on estate maps near **Mains of Leslie** in 1758 (NAS RHP 5199/4), and near **Newbigging** by Clatt (NAS RHP 14753/3/3), while two deserted buildings shown adjacent to the *'Affleck intown'* on a map of Essie in 1776 are annotated *'old stances of cottertoun'* (NAS RHP 2256).

Whatever their origins, relatively few *touns* have retained their pre-improvement layout today, and many of them have been replaced by single farms. Nevertheless, examination of the handful that are still occupied, together with those that appear on 18th-century estate maps and the abandoned examples surviving in the margins, shows that there are two characteristic types. The first type comprises the row villages that exhibit some evidence of planning (pp. 185–6), while the second is made up of what are termed here clustered townships. In comparison to the row villages, the layout of a clustered township is apparently more haphazard, comprising a loose group of houses and yards, but with neither a single dominant street, nor any rows of yards. **Clatt** (Fig. 8.59), which has already been discussed above, is a good example of this type, and **Belhinnie**, **Belnacraig** and **Kirkton of Oyne** (Fig. 8.62) also preserve similar layouts. Others, such as **Upper Coullie**, **Little Collieston**, **Craich**, **Dalmadilly**, **Upperton** and **Pitcandlich** survived in this form on the 1st edition OS 6-inch map, but by far the majority are known only from pre-improvement

Fig. 8.62 **Kirkton of Oyne** *(NJ 6811 2566). The buildings of this village are disposed informally to either side of the B9002 public road. SC1005232*

estate maps. In contrast to the concentration of planned villages in the Garioch (Fig. 8.53), the clustered townships are found throughout Donside, from **Lochans** in Glen Carvie in the west, to **Little Collieston** near the coast at Slains in the east. This type has a much wider distribution, however, extending along the eastern fringes of the Highlands (RCAHMS and HS 2002, 55–7).

Yet even in clustered townships elements of order may be found. The layout of houses and yards typically employs two major axes at right angles to one another, which is often mainly north and south or east and west. This is well illustrated on estate maps at townships like **Auchmenzie** and **Auchlyne** (NAS RHP 14753), or **Upper Coullie** (Figs 8.65; 8.68) and **Todlachie** (Grant MS). These *touns* are amongst the larger examples, but the same tendency is in evidence at smaller *touns* comprising no more than two or three yards and a few houses, such as **Edderlick** (NAS RHP 5199/11), or **Brae of Scurdargue** (NAS RHP 2261). It can also be seen in the archaeological remains of several of the *touns* that have been recorded in the course of the survey, such as **Newton Wood** (Fig. 8.74), **Lynardoch** (Figs 8.63; 8.83), and **Craigs of Longley** (Fig. 8.76).

Examination of the depictions of many *touns* shown on 18th-century estate maps also reveals the third component in the settlement pattern, the individual croft. In contrast to the landless cottar, the crofter held a separate small farm with its own steading, but was generally a dependent sub-tenant of a farmer, rather than an independent farmer in his own right. For example, Simon Ley's croft, which was at **Loanend** near Mains of Leslie, is identified on the maps of 1758 (NAS RHP 5199), while at **Corsehill**, in Rhynie, John Cruikshank's croft on the farm of Newseat is one of several farmsteads that held small pieces of arable on

Fig. 8.63 **Lynardoch** *(NJ 3130 1270). The footings of this farmstead, which was succeeded by the cottage at the top, are accompanied by an extensive system of broad cultivation rigs and terraces. SC961127*

the fringes of the *toun* fields in 1776 (NAS RHP 2261). The dependent status of these crofters may be seen in the documentation elsewhere on the duke of Gordon's estates in Rhynie and Essie, and other examples can be found on the Leslie estate and the Monymusk estate (Hamilton 1945, xxvi). Indeed, of seventeen crofts shown on the Leslie estate in 1758, only four were occupied (e.g. Temple Croft). As dependencies, the land occupied by these crofts could be incorporated back into the farm at the end of their tenancies, effecting their demise as separate entities. At the beginning of the 19th century, old croft land was described as infield by the Board of Agriculture report (Keith 1811, 171, 231–2), which appears to match the designation of most croft land on the earlier estate maps. This leads to the conclusion that such crofts were not a form of long-lived settlement, so much as a method of intake, by which new land was broken in by the crofter under beneficial terms. Evidence of this practice can probably be detected at Garbet (**Craigs of Longley**), where four crofts were established in 1686, apparently as new creations added to the existing *toun* (NAS SC1/60/31). However, no settlements are depicted at Garbet on the estate plan of 1776 (NAS RHP 2257), by which time the lands of the *toun* had reverted to outfields belonging to **Boganclogh**. The area now lies within a mature forestry plantation, but no fewer than three groups of buildings and enclosures have been identified on aerial photographs and from fieldwork (Fig. 8.76). At least some of these buildings may represent the remains of the croft farmsteads of Garbet.

On this evidence the croft was clearly a dynamic element in the Aberdeenshire rural economy in the post-medieval period, and it should perhaps be placed in the wider context of the expanding settlement pattern rather than as a medieval form of settlement. Nevertheless, such an impression may simply reflect the difficulties

of pushing back this component of the settlement pattern, for without direct documentation they are easily overlooked. The earlier documented examples tend to be where crofts were leased directly from the landlord, thus leading to their appearance in rentals. One example is the croft of Auchleck (**Essie**), which is listed as part of the grant of Lesmoir to James Gordon in 1537 (Bulloch 1907, 166). Others are recorded at Fetternear in the bishop of Aberdeen's rental of 1511, which lists fourteen; these include crofts attached to a brewery, a smithy and a mill (Innes 1845, i, 364–7). The earliest reference to a croft dates from 1310, when Ade Chapelane, a burgess of Aberdeen, sold his croft called *'le Spyttalhillis'* (Innes 1845, i, 40). At face value this may be evidence that crofts were also components of the medieval settlement pattern, but this particular croft and some other late medieval holdings of the burgesses may be facets of the burgh's developing hinterland rather than a more general feature of the Aberdeenshire landscape. Elsewhere they do not appear in documentary sources until the 16th century.

Changes in the Settlement Pattern: Expansion, Dispersal and Township Splitting

Crofts were not the only dynamic component of the overall settlement pattern, for it is clear from the estate maps and documentary sources that other processes of change were at work, particularly from the 17th to the early 18th century. Two particular trends can be detected, the one involving the splitting or dispersal of large *touns* into two or more smaller settlements, the other the expansion of settlement into marginal land. These trends are also part of a wider pattern of development in lowland Scotland from the 15th century onwards (Dodgshon 1981, 195; Dixon 2003, 53). In the mid-17th century Robert Gordon of Straloch attributed the changes that had occurred in the settlement pattern during his lifetime to the expansion of arable land and the demands of efficiency:

'Here also I desire to warn my reader that though our kingdom is, generally speaking, populated with few villages, paucity of inhabitants must not be inferred. The reason of this state of matters is as follows. Husbandmen eager for tillage thought from the very first that they were restricted in villages, and that, when they had so many neighbours, too little provision was made for agriculture; for at first the districts were divided into village settlements. To each of these so much of the arable land was allotted as could be tilled with four ploughs. These sections of lands were called in the ancient language dachas, which signifies village allotments. In many places in the higher districts the boundaries still remain, though the homesteads have been separated. But when the woods had been cut down four ploughs were no longer sufficient. Wide extent of bounds was inimical to agriculture, so that the proprietors,

dividing the fields, set limits for each farmer according to his means, in such a way that the homesteads were continuous but not contiguous. I remember seeing instances of this in my early years. The farmers abandoned their villages and removed each to his own possession, where any vein of more fertile soil attracted him. Here the home was fixed, and so it remains at the present day' (Mitchell and Clark 1906–8, ii, 272–3).

In his view at least, the pattern of settlement in the mid-17th century was a relatively recent creation, in which the proliferation of new settlements following the division of farms had led to a dispersal of settlement. Other sources of evidence confirm this general trend. An analysis of the naming protocols in the Poll Tax returns of 1696, for example, reveals that many of the township names are prefixed with Upper and Nether, Easter and Wester, Old and New, or Mickle and Little (Stuart 1844).

Such naming protocols not only imply the splitting of existing townships, but also that the original village sites continued in use. The 'old' prefixes in the Poll Tax are a case in point, thus yielding the locations of some thirty villages in Donside that are potentially medieval in origin, though in every case they continued in occupation until the improvements (Fig. 8.61). Examples of late medieval desertions are rare, but the remains of **Forvie**, which were uncovered by excavation in the sand dunes adjacent to the old parish church, may be a case in point. Here the reason for its final loss may be related to sand-blow rather than any economic trends (p. 44), but the evidence for the date of its abandonment is ambiguous. While medieval pottery was apparently found associated with the buildings, there was still a taxable community at **Forvie** in 1696 (Stuart 1844). Rattray, a little further north, is a more secure example (Murray and Murray 1993), and a few others have been recorded elsewhere in lowland Scotland, such as Springwood Park, in Roxburghshire (Dixon 1998). It remains a possibility that more such sites will be found in Aberdeenshire.

Within the survey area, one of the earliest examples where the division of a township can be inferred is at Pitfoddels in Peterculter. Here it had occurred by 1430 (Robertson and Grubb 1847–62, iii, 264), while at *Knockinblewis* in Chapel of Garioch it had taken place by 1511 (Paul 1984, 775). For the Gordon estates of Rhynie and Essie the rentals of the period 1600 to 1658 record the division of Noth, Merdrum and Forest into Old and New, and they also refer to Gulburn (the alehouse of Noth) and **Milton of Noth** (Harrison 2001b, 18). Of these, only the division of Merdrum dates before the early 16th century (Paul 1984, No. 3599). During the following 150 years many other farms and crofts were established, such as Great and Little Mytice, the four farms of Scurdargue (Brae of Scurdargue, **Howtoun**, Rumfold and Scurdargue itself) and the numerous crofts

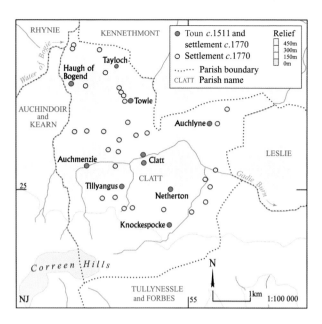

Fig. 8.64 This map of the parish of Clatt reveals the threefold increase in the number of settlements between 1511 and 1770. GV000259

that are depicted on the estate maps of 1776 (NAS RHP 2254). Similar developments can be paralleled in Clatt parish by comparing the 1511 rental (Innes 1845, i, 360–364) with the holdings shown on late 18th-century estate maps (NAS RHP 14753 and 260/2). This reveals a threefold multiplication in the numbers of settlements by the late 18th century (Fig. 8.64).

This general dispersal of settlement is also evident in the population figures recorded for the individual settlements in the Poll Tax returns of 1696 (Stuart 1844). The average number of households per Poll Tax entry is 3.5 (i.e. tenants, sub-tenants, cottars and grassmen, millers, merchants and craftsmen, and lairds) and there was an average taxable population of fourteen per settlement. Only the larger market towns – the burghs of **Inverurie**, **Kintore**, **Old Meldrum** and, on the northern fringes of the survey area, **Ellon** – had taxable adult populations in excess of 100 persons. By far the majority of settlements were much smaller, 87% with less than twenty-five taxable adults, and 97% less than fifteen households. Indeed, some of the largest tax units recorded in the Poll Tax returns are not single townships but include several settlements belonging to one estate, such as the Lesmoir estate in Rhynie and Essie parish, the earl of Errol's lands in Ellon, and the laird of Kinmundy's in New Machar. Be that as it may, about one in ten settlements in Donside had Poll Tax populations of between twenty-five and 100, including *kirktouns* like Culsalmond, Monymusk, Rayne, Bethelnie and Skene, and also townships like **Upper Coullie** (Fig. 8.65) and **Pitmunie** in Monymusk, which were still sizeable settlements in 1774 (Grant MS). The greater number of these larger townships lay in the lowlands, mainly in the Garioch and Buchan, probably reflecting the richer farmland to be found

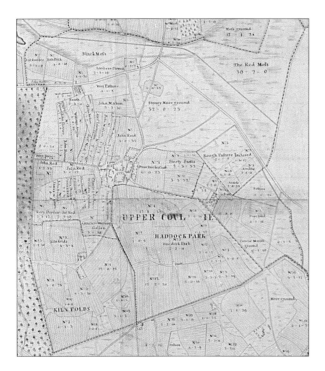

Fig. 8.65 **Upper Coullie** *(NJ 7019 1667). This extract from the plan of the Monymusk estate prepared in 1774 depicts the township at a time when it was still held as a joint tenancy, with its arable land laid out in long narrow strips around the huddle of buildings and yards.* © *Sir Archibald Grant*

there compared with the generally poorer ground of the earldom of Mar.

An examination of the distribution of *toun*-names, which form 10% of the named places in the Poll Tax – mainly *fermtouns, cottouns, kirktouns, milltouns, hattouns, haughtouns, uppertouns* and *nethertouns* – shows that they are distributed right across the area, from Castletoun at Corgarff in the west to Meikletoun of Slains on the coast. Equally widely distributed are the names prefixed Old and New, Over and Nether, Little and Meikle, or Easter and Wester, which account for 20% of the places in the Poll Tax. These serve as the most obvious index of the division of *touns* and the dispersal of settlement. The proportion increases to about 28% if Mains farms are included (sixty-four *in toto*). While the general pattern of dispersal extends throughout the survey area, some differences in the social structure within the settlements can be detected. In the Buchan parishes of Belhelvie, New Machar, Udny, Foveran, Ellon, Tarves and Meldrum, the settlements were predominantly single-tenancy *touns*, in which sub-tenants and cottars were in the majority, but those in the Garioch and Mar were more frequently multiple-tenancy farms.

The process of *toun*-splitting reflects two trends in the settlement record. On the one hand it is a manifestation of the expansion of settlement within the framework of existing townships, but on the other it reflects settlement spreading into marginal areas that were previously unoccupied. Documentary evidence

suggests that the latter took place in the uppermost reaches of Donside in the 16th century, though a note of caution should be sounded, for there is no extant documentation for any individual settlements in the parish of Invernochty until the 15th century. Nevertheless, examination of a rental of the earldom of Mar preserved in the Exchequer Rolls (Burnett 1882, 459–60) suggests that Skellater, lying just above the mouth of Glen Ernan on the north side of the strath, and the Orde, just above the mouth of Glen Conrie on the south, mark the upper limits of settlement in 1451. No places upstream of Skellater are mentioned before 1531–2, but a grant of Glen Carvie, Glen Conrie and the Orde was made to Alexander Forbes of Brux in 1409 (Robertson and Grubb 1862, iv, 381). This suggests that the settlement of the strath was well established as far up as the haugh opposite Skellater by the early 15th century,

Fig. 8.66 **Caldens** *(NJ 3098 1301). This oblique aerial view of the farmstead shows its surrounding enclosure, which overlies the head-dyke on the right of the picture. SC975457*

if not before. The presence of a chapel at **Belniden** at the Orde lends some weight to this argument.

Of the strath between Skellater and Corgarff, nothing is known until 1531–2, when a deed records that the lands of Carryhill (Corriehoul), not far east of Corgarff, were a possession of Agnes Grant, niece of John McAllane of Inverernan (Paul and Thomson 1984, 277). There is also a record of a chapel at **Corriehoul** dedicated to St Machar, but it may have been no more than a holy well. Confirmation that the head of the valley was managed differently may be seen in the grant of a hunting forest at Corgarff in the early 16th century (p. 149), tacit recognition that it was not only unsettled, but there was sufficient woodland for the deer. Although **Corgarff Castle** is said to have originated as a hunting lodge of the earl of Mar (*Stat. Acct.*, xiii, 1794, 182), the tower is first recorded in the 16th century, when it was occupied by members of the Forbes of Towie family (Simpson 1927). General Roy's map (1747–55) is the first to show any places above Corgarff, but it is possible that the relatively large taxable populations for Castletoun (presumed to be Corgarff) and Allargue in the Poll Tax return hide some dependent settlements (Stuart 1844), indicating an expansion of settlement in the late 17th century.

The expansion of settlement is also found in side glens, like that of the Ernan Water or the Kirkney Water, the latter opening off Strathbogie north of Rhynie. In Glen Ernan, the earliest sign of post-medieval expansion is provided by **Lynmore**, first documented in 1631, lying on the south of the river opposite the old established farm of **Lynardoch**. Further additions are documented by the second quarter of the 18th century. These include on the north side of the river: **Rehache** (**Clais Liath**) further up the glen; **Auchnahaich** near **Bressachoil**; **Caldens** and Carnacruie near **Lynardoch** (Figs 8.66; 8.85); Haughton near Edinglassie, and its replacement **Braeside** (Harrison 2001a). On the south side new farms were established at **Deleva** (Fig. 8.84), **Camasour**, **Belnabreck** and **Torrandhu**. Similarly, in the valley of the Kirkney Water, several new settlements are documented, including Stonerives (**Clayshot Hill**), **Backstripes**, Garbet (**Craigs of Longley**; Fig. 8.76) and Longley (**Craigs of Longley**), of which Garbet appears to have been carved out of a hunting forest of the same name (Littlejohn 1906, 258).

18th- and 19th-Century Settlement Reorganisation and Improvement

The 18th century saw the beginning of a reformation of the rural landscape of Donside, led by several lairds who improved their home farms and the policies of their country houses. The tenant farmers rarely followed their lead, and on the whole did not invest in major improvements until the onset of the following century. This does not mean that no changes occurred before the 19th century but, in Aberdeenshire, the wholesale

Fig. 8.67 **Monymusk** *(NJ 6846 1520). This oblique aerial view shows the planned village in the centre, and* **Monymusk House**, *the seat of the Grants, standing on the banks of the River Don in the background. The Grants created the village and were responsible for its subsequent rebuilding and modification throughout the late 18th and 19th centuries. SC961129*

enclosure of the landscape and reorganisation of farms is generally a feature of the early 19th century.

Sir Archibald Grant of Monymusk stands out at the beginning of this process. Unlike the great majority of landowners in Aberdeenshire, he began to improve his estate in the early 18th century, immediately after he took over its management in 1713, and continued until his death in 1778 (pp. 215; 218–19). As well as planting extensive woodlands, he encouraged numerous agricultural changes. These included the construction of enclosures, the clearance of stones and the intake of new land, but he was also interested in the use of legumes and turnips in new crop rotations, leading to the abolition of the division of the land between infield and outfield. In addition, he campaigned to remove sub-tenants and unwanted tenants in order to create unitary farming units, such as at **Tombeg** and **Tillyfourie** during the 1750s and 1760s (Hamilton 1945, xxvi, lxxii-lxxiii). By 1792, the sixty-two families that supplied the labouring population were each provided with a house and garden, and settled in the planned village at **Monymusk** (Fig. 8.67; *Stat. Acct.*, iii, 1792, 73). The removal of sub-tenants, however, did not reduce the population. Indeed, depending on the number of children unaccounted for in the Poll Tax returns of 1696, the population of the parish probably increased during the 18th century from 721 pollable persons in 1696 to 1127 *in toto* in 1792.

A map of the Monymusk estate prepared in 1774 shows the fruits of this first half century of improvement, especially in plantations and new intakes, but enclosed fields laid out in the improved rectilinear

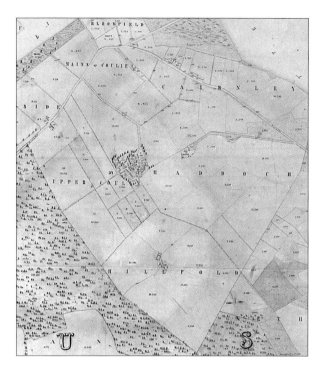

Fig. 8.68 Upper Coullie (NJ 7019 1667). Comparison between the estate plan of 1774 (Fig. 8.65), this extract from the plan of the Monymusk estate surveyed by Alexander Ogg of Aberdeen in 1846, and the 1st edition of the OS 6-inch map, charts the decline of this township. By 1846 its land had been reorganised into small rectangular fields, which in turn had been subsumed into three large fields by 1869. Of the thirty-two roofed buildings that remained then, most had been removed by the end of the 19th century and only four survive today. © Sir Archibald Grant

fashion are limited to the **Home Farm**, parts of East and West Inver, and Enzean, which had been combined with **Delab** to form one large farm. This led to the desertion of **Delab**, but, with this exception, the same settlements listed in the early part of the 18th century largely remained in occupation, and there is little sign of radical change. At **Todlachie**, for example, over the period from 1696 to 1774 the number of tenants actually rose from four to five, and the population from 68 to 70 (Hamilton 1945, lxxvii). And yet, while **Upper Coullie** still lay in runrig, Coullie was now divided into discrete farms, including Nether Coullie, Haddock Park and the Kiln Folds. The eventual demise of the settlement at Upper Coullie, possibly the original nuclear settlement, resulted from the division of the runrig after a survey in 1798 (Hamilton 1945, opp. 148). This led to the creation of several new dispersed crofts, including **Moss-side of Coullie**, Newton Coullie, and **Mains of Coullie**. However, the final desertion of **Upper Coullie** (Fig. 8.68) was a gradual process that was not completed until the 20th century. Here, as on estates elsewhere, settlement rationalisation ranged from the establishment of dispersed steadings on the *toun* lands, leading to the desertion of the *toun*, to the replacement of a *toun* by an improved steading. In the course of the early 19th century new improved farmsteadings were built to replace the multiple-tenancy townships at **Blairdaff**,

Todlachie, **Ardneidly** and **Pitmunie**. A new steading was also erected on the site of the deserted **Delab**.

The apparent increase in the population of Monymusk may be atypical, for during the latter half of the 18th century there is evidence for a widespread decline in the population of rural parishes in Aberdeenshire. At the same time, the population of Aberdeen itself was growing rapidly, as were those of its hinterland parishes of Old Machar, Newhills and Peterculter (*Stat. Acct.*, xix, 1797, 144ff; vi, 1793, 34ff; xvi, 1795, 358ff). Excluding Old Machar, which formed part of the expansion of Aberdeen, there was a general decrease of about 5000 persons in the rural population of Donside between 1755 and the 1790s (Keith 1811, 604–5). Some of the ministers' reports in the *Statistical Account* explain the decline as a product of the amalgamation of small farms and crofts, as at Bourtie and Oyne (*Stat. Acct.*, ix, 1793, 434; xv, 1795, 105), while in Strathdon, Clatt and Auchindoir they attribute it to emigration, mainly to work in the manufacturing industries of the towns (*Stat. Acct.*, xiii, 1794, 171ff; viii, 1793, 535; xii, 1794, 490ff).

This decline in the rural population is manifested in a retreat of settlement from the margins and the loss of the less economically viable small tenants. This may be illustrated by an analysis of the Gordon estates of Rhynie and Essie, which encompasses both upland and lowland terrain. A series of estate maps of 1776 depict abandoned settlements in both upland and lowland contexts, ranging from small townships to crofts and *cottertouns*. In several instances detached outfields are shown where previously documented settlements had already disappeared, such as at Garbet (**Craigs of Longley**; Fig. 8.76) and Stonerives (**Clayshot Hill**), whose lands had been absorbed by the adjacent townships of **Boganclogh** and **New Merdrum** respectively (NAS RHP 2257). At **Essie**, on the lower ground, the 1776 map depicts in one instance the *'stances'* of old houses, and in another the stances of a *cottertoun,* the latter the Intown of Affleck, which is the only indication of the site of the former croft of Auchleck (**Essie**; NAS RHP 2256). Other deserted settlements are depicted, including: one on **Hill of Milduan** in Old Merdrum called the *'Old Stance of Milduan'* (NAS RHP 2258); another on the farm of **Milton of Noth** called the *'Old Stance of Whiteside'* (NAS RHP 2264); and at **Mytice** the *'Old Stance of Little Mytice'* (NAS RHP 2260). The amalgamation of farms continued on the Gordon estates at Rhynie after the 1770s. Some settlements disappeared altogether, like Longley, Gulburn Croft, **Howtoun** and **Smithstown**, while others became settlements for the labourers of the large farms, as at **Raws of Noth** and **Bogs of Noth** (Harrison 2001b, 26). A similar process is also evident in the north part of the lowland parish of Clatt, an area transferred from John Forbes of Newe to the Leith Hall estate in the course of the same period. Here too a number of crofts, farms and cottages were cleared in the process of reorganising the farms (compare RHP 260/2 and Aberdeenshire 1870, sheet xliii).

This sort of evidence for the amalgamation and reorganisation of farms, and the removal of sub-tenants, crofters and cottagers, is not only widespread across Donside, but is also documented throughout the north-eastern counties of Aberdeenshire, Kincardineshire and Banffshire (Gray 1976). It is also a feature of the improvements that occurred in central and southern Scotland in the second half of the 18th century. The difference in the North-east is the way in which the surplus labour force that this created was managed. In southern and central Scotland, some went to manufacturing and industrial enterprises, while many others moved into rural villages (Devine 1994, 146–57). In the North-east, old rural burghs like **Inverurie** provided some scope for manufacturing, but most emigration from the countryside went to Aberdeen. Rural labour, therefore, had to be secured in other ways. Some landowners sought to secure their workforce by planting villages with smallholdings for each tenant, a good example being **Rhynie** on the duke of Gordon's estate, but the solution that sets the North-east apart involved the creation of a new class of crofter. Unlike most of their predecessors, these crofters held their smallholding directly from the landowner. Such crofts were already becoming a reality in the 1790s and are mentioned in the *Statistical Accounts*. In Kemnay, for instance, there were *'a good many small parcels of land, which we call crofts, held immediately of the proprietor'* (*Stat. Acct.*, xii, 1794, 205). The reasons for this development are not hard to find, for the Napoleonic wars had raised fears of revolution. Because few crofts were big enough to provide for a family, the crofters were obliged to labour for wages on the farms, thus not only tying the crofters to the estates, but also suppressing any discontent about the loss of their former status on the pre-improvement farms. It also enabled landowners to invest in the improvement of former common pasture at little direct outlay. The new crofts were predominantly small, taking in less than 20ha (50 acres), and the basic cottages only provided accommodation for the family and a cow (Gray 1976). In economic terms these new smallholdings were marginal, and many have been absorbed into larger holdings. In some cases the ruins of a croft house have survived and have been recorded during the present survey, but others have been simply swept away or replaced by a new steading in the late 19th century.

Other processes were also at work that in some cases led to the clearance and desertion of settlements, in particular the emparkment of the lands around country houses and the creation of Mains farms. The clearance of settlements to make way for new parks is more familiar from the history of the English landscape (Beresford and Hurst 1971, 45), but it is also an aspect

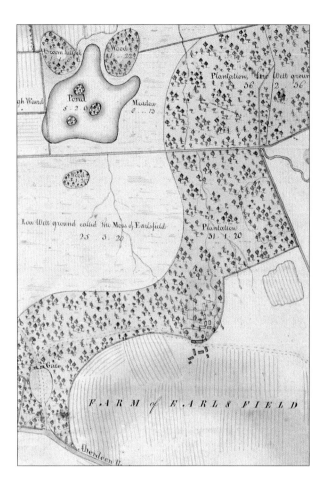

*Fig. 8.69 **Earlsfield** (NJ 5500 2900). This toun was replaced by a steading on a new site prior to 1797 and is shown in a belt of woodland on George Brown's plan of the Mains of Leith Hall. © NTS*

of rural improvement in Scotland. Several instances have been recorded in Donside. In Glen Ernan, for example, the improvement of individual farms in about 1790 went hand in hand with the creation of the policies around the houses at **Edinglassie** and **Inverernan**. This led to the clearance of several *touns*, at Edinglassie including **Braeside** (itself a replacement for Haughton) and Coul (Harrison 2001a, 44), and at **Inverernan** the *toun* of the same name and **Camasour**. In the lowlands several settlements that had taxable populations in 1696 suffered this same fate: **Earlsfield** (Fig. 8.69) was subsumed into the plantations of Leith Hall between 1758 and 1797, and a steading was erected on a new site (NAS RHP 5198 and NTS Leith Hall MS); Little Warthill appears to have been removed in the emparkment of the policies of **Warthill House**; Scotstown was subsumed into the grounds of **Scotstown House**; and **Tonley** and **Tillymair** were also lost in the creation of the policies of their eponymous country houses.

The creation of a Mains or Home Farm near a laird's house was often associated with this phase of emparkments, but some Mains farms are considerably earlier. **Mains of Leslie**, and **Mains of Rhynie**, for example, are amongst about seventy that already existed in 1696, apparently as a result of the dispersal

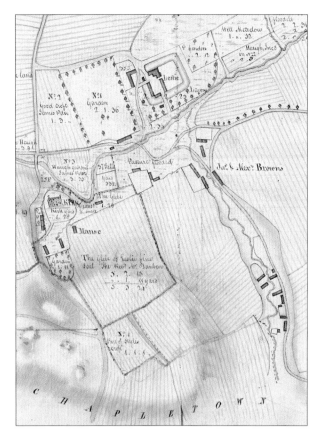

*Fig. 8.70 **Leslie** (NJ 5996 2483). Prepared by George Brown in 1797 as part of the survey of the estate of Leith Hall, this extract shows the site of the medieval estate centre with the tower-house standing on the north side of the moated enclosure. Houses are scattered between the tower and the church to the south-west, and a cottertoun is situated to either side of a burn to the south (bottom right).* © NTS

of settlement and the division of *touns*. However, the separation of the demesne lands from the tenants' lands to create a severalty holding, held by the owner and free of any common rights, was also the first organisational step towards improved agriculture. Many of those established during the improvements are distinguishable by the appellation Home Farm. These were often the vehicle for the landlord to experiment with new crops, rotations, and enclosures.

The pace of improvement accelerated in the early 19th century, when large landowners like the duke of Gordon began to invest more widely in agricultural improvement. At Rhynie enclosure was underway by the turn of the century with the first moves to build a new village at Muir of Rhynie, but it was still in progress in the 1840s. The process of enclosure did not itself lead to the abandonment of farms, but sub-lettings were no longer allowed, leading to the elimination of many of the old crofts, and there was an accompanying process of replacement and improvement of the farm-buildings. Sixteen plots for the new village were laid out in 1803 (NAS GD 44/52/251), and space for a new inn was provided on the site of the old *toun*. A new church was added in 1823, replacing the ruinous old parish church (Harrison 2001b, 27–8). The lands of

Ardglownie and **Mains of Rhynie** were combined in the early 19th century, leading to the desertion of the old Mains farm, and a new improved steading named Mains of Rhynie was erected on the site of **Ardglownie**. The fields on the farm were being dyked and hedged in 1842 (NAS CR 8/65). Further evidence of enclosures comes from estate maps of **Newseat** (1822) and **Blackmiddens** (1827), both depicting the new rectilinear enclosures superimposed on an outline of older fields. Both *touns* were replaced with courtyard steadings, at **Blackmiddens** by 1827.

Evidence of this process of rationalisation as new improved steadings were built is repeated across Donside. On the Gordon estates, for example, some *touns* were deserted altogether, while others were replaced by modern steadings. In a few cases *touns* remained in use, such as the township of **Belhinnie**, which was occupied by crofters. Occasionally, as at **Balhalgardy**, the street plan of the old *toun* is still discernible. The same process may also be seen in the parish of Clatt. There, the *touns* of **Upperton** and **Yonderton of Tullyangus** have progressively declined since the 19th century, replaced by the improved steadings at nearby **Mains of Tullyangus** and **Tullochleys** respectively.

The rationalisation of the settlement pattern and the construction of new steadings during the 19th century was often a two-stage process. The initial improved steading built in the late 18th or early 19th century was in many cases replaced in the late 19th century as estates responded to the changing economic circumstances and reorganised their farms still further. In practice, few marginal farms were able to survive in the tougher economy that developed as world markets began to take advantage of the free trade in corn. This is reflected both in the rarity of surviving *touns* in the modern landscape, and in the abandonment of numerous crofts and small farms between 1870 and 1900 apparent on OS maps, a trend that continued into the 20th century. The settlements along the Craig Burn on the Craig estate, Auchindoir, provide good examples of this process of change. By 1870 some of the *touns* had been replaced by improved steadings, such as **Bogs** (Fig. 8.71), but others retained their pre-improvement layout. **Craik** and nearby **Moss of Tolophin** (Fig. 8.71) fall in the latter category, but in the late 19th century a new courtyard steading and farmhouse was built at **Moss of Tolophin**, and **Bogs** was abandoned altogether. The *toun* of **Craik** was also cleared and replaced by two improved steadings, one of which was given the new name of **Braeside**.

This process was played out throughout the highland fringe, and can equally be seen in Glen Ernan in the parish of Strathdon, where the remains of the settlements have been recorded in some detail in the course of the survey (pp. 208–11; 229–31). The advent of improvement in Strathdon parish has been attributed to Charles Forbes of Newe, who also acquired Edinglassie, Skellater and Bellabeg (*NSA*, xii, Aberdeenshire, 542–3). Work in Glen

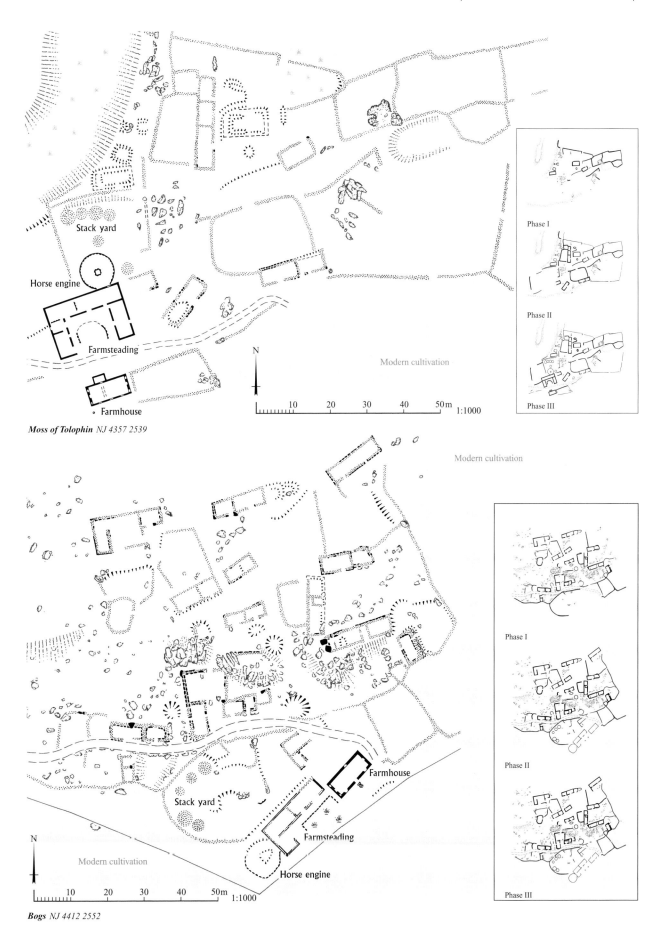

Moss of Tolophin *NJ 4357 2539*

Phase I

Phase II

Phase III

Stack yard

Horse engine

Farmsteading

Farmhouse

Modern cultivation

N

10 20 30 40 50m   1:1000

Modern cultivation

Phase I

Phase II

Phase III

Stack yard

Farmhouse

Farmsteading

Horse engine

N

Modern cultivation

10 20 30 40 50m   1:1000

Bogs *NJ 4412 2552*

Fig. 8.71 Both these touns were replaced by improved steadings that are now abandoned. GV000226

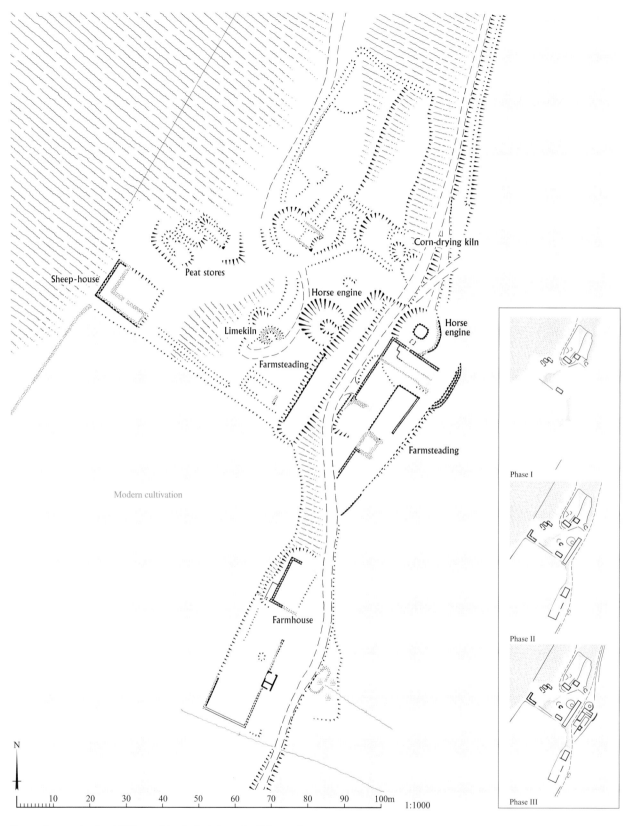

Fig. 8.72 **Bressachoil** (NJ 3056 1290). The remains of this farmstead in Glen Ernan display the transition from pre-improvement toun (Phase I) to improved steading (Phases II & III). The site of the steading was abandoned in the 20th century. GV004152

Ernan began in the 1820s and included the rebuilding of steadings and houses, such as those at **Milton** at the mouth of the glen, and **Lynardoch** and **Relaquheim** further upstream. Of these, only the relatively low-lying farm of **Milton** is still occupied, and the herd's house at **Lynardoch** and the croft at **Relaquheim** (Fig. 8.88) have been abandoned. Further up the glen, the first stage in the improvement of **Bressachoil** (Fig. 8.72), which belonged to another branch of the Forbes family at **Inverernan House**, took place in the early 19th century, following its amalgamation with **Lynmore** and **Auchnahaich** (Fig. 9.15). The latter two farms were deliberately cleared to make **Bressachoil** viable, but even with a further phase of improvement at the end of the 19th century, it was to fail later in the 20th century. On the south side of the glen **Deleva** (Fig. 8.84) and **Belnabreck** were cleared in the 1840s to make **Torrandhu** a more sustainable unit, despite an earlier investment in improving **Deleva**.

Such clearances appear to have been fairly localised, and there is no evidence in Donside for large-scale clearance events affecting whole glens, as happened at Glen Lui on the Mar Lodge estate (RCAHMS 1995). Nevertheless, the long-term effect has been the same, and the general retreat from the margins in the upland glens of Donside is manifested in a scatter of small farms or *touns* deserted in the late 18th or early 19th century (Figs 8.82; 8.86). In only a few cases were these clearances apparently to make way for sheep. One such was at Delnadamph, where the clearance of several small *touns* on the south side of the glen probably preceded the establishment of a sheep station at **Inchmore**. Likewise on the Gordon estates the *toun* of **Boganclogh** had been cleared by 1822 to make way for a sheep farm held directly by the duke of Gordon (NAS CR 8/66). Here a new improved steading was built on the site of the *toun*, but no enclosed fields were laid out for they were not needed. A similar clearance was carried out at **Lynardoch**, in Glen Ernan, probably by Forbes of Newe, in which the *toun* and its dependent holdings (e.g. **Caldens**) were removed. A shepherd's house was eventually built on the site (Harrison 2001a, 50), and the farm was held directly by the estate until the 1870s.

The Archaeology of Rural Buildings and Settlements

The majority of the deserted settlements that have been recorded in Donside (*c.*80%) originate in the agricultural improvements beginning in the early 19th century. As a result most of them are depicted roofed or unroofed on the 1st and 2nd editions of the OS 6-inch map. Nevertheless, a number of other buildings have been discovered singly or in groups, and the absence of any depiction of them on these maps provides a useful guide that some are potentially of earlier date. These latter are mainly found in the fringes of the highland glens, though a scatter has also been discovered in pockets of unimproved ground elsewhere (Figs 8.75; 8.77; 8.82; 8.86). For the purposes of discussion, this wide range of buildings has been divided into broad categories, beginning with some possible examples of medieval

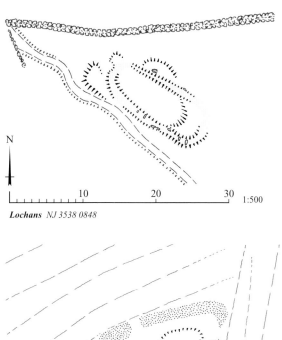

Lochans NJ 3538 0848

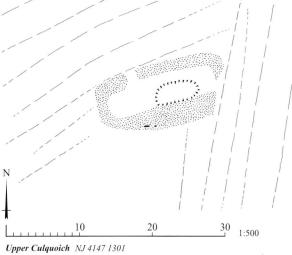

Upper Culquoich NJ 4147 1301

*Fig. 8.73 Several of the buildings that have been recorded may be medieval in date, the example at **Upper Culquoich** apparently pre-dating the adjacent rig-and-furrow cultivation. GV000197*

buildings and the remains of pre-improvement *touns* and shieling groups. This is followed by the more recent remains, which not only include the ruins of improved steadings but also isolated structures, such as sheep-houses and illicit stills.

Medieval Buildings

Possible medieval buildings are few and far between, but they are easily distinguishable from those in the immediately pre-improvement *touns* and farmsteads, both by their architectural features and by the locations in which they are found. Typically, such buildings are not strictly rectangular and are found in moorland outside areas of pre-improvement settlement and cultivation. Examples in Perth & Kinross, the so-called Pitcarmick-type buildings, have been shown to be of early medieval date (RCAHMS 1990, 11–13; Barrett and Downes 1994). No buildings of this specific type, which narrow towards one end and have a partly sunken floor, have been identified in Donside, but occasional examples of large subrectangular buildings have been encountered in locations that are otherwise

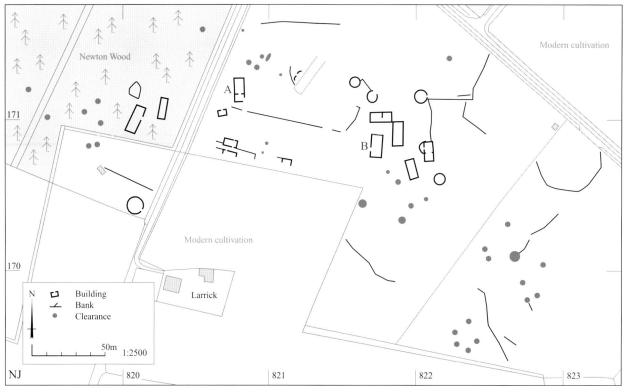

*Fig. 8.74 **Newton Wood** (NJ 8214 1713). At least eight substantial rectangular buildings can be seen in and adjacent to Newton Wood, lying amongst a scatter of hut-circles, small cairns and other rectangular structures. They are probably all dwellings, but the lack of yards and enclosures suggests a cottertoun rather than a fermtoun. GV004136*

occupied by shielings and prehistoric hut-circles. At **Burn of Badnachraskie**, for example, there are three buildings lying in a cluster of clearance heaps. At the time they were recorded, they were under rank heather, making it particularly difficult to see any details of their construction, but the largest measures some 15m by 7m over low footings.

Other buildings that may fall into this category occupy similar positions on the fringes of cultivated ground, but they are not so heavily obscured by vegetation. These include one at **Upper Culquoich**, near Glenkindie, and another at **Lochans**, in Glen Carvie, each of which has stone footings and measures in excess of 15m in overall length by 7m in breadth (Fig. 8.73). While the heavily disturbed **Lochans** building is possibly round-ended, **Upper Culquoich** appears to be

round-cornered. Another large round-ended building that should be considered in this context was discovered in the **Sands of Forvie**. It measured 17.5m in length by up to 8m in breadth from crest to crest of a thick bank, and its interior narrowed slightly towards one end. There are also several rather smaller subrectangular buildings that display evidence of rounded ends or corners, such as two lying some 15m apart on the north face of the Hill of **Bandodle**. Both measure about 11m by 6.4m overall, one with a rounded upper end and a squared lower end, the other rather more round-cornered than round-ended.

Most of the buildings in this category occur singly or in pairs, but at **Newton Wood** (Fig. 8.74) there are the grass-grown footings of eight substantial buildings situated within a scatter of hut-circles and clearance heaps. Most of them are simple rectangular structures with a single entrance in one side, seven of them measuring in excess of 14m in overall length, and in only two cases is there evidence that the interior has been partitioned. The disposition of the buildings resembles that of other pre-improvement townships, with all but one aligned north-east and south-west (p. 189),

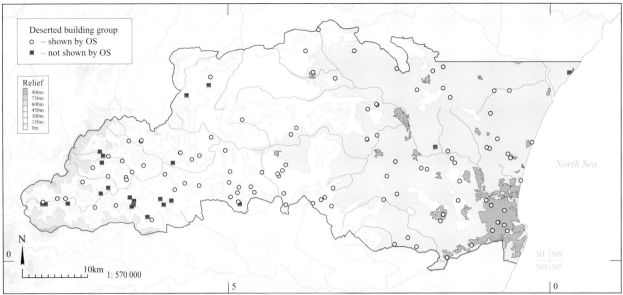

Fig. 8.75 This map shows the distribution of groups of buildings recorded in Donside, some of which may be the remains of small touns. Those lying in the lowlands are mainly known from depictions on the 1st edition of the OS 6-inch map, but the footings of others have been identified by survey, mainly in the upper reaches of the Don. GV000216

but the character of the buildings themselves is very different. Five are more than 7m in overall breadth, and there is no evidence that the buildings served different functions in the manner documented in 18th-century *fermtouns* (p. 203). Indeed, it is likely that they are all dwellings. Coupled with the absence of any yards, this suggests perhaps a *cottertoun* rather than a *fermtoun*, and from the character of the buildings one that is not immediately pre-improvement, but of earlier date.

As yet, there is no reliable basis for placing any of these buildings in a strict chronological horizon, and though some are found amongst scatters of clearance heaps, this is not an indication of an early date so much as a marginal location. Some of the single buildings are perhaps the cottages or *cotts* of landless labourers, others the houses of the small crofters who appear in the documents during the post-medieval period. If so, the *touns* to which they belonged were abandoned well before the preparation of the 1st edition of the OS 6-inch map in the 1870s. Buildings with at least one rounded end in Glen Lui, on the Mar Lodge estate in upper Deeside, are no later than the 18th century in date (RCAHMS 1995, 16, Figs 9 & 12), though these tend to be rather smaller than buildings such as **Upper Culquoich**.

What little excavated evidence there is for rural settlements in north-east Scotland comes from the medieval burgh of Rattray. Here the 13th-century buildings are defined by groups of post-holes and hearths, suggesting a superstructure supported by a framework of earthfast timbers. The walls, it must be presumed, were of entirely perishable materials like turf (*feal*), or wattle and daub, but all trace of them has vanished. In the 14th century the architecture of the buildings changed. Crucks seem to have been employed in place of the earthfast posts, and the walls were built largely of clay with a rubble infill, a technique known as clay and boule (Fenton and Walker 1981, 77). The largest of these cruck-framed buildings measured at least 18m in length by 6m in breadth overall, and it had opposed entrances.

Before the improvements turf or clay was widely used for walls, often rising from the sort of stone footing seen at **Newton Wood**. This raised the crucks off the ground surface so that they were less prone to damp (pp. 203–4). Similar foundations have been found near the old parish church at **Forvie**, where the footings of several small square buildings were of *'roughly-shaped stones and red clay'* (Kirk 1954, 152). A paved area and pottery of 13th- or 14th-century date were also found here.

Pre-improvement Settlements 1650–1750

Most of the pre-improvement settlements that have been recorded lie in the upland fringe at the west end of Donside. On the lower slopes they mainly comprise the remains of small *touns,* but they also include shielings on the summer pastures in the higher reaches of the glens (pp. 204–6; Fig. 8.77). The buildings of these *touns* are usually reduced to low stone footings, typically up to 0.5m in height and 1m in thickness, and they are comparatively narrow in span, ranging from 5m to 6m in overall breadth. Where buildings exceed about 10m in length, they are often partitioned, or have had outshots added at the ends, occasionally forming composite ranges in excess of 20m in length (e.g. **Lynardoch** and **Moss of Tolophin**; Figs 8.71; 8.83). The layouts of the surviving *touns* broadly confirm the patterns observed

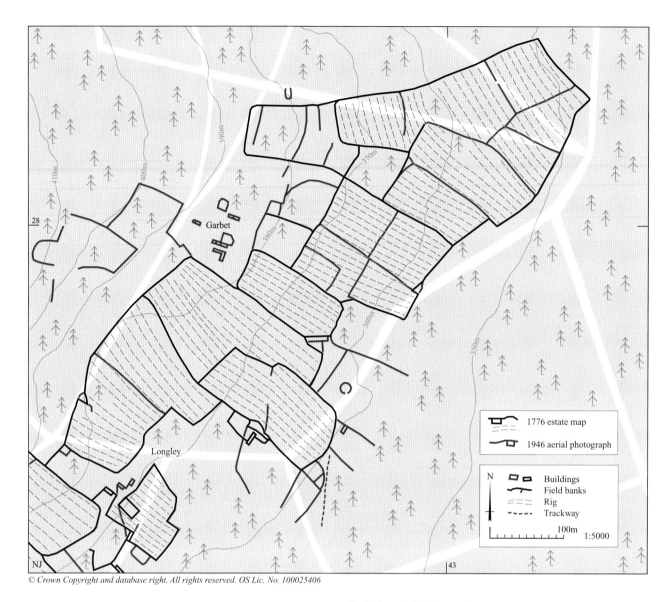

*Fig. 8.76 **Craigs of Longley** (NJ 4270 2797). The layout of the toun of Garbet can be reconstructed from the depiction shown on an estate map of 1776 and the features visible on vertical aerial photographs taken before the area was given over to trees. GV000205*

on estate maps (p. 189), with even the smaller examples tending to display one main axis. To a certain extent this is simply a reflection of local topography, and in many cases there seems to have been a preference to set the long axes of the buildings up and down the slope.

This patterning in the layout can be seen at two small *touns* in Clashindarroch Forest, both of which were probably abandoned before 1776. One lies near **Craigs of Longley** and is named Garbet (Fig. 8.76; NAS RHP 2257); the other is situated on the north face of **Clayshot Hill** and is named Stonerives (NAS RHP 2259). In both cases the names appear on estate maps in 1776, but neither *toun* is depicted, and nor is there documentation to suggest that they were subsequently reoccupied (Harrison 2001b, Sites App.). Each comprises a group of four or five buildings and several enclosures, and Stonerives (**Clayshot Hill**) also

includes a kiln-barn. The buildings, which are aligned on a common axis down the slope, measure up to 18m in length and from 4m to 5m in breadth overall, and are sub-divided into two or three compartments. The *touns* lie adjacent to fields of rig-and-furrow. The latter are enclosed within earthen dykes in a manner that can be seen around farmsteads elsewhere, including those surveyed in a case study of the landscape in Glen Ernan (pp. 229–31). Garbet (**Craigs of Longley**) is documented in the late 17th century, when it was occupied by four crofters, but little is known of Stonerives (**Clayshot Hill**) beyond its appearance as a piece of outfield within the farm of **New Merdrum** on the estate map of 1776 (NAS RHP 2259).

The remains of some other settlements are rather more disparate, and it is harder to determine their status. Four at Inchmore, in the upper reaches of Donside near Delnadamph, will serve by way of example. These settlements are either absent or depicted unroofed on the 1st edition of the OS 6-inch map (Aberdeenshire 1869, sheet lxviii), one lying across the burn at the foot of **Tom Dunan** on the north side of the glen, two on the terrace north of **Inchmore** itself, and the fourth up the **Allt Veannaich** to the south. At the date of survey the two north of **Inchmore** lay in recently felled forestry and it was difficult to distinguish the structures in the piles of cut debris, but the western reveals the character of these settlements. It comprises three buildings disposed over a distance of 90m, and traces of well-developed broad rig can be seen along the edge of the terrace nearby. Attendant enclosures, which are a typical feature of the *touns* depicted on estate maps, are notably absent, though this may be the result of afforestation. Such is the scattered distribution of the buildings here that it is by no means certain that they all belong to the same settlement, but, by way of comparison, the **Tom Dunan** settlement is spread over a distance of about 85m, and **Allt Veannaich** over 100m. In each case three long buildings share roughly the same alignment, accompanied at **Allt Veannaich** by a kiln-barn at right-angles to them. The buildings are relatively narrow, partitioned ranges rather than single long structures, each exceeding 20m in length. Presumably all four settlements represent the remains of small pre-improvement *touns*, the scale of the buildings, the presence of kilns, and the evidence of cultivation, indicating that they are not shielings.

Apart from the general characteristics that allow *touns* such as these to be distinguished from shielings, few buildings display any evidence of their function. Internal drains or midden sumps, which elsewhere serve to identify byres, have not been recorded in Donside, though a hollow has been noted in the end of a building at **Moss of Tolophin**. Fortunately, documentary sources provide some insight into the character and composition of the *touns*. These reveal that byre-houses were not common in the 18th century, and that the domestic and agricultural functions were usually housed separately, if not in free-standing buildings, at the very least in independent compartments. Inventories reveal the types of building that made up the *touns*, listing firehouses, barns, byres, stables, kilns and cotts. The byre is sometimes described as being on the end of the firehouse or barn, but the separation of the functions of the different buildings or compartments is clearly evident in the terminology. Cotts were not necessarily human habitations, and they are often referred to in relation to sheep or goats. An inventory of 1711 for Tillytarmont, lying a little north of the survey area near Gartly, provides a good example of the range of buildings in a *toun*. This lists seven firehouses, six byres, two barns and a kiln-barn, a stable, and a chamber *'before the door'*, suggesting a porch or fore-chamber (NAS GD 44/17/10/13 and Harrison 2001b, 47). The list of units that made up this *toun* certainly accords with some of the ranges that have been examined in the field, where stone partitions divide up the interior into two or three separate compartments, and outshots may have

been added at either end. Both the compartments and the outshots often give the impression that they have been added progressively.

The documentary sources also reveal something of the character of the buildings themselves. The *General View of the Agriculture of Aberdeenshire* (Keith 1811, 129–38), drawn up for the Board of Agriculture even as the countryside was changing, states that the older farmhouses and cottages were usually built with a footing of stone and earth or clay, and a superstructure of turf. Some of the meaner cottages were entirely of turf, but wholly clay-walled construction techniques do not appear to have been in use at this time. As the report states, the buildings were:

> *'generally built about four or five feet high, either with stone and clay, or with stones filled with earth, instead of wrought clay, and one or two feet of turf, (provincially feal) placed above the stones of the side walls, and the gables built of the same perishing materials. The couples, or supporters of the roof, were built in the wall, the feet of them about a yard above the surface of the ground'* (Keith 1811, 129).

It is not clear from this account whether the houses had turf gables rising to the apex of the roof from a stone base, or whether the ends were the same height as the sides below a hipped roof. The roofs, however, were supported on couples, or crucks, which are also mentioned in some inventories. At Monymusk in the early 18th century, for example, inventories of the houses and outbuildings of the tenantry are qualified by the number of couples that they have. Thus, an inventory of Patrick Downey's buildings at Mains of Monymusk in 1738 includes a bere barn (5 couples), an oat barn (6), a kiln barn (4), an ox byre (2), two stirk byres (4), a stable (2) and a firehouse (6), within which there were two partitions separating off a pantry and a chamber (Hamilton 1945, 13). The same style of description is evident in an inventory of William Bruce of *Rumfud* (part of Scurdargue) dating from 1710, which includes a barn and a byre, both of two couples (NAS GD 44/17/10/20), and also one of 1793 for Coul, on the Newe estate, describing a firehouse of four couples, a barn of four couples and a byre of one couple (AUL MS 2769/I/17/3 and Harrison 2001a, 77). Assuming that the bays between the couples were about 2.5m in length, the firehouse at Coul would have been about 12.5m in length, while the byre would have been perhaps 5m in length. The use of this terminology, however, continued after the advent of lime-mortared walls to support the roof, and in some cases a couple may refer to no more than a pair of principal rafters.

Unfortunately, no standing cruck-framed buildings have been identified in Donside in the course of the survey. The example that stood at **Beltimb** in Glenbuchat (Simpson 1942b, 44) has been demolished, and the nearest surviving example is now at Auchtavan

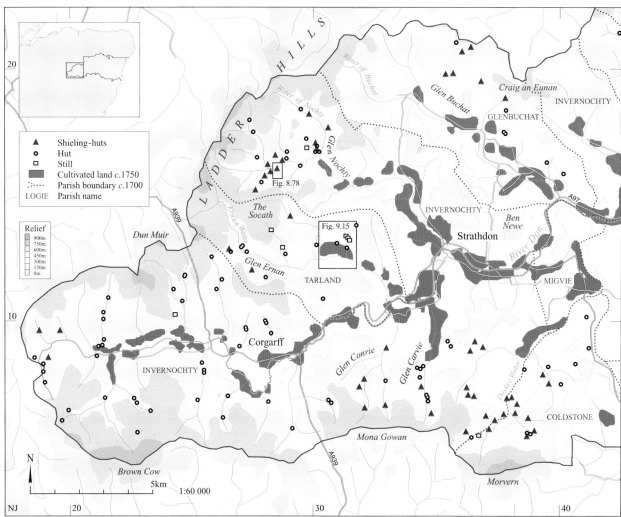

Fig. 8.77 This map shows the distribution of groups of shieling huts in upper Donside. All of them lie well above the extent of cultivated ground in the mid-18th century, which has been drawn schematically from Roy's map (1745–55). The gap in the distribution around Corgarff probably reflects the extent of a hunting reserve, and the solitary huts identified here may be the remains of foresters' lodges, shepherds' bothies and illicit stills. GV000227

on Deeside. Even amongst the ruined buildings that have been recorded, evidence of cruck-slots in the walls is rare, limited to ranges at **Hillockhead** and **Ardler Wood**, and a cottage with clay-bonded walls at **Greencrook** (p. 212). The technique continued to be used after the general introduction of mortared walls, and, as was probably the case at **Greencrook**, was usually employed in a cottage or croft-house that had been built by its occupants. The footings of pre-improvement buildings rarely stand more than 0.3m to 0.5m above the ground, which is well below the level at which the crucks would have been seated. Nevertheless, such footings would have provided firm seats for crucks, raised well up off the ground, and the rest of the walls would have been carried up in turf in the manner described in the Board of Agriculture report.

Shielings

The *touns* that formed the core of the pre-improvement settlement pattern occupied the better land, but many also held rights to graze other areas of pasture during the summer months, often at some remove from the *toun* itself. Known as shielings, some of these pastures can be identified today from clusters of small huts, which would have been occupied by sizeable communities for short periods during the summer. In Donside such huts are mainly to be found in the upper reaches of the highland glens in the parishes of Strathdon, Glenbuchat and Logie-Coldstone (Fig. 8.77), and there is little evidence for shielings east of Kildrummy, either in the post-medieval documents or in the archaeological remains. However, a few of the place-names in the lowland parishes of Midmar, Belhelvie, Old Machar, and Keithhall & Kinkell hint at the former existence of shielings in these areas. Some of these were already farm names by 1696, implying that at least by the post-medieval period, if not before, the shielings had been superseded by permanent settlements. Where this form of transhumance still persisted, it was a long-distance

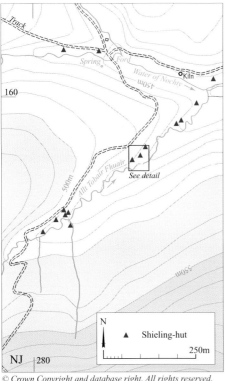

Fig. 8.78 ***Allt Tobair Fhuair*** *(NJ 2826 1583). The shielings strung out along this burn, which include both turf and stone huts, are typical of the groups found in the upper reaches of Glen Nochty. GV00201*

venture in high summer. The tenants of Monymusk, for example, were still sending their cattle in the mid-18th century to the Cabrach, a distance of 35 miles (Hamilton 1945, xli).

The detached portions of lowland parishes found in the highlands (see p. 183) presumably originated in such long-distance transhumance, though in Strathdon this practice had ceased long before the minister recorded the tradition in the *Statistical Account*. Enshrined in the parochial arrangements, this relationship had been established by the mid-12th century, but with the establishment of permanent farms in the same glens during the medieval period, the shieling grounds were presumably displaced into remoter locations. This is certainly implied by the distribution of surviving shielings, in which the clusters of huts lie well beyond the areas that were under cultivation in the mid-18th century (Fig. 8.77).

A large gap in the overall pattern of shielings at the very top of Donside probably reflects the grant of free forest at Corgarff to Lord Elphinstone of Invernochty in the early 16th century. This created an area that was designated for hunting, though it did not prevent the intrusion of three shielings near the watershed

with Strath Avon at **Allt Clach Mheann** (named Ault Clachana Fayn in 1776), **Allt Craig Meann**, and **Cnoc Guibneach** (Cambell's Rive in 1776). These lay in the *'Controverted Land called Fae Vaet'* and were the subject of a survey in 1776 in a dispute about the ownership of the land. The shielings, however, do not appear to have been used by any of the nearby townships on the Don, and it is possible that they belonged to townships in Strath Avon. With the exception of these three, there are no shieling groups for a distance of at least 12km downstream, roughly as far east as Skellater and the mouth of Glen Conrie. As we have seen, this area was probably not settled until the 16th century (pp. 192–3), and there is no evidence that the settlements established then were granted shieling rights within this part of the forest. Indeed, the 18th-century sources indicate that the tenants of the half-*dabhach* of Skellater used Fleuchatts in Glen Ernan (presumably **Meikle Fleuchat**) for shieling rather than going west into what had been the forest. Furthermore, a servitude of common pasture of Corgarff on the north side of the Don gave the four townships of The Luib, Ordachoy, Badinshilloch and Corriehoul common pasturage in Glen Ernan, presumably in place of shielings (Harrison

*Fig. 8.79 **Allt Tobair Fhuair** (NJ 2826 1583). This shieling hut is the south-westernmost of a group of at least three huts on the north side of this burn (see Fig. 8.78). SC961119*

2001a, 63–4). Despite the absence of any shieling groups within the forest, or for that matter shieling place-names, individual huts and structures are dotted along the burns in most of the side glens. None displays any evidence for the rebuilding and re-use that typifies the larger groups of shieling huts, and they are more likely to be the remains of foresters' lodges and shepherds' bothies. In some cases they are perhaps the sites of illicit stills (p. 214).

Further down the strath there are numerous groups of huts in the side glens. On the north these include the groups in Glen Nochty, where shieling is documented from the mid-16th century. In the 18th century shieling was practiced in the upper reaches of the Water of Nochty by the tenants of **Ledmacay**, **Invernochty** and **Drumanettie**, particularly along Allt na Caillach (Harrison 2001a, 64–5 and AUL MS 3175/M/A66). Further east again, there are documentary records of shielings in Glenkindie in the exchequer rental of 1451 (Burnett 1882, 459–60). On the south of the strath there are shieling groups in Glen Conrie, Glen Carvie and the Deskry Water, some of which are shown on the map of Glen Carvie dating from 1766. This labels the various shielings with the names of the farms that used them. Most are on the same estate, such as **Culquharrie** and Brughs near Strathdon church, or **Newe** and **Mains of Newe** a little way to the east, but they also include one belonging to a place called Broughgarrow, which is near Lachlanford in Moray (*c*.NJ 130 609).

The documentary evidence for the shielings in Glen Nochty includes details about the character of the huts. From a document of 1559 it is evident that some were built of perishable materials, such as turf for the walls (*feal*) and a covering of thin turfs or divots for the roof (NAS GD 124/1/218). This accords with some of the structures that have been found in the upper reaches of the **Water of Nochty**, which are apparently entirely of turf. In some cases, these have been reduced to large grass-grown mounds, probably as a result of successive

rebuilding on the same site, but elsewhere there are groups of stone-founded huts, some with walls that were probably carried to the eaves in drystone masonry. An example of the latter occurs on the **Allt Tobair Fhuair** and still stands to a height of 1.2m (Fig. 8.78) where it has been dug back into the slope. Here, as elsewhere, stone huts overlie turf huts. The huts are all relatively small structures with a single entrance, rarely exceeding 9m in overall length and 5m in overall breadth, and they tend to be narrower than the buildings found in the *touns*. On the Mar Lodge estate, Deeside (RCAHMS 1995, 20–22, Fig. 23), and Ben Lawers, north of Loch Tay (Boyle 2003), small ancillary buildings are often found adjacent to huts; probably stores, such structures are absent from Donside. Some huts, however, such as those beside the **Burn of Claisgarbh** in the valley of the Deskry Water, are associated with small oval or subrectangular structures that are too broad to be roofed. These were probably used as pens, but they are by no means universal features of shielings in Donside. It is not clear why some shieling groups have them and others not, unless the more usual technique of building enclosures was to use wattle and stakes in the manner described on the Mar estate in the late 18th century (Cordiner 1780, 26).

By the end of the 18th century, however, the practice of shieling had ceased throughout Donside. This is reflected in contemporary estate surveys, such as that of the Gordon estates of Rhynie and Essie in the 1770s, which records no hint of any shielings, despite taking in a wide swathe of ground in the upper reaches of the Kirkney Water. In Kildrummy, the minister noted that cattle were routinely removed to mountainous ground in the summer months (*Stat. Acct.*, xviii, 1796, 411), but this is perhaps no more than an echo of earlier upland grazing rights being exercised by herdsmen in the parish. The process by which transhumance ceased is discussed below in relation to pre-improvement agriculture (pp. 217–18).

Early Improvement Settlements

Three of the turf-built settlements that have been discovered in the areas that are most typical of upland shieling grounds are quite unlike any of the recorded shielings. Other than on shielings, surviving turf buildings are unusual, though turf was widely used for walls before the improvements and was to remain in use in the meaner cottages (p. 211). Lying at the extremities of the distribution of permanent settlement, each of these three stands within an intake of land that is probably an 18th-century improvement. As such, they are probably the sole survivors of a form of settlement that was once more widespread, characterising many small farmsteads built in the initial stages of occupation on a new intake. In most cases the buildings would have been rapidly replaced as the improvements were carried through.

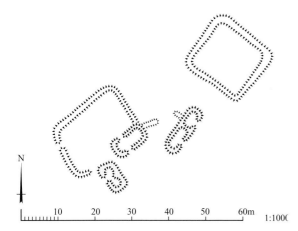

*Fig. 8.80 **Shannach Burn** (NJ 2962 1399). This small turf-built farmstead probably belongs to an early phase of improvement. GV000213*

The first of these settlements (Fig. 8.80) lies at a height of about 480m OD, on a broad terrace above the **Shannach Burn**, a tributary of the Ernan Water, and comprises three turf buildings and two enclosures. The buildings are relatively small and narrow, measuring from 4.5m to 5.5m in overall breadth, and the two smaller ones are a little under 10m in overall length. The third, however, is 14m long and apparently divided into two compartments of unequal size, though these may represent two successive buildings rather than a single structure. The two smaller buildings may also overlie the adjacent enclosure, but all are of a similar character and there is no reason to believe that they are not broadly contemporary. A bank and external ditch bounds the surrounding intake, extending up the hillside to encompass a rectilinear area of some 17.5ha. The only visible evidence that the interior of the enclosure has been improved, however, is restricted to several patches of broad straight rigs on the lower slopes.

A similar enclosure of about 25ha lies at the top of the Don, on the north side of the strath beyond the pre-improvement *toun* of **Tom Dunan** (p. 203), and takes in the ground to either side of the **Allt nan Aighean**. Within it, again at a height of about 480m OD, there is a turf building, an enclosure of two compartments and a circular turf sheepfold. At first sight, the building appears to be divided into three compartments, but each is probably a separate phase of construction, and the individual components are much the same size as the buildings on the **Shannach Burn**. Much of the ground within the enclosure is wet and peaty, but slight traces of rig are visible around the building, and in the mid-18th century Roy's map depicts an area of cultivation to the east of the burn.

The third of these settlements comprises a single turf building and an enclosure on **Breagach Hill**, again lying within a large rectilinear intake. The building is relatively large, measuring overall 13.5m in length by 5.8m in breadth, and there is a midden heap immediately outside its entrance. Although no rig is visible within the

earthen dykes of the surrounding intake, this may be the *'New improvement on Monziefoot'* referred to in a rental of 1757 (AUL MS 3175/928). The dykes, however, were probably built to enclose the grazings, upon which there is also a turf-built sheepfold with a pen or bucht within its interior.

Several other intakes of this type can be identified in the field, such as a rectilinear enclosure defined by earthen dykes to the north of **Lynardoch** in Glen Ernan, which may be the new land identified in a rental of 1733 (Fig. 9.15; NAS GD 124/17/689). Other examples can be found on estate maps. The 1766 map of Glen Carvie, for instance, depicts several large rectilinear enclosures, of which one, the *'Inclosures of Craigydu'* (Craigiedows, NJ 381 092), comprised a five-sided field of 18 acres and contained a single roofed building (AUL MS 2769/I/131/6). The land-use symbols employed indicate that these enclosures were for pasture rather than arable.

The Transition to Improved Steadings

The erection of an improved steading on an old *toun* generally entailed the removal of the earlier buildings. In some cases, however, usually in the uplands, the low grass-grown footings of a *toun* survive side by side with

*Fig. 8.81 **Badenyon** (NJ 3400 1901). Several threshing mills still survive in steadings in the district. SC873272*

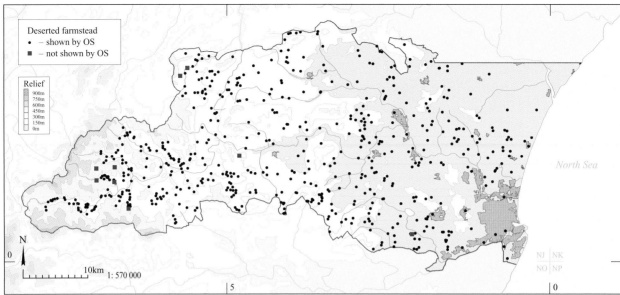

Fig. 8.82 This map shows the distribution of abandoned farmsteads recorded in Donside. Most were still occupied in the 1870s, appearing roofed on the 1st edition of the OS 6-inch map, and in the lowlands many of these have now been removed. A handful of others have been identified in the course of the survey. GV000219

the remains of an improved steading. Good examples can be found on the Craig estate at **Bogs** (Fig. 8.71), **Craik**, **Braeside** and **Moss of Tolophin** (Fig. 8.71). A similar pattern can be seen at **Bressachoil** and **Lynardoch** in Glen Ernan (Figs 8.72; 8.83), and at **Old Morlich** and **Lochans** in Glen Carvie. In each case the buildings of the improved steading readily declare themselves by their construction. They stand on properly levelled stances, forming strictly rectangular shapes, and their lime mortared walls are often of quarried stone, rising to a height of 1.8m or more. The main buildings are also routinely larger than their predecessors, both in length and breadth, but the walls, which were designed to carry the entire weight of the roof, are often as little as 0.6m to 0.7m in thickness.

Many of these new steadings also incorporated a water- or horse-driven threshing mill. This item of machinery, perhaps more than any other, typifies the improved steading, and was a major labour-saving device that fast replaced the ubiquitous threshing flail (Keith 1811, 219). In most cases the threshing machine itself has been removed, but its position is often given away by a lade leading from a pond to the wheel-pit, or a circular platform for the horse engine and an opening for the drive-shaft in the wall of the adjacent building. In a few cases, however, the machine remains substantially intact, good examples including one in the steading at **Badenyon**, in Glen Buchat (Fig. 8.81), and another in a free-standing mill at **Lochans**, in Glen Carvie, both of which bear graffiti dating from the late 19th century.

According to the Board of Agriculture report, 1782 was such a bad season that many landowners decided

to bring in improving farmers from the south. These men were offered inducements, such as a year's rent as an allowance against the cost of constructing a new steading with lime-bonded walls. The use of such incentives in tack agreements was by no means new (e.g. RCAHMS 1995, 9), as can be seen on the Gordon estates of Rhynie and Essie in the tacks drawn up in 1765 for **New Forest**, **Mytice**, **Old Noth**, **Bogs of Noth** and **Boganclogh** (Harrison 2001b, Sites App.). The progress of rebuilding varied from estate to estate and farm to farm, but the implication of the account in the Board of Agriculture report is that by 1811 this process was more-or-less complete.

The courtyard steading and farmhouse constructed at **Wester Fintray** is described in the Board of Agriculture report as an illustration of a model farm (Keith 1811, 134–8). This was designed around a midden yard, and the enclosing ranges housed a water-driven threshing mill, cattle sheds and cow-houses, stables, cartsheds, turnip stores and labourers' apartments. A separate barn was equipped with an iron-plated kiln that is quite different to the circular stone kilns found at pre-improvement *touns* and farmsteads. Despite the idealism espoused by the Board of Agriculture report, the steadings depicted some sixty years later on the 1st edition of the OS 6-inch map display a wide range of layouts. The houses of the larger farms usually stood apart from the farm offices, which lay around the yard containing the midden, but many of the steadings were laid out in an L- or U-shaped arrangement, and the smallest were no more than a single long range, the example at **Bressachoil** (Fig. 8.72) now reduced to a platform some 40m in length.

This diversity must to some extent reflect the way in which the new practices were adopted and the level of investment, particularly in the late 18th and early 19th century, when many of the smaller

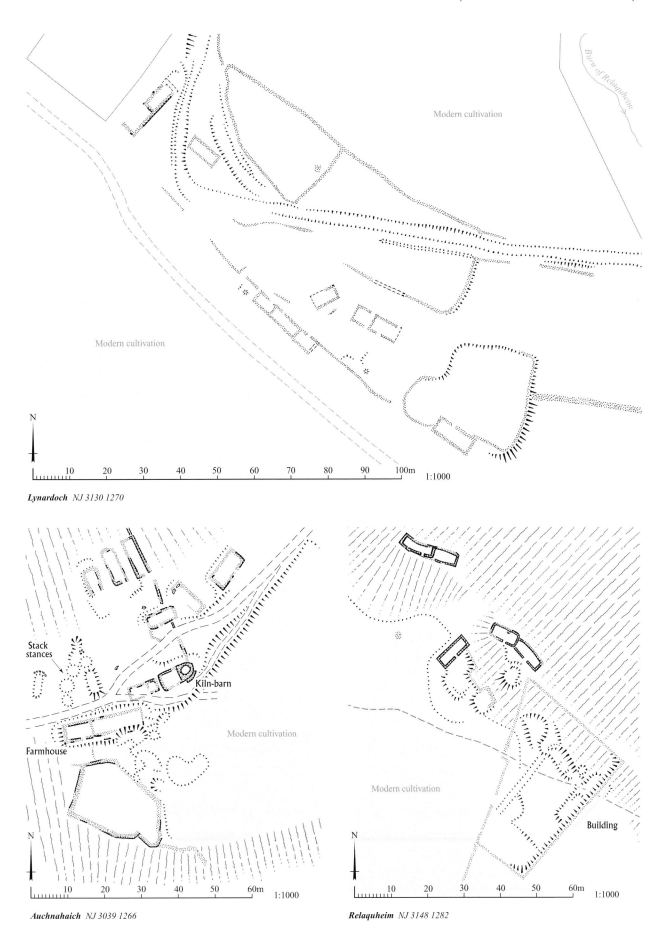

Fig. 8.83 These farmsteads display aspects of improvement architecture, but none was developed into an improved steading. GV000199

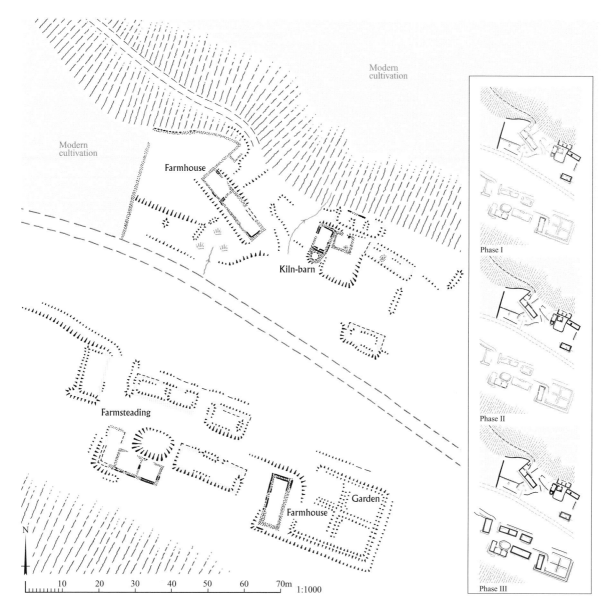

Phase I

Phase I

Phase II

Phase III

*Fig. 8.84 **Deleva** (NJ 3169 1232). This farmstead in Glen Ernan displays a threefold transition from pre-improvement toun (Phase I) to an early improvement farm (Phase II) and a fully developed improvement farm (Phase III). The latter, which was abandoned by 1850, includes an L-shaped byre fronted by the hollow of a midden, and the garden enclosure in front of the dwelling displays the divisions of a parterre. GV000195*

farmsteads incorporated some of the characteristics of improvement, but never developed into fully-fledged improvement steadings. The first stage in the improvement of a steading was often the use of stone and lime for the walls of the buildings, spelling the beginning of the end of cruck-construction, but the arrangement of the buildings would not necessarily follow improvement principles. As the Board of Agriculture report states: *'we too often see the barns in one place, the byres in another, and the stables in a third place, quite detached from each other, while the dung is washed away by the rains, and not attended to as it ought'* (Keith 1811, 134). Kiln-barns

are commonly encountered at the remains of such farmsteads, and there are often limekilns nearby, partly no doubt to provide lime for mortar, but mainly for dressing the fields (pp. 238–9; Harrison 2001a, 103–4).

With further investment, many of the steadings on the better ground were later rebuilt (p. 196), but others were also abandoned, particularly in the highland areas of Donside. There numerous ruined examples have been recorded in the course of the survey, and those in Glen Ernan have been surveyed in detail (Fig. 9.15). A good example of an early improvement farmstead is Rehache (**Clais Liath**), situated where the valley of the Ernan Water abruptly narrows to a highland defile. It is said to have been abandoned after the Muckle Flood of 1828, and is now overgrown with dense juniper thickets (Winram 1986, 47). The layout is irregular and comprises at least one large rectangular building, which probably contained a dwelling, two outbuildings, and a kiln-barn. The walls, which are no more than 1m high,

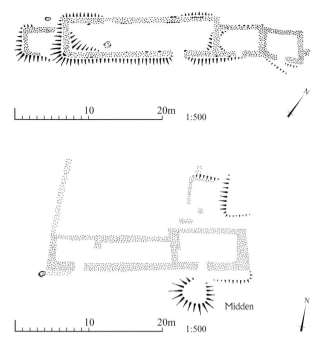

Fig. 8.85 **Caldens** *(NJ 3098 1301) and* **Carnacruie** *(NJ 3088 1301). These two farmsteads are listed under* **Lynardoch** *in a rental of 1735, but whereas the tenant of Caldens (the upper) held a tack for the farm, the occupant of Carnacruie (the lower) was a tenant of Lynardoch who had 'new land' without rent. Carnacruie subsequently disappears from the documentary record, but Caldens retained its independence and the surviving building is much larger than those of pre-improvement touns. GV000181*

are apparently of drystone rubble, though lime pointing may have been washed out from between the stones. The steadings of **Auchnahaich** (Fig. 8.83), **Lynmore** and **Deleva** (Fig. 8.84) in Glen Ernan exhibit the same semi-improved features in their construction, while a less developed variation on this theme can be seen at **Caldens**. There one of two farmsteads has a rectilinear yard overlying the adjacent head-dyke (Fig. 8.66) and a single long range with the sort of low stone footing usually seen at pre-improvement *touns* and farmsteads

(Fig. 8.85). Including the outshots, the range is some 37m in length, but the main portion of the building forms a single compartment over 20m in length and is much larger than might be expected if it dated from before the improvements.

Auchnahaich, **Lynmore** and **Deleva** had ceased to operate as separate farms by 1850, but the surviving remains at **Deleva** preserve the transition from pre-improvement *toun* into developed improvement steading. On the one hand the early improvement buildings overlie pre-improvement structures, on the other a developed improvement steading lies some 50m to the south. The latter includes a farmhouse with a walled garden and parterre, an L-plan byre with a midden, and a long outbuilding.

Crofters' Cottages and Farmhouses

The proliferation of crofts in the late 18th and 19th century (p. 195; Fig. 9.7) led to the construction of huge numbers of cottages in the Aberdeenshire landscape. Many are still occupied today, if heavily altered and extended, but dozens of others have fallen by the wayside, either reduced to ruins or entirely removed (Fig. 8.86). By far the majority were constructed by the crofters themselves, the earlier examples employing crucks and the same building techniques found in pre-improvement cottages. The walls of the latter were described in the Board of Agriculture report as made up of *'stones, filled with earth for three feet, and the rest of the side walls and gables with feal or turf, like the farmer's offices. Sometimes they were built with turf entirely'* (Keith 1811, 138).

Fig. 8.86 This map shows the distributions of isolated buildings discovered in the course of field survey, and those depicted on OS maps that were subsequently abandoned. Many of the latter group have been removed, but most were probably cottages on small crofts that disappeared as the holdings were rationalised during the late 19th and early 20th centuries. GV000215

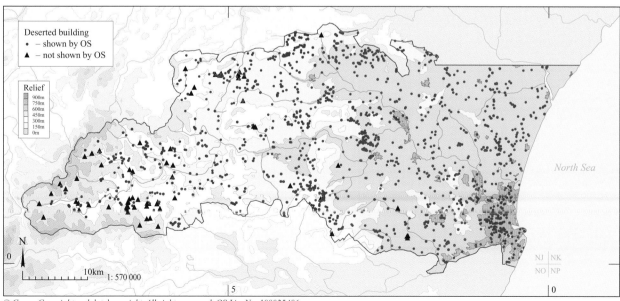

Fig. 8.87 **Badenyon** *(NJ 3403 1902). View of the arched fireplace in the kitchen of the farmhouse. A later fireplace with a corbelled lintel has been inserted into the back of the embrasure. SC957508*

Few of the cottages shown on late 18th-century estate maps now survive, but the remains of one has been identified at **Craigs of Longley**. This measures 10.9m by 5.3m over low stone footings and has an entrance in one side. Likewise most of those depicted on 19th-century estate maps have been removed, usually when the holdings were rationalised later in the 19th century. The attrition is well illustrated by comparing the plan of Balquhain estate prepared by Walker and Beattie in 1838 against successive editions of the OS 6-inch map (pp. 223–4). Fortunately, the Board of Agriculture report provides contemporary descriptions of cottages at the beginning of the 19th century (Keith 1811, 138–9). Typically roofed with thatch, they measured from 7.3m to 11.95m in length by 3.65m in breadth, and by then most had clay-bonded stone walls, sometimes snecked (pointed) with lime. There were generally two windows, though some had three or four. The earthen-floored interior contained two partitions, but no ceilings, and there was a fireplace at each end.

One such cottage has been recorded at **Greencrook**, where the walls also contain two possible cruck-slots (p. 204). Now subsumed into a forestry plantation, the cottage forms one wing of a ruined L-shaped range, and measures 10.7m by 4.9m over clay-bonded walls 0.7m in thickness. The range was described in 1865–6 as a *'dwelling-house, and offices, one storey high, thatched and in good repair'* (Name Book, Aberdeenshire, No. 62, p. 67). It was still roofed at the beginning of the 20th century (Aberdeenshire 1901, sheet lxxii.NW). This and other ruinous cottages recorded in the course of the survey are fairly typical of three-bay cottages built in the 19th century, with a central entrance between two flanking windows at the front. The main rooms were at either end, each with a fireplace in the gable, and a small room between them was sometimes provided with a window at the rear.

This basic design remained in use throughout the 19th century, but slates generally replaced thatch as the typical roofing material, and the attic was often

exploited to create further accommodation. Accessed by a ladder from the hall, the attic could provide sufficient space for two rooms lit by iron-framed skylights or, more occasionally, small windows in the gables. The interiors of the later cottages are usually divided up with stud partitions, and the rooms are lined with lath and plaster or pine panelling. Sprung timber floors also came into general use, though flags were often retained in the kitchen.

In some cottages the kitchen contained a large fireplace some 2.5m across and 0.8m deep, spanned either with a single granite lintel or by a shallow arch. Those with lintels occur quite widely, but the distribution of arched fireplaces is apparently restricted to the glens at the top of the Don. One of the best examples of an arched fireplace occurs in the derelict farmhouse at **Badenyon** (Fig. 8.87), in Glen Buchat (Simpson 1942b, Fig. 39), but others have been recorded at **Stroin**, in Glen Carvie, and **Lynmore**, in Glen Conrie. Numerous others are probably hidden behind plasterwork, as the owners of several cottages in the same neighbourhood have discovered.

While the basic three-bay design remained unchanged, numerous minor alterations and embellishments can be detected in the cottages that remain today. The simplest of such alterations might be the addition of an outshot, such as a scullery opening off the kitchen at the rear, but in the larger cottages the accommodation is altogether more generous. This presumably reflects a greater level of investment as the process of rationalisation of the holdings progressed through the 19th century. This is also reflected in the layout of the steadings on small crofts. These often took on the trappings of an improved farm with a detached farmhouse. One stage in this evolution can be seen at **Relaquheim** (Fig. 8.88), in Glen Ernan, where the small

Fig. 8.88 **Relaquheim** *(NJ 3146 1264). An oblique aerial view of the steading taken in 2000. SC975458*

cottage there today stands to one side of a series of sheds and outbuildings laid out around a small yard. The cottage itself has a central entrance between two flanking windows, though a porch added around the doorway now houses a kitchen. The farmhouse at **Badenyon** is more sophisticated, rising to one and a half storeys, but it still presents the same symmetrical façade. In this case a stair rises from the hall to a second storey lit with half dormers. Not only has the basic design of the cottage been embellished here, but it serves a fully-fledged improved steading ranged around three sides of a yard. A threshing machine still survives in the western wing of the steading (Fig. 8.81).

Sheep-houses and Goat-houses

Some of the ruined buildings that have been recorded in the course of the survey were designed to house sheep or goats, rather than humans (p. 203). Sheep-houses, or sheepcotes and sheepcotts as they are also known, are documented in Aberdeenshire from the late 17th century (Robertson 1843, 386), though the surviving examples usually date from the improvements. Typically they combine a narrow building with an enclosure, or in developed form comprise several buildings set around a closed court. Pre-improvement sheep-houses are less easy to identify, generally being indistinguishable in the field from the remains of cottages belonging to cottars and labourers (see also RCAHMS 2001, 59–60). In some cases, however, estate maps show them. The 1766 map of Glen Carvie, for instance, annotates a series of parallel buildings next to the arable at Mains of Collquharry *'Sheep Cotts of Collquharry'*. Elsewhere, away from the areas of arable, it also annotates several *'Goat Cotts'* (AUL MS 2769/I/131/6).

Notwithstanding the difficulties of identifying undocumented sheep-houses, several good examples have been recorded, notably in Glen Buchat. Of these, two set either side of a narrow yard on the slopes above **Ryntaing**, a deserted farmstead at the top of the glen, exhibit all the typical characteristics (Fig. 8.89). Both measure about 11m by up to 3.2m internally, but

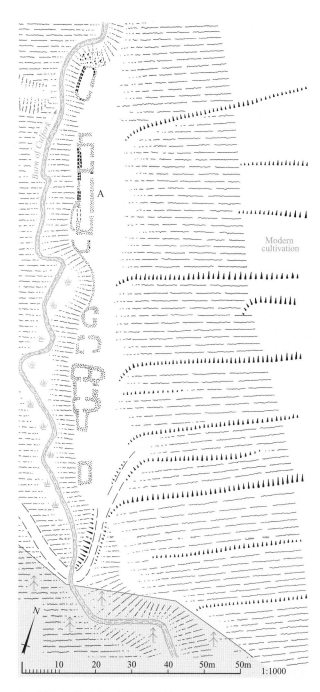

Fig. 8.90 **Culfork** *(NJ 4551 1135). This long, narrow two-compartment building (A) may be the remains of a sheep-house.* GV000194

Fig. 8.89 **Ryntaing** *(NJ 3360 2045). This view from the south-east shows one of the two ruinous sheep-houses that lie at the upper margin of the enclosed fields at the head of Glen Buchat. SC874061*

whereas the walls of a cottage would have stood to at least head height, here they are no more than 1m high, and the gables only stood a little over 2.5m high. Both sheep-houses have an entrance in one end, and one of them also has an entrance opening into the yard. The only other feature visible is a square opening immediately above the lintel of one of the entrances in the gables. No other sheep-house retains low gables like these, but further down the glen, high above Belnaglack on the south-west flank of **Tod Holes**, there is a ruined building displaying some of the same characteristics. In this case it is slightly longer, measuring 13m by 2.5m internally, but again the drystone walls are no more than 1m high, and one of the two entrances is through an end wall.

Other identifications are not so clear-cut, such as one at **Culfork**, Towie, situated at one end of a group of structures strung out along a terrace on the opposite side of the burn from the deserted steading (Fig. 8.90). The majority of the structures are defined by low grass-grown stone footings resembling successive shieling-huts, but the northernmost is a narrow, two-compartment building with drystone walls. At only 4m in overall breadth, this is better interpreted as a sheep-house than a dwelling. Other possible examples include a narrow range around two sides of an old sheepfold at **Bressachoil** in Glen Ernan (Fig. 8.72; Aberdeenshire 1869, sheet lx), and an open-fronted structure on the north-west of the *toun* of **Bogs**.

Stills

In the 18th and early 19th century illicit distilling was rife in the upper reaches of Donside (e.g. Simpson 1942b, 45). During that period, according to the minister of Strathdon, *'To be engaged in distillation, and to defraud the excise, was neither looked upon as a crime, nor considered a disgrace'* (*NSA*, xii, Aberdeenshire, 549). Indeed, the continued presence of a military garrison in **Corgarff Castle** from 1748 until well into the 19th century was concerned more with the maintenance of law and order, and in particular smuggling and illegal distilling, than any suppression of political unrest. The death knell of the illicit trade was signalled by the Act of 1823 to regulate distilling, which was one of the *'vigorous measures adopted by Government, effectively seconded by the proprietors'*, and by 1838 *'the lawless life of the smuggling "bothie" was wholly abandoned'* (*NSA*, xii, Aberdeenshire, 549–50). There was a similar history on the Mar Lodge estate (RCAHMS 1995, 25–6).

During the survey a number of possible stills have been discovered, usually in secluded positions in the upland glens, and often in locations that are more typical of shielings (Fig. 8.77). Unlike shielings, however, the structures most likely to have been stills occur singly. The process itself requires a good source of water, and most possible stills are found tucked in beside a burn, in some cases dug into the foot of an escarpment forming the edge of a meandering stream gully. Set into the folds of such gullies they are effectively hidden in the landscape and may only be visible from the bank directly opposite. The structures

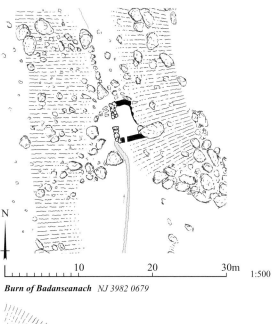

Burn of Badanseanach NJ 3982 0679

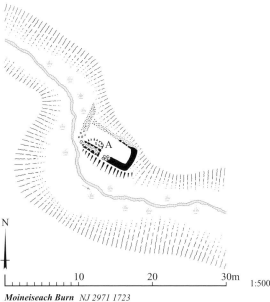

Moineiseach Burn NJ 2971 1723

Fig. 8.91 These examples of stills are typical of such structures, tucked into a secluded gully adjacent to a burn. GV000214

themselves often have drystone walls, and the interior may be oddly proportioned in comparison to a shieling-hut. At **Moineiseach Burn** (Fig. 8.91) a raised bench immediately inside the door probably indicates where the still stood. At **Burn of Badanseanach** (Fig. 8.91) a lade has been dug to bring water into the interior. Such features are rare, however, and the difficulties of distinguishing these structures from herdsmen's huts and the like mean that others may have slipped by unrecognised.

Chapter 9: The Transformation of the Rural Landscape

Piers Dixon and Angela Gannon

The impact of the improvements was as far-reaching upon the appearance of the rural landscape as it was upon the character of the settlement pattern. In Donside this process was set in train in the early 18th century, but the most dramatic period of change was not until the early 19th century, beginning in about 1810 and vividly recalled in the descriptions in the *New Statistical Account*. In practice, however, the landscape continued to evolve throughout the 19th century. Indeed, while the modern landscape of fields and plantations would have been easily recognisable by 1900, economics, politics and world events have combined to ensure that there has been little respite in the pace of change in the 20th century, most recently through grant-aided pasture improvement and blanket afforestation.

This section broadly follows these themes, first describing something of the character of pre-improvement agriculture as it is recorded in the 18th century, and then the transformation of the countryside documented during the 19th century. The discussion of the various features of the landscape created in this process follows the same pattern, beginning with the remains of pre-improvement agriculture and a remarkable case-study of the landscape at the top of the Don in Glen Ernan. It is completed by a brief assessment of the 20th century landscape, including the remains of defences dating from the Second World War.

Pre-improvement Agriculture

There are many accounts of pre-improvement agriculture in Donside, mainly dating from the late 18th century, and ranging from the overview of the county of Aberdeenshire prepared for the Board of Agriculture in 1793 by Dr James Anderson (Keith 1811, 231ff.) to the local descriptions contained within the *Statistical Account*. At that time the pre-improvement field-systems were beginning to disappear, but it should be borne in mind that many of the contemporary practices described had already undergone extensive modification over the preceding century.

Some of the earliest commentaries on pre-improvement agricultural practices are provided by Sir Archibald Grant, whose father bought Monymusk in 1713. In 1716, when Sir Archibald assumed control, *'not one acre upon the whole esteat* [was] *inclosed'* (Hamilton 1945, xlvi) and the ground was described as *'raised and uneven, and full of stones, many of them very large, of a hard iron quality, and all the ridges crooked in the shape of an S, and very high and full of noxious weeds and poor, being worn out by culture, without proper manure or tillage'* (Hamilton 1946, ix). Nor was there *'any timber upon it but a few elms, cycamore and ash'* (Hamilton 1945, xlvi–xlvii).

The age-old use of turf for everything from manure to construction was also a practice that received some adverse criticism. Thomas Winter, an English farmer brought to Monymusk by Grant in 1726, wrote *'The counterry people are very busiey spoiling their land with the foot spade, sum for muck fell, sum to burn and others to repair the houses with, takeing away the earth and leav the stones to produce corn and grass which is certainly a gross errour and hath spoild near half the land'* (Hamilton 1945, 109). The paring of turf to be composted or burnt, *muckfeall* or *muckfaill,* was widely practised, though later writers were as adamant of the result as Winter, that it created *'a short worthless kind of heath'* (*Stat. Acct.*, ix, 1793, 511). Areas of peat moss and peaty soils were also burnt to release nutrients prior to cultivation – the so-called *'burntlands'* that occurred throughout Aberdeenshire (Whyte 1987, 42).

Later accounts give more considered views of the state of pre-improvement agriculture, though in every case the sympathies of the authors unquestionably lay with the improvers. One of the most detailed of these descriptions is provided by the minister of the parish

Fig. 9.1 **Barra Hill** *(NJ 8025 2570). The interlocking pattern of the furlongs of a pre-improvement rig-system can be seen around the fort on the summit of Barra Hill. SC624390*

of Alford, who identified four types of land – infield, outfield, *laigh* land and pasture (*Stat. Acct.*, xv, 1795, 451–70). The infield was in constant cultivation, with a rotation in which one third was manured with dung and sown with barley, and the rest sown with oats. Outfield was not continuously cropped, but was sown at intervals, sometimes after it had been manured by folded cattle on the hoof, a system known as tathing, and at other times simply following on from grass, when it was known as *faugh* land (English – fallow). The beasts used to tathe the outfield were usually pastured elsewhere during the day, and a temporary *feal* dyke was erected to keep them on the area to be cultivated by night. Following harvest, the dyke was knocked down and the land ploughed in preparation for a crop of oats in the spring. This type of outfield was cropped with oats for five seasons before being sown with grass and left fallow for five years. The *faugh* land was cultivated for one or two seasons less and left fallow for one or two more. The *laigh* land had deep soils that were inclined to become waterlogged. They often failed to yield a crop in wet summers. The largest farms had access to all these types of land, but others did not. Small farms and crofts, for example, might only hold infield, while other farms might have infield and outfield, but not *laigh* land and pasture. The general division of the land between infield and outfield, however, persisted until the widespread introduction of turnip breaks in new crop rotations in the late 18th century (Keith 1811, 236).

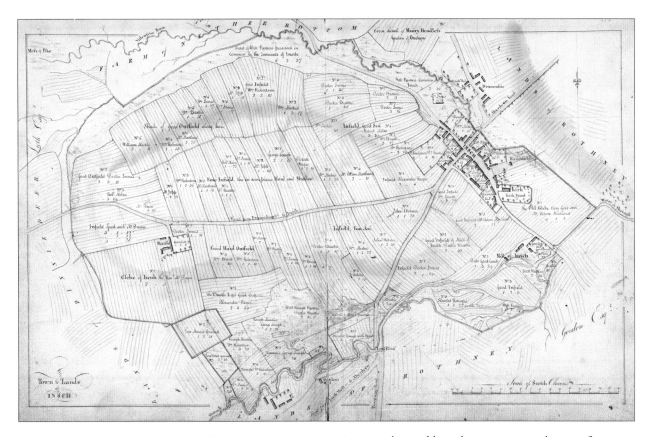

Fig. 9.2 **Insch** *(NJ 63 28). This plan of the village and its lands was prepared in 1797 for the survey of the Leith Hall estate by George Brown. © NTS*

Many estate maps prepared during the second half of the 18th century depict the broad division of the arable land between infield and outfield, but by then relatively few of the farms were held in runrig, the traditional division of the arable lands of a *toun* between multiple tenants. So much so, that the estate maps that have been consulted have produced only five examples where the lands were apparently still in runrig – **Duncanstone** (1758), **Insch** (1797; Fig. 9.2), **Monymusk** (1774), **Upper Coullie** (1774; Fig. 8.65) and **Tillykerrie** (1769). The first two are striking examples of medieval planned villages (pp. 185–6), the third, **Monymusk**, an early 18th-century planned village, and the last two clustered townships. In each case the reverse-S strips lying close to the village are annotated with the names of the tenants, and at **Insch** and **Duncanstone** blocks of outfield are also attributed to them individually. The rarity of runrig in the late 18th century reflects the widespread amalgamation of farms into single holdings, which had already occurred at about 50% of *touns* by 1696. By the onset of the improvements perhaps as few as one third of *touns* had two or more tenants.

The outfields shown on many of the maps were enclosed with folds for tathing, and it is clear that folded outfields were a feature of *touns* throughout the lowlands and uplands, from Castle Fraser in the east to the hills of Rhynie and the Kirkney Water in the west. That said, there was also some variation in the approach to managing arable and pasture, as can be seen from a comparison of the maps of Castle Fraser in 1788 and Glen Carvie in 1766. On the Castle Fraser maps the broad curving rig surrounding the outfield folds on Braeneil and Mains are also styled as outfield (NTS Castle Fraser MS), but the map covering Glen Carvie (AUL MS 2769/I/131/6) makes no distinction between infield and outfield. Nor does it show any enclosed fields, other than some rectilinear intakes at the edge of the rigged land (p. 207). These intakes are not hatched with rigs, and appear to be pasture parks. The overall arrangement in Glen Carvie suggests that the rigged fields are infield, and that no system of folding or tathing was in operation. It may be no coincidence that this map is one of only two in Donside that show any shielings, even where they cover the equivalent areas of upland terrain. The estate maps covering the valley of the Kirkney Water, on the northern fringes of the survey area, for example, give no hint of any shielings, but they do show extensive outfield folds (Fig. 8.76). This contrast with Glen Carvie raises the question of whether the practice of tathing outfields played some part in the demise of the shieling system.

By the late 18th century the greater part of every lowland township had been brought into cultivation, either as infield or outfield, and there was relatively little ground left for pasture. In essence, therefore, tathing was part of a more intensive system of managing arable and pasture, and is likely to have been a response to mounting pressure on the land. The source of this pressure was probably *toun*-splitting and settlement expansion, which saw both the conversion of former outfields to infield, and further inroads into the available pastures for new outfields. In the lowlands this process was evidently at work from the 15th century onwards (pp. 190–3), in the very same areas where shieling had probably died out long before 1696 (p. 204). Thus, the intimate relationship between pasture and arable implicit within tathing systems is likely to have been first developed in areas where the pressure on the land was such that shieling was no longer possible or practical. As can be seen in the valley of the Kirkney Water, it subsequently came into wider usage as a more efficient farming practice, and to some extent formed part of the evolution of improved agriculture.

Agricultural Improvements in the 18th Century

The estate maps that have been cited as evidence of pre-improvement agriculture were also the portents of change, for such surveys were a prerequisite for reform from the very beginning of the 18th century. Sir Archibald Grant, for example, planned his improvements in detail, and as early as 1719 his accounts record the purchase of a compass, rule, theodolite and chain (Hamilton 1945, 72) for measuring the boundaries of the holdings, and laying out new enclosures. In that same year Alexander Jaffray of Kingswells, Grant's friend and right-hand man (Hamilton 1945, xlv), *'marked out a line for inclosing two sides of the moore of Tombegg'* (Hamilton 1945, 79), and throughout the 1730s and 1740s Thomas Winter carried out surveys in advance of enclosure (e.g. Hamilton 1946, opp. 128).

In the second half of the 18th century landowners increasingly employed professional surveyors to prepare detailed plans of their estates. This led to further surveys of Monymusk in 1774 and 1797, but the trend is manifested elsewhere and was often a source of comment to the ministers writing in the *Statistical Account*. By the early 1790s, the neighbouring parishes of Bourtie, and Keithhall & Kinkell, in the arable heartland of Donside, had been *'measured'* (*Stat. Acct.*, ii, 1792, 528; ix, 1793, 434). Likewise the Craig estate in the parish of Auchindoir, where Mr Gordon had *'a farm substantially enclosed, subdivided, and improved, in which the useful and the ornamental are happily united'* (*Stat. Acct.*, xii, 1794, 496).

Grant's own programme of improvement was to last the rest of his life. He planted trees, built walled enclosures, and introduced new crop rotations, becoming widely recognised as a progressive and enlightened landowner. The map prepared by General Roy in the mid-18th century (Roy 1747–55, sheet 29/1) reveals the impact of this work on the landscape around Monymusk. This shows an arrangement of tree-lined

rectilinear parks flanking the approach to the estate from the east-south-east, while, to the south, beyond the **Home Farm** and the policies of the house, a series of irregular enclosures spreads from the township at Inver down to the north bank of the Ton Burn. Several plantations also appear on the map, including Paradise Wood, with its avenues along the south bank of the River Don. No other parklands and policies depicted on General Roy's map in Donside are as extensive as those of Monymusk, nor are any shown with enclosed fields.

Grant implemented his scheme to improve the estate through the leases for the farms. Each one incorporated a string of conditions, as can be seen in a lease for the lands of Afforsk agreed in 1735 with James Moore of Stonywood for a five- or fifteen-year term. Moore was allowed to cast peat locally and provided with sufficient wood to roof a new house, but there were numerous obligations and stipulations, ranging from the management of the arable and pasture to the maintenance of any dykes and ditches. For example, he was obliged *'to keep and preserve from all sheep and cattle, the firr planting upon the said possession, and not to pasture amongst the same, and to plant one hundred trees of ash, elm, allars, birch or plain annually round the said dykes or ditches already upon the said possession, and to plant in the dykes and ditches, which he is hereby bound to erect and make upon the said possession'*. He was allowed only one crofter on the property, and forbidden to *'cast any faile or divete except for the first time nor muck faile nor turfs for fireing upon the said lands'*. He was also under an obligation *'to take in and plough annually from the heath in the park already inclosed or elsewhere within the said lands as he pleases the extent of three bolls of bear at least of new ground, and to inclose the same as it is so taken in with a sufficient dyke or ditch which he is to maintain and plant as aforesaid'* (Hamilton 1945, 31–3).

Measures such as these led to the general improvement of the estate, and paved the way for more fundamental changes in the structure of rural society. Not only were the holdings consolidated into single-tenant farms, but the sub-tenants and cottars were removed from the land (p. 193). And, as this new tier of single tenants improved the farms, so they generated a surplus of wealth that could be reinvested into further improvements. This trend to a more commercial approach to agriculture also brought about a change in the rents, which were now paid solely in money rather than a tripartite combination of money, produce and labour. By the end of the 18th century, however, the status of the sub-tenants and cottars had been reduced to no more than hired hands.

The survey of Monymusk in 1774 captures the estate at a point when such changes had begun to take effect, though the overall character of the landscape had yet to take on the formal framework that exists today. Annotations such as *'New Folds'* and *'Improvements called the Back muir Park'* appear on the map (Hamilton 1946, opp. 1), but nowhere better illustrates the change than the pattern of neat rectangular fields at Inver, to the south-east of the **Home Farm**, which by 1774 had been subdivided into Easter and Wester Inver. Elsewhere, as at Afforsk, the new fields are less regular, while at **Upper Coullie** (Fig. 8.65), on the eastern edge of the estate, the narrow S-shaped plots of the infield were still in runrig. **Upper Coullie** was to remain in runrig until 1798, in which year a map was *'prepared in connection with plans for the abolition of run rig and the creation of consolidated holdings'* (Hamilton 1945, opp. 148).

Several other estates in Donside have two 18th-century surveys, notably those covering the Clatt lands of Towie, the Leith Hall estate, and the former Leslie estates. These provide a rare opportunity to assess the wider impact of 18th-century improvements amongst Grant's Aberdeenshire neighbours. The Leith Hall and Leslie estates were first surveyed in 1758 for John Leith of Leith Hall (NAS RHP 5198 & 5199), and then again in 1797. The Clatt lands were surveyed for Capt. John Forbes of Newe in about 1771 (NAS RHP 260/2), but having passed into the hands of General Hay of Rannes of Leith Hall (*NSA*, xii, Aberdeenshire, 584–5) were resurveyed in 1797.

Superficially the landscape depicted on the later maps appears little altered over this period of 25–40 years, but there are many subtle changes. Several farms had acquired large expanses of moorland, such as **Mains of Leslie**, **Chapelton**, **Edingairoch** and **Auchnagathle**, the result of the divisions of commonty, or intercommoned waste, which were beginning to occur at this time. There was also a general increase in the acreage of infield and outfield land under cultivation, ranging from about 5% to 45%. At two farms on the Leslie estate, **Duncanstone** and **Old Flinder**, the infield and outfield shown on the earlier map were both divided into two parts called *'ploughs'*, and named North and South, and Upper and Nether respectively (NAS RHP 5199). This appears to be a step on the way to the dissolution of runrig, involving the concentration of the rigs of each tenant in one place. Neither division survived to 1797 in this form. By then the outfield at **Duncanstone** was apportioned in severalty blocks between the tenants, while the infields remained in runrig strips. There is also evidence of changes in the status of fields, from infield to outfield (e.g. **New Flinder**) and *vice versa* (e.g. Bank Head or Stony Field), and from arable to pasture. An example of the latter at Blairdinny shows relict rig-and-furrow (NAS RHP 5199 & RHP 260/2; NTS Leith Hall MS). If the hatching within the fields faithfully reproduces the rigs, those within Stony Field No. 3 have even been realigned from east and west to north and south. Fields at Stony Field were also being enlarged and the boundaries straightened, both manifestations of improvements in progress. In doing so, outfield folds were disappearing,

but the furlongs of rig forming the infields are often still recognisable in the later survey.

If the physical alteration of the farming landscape was relatively subtle, the establishment of forestry plantations had a far more dramatic impact on the countryside. From the very outset, Grant had established nurseries within the grounds of Monymusk House and imported seeds from abroad. His intentions were not simply to improve the look of the estate, but to realise the commercial value of timber. The felling of trees and the sales of plants are registered throughout the Monymusk accounts from the mid-1730s and, in a memorandum to his son in 1754, he estimated that there were about two million mature trees on the estate (Hamilton 1945, xlix). Such a figure can hardly be represented in the relatively small plantations shown on Roy's map, but the planted woodlands were certainly extensive by 1774. Two hundred and fifty years later the boundaries of these large plantations are still visible, and the most extensive, on Pitfichie Hill and Millstone Hill, are now in the possession of the Forestry Commission.

Grant was not alone in planting woodlands, and within the survey area he is not even the earliest. What sets him above his peers is the scale of his planting. Most of lowland Aberdeenshire had probably been stripped of woodland long before the 18th century, but from this point on landowners began to restock. Plantations of 13,000 trees had been established by 1703 at Kildrummy (NAS GD 124/17/102), while an area of *'very good fir planting'* referred to near the Hill of New Leslie must also date from the early 18th century (Mitchell and Clark 1906–8, i, 16).

The establishment of many more plantations during the 18th century is evident from the parish entries of the *Statistical Account*. Most seem to have been introduced as a means of utilising land that had either been waste or given over to sheep. Yet the planting does not appear to have been confined simply to the uplands. In Peterculter, one of the more low-lying parishes in the survey area, the minister observed that *'As plantations have increased, sheep have decreased'* (*Stat. Acct.*, xvi, 1795, 367), and on one estate in the parish, the number of sheep fell from in excess of 10,000 to only 100 because *'so much hill has been inclosed and planted'* (*Stat. Acct.*, xvi, 1795, 366). This too is the case on the Monymusk estate, where by the 1790s the number of sheep had dropped by one third over the previous fifty years from a total of almost 4000. According to the minister, *'The cause of the decrease is to be accounted for, from the great number of parks and plantations, which have circumscribed the pasture'* (*Stat. Acct.*, iii, 1792, 71).

With the exception of Monymusk, the largest area of planting mentioned in the *Statistical Account* was on the Craig estate in Auchindoir parish, where 600 acres of *'all kinds of forest trees'* are recorded *'in a very thriving state'*, in the opinion of the minister 'rendering Craig one of the most beautiful places in the country' (*Stat. Acct.*, xii, 1794, 500). The creation of these new woodlands in the 18th century provides a rough guide to the aspirations of at least some of the landowners in the county towards the improvement of their estates. And it is also clear that these plantations were generally but one element in an overall scheme for improvement. Thus, Mr Burnett of Kemnay not only planted 130 acres of mixed woodland on his estate, but also enclosed almost 100 acres of moorland, *'which he broke up, drained, and cleared of stones'* (*Stat. Acct.*, xii, 1794, 202).

Though Aberdeenshire evidently lagged behind the southern lowlands, the seeds of the more radical change that was to follow in the early 19th century can be detected in the observations recorded in the *Statistical Account*. In Premnay parish, for example, one of the proprietors had enclosed his fields and brought cartloads of lime from Aberdeen, and he had also rebuilt the farmhouses on his property (*Stat. Acct.*, xvi, 1795, 639). In the parish of Echt, a few farmers had *'levelled, straighted, and cleaned'* the old infields. They too had brought in lime, and had adopted a rotation of crops that included turnips, grasses and barley. Some of the outfields were also limed and laid out to grass (*Stat. Acct.*, xiii, 1794, 618).

Despite these examples, more often than not the ministers comment on the lack of progress. Some included lists of reasons why this was so, and suggested what might be done to *'draw men from long-confirmed habits'* and kindle *'a spirit of improvement'* amongst the tenantry (*Stat. Acct.*, xii, 1794, 496–7). At the core of the problem lay the lack of finance, but the standard nineteen-year leases offered little incentive to persuade the majority of tenants to introduce crop rotations or enclose their ground (*Stat. Acct.*, xviii, 1796, 415).

The Improved Landscape in the 19th Century

The more radical reorganisation of the countryside in the 19th century followed the development of the communications network. The inadequate road system that existed in the 18th century was cited by some contemporaries as one of the major impediments to agricultural improvement, and Grant himself considered it a *'perpetual bar ... to every kind of internal improvement'* (Anderson 1794, 21). The existing roads were maintained through statute labour, but they continued to be in *'a miserable state'* until the end of the 18th century (Anderson 1794, 21).

Statute labour was evidently inadequate to the task, and many landowners came to realise that a more professional approach to road-building was required. This had already been introduced to good effect further south and across England, involving the establishment

Fig. 9.3 **Monymusk**, *Old Toll House (NJ 6851 1494). Tollhouses often betray the origin of a road as a turnpike. The projecting semi-circular bay contains windows looking both ways along the route. SC874062*

Fig. 9.4 **Glenkindie House**, *West Gates (NJ 4182 1416). Situated at the edge of the A97 public road, this tollhouse was converted into a gate lodge for Glenkindie House at the beginning of the 20th century. SC873277*

of turnpike trusts made up of influential local landowners. The trusts undertook to finance, construct, maintain and repair roads in return for the right to levy tolls on those who used them (West 2000, 67). In 1795 a Turnpike Bill was passed, providing for the construction of toll roads in Aberdeenshire, and in 1798 the first turnpike was opened, running along the north side of the River Dee from Aberdeen to Drum. This was followed in 1800 by roads from Aberdeen to both Ellon and Inverurie. More were to come in the next few decades. By 1811, almost 300 miles of turnpike roads traversed the county, serviced by eighty-seven tollgates (Figs 9.3–4), and by 1857 this had risen to 450 miles.

With local landowners providing much of the finance for the schemes, they were also in a position to influence the proposed routes for the turnpikes. Thus, a section of turnpike that eventually ran from Aberdeen to Corgarff detoured south to serve Rubislaw Quarry, whose owner, James Skene, had subscribed heavily to its construction. In some cases, the new routes bypassed settlements and farms along the existing roads. This fate appears to have befallen Kirkton of Skene, which originally stood on the Old Skene Road at a crossroads with one of the principal routes across the Mounth, but now lies stranded to the north of the main road from Aberdeen to Alford. While some of these settlements withered and died, turnpikes also attracted new developments along their routes. On lower Donside, the industrial suburbs of Aberdeen grew along the turnpike to Inverurie.

Apart from attempting to raise interest in improving the roads, Grant had *'endeavoured to show the practicability of carrying a canal along the banks of the Don'* (Anderson 1794, 23). The scheme came to nothing at the time, but by the early 1790s the idea had been resurrected, and in 1793 plans were drawn up for a canal linking Aberdeen to the Garioch (Anderson 1794, 23). The planned route lay along the south side of the River Don to Monymusk, with a branch along the River Urie as far as Insch, but the scheme was quickly reduced to the stretch from Aberdeen Harbour to the confluence of the two rivers at Inverurie, terminating at what was to become Port Elphinstone (Lindsay 1968, 99). Work was underway by 1797, and it was opened for traffic in 1805. Its construction involved seventeen locks, five aqueducts, fifty-six bridges and twenty culverts, and the canal itself snaked across the countryside for about 19 miles (Lindsay 1968, 104). In so far as the canal had been conceived to *'promote the improvement and better cultivation of the inland parts of the country'*, it was a huge success, carrying lime, coal and bone meal to the Garioch, while at the same time providing an outlet for goods bound for Aberdeen, including granite from the quarries around Kintore. As a consequence, both Inverurie and Kintore grew in size and stature, with the population of Inverurie in particular trebling between 1800 and 1840. In 1854, the canal was superseded by the Great North of Scotland Railway, which used the drained canal bed for much of its length. The best-preserved sections of the canal now lie in **Woodland's Wood**, between Kinaldie and Pitmedden House.

As a consequence of these developments, the first four decades of the 19th century witnessed huge changes, *'not only on the farms in the actual possession of the proprietors, but on those also occupied by their tenancy'* (NSA, xii, Aberdeenshire, 586). Hundreds of acres of waste ground were reclaimed into arable, many more plantations and woodlands were established, countless miles of *'stone fences'* and hedgerows were laid out, fertilisers became more readily available, and the buildings of the tenants were replaced with farmhouses and steadings that were both *'neat and commodious'* and *'constructed of durable materials'* (NSA, xii, Aberdeenshire, 855). The sweeping transformation of the landscape is no better expressed than in the account for the parish of Logie-Buchan, written by a minister who had also prepared an entry for the *Statistical Account: 'When I look around me, I seem to live not only among a new race of men, but in a new world. Cultivation, like the gradual spreading of*

*Fig. 9.5 **Aberdeenshire Canal, Port Elphinstone** (NJ 7770 2051). This section of the canal, which extends from Inverurie Bridge to Ladeside Gardens, still retains its water. SC873288*

a garment, has changed the external face of the earth, and every locality wears a new appearance' (NSA, xii, Aberdeenshire, 816).

By the 1840s, a seven-year cycle had become the standard crop rotation, although a five- or six-year cycle had also been introduced on some of the better soils in the lowland areas of Donside. Extensive tracts of what had been barren ground were also transformed into arable, the greatest impetus dating from the 1810s and early 1820s, though some of the entries in the *New Statistical Account* infer that this had happened piecemeal since the turn of the century. Rising grain prices following the outbreak of war with France provided some of the incentive for progress (NSA, xii, Aberdeenshire, 671).

Waste ground was brought into cultivation by *'trenching, ditching and draining'* (NSA, xii, Aberdeenshire, 110), and it is estimated that in the parishes of Dyce and Belhelvie, almost a third of the arable ground had been reclaimed from moorland. In Dyce parish this amounted to some 600–700 acres, while for Belhelvie it was a staggering 5000 acres. In Skene, where 1000 acres had been brought into cultivation, two new farms had been created on the haughs of the Leuchar Burn at Hillcairnie, *'where farm had never been before'*, by *'straighting, cutting, and deepening the burn at considerable expense'* (NSA, xii, Aberdeenshire, 1096).

The land was also being enclosed with dykes, hedges and *'sunk fences'* (NSA, Aberdeenshire, xii, 246), largely depending on the materials most readily to hand. In Skene parish, where there was a *'superabundance of material for this purpose'*, the new fields were mainly enclosed by *'drystone fences'* (NSA, xii, Aberdeenshire, 1099). In places the

Fig. 9.6 **Cowbyres** *(NJ 7220 2358). The irregular field-pattern at Cowbyres in 1838 can be seen on the plan of the Barony of Balquhain prepared by Walker and Beattie. SC797593*

'*superabundance*' of stones cleared from the land led to the construction of massive consumption dykes, the best-known example built at Kingswells in the 1850s and measuring some 10m in thickness and 2m in height. In Keithhall & Kinkell parish, hawthorn was also used (*NSA*, xii, Aberdeenshire, 745), and Lord Kintore engaged the services of a hedger from Berwickshire. On some of the farms in Meldrum parish double rows of beech and hawthorn hedging were planted, which were both '*ornamental as well as useful*' (*NSA*, xii, Aberdeenshire, 480). The progress of enclosure was uneven, however, and a handful of parishes in the middle reaches of the Don apparently lagged behind the others (*NSA*, xii, Aberdeenshire, 430, 756).

The impact of such enclosures and other improvements on the landscape are quite well charted at Balquhain, where a survey of the estate in 1838 and successive editions of the OS 6-inch map provide a window on the landscape at roughly thirty-year intervals. The survey by Walker and Beattie of Aberdeen in 1838 shows the division of the estate into farms and crofts, and details their occupants and the size of each holding. The only township that remained by this date was **Middleton**, on the north-eastern slopes of Knockinglews.

Closer inspection of the plan reveals that the apparently neat arrangement of fields belies a more irregular pattern, and it is clear that consolidation and improvement had not proceeded uniformly across the whole estate. The plan was evidently prepared for a further stage of change, and while some of the proposed march boundaries of the farms conform to

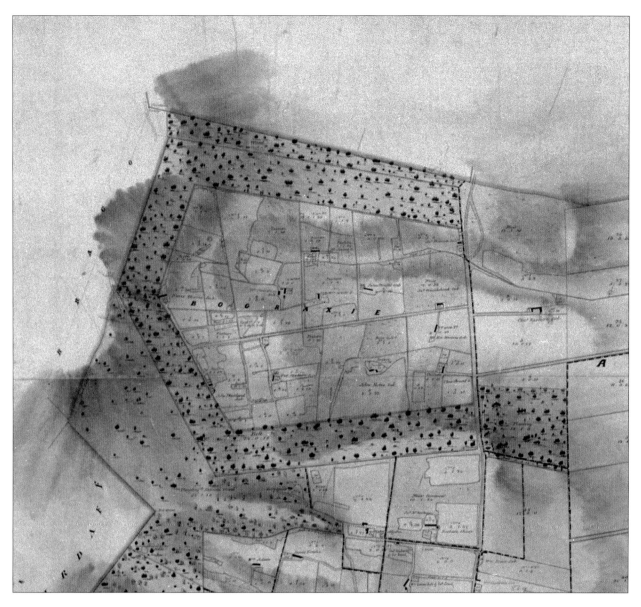

*Fig. 9.7 **Bograxie** (NJ 7117 1992). This area of crofts shown on the plan of the Barony of Balquhain prepared by Walker and Beattie in 1838 can still be detected in the modern field-pattern. SC797593*

blocks of geometric fields, others cut indiscriminately across the field-pattern.

Three particular types of field-pattern can be identified on the plan, reflecting different approaches to improvement and enclosure that are found throughout Donside. The following three examples from Balquhain will serve to illustrate them, namely at **Cowbyres**, **Bograxie** and **Aquhorthies**. **Cowbyres** (Fig. 9.6) is at the north end of the estate, and in 1838 had two small farmsteads. The adjacent fields are rectilinear on the plan, but they lack the regimented geometric pattern that can be observed at **Aquhorthies** in the centre of the estate. Such an irregular field-pattern, in which few of the corners are aligned with each other, suggests that the enclosures of **Cowbyres** developed piecemeal, rather than by any grand design.

Drainage was perhaps a problem in the area, for not only is a large pond depicted to the south-west of the southern farmstead, but the neighbouring farm to the west is called **Boghead**. By the late 1860s, the southern farmstead had emerged as the sole steading (Aberdeenshire 1869, sheet liv). The pond had also disappeared and a drain had been dug across the fields from **Boghead** and through the steading. The boundary of the farm proposed on the 1838 estate plan had been established, but the field-pattern within its bounds had been remodelled, changing once more before the end of the century to create the pattern visible today (Aberdeenshire 1901, sheet xlv.sw; liv.nw). In the mid-20th century **Cowbyres** was renamed **West Balquhain**.

At **Bograxie** (Fig. 9.7), on the west side of the estate, a rather different pattern existed. Here the plan depicts an area of crofts laid out to either side of a track dividing the area into two. Of the buildings scattered across them, at least a dozen appear to have been cottages with named occupants, but the buildings

Fig. 9.8 **Aquhorthies** *(NJ 8327 2940). The regular pattern of large rectilinear fields shown around the House of Aquhorthies on the plan of the Barony of Balquhain prepared by Walker and Beattie in 1838 has remained unchanged to this day. SC797593*

shown at six of these locations had already disappeared by 1869 (Aberdeenshire 1869, sheet liv). Seven of the other locations remained in use, but by this time the earlier buildings at four had been replaced by small steadings equipped with horse-engines or waterwheels. In addition, a fifth steading, a smithy and another cottage had been built on new sites. The basic framework of enclosures and the surrounding shelter belts in 1838 is still recognisable today, though at that time much of the ground had yet to be improved. By 1869, however, virtually all the land appears to have been taken into cultivation and divided up into small fields, forming a pattern that continued to evolve until the end of the 19th century. By then one of the steadings and a row of buildings nearby had been abandoned (Aberdeenshire 1901, sheet liv.sw).

In contrast to **Cowbyres** and **Bograxie**, the field-pattern at **Aquhorthies** (Fig. 9.8) appears to have been laid out in one overall design, and the framework of large rectilinear fields in place in 1838 has remained almost unchanged to this day. The fields are arranged around the policies of the House of Aquhorthies and extend up to the edges of a plantation that covered the west end of a long ridge. The present mansion house was built in 1797–9, originally as a Roman Catholic seminary. Like the surrounding field-pattern, the steading to the north of the house has remained unchanged since 1838.

The improvement of Balquhain also included the planting of extensive woodlands, such as Gallowshill Wood (NJ 717 186) and Cot-town Woods (NJ 728 181). Both of these appear on the plan of 1838, along with various strip plantations and shelter belts, notably around **Fetternear House** and the adjacent Home Farm. By 1869 further plantings had taken place on the hill named Knockinglews (NJ 733 218), though by this time there had also been some loss of woodland with the clearance and improvement of the eastern parts of Gallowshill Wood. Despite this reorganisation of Gallowshill Wood, in general terms there was a huge increase in new plantings throughout Donside during the early 19th century.

This trend is reflected in most of the parish entries in the *New Statistical Account,* which record large acreages going over to trees. Like the other changes in the landscape, planting accelerated in the late 1810s and early 1820s, and in Dyce continued through the 1830s, when more than 75% of the woodland there is said to have been planted (*NSA*, xii, Aberdeenshire, 130). The overall extent of woodland varied, ranging from 600 acres in Fintray to almost 3000 acres of *'thriving plantations'* in Strathdon (*NSA*, xii, Aberdeenshire, 539). Larch and Scots Pine were the most favoured trees, conifers accounting for 930,000 of the trees that had been planted along the sides of the hills in the parish of Monymusk, another 160,000 being made up of oaks and elms. Here the woodlands and plantations were under the management of an experienced forester (*NSA*, xii, Aberdeenshire, 466), but many estates did not have such a long history of woodland management, and some of their woodlands were thought to have been planted too thickly (*NSA*, xii, Aberdeenshire, 504; 539; 824). In the parish of Leochel-Cushnie, where 1500 acres had been planted, the thinnings provided timber for *'both paling and fuel'* (*NSA*, xii, Aberdeenshire, 1107).

With yet more ground given over to trees and arable, sheep farming declined still further, and by the early 1840s, flocks of sheep had more or less disappeared from large parts of Aberdeenshire. In Monymusk, they were almost completely banished on the strength of *'being injurious to the young plantations on the sides of the hills where they formerly pastured'* (*NSA*, xii, Aberdeenshire, 460), and for the same reasons the grazing of sheep on Kintore moor was almost at an end (*NSA*, Aberdeenshire, xii, 661).

The transformation of agriculture that was underway could never have achieved such momentum had it not been for the efforts of various national and local agricultural societies. These produced transactions and journals to disseminate news of the latest techniques and the results of recent trials and experiments. The earliest, The Honourable the Society of Improvers in the Knowledge of Agriculture in Scotland, was founded in Edinburgh in 1723 (Ramsay 1879, 19). Some sixty years later, in 1783, the Royal Highland and Agricultural Society of Scotland was inaugurated, and quickly became the national voice promoting agricultural advance. Amongst other activities, the society awarded *'premiums in money, medals, or otherwise'* (Ramsay 1879, 102) to farmers for essays on subjects such as enclosures, or the cultivation of grasses, and for the improvements on their land. Several farmers in Donside figure amongst the early winners, including the Rev. John Harper of Kildrummy, George Gordon of Ord, Auchindoir, and John Richardson of Mains of Kildrummy, all of whom won prizes over a three-year period between 1798 and 1800 for *'cultivating various kinds of grasses'* and the *'cultivation of turnip'* (Ramsay 1879, 110–11, 124).

Later awards reflect something of the physical alteration of the countryside, such as one for the improvement of *'upwards of 120 acres'* by one of Lord Kintore's tenants (*NSA*, xii, Aberdeenshire, 655), and another for the reclamation of land on the estate of Parkhill in Old Machar parish (*NSA*, xii, Aberdeenshire, 1077). The county society, the Aberdeenshire Agricultural Association, also played its part, and the landowners in the Garioch set up their own Farmers Club in 1808, sponsoring ploughing competitions to create *'a laudable spirit of emulation among the young farm-servants'* (*NSA*, xii, Aberdeenshire, 116).

The key to many of the reclamation schemes was drainage. At its simplest, this might be no more than a system of open ditches, but the improvements also saw the introduction of underground drainage. Prior to the introduction of fired drainage tiles, these drains were

Fig. 9.9 ***Quarry Hill*** *(NJ 485 252). These quarry workings are first mentioned in the Statistical Account and remained in use until the 1930s. SC874004*

little more than trenches loosely filled with *'granite broken to a proper size'* and covered back over with earth (*NSA*, xii, Aberdeenshire, 662). Such techniques were rapidly superseded when drainage tiles became more readily available. The works set up in 1834 at **Westfield of Auchmacoy** was apparently the earliest in the North-east, producing tiles for which the *'quality is approved of, and the demand is considerable'* (*NSA*, xii, Aberdeenshire, 814).

With the introduction of extensive underground drainage, any benefits from maintaining the old rig-and-furrow disappeared. The broad reverse-S rig-and-furrow of the old runrig were synonymous with the old Scotch plough, which was a heavy wooden implement requiring a large team of oxen or horses. According to Anderson, who was unquestionably biased in his view, this *'mode of ploughing is as bad and slovenly as the team is auckward with which it is performed'* (Anderson 1794, 77). In the 1790s, improved types of plough were only to be found on the Mains farms of the larger estates in Donside, but by the 1840s these had been adopted universally, with what must have been dramatic results in the countryside at large. Comparing the new techniques with the old, the minister of Kinellar commented that *'The ridges then raised in the middle, and with deep valleys between, are now straight as an arrow, and as level as a turnpike road'* (*NSA*, xii, Aberdeenshire, 116).

Even as the fields were being drained and enclosed, the steadings were being extensively rebuilt in stone and slate. Much of the stone for the new steadings was gathered locally, cleared from arable land or robbed from ancient monuments, but this period also saw the development of commercial quarrying, particularly for granite. By 1800, several quarries had been opened, producing setts and paving stones (Tyson 1988, 25), and by 1821 some 35,000 tons of granite were being exported to London. Closer to home, granite from Bennachie was favoured for lintels and window mouldings in steadings and country houses (*NSA*, xii,

*Fig. 9.10 **Hill of Tillymorgan** (NJ 6520 3480). The disused slate quarries on the summit and slopes of the hill cast long shadows in this oblique aerial view. SC872643*

Aberdeenshire, 562), while that from the **Correen Hills** was often used for *'pavements and shelves in old kitchens and larders throughout Strathdon'* (Simpson 1942b, 4). Quarries such as **Rubislaw**, the huge crater on the outskirts of Aberdeen (Fig. 1.5), later underpinned the expansion of the city and its distinctive granite architecture.

A freestone quarry had been opened on **Quarry Hill** in the parish of Auchindoir by the end of the 18th century (*Stat. Acct.*, xii, 1794, 493) and remained in operation throughout the 19th century. Another quarry from this parish, on the estate of Druminnor, produced *'a hard and heavy stone'* that was *'susceptible of being split into slabs of great thinness, and of almost any length or breadth'* (*NSA*, xii, Aberdeenshire, 408–9). With slate replacing thatch, there was also a huge surge in demand for roofing slate. As early as 1724, a quarry on the north side of the **Hill of Foudland** supplied the *'Countrey with slate'* (Mitchell and Clark 1906–8, i, 5), though this was most commonly used as floor slabs, hearthstones and shelves. From the beginning of the 19th century, however, more quarries were opened on the hill, and by the 1830s production

of good-quality roofing slates had reached some 900,000 a year, employing a total of sixty-five men (Blaikie 1835, 99–100). A further eight quarries on the **Hill of Tillymorgan** (Fig. 9.10), employed forty men and produced around 300,000 slates a year, while the seven quarries on the **Hill of Corskie** employed thirty-five men and produced up to 500,000 slates. By the early 1840s, however, output from the Foudland quarries had halved, partly as a result of imported slates from Easdale in Argyll, and partly because of rather outdated and inefficient working practices (*NSA*, xii, Aberdeenshire, 757). Nevertheless, the successive editions of the OS 6-inch map (Aberdeenshire 1873, sheet xxxv; 1901) show that the workings here and on the west flank of the **Hill of Tillymorgan** were extended considerably in the closing decades of the 19th century, before all commercial quarrying finally ceased in 1895 (Dean 1998, 63). The poignant epitaph for the industry appears on a gravestone in the burial-ground at Culsalmond. It commemorates the death of Alexander Stuart, who died in February 1901 aged 84, THE LAST OF THE FOUNDLAND QUARRIERS.

The expansion of the quarry workings in the late 19th century was driven by residential building programmes in Aberdeen, but extension and reconstruction can also be detected at many steadings throughout Donside between the 1870s and the turn of the century. Not only can it be seen in the depictions of the steadings on successive editions of the OS 6-inch map, but also in the walls of the buildings that remain today. As such, the scars of the abandoned workings on the **Hill of Foudland** and the **Hill of Tillymorgan**, with their spoil dumps of discarded slate spilling down the slopes, are as much a part of the improved landscape as these steadings.

By the 19th century a small-scale lime industry was also flourishing in the upper Don (see Cruickshank, Nisbet and Greig 2004). In the parish of Strathdon alone, *'8–10 quarries for limestone'* were at work in the 1830s, producing sufficient lime to supply the neighbouring parishes of Kildrummy and Towie (*NSA*, xii, Aberdeenshire, 553). Indeed, according to the *New Statistical Account*, each farm around Corgarff had its own limekiln (xii, Aberdeenshire, 552), while the quarries in Glenbuchat were *'worked to great advantage by the tenants, both for their own use and for sale'* (*NSA*, xii, Aberdeenshire, 436). No less than 110 limekilns have been recorded in Strathdon and Glenbuchat (Cruickshank, Nisbet and Greig 2004), mainly appearing on the 1st edition of the OS six-inch map, but few of them remained in use by the end of the century and many have now been removed (pp. 238–9). Elsewhere, in the Correen Hills and around Newmachar and Oldmeldrum, the exposures of limestone were not sufficiently pure to be used for agricultural purposes, despite attempts to open a limeworks in the parish of Udny (*NSA*, xii, Aberdeenshire, 131).

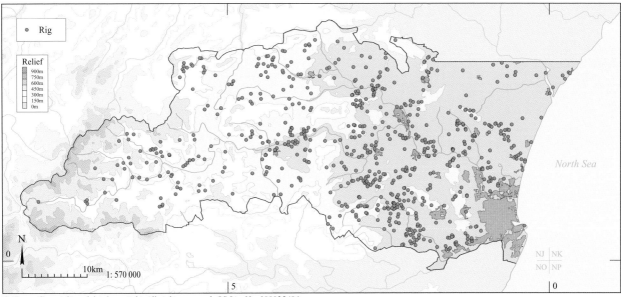

Fig. 9.11 This map shows the distribution of visible rig-and-furrow cultivation in Donside. Most of the examples in the lowlands survive within the bounds of old plantations in the improved landscape. GV000224

The Archaeology of Pre-improvement Agriculture

By their very nature, the remains of pre-improvement agriculture have been largely obliterated. Infields and outfields alike have been drained and ploughed, and in most cases they are now enclosed within the fences, hedges and dykes of the present landscape. With a few notable exceptions (see Glen Ernan, pp. 229–31), glimpses of the pre-improvement landscape are now restricted to the margins of the improved fields, either where the rigs and tathing folds have reverted to pasture, or where they have been subsumed into the shelter belts and woodlands of designed landscapes and policies. On the Monymusk estate, for example, many of the plots of rig that have been recorded are in woodlands created during the 18th century by Sir Archibald Grant, including a system extending to about 5.5ha across the summit of Gallow Hill (**Gallowhill Wood**) on the north side of the River Don opposite **Monymusk House**. Indeed, rig is one of the most common types of visible archaeological remains in Donside, occurring in small patches from the top of the Don at **Allt nan Aighean** to **Balnagask Golf Course** on the south side of Aberdeen (Fig. 9.11). Elsewhere, the furrows separating ploughed-out rigs are occasionally revealed as cropmarks on aerial photographs.

The patches of rig that have been recorded exhibit considerable variety in their forms, and those that are of any great extent invariably reveal evidence of complexity and change. Some of the rig is high-backed, measuring at least 0.5m in height, and may be as much

as 14m in width, displaying a clear reverse-S shape on plan. In the lowlands the best-preserved patches lie in old plantations that have now reverted to islands of pasture in the midst of ploughed farmland. To name but a few, good examples can be seen on **Gallows Hill** above Little Mains of Wardhouse (Fig. 9.12), at **Corsindae** (Fig. 9.14), on the flanks of **Dunnideer**, and filling the interior of the fort on **Barra Hill** (Fig. 9.1). In some of these, the furlongs splay towards one end, leaving wide, flat gaps or baulks between the rigs. At **Wardhouse Home Farm** (Fig. 9.13) the reverse-S rigs are about 6m wide at one end of the furlong, but fan out to as much as 14m at the other, though the flat baulks between the ridges account for some of this breadth.

The evidence of change in these systems shows that they were dynamic, though this is no more than should be expected in view of the documentary evidence for the evolution of the settlement pattern and the depictions of the lands of the *touns* that appear on estate maps. In some cases, such as on **Gallows Hill**, the

*Fig. 9.12 **Gallows Hill** (NJ 590 299). The combination of low winter sunlight and a light covering of snow picks out details of this rig-system preserved in an old plantation enclosure above the modern fields. © AAS*

*Fig. 9.13 **Wardhouse, Home Farm** (NJ 570 303). This oblique aerial view shows a furlong of reverse-S rigs radiating from the centre of the pasture field to the edge of a steep-sided stream gully. The stony banks and small cairns visible beyond the rigs belong to earlier phases of use, one of them probably associated with the two hut-circles visible in the centre of the picture. SC961125*

baulk between high-backed rigs is itself ridged, while in others overlaps and discontinuities in the furlongs indicate multiple phases of cultivation. **Corsindae** provides a good example of the latter (Fig. 9.14), but here there have also been earthen banks enclosing some of the furlongs. These presumably represent the sort of enclosures depicted on the Castle Fraser estate maps as folded outfields (p. 217), the short fragments of banks at the ends of several of the furlongs revealing quite how temporary the arrangement of such folds

might be. Elsewhere in the lowlands the last episode of enclosures on the outfields has generally been reduced to little more than short fragments of banks crossing plantations, but in the upland areas more extensive systems of embanked enclosures at least survived the improvements, even though most have since fallen victim to afforestation. This is the fate that has befallen the systems on **Craigs of Longley** and **Clayshot Hill** in the valley of the Kirkney Water, though it is still possible to piece together their layout from estate maps and aerial photographs. The system on **Craigs of Longley** is presented on Figure 8.76. Formerly named Garbet, four crofts are documented here in 1686 (NAS SC 1/60/31), but the Gordon estate map of 1776 (NAS RHP 2257) shows only the fields, which by then were managed as outfield from **Boganclogh**. The layout of rig

*Fig. 9.14 **Corsindae** (NJ 685 081). This extensive area of rig-and-furrow cultivation reveals evidence of the dynamic nature of such systems, in which the intersections of the furlongs indicate several successive phases of cultivation. The banks represent several periods of construction and probably enclosed tathe folds, some of which have been ploughed out in subsequent phases of cultivation. GV000212*

and enclosures is evidently multi-phase, and compares with the tathed field-systems recorded in Menstrie Glen in the Ochils (RCAHMS 2001, 23 and 43ff), where repeated episodes of enclosure and rig cultivation have left this same characteristic signature. Compared to the broad reverse-S rigs in the unenclosed furlongs at places like **Wardhouse Home Farm**, the rigs in these systems are low and narrow, usually measuring between 3m and 6m in breadth, and often pinching in at the ends.

A Pre-improvement Landscape in Glen Ernan

There are few places in Donside where the documentary and archaeological evidence for pre-improvement settlement and agriculture come together. In the upper part of Glen Ernan, however, there is a rare survival of both settlement and agricultural remains. Glen Ernan, a side glen opening northwards off the main strath a little way above Strathdon, has already figured extensively in the discussion of settlement, shielings and hunting forests (pp. 149; 196–9; 210–11). Documentary evidence indicates that the glen has been used for agriculture and settlement since before the 12th century (p. 183). Palaeoenvironmental work commissioned for

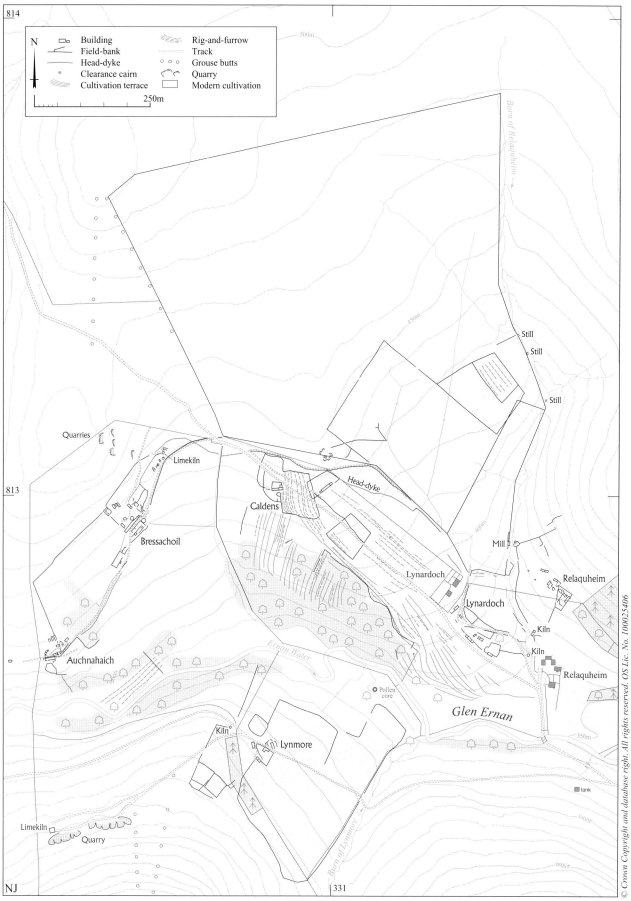

Fig. 9.15 This map shows the disposition of farms and cultivation remains surveyed in Glen Ernan. GV000200

the survey (p. 41) suggests that the glen at Relaquheim, where most of the archaeological remains are situated, has been virtually treeless for the last two thousand years, the present birch woodland being a relatively recent invasion which now cloaks some of the pre-improvement field-system. Over that period the area has been continuously exploited for its grazing and arable potential.

The area within which the field-system lies is divided from the moorland by a head-dyke comprising an externally revetted earthen dyke with a shallow external ditch. This once formed a continuous feature extending from **Lynardoch** round to **Bressachoil** and **Auchnahaich**, where it drops down the steep slope to the Ernan Water. Like other head-dykes around highland townships, it is evidently designed to keep beasts from straying onto the cultivated land. Here, however, there is also a possibility that it was erected when the surrounding area was granted in free forest in the 16th century, in effect defining the *toun* lands within the forest with a deer-dyke. The lands of **Lynmore** are also delimited by a dyke, though in this case it is simply an earthen bank without any evidence of a revetment.

Approached along the track from the east, the most striking features of the field-system are the massive terraces that sweep across the slope below the farmstead at **Lynardoch** (Fig. 9.15), and the lesser terraces dropping obliquely down through the birch woodland to the west. The latter are reverse-S in plan, and are essentially asymmetric rigs, the result of a sustained period of ploughing diagonally across the slope. The massive terraces also owe their inception to reverse-S ploughing, the individual rigs measuring from 8m to 12m in breadth. Aerial photographs reveal that they are disposed in at least three furlongs of reverse-S rigs set end to end between the foot of the slope at **Relaquheim** and the enclosures at **Caldens**. On the ground, however, the pattern of furlongs is more difficult to detect, smoothed by episodes of narrower ridging and later pasture improvements. Nevertheless, the creation of terraces on this scale is the work of many seasons of ploughing, indicating that this component of the field-system is of some antiquity. Whether as early as the cultivation recorded in the pollen diagram at about 1300 remains to be demonstrated. At the neighbouring farms of **Bressachoil**, **Auchnahaich** and **Lynmore**, modern ploughing has virtually obliterated the attendant rig-systems, but it is unlikely that they were as well developed as that below **Lynardoch**.

The individual furlongs of reverse-S rig are apparently unenclosed, but there are also some probable outfield folds at the top of the field-system at **Caldens**, to the west of **Lynardoch**. Some of these small fields are imposed on a furlong of broad rig, which is still visible despite having been ploughed in recent times, and one contains its own furlong of rig defined by shallow sinuous grooves. A series of small intakes

Fig. 9.16 **Lynardoch** *(NJ 3135 1245). This oblique aerial view shows the extent of the rig-system extending along this south-facing slope above the Ernan Water. Protracted cultivation over many seasons has transformed some of the rigs into substantial terraces. SC961122*

bounded by earthen dykes to the west of **Lynmore** are also probably outfield folds. The only other enclosures in the vicinity of **Lynardoch** lie outside the head-dyke to the north and represent several phases of use, elements of which are comparable to the outfield folds around Caldens. These enclosures also include what may have been a pasture park defined by long straight banks forming a large rectilinear enclosure. Lying beyond the head-dyke, these intakes possibly indicate the location of the new land at Lynardoch referred to in 1733 (NAS GD 124/17/689).

The Remains of the 19th-Century Landscape

Glen Ernan has been presented as a case-study of the pre-improvement agricultural remains, but it is, of course, also an example of a working 19th- and 20th-century landscape. The farmstead at **Bressachoil**, for example, not only displays the transition from *toun* to a small improved steading, but also its replacement with a more substantial steading and a detached farmhouse (Fig. 8.72). This later arrangement was only abandoned in the 1960s. Upland locations such as this lie on the

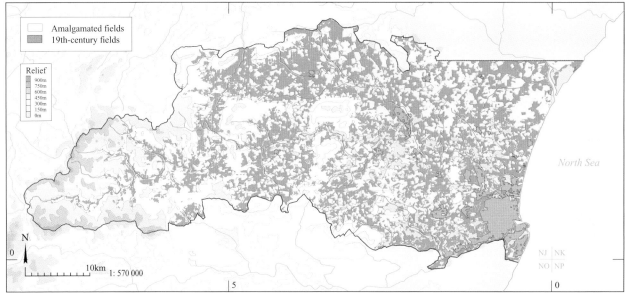

Fig. 9.17 This map shows the areas where the field-pattern in Donside has changed since the 1870s. Some of the changes came about through the continued expansion of improved ground before 1900, but others are the result of more recent changes in agricultural practice and the amalgamation of fields into larger arable units. GV000105

margins of the agricultural landscape and there has been little investment here in the construction of stone fields-walls, yet the surrounding ground has all been improved, as it has around **Lynmore** and **Relaquheim**. The limekilns near **Bressachoil** and **Lynmore** form part of this improved landscape, and the area continues to provide pasture for a herd of cattle.

This more recent farming landscape has not formed part of the present survey, but an Historic Land-use Assessment has also been carried out in Donside. This has combined information from successive editions of the OS 6-inch survey and vertical aerial photographs to map the historical character of the countryside as it is today. Blocks of rectilinear enclosures can be recognised in the present field-pattern, for example, betraying not only something of the history of enclosure in the area, but also the evolution of the landscape thereafter. The extent of the plantations and parks of designed landscapes can equally be recognised, identifying the areas in the lowlands where most traces of the pre-improvement landscape are to be found (Figs 9.11; 9.19).

The most common type of field in Donside is rectilinear in shape, variously bounded by drystone dykes, stone-faced banks, hedges, fences and earthen banks with ditches. This type of field occurs widely, though many have been amalgamated into more open arable landscapes (Fig. 9.17), particularly in the eastern half of the area. Nevertheless, the rectilinear fields are often laid out in co-axial blocks with parallel boundaries, and they evidently manifest the planned enclosures depicted on some later estate maps. In some cases these blocks comprise as few as four fields, but in others they

are formed into much larger systems. Of the latter, the area around Myreton, north of Insch in the Garioch, is particularly striking. The fields are bounded with hedges, low walls and belts of trees, and the roads cutting through them are closely lined with beech trees. The latter appear as little more than saplings above closely trimmed hedges and neatly built walls on James Ritchie's photographs of the **Picardy Stone**, a Pictish symbol stone, probably taken in the early 20th century. They were presumably only planted at the turn of the 19th century, but now form a dense arched canopy above the road.

Equally striking in the field-pattern are the crofts and smallholdings (Fig. 9.18), which include allotments laid out during the improvements around planned villages such as **Rhynie**. Most of the croftlands tend to be on the margins of the better land, but the pockets of small fields around the closely spaced cottages and steadings contrast with the larger fields around the principal farms. Thus, most of the quarrymen's crofts around the Hill of Foudland are still recognisable in the field-pattern, though with the closure of the quarries many of the croft houses now lie abandoned and only one group remains occupied. In other cases, however, the consolidation of the holdings has removed all trace of a group of crofts. At **Rowanbush**, north-west of Midmar, for example, a new farm and a block of fields replaced a group of crofts before the end of the 19th century.

The parks and policies of country houses are also an important component of this landscape (Fig. 9.19). The origins of some of these go back into the 17th and 18th centuries, the earlier examples appearing on Roy's map (1747–55). By far the majority of those appearing on Roy's map are depicted with only one or two rectilinear enclosures lined with trees, but a few were evidently quite extensive, combining formal avenues with a chequerboard of enclosed parks and plantations.

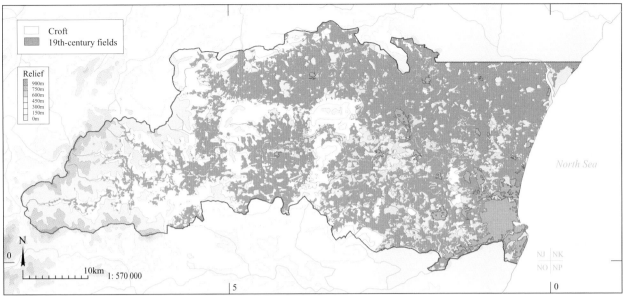

Fig. 9.18 The crofts that formed such a significant component of the 19th-century settlement pattern can often still be detected in the field-pattern. GV000104

Monymusk is one of the prime examples of the latter, but others include **Westhall** and **Wardhouse**, the latter then named Gordonhall. In the second half of the 18th century such regimented plans were supplanted by more free-flowing designs to enhance the natural beauty of the landscape. Thereafter, the diversification of ideas was to see some return to more formal layouts, as is shown by the contrasting depictions of policies appearing on the 1st edition of the OS 6-inch map. These maps reveal a wide range of forms, which are still embedded in the present landscape. On the one hand there are the softened, naturalistic lines of the emparking around **Castle Forbes**, or the curvilinear parks and plantations of **Wardhouse**, on the other the strictly geometric avenues, parks and strip plantations of **Freefield**.

By this time the majority of the older policies had been extensively redesigned, and it is rarely possible to transpose a formal layout shown on Roy's map to the depiction on the 1st edition of the OS 6-inch map. The broad layout of the policies at **Kemnay House** is a rare exception, but more often than not the earlier design is barely recognisable. This said, some of these redesigned policies preserve fragments of earlier parks and plantations, together with rig-and-furrow and tathing folds from the pre-improvement farming landscape. At **Wardhouse** (Fig. 9.20), for example, elements of earlier designs can be seen in the rough pasture to the north of the Palladian mansion. This area lay beneath a plantation shown on the 1st edition OS map, forming

Fig. 9.19 This map shows the extent of the designed landscapes and parklands identified in the Historic Land-use Assessment of Donside. Many of the traces of earlier land-use in the lowlands are preserved in the parklands and policies of country houses. GV000106

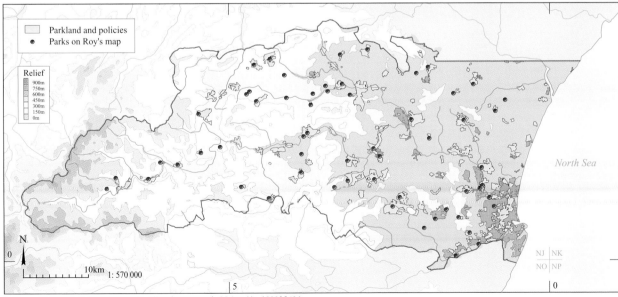

*Fig. 9.20 **Wardhouse** (NJ 5666 3077). This oblique aerial view shows the shell of this Palladian mansion standing in the remains of its policies. SC1004889*

an angular block of woodland on the slopes above the house. At this time the house itself stood within a roughly square wooded enclosure, which was laid out with five improved fields in a row along the foot of the hill. This rectilinear arrangement contrasts with the more decorative curvilinear lines of the plantations in front of the house to the south and south-east, and may be an echo of the rectilinear, tree-lined parks shown on Roy's map (1747–55) to either side of an avenue leading up to the house. Unfortunately, the existing house was built in 1757, some years after the preparation of the map, and it is difficult to be certain where it stands in relation to these earlier policies.

*Fig. 9.21 **Glenkindie House** (NJ 4226 1445). This oblique aerial view shows the house standing in its policies on the northern bank of the River Don. SC873292*

Time has taken its toll on **Wardhouse**. The mansion is now a roofless shell, the parks have been taken back into cultivation, and many of the plantations have been felled, but it is the removal of the trees that has revealed traces of at least two earlier designs: one comprises banks and ditches enclosing two strips extending up the slope above the house, the other a curvilinear boundary comparable to those enclosing the parks to the south. The banks defining the two strips have internal ditches, suggesting that they were not themselves planted enclosures, but formed open avenues through the woodland. It is by no means certain that these avenues are contemporary with each other, but both display

similar features, and the western is aligned squarely on the existing house. Each has a semi-circular terminal at its upper end, and a geometrically shaped expansion midway along its length.

The parks and plantations of these designed landscapes are essentially monuments in their own right, projecting the wealth and aspirations of the owners of the houses they enclose. Some of those in the lowlands are also remarkably extensive. At **Castle Fraser** the design takes in an area at least 1.5km across, and the belts of woodland enclosing the parks in the immediate vicinity of the house extend out westwards to embrace the improved fields of West Mains. A tree-lined avenue, possibly one of those shown on Roy's map, also leads down to the West Mains. Most of the major country houses in the lowlands lie within equally extensive

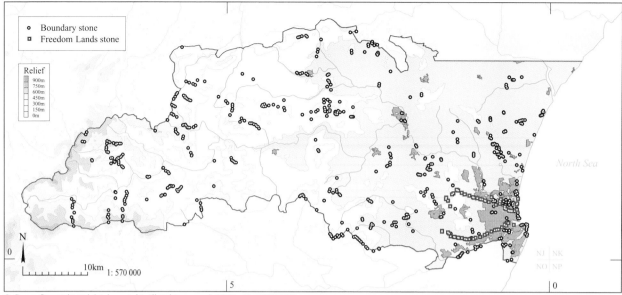

Fig. 9.22 This map shows the distribution of boundary stones recorded in Donside, including those delineating the Freedom Lands and Marches of Aberdeen (see Fig. 1.4). GV000109

Fig. 9.23 **Knock Saul** *(NJ 5795 2308). This boundary stone stands adjacent to a Bronze Age burial-cairn on the summit of Knock Saul, straddling the boundary between the parishes of Leslie and Tullynessle and Forbes. SC957507*

designs, including **Dunecht House**, **Fetternear House** and **Keith Hall**, though there are numerous other houses where the policies are of more modest proportions. These include many of the houses in the uplands, such as **Glenkindie** (Fig. 9.21), **Edinglassie** and **Inverernan**, but here the grandeur of the highland scenery was also enhanced by major plantings of conifers on the overlooking hills.

By the late 19th century the interests of these highland estates were mainly focused on hunting and fishing, and had shifted away from agriculture. Indirectly this has led to the preservation of numerous earlier archaeological monuments, but sporting estates also have their own characteristic architecture and archaeology. The country houses and shooting lodges alone are worthy of a survey in their own right, though they fall outside the scope of the present work. Likewise the numerous other features, from the kennels and keepers' cottages, to game larders and shooting butts. The moors themselves form a patchwork of burnt and regenerating strips of heather, and on some estates the rows of butts take on an almost monumental character. In Glen Ernan, for example, the present butts are well-built structures, often with an internal drystone lining encased within a mound of turf and sods. These are routinely maintained and have been in use for many years, but in some places the decayed remains of earlier butts can also be detected. These may be little more than a low mound or a small patch of disturbed ground, but their position and spacing across a hillside betray their purpose. Some of the narrow hollowed trackways that ascend these hills, often interwoven beneath modern access tracks, are a relict of a period when access to the moors was more often by foot or on horseback, and a day's shooting was rather more strenuous than it is today.

While these features have not been surveyed, the boundary stones that are found on the marches of

Fig. 9.24 **Hill of Blackford** *(NJ 7067 3464). Situated in the saddle between the Hill of Blackford and the Hill of Kinbroon, this stone is one of several marking the boundary between the estates of Blackford and Warthill. The groove cut in the flat top indicates the line of the march at this point. SC957503*

Fig. 9.25 **Cairntradlin** *(NJ 8116 1389). This three-sided boundary marker is situated at the intersection of three estates. SC957509*

Fig. 9.26 **Hill of Rhinstock** *(NJ 3262 1734). This boundary stone stands near a commemorative cairn on the southern shoulder of the hill. Unlike the other boundary stones shown here, it is a roughly hewn cylindrical pillar and its top has been cut to form two sloping facets, one bearing the word MARCH, the other STONE. SC957510*

many of the estates have been recorded. Topographical features define most of the marches, but these have been supplemented with built marker cairns, low piles of stones and hewn pillars. The use of stones to mark boundaries goes back to the medieval period (p. 142), but comparison of successive editions of the OS 6-inch map shows that this form of marker became increasingly fashionable between 1870 and 1900, often in numbered or lettered sequences, with initials to identify the adjoining estates. In Donside no less than 680 marker stones have been identified, mainly surviving in the uplands (Fig. 9.22), but also scattered across the lowlands. Some of them are no more than rough granite pillars, such as those at **Greenmoss** now incorporated into a stone dyke on the boundary between the parishes of Kinellar and Kintore, but many are dressed, including some in polished granite. Where sequences of letters and numbers have been recorded, they often imply a series of missing stones. Thus the sequence from M to T on the moorland march between Glenkindie and Kildrummy perhaps indicates that a sequence from A to L has been removed from the low-lying ground.

Most of these stones were probably supplied from local quarries, which are found throughout the improved landscape (Fig. 3.3). Many of the pits are shown on the 1st edition of the OS 6-inch map, though not all of

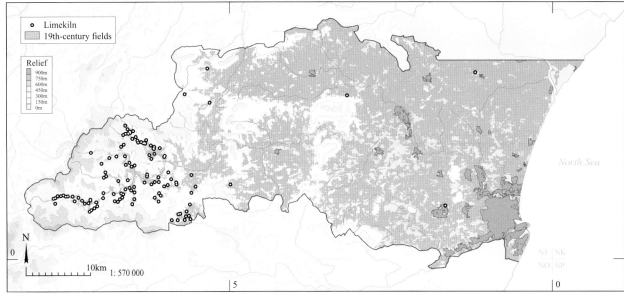

Fig. 9.27 The distribution of limekilns in Donside is restricted to the principal outcrops of limestone, the most important of which occur between Glenbuchat and Corgarff. GV000220

them were in use. Some are annotated as disused, and others are merely outlined with a hachured symbol. Some of these workings were small-scale, and a visit today reveals no more than a shallow pit, more often than not filled with field-cleared stones or covered back over. Presumably these were sunk to provide the stone, sand and gravel for specific building projects, in contrast to some of the more extensive workings. The latter were large enterprises supplying markets both at home and abroad. Granite was especially important in the growth of Aberdeen, earning it the title of The Granite City. The expansion of the industry can be traced on successive editions of the OS 6-inch map, and has led to the creation of some gaping scars in the landscape, such as the **Rubislaw Quarry**, now closed, on the western outskirts of Aberdeen. The remains of the slate quarries on **Hill of Foudland** and the **Hill of Tillymorgan** (Fig. 9.10) are equally impressive monuments to the commercial enterprises that developed side by side with the transformation of agriculture. Exploiting outcrops on the north side of the Garioch, the workings and spoil dumps sprawl across the hillsides to either side of the A96 public road. Many of the quarrymen occupied crofts nearby, but several shelters and bothies can also be found built into the spoil dumps amongst the workings. Constructed with corbelled walls, they include such features as aumbries, and one has a narrow entrance passage leading into its interior.

The workings of the lime industry, which were so important in the improvement of the new fields, are less prominent. Nonetheless, a rash of small quarries can be seen on the limestone outcrops in the upper reaches of the Don, often with a the remains of a kiln in close

attendance. Between the two parishes of Strathdon and Glenbuchat there are records for no less than 110 limekilns (see Cruickshank, Nisbet and Greig 2004). Many have been demolished, but some remarkable examples survive almost intact. Typically they are built on a slope to allow easy access to the top, and form a drum of masonry between 3m and 4m high, with a distinctive lintelled draw-hole at the bottom. The pot of the kiln was charged from the top with alternate layers of limestone and fuel, and the burnt lime was raked out at the bottom. The kiln at **Bressachoil**, in Glen Ernan, is

*Fig. 9.28 **Water of Buchat** (NJ 3673 1755). This limekiln is one of the best-preserved in upper Donside. GV004084*

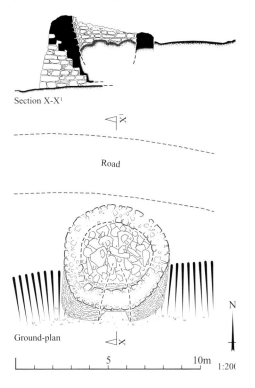

Section X-X¹

Road

Ground-plan

N

5   10m
1:200

of this type, but a better-preserved example can be seen at **Hillockhead**, in Strathdon, and stands 3.2m in height, the mouth of its draw-hole some 2m high and its outer face buttressed with a thick boulder revetment. Other fine examples are situated overlooking the floodplain of the **Water of Buchat** (Figs 9.28–9). The one at **Badenyon** (Fig. 9.30) is almost 4m high and its draw-hole is also flanked by buttresses. A terraced trackway that served the loading platform zig-zags up the slope to the top of the escarpment into which the kiln is built. This particular kiln is first depicted on the 2nd edition of the OS 6-inch map (Aberdeenshire 1903, sheet l), by which time it was out of use.

With one exception, the kilns of upper Donside are apparently built to this drum-shaped design. The exception lies in Glen Ernan on **Sron Aonghais** above Lynmore (Fig. 9.15), and is square on plan, standing at the west end of an extensive quarry some 150m in length. This is presumably the limestone quarry documented at Lynmore in the 18th century, first appearing in 1737 in Alexander Steuart's sasine of Edinglassie (see Harrison 2001a, 103–4). It appears to have gone out of use at the beginning of the 19th century, and by the 1820s lime for building work was being brought in from Corgarff and elsewhere. In an arbitration

*Fig. 9.30 **Badenyon** (NJ 3423 1894). This limekiln, which is built into the escarpment overlooking the flood-plain of the Water of Buchat, is reinforced with buttresses to either side of the draw-hole. An unusual aperture can be seen immediately above the draw-hole. SC958751*

*Fig. 9.29 **Water of Buchat** (NJ 3673 1755). Set into the steep south-facing edge of the river-terrace, this circular kiln has a well-preserved draw-hole. It probably dates from the early 19th century. SC957506*

of 1796, the owners of Edinglassie and Skellater were entitled to *'dig for limestone, erect huts for holding lime, built peat stacks in convenient locations for burning the said lime at the said limekiln'* (Harrison 2001a, 103).

Other important industries for the agricultural improvements are even less prominent in the landscape. These include the works manufacturing drainage tiles. The tileworks at **Westfield**, which is the earliest in the district, continued in operation until at least the early 1870s, and its depiction on the 1st edition of the OS 6-inch map includes a clay-pit, two kilns, and drying sheds (Aberdeenshire 1871, sheet xxxix; 1870, sheet xlviii). By this time several other brick- and tileworks were in production, including one at **Tipperty**, a short distance to the south-west of Westfield, and the **Seaton** works in Old Aberdeen. Unlike Westfield, which was out of use by the turn of the century, the **Tipperty** and **Seaton** works continued to operate until quite recently, closing in 1980 and 1967 respectively (Douglas and Oglethorpe 1993, 52). At **Tipperty** the three buildings shown on the 1st edition of the OS 6-inch map had been replaced by the end of the 19th century by an H-shaped range (Aberdeenshire 1870, sheet xlvii; 1901, sheet xlvii. ne), and in 1977, three years before the works closed, it comprised a range of four round downdraught kilns with three circular chimneys. The kilns were enclosed within a two-storey building, and the tiles were dried both on its upper floor and in single-storey louvred sheds. Linking the works to the clay-pit, there was a narrow-gauge railway. The site is now in use as an industrial estate and most of the works has been levelled, but at least one large brick building and a tall chimney still survive. At **Seaton** excavation has shown that extensive remains of the works have survived demolition, now lying buried beneath between 1.5m and 2m of sandy soil (*DES 2002*, 7; *2003*, 12).

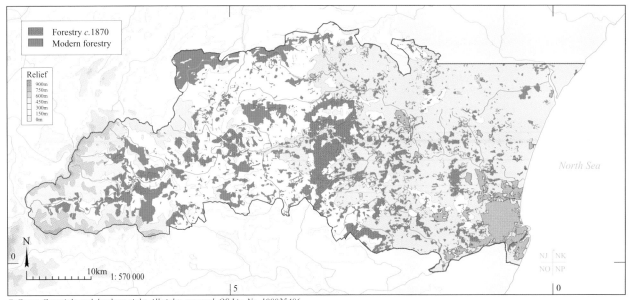

Fig. 9.31 This map shows the expansion of forestry in Donside since 1870. Many of the 19th-century plantations have also been restocked. GV000103

The 20th-Century Landscape

If the 19th century was characterised by the creation of the improved landscape, the signature of the 20th century is probably written in its attrition. The general expansion of improved ground had reached its peak at the beginning of the 20th century, and had increased from about 555,000 in the 1860s to 631,015 acres in 1901 (Carter 1979, 53). By this time the framework of the present landscape was essentially in place, and the pattern of plantations and enclosed fields was firmly established.

Despite the improved efficiency of agriculture, however, the viability of many farms has been tested by the more stringent agricultural economy of the 20th century, particularly along the highland edge. The drive for self-sufficiency in the First World War may have seen long-established pastures ploughed up, but the depression that followed in its wake brought hard times to landowners and tenants alike, eventually forcing the sale of a number of large estates. One of the main beneficiaries was the National Trust, with the acquisition of properties like **Leith Hall**, **Craigievar** and **Castle Fraser**, but many estates were broken up at this time and the farms sold off. This was the fate of Balquhain, which was auctioned by Messrs H E Foster and Cranfield in 1932. The accompanying sales brochure divides the estate into a series of lots, and provides the particulars of each farm and croft, together with details of the acreage, the annual rent, the tenant's name, and the layout and function of the buildings.

The newly formed Forestry Commission was also to benefit. Set up in 1919 to help restock the timber felled during the First World War, the Forestry Commission acquired a rash of marginal agricultural land. In theory, improved farmland was not to be planted with trees, a principle that has generally been adhered to, but the exceptions were invariably highland-edge farms. One of the earliest blocks of farmland to be planted, which was also one of the largest, lies in the valley of the Kirkney Water, which was acquired by the Forestry Commission on the sale of the duke of Gordon's estates and is now called Clashindarroch Forest. Amongst other farms, the plantings included all the improved fields at **Old Forest**, and the ruins of the field-walls and the steading may still be traced amongst the trees.

The costs of restocking the older plantations often proved beyond the means of owners, and led to the piecemeal sales of hill ground for new plantings. These included 6000 acres of the Monymusk estate, sold to the Forestry Commission in 1946, which took in all the hill ground to the north of Pitfichie and the slopes of Millstone Hill. Perhaps the most dramatic impact of such planting can be seen at **Auchernach**, at the head of the Nochty Water, where not only the improved farmland went under trees, but also the site of the lodge, the policies and the walled garden, the latter modelled on an Indian fort. Various incentive schemes to promote private forestry in the second half of the 20th century have seen even more afforestation, with vast tracts of moorland turned over to commercial plantations (Fig. 9.31). But, with their hill grazings sold and under trees, yet more farms are no longer viable for traditional agricultural enterprises and their steadings now lie derelict. The final codicil to this general process of agricultural retreat has come in the last decade of the 20th century with a notable shift in planting policy towards better ground. This has led to entire lowland farms being turned over to woodland, such as those at **Auchnacant** and **Fornety** to the south of Ellon.

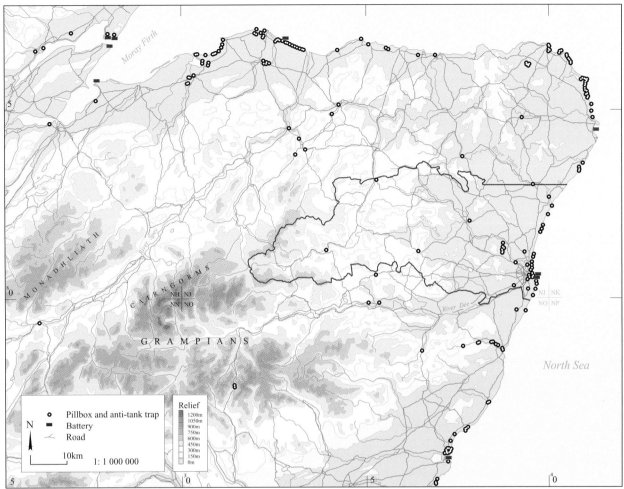

Fig. 9.32 Most of the visible remains of defence installations dating from the Second World War are distributed around the coast, comprising pillboxes, anti-tank traps and coastal batteries. GV000107

While there has been a dramatic shift in the balance between forestry and agriculture, agricultural production has itself been revolutionised over the 20th century. The demands for efficiency in particular have led to the progressive mechanisation and industrialisation of farming, which in turn are manifested in a wide range of changes in the countryside. In some cases the maintenance of the hedges and walls of the old fields has simply lapsed, but in others the boundaries have been removed to create new and more open field-patterns (Fig. 9.17). The steadings have fared no better, and their byres, stables and cartsheds are now redundant, supplanted by the large open sheds that are required for modern farming. Just as the earlier *touns* were overtaken by the improvements of the 18th and 19th centuries, so the farms that replaced them are being overtaken by another stage of agricultural development.

Most of these changes through the 20th century have tended to remove earlier features of the landscape rather than create their own archaeological monuments. The one notable exception relates to a brief period after the fall of France in 1940, when Britain was

under serious threat of invasion. Major batteries already defended the seaward approaches to Aberdeen harbour, but this stretch of coastline from the Dee to the Ythan was particularly vulnerable to sea-borne assault, and the beaches were invested with pillboxes and lines of anti-tank blocks (Fig. 9.32). Inland, pillboxes were constructed to defend nodal points in the communication network, or airfields, such as Dyce, now Aberdeen International Airport. Many are still to be found in key roadside positions controlling river and railway crossings, or in the dunes along the coast, sometimes canted at extraordinary angles as a result of erosion (Figs 9.33–6). These pillboxes have proved the most enduring monuments of this conflict, yet there is evidence of many other installations on contemporary vertical and oblique aerial photography taken by the RAF between 1941 and 1943. These reveal anti-glider obstructions on the flat land at the mouth of the Don, a Z-battery on the sea-front near Pittodrie, and further anti-glider defences in the shape of trenches along the promenade. Perhaps, most striking is the **Torry Battery** (Fig. 9.37), originally built in 1860, which commands the approaches to the harbour and the beach northwards to the mouth of the Ythan. Here the aerial photographs show a deep belt of barbed wire enclosing the concrete

Fig. 9.33 **Tillybrig Cottage** (NJ 8744 1460). This brick-built pillbox guards the bridge over the railway at Tillybrig Cottage, to the north of Aberdeen Airport, Dyce. SC857890

Fig. 9.34 **Balgownie Links** (NJ 9570 1093). Coastal erosion has undermined the large concrete plinth beneath this hexagonal pillbox and the concrete anti-tank blocks that accompanied it. SC674806

Fig. 9.35 **Drums Links** (NJ 9980 2225). Coastal erosion has exposed the concrete plinth and piles of this pillbox. SC857886

Balmedie Links, Type 24 variant
NJ 9807 1836

Garpelhead, Type 22
NK 0006 2684

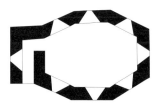

Tilliefourie, Type 24 variant
NJ 6417 1246

Balmedie Links,
Machine-gun emplacement
NJ 9769 1764

Slack, Type 24 variant
NJ 5255 0623

Cults, Arnlee Lodge
NJ 9041 0339

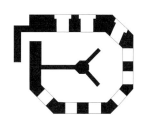

Balmedie Links, Type 24 variant
NJ 9766 1756

Aberdeen, King's Links, Type 27
NJ 9529 0873

5   10m
1:200

Fig. 9.36 Plans of a selection of pillboxes found in Donside. On account of their robust construction, these have proved the most durable component of the Second World War defences. They were constructed in accordance with military specifications, most of those in Donside corresponding to Types 22, 24 and 27. GV000119

gun emplacements and an encampment of Nissen huts occupied by the garrison. Substantial portions of the 19th-century battery survive intact, but there is little to show that this was such a key position in the chain of coastal defences in 1940. The gun emplacements on the seaward side have been demolished, and, save for a few concrete plinths on the south, all the Nissen huts have been removed. The visitor today is more likely to have come for a breath of sea air and the panoramic views than for any sense of history.

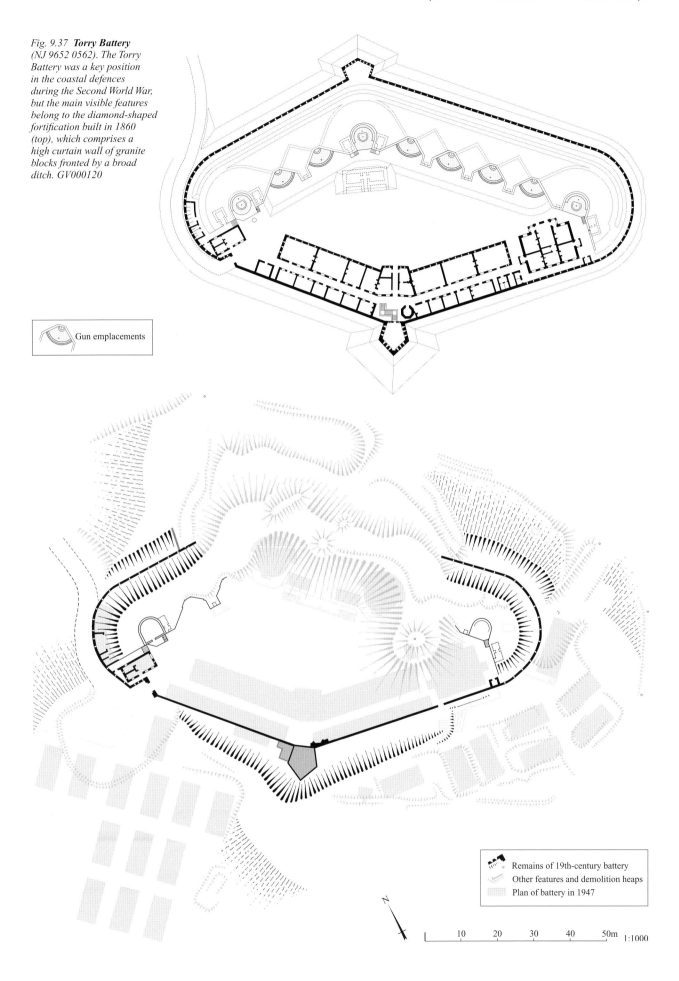

Fig. 9.37 **Torry Battery** (NJ 9652 0562). The Torry Battery was a key position in the coastal defences during the Second World War, but the main visible features belong to the diamond-shaped fortification built in 1860 (top), which comprises a high curtain wall of granite blocks fronted by a broad ditch. GV000120

Gun emplacements

Remains of 19th-century battery
Other features and demolition heaps
Plan of battery in 1947

N

10   20   30   40   50m
1:1000

*Fig. 9.38 This view looking across the site of the **Torry Battery** to Girdle Ness lighthouse shows how this key strategic position defending the approaches to Aberdeen harbour is now an important recreational asset, with car parks along the coast road and the golf course extending away to the south. SC1066199*

Nevertheless, monuments such as this are important resources that underpin the expansion of new industries founded on tourism and recreation. Urban expansion around Aberdeen and its satellites has created large centres of population for whom the countryside has acquired new values. Where the *touns* were torn down and swept away, many steadings are now converted for private housing. And where field-boundaries and old shelter belts might once have been removed, now they are seen as important components of the rural habitat. Legislation and planning controls have shifted inexorably to a presumption for conservation. The countryside has become a valued resource for the nation, in the North-east combining its scenery, its habitats and its architecture in a distinct regional identity. The challenge of today is to ensure that its conservation can move forwards in harmony with the harsh realities of the rural economy.

Chapter 10: Conclusion

The results of this survey of Donside have revealed a wealth of information about the history of settlement in north-east Scotland. For prehistory this wealth is represented by monuments that are unequivocally spectacular, such as the recumbent stone circles, or the forts on the summits of **Tap o' Noth** and the **Mither Tap o' Bennachie**, but it also includes a range of lesser structures, from hut-circles to small burial cairns. On the one hand these monuments reflect history that is uniquely north-eastern, on the other they reflect patterns found much more widely to the north and south. A comparable balance of monuments represents medieval and later times, supplemented from the 12th century onwards by a rich vein of documentary evidence. Again, there is a sense of local history played out in the character of the various types of monument, but equally the evidence has a much wider resonance.

The character of the information, however, is uneven from period to period. The first challenge for any archaeological survey is to understand the factors that lie behind the patterns of survival that have created this unevenness. For the archaeological remains, the principal agent that dominates the pattern of survival is successive episodes of arable agriculture, which have variously destroyed, modified, revealed and preserved earlier structures. This challenge in Donside is particularly acute, for the agricultural improvements initiated in the early 18th century continued throughout the 19th century, reshaping the entire landscape from the coastal plain right up to the foothills of the Grampian Mountains. Relatively few stones were left unturned, leading to the wholesale attrition of any tangible prehistoric landscape and the removal of huge numbers of monuments. The impact of this process is perhaps most graphically seen in the way large numbers of the cottages, crofts and steadings shown roofed on the 1st edition of the OS 6-inch map have been erased from the face of the landscape, many of them disappearing before 1900.

The improvements of the 18th and 19th centuries, however, are only part of the story, for the settlement pattern has probably been expanding continuously since the 12th century, and with it the extent of agricultural land. This has progressively removed early medieval and prehistoric monuments over a period of at least 500 years before the reorganisation of the landscape in the 19th century. The relatively small number of deserted *touns* shown on 18th-century estate maps – and indeed of prehistoric monuments – stands tacit witness to this process. The remarkably high incidence of rig-and-furrow cultivation in rough and rocky ground beneath plantations in the lowlands (Fig. 9.11) provides the physical evidence of the extent of pre-improvement agriculture; in some respects it is remarkable that any prehistoric monuments have survived in the lowlands at all. It would also be unwise to underestimate the impact of successive phases of prehistoric agriculture on the character of the remains surviving from earlier periods (see Lairg, Sutherland, in McCullagh and Tipping 1998).

This intensity of land-use should come as no surprise. The Garioch is not simply the 'meal girnal' of medieval and later Aberdeenshire, but lies at the heart of the distributions of monuments throughout prehistory. Donside has always been extensively and relatively heavily settled. In this sense, the survey of any area of rich farmland will always pose problems, for the prime settlement locations will be in relatively continuous occupation, and the visible remains of most periods will usually be restricted to the margins. In areas such as Angus or East Lothian, this is compensated for by a rich cropmark record, reflecting the coincidence of favourable patterns of sunshine, rainfall and freely draining soils. In Donside, the situation is merely compounded by the unfavourable

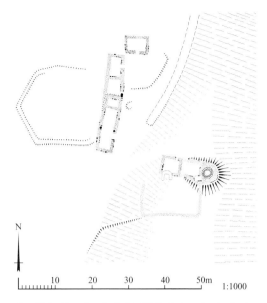

Fig. 10.1 **Glen Carvie** *(3483 0937). Reduced to its footings, this small farmstead with its kiln-barn probably relates to an early 19th-century phase of improvement on the east side of the glen. GV004153*

conditions for the formation of cropmarks, which are three to four times less frequent than in equivalent areas south of the Mounth or along the Moray Plain.

With such wide-ranging constraints, future fieldwork programmes need to focus on other forms of survey, in particular arable field-walking to identify artefact scatters in ploughsoil. This was not a practical approach for the small team engaged in the survey over such a large area, but a small area investigated on behalf of RCAHMS by Reading University clearly reveals the potential for this sort of work (Phillips 2005).

Given these general circumstances, the number of new monuments discovered is remarkably high, albeit heavily weighted to features relating to the last two centuries or so; the proliferation of farmsteads, crofts and cottages, followed by their widespread abandonment, has left a rash of ruined buildings throughout the uplands (Fig. 10.1). Nevertheless, a significant number of prehistoric monuments has also been recovered. Previously unknown burial-cairns, for example, have been discovered throughout Donside, which is particularly welcome when so many others were removed in the 19th century. That some of these large mounds have apparently passed unnoticed in the lowlands is always surprising, and yet repeats a pattern that is often encountered elsewhere. The hut-circles that have been located in small patches of rough ground in the lower reaches of the valley are an equally important resource, providing new examples of this type of prehistoric settlement throughout the catchment, from marginal locations on the upper fringes of any contemporary settlement pattern down to virtually sea level. The lower-lying examples are especially valuable, potentially preserving deposits that would have been long since removed had they been under plough and recorded as cropmarks.

With the emphasis on visible monuments rather than artefact scatters, the survey has made little contribution to the recording of the Mesolithic archaeology. No attempt has been made to map the distribution of Mesolithic artefacts, if only because such a distribution currently has more to say about patterns of collection and the activities of antiquarian collectors than any pattern of Mesolithic activity. Progress in this field requires a systematic approach to collection, in which the poorly catalogued material that currently exists can indicate no more than the general areas in which material has already been found. The palaeoenvironmental record offers some potential for a broader view of the impact of hunter-gatherer groups on the landscape, but here research is hamstrung by the dearth of modern analyses. At present the discussion of anthropogenic impacts is heavily dependent on work in the Howe of Cromar, in Deeside, and it is not known whether this is equally representative of the rest of Donside.

Palaeoenvironmental data are equally sparse for succeeding periods and, until more cores are analysed, any understanding of the evolution of the landscape will be thrown back onto the archaeological remains. For the Neolithic, the monumental record in Donside is particularly thin, but the distribution of artefacts reveals that people were active throughout the catchment of the Don. Stone axes have been used as the signature of this period of activity, despite the problems of provenancing much of the material held in museum collections. The concentration of axes apparently provenanced to Inverurie, for example, is perhaps referencing the museum collection there rather than a focus of Neolithic activity, despite the existence of the henge at **Broomend of Crichie**. Unquestionably there was a ceremonial centre here, perpetuated by other monuments and burials into the Early Bronze Age, but, with the limited distribution of cropmarks, it is impossible to be certain whether it is of regional significance, or simply one of a number of more local centres. The cursus monuments at **Mill of Fintray** and **Myreton**, and the two long barrows near Kintore, at **Forest Road** and **Midmill**, perhaps suggest the latter. Certainly the weight of the stone axe distribution, and indeed stone balls, Bronze Age tools and cist-burials, sweeps up the Don to Inverurie and the Garioch. The discovery of the long barrow at **Forest Road**, **Kintore**, also holds the possibility that this wider distribution may yet be populated with Neolithic monuments. Pits containing Neolithic material are regularly discovered as a result of area excavations ahead of development, as indeed happened at **Forest Road**, but the discovery of such a large monument, still partly upstanding, was entirely unexpected.

With the Early Bronze Age, the pattern of monuments becomes much denser and more extensive. Not only are numerous burial-cairns distributed

*Fig. 10.2 **Ardlair** (NJ 5527 2794). The site of the recumbent stone circle on the summit of this hill commands panoramic views, in this direction looking towards the Hill of Noth. SC851562*

throughout the catchment, but the work of Professor Richard Bradley has shown that the recumbent stone circles were part of their contemporary monumental repertoire (Fig. 10.2). The other stone circles in the area have received less attention, in part because they have proved less durable, but these demonstrate an even wider vocabulary. A separate gazetteer volume of recumbent stone circles is planned, in which these spectacular monuments will be considered in more detail. Suffice it to say here that the survey has demonstrated recurring patterns of design and construction in which architectural devices have been employed to lead any observer, ancient or modern, to confront the setting of stones on the southern arc from outside the circle. What is surely of significance is that, despite extensive fieldwork, these monuments remain stubbornly absent from the upper reaches of the Don. These are essentially lowland monuments, even though they are usually built in elevated locations.

Tangible evidence of settlement in Donside also emerges during the Bronze Age, as has been demonstrated in the radiocarbon dating programme for the excavations at **Forest Road**, **Kintore**. Here, well over thirty round-houses have now been excavated, ranging from simple post-rings to partly sunken-floored structures, the so-called ring-ditch houses. Elsewhere in eastern Scotland, these sunken-floored round-houses make up the mainstay of the cropmark record, forming disk- and crescent-shaped maculae in ripening cereal crops. For the reasons already outlined, such markings are more thinly scattered in Donside, which serves to underline the significance of the excavations at **Forest Road**, **Kintore**; with the exception of one or two of the round-houses on the line of the bypass nearby at **Deer's Den**, the rest were only identified as a result of the excavations. If nothing else, these excavations have demonstrated the importance of invasive sampling strategies in advance of development work, but the discovery of so many ploughed-out hut-circles shows how poorly served prehistorians are by traditional survey techniques in an area such as Donside. The distributions drawn from aerial photography, terrestrial survey and the antiquarian record will always be relatively thin.

Despite these problems, the fieldwork for the survey has roughly doubled the number of hut-circles in Donside, both extending the upper margin of the distribution into the foothills of the Grampian Mountains and recovering a scatter of survivors from small pockets of unimproved ground in the lowlands. To these can be added a series of structures in the lowlands that appear in the antiquarian record following their removal in the course of agricultural improvements; these range from three *camps* on the **Hill of Boghead** (Fig. 6.4) and the *turrets* of the *fort* at **Damil**, to a series of supposed stone circles, several of which almost certainly accompanied souterrains (e.g. **Nether Balfour**, **Bankhead** and **Newbigging**). Cropmarks add a further dimension to the pattern in the lowlands, revealing a scatter of ploughed-out settlements in the middle reaches of the Don and in the Garioch. The gaps between all these settlements in the lowlands tend to be in the order of 2km to 5km. The briefest comparison of the scatter of lowland settlements against the dense concentration of hut-circles on the hills between the upper Don and the Howe of Cromar clearly reveals that the overall distribution has far more to say about the loss of visible settlement remains in the improved land than their presence. Hundreds of hut-circle groups must have been removed, in the first place to make way for the expansion of medieval agriculture and, in the second, for the creation of the present landscape. The presence of several clusters of round-houses in the excavations at **Forest Road**, within a few hundred metres of those photographed as cropmarks at **Deer's Den**, essentially proves the point.

The excavations around Kintore also have a much wider significance, for they will in due course provide an unparalleled insight into the history of settlement in the North-east. The earliest domestic structures appear to be of Late Neolithic date, but a series of large round-houses were erected from the beginning of the 2nd millennium BC until the end of the 1st millennium BC. The sequence appears to end well before the arrival of the Roman army and the construction of a temporary camp, and heralds a period of some 500 years before any evidence of settlement reappears within the area that has been excavated to date. This lacuna in the settlement record is at once unfortunate and interesting. Unfortunate in that the 1st and 2nd centuries AD are a period when settlements in eastern Scotland apparently take on a characteristic form, typically including at least one souterrain; interesting in that this particular area was not occupied during this period, the more so for the density of such settlements recorded around Kildrummy (Fig. 6.11). The nature of a souterrain – essentially constructed in a trench and covered over – lends itself to discovery, for on the one hand the capstones of roofed souterrains were frequently encountered during the agricultural improvements, on the other the trench creates the potential for cropmarks to form in arable crops growing above them. As a result, the record of the settlement pattern, though patently threadbare, is more complete for this period than for any other. In Donside

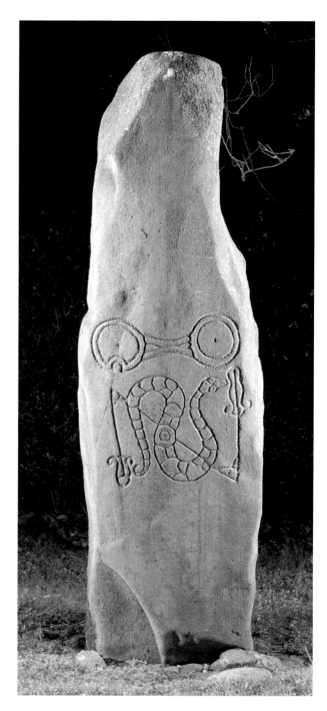

Fig. 10.3 **Newton House** *(NJ 6623 2972). Now in the grounds of Newton House, this Class I symbol stone originally stood near Pitmachie, about 1km to the south-west, close to the sites of several graves. The stone is incised with a double-disc, and a serpent and Z-rod. SC636521*

the discoveries by aerial photography are relatively few, but they complement the set of discoveries made through the agricultural improvements, and further examples can be added by reinterpreting some cryptic descriptions of monuments contained in the antiquarian record. A fresh analysis demonstrates that the Aberdeenshire souterrains are indistinguishable in either character or date from those found south of the Mounth. This is an important advance, for the latter are commonly treated as a discrete group (Wainwright 1963; Armit 1999). The density of the distribution north of Kildrummy also implies that souterrain settlements are probably as common in Aberdeenshire as they are in Angus and Perth & Kinross. Thus, it is interesting that no examples should have turned up in the excavations at **Forest Road**, **Kintore**. Occupation here was brought to a close at the end of the 1st millennium BC, following which this particular area seems to have been set aside for some other purpose. It remains to be seen whether this is any more than a local change in the pattern of settlement, or whether it reflects a wider reorganisation of the landscape, in which the areas given over to settlement, arable, pasture and forest were more closely defined.

With the abandonment of souterrain settlements, probably at the beginning of the 3rd century AD, archaeological traces of settlements in Donside become few and far between until the post-medieval period. This is a common phenomenon throughout eastern Scotland, and indeed elsewhere, essentially reflecting the uneven nature of the survival patterns. In essence, the expansion of settlement from the 12th century onwards, with the consequential expansion of agricultural land, has hidden the settlement remains until the very end of this span. From the 12th century there are various clues to the locations of some components of the settlement pattern, but for the preceding early medieval period there is little trace of any tangible sense of landscape. By far the majority of the Pictish symbol stones (Fig. 10.3), which are such evocative monuments of this period, have been moved from their original positions, and the four in Donside that have not now stand isolated in ploughed fields. Nevertheless, it is reasonably clear that the pattern of secular estates and parishes that emerges in the 12th century is firmly rooted in the early medieval period. In Moray, Alisdair Ross has mapped the pattern of *dabhachs*, sub-parochial territorial units which, he argues, were already ancient by the time they first come on record in the 12th century (Ross 2006). *Dabhachs* are also present in Donside, such as Resthivet in Chapel of Garioch, and Glen Ernan in Strathdon, but it has been beyond the means of the survey to exhaustively search post-medieval documentation for others in the way Ross has achieved for Moray. The discussion that has been presented focuses on the parochial structure, which provides a useful framework against which to analyse the distributions of early sculpture and place-names.

The Pictish symbol stones in Donside form an important corpus in their own right, but the survey has sought to put them in a landscape context, both in terms of their topographical position and in relationship to the parochial structure. Though all bar four of the stones have been moved from their original positions, the locations at which most of the stones were first discovered tend to be close to watercourses that were employed as the marches of the units forming the

Fig. 10.4 **Peel of Fichlie** *(NJ 4600 1390). Earthwork castles such as this served as the caputs of estates and are important components of the medieval landscape. This oblique aerial photograph shows the way such earthworks in Donside were often fashioned from a natural hillock. SC961124*

medieval parishes. The latter, however, evidently represents a pattern in transition. On the one hand they seem to represent relatively small units, such as Leslie or Insch in the Garioch, which appear to originate as subdivisions of a larger unit known as *Garviach* in the 12th century; on the other they include large territories like the parish of Kinkell, which was coterminous with the thanage of Kintore and was not broken up into smaller parishes until much later. The churches of these new parishes originated as dependent chapels of Kinkell, and it is argued that the new parishes reflect the earlier secular organisation of the thanage. Invernochty, in the uplands, seems to represent an intermediate stage, in which a number of smaller units that fall within its topographical compass had been granted to neighbouring parishes in the Howe of Cromar. One of these smaller units is the *dabhach* of Glen Ernan, which formed part of the parish of Tarland.

Kintore, *Garviach* and Invernochty were perhaps the typical territorial units in Donside prior to the 12th century. Each was subdivided into what were to become the smaller parish-sized units, and, on the strength of place-name evidence, subdivided again into a raft of smaller estates. The apparent relationship between the sculptured stones and the framework of parish boundaries may be no more than a coincidence, created by a topographical preference for locations adjacent to watercourses and confluences. Nevertheless, long

*Fig. 10.5 **Glenkindie Home Farm** (NJ 4245 1455). The ornate central bay that projects into the courtyard from the south range, with its clock and decorative ventilator, incorporates a recessed panel bearing the initials A.H.L. and the date 1897. It is probably an addition to the rest of the steading. SC873293*

cist cemeteries and Roman Iron Age burials elsewhere appear to display a similar relationship, and the pattern is certainly worthy of further research. Progress in Donside must await investigation into the pattern of *dabhachs* across the district.

The lack of visible settlement remains relating to the early medieval landscape carries on through the medieval period, but from the 12th century onwards charter evidence begins to illuminate the pattern of settlement, and earthwork castles serve to identify some of the medieval estate centres (Fig. 10.4). The latter range from major castles, such as the **Bass of Inverurie** and the **Doune of Invernochty**, to the *caputs* of lesser nobles. A good example of one of these lesser *caputs* is the moated enclosure at **Leslie**, which continued in use with the erection of a tower-house on the same site. It has been estimated that within the Garioch lordship there were at least forty principal landholders, each of whom would have required some form of administrative centre. While it is possible to reconstruct a number of these smaller estates in some detail from charter evidence, most of their *caputs* are now lost.

The documentary evidence not only allows the pattern of lordship at the end of the 12th century to be established, but also provides evidence that new settlements were planted following the grant of the Garioch lordship to Earl David of Huntingdon. Some of the new settlements are row villages when they first appear on 18th-century estate maps, and their apparent concentration in the area of the Garioch lordship, it

is argued here, betrays origins as medieval planned villages planted in the 12th century. This highlights the role of many of the villages in the modern landscape as components of the medieval settlement pattern. These villages, particularly where they are clustered around a medieval parish church, sometimes, as at **Leslie**, with an estate centre nearby, offer the same potential as medieval villages anywhere else in the British Isles. They are an important archaeological resource that requires detailed study and excavation if medieval settlement studies are to be advanced.

Other named places in documentary sources, such as the *touns* whose names are prefixed with 'Old' in the Poll Tax returns of 1696, offer a similar potential, but it is more difficult to be certain where the settlement stood. This is a problem until the first depictions of settlements on 18th-century estate maps. The evidence of *toun*-splitting contained in documentary sources reveals the general trend towards dispersal and expansion of the settlement pattern from at least the 15th century, but the radical and dramatic reorganisation of the landscape during the 18th and 19th centuries has dislocated the relationship between the modern farms and more ancient settlements of the same name. In some cases they may occupy the same site, but it can also be demonstrated that in others the modern farm has moved some distance. There are also examples where a long-established name has been applied to an improved farm standing on the site of a *toun* that held an entirely different name. Despite these problems, Donside has much to offer the student of medieval and post-medieval settlement. Indeed, the tendency for archaeological studies to concentrate on marginal areas where the state of preservation is apparently better is misguided. Marginal areas, in whatever way they are defined, merely provide evidence of marginal settlement responses at times when settlement has expanded. Areas of rich farmland such as the Garioch not only lie at the heart of the medieval settlement pattern, but they are also more likely to contain evidence of continuous settlement and land-use from prehistory to the present day.

The lowland areas also contain the greater number of architectural monuments dating from the medieval period. These have largely fallen outside the scope of the present work, which has been more concerned with the role of such sites as estate centres, backed up by the detailed survey of a handful of ruinous examples of castles, tower-houses and laird's houses to illustrate the general trend of fortified and domestic architecture. This may appear an idiosyncratic approach, particularly in a region blessed with such a spectacular set of tower-houses and country houses, but was adopted as a practical approach to the resourcing of the project. Many of the towers and houses concerned are listed buildings and some at least have been embraced by other RCAHMS survey programmes (e.g. **Skellater**

*Fig. 10.6 **Craik** (NJ 4618 2553). Ruined and derelict farmsteads such as this are a common feature of the upland landscape. SC874015*

House, **Leith Hall** and **Craigievar Castle**). The combination of fieldwork and documentary search adopted for Donside resulted in the discovery of a number of 'lost' laird's houses of late 17th- and early 18th-century date.

The weakness of omitting standing buildings is more exposed in the recording of the monuments of the improved landscape. This has been directed exclusively to what are in effect the failed components of that landscape. Hundreds of ruined farmsteads, crofts and cottages have been visited and recorded, and yet there are unaltered examples of the same types of buildings still occupied and in use throughout the landscape (Fig. 10.6). Again the survey has focused for practical reasons on the general trend of settlement in the landscape, while another national survey programme has recorded a selection of farmsteadings (Fig. 10.5). Unquestionably, a parallel recording programme to assess the hundreds of improved steadings that remain in use would have produced a mass of detailed information about the development of agriculture through the 19th and 20th centuries, though its publication would probably have entailed a separate volume.

This commentary should not detract from the importance of the ruined farmsteads that have been recorded. These are important cultural relics in their own right, which not only contribute to the character of the north-eastern landscape, but also maintain a resonance for the communities that still live around them. As such they stand shoulder to shoulder with the recumbent stone circles, arguably representing a far more tangible and accessible past. Like the recumbent stone circles, they reflect a regional history, but the ruins of deserted steadings are much more than this. They reflect national and international histories. The abandonment of each is a manifestation of particular components in a cocktail of far-flung political and economic events.

A survey such as this cannot hope to embrace every aspect of the landscape and its history. It is unequivocally a field archaeology, dealing with field monuments and constrained by the patterns of survival and the problems of discovering and recognising the diverse traces of man's impact on the landscape. To this end it relies heavily on maps for its presentation, placing the different categories of information in the framework of an historical geography of Donside. The possibilities for further research are endless. The potential of the standing architecture has already been mentioned, as has the investigation of the palaeoenvironmental record. The extensive museum collections relating to Aberdeenshire have also fallen outside the scope of the survey, but the artefactual record of prehistory, for example, is second to none (e.g. Cowie 1988; Shepherd 1986). The field archaeology is itself far from exhausted. Visible traces of human activity can only be recognised within the limits of current knowledge and experience, and there may yet be types of monuments that are visible but have so far escaped notice. The patches of deepened soils identified in the Garioch (p. 42; Glentworth 1944) are a case in point. These may simply provide an insight into relatively recent agricultural practices, but artificial soils created by high inputs of manure and domestic debris have a long history (Davidson and Simpson 1994). Such soils may well have subsumed and buried a range of prehistoric and medieval settlement remains, and the very character of these deposits may mask such remains from conventional survey. The soils, however, are as valid a monument as any other form of field-system, and should perhaps be treated as such.

Surveying monuments is, of course, merely the starting point in managing the long-term conservation and investigation of our cultural heritage. This is an arena fraught with competing demands, ranging from the local economy to amenity, recreation and habitat. Fortunately, Aberdeenshire Council's role in this respect is long-established, as can be seen in the far-sighted archaeological response to the development of housing around Kintore. This sets a new standard in Scotland for remedial work in advance of extensive development. In an area where little more than the ditch of the Roman temporary camp was known previously, the results have been more than justified. A wealth of evidence that might otherwise have been lost has been recovered by the excavations. In areas like Donside, where it is relatively difficult to identify the remains of prehistoric settlements by other means, this extensive invasive approach will be essential to the development of knowledge about the people who have inhabited our landscape for some 10,000 years.

Bibliography

Abercromby, J 1904
Exploration of circular enclosures and an underground house near Dinnet, on Deeside, *Proc Soc Antiq Scot* 38 (1903–04), 102–22

Agricola
Tacitus. Agricola and Germany, translated by A R Birley, Oxford World Classics, Oxford

Aitken, J F 1991
Sedimentology and Palaeoenvironmental Significance of Late Devensian to mid-Holocene Deposits in the Don Valley, Unpublished PhD thesis, University of Aberdeen, Aberdeen

Alcock, E 1991
Pictish stones Class I: where and how?, *Glasgow Archaeol J* 15 (1988–9), 1–21

Alexander, D 2000
Excavation of Neolithic pits, later prehistoric structures and a Roman temporary camp along the line of the A96 Kintore and Blackburn Bypass, Aberdeenshire, *Proc Soc Antiq Scot* 130 (2000), 11–75

Alexander, D 2005
Redcastle, Lunan Bay, Angus: the excavation of an Iron Age timber-lined souterrain and a Pictish barrow cemetery, *Proc Soc Antiq Scot* 135 (2005), 41–118

Alexander, D and Ralston, I B M 1999
Survey work on Turin Hill, Angus, *Tayside Fife Archaeol J* 5 (1999), 36–49

Alexander, W M 1952
The Place-Names of Aberdeenshire, Third Spalding Club, Aberdeen

Allen, J R 1883
On the discovery of a sculptured stone at St Madoes, with some notes on interlaced ornament, *Proc Soc Antiq Scot* 17 (1882–3), 211–72

Allen, J R and Anderson, J 1903
The Early Christian Monuments of Scotland. A classified, illustrated, descriptive list of the Monuments, with an Analysis of their Symbolism and Ornamentation, Edinburgh

Alley, R B 2000
The Younger Dryas cold interval as viewed from central Greenland, *Quaternary Sci Rev* 19, 213–26

Ammianus Marcellinus
Res Gestax, xx, 1, see Ireland 1996, 254–5

Anderson, A O 1922
Early Sources of Scottish History AD 500 to 1286, Edinburgh

Anderson, J 1779
An account of ancient monuments and fortifications in the highlands of Scotland. In a letter ... to George Wilson, Esq; of Lincoln's-Inn, *Archaeologia* 5 (1779), 241–66

Anderson, J 1782
A further description of ancient fortifications in the north of Scotland, *Archaeologia* 6 (1782), 87–99

Anderson, J 1794
General view of the Agriculture of the county of Aberdeen, Edinburgh

Anderson, J 1880
Notice of an ancient Celtic reliquary exhibited to the Society by Sir Archibald Grant, Bart., of Monymusk, *Proc Soc Antiq Scot* 14 (1879–80), 431–5

Anderson, J 1881a
Scotland in Early Christian Times – The Rhind Lectures in Archaeology – 1879, Edinburgh

Anderson, J 1881b
Scotland in Early Christian Times (Second Series) – The Rhind Lectures in Archaeology for 1880, Edinburgh

Anderson, J 1883
Scotland in Pagan Times: The Iron Ages – The Rhind Lectures for 1881, Edinburgh

Apted, M R 1963
Excavation at Kildrummy Castle, 1952–1962, *Proc Soc Antiq Scot* 96 (1962–3), 208–36

Armit, I 1999
The abandonment of souterrains: evolution, catastrophe or dislocation, *Proc Soc Antiq Scot* 129 (1999), 577–96

Ash, M 1976
The diocese of St. Andrews under its 'Norman' bishops, *Scot Hist Rev* 55 (1976), 106–26

Ash, M 1981
'A fine, genial, hearty band': David Laing, Daniel Wilson and Scottish Archaeology, in Bell (ed) 1981, 86–112

Ash, M 1999
Old books, old castles, and old friends: the making of Daniel Wilson's 'Archaeology and Prehistoric Annals of Scotland', in Hulse (ed) 1999, 60–80

Ashmore, P J 1981
Low cairns, long cists and symbol stones, *Proc Soc Antiq Scot* 110 (1978–80), 346–55

Atkinson, T C, Briffa, K R & Coope, G R 1987
Seasonal temperatures in Britain during the past 22,000 years, reconstructed from beetle remains, *Nature* 325, 587–92

Aubrey, J 1980
Monumenta Britannica; or a Miscellany of British Antiquities by John Aubrey illustrated with Notes by Thomas Gale and John Evelyn (Legg, R and Fowles, J eds), Sherborne

AUL
University of Aberdeen Library Special Collections

AUL MS 2499
Gordon of Craig Collection

AUL MS 2769
Davidson and Garden Collection

AUL MS 2769/I/131/6
Plan of Glen Carvy and Bunzeach 1766

AUL MS 3175
Duff House (Montcoffer) Papers

AUL MS 3528/11
Plan of the Barony of Balquhain Lying in the Parishes of Inverurie and Chapel of Garioch

B, H W 1913
Thomas Francis Jamieson, *The Geological Magazine*, Decade 5: 10 (1913), 332–3

Baldwin, J R (ed) 1986
Firthlands of Ross and Sutherland, Scottish Society for Northern Studies

Balfour, J (ed) 1900
Accounts of the Lord High Treasurer of Scotland, 1500–1504, Vol. 2, Edinburgh

Ballantyne, C K & Harris, C 1994
The Periglaciation of Great Britain, Cambridge

Barber, J W & Crone, B A 2001
The duration of structures, settlements and sites: some evidence from Scotland, in Raftery and Hickey (eds) 2001, 69–86

Barber, J W (ed) 1997
The Archaeological Investigation of a Prehistoric Landscape: Excavations on Arran 1978–81, Scottish Trust for Archaeological Research Monograph 2, Edinburgh

Barber, K E, Maddy, D, Rose, N, Stevenson, A C, Stoneman, R E & Thompson, R 2000
Replicated proxy-climate signals over the last 2000 years from two distant UK peat bogs: new evidence for regional palaeoclimate teleconnections, *Quaternary Sci Rev* 18, 471–9

Barclay, G J 1983
Sites of the third millennium bc to the first millennium ad at North Mains, Strathallan, Perthshire, *Proc Soc Antiq Scot* 113 (1983), 122–281

Barclay, G J 1993
The excavation of pit circles at Romancamp Gate, Fochabers, Moray, 1990, *Proc Soc Antiq Scot* 123 (1993), 255–68

Barclay, G J 2000
Between Orkney and Wessex: the search for the regional Neolithics of Britain, in Ritchie (ed) 2000, 275–85

Barclay, G J & Maxwell, G S 1998
The Cleaven Dyke and Littleour: monuments in the Neolithic of Tayside, Soc Antiq Scot Monogr 13, Edinburgh

Barclay, G J, Brophy, K & MacGregor, G 2002
Claish, Stirling: an early Neolithic structure in its context, *Proc Soc Antiq Scot* 132 (2002), 65–137

Barrett, J C & Downes, J M 1994
Excavations and Fieldwork at North Pitcarmick 1994: Interim Report, privately circulated

Barrow, G W S (ed) 1960
Regesta Regum Scottorum, Acts of Malcolm IV, King of Scots 1153–65, Vol. 1, Edinburgh

Barrow, G W S 1973
The Kingdom of the Scots, London

Barrow, G W S 1975
Macbeth and other mormaers of Moray, in Maclean (ed) 1975, 109–22

Barrow, G W S 1980
The Anglo-Norman Era in Scottish History, Oxford

Barrow, G W S 1983
The childhood of Scottish Christianity: a note on some place-name evidence, *Scot Stud* 27 (1983), 1–15

Barrow, G W S & Scott, W W (eds) 1971
Regesta Regum Scottorum, Acts of William I, King of Scots 1165–1214, Vol. 2, Edinburgh

Barton, N, Roberts, A J & Roe, D A (eds) 1991
The Late Glacial in North-west Europe, Council for British Archaeology, London

Baxter, J M *et al.* (eds) 1998
Scotland's Living Coastline, Edinburgh

Behre, K-E 1981
The interpretation of anthropogenic indicators in pollen diagrams, *Pollen et Spores* 23, 225–45

Bell, A S (ed) 1981
The Scottish Antiquarian Tradition: Essays to Mark the Bicentenary of the Society of Antiquaries of Scotland and its Museum, 1780–1980, Edinburgh

Bennett, K D 1984
The post-glacial history of Pinus sylvestris in the British Isles, *Quaternary Sci Rev* 3, 133–55

Bennett, K D & Birks, H J B 1990
Postglacial history of alder (*Alnus glutinosa (L.) Gaertn.*) in the British Isles, *J Quaternary Sci* 5, 123–34

Bennett, K D, Birks, H J B & Willis, K 1998
Vegetation history, in Richardson (ed) 1998, 27–51

Bennett, M R & Glasser, N F 1991
The glacial landforms of Glen Geusachan: a reinterpretation, *Scot Geogr Mag* 107, 116–23

Beresford, M & Hurst, J G (eds) 1971
Deserted Medieval Villages, London

Binney, H 1997
Holocene environmental change in the Scottish Highlands: multi-proxy evidence from blanket peats, Unpublished PhD thesis, Guildhall University, London

Birks, H H 1975
Studies in the vegetational history of Scotland. IV. Pine stumps in Scottish blanket peats, *Phil Trans Roy Soc London* B270, 181–226

Birks, H J B 1989
Holocene isochrone maps and patterns of tree-spreading in the British Isles, *J Biogeography* 16, 503–40

Birse, E L & Robertson, J S (eds) 1976
Plant Communities and Soils of the Lowland and Southern Upland Regions of Scotland, Macaulay Institute for Soil Research, Aberdeen

Bjorck, S *et al.* 1998
An event stratigraphy for the last termination in the North Atlantic region based on the Greenland ice-core record: a proposal by the INTIMATE Group, *J Quaternary Sci* 13, 283–92

Blackford, J 1993
Peat bogs as sources of proxy climatic data: past approaches and future research, in Chambers (ed) 1993, 47–56

Blaikie, J 1835
On the slate quarries of Aberdeenshire, *Prize Essays and Trans Highland and Agric Soc Scotland*, New Ser 4, 98–106

Boardman, J (ed) 1987
Periglacial Processes and Landforms in Britain, Cambridge

Bond, G C *et al.* 1993
Correlations between climate records from North Atlantic sediments and Greenland ice, *Nature* 365, 143–7

Bonney, D 1972
Early boundaries in Wessex, in Fowler (ed) 1972, 168–86

Bonsall, C (ed) 1989
The Mesolithic in Europe, Edinburgh

Boyd, W E & Kenworthy, J B 1992
The use of wood as a natural resource at a Scottish Mesolithic site, *Glasgow Archaeol J* 17, 11–19.

Boyle, S 2003
Ben Lawers: an improvement period landscape on Lochtayside, Perthshire, in Govan (ed) 2003, 17–29

Bradley, R 2000
The Good Stones: A New Investigation of the Clava Cairns, Soc Antiq Scotland Monograph Series 17, Edinburgh

Bradley, R 2001
Excavations at recumbent stone circles and related sites in Aberdeenshire, 2001: Interim Report

Bradley, R 2002a
The land, the sky and the Scottish stone circle, in Scarre (ed) 2002, 123–37

Bradley, R 2002b
The stone circles of northeast Scotland in the light of excavation, *Antiquity* 76 (2002), 840–8

Bradley, R 2005
The Moon and the Bonfire: An Investigation of Three Stone Circles in North-east Scotland, Society of Antiquaries Monograph, Edinburgh

Bradley, R S & Jones, P D 1995
Climate Since AD 1500, Cambridge

Brazier, V, Gordon, J E, Hubbard, A & Sugden, D E 1996
The geomorphological evolution of a dynamic landscape: the Cairngorm Mountains, Scotland, *Bot J Scotland* 48, 13–30

Bremner, A 1942
The origin of the Scottish river systems. Part II, *Scot Geogr Mag* 58, 54–99

Bridge, M C, Haggart, B A & Lowe, J J 1990
The history and palaeoclimatic significance of subfossil remains of *Pinus sylvestris* in blanket peats from Scotland, *J Ecology* 78, 77–99

Broecker, W S 2001
Was the Medieval Warm Period global?, *Science* 291, 1497–9

Brogden, W A 1998
Aberdeen: An Illustrated Architectural Guide, 2nd ed, Edinburgh

Brooks, S J 1996
Three thousand years of environmental history in a Cairngorms lochan revealed by analysis of non-biting midges (Insecta: Diptera: Chironomidae), *Bot J Scotland* 48, 89–98

Broun, D 2000
The seven kingdoms in *De situ Albanie*: a record of Pictish political geography or imaginary map of ancient Alba?, in Cowan and McDonald (eds) 2000, 24–42

Brown, A G 1997
Alluvial Geoarchaeology, Cambridge

Brown, I M 1993
Pattern of deglaciation of the last (Late Devensian) Scottish ice sheet: evidence from ice-marginal deposits in the Dee valley, northeast Scotland, *J Quaternary Sci* 8, 235–50

Browne, G F 1921
On Some Antiquities in the Neighbourhood of Dunecht House Aberdeenshire, Cambridge

Browne, G J (ed) 1923
Echt-Forbes Charters 1345–1727, records of the Forest of Birse, notarial signs 926–1786, Edinburgh

Brück, J 2004
Early Bronze Age burial practices in Scotland and beyond: differences and similarities, in Shepherd and Barclay (eds) 2004, 179–88

Bulloch, J M (ed) 1907
The House of Gordon, Spalding Club, Vol. 2, Aberdeen

Burl, H A W 1970
The recumbent stone circles of north-east Scotland, *Proc Soc Antiq Scot* 102 (1969–70), 56–81

Burl, H A W 1979
Rings of Stone: The Prehistoric Stone Circles of Britain and Ireland, London

Burl, H A W 1980
Science or symbolism: problems of archaeo-astronomy, *Antiquity* 54 (1980), 191–200

Burl, H A W 1985
Report on the excavation of a Neolithic mound at Boghead, Speymouth Forest, Moray, 1972 and 1974, *Proc Soc Antiq Scot* 114 (1984), 35–73

Burl, H A W 1993
From Carnac to Callanish: the prehistoric stone rows and avenues of Britain, Ireland and Brittany, New Haven and London

Burl, H A W 1995
A Guide to the Stone Circles of Britain, Ireland and Brittany, Newhaven and London

Burl, H A W 2000
The Stone Circles of Britain, Ireland and Brittany, London

Burnett, G (ed) 1882
The Exchequer Rolls of Scotland 1437–54, Vol. 5, Edinburgh

Burnett, G (ed) 1889
The Exchequer Rolls of Scotland 1502–07, Vol. 12, Edinburgh

Burnett, J H (ed) 1964
The Vegetation of Scotland, Edinburgh

Callander, J G 1903
Notice of a collection of perforated stone objects, from the Garioch, Aberdeenshire, *Proc Soc Antiq Scot* 37 (1902–3), 166–77

Callander, J G 1904
Notice of a stone mould for casting flat bronze axes found in the parish of Insch, Aberdeenshire, with notes on the occurrence of flat axe moulds in Europe, *Proc Soc Antiq Scot* 38 (1903–4), 487–505

Callander, J G 1905
Notices of two cinerary urns and a pendant of slate found at Seggiecrook, in the parish of Kennethmont, Aberdeenshire, *Proc Soc Antiq Scot* 39 (1904–5), 184–9

Callander, J G 1906
Notices of (1) two cists from Oyne and Skene; (2) a late Celtic harness mounting of bronze from Culsalmond; (3) a stone mould for casting flat axes from Auchterless; and (4) two star-shaped beads from Aberdeenshire, *Proc Soc Antiq Scot* 40 (1905–6), 23–39

Callander, J G 1907
Notice of (1) a stone cist containing a skeleton and a drinking-cup discovered at Mains of Leslie, Aberdeenshire; (2) a small cinerary urn from Mill of Wardes, Insch, Aberdeenshire; (3) of cinerary urns and other remains from the estate of Logie Elphinstone, Aberdeenshire; and (4) a bronze sword from Grassieslack, Daviot, Aberdeenshire, *Proc Soc Antiq Scot* 41 (1906–7), 116–29

Callander, J G 1908
Notices (1) of the discovery of a fourth cinerary urn, containing burnt human bones and other relics at Seggiecrook, Kennethmont, Aberdeenshire, and (2) two small polished stone axes and a flanged spearhead of bronze from Asia Minor, *Proc Soc Antiq Scot* 42 (1907–8), 212–33

Callander, J G 1909
Notice of the discovery in Aberdeenshire of five cists, each containing a drinking-cup urn, *Proc Soc Antiq Scot* 43 (1908–9), 76–92

Callander, J G 1912
Notice of the discovery of two drinking-cup urns in a short cist at Mains of Leslie, Aberdeenshire, *Proc Soc Antiq Scot* 46 (1911–12), 344–8

Callander, J G 1913
Notices of (1) a bronze socketed axe from Daviot, Aberdeenshire, and (2) a stone mould for casting whorls, from Insch, Aberdeenshire, with (3) notes on lead whorls, lead brooches and button moulds, *Proc Soc Antiq Scot* 47 (1912–13), 450–62

Callander, J G 1916
Notices of (1) three stone cups in a cairn in Aberdeenshire, and (2) a short cist containing a Beaker urn found at Boglehill Wood, Longniddry, East Lothian, *Proc Soc Antiq Scot* 50 (1915–16), 145–51

Callander, J G 1917

A flint workshop on the Hill of Skares, Aberdeenshire, *Proc Soc Antiq Scot* 51 (1916–17), 117–27

Callander, J G 1923

Scottish Bronze Age hoards, *Proc Soc Antiq Scot* 57 (1922–3), 123–66

Callander, J G 1925

A long cairn and other prehistoric monuments in Aberdeenshire and Banffshire, and a short cist at Bruceton, Alyth, Perthshire, *Proc Soc Antiq Scot* 59 (1924–5), 21–8

Callander, J G 1927

A symbol stone from Fiscavaig, Skye; an early Iron Age hoard from Crichie, Aberdeenshire; and cinerary urns from Seamill, West Kilbride, Ayrshire, *Proc Soc Antiq Scot* 61 (1926–7), 241–51

Callander, J G 1929

Scottish Neolithic pottery, *Proc Soc Antiq Scot* 63 (1928–9), 29–98

Callander, J G 1933

A short cist containing a Beaker at Newlands, Oyne, Aberdeenshire, and sundry archaeological notes, *Proc Soc Antiq Scot* 67 (1932–3), 228–3

Camden, W (Gibson, E ed) 1695

Camden's Britannia, Newly Translated into English with Large Additions and Improvements, London

Cameron, K 1999

Excavation of an Iron Age timber structure beside the Candle Stane recumbent stone circle, Aberdeenshire, *Proc Soc Antiq Scot* 129 (1999), 359–72

Carter, I 1979

Farm Life in North-east Scotland 1840–1914: The Poor Man's Country (2nd ed 2003), Edinburgh

Carter, S 1993

Tulloch Wood, Forres, Moray: the survey and dating of a fragment of a prehistoric landscape, *Proc Soc Antiq Scot* 123 (1993), 215–33

Carter, S 1999

The burgh of Inverurie, Aberdeenshire: archaeological evidence from a medieval lordship, *Proc Soc Antiq Scot* 129 (1999), 649–61

Caruana, I D 1992

Carlisle: excavation of a section of the annexe ditch of the first Flavian fort, 1990, *Britannia* 23, 45–109

Carver, M 1998

Sutton Hoo: Burial Ground of Kings, Philadelphia

Cassius Dio

Roman History; for relevant passages see Ireland 1996, 108–111

Chalmers, G 1807

Caledonia, or, An Account, Historical and Topographical, of North Britain from the Most Ancient to the Present Times: with a Dictionary of Places, Chorographical and Philological, Vol. 1, London

Chalmers, G 1887–1894

Caledonia: or A Historical and Topographical Account of North Britain from the Most Ancient to the Present Times, with a Dictionary of Places Chorographical and Philological, 2nd ed, Paisley

Chambers, F M (ed) 1993

Climate Change and Human Impact on the Landscape, London

Chapman, J C & Mytum, H C (eds) 1983

Settlement in North Britain 1000 BC – AD 1000, BAR British Series 118, Oxford

Childe, V G 1933

Trial excavations at the Old Keig stone circle, Aberdeenshire, *Proc Soc Antiq Scot* 67 (1932–3), 37–53

Childe, V G 1934

Final report on the excavation of the stone circle at Old Keig, Aberdeenshire, *Proc Soc Antiq Scot* 68 (1933–4), 372–93

Childe, V G 1935

Excavation of the vitrified fort of Finavon, Angus, *Proc Soc Antiq Scot* 69 (1934–5), 49–80

Childe, V G 1936

(1) Carminnow Fort; (2) supplementary excavations at the vitrified fort of Finavon, Angus; and (3) some Bronze Age vessels from Angus, *Proc Soc Antiq Scot* 70 (1935–6), 341–56

Chippindale, C 1983

The making of the first ancient monuments act, 1882, and its administration under General Pitt-Rivers, *J Brit Archaeol Assoc* 136 (1983), 1–55

Christison, D 1898

Early Fortifications in Scotland: Motes, Camps, and Forts, London

Christison, D 1900

Report on events of last season, 1899; in anniversary meeting, 30th November 1899, *Proc Soc Antiq Scot* 34 (1899–1900), 1–14

Clancy, T O 1995

Annat in Scotland and the origins of the parish, *Innes Review* 46 (pt 2), 91–115

Clapperton, C M 1997

Greenland ice cores and North Atlantic sediments: implications for the last glaciation in Scotland, in Gordon (ed) 1997, 45–58

Clapperton, C M & Sugden, D E 1975

The glaciation of Buchan: a reappraisal, in Gemmell (ed) 1975, 19–22

Clapperton, C M & Sugden, D E 1977

The Late Devensian glaciation of north-east Scotland, in Gray and Lowe (eds) 1977, 1–15

Clapperton, C M, Gunson, A R & Sugden, D E 1975

Loch Lomond Readvance in the eastern Cairngorms, *Nature* 253, 710–12

Clarke, D 1978

Mesolithic Europe: the Ecological Basis, London

Clarke, D V 1981
Scottish archaeology in the second half of the nineteenth century, in Bell (ed) 1981, 114–41

Clarke, D V 2002
'The foremost figure in all matters relating to Scottish archaeology': aspects of the work of Joseph Anderson (1832–1916), *Proc Soc Antiq Scot* 132 (2002), 1–18

Close-Brooks, J 1981
Excavations in the Dairy Park, Dunrobin, Sutherland, 1977, *Proc Soc Antiq Scot* 110 (1978–80), 328–45

Clough, T H McK & Cummins, W A (eds) 1988
Stone Axe Studies, Vol. 2, Council Brit Archaeol Res Rep, 67, London

Coles, F R 1900
Report on stone circles in Kincardineshire (north) and part of Aberdeenshire, with measured plans and drawings, obtained under the Gunning Fellowship, *Proc Soc Antiq Scot* 34 (1899–1900), 139–98

Coles, F R 1901
Report on the stone circles of the north-east of Scotland, Inverurie District, obtained under the Gunning Fellowship, with measured plans and drawings, *Proc Soc Antiq Scot* 35 (1900–1), 187–248

Coles, F R 1902
Report on stone circles in Aberdeenshire (Inverurie, eastern parishes, and Insch districts), with measured plans and drawings, obtained under the Gunning Fellowship, *Proc Soc Antiq Scot* 36 (1901–2), 488–581

Coles, F R 1903a
Report on the stone circles of north-eastern Scotland, chiefly Auchterless and Forgue, with measured plans and drawings, obtained under the Gunning Fellowship, *Proc Soc Antiq Scot* 37 (1902–3), 82–142

Coles, F R 1903b
Notices of (1) The Camp at Montgoldrum and other antiquities in Kincardineshire; (2) a stone circle called the Harestones in Peebleshire; (3) a cairn and standing stones at Old Liston, and other standing stones in Midlothian and Fife; (4) some hitherto undescribed cup- and ring-marked stones; and (5) recent discoveries of urns, *Proc Soc Antiq Scot* 37 (1902–3), 193–232

Coles, F R 1905
Record of the excavation of two stone circles in Kincardineshire – (1) in Garrol Wood, Durris; (2) in Glassel Wood, Banchory-Ternan; and (II) report on stone circles in Aberdeenshire, with measured plans and drawings; obtained under the Gunning Fellowship, *Proc Soc Antiq Scot* 39 (1904–5), 190–218

Coles, F R 1910
Report on the stone circles surveyed in Perthshire (Aberfeldy District): with measured plans and drawings (obtained under the Gunning Fellowship), *Proc Soc Antiq Scot* 44 (1909–10), 117–68

Coles, J M & Simpson, D D A 1965
The excavation of a Neolithic round barrow at Pitnacree, Perthshire, Scotland, *Proc Prehist Soc* 121 (1965), 34–57

Connell, E R & Hall, A M 1987
The periglacial history of Buchan, north-east Scotland, in Boardman, J (ed) 1987, 277–85

Cook, M & Dunbar, L 2004
Kintore, *Current Archaeology* 194 (Oct/Nov 2004), 84–9

Cook, M, Dunbar, L & Crone, B A forthcoming
Rituals, Roundhouses and Romans: Excavations at Kintore 2000–2006, Volume 1: Forest Road, Scottish Trust for Archaeological Research, Edinburgh

Cooper, J (ed) 1888–92
Cartularium Ecclesiae Sancti Nicholai Aberdonensis recognovit Jacobus Cooper, New Spalding Club, Aberdeen

Cordiner, C 1780
Antiquities and Scenery of the North of Scotland in a Series of Letters to Thomas Pennant, Esq., London

Cordiner, C 1795
Remarkable Ruins, and Romantic Prospects, of North Britain, with Ancient Monuments and Singular Subjects of Natural History, London

Courtenay, E H 1868
Account of the recent discovery of a Roman camp at Kintore, Aberdeenshire, *Proc Soc Antiq Scot* 7 (1866–8), 387–94

Cowan, E J and McDonald, R A (eds) 2000
Alba: Celtic Scotland in the Medieval Era, East Linton

Cowan, I B 1967
The Parishes of Medieval Scotland, Scottish Record Society, Edinburgh

Cowan, I B & Easson, D E 1976
Medieval religious houses, Scotland: with an appendix on the houses in the Isle of Man, 2nd ed, London

Cowie, T G 1988
Magic Metal: Early Metalworkers in the North-east, Anthropological Museum, University of Aberdeen, Aberdeen

Craig, G Y (ed) 1983
Geology of Scotland, Edinburgh

Crawford, B E (ed) 1996
Scotland in Dark Age Britain, St John's House Papers No. 6, St Andrews

Crawford, B E (ed) 1999
Church, Chronicle and Learning in Medieval and Early Renaissance Scotland: Essays Presented to Donald Watt on the Occasion of the Completion of the Publication of Bower's 'Scotichronicon', Edinburgh

Crawford, O G S 1939
Air reconnaissance of Roman Scotland, *Antiquity* 13 (1939), 280–92

Crawford, O G S 1949
Topography of Roman Scotland North of the Antonine Wall, Cambridge

Creighton, J D & Wilson, R J A (eds) 1999
Roman Germany: Studies in Cultural Interaction, J Roman Archaeol Supplementary Series no. 32, Portsmouth, Rhode Island

Cruden, S 1960
The Scottish Castle, Edinburgh

Cruickshank, J (ed) 1935
Court Book of the Barony of Fintray 1711–1726, Third Spalding Club, Aberdeen

Cruickshank, J (ed) 1941
Logan's Collections, Third Spalding Club, Aberdeen

Cruickshank, J 1926
Newhills cross, Aberdeenshire, *Proc Soc Antiq Scot* 60 (1925–6), 269–73

Cruickshank, J & Gunn, D B 1929
The Freedom Lands and Marches of Aberdeen, 1319–1929, Aberdeen

Cruickshank, K, Nisbet, J & Greig, M 2004
The Limekilns of Upper Donside: A Forgotten Heritage, Aberdeenshire Council, Aberdeen

Cullingford, R A, Davidson, D A & Lewin, J (eds) 1980
Timescales in Geomorphology, Chichester

Curle, A O 1919
Note on a pottery mask and sherds of medieval pottery found at the Bass of Inverurie, with some particulars of the Bass, *Proc Soc Antiq Scot* 53 (1918–19), 46–50

Dalrymple, C E 1866
Notes on the excavation of two shell-middens on the eastern coast of Aberdeenshire, *Proc Soc Antiq Scot* 6 (1864–6), 423–6

Dalrymple, C E 1884
Notes of the excavation of the stone circle at Crichie, Aberdeenshire, *Proc Soc Antiq Scot* 18 (1883–4), 319–25

Davidson, C B 1870
Additional note on the supposed 'leather lamp' found in an urn in a short cist at Broomend, Inverurie, Aberdeenshire, *Proc Soc Antiq Scot* 7 (1866–8), 561–2

Davidson, D A & Simpson, I A 1994
Soils and landscape history: case studies from the Northern Isles of Scotland, in Foster and Smout (eds) 1994, 66–75

Davidson, Rev. J 1878
Inverurie and The Earldom of the Garioch: A Topographical and Historical Account of the Garioch, Edinburgh and Aberdeen

Davies, A L & Tipping, R 2001
Late Prehistoric and Historic Vegetation and Land-Use Change at Relaquheim, Strathdon, Aberdeenshire, Unpublished archive report, RCAHMS

Davies, A L, Tisdall, E & Tipping, R 2004
Holocene climatic variability and human settlement in the Scottish Highlands: fragility and robustness, in Housley and Coles (eds) 2004, 2–11

Dawson, J 1997
Early to mid-Holocene Vegetation Change at Kennethmont, north-east Scotland, Unpublished BSc dissertation, University of Stirling

Dean, A 1998
Foudland: Slate Quarriers and Crofters in Aberdeenshire, Insch

Dennison, E P, Ditchburn, D & Lynch, M (eds) 2002
Aberdeen before 1800: A New History, Aberdeen

DES (date)
Discovery and Excavation in Scotland, Council for Scottish Archaeology

Devine, T M 1994
The Transformation of Rural Scotland: Social Change and the Agrarian Economy, 1660–1815, Edinburgh

Diack, F C (Alexander, W M and Macdonald, J eds) 1944
The Inscriptions of Pictland: An Essay on the Sculptured and Inscribed Stones of the North-East and North of Scotland: with Other Writings and Collections, Third Spalding Club, Aberdeen

Dickson, T (ed) 1877
Accounts of the Lord High Treasurer of Scotland, 1473–1498, Vol. 1, Edinburgh

Dixon, P J 1998
Rural medieval settlement in Roxburghshire: excavations at Springwood Park, Kelso, *Proc Soc Antiq Scot* 128 (1998), 671–751

Dixon, P J 2003
Champagne country: a review of medieval settlement in lowland Scotland, in Govan (ed) 2003, 53–64

Dodgshon, R A 1981
Land and Society in early Scotland, Oxford

Donner, J J 1957
The geology and vegetation of Late-glacial retreat stages in Scotland, *Trans Roy Soc Edinburgh* 63, 221–64

Douglas, G & Oglethorpe, M 1993
Brick, Tile and Fireclay Industries in Scotland, RCAHMS, Edinburgh

Dowden, Rev. J (ed) 1903
Chartulary of the Abbey of Lindores 1195–1479, Scottish History Society, Edinburgh

Driscoll, S T 1987

The Early Historic Landscape of Strathearn, Unpublished PhD thesis, University of Glasgow

Driscoll, S T 1991

The archaeology of state formation, in Hanson and Slater (eds) 1991, 81–111

Dubois, A D 1984

On the climatic interpretation of the hydrogen isotope ratios in recent and fossil wood, *Bulletin de la Société Belge de Géologie* 93, 267–70

Dubois, A D & Ferguson, D K 1985

The climatic history of pine in the Cairngorms based on radiocarbon dates and stable isotope analysis, with an account of events leading up to its colonization, *Rev Palaeobotany and Palynology* 46, 55–80

Dubois, A D & Ferguson, D K 1988

Additional evidence for the climatic history of pine in the Cairngorms, based on radiocarbon dates and tree ring D/H ratios, *Rev Palaeobotany and Palynology* 54, 181–5

Dugmore, A J, Larsen, G & Newton, A J 1995

Seven tephra isochrones in Scotland, *The Holocene* 5, 257–66

Dumville, D N 1981

Primarius cohortis in Adomnan's Life of Columba, *Scottish Gaelic Studies* 13 (1978–81), 130–31

Duncan, A A M (ed) 1988

Regesta Regum Scotorum, The Acts of Robert I, King of Scots 1306–29, Vol. 5, Edinburgh

Durno, S E 1956

Pollen analysis of peat deposits in Scotland, *Scot Geogr Mag* 72, 177–87

Durno, S E 1957

Certain aspects of vegetational history in north-east Scotland, *Scot Geogr Mag* 73, 176–84

Durno, S E 1959

Pollen analysis of peat deposits in the eastern Grampians, *Scot Geogr Mag* 75, 102–11

Durno, S E 1961

Evidence regarding the rate of peat growth, *J Ecology* 49, 347–51

Durno, S E 1970

Pollen diagrams from three buried peats in the Aberdeen area, *Trans Bot Soc Edinburgh* 41, 43–50

Durno, S E 1976

Post-glacial change in vegetation, in Birse and Robertson (eds) 1976, 20–36

Durno, S E & Romans, J C C 1969

Evidence for variations in the altitudinal zonation of climate in Scotland and northern England since the Boreal period, *Scot Geogr Mag* 85, 31–3

Edwards, K J 1978a

Palaeoenvironmental and Archaeological Investigations in the Howe of Cromar, Grampian Region, Scotland, Unpublished PhD thesis, University of Aberdeen

Edwards, K J 1978b

Excavation and environmental archaeology of a small cairn associated with cultivation ridges in Aberdeenshire, *Proc Soc Antiq Scot* 109, 22–9

Edwards, K J 1979a

Palynological and temporal inference in the context of prehistory, with special reference to the evidence from lake and peat deposits, *J Archaeol Sci* 6, 255–70

Edwards, K J 1979b

Environmental impact in the prehistoric period, *Scot Archaeol Forum* 9 (1979), 27–42

Edwards, K J 1989

Meso-Neolithic vegetation impacts in Scotland and beyond – palynological considerations, in Bonsall (ed) 1989, 143–63

Edwards, K J 1990

Fire and the Scottish Mesolithic: evidence from microscopic charcoal, in Vermeesch and van Peer (eds) 1990, 71–9

Edwards, K J & Hirons, K R 1984

Cereal pollen grains in pre-elm decline deposits: implications for the earliest agriculture in Britain and Ireland, *J Archaeol Sci* 11, 71–80

Edwards, K J & Ralston, I B M 1984

Postglacial hunter-gatherers and vegetational history in Scotland, *Proc Soc Antiq Scot* 114 (1984), 15–34

Edwards, K J & Rowntree, K M 1980

Radiocarbon and palaeoenvironmental evidence for changing rates of erosion at a Flandrian Stage site in Scotland, in Cullingford, Davidson and Lewin (eds) 1980, 207–23

Edwards, K J & Whittington, G 2001

Lake sediments, erosion and landscape change during the Holocene in Britain and Ireland, *Catena* 42, 143–73

Edwards, K J, Whittington, G & Tipping, R 2000

The incidence of microscopic charcoal in late glacial deposits, *Palaeogeography, Palaeoclimatology, Palaeoecology* 164, 247–62

Eeles, F C 1909

Two incised slabs at Foveran, Aberdeenshire, and Oathlaw, Forfarshire, *Proc Soc Antiq Scot* 43 (1908–9), 308–16

Eeles, F C 1956

King's College Chapel, Aberdeen: Its Fittings, Ornaments, and Ceremonial in the Sixteenth Century, Edinburgh

Eogan, G 1994

The Accomplished Art: Gold and Gold-working in Britain and Ireland During the Bronze Age (c.2300–650 B.C.), Oxbow Monograph, Oxford

Epstein, S & Yapp, C J 1977

Isotope tree thermometers, *Nature* 266, 477–8

Ewan, L A 1981

A Palynological Investigation of a Peat Deposit near Banchory: some Local and Regional Environmental Implications, O'Dell Memorial Monograph No. 11, Department of Geography, University of Aberdeen, Aberdeen

Fairweather, A D & Ralston, I B M 1993

Neolithic plant macrofossils from the Balbridie timber hall, Grampian Region, Scotland: the building, the date, the plant macrofossils, *Antiquity* 67 (1993), 313–23

Fawcett, R 1994

Scottish Architecture from the Accession of the Stewarts to the Reformation, 1371–1560, Vol. 1, Edinburgh

Feachem, R W 1955

Fortifications, in Wainwright (ed) 1955, 66–86

Feachem, R W 1966

The hillforts of northern Britain, in Rivet (ed) 1966, 59–87

Feachem, R W 1971

Unfinished hill-forts, in Jesson and Hill (ed) 1971, 19–39

Feachem, R W 1977

Guide to Prehistoric Scotland, 2nd ed, London

Fenton, A & Walker, B 1981

The Rural Architecture of Scotland, Edinburgh

Fitzpatrick, E A 1963

An interglacial soil at Teindland, Morayshire, *Nature* 207, 621–2

Fleet, H 1938

Erosion surfaces in the Grampian Highlands of Scotland, *Amsterdam: Union Géographique Internationale – Commission Cartographie des surfaces d'Aplanissement Tertiaries*, 91–4

Forsyth, K 1997

Language in Pictland, Studia Hameliana 2, Utrecht

Fossitt, J A 1994

Late-glacial and Holocene vegetation history of western Donegal, Ireland, *Proc Roy Irish Acad* 94B, 1–31

Foster, S & Smout, T C (eds) 1994

The History of Soils and Field Systems, Aberdeen

Foster, S M 1996

Picts, Gaels and Scots, London

Fowler, P J (ed) 1972

Archaeology and the Landscape: Essays for L V Grinsell, London

Fraser, D M 1998

An investigation into distributions of ach?, bal? and pit? Place-Names in North East Scotland, Unpublished M.Litt thesis, University of Aberdeen

Fraser, G K & Godwin, H 1955

Two Scottish pollen diagrams: Carnwath Moss, Lanarkshire, and Strichen Moss, Aberdeenshire, *New Phytologist* 54, 216–21

Fraser, G M 1905

Historical Aberdeen: the Castle and the Castle-Hill, the Snow Church, the Woolmanhill and neighbourhood, and the Guestrow, Aberdeen

Fraser, I 1989

The later mediaeval burgh kirk of St Nicholas, Aberdeen, Unpublished PhD thesis, University of Edinburgh

Fraser, I A 1986

Norse and Celtic place-names around the Dornoch Firth, in Baldwin (ed) 1986, 23–32

Fraser, J 2005

The Roman Conquest of Scotland: The Battle of Mons Graupius AD 84, Stroud

Frere, S S 1990

Roman Britain in 1989. I. Sites explored, *Britannia* 21 (1990), 304–64

Garden, J 1770

A Letter from the Reverend Dr. James Garden, Professor of Theology in the King's College at Aberdeen, to John Aubrey, Esq. on the circular stone monuments in Scotland, *Archaeologia* 1 (1770), 314–21

Gardiner, V (ed) 1987

International Geomorphology 1986 Volume II, Chichester

Gemmell, A M D (ed) 1975

Quaternary Studies in North East Scotland, Department of Geography, University of Aberdeen, Aberdeen

Gentles, D 1993

Vitrified forts, *Current Archaeology* 133 (1993), 18–20

Gibb, A W 1910

The relation of the Don to the Avon at Inchrory, Banffshire, *Trans Edinburgh Geol Soc* 9, 227–9

Gibson, A & Simpson, D D A (eds) 1998

Prehistoric Ritual and Religion: Essays in Honour of Aubrey Burl, Stroud

Gilbert, J M 1979

Hunting and Hunting Reserves in Scotland, Edinburgh

Giles, J (Simpson, W D ed) 1936

Drawings of Aberdeenshire Castles, Third Spalding Club, Aberdeen

Gillan, J 1863

Notes of some antiquities in the parish of Alford, Aberdeenshire, *Proc Soc Antiq Scot* 4 (1860–62), 382–6

Gimingham, C H 1964

Maritime and sub-maritime communities, in Burnett (ed) 1964, 67–143

Glasser, N F & Bennett, M R (eds) 1996

The Quaternary of the Cairngorms: Field Guide, Quaternary Research Association, London

Glendinning, B D & Dunwell, A J 2000
Excavations of the Gask frontier tower and temporary camp at Blackhill Wood, Ardoch, Perth and Kinross, *Britannia* 31 (2000), 255–90

Glentworth, R 1944
Studies on the soils developed on basic igneous rocks in central Aberdeenshire, *Trans Roy Soc Edinburgh* 61, 149–56

Glentworth, R & Muir, J W 1963
The Soils of the Country round Aberdeen, Inverurie and Fraserburgh, Edinburgh

Godwin, H & Willis, E H 1959
Cambridge University natural radiocarbon measurements I, *Radiocarbon* 1, 63

Godwin, H 1975
History of the British Flora, 2nd ed, Cambridge

Gordon, A 1726
Itinerarium Septentrionale, London

Gordon, C A 1960
Professor James Garden's Letters to John Aubrey, 1692–1695, in *The Miscellany of the Third Spalding Club*, III, Third Spalding Club, Aberdeen

Gordon, J 1842
Aberdoniae Utriusque Descriptio. A Description of Both Touns of Aberdeen, Spalding Club, Edinburgh

Gordon, J E (ed) 1997
Reflections on the Ice Age in Scotland, Scottish Association of Geography Teachers and Scottish Natural Heritage, Glasgow

Gordon, J E & Sutherland, D G 1993
The Quaternary of Scotland, London

Gough, R (ed) 1789 and 1806
Britannia, London

Govan, S (ed) 2003
Medieval or Later Rural Settlement in Scotland: 10 Years On, Historic Scotland, Edinburgh

Graham, A 1976
The archaeology of Joseph Anderson, *Proc Soc Antiq Scot* 107 (1975–6), 279–98

Grant MS
Plan of Lands & Barony's of Monymusk …belonging humbly to Sir Archibald Grant Baronet of [Monymusk] …Anno 1774, Unpublished photographic copy RCAHMS D49151CN

Grant, A 1993
Thanes and thanages from the eleventh to the fourteenth centuries, in Grant and Stringer (ed) 1993, 39–81, Edinburgh

Grant, A 1996
Baronies, lordships and earldoms in the early 15th century, in McNeill and MacQueen (ed) 1996, 201–7

Grant, A & Stringer, K J (ed) 1993
Medieval Scotland: Crown, Lordship and Community, Essays Presented to G W S Barrow, Edinburgh

Gray, J M & Lowe, J J (eds) 1977
Studies in the Scottish Lateglacial Environment, Oxford

Gray, M 1976
North-east agriculture and the labour force 1790–1875, in Maclaren (ed) 1976, 86–104

Gregory, R A 2001
Excavations by the late G D B Jones and C M Daniels along the Moray Firth littoral, *Proc Soc Antiq Scot* 131 (2001), 177–222

Greig, C, Greig, M & Ashmore, P 2000
Excavation of a cairn cemetery at Lundin Links, Fife, in 1965–6, *Proc Soc Antiq Scot* 130 (2000), 585–636

Grieve, I C, Davidson, D A & Gordon, J E 1995
Nature, extent and severity of soil erosion in upland Scotland, *Land Degradation & Rehabilitation* 6, 41–55

Hale, A 2003
Prehistoric rock carvings in Strath Tay, *Tayside Fife Archaeol J* 9 (2003), 6–13

Hall, A M 1984
The Quaternary of Buchan: Field Guide, Quaternary Research Association, Cambridge

Hall, A M 1986
Deep weathering patterns in north-east Scotland and their geomorphological significance, *Zeitschrift für Geomorphologie* 30, 407–22

Hall, A M 1987
Weathering and relief development in Buchan, Scotland, in Gardiner (ed) 1987, 991–1005

Hall, A M 1991
Pre-Quaternary landscape evolution in the Scottish Highlands, *Trans Roy Soc Edinburgh: Earth Sci* 82, 1–26

Hall, A M 1996
The paleic relief of the Cairngorm Mountains, in Glasser and Bennett (eds) 1996, 13–27

Hall, A M 1997
Landscape evolution in Scotland before the ice age, in Gordon (ed) 1997, 31–7

Halliday, S P 1995
The Borders in prehistory, in Omand (ed) 1995, 21–38

Halliday, S P 2000
Hut-circle settlements in the Scottish landscape, *Northern Archaeology* 17/18 (1999), 49–65

Halliday, S P 2006
Into the dim light of history: more of the same or all change?, in Woolf (ed) 2006, 11–27

Halliday, S P 2007
Unenclosed Roundhouses in Scotland: occupation, abandonment, and the character of settlement, in Burgess, C, Topping, P and Lynch, F (eds), *Beyond Stonehenge: Essays on the Bronze Age in Honour of Colin Burgess*, Oxbow Monograph

Hamilton, H (ed) 1945

Selections from the Monymusk Papers (1713–1755), Scottish History Society, Ser 3, Edinburgh

Hamilton, H (ed) 1946

Life and Labour on an Aberdeenshire Estate 1735–1750 (Being selections from the Monymusk Papers), Third Spalding Club, Aberdeen

Hansom, J 1998

The coastal geomorphology of Scotland: understanding sediment budgets for effective coastal management, in Baxter *et al.* (eds) 1998, 34–44

Hanson, W S 1978

Roman campaigns north of the Forth-Clyde isthmus: the evidence of the temporary camps, *Proc Soc Antiq Scot* 109 (1977–8), 140–50

Hanson, W S & Slater, E A (eds) 1991

Scottish Archaeology: New Perceptions, Aberdeen

Harbottle, B & Ellison, M 1981

An excavation in the castle ditch, Newcastle-upon-Tyne, 1974–6, *Archaeologia Aeliana*, Ser 5, 9 (1981), 75–250

Harkness, D D & Wilson, H W 1979

Scottish Universities Research and Reactor Centre radiocarbon measurements III, *Radiocarbon* 21, 203–56

Harris, D R (ed) 1994

The Archaeology of V Gordon Childe, London

Harrison, J G 2001a

Glenernan: A Report for RCAHMS, Unpublished manuscript, RCAHMS MS1155/4

Harrison, J G 2001b

Rhynie and Essie: A Report for RCAHMS, Unpublished manuscript, RCAHMS MS1155/5

Hawke-Smith, C F 1980

Two Mesolithic sites near Newburgh, Aberdeenshire, *Proc Soc Antiq Scot* 110, 497–534

Haws, C H 1972

Scottish parish clergy at the Reformation 1540–1574, Scottish Record Society, Edinburgh

Henderson, I 1958

The origin centre of the Pictish symbol stones, *Proc Soc Antiq Scot* 91 (1957–8), 44–60

Henderson, I 1967

The Picts, London

Henderson, I 1972

The Picts of Aberdeenshire and their monuments, *Archaeol J* 129 (1972), 166

Henry, D (ed) 1997

The worm, the germ and the thorn: Pictish and related studies presented to Isabel Henderson, Balgavies

Henshall, A S 1983

The Neolithic pottery from Easterton of Roseisle, Moray, in O'Connor and Clark (eds.) 1983, 19–44

Hibbert, S 1857

Collections relative to vitrified sites, *Archaeologia Scotica* 4 (1857), 280–97

Hingley, R, Moore, H L, Triscott, J E & Wilson, G 1997

The excavation of two later Iron Age fortified homesteads at Aldclune, Blair Atholl, Perth & Kinross, *Proc Soc Antiq Scot* 127 (1997), 407–66

Hirons, K R & Edwards, K J 1986

Events at and around the first and second *Ulmus* declines: palaeoecological investigations in Co. Tyrone, Northern Ireland, *New Phytologist* 104, 131–53

Histories

See *Tacitus: The Histories*, Penguin Classics (2004), translated by K Wellesley

Hope-Taylor, B 1977

Yeavering. An Anglo-British centre of early Northumbria, Dept Env Archaeol Rep No. 7, London

Housley, R A & Coles, G M (eds) 2004

Atlantic Connections & Adaptations, Oxford

Howard, D 1995

Scottish Architecture from the Reformation to the Restoration, 1560–1660, Vol. 2, Edinburgh

Hughes, M K & Diaz, H F 1994

Was there a 'medieval warm period', and if so, where and when?, *Climatic Change* 26, 109–42

Hulse, E (ed) 1999

Thinking with Both Hands: Sir Daniel Wilson in the Old World and the New, Toronto

Hunter, F 2002a

Roman Britain in 2001. I. Sites explored 2. Scotland, *Britannia* 33 (2002), 284–90

Hunter, F 2002b

Birnie; buying peace on the northern frontier, *Current Archaeology* 181 (2002), 12–16

Hunter, J R 1997

A persona for the northern Picts, Groam House Lecture 7, Rosemarkie

Hunter, M 1975

John Aubrey and the Realm of Learning, London

Hunter, M 2001

The Occult Laboratory: Magic, Science and Second-Sight in Late Seventeenth-Century Scotland, Woodbridge

Huntley, B 1993

Rapid early Holocene migration and high abundance of hazel *(Corylus avellana* L.*)*: alternative hypotheses, in Chambers (ed) 1993, 205–15

Huntley, B 1994

Late Devensian and Holocene palaeoecology and palaeoenvironments of the Morrone Birkwoods, Aberdeenshire, Scotland, *J Quaternary Sci* 9, 311–36

Huntly, C Marquis of (ed) 1894

Records of Aboyne 1230–1681, Aberdeen

Inglis, J 1987

Patterns in stone, patterns in population: symbol stones seen from beyond the Mounth, in Small (ed) 1987, 73–9

Innes, C N (ed) 1845

Registrum Episcopatus Aberdonensis. Ecclesie Cathedralis Aberdonensis Regesta Que Extant in Unum, Spalding Club, Edinburgh

Ireland, S 1996

Roman Britain: A sourcebook, 2nd ed, London

Jervise, A 1864

Notice of the 'eirde house', or underground chamber, at Migvie, Aberdeenshire, with plans, *Proc Soc Antiq Scot* 5 (1862–4), 304–6

Jesson, M & Hill, D (eds) 1971

The Iron Age and its Hill-Forts, papers presented to Sir Mortimer Wheeler, Southampton

Johnson, M R W 1983

Dalradian, in Craig (ed) 1983, 77–104

Jolly, W 1882

On cup-marked stones in the neighbourhood of Inverness; with an appendix on cup-marked stones in the Western Islands, *Proc Soc Antiq Scot* 16 (1881–2), 300–401

Jones, B, Keillar, I, & Maude, K 1993

The Moray aerial survey: discovering the prehistoric and proto-historic landscape, in Sellar (ed) 1993, 47–74

Jones, R H 2006

The Temporary Encampments of the Roman Army in Scotland, Unpublished PhD thesis, University of Glasgow

Jones, V J *et al*. 1993

Palaeolimnological evidence for the acidification and atmospheric contamination of lochs in the Cairngorm and Lochnagar areas of Scotland, *J Ecology* 81, 3–24

Keiller, A 1927

Interim Report upon Such of the Stone Circles of Aberdeenshire and Kincardineshire as have been Scheduled as Ancient Monuments, London

Keiller, A 1928

Final Report upon Such of the Megalithic Monuments of Aberdeenshire as have been Scheduled as Ancient Monuments, London

Keiller, A 1934

Megalithic Monuments of North-East Scotland: Being a Paper Read on September 7th, 1934, at the Meeting of the British Association at Aberdeen, London

Keith, G S 1811

A General View of the Agriculture of Aberdeenshire; drawn up under the direction of the Board of Agriculture, Aberdeen

Kemp, D W 1887

Tours in Scotland 1747, 1750, 1760, by R Pococke, Bishop of Meath, Scottish Hist Soc, Edinburgh

Kennedy, W 1818

Annals of Aberdeen, Vols 1–2, London

Kenworthy, J B 1975

The prehistory of north-east Scotland, in Gemmell (ed) 1975, 74–81

Kenyon, J R 1990

Medieval Fortifications, Leicester

Kilbride-Jones, H 1994

In postscript: three Recollections of Childe the man, in Harris (ed) 1994, 135–9

Kilbride-Jones, H E 1935

An account of the excavation of the stone circle at Loanhead of Daviot, and of the standing-stones of Cullerlie, Echt, both in Aberdeenshire, on behalf of HM Office of Works, *Proc Soc Antiq Scot* 69 (1934–5), 168–223

Kilbride-Jones, H E 1936

Late Bronze Age cemetery: being an account of the excavations of 1935 at Loanhead of Daviot, Aberdeenshire, on behalf of HM Office of Works, *Proc Soc Antiq Scot* 70 (1935–6), 278–303

Kirk, W 1954

Prehistoric sites at the Sands of Forvie, Aberdeenshire, *Aberdeen Univ Rev* 35 (1953–4), 150–71

Kullman, L 1988

Holocene history of the forest-alpine tundra ecotone in the Scandes Mountains (central Sweden), *New Phytologist* 108, 101–10

Laing, A 1828

The Donean tourist: giving an account of the battles, gentlemen's seats, families, with their origin, armorial ensigns, badges of distinction, carefully selected from the best authorities; and interspersed with anecdotes, and ancient national ballads, Aberdeen

Leith-Hay, Sir A 1849

The Castellated Architecture of Aberdeenshire, Aberdeen

Leivers, M, Roberts, J & Petersen, R 2000

The cairn at East Finnercy, Dunecht, Aberdeenshire, *Proc Soc Antiq Scot* 130 (2000), 183–95

Leslie, A 1995

Roman temporary camps in Britain, Unpublished PhD thesis, University of Glasgow

Lewis, A L 1888

Stone circles near Aberdeen, *J Roy Archaeol Inst* 17 (1888), 44–57

Lewis, A L 1900

The stone circles of Scotland, *J Anthrop Inst* 30 (1900), 56–73

Lewis, C, Mitchell-Fox, P & Dyer, C 2001

Village, Hamlet and Field: Changing Medieval Settlements in Central England, Macclesfield

Lindsay, J 1968

The canals of Scotland, Newton Abbot

Linton, D L 1951

Watershed breaching by ice in Scotland, *Trans Inst British Geogr* 15, 1–15.

Linton, D L 1954
Some Scottish river captures re-examined. III. The beheading of the Don, *Scot Geogr Mag* 70, 64–78

Littlejohn, D 1906
Records of the Sheriff Court of Aberdeen, 1598–1649, New Spalding Club, Vol. 2, Aberdeen

Lockyer, Sir N 1909
Stonehenge and Other British Stone Monuments Astronomically Considered, London

Logan, J 1829a
Two drawings of druidical circles in Aberdeenshire, accompanied by some remarks, *Archaeologia* 22 (1829), 409–11

Logan, J 1829b
Observations on several circles of stones in Scotland, presumed to be druidical ... in a letter addressed to the Right Honourable the Earl of Aberdeen, KT President, *Archaeologia* 22 (1829), 198–203

Logan, J 1829c
Observations on several monumental stones in the north of Scotland, *Archaeologia* 22 (1829), 55–8

Logan, J 1831a
The Scottish Gael; or, Celtic Manners, as Preserved among the Highlanders: Being an Historical, and Descriptive Account of the Inhabitants, Antiquities, and National Peculiarities of Scotland, London

Logan, J 1831b
Ecclesiastical Collections for Aberdeenshire, *Archaeologia Scotica* 3 (1831), 4–16

Loveday, R 2006
Inscribed across the landscape. The Cursus Enigma, Stroud

Low, A 1866
Notices of the localities in a grant of the lands of Keig and Monymusk by Malcolm, King of Scots, to the church of St Andrews; and a sketch or history of the priory of Monymusk, *Proc Soc Antiq Scot* 6 (1864–6), 218–32

Low, A 1936
A short cist containing a Beaker and other relics at Newlands, Oyne, Aberdeenshire, *Proc Soc Antiq Scot* 70 (1935–6), 326–31

Lowe, J J & Walker, M J C 1997
Reconstructing Quaternary Environments, 2nd ed, London

Lowe, J J, Coope, G R, Sheldrick, C, Harkness, D D & Walker, M J C 1995
Direct comparison of UK temperatures and Greenland snow accumulation rates, 15,000–12,000 yrs ago, *J Quaternary Sci* 10, 175–80

Lukis, W C 1885
Survey of certain megalithic monuments in Scotland, Cumberland and Westmoreland, executed on behalf of the Society of Antiquaries of London in the summer of 1884, *Proc Soc Antiq London*, Ser 2, 10 (1883–5), 302–20

Lumsden, H G 1878
Notes of the opening of two eirde-houses at Clova, Kildrummy, Aberdeenshire, and of a cist with an urn and flint implements at New Leslie, *Proc Soc Antiq Scot* 12 (1876–8), 356–8

Lynch, F & Ritchie, J N G 1975
Small cairns in Argyll: some recent work (ii) Kerb-cairns, *Proc Soc Antiq Scot* 106 (1974–5), 30–3

McCullagh, R P J & Tipping, R (eds) 1998
The Lairg Project 1988–96: The Evolution of an Archaeological Landscape in Northern Scotland, Scottish Trust for Archaol Res Monograph 3, Edinburgh

MacDonald, A 1973
'Annat' in Scotland: a provisional review, *Scot Stud* 17 pt 2 (1973), 136–46

MacDonald, J 1891
Place Names in Strathbogie, Aberdeen

MacGibbon, D & Ross, T 1887–92
The Castellated and Domestic Architecture of Scotland from the Twelfth to the Eighteenth Century, Vols 1–5, Edinburgh

MacGibbon, D & Ross, T 1896–7
The Ecclesiastical Architecture of Scotland from the Earliest Christian Times to the Seventeenth Century, Vols 1–3, Edinburgh

McKean, C 2001
The Scottish Chateau: the Country House of Renaissance Scotland, Stroud

MacKie, E 1969
Radiocarbon dates and the Scottish Iron Age, *Antiquity* 43 (1969), 15–26

Macklin, M G 1999
Holocene river environments in prehistoric Britain: human interaction and impact, *J Quaternary Sci* 14, 521–30

Maclagan, C 1875
The Hill Forts, Stone Circles and Other Structural Remains of Ancient Scotland, Edinburgh

Maclagan, C 1880
Notice of the discovery of two sculptured stones, with symbols, at Rhynie, Aberdeenshire, *Proc Soc Antiq Scot* 14 (1879–80), 11–13

Maclaren, A A (ed) 1976
Social Class in Scotland: Past and Present, Edinburgh

Maclean, L (ed) 1975
The Hub of the Highlands, The Book of Inverness and District, The Centenary Volume of Inverness Field Club, 1875–1975, Inverness

McNeill, P G B & MacQueen, H L (eds) 1996
Atlas of Scottish History to 1707, The Scottish Medievalists and Department of Geography, University of Edinburgh, Edinburgh

Macpherson, W M 1895
Materials for a history of the church and priory of Monymusk, Aberdeen

Mack, A 1997
The Rhynie cluster – or clusters?, *Pictish Arts Soc J* 11 (Summer 1997), 2–5

Maitland, W 1757
The History and Antiquities of Scotland from the Earliest Account to the Death of James I, Vol. 1, London

Maizels, J & Aitken, J 1991
Palaeohydrological change during deglaciation in upland Britain: a case study from northeast Scotland, in Starkel, Gregory and Thornes (eds) 1991, 105–46

Malone, C 2001
Neolithic Britain and Ireland, Stroud

Marshall, D N 1977
Carved stone balls, *Proc Soc Antiq Scot* 108 (1976–7), 40–72

Maxwell, G S 1990
A Battle Lost: Romans and Caledonians at Mons Graupius, Edinburgh

Mercator, G 1578
Tabulae Geographicae Cl. Ptolemei Admentem Autoris Restitutae & Emendate Per Gerardum Mercatorem, Cologne

Mercer, R J 1978
The Castle Frazer (Balgorkar) Stone Circle: A Further Note, in Slade 1978, *Proc Soc Antiq Scot* 109 (1977–8), 273–7

Merritt, J W, Connell, E R & Bridgland, D R (eds) 2000
The Quaternary of the Banffshire Coast and Buchan: Field Guide, Quaternary Research Association, London

Miller, M 1975
Stilicho's Pictish war, *Britannia* 6 (1975), 141–5

Mills, C M & Coles, G (eds) 1998
Life on the Edge: Human Settlement & Marginality, Oxford

Milne, J 1892
Traces of early man in Buchan, *Trans Buchan Fld Club* 2 (1891–2), 97–108

Mitchell, A 1862
Notice of the recent excavation of an underground building at Buchaam, Strathdon, on the property of Sir Charles Forbes, Baronet, of Newe and Edinglassie, *Proc Soc Antiq Scot* 4 (1860–2), 436–40

Mitchell, Sir A & Clark, J T (eds) 1906–8
Geographical Collections Relating to Scotland Made by Walter Macfarlane, Vols 1–3, Scottish History Society 51–3, Edinburgh

Moir, J (ed) 1894
Boece's Bishops of Aberdeen, Aberdeen

Morrison, A 1979
A Bronze Age burial site at South Mound, Houston, Renfrewshire, *Glasgow Archaeol J* 6 (1979), 20–45

Munro, M 1986
Geology of the Country around Aberdeen. Memoir of the British Geological Survey, Sheet 77 (Scotland), London

Murdoch, W 1975
The geomorphology and glacial deposits of the area around Aberdeen, in Gemmell (ed) 1975, 14–18

Murray, D M & Ralston, I B M 1997
The excavation of a square-ditched barrow and other cropmarks at Boysack Mills, Inverkeilor, Angus, *Proc Soc Antiq Scot* 127 (1997), 359–86

Murray, H 2002
Late prehistoric settlement, Berryhill, Aberdeenshire, *Proc Soc Antiq Scot* 132 (2002), 213–27

Murray, H K & Murray, J C 1993
Excavations at Rattray, Aberdeenshire. A Scottish deserted burgh, *Med Archaeol* 37, 109–218

Murray, H K, Murray, J C, Shepherd, A N & Shepherd, I A G 1992
Evidence of agricultural activity of the later second millenium BC at Rattray, Aberdeenshire, *Proc Soc Antiq Scot* 122, 113–25

Murray, L J 1999
A Zest for Life: the Story of Alexander Keiller, Swindon

Name Book (County)
Original Name Books of the Ordnance Survey

NAS
The National Archives of Scotland

NAS CR 8
Crown Estate Records for the Duke of Gordon's estates

NAS GD 124
Mar and Kellie Papers

NAS GD 44
Gordon Castle Manuscripts

NAS RHP 232
Plan of Kincraigie Estate, Tough 1769

NAS RHP 260/1
Plan of that part of the lands of Forbes comprehending the parish of Kearn. Property of Capt. John Forbes of Newe. Surveyor John Home [*c.*1771]

NAS RHP 260/2
Plan of that part of the lands of Forbes comprehending the parish of Clatt. Property of Capt. John Forbes of Newe. Surveyor John Home [*c.*1771]

NAS RHP 2254
Plan of part of the Lordship of Huntly lying within the parishes of Rhynie, Essie and Gairtly ... Property of the Duke of Gordon. Survey by Thos. Milne Anno 1776

NAS RHP 2256
Plan of the lands of Essie and Lesmoir. Surveyor Thomas Milne [*c.*1776]

NAS RHP 2257
Plan of Longley, Garbet and Boganclogh. Surveyor Thomas Milne [*c.*1776]

NAS RHP 2258

Plan of Old Merdrum. Surveyor Thomas Milne
[*c*.1776]

NAS RHP 2259

Plan of New Merdrum, Ward, Stonerives and
Backstrypes. Surveyor Thomas Milne [*c*.1776]

NAS RHP 2260

Plan of Over Mytts and Nether Mytts. Surveyor
Thomas Milne [*c*.1776]

NAS RHP 2261

Plan of Brae of Scurdargue, Howtown, Scurdargue
and Newseat. Surveyor Thomas Milne [*c*.1776]

NAS RHP 2262

Plan of the Farm of Newseat 1822

NAS RHP 2264

Plan of Windyfield and Miltown of Noth. Surveyor
Thomas Milne [*c*.1776]

NAS RHP 2265

Plan of the Farm of Blackmiddens as now divided
for Enclosing and Improvements by Archd Shier
1827

NAS RHP 2266

Plan of New Forrest and Old Forrest [*c*.1776]

NAS RHP 2267

Plan of Cran's Mill and Finglenny. Surveyor Thomas
Milne [*c*.1776]

NAS RHP 4156

Plan of contraverted ground called Feith Bhait (Fae
Vaet), 1776

NAS RHP 5198

Book of six plans of the estates of Leith Hall
belonging to John Leith Esq. showing the extent of
each farm likewise the different quality of each field:
1758

NAS RHP 5199

Book of thirteen plans of the estates of Leslie
belonging to John Leith Esq. showing the extent of
each farm likewise the different quality of each field:
1758

NAS RHP 14753

Plan of the estate of Knockespock, Terpersie ...
belonging to James Gordon of Moorplace [late 18th
century]

NAS SC 1

Sheriff Court Records for Aberdeenshire

Needham, S 2004

Migdale – Marnoch: sunburst of Scottish metallurgy,
in Shepherd and Barclay (eds) 2004, 217–45

Nicolaisen, W F H 1976

Scottish Place-names: their study and significance,
London

Nicolaisen, W F H 1997

On Pictish rivers and their confluences, in Henry
(ed) 1997, 113–18

NLS

National Library of Scotland

NLS Gordon MS

Formarten and part of Marr and Buquhan by Robert
Gordon, *c*.1636–52, NLS, Gordon 32 manuscript

NSA 1845

The New Statistical Account of Scotland, Edinburgh

NTS

National Trust for Scotland

NTS Castle Fraser MS

Castle Fraser: historic landscape survey by Peter
McGowan Associates with AOC (Scotland) Ltd and
Patricia Thompson 1996, Unpublished report

NTS Leith Hall MS

Survey of the lands of Leith Hall 1797

O'Connor, A & Clark, D V (eds) 1983

*From the Stone Age to the Forty Five: studies
presented to RBK Stevenson*, Edinburgh

Ogston, Sir A (Simpson, W D ed) 1931

The Prehistoric Antiquities of the Howe of Cromar,
Third Spalding Club, Aberdeen

Omand, D (ed) 1987

The Grampian Book, Golspie

Omand, D (ed) 1995

The Borders Book, Edinburgh

Orem, W 1830

*A description of the Chanonry, Cathedral and King's
College of Old Aberdeen, in the years 1724–5*,
Aberdeen

Ortelius, A 1590

*Britannicarum Insularum Vetus Descriptio;
Additamentum IV. Theatri Orbis Terrarum*, Antwerp

Pan Lat Vet

Panegyrici Latini Veteres, Mynors, R A B (ed) 1934,
Oxford

**Parker, A G, Goudie, A S, Anderson, D E,
Robinson, M A & Bonsall, C 2001**

A review of the mid-Holocene elm decline in the
British Isles, *Progress in Physical Geography* 26,
1–45

Paterson, H M L & Lacaille, A D 1936

Banchory microliths, *Proc Soc Antiq Scot* 70,
419–34

Paul, J B (ed) 1984

*Registrum Magni Sigilli Regum Scotorum,
1424–1513*, Vol. 2, Edinburgh

Paul, J B 1908

*The Scots Peerage, Founded on Wood's Edition of Sir
Robert Douglas's Peerage of Scotland, containing an
historical and genealogical account of the nobility of
that kingdom*, Vol. 5, Edinburgh

Paul, J B & Thomson J M (eds) 1984

*Registrum Magni Sigilli Regum Scotorum,
1513–1546*, Vol. 3, Edinburgh

Pears, N V 1975a

Radiocarbon dating of peat macrofossils in the
Cairngorm Mountains, Scotland, *Trans Bot Soc
Edinburgh* 42, 255–60

Pears, N V 1975b
The growth rate of hill peats in Scotland, *Geologiska Foreningens I Stockholm Forhandlingar* 97, 265–70

Pears, N V 1988
Pine stumps, radiocarbon dates and stable isotope analysis in the Cairngorm Mountains: some observations, *Rev Palaeobotany and Palynology* 54, 175–85

Pennant, T 1776
A Tour in Scotland 1772, Vol. 2, London

Phillips, T 2003
Fieldwalking on Donside, Aberdeenshire, 2002, Typescript report, Department of Archaeology, University of Reading

Phillips, T 2005
The results of fieldwalking at Tarland and Castle Forbes, in Bradley 2005, 87–97

Piggott, S 1972
Excavation of the Dalladies long barrow, Fettercairn, Kincardineshire, *Proc Soc Antiq Scot* 104 (1971–2), 23–47

Pinkerton, J 1814
An Enquiry into the History of Scotland, Preceding the Reign of Malcolm III, or the Year 1056, Including the Authentic History of that Period, Edinburgh

Pollard, A & Morrison, A (eds) 1996
The Early Prehistory of Scotland, Edinburgh

Preece, R C, Bennett, K D & Robinson, J E 1984
The biostratigraphy of an early Flandrian tufa at Inchrory, Glen Avon, Banffshire, *Scottish J Geol* 20, 143–59

Raftery, B & Hickey, J (eds) 2001
Recent Developments in Wetland Research, Seandálaíocht: Mon 2, Dept Archaeol, UCD, and WARP (Wetland Archaeol Res Proj) Occasional Paper 14, Dublin

Ralston, I B M 1980
The Green Castle and the promontory forts of north-east Scotland, *Scot Archaeol Forum* 10 (1980), 27–40

Ralston, I B M 1982
A timber hall at Balbridie Farm, *Aberdeen Univ Rev* 168 (1982), 238–49

Ralston, I B M 1987
Portknockie: promontory forts and Pictish settlement in the North-East, in Small (ed) 1987, 15–26

Ralston, I B M 1996
Four short cists from north-east Scotland, *Proc Soc Antiq Scot* 126 (1996), 121–55

Ralston, I B M 2004
The Hillforts of Pictland since 'The Problem of the Picts', Groam House Museum Academic Lecture Series, Rosemarkie

Ralston, I B M & Sabine, K A 2000
Excavations of second and first millennia BC remains on the sands of Forvie, Slains, Aberdeenshire, Dept Geogr & Environment,

University of Aberdeen, Aberdeen, O'Dell Memorial Monograph No. 28

Ramsay, A 1879
History of the Highland and Agricultural Society of Scotland, Edinburgh and London

Rapson, S C 1985
Minimum age of corrie moraine ridges in the Cairngorm Mountains, Scotland, *Boreas* 14, 155–9

RCAHMS
Royal Commission on the Ancient and Historical Monuments of Scotland

RCAHMS 1956
An Inventory of the Ancient and Historical Monuments of Roxburghshire, Edinburgh

RCAHMS 1963
Stirlingshire: an Inventory of the Ancient Monuments, Edinburgh

RCAHMS 1990
North-east Perth: an archaeological landscape, Edinburgh

RCAHMS 1994
South-east Perth: an archaeological landscape, Edinburgh

RCAHMS 1995
Mar Lodge Estate, Grampian: An Archaeological Survey, Edinburgh

RCAHMS 1997a
Eastern Dumfriesshire: An Archaeological Landscape, Edinburgh

RCAHMS 1997b
Aberdeen on Record, Edinburgh

RCAHMS 2001
'Well Shelterd and Waterd': Menstrie Glen, a farming landscape near Stirling, Edinburgh

RCAHMS and Historic Scotland 2002
But the Walls Remained: a survey of unroofed rural settlement depicted on the first edition of the Ordnance Survey 6-inch map of Scotland, Edinburgh

RCAHMS Marginal Lands
Typescript of RCAHMS Survey of Marginal Lands

RCAHMS MS:SAS 39
Society of Antiquaries of Scotland: A collection of annotated plans of stone circles in Kincardineshire and Aberdeenshire: plans by J Rait and A Crease, redrawn by H Dryden

Reid, R W 1924
Illustrated catalogue of specimens from prehistoric interments found in the north-east of Scotland and preserved in the Anthropological Museum, Marischal College, University of Aberdeen, Aberdeen

Richardson, D M (ed) 1998
Ecology and Biogeography of Pinus, Cambridge

Rideout, J 1995
Carn Dubh, Moulin, Perthshire: survey and excavation of an archaeological landscape, *Proc Soc Antiq Scot* 125 (1995), 139–95

Ritchie, A 2000 (ed)
Neolithic Orkney in its European Context,
Cambridge

Ritchie, J 1910
The sculptured stones of Clatt, Aberdeenshire, *Proc
Soc Antiq Scot* 44 (1909–10), 203–15

Ritchie, J 1911
Some old crosses and unlettered sepulchral
monuments in Aberdeenshire, *Proc Soc Antiq Scot* 45
(1910–11), 333–53

Ritchie, J 1912
An account of the watch-houses, mortsafes, and
public vaults in Aberdeenshire churchyards,
formerly used for the protection of the dead from the
Resurrectionists, *Proc Soc Antiq Scot* 46 (1911–12),
285–326

Ritchie, J 1915
Notes on some Aberdeenshire sculptured stones and
crosses, *Proc Soc Antiq Scot* 49 (1914–15), 33–49

Ritchie, J 1916
Description of sculptured symbol stone at Rayne and
small cross at Culsalmond, Aberdeenshire, *Proc Soc
Antiq Scot* 46 (1915–16), 285–326

Ritchie, J 1917
Notes on some stone circles in central Aberdeenshire,
Proc Soc Antiq Scot 51 (1916–17), 30–47

Ritchie, J 1918
Cup-marks on the stone circles and standing-stones
of Aberdeenshire and part of Banffshire, *Proc Soc
Antiq Scot* 52 (1917–18), 86–121

Ritchie, J 1919
Notes on some stone circles in the south of
Aberdeenshire and north of Kincardineshire,
Proc Soc Antiq Scot 53 (1918–19), 64–75

Ritchie, J 1920
The stone circle at Broomend of Crichie,
Aberdeenshire, *Proc Soc Antiq Scot* 54 (1919–20),
154–72

Ritchie, J 1921
Relics of the body-snatchers: supplementary notes on
mortsafe tackle, mortsafes, watch-houses and public
vaults, mostly in Aberdeenshire, *Proc Soc Antiq Scot*
55 (1920–21), 221–9

Ritchie, J 1925
Whin-mills in Aberdeenshire, *Proc Soc Antiq Scot* 59
(1924–25), 128–42

Ritchie, J 1926
Folklore of the Aberdeenshire stone circles and
standing-stones, *Proc Soc Antiq Scot* 60 (1925–6),
304–13

Ritchie, J 1927
Some Antiquities of Aberdeenshire and Its Borders,
Edinburgh

Ritchie, J N G 1998
Tyrebagger recumbent stone circle, Aberdeenshire:
a note on recording, in Gibson and Simpson (eds)
1998, 176–82

Ritchie, P R & Scott, J G 1988
The petrological identification of stone axes from
Scotland, in Clough and Cummins (eds) 1988, 85–91

Ritchie, W 1992
Scottish landform examples 4 – coastal parabolic
dunes of the Sands of Forvie, *Scot Geogr Mag* 108,
39–44

Rivet, A L F (ed) 1966
The Iron Age in Northern Britain, Edinburgh

Rivet, A L F & Smith, C 1979
The Place-names of Roman Britain, London

Roberts, B K & Glasscock, R E (eds) 1983
*Villages, Fields and Frontiers: Studies in European
Rural Settlement in the Medieval and Early Modern
Periods*, BAR International Series 185, Oxford

Robertson, J (ed) 1843
*Collections for a history of the shires of Aberdeen
and Banff*, Spalding Club, Aberdeen

Robertson, J & Grubb, G (eds) 1847–62
*Illustrations of the topography and antiquities of the
shires of Aberdeen and Banff*, Vols 1–4, Spalding
Club, Aberdeen

Rogers, J M 1992
The formation of the parish unit and community in
Perthshire, Unpublished PhD thesis, University of
Edinburgh

Romans, J C C & Robertson, L 1983
The environment of north Britain: soils, in Chapman
and Mytum (eds) 1983, 55–82

Ross, A 2003
The Province of Moray *c.*1000–1230, Unpublished
PhD thesis, University of Aberdeen

Ross, A 2006
The dabhach in Scotland: a new look at an old tub,
in Woolf (ed) 2006, 57–74

Roy, W 1747–55
Military Survey of Scotland

Roy, W 1793
*The Military Antiquities of the Romans in North
Britain*, London

Royan, N 1999
'Scotichronicon' rewritten? Hector Boece's debt to
Bower in the 'Scotorum Historia', in Crawford (ed)
1999, 57–71

Ruggles, C 1999
Astronomy in Prehistoric Britain and Ireland, New
Haven and London

Russell-White, C J 1995
The excavation of a Neolithic and Iron Age
settlement at Wardend of Durris, Aberdeenshire,
Proc Soc Antiq Scot 125 (1995), 9–27

St Joseph, J K 1958
Air reconnaissance in Britain, 1955–57, *J Roman
Stud* 47 (1958), 86–101

St Joseph, J K 1969
Air reconnaissance in Britain, 1965–68, *J Roman
Stud* 59 (1969), 104–28

St Joseph, J K 1970

The camps at Ardoch, Stracathro and Ythan Wells: recent excavations, *Britannia* 1 (1970), 163–78

St Joseph, J K 1973

Air reconnaissance in Roman Britain, 1969–72, *J Roman Stud* 63 (1973), 214–46

St Joseph, J K 1977

Air reconnaissance in Roman Britain, 1973–76, *J Roman Stud* 67 (1977), 125–61

St Joseph, J K 1978

The camp at Durno, Aberdeenshire, and the site of Mons Graupius, *Britannia* 9 (1978), 271–87

Sanderson, D, Placido, F & Tate, J O 1988

Scottish vitrified forts: TL results from six study sites, *Int J Radiat Appl Instrum, Part D, Nucl Tracks Radiat Meas* 14 (1988), 307–16

Saville, A 1995

Prehistoric exploitation of flint from the Buchan Ridge Gravels, Grampian Region, north-east Scotland, *Archaeologia Polona* 33, 353–68

Scarre, C (ed) 2002

Monuments and Landscape in Atlantic Europe: Perception and Society During the Neolithic and Early Bronze Age, London

Schlüter, W 1999

The Battle of the Teutoburg Forest: archaeological research at Kalkriese near Osnabrück, in Creighton and Wilson (eds) 1999, 125–59

Scott, J D G 1956

Memoir of Dr F C Eeles, in Eeles 1956, ix–xxii

Scott, N 1926

Fasti Ecclesiae Scoticanae: the succession of ministers of the Church of Scotland from the Reformation, Edinburgh, Vol. 6, Synods of Aberdeen and of Moray

Scull, C J and Harding, A F 1990

Two early medieval cemeteries at Milfield, Northumberland, *Durham Archaeol J* 6 (1990), 1–29

Sellar, W D H (ed) 1993

Moray: Province and People, Edinburgh

Sharpe, R (ed) 1995

Adomnan of Iona: Life of St Columba, London

Shepherd, A N 1986

Excavations at Kintore Roman temporary camp, 1984, *Proc Soc Antiq Scot* 116 (1986), 205–9

Shepherd, A N 1996

A Neolithic ring-mound at Midtown of Pitglassie, Auchterless, Aberdeenshire, *Proc Soc Antiq Scot* 126 (1996), 17–51

Shepherd, I A G 1983

A Grampian stone circle confirmed, *Proc Soc Antiq Scot* 113 (1983), 630–4

Shepherd, I A G 1986

Powerful Pots: Beakers in North-east prehistory, Aberdeen

Shepherd, I A G 1987

The early peoples, in Omand (ed) 1987, 119–130

Shepherd, I A G 1994

Gordon: An Illustrated Architectural Guide, Edinburgh

Shepherd, I A G & Barclay, G J (eds) 2004

Scotland in Ancient Europe: The Neolithic and Early Bronze Age of Scotland in their European Context, Soc Antiq Scot, Edinburgh

Shepherd, I A G & Greig M K 1996

Grampian's Past: Its Archaeology from the Air, Grampian Regional Council

Shepherd, I A G & Shepherd, A N 1978

An incised Pictish figure and a new symbol stone from Barflat, Rhynie, Gordon District, *Proc Soc Antiq Scot* 109 (1977–8), 211–22

Sheridan, A 2002

Pottery and other ceramic finds, in Barclay *et al.* (2002), 79–88

Sheridan, A 2003

The National Museums of Scotland dating cremated bones project: results obtained during 2002/3, *Disc Exc Scotland, J of the Council for Scottish Archaeology*, New Ser, 4 (2004), 167–9

Sherriff, J R 1995

Prehistoric rock-carving in Angus, *Tayside Fife Archaeol J* 1 (1995), 11–22

Sherriff, J R 1999

Five Neolithic carved stones from Angus, *Tayside Fife Archaeol J* 5 (1999), 7–11

Simpson, W D 1919

The Doune of Invernochty, *Proc Soc Antiq Scot* 53 (1918–19), 34–45

Simpson, W D 1920

Note on recent excavations at Kildrummy Castle, *Proc Soc Antiq Scot* 54 (1919–20), 134–45

Simpson, W D 1921

Notes on Five Donside Castles, *Proc Soc Antiq Scot* 55 (1920–1), 135–49

Simpson, W D 1923a

The Castle of Kildrummy: Its Place in Scottish History and Architecture, Aberdeen

Simpson, W D 1923b

Hallforest Castle, *Scottish Notes & Queries*, Ser 3, 1 (1923), 164–7

Simpson, W D 1924

The excavation of Coull Castle, Aberdeenshire, *Proc Soc Antiq Scot* 58 (1923–4), 45–99

Simpson, W D 1925

The Augustinian priory and parish church of Monymusk, Aberdeenshire, *Proc Soc Antiq Scot* 59 (1924–5), 34–71

Simpson, W D 1927

Corgarff Castle, Aberdeenshire, *Proc Soc Antiq Scot* 61 (1926–7), 48–103

Simpson, W D 1928a

A new survey of Kildrummy Castle, *Proc Soc Antiq Scot* 62 (1927–8), 36–80

Simpson, W D 1928b
The early castles of Mar, *Proc Soc Antiq Scot* 62 (1927–8), 102–38

Simpson, W D 1930
Craig Castle and the kirk of Auchindoir, Aberdeenshire, *Proc Soc Antiq Scot* 64 (1929–30), 48–96

Simpson, W D 1932
Lesmoir Castle and the church of Essie: with some further notes on Auchindoir, *Proc Soc Antiq Scot* 66 (1931–2), 86–107

Simpson, W D 1936a
Excavations at the Doune of Invernochty, *Proc Soc Antiq Scot* 70 (1935–6), 170–81

Simpson, W D 1936b
Balquhain Castle, Aberdeenshire, *Aberdeen Univ Rev* 23 (1936), 1–5

Simpson, W D 1938
John Graham Callander, LLD, *Aberdeen Univ Rev* 25 (1937–8), 247–8

Simpson, W D 1942a
Two Donside castles, *Proc Soc Antiq Scot* 76 (1941–2), 93–102

Simpson, W D (ed) 1942b
The Book of Glenbuchat, Spalding Club, Aberdeen

Simpson, W D 1943
The Province of Mar: Being the Rhind Lectures in Archaeology, 1941, Aberdeen University Studies 121, Aberdeen

Simpson, W D 1944
The excavation of Esslemont Castle, Aberdeenshire, *Proc Soc Antiq Scot* 78 (1943–4), 100–5

Simpson, W D 1949
The Earldom of Mar: Being a Sequel to 'The Province of Mar', 1943, Aberdeen University Studies 124, Aberdeen

Simpson, W D 1960
The development of Castle Fraser, in *The Miscellany of the Third Spalding Club*, III, Third Spalding Club, Aberdeen

Sissons, J B 1967
The Evolution of Scotland's Scenery, Edinburgh

Sissons, J B 1976
The Geomorphology of the British Isles: Scotland, London

Sissons, J B 1979a
Loch Lomond Advance in the Cairngorm Mountains, *Scot Geogr Mag* 95, 66–82

Sissons, J B 1979b
Palaeoclimatic inferences from Loch Lomond Stadial glaciers in Scotland and the Lake District, *Nature* 278, 518–21

Skene, J 1822
An account of the hill fort of the Barmekyne in Aberdeenshire, *Archaeologia Scotica* 2 (1822), 324–7

Skene, W F (ed) 1871–2
Johannis de Fordun Chronica Gentis Scotorum (John of Fordun's Chronicle of the Scottish nation. Translated from the Latin text by Felix J H Skene), Vols 1–2, Edinburgh

Slade, H G 1967
Druminnor, formerly Castle Forbes, *Proc Soc Antiq Scot* 99 (1966–7), 148–66

Slade, H G 1978
Castle Fraser: a seat of the ancient family of Fraser, *Proc Soc Antiq Scot* 109 (1977–8), 233–300

Slade, H G 1982
Tillycairn Castle, *Proc Soc Antiq Scot* 112 (1982), 497–517

Slade, H G 1985
The Tower and House of Drum, Aberdeenshire, *Proc Soc Antiq Scot* 115 (1985), 297–356

Small, A (ed) 1987
The Picts: a new look at old problems, Dundee

Smellie, W 1782
Account of the Institution and Progress of the Society of Antiquaries of Scotland, Edinburgh

Smellie, W 1792
An historical account of the Society of the Antiquaries of Scotland, *Archaeologia Scotica* 1 (1792), iii–xxxiii

Smith, A G 1970
The influence of Mesolithic and Neolithic man on British vegetation: a discussion, in Walker and West (eds) 1970, 81–96

Smith, A G & Pilcher, J R 1973
Radiocarbon dates and vegetational history of the British Isles, *New Phytologist* 72, 903–14

Smith, D E 2002
The Storegga disaster, *Current Archaeology* 179, 468–71

Smith, D E, Cullingford, R A & Brooks, C L 1983
Flandrian relative sea level changes in the Ythan valley, northeast Scotland, *Earth Surface Processes & Landforms* 8, 423–38

Smith, D E, Cullingford, R A & Seymour, W P 1992
Flandrian relative sea level changes in the Philorth valley, north-east Scotland, *Trans Inst British Geogr*, New Ser 7, 321–36

Smith, D E, Firth, C R, Brooks, C L, Robinson, M & Collins, P E F 1999
Relative sea-level rise during the Main Postglacial Transgression in NE Scotland, UK, *Trans Roy Soc Edinburgh: Earth Sci* 90, 1–27

Smith, I F 1965
Windmill Hill & Avebury. Excavations by Alexander Keiller, 1929–35, Oxford

Smith, I M 1985
Balsarroch House, Wigtownshire, *Trans Dumfries and Galloway Natur Hist Antiq Soc*, Ser 3, 60 (1985), 73–81

Smith, J A 1874
Notice of a Silver Chain or Girdle, the Property of Thomas Simson, of Blainslie, Esq., Berwickshire; Another in the Possession of the University of Aberdeen and of Other Ancient Scottish Silver Chains, *Proc Soc Antiq Scot* 10 (1872–4), 321–47

Smith, J S & Stevenson, D (eds) 1988
Aberdeen in the Nineteenth Century: The Making of the Modern City, Aberdeen

Starkel, L, Gregory, K J & Thornes, J B (eds) 1991
Temperate Palaeohydrology, Chichester

Stat. Acct.
The Statistical Account of Scotland, Sinclair, J (ed) 1791–9, Edinburgh

Steers, J A 1976
The Coastline of Scotland, Cambridge

Steven, H M & Carlisle, A 1959
The Native Pinewoods of Scotland, Edinburgh

Stevenson, R B K 1948
Notes on some prehistoric objects, *Proc Soc Antiq Scot* 82 (1947–8), 292–5

Stevenson, R B K 1955
Pictish art, in Wainwright (ed) 1955, 97–128

Stevenson, R B K 1964
The Gaulcross hoard of Pictish Silver, *Proc Soc Antiq Scot* 97 (1963–4), 206–11

Stewart, J M & Durno, S E 1969
Structural variations in peat, *New Phytologist* 68, 167–82

Stringer, K J 1985
Earl David of Huntingdon 1152–1219: A Study in Anglo-Scottish History, Edinburgh

Stuart, A (ed) 1846
Essays, Chiefly on Scottish Antiquities by the Late John Stuart, Esquire, of Inchbreck, Professor of Greek in the Marischal College and University of Aberdeen. With a Brief Sketch of the Author's Life, Aberdeen

Stuart, J (ed) 1844
List of Pollable Persons within the Shire of Aberdeen, 1696, Vols 1–2, Spalding Club, Aberdeen

Stuart, J 1822a
An account of some subterraneous habitations in Aberdeenshire, *Archaeologia Scotica* 2 (1822), 53–8

Stuart, J 1822b
Observations upon the various accounts of the progress of Roman arms in Scotland and of the scene of the great battle between Agricola and Galgacus, *Archaeologia Scotica* 2 (1822), 289–313

Stuart, J 1822c
An account of some sculptured pillars in the northern part of Scotland addressed to the Edinburgh Society of Antiquaries, *Archaeologia Scotica* 2 (1822), 314–23

Stuart, J 1856
The Sculptured Stones of Scotland, Aberdeen

Stuart, J 1866
Notice of cairns recently examined on the estate of Rothie, Aberdeenshire, *Proc Soc Antiq Scot* 6 (1864–6), 217–18

Stuart, J 1867
The Sculptured Stones of Scotland, Vol. 2, Spalding Club, Aberdeen

Stuart, J 1868
Notice of cists and other remains discovered in 'Cairn Curr', on the farm of Warrackstone, in Aberdeenshire, *Proc Soc Antiq Scot* 7 (1866–8), 24–5

Stuart, J 1871
Notices of the Spalding Club with the Annual Reports, List of Members and Works Printed for the Club, 1839–71, Spalding Club, Edinburgh

Stuart, J & Burnett, G (eds) 1878
The Exchequer Rolls of Scotland 1264–1359, Vol. 1, Edinburgh

Sugden, D E 1970
Landforms of deglaciation in the Cairngorm Mountains, Scotland, *Trans Inst British Geogr* 51, 201–19

Sugden, D E 1971
The significance of periglacial activity on some Scottish mountains, *Geogr J* 137, 388–92

Sugden, D E & Clapperton, C M 1975
The deglaciation of upper Deeside and the Cairngorm mountains, in Gemmell (ed) 1975, 30–8

Sutherland, D G 1984
The Quaternary deposits and landforms of Scotland and the neighbouring shelves: a review, *Quaternary Sci Rev* 3, 157–254

Taylor, C 1983
Village and Farmstead, London

Taylor, J J 1980
Bronze Age Goldwork of the British Isles, Cambridge

Taylor, S 1994
Some early Scottish place-names and Queen Margaret, *Scottish Language* 13 (1994), 1–17

Taylor, S 1995
Settlement Names in Fife, Unpublished PhD thesis, University of Edinburgh

Taylor, S 1996
Place-names and the early church in Eastern Scotland, in Crawford (ed) 1996, 93–110

Thomson, J M (ed) 1984a
Registrum Magni Sigilli Regum Scotorum, 1306–1424, Vol. 1, Edinburgh

Thomson, J M (ed) 1984b
Registrum Magni Sigilli Regum Scotorum, 1546–1580, Vol. 4, Edinburgh

Tipping, R 1991
Climatic change in Scotland during the Devensian Late Glacial: the palynological record, in Barton, Roberts and Roe (eds) 1991, 7–21

Tipping, R 1994
The form and fate of Scotland's woodlands, *Proc Soc Antiq Scot* 124, 1–55

Tipping, R 1996
Microscopic charcoal records, inferred human activity and climate change in the Mesolithic of northernmost Scotland, in Pollard and Morrison (eds) 1996, 39–61

Tipping, R 1998a
The chronology of Late Quaternary fluvial activity in part of the Milfield Basin, northeast England, *Earth Surface Processes & Landforms* 23, 845–56

Tipping, R 1998b
Cereal cultivation on the Anglo-Scottish Border during the 'Little Ice Age', in Mills and Coles (eds) 1998, 1–12

Tipping, R & Milburn, P 2000a
Palaeoenvironmental significance of peat beneath the floor of the Den of Boddam, in Merritt, Connell and Bridgland (eds) 2000, 116–25

Tipping, R & Milburn, P 2000b
The mid-Holocene charcoal fall in southern Scotland: spatial and temporal variability, *Palaeogeography, Palaeoclimatology, Palaeoecology* 164, 193–209

Tipping, R & Tisdall, E 2004
Continuity, crisis and climate change in the Neolithic and early Bronze periods of north west Europe, in Shepherd and Barclay (eds) 2004, 71–82

Tipping, R, Davies, A L & McCulloch, R 2006
Introduced oak woodlands in northern Scotland: pollen-analytical evidence for early historic plantations, in Woolf (ed) 2006, 29–47

Tyson, R E 1988
The economy of Aberdeen, in Smith and Stevenson (eds) 1988, 19–36

Vasari, Y 1977
Radiocarbon dating of the lateglacial and early Flandrian vegetation succession in the Scottish Highlands and the Isle of Skye, in Gray and Lowe (eds) 1977, 143–62

Vasari, Y & Vasari, A 1968
Late- and Post-glacial macrophytic vegetation in the lochs of northern Scotland, *Acta Botanica Fennici* 80, 1–120

Vermeesch, P M & van Peer, P (eds) 1990
Contributions to the Mesolithic in Europe, Leuven

Wainwright, F T (ed) 1955
The Problem of the Picts, Edinburgh

Wainwright, F T 1963
The Souterrains of Southern Pictland, London

Walker, D & West, R G (eds) 1970
Studies in the Vegetational History of the British Isles, Cambridge

Walker, M J C, Bohncke, S J P, Coope, G R, O'Connell, M, Usinger, H & Verbruggen, C 1994
The Devensian/Weichselian Late-glacial in northwest Europe (Ireland, Britain, north Belgium, The Netherlands, northwest Germany), *J Quaternary Sci* 9, 109–18

Walton, K 1950
The population of Aberdeenshire 1696, *Scot Geogr Mag* 66, 17–25

Watson, G (ed) 1946
The Mar Lodge Translation of the History of Scotland by Hector Boece, Vol. 1, Scottish Text Society, Ser 3, 17, Edinburgh

Watson, W J 1926
The History of the Celtic Placenames of Scotland, Edinburgh and London

Watt, A 1865
The Early History of Kintore; with an account of the rights and privileges belonging to the heritors and the community of the burgh; extracted from old records and charters, Aberdeen

Webster, B (ed) 1982
Regesta Regum Scotorum, The Acts of David II, King of Scots 1329–71, Vol. 6, Edinburgh

Wells, P S 2003
The Battle that Stopped Rome. Emperor Augustus, Arminius, and the slaughter of the legions in the Teutoburger forest, New York

West, G 2000
The technical development of roads in Britain, Aldershot

Whittington, G 1975
Placenames and the settlement pattern of dark-age Scotland, *Proc Soc Antiq Scot* 106 (1974–5), 99–110

Whittington, G & Edwards, K J 1993
Ubi solitudinem faciunt pacem appellant: the Romans in Scotland, a palaeoenvironmental contribution, *Britannia* 24 (1993), 13–25

Whittington, G & Soulsby, J A 1968
A preliminary report on an investigation into pit placenames, *Scot Geogr Mag* 84 (1968), 117–25

Whyte, I 1987
Agriculture in Aberdeenshire in the seventeenth and eighteenth centuries: continuity and change, *Rev Scottish Culture* 3 (1987), 39–51

Wilson, D 1851
The Archaeology and Prehistoric Annals of Scotland, Edinburgh

Wilson, D 1863
Prehistoric Annals of Scotland, 2nd ed, London

Wilson, D & Laing, D 1874
An account of Alexander Gordon, AM, author of the 'Itinerarium Septentrionale', 1726; with additional notes concerning Gordon and his works, *Proc Soc Antiq Scot* 10 (1872–4), 363–82

Winram, R 1986
  The Land o' Lonach, Aberdeen
Woolf, A (ed) 2006
  Landscape and Environment in Dark Age Scotland,
  St John's House Papers No. 11, University of St
  Andrews
Woolliscroft, D J 2002
  *The Roman Frontier on the Gask Ridge, Perth and
  Kinross: An interim report on the Roman Gask
  Project 1995–2000*, BAR British Series 335, Oxford

Yeoman, P 1984
  Excavations at the Castlehill of Strachan, *Proc Soc
  Antiq Scot* 114 (1984), 315–64
Yeoman, P 1998
  Excavations at Castle of Wardhouse,
  Aberdeenshire, *Proc Soc Antiq Scot* 128 (1998),
  581–617
Young, A 1993
  The earls and earldom of Buchan in the thirteenth
  century, in Grant and Stringer (eds) 1993, 174–202

Index

Abbey of Lindores: *see* Lindores Abbey
aber place-names 124
Abersnithock: *see* Braehead, Monymusk
Aberdeen 1, 24, 195, 226
    Archaeological Unit 163
    bishop's palace [NJ90NW 9.03] 162–3
    burghs of Old and New Aberdeen [NJ90NW 201]
        4–6, 164 (Fig. 8.27), 169, 184
    cathedral *see* St Machar's
    cross-marked stones 125 (Fig. 7.11), 142
    free forest grant, 146: *see also* Stocket Forest
    Freedom Lands 5, *6*, 142, 236 (map Fig. 9.22)
    harbour defences [NJ90NE 19, 22, 31, 61–71, 90 &
        211] 241–4 (Figs 9.36–37)
    hospitals [NJ90NW 9.02, 13, 16.01, 47, 163 & 416]
        11, 142, 148, 164
    King's Links, pillbox [NJ90NE 25] 242 (Fig. 9.36)
    parish church: *see* St Nicholas, Church of
    Pittodrie, Z-battery [NJ90NE 68] 241
    thanage 134, 139, 145, 146, 161
    see also Nelson Street; Meston Walk
Aberdeen Castle [NJ90NW 22] 154–5, 163, 164
Aberdeenshire Agricultural Association 225
Aberdeenshire Canal 221: *see also* Woodland's Wood
Aberdeenshire Council Archaeological Services 16, 251
Abernethy, Perth & Kinross, *pit-* place-names 132
Aboyne, Coull, Aberdeenshire
    souterrain and bronze armlets [NJ40SE 13] 92, 139
    thanage 139
achadh- place-names 132–3
Achynaterman, Dyce, place-name 147
Adrian, Pope 139
Aed, king of Picts 116
aerial photography 16, 23, 81, 85–7, 88–9, 91, 93–5,
        121–2, 248: *see also* cropmarks
Affleck, Rhynie, cottertoun 189
Afforsk, Oyne, lease 219: *see also* Mains of Afforsk
Agricola, Gnaeus Julius 110, 111–12, 113–14

agricultural improvements
    impact on prehistoric monuments 20, 47, 74, 80, 81
    drainage 23
    dykes 2, 20, 66, 149, 207, 221–2, 231–2
    18th century 2, 17, 215, 218–20
    New Statistical Account 19–20, 137, 215
    settlements 130–3, 138–9, 183–8, 193–9, 201–4,
        206–7, 245
    Statistical Account 19–20, 215
    see also drainage
agriculture
    palaeoenvironmental evidence 39–44
    prehistoric 39–40, 41–2, 43, 44, 47, 75, 80, 83
        (map Fig. 6.5), 109, 110
    pre-improvement 215–18, 227–31
    see also assarting; rig-and-furrow; tathing
Aikey Brae, Aberdeenshire, recumbent stone circle
        [NJ94NE 4] 66, 67
Aldachie, Strathdon, *achadh-* place-name, 133
Aldclune, Perth & Kinross, stone-walled enclosures
        [NN86SE 1] 101
alder 38, 39, 43
Aldnakist, Towie, forest grant 149
Alexander, W M, *Place-Names of Aberdeenshire* 15
Alexander II, King of Scots 157
Alexander III, King of Scots 146–7
Alford, 3, 18, 141, 142, 147, 179
    Battle of 18
    burgh of barony [NJ51NE 44] 188
    earthwork [NJ51NE 7] 80, 154
    Elrick, place-name 147
    parish church [NJ51NE 10] 154
    pre-improvement agriculture 215–16
Allargue, Strathdon, Poll Tax 193
Allanshaw, Kintore, cist, clay-luted [NJ71NE 101] 53
Allen, Romilly 12–13
Allt Clach Mheann (Ault Clachana Fayn), Strathdon,
        shieling [NJ10NE 20] 205

enclosures
agricultural 17–18, 20, 109, 196, 217, 218, 221, 222–4
settlement earthworks 92–6 (Figs 6.17–23): *see
also* Glenkindie; Hill of Christ's Kirk; Little Hill;
Quarry Wood; Sleepieshill Wood; Tillymuick
cropmark 86, 92 (Fig. 6.17), 93–5 (map Fig. 6.18
& Figs 6.19–22), 96 (Fig. 6.23), 111 (map
Fig. 6.35), 122 (Fig. 7.8): *see also* Ardmorn;
Arnbog; Auchrynie; Barflat; Batchart; Braehead,
Insch; Bridestonefold; Candieshill; Castlehill,
Auchindoir; Colpy; Cowhythe; Dallyfour; East
Mains of Arboyne; Easter Calcots; Foggieburn;
Fullerton; Greenhaugh; Hillhead of Gask;
Inverurie; Kintocher; Lawfolds; Legatesden;
Lochhills; Maryfield; Middleton; Millbank;
Netherton of Mounie; Park of Logie; Pyke;
Riverbank Wood; Suttie; Templestone; West
Balhalgardy; West Cockmuir; Wester Fintray;
Wester Tulloch; Whitestripes
moated 150, 151, 154, 161, 163, 174–5 (Fig. 8.40),
250: *see also* moated sites
palisaded 93–5, 100 (map Fig. 6.26): *see also*
Braehead, Insch; Colpy; Durn Hill; Hill of Christ's
Kirk; East Mains of Aboyne; Millbank; Suttie;
Templestone; Wardend of Durris
stone-walled 92–3, 98 (Fig. 6.25), 100–101
(map Fig. 6.26), 108, 110: *see also* Aldclune;
Hill of Keir; Maiden Castle; Stot Hill; Turin Hill;
White Hill; Widdie Hillock
rectilinear 96 (Fig. 6.23): *see also* Auchtydonald;
Boyndie; Chapelton, Dunottar; Easter Galcantray;
Hindwells; Kirkhill; Middleton; Newton of
Lewesk
see also henges
Ennets, Lumphanan, Aberdeenshire, *annait* place-name
129
Ennot Hillocks, Strathdon, *annait* place-name 129
Enzean, Monymusk, farm 194
episcopal baronies 142, 172
Ernan Water 37, 41, 193, 207, 210, 231: *see also* Glen
Ernan
Erskine family 141, 142
Essie, Rhynie
farmstead, cottertoun and croft [NJ42NE 155] 190,
191, 194
Lulach killed 115, 121
old parish church [NJ42NE 7] 15
shielings 206
Esslemont: *see* Castle of Esslemont
estates
centres, medieval 137, 150–63, 172–83, 250
maps 81, 138, 185 (Fig. 8.55), 186, 188, 189, 190,
191, 194, 196, 201–2, 207, 212, 213, 217 (Fig. 9.2),
218–19, 222–4 (Figs 9.6–8), 227–8, 245
medieval 130, 133–5, 139–41, 142–3, 145–6, 183, 249
see also boundaries; *dabhachs*
Eystein of Norway 5

farmsteads 138, 198–9 (Fig. 8.72), 208–11 (map
Fig. 8.82 & Figs 8.83–85), 213, 231, 246
(Fig. 10.1), 251
faugh land 216
Fentoun, William de, lands of Over and Nether Towy
and Culfork 141
fermtouns 188–9, 192, 201: *see also touns*
Fernybrae, Chapel of Garioch, Neolithic pottery
[NJ72NW 40] 14, 46
Fetternear, Chapel of Garioch 144
bishop's palace and moated site [NJ71NW 7.01] 151,
162, 163
country house and policies [NJ71NW 7] 176, 178,
180, 181 (Fig. 8.49), 224, 236
ecclesiastical estate 139, 161, 190
Elrick place-name 147
forest grant 146
Fetternear, Chapel of Garioch, crofts 190
Fichlie, grange of Strathdon 153: *see also* Peel of Fichlie
field-systems
prehistoric 15, 17, 80–1 (Figs 6.2–3), 83 (map
Fig. 6.5), 109: *see also* cairns, cairnfields
improvement 221–4 (Figs. 9.6–8), 232 (Fig. 9.17),
233 (Fig. 9.18), 241
pre-improvement 227–31 (map Fig. 9.11 &
Figs 9.12–16), 251: *see also* rig-and-furrow
see also agricultural improvements; agriculture
Finavon, Angus, vitrified fort [NO55NW 32] 100, 102
Finglenny Hill, Rhynie, flat axe hoard [NJ43SE 1] 57,
76
Fintray
church and burial ground: *see also* Hatton of Fintray
ecclesiastical estate 146, 151, 161: *see also* Hatton of
Fintray
forest grant 146
lordship of Garioch 140
plantations 224
St Meddan's, old parish church, medieval graveslabs,
sacrament house [NJ81NE 11] 146, 151, 167
(Fig. 8.32), 170–1 (Fig. 8.36)
tref- place-name 130
Fir Bog, Grampian Foothills, soil development 30
(Table 2)
Flandres: see Flinder
flat cemeteries, Bronze Age 52–5 (maps Figs 5.9 & 14)
flax *(Linum usitatissimum)* 40
Flemings: *see* Flinder
Fleuchatts, Strathdon, shielings 205: *see also* Meikle
Fleuchat
Flinder, Leslie, Fleming settlement 140, 185: *see also*
Little Flinder; New Flinder; Old Flinder
Flint 27
tools 14, 24, 36, 47, 48, 54, 55
mines 39 (Fig. 4.6), 43
floodplain terraces 36–7, 43
Foggieburn, Insch, enclosure [NJ52NE 32] 94
(Fig. 6.20), 95

St Colm's Chapel, Monykebbuck, chapel [NJ81NE 1]
144: *see also* New Machar

St Fergus, Dyce, pollen diagram 29 (Table 1), 36, 43

St John's Episcopal Church, Aberdeen, font from
Kinkell [NJ90NW 793] 169

St Katherine's Hill, Aberdeen, possible earthwork castle
[NJ90NW 2621] 154

St Luke's Chapel, Kildrummy, chapel and cross-shaped
stones [NJ42SE 11] 15, 129 (Fig. 7.15), 130

St Machar
cathedral, effigies and monumental brasses
[NJ90NW 9] 5, 11, 163, 164 (Figs 8.27–28), 167,
169, 171
parish 144, 142
see also Corriehoul, chapel

St Mary's Church, Monymusk 165–6 (Figs 8.31–32):
see also Monymusk

St Mary's Chapel, Auchenhuive, Udny, chapel
[NJ82NW 38] 167 (Fig. 8.32)

St Mary's Chapel, Stoneywood: *see* Stoneywood

St Meddan's, Fintray: *see* Fintray

St Moluag 15: *see also* Clova, *monasterium*

St Nicholas, Aberdeen, church, effigies and monumental
brasses [NJ90NW 42] 11, 164, 165 (Fig. 8.30),
170–1 (Fig. 8.36)

St Peter's, Aberdeen
Hospital and lands 142, 148: *see also* Aberdeen,
hospitals
parish 142

St Wallach, dedication, Glenbuchat 129

salt marshes 38, 43

sand, wind-blown 43, 44, 191

Sands of Forvie, Slains 12, 43
kerb cairns [NK02NW 13] 51
ring-cairn [NK02NW 3] 15, 51 (Fig. 5.8)
round-ended building [NK02NW 14] 200
shell middens 12 (Fig. 2.6), 43–4
see also Forvie

Scandinavian Three Age System 12

Scotstown House, Old Machar, country house, policies
and *toun* [NJ91SW 160] 195

Scurdargue, Rhynie
cup-and-ring marks [NJ42NE 8] 73, 74
township [farmsteading NJ42NE 74] 191, 203

sea level 37, 38, 43

Seaton, Aberdeen, pottery, brick and tileworks
[NJ90NW 331] 239

Seggiecrook, Kennethmont, Cinerary Urns, slate
pendant, pinheads and bead [NJ52NE 27] 14, 55

Seggieden, Kennethmont, lands 143: *see also*
The Sunken Kirk

Semple, Master of 16

settlements
Neolithic 40, 46–7, 78: *see also* Neolithic
Bronze Age 47, 80–7: *see also* Bronze Age
Iron Age 87–109: *see also* Iron Age; forts;
hut-circles; souterrains

early medieval, place-names 130–3

medieval 140, 183–6, 188, 190, 199–201

post-medieval 138–9, 186–99, 201–4, 231

shielings 204–6, 218

improved farmsteads 206–13, 231

see also buildings; cottages; crofts; cropmarks;
farmsteads; *touns*

Severus, Septimius, Roman emperor 112–13

Sgur Mor, Cairngorms, pollen diagram 30 (Table 2)

Shand, Colonel Alexander 9

Shannach Burn, Strathdon, turf buildings and intake
[NJ21SE 19] 207 (Fig. 8.80)

sheep-houses 199, 203, 213–14 (Figs 8.89–90)

Shelden, Bourtie, stone circle, cairn, cist and standing
stones [NJ82SW 1] 69, 70, 71 (Fig. 5.37), 72

shell middens 12, 43–4

Shevock, burn, floodplain terrace 36

shielings 138, 149, 204–6 (map Fig. 8.77 &
Figs 8.78–9), 214, 217–8

shires 142–3, 145–6, 161

Sibbald, Sir Robert, antiquary 8

silver, Pictish
chains 12, 133
hoard 119

Simpson, Douglas, historian 15, 156, 158, 159, 160, 175

Sinclair, Sir John, statistician 8

Skellater, Strathdon
laird's house [NJ31SW 6] 180 (Fig. 8.48), 250–1
lands 141, 192–3, 196
lime 239
shielings 205

Skene, parish
agricultural improvements 221
barony 172
Elrick place-name 147
parish church, chapel of Kinkell [NJ80NW 3] 130,
145
pollen diagram 31 (Table 2), 34
stone circle and cupmarks [NJ70NE 3] 73
stone circles 21
see also Kirkton of Skene

Skene, James, antiquary 10, 11 (Fig. 2.4), 121
(Fig. 7.6), 220

Skene family 142

Skene Lowland 27–8, 31 (Table 2) 40, 42–3

Slack, Coull, pillbox [NJ50NW 19] 242 (Fig. 9.36)

The Slacks, Dyce, hut-circles [NJ81SW 48] 84
(Fig. 6.6)

slate quarries 226 (Fig. 9.10), 238

Sleepieshill Wood, Moray, enclosure, earthwork
[NJ26SE 29] 96

Smithstown, Rhynie, township [NJ52NW 74] 194

Society of Antiquaries of London 12

Society of Antiquaries of Scotland 8, 9, 10, 12, 13, 14,
16, 19, 21–2, 23

soil acidification 40–1

soil erosion 37, 41–2, 110